W9-CNN-918

fourth edition

Writing in the Disciplines

A Reader for Writers

Mary Lynch Kennedy
SUNY Cortland

William J. Kennedy
Cornell University

Hadley M. Smith
Ithaca College

PRENTICE HALL
Upper Saddle River, NJ 07458

Library of Congress Cataloging-in-Publication Data

Kennedy, Mary Lynch
    Writing in the disciplines : a reader for writers / Mary Lynch
Kennedy, William J. Kennedy, Hadley M. Smith. – 4th ed. p. cm.
    Includes index.
    ISBN 0-13-021027-7
    1. College readers. 2. Interdisciplinary approach in education Problems, exercises,
etc. 3. English language--Rhetoric Problems, exercises, etc. 4. Academic writing
Problems, exercises, etc. I. Kennedy, William J. (William John), 1942- II. Smith,
Hadley M., 1950- III. Title.
    PE1417 .K45 1999
    808'.0427--dc21
                                        99-27630
                                          CIP

Editor-in-Chief: *Charlyce Jones Owen*
Senior Acquisitions Editor: *Leah Jewell*
Director of Production and Manufacturing: *Barbara Kittle*
Senior Managing Editor: *Bonnie Biller*
Senior Project Manager: *Shelly Kupperman*
Manufacturing Manager: *Nick Sklitsis*
Prepress and Manufacturing Buyer: *Mary Ann Gloriande*
Director of Marketing: *Gina Sluss*
Marketing Manager: *Sue Brekka*
Interior Designer: *Amy Rosen*
Cover Designer: *Bruce Kenselaar*
Editorial Assistant: *Patricia Castiglione*

This book was set in 11/13 Caledonia by Typographics and printed by R R Donnelley—
Harrisonburg. The cover was printed by Phoenix Color Corp.

© 2000, 1996, 1990, 1987 by Prentice Hall, Inc.
Upper Saddle River, New Jersey 07458

All rights reserved. No part of this book may be reproduced, in any form or by any
means, without permission in writing from the publisher.

Printed in the United States of America
10 9 8 7 6 5 4 3

ISBN 0-13-021027-7

Prentice-Hall International (UK) Limited, *London*
Prentice-Hall of Australia Pty. Limited, *Sydney*
Prentice-Hall Canada, Inc., *Toronto*
Prentice-Hall Hispanoamericana, S.A., *Mexico*
Prentice-Hall of India Private Limited, *New Delhi*
Prentice-Hall of Japan, Inc., *Tokyo*
Pearson Asia Pte. Ltd., *Singapore*
Editora Prentice-Hall do Brasil, Ltda., *Rio de Janeiro*

B R I E F
c o n t e n t s

Humanities   507

contents

2 Writing an Essay in Response to a Source: An Illustration of the Writing Process 36

3 Composing Essays Drawing from Two or More Sources: Comparison and Contrast and Synthesis 77

4   Essays of Argument, Analysis, and Evaluation   103

5   Writing Research Papers   142

P A R T   T W O

An Anthology of Readings   191

Natural Sciences and Technology   193

6   Cloning and Reproductive Technology   197

NINE LIVES • Ursula K. Le Guin   198
Describes how a "family" of clones function in a futuristic society. An excerpt from a short story.

7 Interaction Between Machines and Humans   246

8 Technology and Civil Liberties   296

Social Sciences   359

9 Redefining the American Family   364

10 Social Class and Inequality   429

Humanities   507

11 The Community and the Individual   513

13 Literatures of Diaspora: Fiction and Nonfiction   631

preface

TO OUR READERS IN APPRECIATION

In preparing the fourth edition of *Writing in the Disciplines: A Reader for Writers,* we listened closely to students and instructors who had used the third edition, and we followed their advice. As requested, we reworked the first part of the book. We added a new student essay to Chapter 2, rearranged Chapters 3 and 4, and made extensive revisions to Chapter 5, "Writing Research Papers." We have also made changes to the second half of the book. A number of the readings are new, and in Chapter 12, we have introduced a new topic. To the readers who suggested these changes, we say "thank you" for helping us strengthen this book.

ORGANIZATION AND APPROACH

Writing in the Disciplines: A Reader for Writers serves two functions. It explains how to use reading sources as idea banks for college papers, and it teaches fundamental academic writing strategies: reading, paraphrasing, summarizing, quoting, organizing, drafting, revising, editing, synthesizing, analyzing, researching, and developing arguments. It also provides an anthology of readings in the humanities, the natural sciences and technology, and the social sciences which contains articles representing various rhetorical approaches across academic disciplines. These articles, along with the accompanying instructional apparatus, help develop students' abilities to think critically and reason cogently as they read, compose, and revise. The activities and questions that accompany each reading encourage students to approach academic writing as a process: to preview the source, set reading goals, and ponder the general topic before reading; to annotate the text and think critically while reading; and to reflect on the source and identify information content, form, organization, expository and stylistic features, and rhetorical elements after reading. Students are also shown how to draw on annotations, notes, and preliminary writing to produce first drafts of academic essays and how to revise essays at the drafting stage as well as later in the writing process. Additional activities help students to use ideas from different sources to produce synthesis essays and research papers.

Chapter 1 presents active reading strategies that help students engage the ideas in academic texts and incorporate them in their own writing by paraphrasing, summarizing, and quoting. Chapter 2 presents the writing process, including analyzing the assignment, planning, organizing, drafting, revising, and editing. In addition, Chapter 2 examines essay structures, from the introduction and thesis statement through the body of the essay to its conclusion, and teaches students to write essays of response to a source. Chapter 3 focuses on essays that draw on two or more sources, including compare-and-contrast essays and synthesis. Chapter 4 covers essays of argumentation, analysis, and evaluation, with the special attention to literary analysis; and Chapter 5 focuses on library research strategies and writing research papers. In the eight succeeding chapters, we provide forty-seven reading selections. We have organized the anthology in Chapters 6 through 13 by dividing the academic curriculum into three major fields: the natural sciences and technology, the social sciences, and the humanities. Each chapter in *Writing in the Disciplines* deals with a topic that is widely studied in the field. For example, the social sciences section has chapters on redefining the American family and social class and inequality. The reading selections help students view each topic from a range of perspectives, and they provide diverse views from experts within the discipline and from journalists and specialists in other academic fields. Most of the articles are written for nonspecialized readers, not for majors in particular fields. We believe these articles, from popular as well as scholarly sources, represent the types of readings many professors assign in introductory and lower-level courses. Psychology professors, for instance, know that first-year students cannot interpret most psychological research reports until they acquire a basic knowledge of the discipline and learn its principles of experimental methodology and statistical analysis. However, first-year students can read summaries and analyses of psychological research written for nonspecialists. For *Writing in the Disciplines,* we chose readings that might appear on a reserve list as supplements to an introductory-level textbook. We make no assumptions about students' prior knowledge. Our intent is to model first-year-level reading assignments, not to exemplify professional standards within the disciplines.

In the introduction to each of the sections, we characterize the field of study with a discussion of its subdisciplines, methodology, logic, and vocabulary. We then describe writing within the field by examining authors' perspectives, goals, organizational patterns, literary devices, and rhetorical styles. We recognize that there is no absolute standard for categorizing intellectual activities. For example, although we have classified history as a discipline within the humanities, we could as well have placed it within the social sciences, depending on the methodology the historians use. Throughout the book, we not only point out overlaps among disciplines but also capitalize on them in synthesis assignments at the end of each chapter. Despite the imprecision of these categories, we believe that important differences in approaches to scholarship and writing do exist among the three main academic areas. Students who understand these differences will read more critically and write more persuasively.

IMPROVEMENTS IN THE FOURTH EDITION

In the fourth edition of *Writing in the Disciplines,* we have revised the initial section on academic writing. Chapter 2 contains a new student essay. We have moved argumentation from Chapter 3 to Chapter 4, and in Chapter 4 we have collapsed the material on analysis and evaluation. Chapter 5 has changed dramatically in response to advances in computerized information retrieval systems. Chapter 5 also includes a new research paper written in American Psychological Association (APA) style. In the anthology section, Chapter 6 has been revised to focus on the current controversy over human cloning, and Chapter 12 features a new topic, "Rock Music and Cultural Values." We also added new articles and fiction excerpts to Chapters 7 and 8. We continue to accompany each article with activities and questions that promote critical thinking. Each reading is preceded by a prereading activity and followed by groups of questions that encourage students to grasp information and decide what form, organization, and expository features the author uses. Additional questions ask students to analyze rhetorical concerns, such as the context and the author's purpose (Haas and Flower). As in previous editions, several writing assignments accompany each reading and each topically related chapter.

Finally, we have refined and expanded the guide to documentation and the comparison of the MLA (Modern Language Association) and APA styles in the Appendix.

COLLABORATIVE LEARNING ACTIVITIES

Writing in the Disciplines provides a series of collaborative learning activities that require students to work together in groups to clarify and extend their understanding of material presented in Chapters 1 through 5. We have constructed pairs of individual and collaborative exercises for each chapter subsection, so for any particular concept, instructors may assign out-of-class work and follow with in-class collaborative activities. Some instructors may use the collaborative exercises to emphasize points they or their students deem particularly important or problematic.

It is important to prepare students for group work by teaching them the collaborative skills they need in order to work together—requisite social skills, group dynamics, methods of interaction, and strategies for learning from each other as well as from the teacher. Some instructors pair off students at first. Then, when they move the students into groups, they give them time to become acquainted. Another technique is to re-define the groups frequently until everyone in the class has gotten to know each other.

Each of the collaborative exercises in this textbook requires students to divide into work groups. Experiment with different ways of grouping students together. You might allow them to choose their groups, or you might assign them to groups on the basis of working style, personality types, or role. We have found Kenneth Bruffee's methods for conducting collaborative learning groups particularly useful (28–51). The following procedure, which draws heavily on Bruffee's *Collaborative Learning: Higher Education, Interdependence, and the Authority of Knowledge*, is applicable to all the collaborative exercises in this textbook.

WORKING IN COLLABORATIVE LEARNING GROUPS

1. Students form groups of five or six by counting off. (Bruffee maintains that groups of five are particularly effective for collaborative activities.)

2. Each group selects a recorder who will write down the results of the group's deliberation and will eventually report to the entire class.

3. Each group selects a reader who then reads the collaborative task from the textbook.

4. Group members attempt to achieve a consensus on the question or issue posed by the collaborrative task. All viewpoints should be heard and considered. (Bruffee recommends that instructors refrain from taking part in or monitoring collaborative learning groups. He believes that teacher interference in groups "inevitably destroys peer relations among students and encourages the tendency of well-schooled students to focus on the teacher's authority and interests" [29].)

5. When a consensus is reached, the recorder reads her or his notes back to the group, and they are revised to make sure they reflect the group's decision. Differences of opinion are also included in the notes.

6. When all groups have completed the assignment, recorders read their notes to the entire class. The instructor may choose to summarize each group's report on the chalkboard. A discussion involving the entire class may follow.

Other methods of forming and conducting collaborative learning groups will also work with the exercises in Chapters 1 through 5. Although we have had success with Bruffee's technique, we encourage instructors to pick the methods that work best for them and their students. The following resources will be helpful:

Angelo, T. A., and K. P. Cross. *Classroom Assessment Techniques: A Handbook for College Teachers.* San Francisco: Jossey-Bass, 1993.

Goodsell, Anne, Michelle Maher, and Vincent Tinto. *Collaborative Learning: A Sourcebook for Higher Education.* University Park, PA: NCTLA, 1992.

Johnson, David W., Roger T. Johnson, Karl A. Smith, and E. Holubec. *Circles of Learning: Cooperation in the Classroom.* Edina, MN: Interaction, 1993.

ACKNOWLEDGMENTS

Once again, in the fourth edition we have relied on the work of many researchers and scholars in composition and reading. We are particularly grateful to Ann Brown, Kenneth Bruffee, Linda Flower, Christina Haas, John Hayes, and Bonnie Meyer. We used pilot versions of *Writing in the Disciplines* in first-year-level writing courses at Cornell University, Ithaca College, and SUNY at Cortland, and we are indebted to our students for their comments and suggestions. Liam and Maura Kennedy deserve special thanks for their important contributions to Chapter 1, 2, 3, and 4. Hadley Smith would like to acknowledge David Flanagan's and Marlene Kobre's suggestions for articles for Chapters 6, 7, and 8 as well as their collegiality over the years.

At Prentice Hall, Senior English Acquisitions Editor Leah Jewell supervised our project with skill and professionalism. We also appreciate the assistance we received from Company President Phil Miller, and Editorial Assistant Patricia Castiglione. Special thanks to our Senior Production Editor Shelly Kupperman for her expert work and to our meticulous copy editor Diane Garvey Nesin. We are indebted to our reviewers who contributed their ideas and insightful analysis: Jia-Yi Cheng-Levine, Indiana University of PA; Jean H. Wilson, Indiana University of PA; Patricia Coward, Frostburg State University; Phillip Sipiora, University of South Florida; James Allen, College of DuPage; Charles Baker, Indiana University of PA; Chad Beck, North Carolina State University; Peter Stokes, Tufts University; Alma G. Bryant, University of South Florida.

Finally, we are grateful to Liam and Maura Kennedy, Nancy Siegele, and Annie, Colin, and Timm Smith for their patience, support, and understanding.

WORKS CITED

Bruffee, Kenneth. *Collaborative Learning: Higher Education, Interdependence, and the Authority of Knowledge.* Baltimore: Johns Hopkins UP, 1993.

Haas, Christina, and Linda Flower. "Rhetorical Reading and the Construction of Meaning." *College Composition and Communication* 39 (1988): 167–83.

Mary Lynch Kennedy

William J. Kennedy

Hadley M. Smith

P A R T

one

Reading
and Writing
in the Academic
Disciplines

one

Preparing to Write:
Active Reading

ACADEMIC WRITING: AN INTRODUCTION

In college, you sometimes find the language used is quite different from what you have encountered in the past. This textbook will prepare you to present your ideas to professors and fellow students by using the conventions of *academic* writing. Academic reading and writing follow a distinct process that we have briefly outlined in the box that follows.

OVERVIEW OF THE ACADEMIC READING-WRITING PROCESS

Active Reading

Prereading.　Preview the reading sources, freewrite about your topic, and set your goals.

Close reading.　Mark, annotate, elaborate on, and pose questions about the reading. Questions address three areas: (1) information; (2) textual form, organization, and expository features; and (3) rhetorical concerns.

Postreading.　Record comments, reactions, quotations, paraphrases, and summaries about the readings.

(continued on the next page)

Planning

Formulating a thesis.   Arrive at a preliminary understanding of the point you want to make in your paper.

Organizing.   Decide how you will use sources in the paper and how you will develop your argument.

Drafting

Drafting.   Weave source material (usually in the form of quotations, paraphrases, and summaries) with your own ideas to create paragraphs and, ultimately, a complete paper, typically with an introduction, a body, and a conclusion.

Reworking

Revising.   Lengthen, shorten, or reorder your paper; change your prose to make it more understandable to your reader; make sentence-level, phrase-level, and word-level stylistic changes; or, in some cases, make major conceptual or organizational alterations to incorporate what you learned during the process of drafting.

Editing.   Proofread your paper for errors in sentence structure, usage, punctuation, spelling, and mechanics and check for proper manuscript form.

Writers do not proceed through the stages of this process in lock-step fashion, beginning with prereading and ending with editing. The movement is recursive, and the processes may be intermixed. You may find yourself revising *while* you draft as well as after you have finished the piece. Even though you will read the sources before you write, you will probably reread portions of them during and after the drafting phase. And writing can occur at any point in the process. You can do freewriting on the assigned topic before you read sources, annotate as you read, or rewrite parts of the paper after you have produced a draft of it.

The first two chapters of this textbook are devoted to describing and illustrating the various stages in the academic reading-writing process. Although we do not apply the actual process sequentially, we will, for convenience, begin with reading and proceed through the phases in the order outlined in the preceding box.

ACTIVE READING STRATEGIES

Effective reading is essential because academic writing is frequently based on "outside sources." College writers rarely have the luxury of choosing a topic that interests them or of composing an essay based entirely on their own ideas and personal experiences. Typically, professors specify topics and expect students to formulate a thesis or a position and support it by drawing on published sources—textbooks, reserve readings, scholarly books, journals, newspapers, and magazines—along with lecture notes, interviews, and other forms of information. To use outside sources in your papers, you need to practice effective methods of paraphrasing, summarizing, and quoting. In other words, you have to become a skilled reader as well as an accomplished writer.

Skilled readers are *active readers.* They connect what they are reading to texts they have read before and to prior knowledge and personal experiences. Usually when readers have difficulty understanding texts, it is because they lack the appropriate background and cannot make those connections.

To become a more active reader, try some of the strategies listed in the box that follows.

ACTIVE READING STRATEGIES

Prereading

1. Preview the source and derive questions that will help you set goals for close reading.
2. Freewrite or brainstorm to recall your prior knowledge or feelings about the reading topic.

Close Reading

1. Annotate and elaborate on the source.
2. Take content notes.
3. Pose and answer questions about three aspects of the source: information; textual form, organization, and expository features; and rhetorical concerns.

Postreading

1. Review the source and your notes.
2. Compose paraphrases and summaries and record quotations that may be useful at a later date.

PREREADING

Prereading lays the groundwork for comprehension and understanding. Just as you wouldn't plunge into an athletic activity "cold," you wouldn't set out to read a difficult text without preparation. The more challenging the reading, the more important the prereading activities become. The prereading strategies you select depend on the reading source's character and level of difficulty. Two useful techniques are (1) previewing the source and deriving questions that will help you set goals for close reading, and (2) freewriting or brainstorming to recall your prior knowledge or feelings about the reading topic.

Preview the Source and Derive Questions That Will Help You Set Goals for Close Reading

Before you do a close reading of the source, thumb through it for a quick inspection. This overview will give you a general idea of the content and organization and enable you to understand it better. As you preview the reading, ask yourself the following questions:

1. What does the title indicate the piece will be about?
2. Is there any biographical information about the author? What does this information tell me about the piece?
3. How do the subtitles and headings function? Do they reveal the author's organizational format (for example, introduction, body, conclusion)?
4. Do any topic sentences of paragraphs seem especially important?
5. Does the author provide any other organizational signals, such as enumeration, italics, indention, diagrams, or footnotes?
6. Does the reading end with a summary? What does it reveal about the content of the piece?

Another useful previewing technique is to turn the title and the subheadings into questions that you can try to answer before reading the piece. Consider how one of our students used this technique to preview Warren Robinett's "Electronic Expansion of Human Perception" (Chapter 7). The first subheading was "Expansion of Perception."

STUDENT'S CONVERSION OF SUBHEADING INTO QUESTIONS

In what ways could virtual reality expand human perception?

STUDENT'S ANSWER (BASED ON SUBSEQUENT CLOSE READING)

Virtual reality systems can visually display stimuli that come through other sensory pathways. For example, VR units coupled with ultrasound could allow doctors to "see" inside their patients as they examine them. Similarly, scientists could use VR to "see" radioactive decay, the structure of microscopic molecules, or the pattern of a data set.

Continue where our student left off. Turn to pages 278–281 and convert the subheadings into questions. Answer them as best you can.

Freewrite or Brainstorm to Recall Your Prior Knowledge or Feelings About the Reading Topic

The knowledge and experiences you bring to bear on a text affect your understanding of it. While you read, you are constructing new knowledge by relating what you already know to the new material. Prior knowledge paves the way for understanding. For example, if you are reading about alternatives to the traditional nuclear family, as in Frances Goldschneider and Linda Waite's "Alternative Family Futures" (pp. 365–373), it may help you to process the argument if you first think about kinds of families that you are familiar with: two-parent families, single-parent families, families that include stepparents, families with stepsiblings, and so forth. Or if you are reading about the arrival of Asian immigrants in America, as in Ronald Takaki's "A Different Mirror" (pp. 653–664), it may help you to imagine some of the situations you or your own family might have experienced in coming to the United States.

Two ways to trigger prior knowledge and experiences are *freewriting* and *brainstorming*. To freewrite, jot down anything that comes to mind about a topic. Write nonstop for five or ten minutes without worrying about usage or spelling. Put down whatever you want. Brainstorming uses a process of free association. Start the process by skimming the reading source and listing key words or phrases. Then run down the list and record associations that come to mind when you think about these target concepts. Don't bother to write complete sentences; just write down words and phrases. Give your imagination free rein.

For an example, look at the freewriting and brainstorming of our student as she proceeded.

EXCERPT FROM FREEWRITING

I wonder how Robinett thinks virtual reality could "expand human perceptions." I tried a virtual reality system in a shopping mall arcade last summer; it was sort of a fancy video game where you tried to hunt down and shoot your opponent while avoiding a huge flying dinosaur. While the graphics were no better than my home video game, the system gave me the sense that I actually <u>was</u> a character in the game rather than merely controlling a character on the screen. It was almost like stepping inside the television screen and taking part in the action yourself. I guess that this could be a form of expanded perceptions since you actually perceive the artificial world of the computer game from the perspective of a game character. Is this what is meant by the term "cyberspace"?

EXCERPT FROM BRAINSTORMING LIST

1. Virtual reality (def. in 1st sentence of article)
2. Head-Mounted Display (I wore one of these in the arcade)
3. "Expansion of perception" (Does this refer to sensory perception?)
4. Ultrasound scanners (Ultrasound is used to examine fetuses)
5. Real-Space Databases (????????? I can't imagine a database in "real space")
6. Remote Presence (same as telepresence?)
7. Green Man project (Isn't Green Man a Celtic wood sprite?)

Once you use freewriting or brainstorming to tap into what you already know about a topic, you will better understand the material and read more objectively. You will also be more conscious of your opinions and biases and less likely to confuse them inadvertently with those of the author. You may also find that freewriting helps break ground for the paper that you will eventually write. The ideas that you summon in freewriting can generate ideas for comparison, contrast, reinforcement, or contestation in your paper. As an argumentative "other" voice that helps to test the claims of your reading, a piece of freewriting can show the direction that your further reading and rewriting might take.

CLOSE READING

When you read, you are actively constructing meaning. You are not a passive decoder who transfers graphic symbols from the written page to your mind. You are taking part in two-way communication. Visualize and "talk" directly to the author. Let the author know what you are thinking, and ask questions when you need more information or have difficulty understanding.

To keep the interaction between you and the author dynamic, read with pencil in hand, annotating and elaborating on particular ideas, taking separate notes, and posing and answering questions. To illustrate, we will apply these strategies to Warren Robinett's article in the examples that follow.

Annotate and Elaborate on the Source

Annotate by making marginal notes, underlining, or highlighting important concepts and your own responses to them. *Elaborate* on the sources by drawing on your knowledge and experiences to extend, illustrate, or evaluate the particular ideas. You can apply ideas in the text to situations the writer does not envision or you can provide analogies, examples, or counter examples of ideas. Note how one of our students annotated and elaborated on a passage from Warren Robinett's "Electronic Expansion of Human Perception."

Passage from Robinett	*Student Annotations*
Virtual reality will prove to be a more compelling fantasy world than Nintendo, but even so, the real power of the Head-Mounted Display is that it can help you perceive the world in ways that were previously impossible. To see the invisible, to travel at the speed of light, to shrink yourself into microscopic worlds, to relive experiences— these are the powers that the Head-Mounted Display offers you. Though it sounds like science fiction today, tomorrow it will seem as commonplace as talking on the telephone.	Is fantasy a good thing? The author's conclusion Examples ??? No way!!!

ELABORATION OF THE ROBINETT PASSAGE

I don't doubt that virtual reality can provide "a more compelling fantasy," but is this a good idea? My younger cousin is so obsessed with Nintendo that he ignores school work, physical activity, and friendships. Virtual reality, if it is even "more compelling," might intensify his addiction. We studied addictive behaviors in my high school psychology class, and the psychological profiles of those obsessed with video games are similar, in several ways, to those of substance abusers.

You might want to record your elaborations in a notebook or reading journal. This record will be particularly useful if you intend to write a paper that gives your view on the ideas in the source. It will certainly help your critical analysis of the reading material by pointing to passages that raised questions, offered insights, and provoked your responses the first time you read them.

When you annotate, do not overuse highlighting markers. It is hard to decide what is important as you read through a text for the first time. Every concept may seem significant. But if you highlight a large percentage of the text, you will have a lot to reread when you study for an exam or look for ideas to put in a paper. Another problem with highlighting is that it is a mechanical process that does not actively engage you with the text. It merely gives the illusion that you are reading effectively. Write out summary statements and reactions instead of just highlighting important ideas. Writing makes you process the information, restate it in your own words, and react to it. The ultimate goals of any annotating process are to involve you intellectually with the text and to give you access to it without rereading. Writing out marginal or separate notes is the best way to accomplish this.

Take Content Notes

When you encounter difficult sources, you may want to take separate notes that will supplement your annotations and elaborations. These notes can be in the form of outlines, summaries, or paraphrases of key passages, lists of particularly significant pages or paragraphs, or any combination of these elements.

When you are taking notes, pay special attention to *thesis statements* and *topic sentences*. The thesis is the focal point of the entire piece: the major point, position, or objective the author demonstrates or proves. The main idea of a paragraph or another subdivision of the text is often expressed in a topic sentence. Both the thesis and the topic sentences may include more than one sentence, so do not assume that you should always search for a single sentence. Nor should you make assumptions about their location. The thesis statement is typically in the introductory paragraph, but it can also appear elsewhere in the piece. Topic sentences are not always at the beginnings of paragraphs; they can appear in the middle or at the end as well. Some paragraphs do not contain explicit topic sentences; the main idea is implied through an accumulation of details, facts, or examples.

If sources are easy to read and have straightforward content, you can streamline note-taking and annotating procedures to capture only the most basic ideas. But remember that it is natural to forget much of what you have read; even relatively simple ideas can slip from your memory unless you record them in notes or annotations. And of course, when you are working with library sources, note taking is indispensable.

Pose and Answer Questions About the Source

A useful method for note taking is to pose questions about the text and attempt to answer them as you read. Questions provide you with goals for obtaining information from the reading source. If you are reading a textbook chapter, first look at the reader aids: the preview outline at the beginning, the introductory or concluding sections, and the review questions at the end. Also check out chapter or section headings for the concepts or issues that the chapter covers. Using these reader aids, generate some questions about what the chapter will be about, and answer them as you read. This strategy works best if you record your answers as you locate the relevant material. Write your answers in a reading journal so that you can return to them later and find the important ideas you took away from the reading. Too often, students spend hours reading only to find several days later that they remember virtually nothing and must reread all the material. Although it takes extra time to pose and answer questions, it can reduce time spent rereading texts.

A powerful strategy that will increase your chances of understanding even difficult reading sources is to ask questions about three specific aspects of the source: (1) information, (2) form, organization, and expository features, and (3) rhetorical concerns. When you ask these questions, you will be reading in three different but not necessarily separate ways. Skilled readers use all three strategies simultaneously and harmoniously.

Reading for Information

To read for information, ask the following questions:

> What has the author written?
> What is the main idea?
> What other content is important?

To ask pointed questions about information or content will enable you to set specific goals, to read with an active purpose rather than merely trying to get through all the words on the page. An example of assertive reading is the strategy that our student Sarah Allyn used when she wrote a paper on "Communitarianism Contested" (see pp. 115–120). Instead of accepting the positions of Etzioni, Little, and Walzer in their essays on communitarianism in this anthology (see Chapter 11), Sarah developed the opposite position that "communitarians are working to realize a society bereft of many of the hard-fought liberties achieved in our national Constitution." She began to formulate her ideas at the stage of close reading when, as her notes reveal, she started to question Etzioni's remarks about coercion as he presents them on pages 514–521. Her questioning led to a series of rebuttals that finally enabled her to produce a statement of her own position.

Reading for Form, Organization, and Expository Features

To identify form, organization, and expository features, you will want to ask questions about how the text functions and what the author is *doing* as well as saying; for example:

> How has the author written the piece?
> Is the author using an identifiable form or genre?
> How do the different parts function?
> How is the text organized?
> What are the text's distinctive characteristics?
> Does the author use any special conventions?

Often it is easy to categorize or classify a piece of writing because it has certain regularities. We all recognize the distinguishing characteristics of literary genres, such as short stories, novels, and poems, and the conventions of nonliterary forms, such as thank-you notes, do-it-yourself manuals, or gossip columns. Academic writing also takes identifiable forms. Some, such as the psychological research article, the scientific lab report, and the philosophical essay of reflection, are quite specialized. Others, such as the forms listed here, are more generic.

Response	Essay using comparison and contrast
Synthesis	Analysis
Argument	Evaluation
Research paper	Literature review

We will describe each of these forms in detail in Chapters 2 through 5.

Just as you already know something about the different forms that texts take, you are probably aware that many texts regularly have recognizable parts, such as introductions, conclusions, theses or main-idea statements, topic sentences, and paragraphs. Texts are also arranged in identifiable patterns. Most likely, you have organized your own essays using some of the common patterns listed here:

Time order, narration, process	Example
Antecedent-consequent, cause-effect	Analysis/classification
	Definition
Description	Analogy
Statement-response	Argument/evaluation,
Comparison/contrast	problem-solution

As you read, be mindful of the text's form, parts, and organizational pattern. Continually ask yourself such questions as "Where does this introduction end?" "What point is the author making in this paragraph?" "Will the author explain the causes after having described the effects?"

In addition to identifying form and organizational patterns, proficient readers pay attention to the distinctive expository features, stylistic qualities, and particular characteristics of texts. They will observe, for example, that scholarly writers often draw extensively on evidence from published sources or original research that they carefully document. Such readers will expect academic writers to adopt rather formal voices and use sentences with a number of coordinated and parallel elements. They will notice when academic writers use conversational, less formal styles or deviate from accepted conventions.

As you become more familiar with academic writing, you will expect particular texts to be organized in certain ways and you will look for special textual features. For example, once you are acquainted with writing on technological innovation, the subject of the first three chapters in our anthology, you will automatically look for discussions of the costs and benefits of new technologies whenever you read articles on this topic. You will know from your past experiences as a reader that articles on new technology often include, or are entirely structured as, a costs/benefits analysis. You will also take note of any special terminology associated with the technology because you will know that technical vocabulary changes constantly and that mastering the current "buzzwords" is crucial. You will also try to find experimental verification of any new, startling conclusions or look for references to other work in the field. These are just a few of the strategies that skilled readers of technical literature might use.

Reading for Rhetorical Concerns

Skilled readers are interested in rhetorical concerns as well as in information and textual features (Haas and Flower 167–83). When we speak of rhetoric in this book, we mean an author's attempt to use language to achieve an intended effect. An important word here is "intended." Both writing and reading are intentional. They are deliberate actions, and each is guided by a purpose or goal. As you read to discover the rhetorical context, ask yourself five questions:

> What prompted the author to write?
>
> What community of readers is the piece intended for?
>
> What impact does the author want to have on the reader?
>
> What role does the author assume with regard to the audience, the subject matter, and his or her own voice?
>
> How does the author view what others have said on the topic?

Answers to these questions help define the rhetorical purpose and the context of the piece. The writer's purpose may not be obvious, but if you ask the right questions, you will be able to discover the imperative— the feeling, view, incident, or phenomenon—that inspired the author to write. For example, consider once again Warren Robinett's "Electronic

Expansion of Human Perception." Robinett's biography suggests that he has a professional commitment to virtual-reality technology, and the text of his article refers frequently to work on virtual reality being done at his workplace. It seems reasonable to infer that at least part of his goal as a writer is to promote the research that he and his colleagues are doing. This does not mean that Robinett is distorting the truth in any way. But, if we were contrasting Robinett's article with one that is less enthusiastic about virtual reality, it might be useful to take into consideration each writer's rhetorical goals.

INDIVIDUAL EXERCISE ON ACTIVE READING

Read Jeremy Rifkin's "The Age of Simulation" on pages 284–294 (or another article of your choice from Chapter 7 or 8) using the active reading strategies described on pages 5–15. Write out answers to the questions on information (p. 12); form, organization, and expository features (p. 12); and rhetorical concerns (p. 14).

COLLABORATIVE EXERCISE ON RHETORICAL READING

1. In preparation for class, each student should read Gene Stephens's "High-Tech Crime Fighting: The Threat to Civil Liberties" on pages 313–322 (or another article from Chapter 7 or 8).
2. Form collaborative learning groups of five students each, as described in the Preface, or fashion groups according to a method of your own.
3. Work collaboratively to answer the following questions about the author's rhetorical purpose. The group recorder should write out your answers.
   a. What prompted the author to write?
   b. What community of readers is the piece intended for?
   c. What impact does the author want to have on the reader?
   d. What role does the author assume with regard to the audience, the subject matter, and his or her own voice? How does the author view what others have said on the topic?
4. Reconvene the entire class. Have each group recorder read the group's answers to the four rhetorical reading questions. After all have been heard from, the entire class can discuss any points on which various groups disagree.

POSTREADING

Review the Source and Your Notes

Once you have finished the last page of reading, resist the temptation to lay the book aside and move on to another activity. Take a few minutes to reinforce your understanding by briefly reviewing the source, scanning through your annotations, and looking through your elaborations and notes. Don't hesitate to revise or add to your annotations, elaborations, and notes as you review them. Remember that you can best perform this review activity immediately after reading the text.

Compose Paraphrases and Summaries and Record Quotations That May Be Useful at a Later Date

Whenever you intend to draw on reading sources in your future writing, take some time immediately after reading to paraphrase, summarize, or quote passages that may be particularly useful. You will continue to paraphrase, summarize, and quote as you compose and revise your essay, but you are best prepared to do this while the reading is still fresh in your mind. Remember that one of the chief goals of active reading is to eliminate the need for rereading the source when you sit down to draft your essay.

Paraphrasing

When you *paraphrase* a sentence, a paragraph, or some other segment from a reading, you translate the entire piece into your own words. Paraphrasing is a powerful operation for academic writing, but often students do not use it enough. Too many beginning academic writers use direct quotations whenever they refer to information from a reading source. Direct quotations are necessary only when you need the precise wording of the original. We will discuss some of the reasons for quoting later in this chapter. Because paraphrasing is an active process that forces you to grapple with the author's ideas, it promotes comprehension. It is no wonder that many professors ask students to paraphrase rather than quote. They know that if you can paraphrase the material in a reading source, then you must be able to understand it.

A paraphrase differs from a summary in that a paraphrase includes *all* the information in the original, whereas a summary contains only the *most important* information. Paraphrase when you want to record the total, precise meaning of a passage. If you are interested in only the gist, summarize it. In general, relatively small sections of the original, often a sentence or two, are paraphrased, and larger chunks of information are summarized.

Paraphrasing requires you to make substantial changes to the vocabulary and sentence structure of the original. It is not enough to substitute a few synonyms and keep the same sentence structure and order of ideas. The following examples, based on an excerpt from Michael Heim's "From Interface to Cyberspace," show adequate and inadequate paraphrases.

> *Original Sentence:* Virtual-reality systems can use cyberspace to represent physical space, even to the point that we feel telepresent in a transmitted scene, whether Mars or the deep ocean.
>
> *Inadequate Paraphrase:* Virtual-reality systems can represent physical space by using cyberspace, even to the extent that people feel telepresent in a scene that is transmitted, perhaps Mars or the deep ocean (Heim 80).
>
> *Adequate Paraphrase:* We can achieve the illusion of being present in remote locations, for example the planet Mars or deep parts of the ocean, by using virtual-reality equipment that creates a cyberspace representation of real-world space (Heim 80).

The writer of the inadequate paraphrase reshuffled the words in the original sentence but retained the vocabulary, sentence structure, and order of ideas. If you do not intend to make major changes to the passage, then quote it word for word. There is no acceptable middle ground between a paraphrase and a direct quotation. An inadequate paraphrase is considered a form of *plagiarism*, since it is interpreted as an attempt to pass off another writer's sentence structure and words as one's own.

You can sometimes paraphrase simply by rewriting the original passage for a new audience. To illustrate, look at an excerpt from "Being and Believing: Ethics of Virtual Reality," a medical journal editorial. The sentence describes a computer-based system (virtual reality) designed to simulate a real-world situation.

> The overall effect was that the observer experienced a computer-generated artificial or virtual reality (VR) whose credibility depended largely on the agreement between the simulated imagery and the familiar sensible world. (283)

Suppose that your objective is to paraphrase the sentence for an audience of high school students. Because you do not want to talk over the students' heads, you put the sentence into simpler language.

> The effectiveness of a virtual reality system depends upon the extent to which it can create an environment of computer images that appear life-like ("Being and Believing" 283).

You should notice that in this example the parenthetical documentation gives an abbreviated article title rather than an author's name. That is because the article was written by the medical journal's editorial staff and was not attributed to a specific author. To learn more about documentation conventions, see the Appendix.

As the example demonstrates, paraphrasing will often require you to express abstract ideas in a more concrete form. When a passage includes difficult concepts or complex language, it may be hard to reword it and still preserve the original meaning. You will need a more systematic paraphrasing procedure, such as the one in the following box:

PARAPHRASING STRATEGIES

1. Locate the individual statements or major idea units in the original.
2. Change the order of major ideas, maintaining the logical connections among them.
3. Substitute synonyms for words in the original, making sure the language in your paraphrase is appropriate for your audience.
4. Combine or divide sentences as necessary.
5. Compare the paraphrase with the original to assure that the rewording is sufficient and the meaning has been preserved.
6. Weave the paraphrase into your essay in accordance with your rhetorical purpose.
7. Document the paraphrase.

Keep in mind that paraphrasing is not a lockstep process that always follows the same sequence. You may use fewer than all seven strategies, and you can vary the order in which you apply them. For illustration, however, we are going to paraphrase a sentence from Carl Sagan's article

"In Defense of Robots," using all the strategies in approximately the order given in the box. Let's assume that we are writing for an audience of first-year college students. The excerpt is taken from page 257.

> There is nothing inhuman about an intelligent machine; it is indeed an expression of those superb intellectual capabilities that only human beings, of all the creatures on our planet, now possess.

Locate the individual statements or major idea units

First, we will determine how many major ideas are presented in the passage. We find two central units of information: (1) an assertion about intelligent machines (they are not "inhuman") and (2) an argument to back up the assertion (that the ability to produce these machines demonstrates humans' unique intelligence).

1. There is nothing inhuman about an intelligent machine;
2. it is indeed an expression of those superb intellectual capabilities that only human beings, of all the creatures on our planet, now possess.

Change the order of major ideas, maintaining the logical connections among them

Now we will change the order of the two units of information, placing the second before the first. To accomodate this switch, we substitute the noun phrase "an intelligent machine" for "it" so the subject is clear at the outset of the sentence. Then we add "which demonstrates that" to indicate the logical relationship between the two units.

1. An intelligent machine is indeed an expression of those superb intellectual capabilities that only human beings, of all the creatures on our planet, now possess;
2. which demonstrates that there is nothing inhuman about an intelligent machine.

Substitute synonyms for words in the original

Think about your audience at this stage. Sagan's original language is relatively easy to understand, but when the words in the original source are too formal or sophisticated, you may want to choose vocabulary more accessible to your readers.

Begin your search for synonyms *without* consulting a dictionary or a thesaurus. Many students rush to such reference books and copy synonyms without considering how they fit into the general sense of the sentence. Paraphrases filled with synonyms taken indiscriminately from a dictionary or a thesaurus can be awkward and confusing.

As a rule of thumb, do not repeat more than three consecutive words from the original. You may occasionally need to repeat a word or a phrase, but whenever possible, substitute synonyms for the original words. It is not necessary to locate a substitute for every word in the sentence you are paraphrasing. Repeat words that are central to the meaning or have no appropriate synonyms, such as the term "inhuman" in our example.

As we return to our example, by substituting synonyms, doing a little more rearranging, and providing context where necessary, we arrive at the following paraphrase.

> Since artificial intelligence results from humans beings' unique intellectual talents, the technology should not be regarded as inhuman (Sagan 292).

Combine or divide sentences as necessary

Although there is no particular need to divide our paraphrase, for illustration we will split it into two short sentences.

> Artificial intelligence results from humans beings' unique intellectual talents. Thus, the technology should not be regarded as inhuman (Sagan 292).

Compare the paraphrase with the original

Compare the paraphrase with the original sentence to see if you have reworded sufficiently yet have retained the meaning of the original.

> *Original:* There is nothing inhuman about an intelligent machine; it is indeed an expression of those superb intellectual capabilities that only human beings, of all the creatures on our planet, now possess.
>
> *Paraphrase:* Since artificial intelligence results from humans beings' unique intellectual talents, the technology should not be regarded as inhuman (Sagan 292).

In this case, the paraphrase seems adequate. In other cases, you might need to revise the paraphrase, possibly by reapplying one of the strategies we have already discussed.

Weave the paraphrase into your essay

Weave the paraphrase into your essay in a way that helps further your rhetorical purpose. Consider the following example.

EXCERPT FROM ESSAY

> Even though we live in a technologically advanced society, many Americans still feel uncomfortable with the idea of machine intelligence. Science fiction abounds with stories of computers whose "inhuman" logic poses a threat to human values. But as Sagan points out, since artificial intelligence results from humans beings' unique intellectual talents, the technology should not be regarded as inhuman (292). These thinking machines are an extension of our own abilities rather than a challenge to our humanity.

Notice that we did not plop the paraphrase into the paragraph. Since Sagan's view contrasts with the preceding sentence, we began with the word "But." Then, we attributed the material to Sagan by writing "as Sagan points out." At the end of the sentence, we provided the page number in parentheses. We cannot be sure that a paraphrase is successful unless we see that it fits smoothly into the essay for which it was intended.

Document your paraphrase

Failing to document a paraphrase is considered plagiarism, an offense that can lead to failure and permanent expulsion. Always cite the author of the source, enclose in parentheses the page numbers of the information you paraphrased, and provide an entry on the Works Cited page. Notice how we documented the paraphrase in the preceding example.

INDIVIDUAL EXERCISE ON PARAPHRASING

1. Apply the steps in the Paraphrasing Strategies box (p. 18) to the following passage taken from Gary Marx's "Privacy and Technology" (Chapter 8). Work through the steps in the process one by one and record the results of each step, just as we did on pages 19–21 with the sentence from Carl Sagan's article. Write your paraphrase for an audience of first-year college students who have not read the article.

   > Just as free association led to discovery of the unconscious, new techniques reveal bits of reality that were previously hidden or contained no informational clues. When their privacy is invaded, people are in a sense turned inside out, and what was previously invisible and meaningless is made tangible and significant (paragraph 6).

2. Revise your paraphrase.
3. Submit not only the final paraphrase but also all the preliminary work produced at each stage of the paraphrasing process.

COLLABORATIVE EXERCISE ON PARAPHRASING

1. Form collaborative learning groups of three students each, as described in the Preface, or fashion groups according to a method of your own.

2. Have each group member take responsibility for one of the following sentences from Gary Marx's "Privacy and Technology" (Chapter 8). *Do not read any sentences other than the one you are responsible for.*

    a. Those unconcerned about privacy remind us that we live in an open society that believes that visibility in government brings accountability (paragraph 24).

    b. Noting the social functions of privacy certainly is not to deny that privacy taken to an extreme can be harmful (paragraph 26).

    c. The private subversion of public life carries dangers, as does the public intrusion into private life (paragraph 27).

3. Use the steps listed in the Paraphrasing Strategies box to come up with a paraphrase of your sentence. Write your paraphrase for an audience of first-year college students who have not read the article.

4. When all group members have finished their paraphrases, pass the sheet with your paraphrase to the person on your left and receive the paraphrase of the person on your right. On a new sheet of paper, paraphrase the sentence you received from the person on your right. *Do not refer to the original sentence in the book.*

5. When all group members have finished their paraphrases, pass sheets once more to the left and once again paraphrase the sentence you receive.

6. Your group should now have serial paraphrases that have gone through three versions for each of the sentences from Marx. Working together, compare the original of each sentence with the final version of the paraphrase. Does the paraphrase preserve the meaning of the original? If not, where did the meaning get lost? Which steps in the paraphrasing process worked well and which were problematic? Make sure your group recorder notes the conclusions the group comes to.

7. When the class reconvenes, have the recorders explain the conclusions groups came to about the paraphrasing process.

Summarizing

Whether you are writing a synopsis of a piece of literature, an abstract of a journal article, a précis of an argument, or some other type of summary, the fundamental task is to shorten the original without changing its meaning. Whether summaries are brief or comprehensive, they are attempts to capture the overall gist of the source.

SUMMARIZING STRATEGIES

1. Preview the source and recall your prior knowledge of the topic.
2. Read the source using active reading strategies (annotating, elaborating, taking content notes, and posing and answering questions).
3. Identify and emphasize the most important ideas and the significant connections among those ideas.
4. Construct a graphic overview.
5. Delete unimportant detail, irrelevant examples, and redundancy.
6. Combine ideas in sentences and paragraphs.
7. Identify and imitate the organizational pattern of the source.
8. Identify and incorporate the rhetorical context and the author's rhetorical purpose.
9. Document your summary.

You need not apply these strategies in any particular order. Nor do you have to use all seven of them for each summary you write. Simply choose ones that are appropriate for the source you are working with. You can write a short summary simply by explaining the context and the author's rhetorical purpose. Lengthy or complex summaries may require the full range of strategies.

Preview the source and recall your prior knowledge of the topic, and read the source using active reading strategies

The first two summarizing strategies recap the active reading techniques that we covered earlier in this chapter. Assertive reading is imperative for summarizing. Annotating the text to draw your attention to main ideas, taking content notes, and identifying the author's organization plan and rhetorical goal are particularly helpful preparation.

Identify and emphasize the most important ideas and the significant connections among those ideas

Your annotations and notes should direct you to the most important ideas in the text. Write out the main ideas and explain how they are related to each other. A summary is more than a retelling of main ideas; it should indicate relationships between the ideas and tie them together in coherent paragraphs.

Construct a graphic overview

Another way of identifying the principal ideas and of determining how they tie together is to *construct a graphic overview.* A graphic overview is a diagram that represents the central ideas in a reading source, shows how they are related, and indicates the author's overall purpose. You might think of it as a blueprint charting the source's main ideas.

Let's walk through the process of creating a graphic overview. First, review your reading notes and annotations and select key words and concepts. Then, try to depict the relationships among those ideas by drawing circles and boxes connected by lines and arrows. Use labels to show how the various points are interrelated. Be creative!

The graphic overview shown in Figure 1-1 was drawn by one of our students to represent the principal content of Gene Stephens's article "High-Tech Crime Fighting: The Threat to Civil Liberties," which appears in Chapter 8. You may want to read the article to get the most out of this example. As you study the example, keep in mind that creating a graphic overview is a highly individual process. A single, definitive graphic overview does not exist for each text. Countless variations are possible.

The graphic overview forces you to think about the big picture. You have to manipulate chunks of information like pieces in a puzzle and determine how they best fit together. The graphic overview allows you to visualize relationships among main ideas and perceive the web of meaning in a form other than sentences and paragraphs. Notice that the overview of Stephens's article clarifies its focus on the conflict between individual rights and societal control. This conflict is represented at the top of the diagram. Lower down in the diagram are specific examples of technologies that contribute to the conflict. You should find it easy to

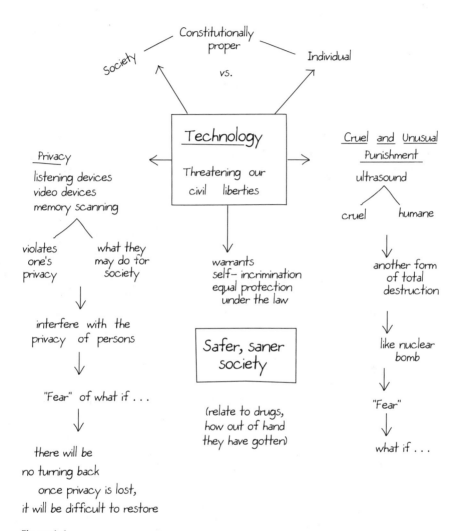

Figure 1-1

summarize this source after you have seen all its main ideas diagrammed on a single page. A special advantage of the graphic overview is that it distances you from the author's exact words and thus helps you avoid plagiarizing. You won't fall back on the author's language as you write out your summary.

Delete unimportant detail, irrelevant examples, and redundancy

Cross out or label as nonessential any material that is repetitive, excessively detailed, or unrelated to the main idea. Academic sources are often highly redundant because authors repeat or illustrate complex concepts in order to give the reader more than one chance to understand them.

Combine ideas in sentences and paragraphs

After you delete nonessential material and categorize bits of information, you are often left with disjointed pieces of text. If you want your summary to flow clearly, you have to rearrange these key ideas, make elements parallel, or add logical connectors. You may also want to compress several words or phrases into fewer words and to reduce items in the same class to a single category.

Identify and imitate the organizational pattern of the source

On page 12, we identified ten organizational plans for academic writing: (1) time order, narration, process; (2) antecedent-consequent, cause-effect; (3) description; (4) statement-response; (5) problem-solution; (6) comparison/contrast; (7) example; (8) analysis/classification; (9) definition; (10) analogy; (11) argument. Rarely do authors restrict themselves to a single plan; they usually use these plans in combination.

Once you identify how the author arranges and orders the piece, you can use a comparable pattern as the skeleton for your summary. Organization conveys meaning, so you will be helping your reader to follow the train of thought.

Identify and incorporate the rhetorical context and the author's rhetorical purpose

You may want to include in your summary information about the rhetorical context of the source and the author's rhetorical purpose. This is particularly appropriate when you are writing a summary that will stand alone rather than one that will become a part of a longer essay. To determine the rhetorical context, ask yourself the questions in the box on the next page.

Rhetorical purpose or *intention* refers to how the author tries to affect or influence the audience. Sometimes the purpose is easily identified because it emerges as a controlling feature of the piece, such as in an argumentative text or a highly opinionated editorial. At other times the author's purpose may not be self-evident.

QUESTIONS FOR DETERMINING RHETORICAL CONTEXT

1. What is the author's background? Is he or she an acceptable, credible authority?
2. What feeling, view, incident, or phenomenon brought about the need or motivated the author to write?
3. What role does the author assume in relation to the audience?
4. In what type of publication does the piece appear? If the publication is a journal, magazine, or newspaper, what is the readership?
5. When was the piece published? Is it current or dated?

Document your summary

Even when you have summarized a text in your own words, you must acknowledge the title and the author. As with paraphrasing, summarizing a source without proper documentation is considered plagiarism. Always cite the source at the point where you use it in your writing and include a complete reference in the Works Cited list at the end of your paper. We explain how to set up a Works Cited list on page 57.

We will draw on several of the strategies described above to illustrate the process of writing a brief summary. Let's assume that as you are preparing to write an essay on recent controversies over the constitutional right to privacy, you locate Gene Stephens's article "High-Tech Crime Fighting: The Threat to Civil Liberties" (Chapter 8). First, you read the article using the active strategies we have described in this chapter—carefully previewing, annotating, taking content notes, and posing and answering questions as you read. Before summarizing relevant parts of the article, you want to be sure you have a good sense of its global structure, so you decide to construct a graphic overview. Let's assume you produced the overview shown in Figure 1-1. The graphic overview makes plain Stephens's central assertion that a number of new technologies threaten civil liberties, and it shows how Stephens supports this assertion by referring to particular civil liberties and the specific technologies that endanger them. You begin your summary by writing the following account of Stephens's central assertion:

Stephens claims that certain new technologies threaten our civil liberties, and he predicts that this danger will increase in the future.

Consider next which examples are important enough to include in your summary. At this point, as the summarizing strategy suggests, you are identifying and emphasizing the most important ideas. This process also involves another summarizing strategy—deleting peripheral detail, parallel examples, and redundancy.

Next, you need to decide on an organizational plan for ordering the material you have selected from the graphic overview. Recalling the summarizing strategy of identifying and imitating the organizational pattern of the source, you return to your annotations and notes to figure out Stephens's organizational plan. A strong candidate is the cause-effect plan since Stephens describes how a variety of new technologies (cause) will endanger citizens' civil liberties (effect). You could present the relevant examples by first describing the new technologies and then relating the consequences Stephens envisions.

Finally, you locate in your question-answer notes a statement about Stephens's rhetorical purpose, which is to alert readers to the threat that technology poses to their civil liberties and to encourage them to resist intrusive technology. Here you are applying the summarizing strategy that identifies and incorporates the rhetorical context and the author's rhetorical purpose.

After adding selected examples to your paraphrase of Stephens's central idea, indicating the logical relationship between them, and ending with a statement about Stephens's rhetorical purpose, you come up with the following rough summary:

> Stephens claims that certain new technologies threaten our civil liberties, and he predicts that this danger will increase in the future. While Stephens discusses a range of civil liberties issues, the thrust of his article is on issues of personal privacy. Some of the specific technologies he mentions are ultrasensitive listening and video devices that can penetrate private homes, private computer records that can be accessed by the government, and electronic monitoring to enforce "house arrest." Stephens believes that these technologies may lead to violations of our constitutional right to privacy and protection against unwarranted search and seizure. Stephens's goal is to alert the reader to the threat technology poses to our civil liberties and encourage the reader to resist intrusive technology (20–25).

Note that we have documented the summary by using Stephens's name in the text and ending with the inclusive page numbers in parentheses.

INDIVIDUAL EXERCISE ON SUMMARIZING

1. Read an article of your choice (other than Gene Stephens's article) from Chapter 8 using the active reading strategies described on pages 5–15.
2. Decide which summarizing strategies will work best for the article.
3. Locate in this chapter the steps for the summarizing strategy you chose.
4. Work through the process to produce a 250-word summary of the article. Write for an audience of first-year college students who have not read the article.
5. Submit not only the final summary but all the preliminary work produced at each stage of the summarizing process.

COLLABORATIVE EXERCISE ON SUMMARIZING

First-Day Activities:

1. Form collaborative learning groups of five students each, as described in the Preface, or fashion groups according to a method of your own.
2. Assign to each group one of the articles from Chapter 8 (other than Gene Stephens's article). Each group should work with a different article. Group members should read their articles outside class.

Second-Day Activities:

1. Divide into collaborative groups.
2. Identify a summarizing strategy that your group agrees will work best for your article.
3. Apply the summarizing strategy, working as a group and following the steps outlined in this chapter, to produce a 250-word summary of your article. You may want to work through each step in the process together with the recorder noting the results of your discussion, or you may prefer to subdivide the task among group members and then pool your work. Write for an audience of first-year college students who have not read the article.
4. Reconvene the entire class. Each group recorder should explain what summarizing strategy the group chose and why that choice made sense, and the recorder should describe any problems that the group encountered using the strategy.

Quoting

When you compose essays based on sources, try summarizing or paraphrasing rather than stringing together endless quotations. Pack your postreading notes with paraphrases and summaries, not quotations. As a general rule, repeat passages word for word only if they are exceptionally well expressed or contain special forms of writing, such as definitions, key concepts, clever sayings, testimonials, or poetic language. When you take notes on facts and data, paraphrase the original instead of quoting it, unless its wording is particularly striking.

For convenience, we will discuss in this section how to incorporate quotations in drafts of your essay as well as how to select quotations for inclusion in your postreading notes.

Selecting quotations

A typical reason for quoting is *to retain the meaning or authenticity of the original source*. Assume you are writing about Gene Stephens's "High-Tech Crime Fighting: The Threat to Civil Liberties" (Chapter 8), an article that discusses individuals' constitutional rights. In your essay, you decide to quote directly from relevant parts of the United States Constitution. It would not be wise to paraphrase the Constitution, since the exact wording is crucial to its interpretation. When precise wording affects your argument, you need to quote.

Another purpose for quoting is *to lend support to a literary analysis*. When you analyze literature, you need to identify the specific passages that support your interpretation. To illustrate, look at how one of our students used a direct quotation to support his analysis of Mary Ann Rishel's short story "Steel Fires."

> The distinction is blurred between workmen and the steel they are producing. When Mike and Rebb, after working hard, begin to tire and lose their momentum, their fatigue is described in terms of the steel production process: "Working metal doesn't always mean it comes out strong" (11).

If the student had paraphrased Rishel's words instead of quoting them directly, the point would not come across as well.

A third purpose for quoting is *to capture exactly language that supports your point*. In his article on implanting electronic devices in humans, Gareth Branwyn quotes John Anderson, a man who had been totally deaf, about the importance of the electronic hearing implant he received.

"The silence of those three years when I was totally deaf is still deafening to me these many years later. My life was in the hearing world and it was critical for me to be able to hear like 'everyone else.' " (Branwyn 64)

This quotation lends a sense of reality to Branwyn's discussion. Anderson's exact language tells the reader much more about his attitudes than a paraphrase would reveal.

Another reason to use a direct quotation is *to employ it as a stylistic device*—for example, to open or close a paper. Michael Heim ends his article on human-machine interfaces with a quotation that makes the audience contemplate the future impact of this technology.

> In the 1960s, Jim Morrison saw the danger to sensibility in *The Lords and the New Creatures,* in which he warned: "There may be a time when we'll attend Weather Theatre to recall the sensation of rain." Back then, Morrison could not know that the Weather Theatre will soon be everywhere and that we will need lessons in recalling why we love the sensation of the rain.

A final reason for quoting is *to capture language that you find especially effective or memorable.* Notice how our student Karla Allen employs Charles Dickens's memorable lines:

> In Charles Dickens' words, "It was the best of times, it was the worst of times" (3). While big corporations were reaping larger profits than ever before, many smaller companies and individuals found themselves out of work.

Altering quotations

It is permissible to alter direct quotations, either by deleting some of the author's words or by inserting your own words, as long as you follow conventions that alert your audience to what you are doing. The sentence below, taken from an editorial in *The Lancet* entitled "Being and Believing: Ethics of Virtual Reality," was quoted in a student paper. The student used an *ellipsis,* a set of three spaced periods, to show where words were left out.

> *Editorial:* Although the motives behind clinical VR experimentation may be praiseworthy—e.g., it may replace the prescription of harmful psychotropics—the fact that experimentation may be well intended does not preclude early examination of ethical issues.

> *Student:* Using virtual reality to help disabled people extend their physical capabilities seems attractive, but it is not without pitfalls. As the editors of the medical journal *The Lancet* state, "Although the motives

```
                                                          Nelson 3

   At the end of his article Stephens reminds us of both the
   promise and threat of high-tech crime fighting.
              Once privacy is gone it will be difficult to
              restore. Once mind control is accomplished it will
              be difficult to reestablish free thought. But with
              proper safeguards the superior investigative
              techniques and more effective treatment of
              offenders that new technology offers promise a
              safer saner society for us all. (25)
         Unfortunately, Stephens overlooks important
   advantages of crime fighting technology and the
```

Figure 1-2

behind clinical VR experimentation may be praiseworthy . . . the fact that experimentation may be well intended does not preclude early examination of ethical issues" (283).

To show omission at the end of quoted material, a normal period is followed by the three spaced periods.

When you insert your own words into a quotation, signal your insertion by placing the words within brackets. Notice how our student uses this convention when she quotes from Rishel's story "Steel Fires:"

> *Rishel:* They had a hand in it. Helped make the steel. Forged. Pressed. Rolled. Cast. Hammered steel. But they didn't invent steel. They didn't design a bridge. They didn't think up new uses for steel. They weren't idea men.
>
> *Student:* But in the end, Mike does not value his own contribution to the industry. "They [laborers] had a hand in it. . . . But they didn't invent steel. . . . They weren't idea men" (13).

By inserting the bracketed word "laborers," the student clarifies the meaning of the pronoun "they."

Documenting quotations

If the quotation occupies no more than four typed lines on a page, enclose it in double quotation marks. If it is longer, set the entire quotation apart from your text by indenting it ten spaces (see Fig. 1-2).

Notice that in the long, set-off quotation in Figure 1-2, the parenthetical citation goes outside the final punctuation. For short quotations, place the parenthetical citation *between the final quotation marks and the closing punctuation.* The following example draws on Warren Robinett's article "Electronic Expansion of Human Perception" (Chapter 7).

> Robinett states, "Though it [virtual reality] sounds like science fiction today, tomorrow it will seem as common as talking on the telephone" (21).

The phrase "Robinett states" leads into the quotation and acknowledges the author. Other words to use to introduce quotations:

VERBS FOR ACKNOWLEDGING SOURCES

acknowledges, admits, adds, ascertains, asks, analyzes, assesses, argues, agrees (disagrees), addresses, answers, believes, categorizes, compares (contrasts), critiques, considers, concurs, concludes, cites, defines, delineates, describes, determines, demonstrates, discovers, evaluates, explores, examines, expounds on, emphasizes, envisions, finds, furnishes, investigates, inquires, identifies, lists, makes the case, measures, notes, observes, points out, postulates, presents, proposes, proves, questions, rationalizes, remarks, replies, refers to, reviews, reports, says, shows, states, stipulates, stresses, suggests, summarizes, surveys, synthesizes, traces, views, warns, writes

---

Of course, you can use such introductory phrases and words as lead-ins to summaries and paraphrases as well as to quotations.

Weaving quotations into your essay

You can weave a quotation into your writing in several ways. You can refer to the author in the text itself or you can place the last name within parentheses. When you refer directly to the author, you can cite the name before the quotation, within the quotation, or after it. Consider these examples from a student paper; the page numbers refer to the journal in which the article originally appeared, not to its reprinting in this anthology.

WEAVING QUOTATIONS INTO YOUR ESSAY

Here are five options:

Option a—Quotation followed by author's name:
> "Virtual reality, as its name suggests, is an unreal, alternate reality in which anything could happen" (Robinett 17).

Option b—Acknowledgment of author before the quotation:
> Robinett writes, "Virtual reality, as its name suggests, is an unreal, alternate reality in which anything could happen" (17).

Option c—Acknowledgment of author within a quotation:
> "Virtual reality, as its name suggests," states Robinett, "is an unreal, alternate reality in which anything could happen" (17).

Option d—Acknowledgment of author after a quotation:
> "Virtual reality, as its name suggests, is an unreal, alternate reality in which anything could happen," observes Robinett (17).

Option e—Acknowledgment of author in complete sentence followed by a colon:
> Robinett provides us with a concise definition of this new technology: "Virtual reality, as its name suggests, is an unreal, alternate reality in which anything could happen" (17).

Note that all five options require you to cite the page numbers in parentheses. If you are using Modern Language Association (MLA) style, the foregoing method of documentation will suffice. The style of the American Psychological Association (APA) is slightly different in that the publication date follows the author's name, and the abbreviation for *page* is always included. For example, for option *a* you would write (Robinett, 1991, p. 17) and for options *b, c, d,* and *e* (1991, p. 17).

When you use option *a*, don't forget to provide transitions between your own ideas and those of the source author. Inexperienced writers sprinkle their papers with direct quotations that have little connection with the rest of the text. You can avoid this problem by leading *into* quotations with the verbs listed on page 33.

INDIVIDUAL EXERCISE ON QUOTING

Scan Jeremy Rifkin's "The Age of Simulation" (Chapter 7) for places where the author has quoted directly. Can you make any generalizations about how Rifkin uses direct quotations to build his argument?

COLLABORATIVE EXERCISE ON QUOTING

1. Form collaborative learning groups of five students each, as described in the Preface, or fashion groups according to a method of your own.

2. Assume that your group is preparing to write a collaborative essay about interaction between humans and machines. (You will not, in fact, write the essay.)

3. Choose one group member to read aloud the first five paragraphs of Carl Sagan's article "In Defense of Robots" (Chapter 7).

4. After each paragraph, decide which sentences, if any, contain information that you might use in your essay. Which of these sentences would you paraphrase and which would you quote? Explain your decisions.

5. At the end of the small-group session, the recorder should have a list of sentences and, for each sentence, an indication of whether it would be quoted or paraphrased and why.

6. Reconvene the entire class. Have each group recorder read the list of sentences and explanations. Discuss points of agreement and difference.

WORKS CITED

"Being and Believing: Ethics of Virtual Reality." Editorial. *The Lancet* 338 (1991): 283–84.

Branwyn, Gareth. "Desire to Be Wired." *Wired* Sept./Oct. 1993: 62+.

Dickens, Charles. *A Tale of Two Cities.* New York: Pocket Library, 1957.

Haas, Christina, and Linda Flower. "Rhetorical Reading and the Construction of Meaning." *College Composition and Communication* 39 (1988): 167–83.

Heim, Michael. "From Interface to Cyberspace." *The Metaphysics of Virtual Reality.* New York: Oxford UP, 1993. 72–81.

Rishel, Mary Ann. "Steel Fires." Unpublished short story, 1985.

C H A P T E R

t w o

Writing an Essay in Response to a Source: An Illustration of the Writing Process

THE READING-WRITING PROCESS

In Chapter 1, we brought you through the first part of the academic reading-writing process by describing strategies for active reading: pre-reading, close reading, and postreading. In this chapter, we will guide you through the remainder of the process by showing you how to plan, draft, and rework essays.

OVERVIEW OF THE ACADEMIC READING-WRITING PROCESS

Active Reading

Prereading.   Preview the reading sources, freewrite about your topic, and set your goals.

Close reading.   Mark, annotate, elaborate on, and pose questions about the reading. Questions address three areas: (1) information, (2) textual form, organization, and expository features, and (3) rhetor-ical concerns.

Postreading.   Record comments, reactions, quotations, paraphrases, and summaries about the readings.

(continued on the next page)

Planning

Formulating a thesis.   Arrive at a preliminary understanding of the point you want to make in your paper.

Organizing.   Decide how you will use sources in the paper and how you will develop your argument.

Drafting

Drafting.   Weave source material (usually in the form of quotations, paraphrases, and summaries) with your own ideas to create paragraphs and, ultimately, a complete paper, typically with an introduction, a body, and a conclusion.

Reworking

Revising.   Lengthen, shorten, or reorder your paper; change your prose to make it more understandable to your reader; make sentence-level, phrase-level, and word-level stylistic changes; or, in some cases, make major conceptual or organizational alterations to incorporate what you learned during the process of drafting.

Editing.   Proofread your paper for errors in sentence structure, usage, punctuation, spelling, and mechanics and check for proper manuscript form.

As we mentioned in Chapter 1, rarely do writers methodically work their way through the reading and writing process, beginning with pre-reading and ending with editing. Sometimes they vary the sequence, or they may return repeatedly to work out particular phases. On page 8, for example, we suggested that some of your freewriting before close reading may provide a basis for your later writing about what you've read. On pages 16–21, we saw that the decision to incorporate a paraphrase rather than a direct quotation may come after you have already drafted your argument and included several quotations, or that you may later rework your paraphrase so that it sounds less like the original to which it refers. On page 28, we saw that you might add illustrative examples to your writing after you have completed substantial parts of your paper. Allow yourself flexibility, but keep in mind that some approaches to the writing process can be more productive than others. While you are drafting your essay, it would be unwise to stop every few minutes to check spelling, punctuation, or the correct usage. The result could be disjointed, disconnected prose. While drafting, you should concentrate on generating ideas. Save editing for later.

You should also be aware that writers may use different composing styles depending on their purposes. A writer completing a complex history assignment may spend much more time on prewriting activities—reading, underlining, and annotating the materials and taking notes—than a writer who is composing an essay that recalls prior knowledge or personal experience.

INDIVIDUAL EXERCISE ON THE WRITING PROCESS

1. Write a one-paragraph description of how you have composed essays in the past. You might consider the following questions: How did you come up with ideas for your writing? What organizational plans did you use? Did you create outlines? Did you write first drafts with or without summaries, paraphrases, or quotations, with or without notes? Did you ask friends, family members, or teachers to read your rough drafts? If so, what types of feedback did you receive and how did you respond? When you proofread, what specific issues of usage, spelling, punctuation, and mechanics did you focus on?

2. Now consider the overall writing process you used in the past. Over how many days did the process extend? What were the strengths of your approach to writing assignments? What were its weaknesses? What parts of the process were the easiest for you and what parts were the hardest? Write another paragraph in response to these questions.

COLLABORATIVE EXERCISE ON THE WRITING PROCESS

1. Form collaborative learning groups of five students each, as described in the Preface, or fashion groups according to a method of your own.

2. Allow ten minutes for each group member to freewrite in response to the first set of questions provided for the Individual Exercise on the Writing Process.

3. Convene your group and have each member read his or her freewriting piece. After each reading, the group should identify strengths and weaknesses in the writer's approach to the composing process. The group recorder should compile lists of strengths and weaknesses.

4. Reconvene the class. Have each group recorder read the lists of individual strengths and weaknesses. Discuss any variations in the lists.

PERSONAL RESPONSE IN ACADEMIC WRITING

Though the types of writing you usually associate with undergraduate assignments—summaries, research reports, arguments, syntheses of readings, and the like—will determine most of your activities, occasionally you will be assigned papers that are less factual and impersonal. One such typical assignment calls for a personal reaction to designated readings. Consider the following example:

> Write a brief essay in response to one of the reserve readings on the topic of immigration.

Notice that this assignment is not asking you to draw on personal experiences. Nor does it require you to refer only to the source and make minimal use of your own ideas. It asks you to relate two materials—your own views and the views of the author of the text—and in so doing to present an *informed* outlook. (Response)

The writing tasks that we will focus on in this chapter require a balance between personal expression and textual content. You could fulfill these assignments in an elementary fashion by summarizing the source and tacking on a few sentences of commentary or reaction. But there are much more interesting approaches.

To react and respond to a text, you have to explore the topic and bring your personal experience and knowledge to bear on it in a pertinent way. *Personal response* essays are sometimes called *exploratory* essays because they allow you to probe a topic and examine it by turning it around in the laboratory of your mind. You can use the topic as a catalyst for unraveling personal meaning, uncovering personal relationships, and recalling relevant memories.

You need to frame the author's message in your own context, to carry on a dialogue with the author, and to expand meaningfully on the author's ideas. Your reactions can take a number of forms. You can agree or disagree with the author's ideas, call them into question, express satisfaction or dissatisfaction with them, approve or disapprove of them, elaborate on their consequences, or speculate about them. But you must always take care to treat authors fairly and represent their ideas accurately. The assignment requires you to react in order to learn more about the issues raised in the sources, not just to get your licks in. In academic papers, personal responses should clarify issues rather than cloud the truth or manipulate readers.

ACTIVE READING STRATEGIES FOR RESPONSE ESSAYS

The active reading strategies we described in Chapter 1 work for all academic essays, including essays of response. We will not repeat those strategies here, but we will discuss a task that precedes them. It is the task of analyzing the assignment, an activity that initiates the reading and writing process but that we postponed explaining until we were ready to work with an actual writing task. We will also discuss additional elaborating techniques that are particularly useful for response essays. They include strategies for exploring the topic, expressing agreement or disagreement, comparison and contrast, criticism or interpretation, and the like.

Analyze the Assignment

Throughout your college career, you will receive a variety of writing assignments. Some will include detailed directions and explicit criteria; others will be more loosely structured and open-ended. After you read the assignment two or three times, underline key words that are crucial to your aim and purpose and ask yourself these questions:

1. What is the topic of the paper? Has the professor specified the topic and supplied all the readings? Do I have to select the readings and define and limit the topic myself?
2. What task do I have to perform? What words serve as clues to the nature of this task? The box that follows lists typical directives for assignments. As you read each directive, speculate about what you would have to do.

DIRECTIVES FOR ACADEMIC ASSIGNMENTS

abstract, agree (or disagree), analyze, appraise, argue, assess, classify, compare/contrast, convince, criticize, critique, defend, define, describe, delineate, demonstrate, differentiate, discuss, distinguish, establish cause-effect, estimate, evaluate, exemplify, explain, explore, expound on, furnish evidence, give examples, identify, illustrate, judge, list, make a case for or against, paraphrase, picture, predict, present, prove, recount, refute, relate, report, respond to, restate, review, show, solve, state, suggest, summarize, support, survey, trace

---

3. What type of paper do I have to write? Does the assignment call for a specialized form of academic writing, such as a research essay, book review, case study, or laboratory report?

4. For whom am I writing—for the professor, classmates, or some other audience? What are the audience's expectations? How much knowledge does my audience have about the topic? Is the audience familiar with the reading source? Will I have to supply background information?

5. What reading sources will I use? Will the professor allow me to include personal reactions, experiences, and subjective interpretations? Does the professor expect me to demonstrate knowledge I have acquired from lectures, discussions, or experiments as well as from readings? Am I limited in the number and kind of reference materials I can use?

6. How shall I document and list my sources? Which style sheet shall I use?

7. What is the approximate length of the paper?

8. Does the professor expect me to submit preliminary drafts as well as the final copy?

These questions will help you develop a mind-set for the assignment and define a rhetorical purpose that will direct your work. If you are unable to answer them, ask your professor for additional information. Recall the assignment we examined earlier.

> Write a brief essay in response to one of the reserve readings on the topic of immigration.

Maura Grady, one of our students who was working on this assignment, chose to respond to Ronald Takaki's "A Different Mirror" (Chapter 13). As Maura looked over the source and reread the assignment, she was able to answer most of the questions listed above, but she was unsure about how to balance the summary of the source against the personal reaction. When she discussed this issue with her professor, he cautioned her against letting the summary dominate her essay and told her to highlight her own thinking.

After analyzing the assignment once more, Maura turned her attention to her purpose for reading: to explore the topic and generate reactions to the author's ideas. She previewed Takaki's article by asking the set of questions we presented on page 6, and then she spent fifteen minutes freewriting about the issues surrounding American diversity and immigration. Next, she did a close reading of the article by underlining, annotating, and taking down notes in which she elaborated on some of

Takaki's points. These prereading, close reading, and postreading strategies are discussed in Chapter 1. Finally, she moved on to the task of elaborating on her reactions to the text so that she could draft an essay in response to the author's ideas.

Elaborate on Reading Sources

As we explained earlier, elaborating involves probing your memory and making associations between prior knowledge and the propositions in the text. Elaborations can be written as annotations in the margins of the text or as separate notes. Response essays call for a wider repertoire of elaboration strategies than we provided in Chapter 1. A complete set is presented in the box that follows.

STRATEGIES FOR ELABORATING ON READING SOURCES

1. Agree or disagree with a statement in the text, giving reasons for your agreement or disagreement.
2. Compare or contrast your reactions to the topic (for example, "At first I thought . . . , but now I think . . .").
3. Extend one of the author's points.
4. Draw attention to what the author has neglected to say about the topic.
5. Discover an idea implied by the text but not stated by the author.
6. Provide additional details by fleshing out a point made by the author.
7. Illustrate the text with an example, an incident, a scenario, or an anecdote.
8. Embellish the author's point with a vivid image, a metaphor, or an example.
9. Test one of the author's claims.
10. Compare one of the author's points with your own prior knowledge of the topic or with your own or others' experiences.
11. Interpret the text in the light of your own knowledge or experiences.
12. Personalize one of the author's statements.
13. Question one of the author's points.
14. Speculate about one of the author's points by
    a. Asking questions about the direct consequences of an idea
    b. Predicting consequences

(continued on the next page)

c. Drawing implications from an idea
d. Applying the idea to a hypothetical situation
e. Giving a concrete instance of a point made in the text
15. Draw comparisons between the text and books, articles, films, or other media.
16. Classify items in the text under a superordinate category.
17. Discover in the text relations unstated by the author.
18. Validate one of the author's points with an example.
19. Criticize a point in the text.
20. Outline hierarchies of importance among ideas in the text.
21. Make a judgment about the relevance of a statement that the author has made.
22. Impose a condition on a statement in the text. (For example, "If . . . , then. . . .")
23. Qualify an idea in the text.
24. Extend an idea with a personal recollection or reflection.
25. Assess the usefulness and applicability of an idea.

In the following example, notice how Maura embellishes Takaki's points with examples. She draws connections between this selection and the literature she has read in English class and a novel she read the previous summer.

Takaki's Article

Questions like the one my taxi driver asked me are always jarring, but I can understand why he could not see me as American. He had a narrow but widely shared sense of the past—a history that has viewed American as European in ancestry. "Race," Toni Morrison explained, has functioned as a "metaphor" necessary to the "construction of Americanness": in the creation of our national

Maura's Elaborations

Takaki's experience is summed up in an incisive little poem I just read in English class:

It must be odd
to be a minority
he was saying.
I looked around
and didn't see any.
So I said
Yeah.

Like Takaki, the poet, Mitsuye Yamada, is Japanese. I'm also reminded of identity. "America" has been defined as "white."

Snow Falling on Cedars, the novel about Japanese Americans who were interned in concentration camps during the war.

When you are preparing to write a response essay, it is best to elaborate as fully as you can by annotating the text or taking separate notes. Even if you don't use all these elaborations in your later writing, you will have a rich pool of resources at your disposal.

INDIVIDUAL EXERCISE ON ELABORATING ON READINGS

Assume that you are working on the following essay assignment:

> In her article "Designing Better Humans," Carol Foote outlines a debate over whether our society should employ eugenics to improve the human species. In a three-page essay, summarize and respond to this debate.

Turn to "Designing Better Humans" (Chapter 6). As you read the article, elaborate on your reactions in some of the ways we described on pages 42–43. Jot down your elaborations on a separate sheet of paper and submit them to your instructor.

COLLABORATIVE EXERCISE ON ELABORATING ON READINGS

1. Form collaborative learning groups of five students each, as described in the Preface, or fashion groups according to a method of your own.
2. Select a group member to read aloud, one paragraph at a time, Charles Platt's "Nowhere to Hide: Lack of Privacy Is the Ultimate Equalizer" (Chapter 8).
3. After each paragraph is read, group members should suggest elaborations, drawing on the suggestion in the Strategies for Elaborating on Reading Sources box that appears on pages 42–43. The group recorder should compile a list of these elaborations.
4. Reconvene the entire class. Each group recorder should read the group's list of elaborations. Discuss similarities and differences among the lists.

PLANNING

Active reading strategies such as freewriting, brainstorming, taking content notes, annotating, and elaborating on the text will provide you with raw materials for an essay. Your next challenge is to give form to those raw materials by finding common threads among them, organizing them, deleting extraneous or inappropriate items, and, if necessary, returning to the sources to extract more information. This is the work of planning, the stage when you impose your own rhetorical goal and begin to exercise control over the material you have collected and generated.

Formulating a Thesis

Your first move should be to establish your *preliminary* or *working thesis,* the central idea you intend to develop in your paper. Have it reflect your rhetorical purpose, the effect you want to have on the audience, and perhaps your organizational plan. In a response essay, the thesis expresses the writer's general reaction to the source, his or her agreement and disagreement, criticism and speculation, qualifications and extensions, and the like. We call the thesis "preliminary" at the prewriting stage because writers often revise their thesis statements later in the writing process.

To form a preliminary thesis, review your reading and elaboration notes as follows:

1. *See if any one type of elaboration predominates.* Are a good portion of your elaborations drawn from your personal experiences? If so, your essay could show how your experiences either validate or contradict the author's claims.

2. *See if several elaborations were triggered by one or two particular ideas in the reading.* Did you elaborate at length on a specific point in the source? If you wish, you can focus your paper on that single aspect of the topic.

3. *Classify your elaborations.* Can you sort your elaborations into workable categories and discard the rest? For example, you could star all the elaborations in which you agree or disagree with the author of the source and then work only with those as you draft your essay.

As our student Maura Grady sorts through her elaborations, she finds a predominance of instances in which she interprets Takaki's text in the light of her own experiences. She jots down the following preliminary thesis:

> Well, I agree that our history books should tell us more about the lives and accomplishments of the diverse groups that settled in the United States. But I also hope the revisionist historians give a strong voice to women, even if evidence about women's lives complicates the account of immigration.

Organizing

After you come up with a preliminary thesis, your next step is to decide what organizational format you will use. Systematically examine your freewriting, brainstorming, content notes, annotations, and elaborations. Try to derive one or more possible plans by categorizing this information and grouping related information together, to see what patterns appear. Try several different grouping schemes to find what works best. Many of the organizational plans that we presented in Chapter 1 are appropriate for response essays.

Time order, narration, process	Example
Antecedent-consequent, cause-effect	Analysis/classification
	Definition
Description	Analogy
Statement-response	Argument/evaluation,
Comparison/contrast	problem-solution

For example, if your purpose is to show the negative consequences of what an author has proposed, you might develop your essay in a cause-and-effect format. If you want to discuss the similarities and differences between the author's points and your own knowledge or experiences, you could use a plan for comparison/contrast.

Especially useful for a response essay are two variations of the statement-response plan: (1) the summary-response and (2) the point-by-point response. The procedure for each is outlined in the following boxes.

SUMMARY-RESPONSE PATTERN

Introduction

1. Identify briefly the issue(s) in the reading source that you intend to focus on.
2. Explain briefly your own view on the issue(s).

Body Paragraphs

1. Summarize the source, making sure to explain the issue(s).
2. Give reasons to support your position on the issue(s).

Conclusion

See the technique on page 56.

POINT-BY-POINT ALTERNATING PATTERN

Introduction

1. Identify briefly the issue(s) in the source that you intend to focus on.
2. Explain briefly your own view on the issue(s).

Body Paragraphs

1. Mention one issue, one subsection, or one main point from the source.
2. Respond to the material that was just summarized.
3. Repeat steps 1 and 2 for as many aspects of the source as you intend to treat.

Conclusion

See the technique on page 56.

As Maura studies her elaborations and other reading notes, she realizes that she wants to respond to specific points that Takaki makes with regard to women. She decides that the point-by-point alternating plan best suits her purpose, so she looks back over the annotated article and sketches out the following loose plan:

> Bring personal experience to bear on the main point I want to cover: that revisionist historians should give a strong voice to women.
>
> 1. <u>Point from Takaki</u>: In the 1800s, Chinese immigrants were predominantly male.
> 2. <u>My response</u>: This was because they were not allowed to bring wives to the U. S. Nor were they allowed to marry. What was life like for the women they left behind?
> 1. <u>Point from Takaki</u>: The Japanese men imported women as picture brides.
> 2. <u>My response</u>: Women are still imported to the United States, as brides and as childcare workers. These women's stories are worth telling.
> 1. <u>Point Takaki has neglected to mention:</u> Many immigrant women are still marginalized today.
> 2. <u>My response</u>: Let's hear their stories.

This loose plan suggests that the body of Maura's essay will contain a brief summary of Takaki's main points followed by three point-response units, the first and second beginning with a point made by Takaki and the third beginning with a point that, in Maura's view, Takaki has left out.

You might prefer to organize your notes with the *graphic overview* technique we described in Chapter 1 or with a formal outline. The graphic overview will diagram major ideas and show how they are related. It functions as an idea map for your essay. In Figure 2-1, on the next page, we have produced a graphic overview of Maura's work.

Some students are more comfortable with a *formal outline* than with graphic overviews or loose plans. Traditional outlines are based on the following structure.

    I.
        A.
           1.
               a.
                    i.
                    ii.
               b.
           2.
        B.
    II.

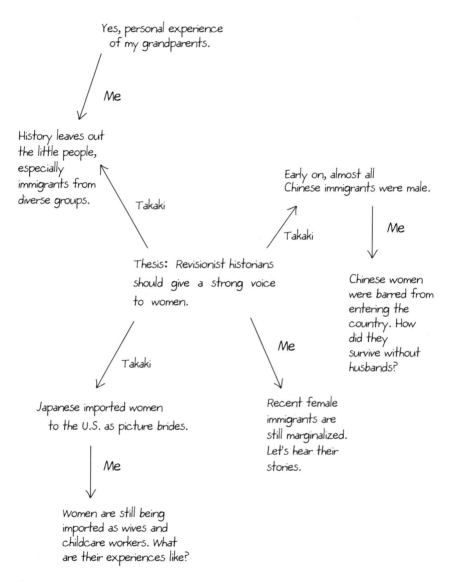

Yes, personal experience
of my grandparents.

Me

History leaves out
the little people,
especially
immigrants from
diverse groups.

Takaki

Early on, almost all
Chinese immigrants were male.

Takaki

Me

Thesis: Revisionist historians
should give a strong voice
to women.

Takaki

Chinese women
were barred from
entering the
country. How
did they
survive without
husbands?

Me

Takaki

Japanese imported women
to the U.S. as picture brides.

Recent female
immigrants are
still marginalized.
Let's hear their
stories.

Me

Women are still being
imported as wives and
childcare workers. What
are their experiences like?

Figure 2-1

The formal outline provides a clear hierarchical structure useful for imposing order on a topic that is complicated and has a number of discrete subtopics. The following is a segment of a formal outline for Maura's paper on immigration and women.

   B. Women are imported to the United States.
      1. Japanese picture brides
      2. Russian picture brides
      3. Au pairs and nannies
   C. Poor immigrant women are still marginalized.
      1. Women of color
      2. Female heads of households

DRAFTING

When you sit down to write your essay, you will find that you have already generated a fair amount of material: the freewriting you produced before reading; the annotations and elaborations you wrote in response to the source; the content notes, including summaries, paraphrases, and quotations, that you extracted from the source; and the outline or the graphic overview that you drew up when you planned your paper. Now comes the challenge. As you weave together bits of information from the reading source and your own thoughts on the topic, you may find it necessary to change, rearrange, or eliminate some of the material you have assembled. This process will be less daunting if you observe the guidelines listed in the following box.

ROUGH-DRAFT GUIDELINES

1. You need not include all your notes in your draft.
2. You don't have to follow your outline religiously or incorporate it completely.
3. You don't have to—and probably shouldn't—begin at the beginning. Many writers start with the body paragraphs and then work on the introduction and the conclusion. After all, you can't introduce a person until he or she is present, so you shouldn't expect to introduce a paper until you've written it.
4. As you revise, you should focus on higher-order concerns, such as ideas and organization, and not get bogged down with spelling, punctuation, and word choice. You can return to these lower-level concerns when you have completed the draft.

Keep these guidelines foremost in mind as you consider the six strategies for drafting, shown in the following box. Apply these strategies liberally and flexibly; drafting does not necessarily follow a set procedure or a fixed sequence.

DRAFTING STRATEGIES

1. Select and use organizational plans for individual paragraphs.
2. Weave direct quotations, paraphrases, and summaries in with your own ideas and supply proper documentation.
3. Decide on an introductory paragraph.
4. Construct a conclusion.
5. Develop a list of references or works cited.
6. Title your essay.

For convenience, we will describe the strategies in the order in which they appear in the boxed outline. We reemphasize that you need not apply them in that order. For instance, you may find it easier to begin with the introduction and then compose the body of the essay. Whatever you do, don't get stymied by a particular sequence. Try another approach if you find yourself staring at the blank page or waiting for sentences to come to you. Move on to sections you can write readily. Later you can return to the parts that caused difficulty.

Planning Individual Paragraphs

As you draft the body of your response essay, follow the organizational plan you chose at the prewriting stage: summary-response, point-by-point, or some other format. Develop each paragraph in accordance with this top-level structure. Needless to say, as you compose individual paragraphs, other organizational patterns will come into play. Most writers use multiple patterns to organize their prose. Again, we should point out that if your prewriting plan proves unworkable, or if you discover a new direction for the paper in the process of drafting, don't hesitate to rethink your organizational strategy.

Your paragraphs should be *unified* and *coherent*. Each should develop a central idea, and all the sentences should contribute to that idea in some way. Often, one or more *topic sentences* in each paragraph express the paragraph's dominant ideas. You can achieve coherence by repeating words and ideas, rewording ideas, and using transitional expressions ("also," "for example," "thus," "similarly," "consequently," and so on). All these devices show readers the logical links among sentences.

Notice how Maura Grady unifies the body paragraphs in her final draft with strong topic sentences that add coherence to the essay. Maura intentionally uses repetition to reinforce her thesis: The same topic sentence ends each paragraph. This stylistic device is called anaphora. You may recall Martin Luther King's use of anaphora in his famous refrain, "I have a dream."

Takaki tells us that more women emigrated from Japan than China because Japan had a strong government which was able to promote female emigration. Though this may be the case, when I read Takaki's account of the "predominantly male Chinese community in the United States" (248), I am reminded that these young Chinese men were segregated in all-male ghettos because exclusion laws prohibited them from bringing wives to the United States and forbade them from marrying Caucasians. Is it any wonder they turned to "prostitution, gambling, and drunkeness" (248)? How lonely it must have been for these men and how devastating for the wives they left behind in China. Few of these women ever saw their loved ones again. What hardships these impoverished women must have endured as they struggled to raise their children. I would like to hear these women's stories.

It seems the Japanese resolved the problem of male isolation by negotiating the Gentlemen's Agreement and thus paving the way for over 60,000 women to enter the United States, "many as 'picture brides'" for men they had never met (248). Though arranged marriages were consistent with Japanese custom, the prospect of crossing the Pacific to wed an older man, whom she had seen only in a picture, must have been daunting and traumatic to a young Japanese woman. Such arrangements still exist. An acquaintance of my father recently "sent for" and married a Russian woman he had selected from a catalog of picture brides. A more common practice is for professional couples to recruit au pair girls and nannies from other countries. Employment agencies have placed thousands in American families, sometimes as illegal aliens in inadequate conditions earning inadequate pay. I would like to hear these women's stories.

Despite great strides in many areas, poor women, especially immigrants, are marginalized today. Women of color are still in the lowest paid jobs in the nation, and

```
female heads of families and their children constitute the
poorest of the poor. New welfare legislation will require
millions of these women to join the workforce, yet
childcare facilities are dreadfully scarce. I would also
like to hear these women's stories.
```

If you are using the point-by-point pattern to structure your essay, you might not need to include a summary of the source. Instead, simply mention the main points to which you are reacting. If you include a summary, the length depends on your purpose. You may want to provide your readers with a comprehensive summary that covers all the major aspects of the source, or you may want just to focus in on the aspects that concern you most. Refer to the summarizing strategies in Chapter 1. You will find them very helpful.

Remember that your objective is to integrate the summary of the source with your own ideas on the topic. Once you order and classify your ideas and establish your direction, adapt the summary to your purpose. You need not summarize the entire article, only the sections that relate to your purpose. The summary should highlight the passages that prompted your reaction and refer only incidentally to other portions of the text.

Using Quotations, Paraphrases, and Summaries

Quotations, paraphrases, and summaries are the principal ways to integrate material from sources into an essay. In Chapter 1, we covered in detail how to compose paraphrases and summaries and how to extract quotations as you take content notes. If you need to supplement your content notes with additional paraphrases, summaries, and quotations, return to those procedures. Remember that the reading-writing process is recursive. It is not uncommon for writers to read the source texts at the drafting stage.

When you employ quotations, paraphrases, or summaries at the drafting stage, be sure to differentiate them from your own words and to cite the sources, as we described in Chapter 1. Always provide your readers with some identification of the source, usually the author and the page number and, if necessary, the title. The reason for including this information is to allow interested readers to locate the complete reference in the list of sources at the end of the paper. Be sure you are aware of the documentation style that your professor requires.

Writing Introductory Paragraphs

A strong introduction ought to interest readers, announce the topic, disclose a thesis or an attitude toward the topic, and establish the writer's voice. It may also, when appropriate, present background information essential to understanding the topic and indicate the writer's plan.

The opening sentences of an essay are crucial. They should engage the readers and encourage them to read on. These initial sentences also establish the writer's voice as formal or informal, academic or conversational. Some forms of academic writing require you to write in a very professional voice and open your paper in a designated way. For instance, research studies often begin with a one-paragraph abstract or summary of the study's principal findings, which is written in formal, objective language. Response essays give you much more freedom. If you wish, you can use an informal opening that speaks directly to the reader.

There are several openers you could use. For example, if you were writing an essay on cloning human beings, you could open it with a quotation from the reading source.

> "Human embryos are life-forms, and there is nothing to stop anyone from marketing them now, on the same shelves with Cabbage Patch dolls" (Ehrenreich 86). Perhaps we are headed for a future where, as Ehrenreich suggests, we will purchase rather than bear our children?

Or you could start out with an anecdote, a brief story, or a scenario.

> Imagine that you are a clone, an exact copy, of either your mother or your father rather than a combination of genetic material from both of them.

Alternatively, you might begin by providing background information.

> Cloning, a genetic process that makes it possible to produce an exact, living replica of an organism, has been applied to simple organisms for years. Now it is possible to clone complex animals, even human beings.

Other opening strategies might begin with a question, a fact or a statistic, a generalization, a contradiction, or a thesis statement. Avoid opening with clichés or platitudes ("As we contemplate cloning, we should remember that fools rush in where angels fear to tread"), dictionary definitions ("According to *Webster's International Dictionary*, 'cloning' is . . . "), or obvious statements ("Cloning is a very controversial topic").

As you work on the introduction, leave open the possibility of revising the preliminary thesis that you derived at the planning stage (p. 45). Make sure that it still expresses your main idea. You don't have to situate the thesis in any particular place. Although the thesis statement often occurs toward the end of the introduction, after the opening explanation of the general topic and identification of the source, it can occur elsewhere, even at the beginning of the introductory paragraph. Wherever you place it, be sure that you express it adequately and provide your reader with enough context to understand it fully. In academic writing, a thesis statement may occupy several sentences. The complex issues that academic essays deal with cannot always be formulated adequately in a single sentence.

Just as the thesis statement can consist of more than one sentence, the introduction can comprise more than one paragraph. Notice how Maura Grady opens the final draft of her essay with two introductory paragraphs. The first stresses the significance of her personal experience; the second identifies the key topic the paper will address and presents Maura's thesis statement.

> I am a second-generation American. My grandparents emigrated to the United States from the west of Ireland in the 1920s to pursue the American Dream and make a better life for their children. Like most immigrants, they came to this country to labor in low-paying jobs, the Kellys as cab driver and domestic worker, the Gradys as longshoreman and laundress. I never read about "little people" like them in my history textbooks. Textbook writers must think along the same lines as the Irish maid in Ronald Takaki's A Different Mirror: " 'I don't know why anybody wants to hear my history. . . . Nothing ever happened to me worth tellin'" (15).
>
> Historically, women fortunate enough to gain entry into the United States, women like my grandmothers--Irish maids, Chicana cleaners, and Japanese "wives who [did] much of the work in the fields"(251)--have been even more silenced than their male counterparts. The women whom male immigrants left behind--wives and lovers barred from entering the country-- have never had the opportunity to tell their tales. As revisionist historians, Takaki and others, relate the stories of the "little people," I hope they remember to give

```
women a strong voice. I want my daughters to be able to look
into the " 'mirror' of history" and through the lens of the
present to see "who [women] have been and hence are" (16) and
what they have the potential to become.
```

Lengthy articles in scholarly journals often have a multiparagraph subsection labeled "Introduction" that includes information needed to understand the thesis statement. Sometimes a complex paper opener requires a separate paragraph. For instance, an essay that evaluates the social consequences of cloning human beings might begin with a dramatized scenario, perhaps a description of a family in which the children were clones of their parents, to provide a test case for the author's argument. The details of this scenario might require one or more paragraphs. These opening paragraphs would be followed by a paragraph that zeroes in on the topic and presents the thesis.

Writing Conclusions

The concluding paragraph should do more than recapitulate the high points of the discussion that precedes it. A summary of the main points is justified, but you should also use techniques such as (1) stressing the significance of your thesis rather than simply repeating it; (2) predicting the consequences of your ideas; (3) calling your readers to action; and (4) ending with a question, an anecdote, or a quotation.

Notice how Maura closes her final draft with a quotation from Takaki and a prediction about the consequences of her proposal.

```
Takaki quotes Leslie Marmon Silko's precaution:
    I will tell you something about stories . . .
    They aren't just entertainment.
        Don't be fooled (15).
As readers, it may be difficult for some of us to step outside
the familiar histories we learned in school to enter the
stories of women whose lives are "worth tellin'." To identify
with the storyteller, we will have to cross barriers of race,
gender, and class. Our reward will be a better understanding
of history and ourselves.
```

Preparing Lists of References or Works Cited

At the end of your paper, construct a list of sources that includes complete information on anything you quote, paraphrase, summarize, or allude to in the text of your essay. The list should contain an entry for every source you use, and it should be alphabetized according to the authors' last names. The Appendix includes detailed information for setting up source lists. Maura's Work Cited list, constructed according to MLA guidelines, contains only one source since she draws only on Takaki's article.

Work Cited

Takaki, Ronald. <u>A Different Mirror: A History of</u>
    <u>Multicultural America</u>. Boston: Little, Brown, 1993.

Titling the Essay

Your title should indicate your perspective and, if possible, capture the spirit of the issue you are addressing. The title "A Response to Barbara Ehrenreich's 'The Economics of Cloning'" identifies the subject, nothing more. If you prefer a title that is less straightforward, you can choose from a number of options for deriving titles. One alternative is to let the title reflect your organizational plan. An essay that develops according to the comparison/contrast pattern might be titled thus:

The Anti-Cloning Lobby: Humanists or Hypocrites?

You could also title your paper with an apt phrase from the reading source or from your essay itself. Ehrenreich's phrase "genetic immortality" could be used to title an essay that focuses on the implications of cloning for the future of humanity. A catchy saying or a relevant quotation from some other source could also be used:

Cheaper by the Dozen: Cloning and Human Reproduction

The possibilities for titles are limited only by your creativity.

At this point, you will have finished a complete draft of your paper. Congratulations! You are now entitled to take a break from your assignment. But remember that a paper presented only in first-draft form is unlikely to earn you a high grade. A conscientiously revised paper, however, will display your writing to its best advantage. So, you must now turn to a full-scale revision of your paper before you hand it in. This last phase includes both reworking your ideas and your presentation of them and copyediting your paper for errors in standard form or usage. It can be the most rewarding phase because you will see your ideas take stronger, clearer shape and hear your voice emerge with confidence and authority. You will also find that cleaning up your grammar, spelling, punctuation, and other mechanics will reassure you about having written a good paper. First, however, it would be wise to set your first draft aside for some time before you revise it. Experience shows that you will come back to it with freshness and alertness, keen to spot weak arguments, poor evidence, awkward transitions, and stylistic mistakes that you did not realize you had made.

REVISING THE PRELIMINARY DRAFT

To varying degrees, writers revise *while* they are drafting as well as after they have produced full-blown papers. Those who do a great deal of revision as they are composing their drafts may come up with polished products that require minimal changes. Those who prefer to scratch out rough first drafts may make substantial changes as they rewrite in multiple versions. Whether you are an in-process reviser or a post-process reviser, you should keep in mind certain effective principles of revision.

Do not allow your in-process revision to interfere with your draft. Restrict in-process revising to important elements, such as ideas and organization. Check that you have a clear thesis and convincing support, and as you move from one part of the paper to another, be sure you are progressing logically, maintaining your focus, and supplying appropriate transitions. Be sensitive to your readers' needs. But leave concerns like word choice, sentence structure, punctuation, spelling, and manuscript format until after you have finished a full draft of the paper.

The best revisions do more than correct errors in usage, punctuation, and spelling. Notice how Maura revises the first version of her paper.

EXCERPT FROM MAURA'S FIRST DRAFT

```
Historically, women like my grandmothers, Irish maids,
Chicana cleaners, and Japanese "wives who [did] much of the
work in the fields" (251), have been even more silenced than
their male counterparts. As revisionist historians, Takaki
and others relate the stories of the "little people," I hope
```

they give these women a strong voice. I want my daughters to
be able to look into the "'mirror' of history" and through
the lens of the present to see "who [women] have been and
hence are" (16) and who we have the potential to become. When
I read Takaki's account of the "predominantly male Chinese
community in the United States" (248), I am reminded that
these young Chinese men were segregated in all male ghettos
because exclusion laws prohibited them from bringing wives to
the United States and forbade them from marrying Caucasians.
How lonely it must have been for these men and how
devastating for the women they left behind in China. Few of
these women ever saw their loved ones again. I would like to
hear these women's stories. It seems the Japanese resolved
the problem of male isolation by arranging marriages via
photographs. Though arranged marriages were consistent with
Japanese custom, the prospect of crossing the Pacific to wed
an older man whom one had seen only in a picture must have
been daunting and traumatic to a young Japanese woman. Such
arrangements still exist. An acquaintance of my father
recently "sent for" and married a Russian woman he had
selected from a catalog of picture brides. A more common
practice is for professional couples to recruit au pair girls
and nannies from other countries. Employment agencies have
placed thousands of them in American families, sometimes in
inadequate conditions earning inadequate pay. I would like to
hear these women's stories.

> women fortunate enough to gain entry into the United States,

> The women male immigrants left behind -- wives and lovers barred from entering the country -- have never had an opportunity to tell their tales.

Historically, women like my grandmothers--
Irish maids, Chicana cleaners, and Japanese "wives who
[did] much of the work in the fields" (251)—-have
been even more silenced than their male counterparts.
As revisionist historians, Takaki and others, relate
the stories of the "little people," I hope they remember to
give ~~these~~ women a strong voice. I want my daughters

to be able to look into the "'mirror' of history" and through the lens of the present to see "who [women] have been and hence are" (16) and who ~~we~~ they have the potential to become.

> Takaki tells us that more women emigrated from Japan than China because Japan had a strong government which was able to promote female emigration. Though this may be the case,

~~W~~When I read Takaki's account of the "predominantly male Chinese community in the United States" (248), I am reminded that these young Chinese men were segregated in all-male ghettos because exclusion laws prohibited them from bringing wives to the United States and forbade them from marrying Caucasians. How lonely it must have been for these

> Is it any wonder they turned to "prostitution, gambling, and drunkeness" (248)?

men and how devastating for the ~~women~~ wives they left behind ~~in China~~. Few of these women ever saw their loved ones again. I would like to hear these women's stories.

> What hardships these impoverished women must have endured as they struggled to raise their children ⊙

Maura revises the first paragraph by adding two qualifications that allow her to draw a distinction between women "fortunate enough to gain entry into the United States" and women "barred from entering the country." Realizing that the second paragraph begins with a vague reference to male immigration from China, she summarizes Takaki's contrasting point about female immigration policies from Japan. Then she re-words the second sentence to provide a smoother transition to the preceding sentence about immigrant women. In order to flesh out the paragraph's focus on women, she adds two additional sentences, one which draws upon the source and another which expresses her reaction. In both paragraphs, Maura also revises awkward or imprecise word choice and combines related sentences to improve unity and coherence.

Revising Ideas

When you revise your paper, your first priority should be to make changes in meaning by reworking your ideas. You might add information, introduce a new line of reasoning, delete extraneous information or details, or rearrange the order of your argument. Revision should always serve to sharpen or clarify meaning for your readers. Consider the strategies shown in the following box.

REVISING IDEAS

1. Is your paper an adequate response to the assignment?
2. Is your rhetorical purpose clear? How are you attempting to influence or affect your readers?
3. Does everything in the draft lead to or follow from one central thesis? If not, which ideas appear to be out of place? Should you remove any material?
4. Do individual passages of your paper probe the issues and problems implied by the thesis in sufficient detail? What do you need to add?
5. Will the reader understand your central point?

The process of drafting stimulates your thinking and often brings you to new perspectives. You may see links among pieces of information and come to conclusions that had not occurred to you at the planning stage. As a result, first drafts are often inconsistent; they may start with one central idea but then depart from it and head in new directions.

Do allow yourself to be creative at the drafting stage, but when you revise, make sure that your paper expresses a consistent idea throughout the entire piece. Check to see if you have drifted away from your thesis in the subsequent paragraphs or changed your mind and ended up with another position. If you have drifted away from your original goal, examine each sentence to determine how the shift took place. You may need to eliminate whole chunks of irrelevant material, add more content, or re-order some of the parts. After you make these changes, read over your work to be sure that the new version makes sense, conforms to your organizational plan, and shows improvement.

Revising Organization

When you are satisfied that your draft expresses the meaning you want to get across to your reader, check that your ideas connect smoothly with each other. Your readers should be able to follow your train of thought by referring back to preceding sentences, looking ahead to subsequent sentences, and paying attention to transitions and other connective devices. Keep in mind the organizational concerns shown in the following box.

REVISING ORGANIZATION

1. Is your organizational plan or form appropriate for the kind of paper you've been assigned? If not, can you derive another format?
2. Do you provide transitions and connecting ideas? If not, where are they needed?
3. Do you differentiate your own ideas from those of the author?
4. What should you add so that your audience can better follow your train of thought?
5. What can you eliminate that does not contribute to your central focus?
6. What should you move that is out of place or needs to be grouped with material elsewhere in the paper?
7. Do you use a paper opener that catches the reader's attention?
8. Does each paragraph include a topic sentence(s) and does all the material in this paragraph support it?
9. Does your conclusion simply restate the main idea or does it offer new insights?
10. Does your essay have an appropriate title?

Revising Style

With reference to writing, you may associate the term "style" with high works of literary art—the style, say, of a poem by John Keats or a novel by Emily Brontë. In actuality, however, every piece of writing displays a style of its own, whether it be a business report by a professional analyst or a note of reminders by a roommate or a family member. A style, a tone, a sense of voice and attitude, and above all a sense of liveliness and energy (or their absence) emerge from the writer's choice and use of words, the length and complexity of the writer's sentences, and the writer's focus on sharp, meaningful reader-based expression.

When you revise for style, you consider the effect your language choices have on your audience. Here are five ways to improve your writing style:

1. Move from writer-based prose to reader-based prose.
2. Add your own voice.
3. Stress verbs rather than nouns.
4. Eliminate ineffective expressions.
5. Eliminate sexist language.

Moving from Writer-Based Prose to Reader-Based Prose

Throughout this book, we continually stress the importance of audience. It is imperative to keep your readers in mind throughout the entire reading-writing process, especially at the revising stage. Making a distinction between writer-based prose and reader-based prose will help you attend to audience needs as you revise (Flower 19–37). Writer-based prose is egocentric because the writer records ideas that make sense to him or her but makes minimal if any effort to communicate those ideas to someone else. You can compare writer-based prose to a set of personal notes in which the writer puts down information that is meaningful personally but may not make sense to a larger audience. In contrast, reader-based prose clearly conveys ideas to other people. The writer does not assume that the reader will understand automatically but, rather, provides information that will facilitate the reader's comprehension. It is easy to forget about the audience amid all the complications in producing the first draft of an academic essay. That's why first drafts are quite often writer-based. An important function of revising is to convert this writer-based prose to something the reader can readily understand.

To illustrate writer-based prose, we have reproduced a student's reaction to two articles on computer intelligence. As you read the student essay, place checks next to the sentences that are writer-based.

Both of these articles deal with the future and the present status of the computer. Carl Sagan the author of the article "In Defense of Robots," tends to agree with Ulrich Neisser who is the author of the article "The Imitation of Man by Machine." However, one way they disagree is that Sagan thinks the present state of computers will only remain for a short time. On the other hand, Neisser believes that the status of the computer will remain the same for quite some time.

Both of these articles deal with the issue that computer intelligence is different from human intelligence. To prove that human intelligence is different, Sagan uses the example with a U.S. Senator. Neisser also agrees with Sagan by stating that a computer has no emotions, no motivation, and does not grow. Because of this, Neisser feels that this is where humans have the advantage over computers. As stated in the introductory paragraph, the authors have one contrasting belief. Sagan thinks that the computer's ability will change soon while Neisser thinks that it will be some time before that happens.

The other issue that is discussed in the articles is about the making of important social decisions. Both the writers feel that the computer being in the stage it is in should not be allowed to make social decisions. Sagan also proves this by his past example. He believes a computer shouldn't make social decisions if it can't even pass the test in the example. Neisser also goes back to his example. He also states that the computer only deals with the problems that it is given, and that it has no room for thought since it is confined just to finding the answer. Once again, the only place they seem to contrast is about the length of time it will take for the computer to be able to make social decisions.

My reaction to the articles is a positive one. I tend to agree more with Sagan than with Neisser. I feel that the rapid growth of computers will continue. And therefore it is more likely for both these issues to change.

Notice that our writer assumes the audience is familiar with both the assignment and the articles on which it is based. For example, the introduction begins "Both of these articles . . ." as if the reader knows in advance which articles will be discussed. The first sentence tells us only that the articles discuss the computer's "status," a term that conveys little to anyone who has not read the articles. The second sentence states that Neisser and Sagan agree on something but it does not indicate what ideas they supposedly share. The writer has simply failed to take into account that the reader may or may not be able to follow the train of thought. Similar failures to consider the audience occur throughout the essay. Below, we have transformed its introduction from writer-based prose to reader-based prose.

```
The articles "In Defense of Robots" by Carl Sagan and
"The Imitation of Man by Machine" by Ulrich Neisser both
deal with the computer's potential to match the intellectual
accomplishments of humans. Sagan and Neisser agree that
there is currently a wide gap between machine and human
intelligence. However, Sagan argues that the gap will
quickly narrow, whereas Neisser maintains that computer and
human intelligence will always be significantly different.
```

As you revise your first drafts, make sure that you have provided the necessary context or background for any material that you include from sources. Unless the assignment indicates that the audience has read the sources, do not assume that your readers will share your prior knowledge and experience.

Adding Your Own Voice

After you've written your paper, read it aloud. Better still, ask a friend to read it aloud to you. Does your writing sound like it's really yours? Or does it sound stiff, wooden, impersonal, colorless? Would your paper be better if it resonated with some of your spoken personality? Richard Lanham devoted his book *Revising Prose* to helping writers project their own voices and breathe life into their writing. Among his suggestions are the following:

1. If too many of the sentences wind endlessly around themselves without stopping for air, try dividing them into units of varying length.

2. Give a rhythm to your prose by alternating short sentences with longer ones, simple sentences with complex ones, statements or assertions with questions or exclamations.

3. Bring your readers into the essay by addressing them with questions and commands, expressions of paradox and wonderment, challenge and suspense.

Try these strategies. They can bring the sound of your own voice into otherwise silent writing and liven it considerably. Be careful, though. Some college instructors prefer a relentlessly neutral style devoid of any subjective personality. Proceed cautiously.

Stressing Verbs Rather Than Nouns

Pack the meaning in your sentences into strong verbs rather than nouns or weak verbs. See how the following example uses verbs and nouns. We have underlined the nouns and italicized the verbs.

> *Original:* The <u>creation</u> of multiple <u>copies</u> of an <u>individual</u> through the <u>process</u> of <u>cloning</u> *is* now an actual <u>feasibility</u>.
>
> *Revision:* <u>Scientists</u> *can* now *clone* multiple <u>copies</u> of a <u>human</u>.

The first version uses nouns to get the message across, but the revised version uses verbs. Notice that the first version contains only a single verb, *is*. *Is* and other forms of the verb *be* (*are, was, were, be, being, been*) are weak and lifeless because they draw their meaning from the nouns preceding and following them. Sentences that are structured around *be* verbs depend heavily on nouns to convey their central ideas. These "noun-style" sentences are characterized by forms of the verb *be* (*is, are,* and so on) and by nominalization. Nominalization is the practice of making nouns from verbs or adjectives by adding suffixes (*-ance, -ence, -tion, -ment, -sion, -ity, -ing*). The nouns in such sentences often appear in prepositional phrases. An additional sign of nominalization is frequent use of prepositions. In the following example, we have underlined the *be* forms, the instances of nominalization, and the prepositions in the sentence we considered earlier. Notice that the revision does not rely on *be* verbs or nominalization.

> *Original:* The <u>creation</u> <u>of</u> multiple copies <u>of</u> an individual <u>through</u> the process <u>of</u> <u>cloning</u> <u>is</u> now an actual <u>feasibility</u>.
>
> *Revision:* Scientists can now clone multiple copies <u>of</u> a human.

Of course, there are occasions when it is appropriate to use *be* verbs or nominalization. Problems arise only when these forms are overused. Although there is no absolute rule, you should look closely when you find more than one *be* verb or one nominalization per sentence. You need not analyze the nouns and verbs in every paper you write, but it is a good idea to check periodically the direction in which your style is developing. Over time, you will find that less analysis is necessary since you will tend to use more active verbs and fewer prepositions and nominalizations.

Eliminating Ineffective Expressions

Avoid ineffective expressions and words that do not contribute directly to the meaning of your paper. Notice how the underlined words and phrases in the following passage do not advance the writer's goals.

> <u>Basically</u>, those in support of surrogate motherhood claim that this <u>particular</u> method of reproduction has brought happiness to countless infertile couples. It allows a couple to have a child of their own <u>despite the fact that</u> the woman cannot bear children. In addition, it is <u>definitely</u> preferable to waiting for months and sometimes years on <u>really</u> long adoption lists. <u>In my opinion</u>, however, surrogate motherhood exploits the woman and can be <u>especially</u> damaging to the child. <u>Obviously</u>, poor women are affected most. <u>In the event that</u> a poor couple cannot have a child, it is <u>rather</u> unlikely that they will be able to afford the services of a surrogate mother. <u>Actually</u>, it is fertile, poor women who will become "breeders" for the infertile rich. In any case, the child is <u>especially</u> vulnerable. The <u>given</u> baby may become involved in a custody battle between the surrogate mother and the adopting mother. If the <u>individual</u> child is born handicapped, he or she may be <u>utterly</u> rejected by both mothers. <u>Surely</u>, the child's welfare should be <u>first and foremost</u> in everyone's mind.

The underlined elements are either overused, hackneyed words and phrases or unnecessary qualifiers, intensifiers, or modifiers. None of these words further the writer's intentions. They are inherently vague. Check to see if ineffective expressions occur frequently in your writing.

Eliminating Sexist Language

Always reread your drafts to check that you have avoided sexist language. Use the masculine pronouns "he" and "his" and nouns with *-man* and *-men* (mail*man,* police*men,* and so on) only when they refer to a male or a group composed entirely of males. Don't use these forms to refer to women. Instead, use the techniques listed in the following box.

TECHNIQUES FOR AVOIDING SEXIST LANGUAGE

1. Use pronouns that recognize both sexes ("his or her" or "her or his").
2. Use the plural rather than the singular. Plural pronouns by their very nature do not specify gender ("they" and "their").
3. Use nouns that are not gender-specific ("mail carrier" and "police officer").

Observe how we used these techniques in the following example.

ORIGINAL DRAFT WITH SEXIST LANGUAGE

A physician must consider the broader social consequences of supplying new reproductive technologies to <u>his</u> patients. Likewise, each scientist working on genetic engineering must be aware of the potential social impact of <u>his</u> research.

REVISION OF SEXIST LANGUAGE

Physicians must consider the broader social consequences of supplying new reproductive technologies to their patients. Likewise, scientists working on genetic engineering must be aware of the potential social impact of their research.

INDIVIDUAL EXERCISE ON REVISION

1. Obtain a copy (photocopy or extra computer-generated copy) of at least two pages of a paper you have written. Select a paper written for any course, either a final draft or a rough draft. (Your instructor may elect to distribute a single essay to the entire class.)
2. Apply the questions listed in the Revising Ideas and Revising Organization boxes to the piece of writing. Ask yourself each question and handwrite on the essay any revisions that seem necessary.
3. Submit the original essay along with your revised version.

COLLABORATIVE EXERCISE ON REVISION

1. In preparation for this exercise, the instructor needs to copy a short student essay (not more than two pages) for each class member. A preliminary draft will work best.

2. Form collaborative learning groups of five students each, as described in the Preface, or fashion groups according to a method of your own.

3. Select one student to read the essay aloud. Other group members should follow along on their own copies.

4. Select another student to read aloud the questions from the Revising Ideas and Revising Organization boxes. After each question is read, discuss whether it suggests any revisions that might improve the essay, and have the recorder write out the changes that the group agrees on.

5. Reconvene the entire class. Each group recorder should report the revisions the group made and explain why they are necessary. Try to account for differences in revisions.

EDITING

When you have finished your revision, read your paper aloud once again to catch any glaring errors. Then reread the essay line by line and sentence by sentence. Check for correct usage, punctuation, spelling, mechanics, manuscript form, and typos. If you are using a word processing program, apply the spell checker. If you are especially weak in editing skills, and if it is all right with your instructor, go to your campus writing center or get a friend to read over your work.

This stage of revision encompasses all the rules for usage, punctuation, spelling, and mechanics. We cannot begin to review all that material in this textbook. You should think seriously about purchasing a few good reference books, such as a good dictionary; a guide to correct usage, punctuation, and mechanics; and a documentation manual like the *MLA Handbook for Writers of Research Papers* or the *Publication Manual of the American Psychological Association*. Your campus bookstore and your college library may have a variety of self-help books for improving spelling, vocabulary, and usage. Browse through them and select the ones that best serve your needs.

Here is a list of some features to note as you edit your paper, but remember that you need to keep in mind all the rules of standard written English.

1. Are all your sentences complete?

   Original: Certain feminists claim that the new reproductive technologies exploit women. While other feminists argue that these same technologies help liberate women from traditional, oppressive roles.

   Revision: Certain feminists claim that the new reproductive technologies exploit women, while other feminists argue that these same technologies help liberate women from traditional, oppressive roles.

2. Have you avoided run-on sentences, both fused sentences and comma splices?

   Original: Science fiction writers have long been fascinated with the prospect of cloning, their novels and short stories have sparked the public's interest in this technology.

   Revision: Science fiction writers have long been fascinated with the prospect of cloning, and their novels and short stories have sparked the public's interest in this technology.

3. Do pronouns have clear referents, and do they agree in number, gender, and case with the words for which they stand?

   Original: A scientist who works on new reproductive technologies should always consider the social consequences of their work.

   Revision: A scientist who works on new reproductive technologies should always consider the social consequences of his or her work.

4. Do all subjects and verbs agree in person and number?

   Original: Not one of the new reproductive technologies designed to increase couples' fertility have failed to incite controversy.

   Revision: Not one of the new reproductive technologies designed to increase couples' fertility has failed to incite controversy.

5. Is the verb tense consistent and correct?

   Original: Some futurists claim that only eugenics can provide the answers needed to ensure the survival of the human race. They predicted that by the year 2050, human reproduction will be controlled by law.

   Revision: Some futurists claim that only eugenics can provide the answers needed to ensure the survival of the human race. They predict that by the year 2050, human reproduction will be controlled by law.

6. Have you used modifiers (words, phrases, subordinate clauses) correctly and placed them where they belong?

   Original: Currently, scientists across the nation work to clone various species with enthusiasm.

   Revision: Currently, scientists across the nation work enthusiastically to clone various species.

7. Have you used matching elements within parallel construction?

Original: Proposed reproductive technology projects include creating ways for sterile individuals to procreate, developing cures for genetic disease, and eugenic programs designed to improve the human species.

Revision: Proposed reproductive technology projects include creating ways for sterile individuals to procreate, developing cures for genetic disease, and designing eugenic programs to improve the human species.

8. Are punctuation marks used correctly?

Original: The potentially dire social consequences of genetic engineering, must be examined carefully, before we embrace this powerful new frightening technology.

Revision: The potentially dire social consequences of genetic engineering must be examined carefully before we embrace this powerful, new, frightening technology.

9. Are spelling, capitalization, and other mechanics (abbreviations, numbers, italics) correct?

Original: Research on Reproductive Technology is not often funded by The Government since these innovations are so controversial.

Revision: Research on reproductive technology is not often funded by the government since these innovations are so controversial.

Manuscript Format

For this stage of revision, you need a great deal of patience and a good pair of eyes. Here is a checklist of features to note.

MANUSCRIPT CHECKLIST

_____ Have you double-spaced and left one-inch margins on all sides?

_____ Are all typed words and corrections legible?

_____ Will your audience be able to tell which thoughts are yours and which are derived from sources?

_____ Are all quotations enclosed in quotation marks and properly punctuated?

_____ Have you properly documented all quotations, paraphrases, and summaries?

_____ Do you include all sources in a Works Cited list or References list?

The *MLA Handbook for Writers of Research Papers* describes particular guidelines for manuscript preparation. In Figure 2-2, we annotate Maura's final draft to show the important features of MLA manuscript format.

SAMPLE RESPONSE ESSAY

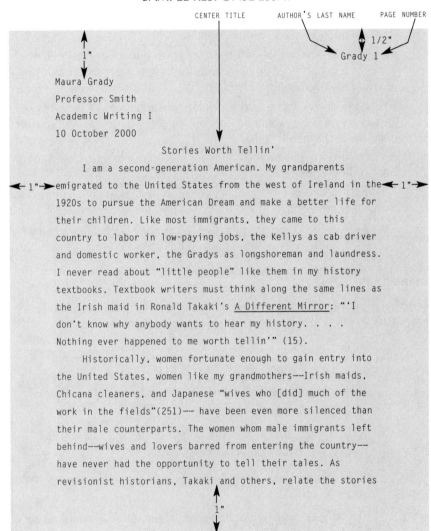

CENTER TITLE   AUTHOR'S LAST NAME   PAGE NUMBER

1/2"

Grady 1

1"

Maura Grady
Professor Smith
Academic Writing I
10 October 2000

Stories Worth Tellin'

1"→ I am a second-generation American. My grandparents emigrated to the United States from the west of Ireland in the ←1"→ 1920s to pursue the American Dream and make a better life for their children. Like most immigrants, they came to this country to labor in low-paying jobs, the Kellys as cab driver and domestic worker, the Gradys as longshoreman and laundress. I never read about "little people" like them in my history textbooks. Textbook writers must think along the same lines as the Irish maid in Ronald Takaki's A Different Mirror: "'I don't know why anybody wants to hear my history. . . . Nothing ever happened to me worth tellin'" (15).

Historically, women fortunate enough to gain entry into the United States, women like my grandmothers—Irish maids, Chicana cleaners, and Japanese "wives who [did] much of the work in the fields"(251)— have been even more silenced than their male counterparts. The women whom male immigrants left behind—wives and lovers barred from entering the country— have never had the opportunity to tell their tales. As revisionist historians, Takaki and others, relate the stories

1"

USE 8 ½" BY 11" PAPER FOR EACH PAGE. USE DOUBLE SPACES BETWEEN ALL LINES. LEFT JUSTIFY ALL LINES IN THE TEXT OF THE PAPER. DO NOT RIGHT JUSTIFY, EVEN IF YOUR WORD PROCESSOR PROVIDES THIS FEATURE.

Figure 2-2

INDENT
FIVE SPACES

1/2"

1"

Grady 2

of the "little people," I hope they remember to give women a strong voice. I want my daughters to be able to look into the " 'mirror' of history" and through the lens of the present to see "who [women] have been and hence are" (16) and what they have the potential to become.

Takaki tells us that more women emigrated from Japan than China because Japan had a strong government which was able to promote female emigration. Though this may be the

◄1"► case, when I read Takaki's account of the "predominantly male ◄1"► Chinese community in the United States" (248), I am reminded that these young Chinese men were segregated in all-male ghettos because exclusion laws prohibited them from bringing wives to the United States and forbade them from marrying Caucasians. Is it any wonder they turned to "prostitution, gambling, and drunkeness" (248)? How lonely it must have been for these men and how devastating for the wives they left behind in China. Few of these women ever saw their loved ones again. What hardships these impoverished women must have endured as they struggled to raise their children. I would like to hear these women's stories.

It seems the Japanese resolved the problem of male isolation by negotiating the Gentlemen's Agreement and thus paving the way for over 60,000 women to enter the United States, "many as 'picture brides'" for men they had never met (248). Though arranged marriages were consistent with Japanese custom, the prospect of crossing the Pacific to wed an older man, whom she had seen only in a picture, must have been daunting and traumatic to a young Japanese woman. Such arrangements still exist. An acquaintance of my father recently "sent for" and married a Russian woman he had selected from a catalog of picture brides. A more common practice is for professional couples to recruit au pair girls and nannies from other countries. Employment agencies have

1"

Grady 3

placed thousands in American families, sometimes as illegal
aliens in inadequate conditions earning inadequate pay. I
would like to hear these women's stories.

Despite great strides in many areas, poor women,
especially immigrants, are marginalized today. Women of color
are still in the lowest paid jobs in the nation, and female
heads of families and their children constitute the poorest of
the poor. New welfare legislation will require millions of
these women to join the workforce, yet childcare facilities
are dreadfully scarce. I would also like to hear these women's
stories.

Takaki quotes Leslie Marmon Silko's precaution:

I will tell you something about stories . . .

They aren't just entertainment.

Don't be fooled (15).

As readers, it may be difficult for some of us to step outside
the familiar histories we learned in school to enter the
stories of women whose lives are "worth tellin'." To identify
with the storyteller, we will have to cross barriers of race,
gender, and class. Our reward will be a better understanding
of history and ourselves.

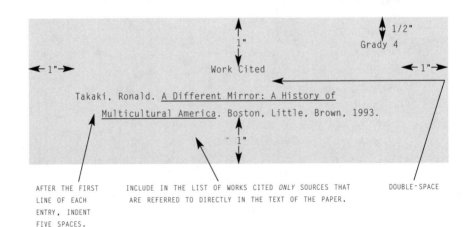

1/2"

↑
1"
↓

Grady 4

←1"→

Work Cited

←1"→

Takaki, Ronald. _A Different Mirror: A History of_
Multicultural America. Boston, Little, Brown, 1993.

↑
1"
↓

AFTER THE FIRST
LINE OF EACH
ENTRY, INDENT
FIVE SPACES.

INCLUDE IN THE LIST OF WORKS CITED _ONLY_ SOURCES THAT
ARE REFERRED TO DIRECTLY IN THE TEXT OF THE PAPER.

DOUBLE-SPACE

INDIVIDUAL EXERCISE ON REVISING STYLE AND EDITING

1. Obtain a copy (photocopy or extra computer-generated copy) of at least two pages of a paper you have written. Select a paper written for any course, either a final draft or a rough draft. (Your instructor may elect to distribute a single essay to the entire class.)

2. Revise the draft according to the advice in this chapter, keeping in mind the following concerns:

   a. Moving from writer-based to reader-based prose

   b. Varying sentence length

   c. Stressing verbs rather than nouns

   d. Using words effectively

   e. Detecting sexist language

   f. Adding your own voice

   g. Editing for complete sentences, run-on sentences, pronoun reference, subject-verb agreement, verb tense, use of modifiers, parallel structure, punctuation, and mechanics

   Handwrite on the essay any revisions that seem necessary.

3. Submit the original version of the essay along with your revised version.

COLLABORATIVE EXERCISE ON REVISING STYLE AND EDITING

1. In preparation for this exercise, the instructor will need to copy a short student essay (not more than two pages) for each class member. A preliminary draft will work best.

2. Form collaborative learning groups of five students each, as described in the Preface, or fashion groups according to a method of your own.

3. Select one student to read the essay aloud. Other group members should follow along on their own copies.

4. Select another student to read aloud the following list of revising and editing concerns:

   a. Moving from writer-based to reader-based prose

   b. Varying sentence length

   c. Stressing verbs rather than nouns

   d. Using words effectively

   e. Detecting sexist language

   f. Adding your own voice

g. Editing for complete sentences, run-on sentences, pronoun reference, subject-verb agreement, verb tense, use of modifiers, parallel
structure, punctuation, and mechanics

After each concern is read, discuss any revisions to the essay that it suggests, and have the recorder write out the changes the groups agrees on.

5. Reconvene the entire class. Each group recorder should report the revisions the group made and explain why they are necessary. Try to
account for differences in revisions.

WORKS CITED

Flower, Linda. "Writer-Based Prose: A Cognitive Basis for Problems in Writing." *College English* Sept. 1979: 19–37.

Lanham, Richard A. *Revising Prose.* 2nd ed. New York: Macmillan, 1987.

Neisser, Ulrich. "The Imitation of Man by Machine." *Science* 139 (1963): 193–97.

three

Composing Essays Drawing from Two or More Sources: Comparison and Contrast and Synthesis

Up to now we have focused on assignments in which the writer is working chiefly with a single reading source. Now you will tackle assignments that expect you to draw on two or more sources, such as books, journal articles, and newspaper reports. This is a complex task because you have to locate consistencies among the sources and then integrate the relevant information with your own ideas on the topic. In this chapter, we will show you how to write two types of papers that draw on multiple sources:

1. An essay comparing and contrasting sources
2. A synthesis

COMPARISON AND CONTRAST ESSAY

Writers use comparison and contrast to explore similarities and differences between two or more objects of study. With this organizational pattern, you might discuss the relationships between two authors' views on the causes of homelessness, for example, or you might attempt to persuade your readers that two authors who represent different political positions have come to synonymous conclusions on a topic.

Usually, the object of comparison and contrast is not simply to list and report similarities and differences as an end in itself. There is nothing intrinsically wrong with this pattern, but when it is your only goal, you may fall into the trap of doing too much summarizing, giving a synopsis of each author's views, and then explaining how the authors are alike and different. For maximum impact, you should take the process a step further. Strive to make some point about the two subjects you are comparing. This will be easy if, after you locate the similarities and differences, you step back and ask yourself what they represent, reveal, or demonstrate. Why are they interesting, relevant, eventful, or meaningful? What angle or point of view emerges with regard to the material? Answering these questions will help you decide how to write an assignment that shapes or expands on your ideas in an engaging way.

Identifying Comparisons and Contrasts

When you first read the materials that you intend to compare and contrast, jot down any connections you can make between your previous knowledge and the ideas in the reading sources. As you read, annotate the two sources to highlight correspondences between them. Then do a second reading for the purpose of identifying as many similarities and differences as you can. If you have difficulty elaborating on the reading sources, refer to the suggestions in the Strategies for Elaborating on Reading Sources box on pages 42–43. Here are some additional strategies that will help you discover how two reading sources are similar and different.

ELABORATING TO UNCOVER COMPARISONS AND CONTRASTS

1. Identify points where one source author
   a. Agrees or disagrees with the other author;
   b. Says something relevant about the topic that the other author has neglected to say;
   c. Qualifies ideas stated by the other author;
   d. Extends a proposition made by the other author.
2. Validate one author's assertion with information provided by the other author.
3. Subsume similarities and differences between the sources under subordinate categories.
4. Create hierarchies of importance among ideas that are similar or different.
5. Make judgments about the relevance of one author's view in relation to the other's view.

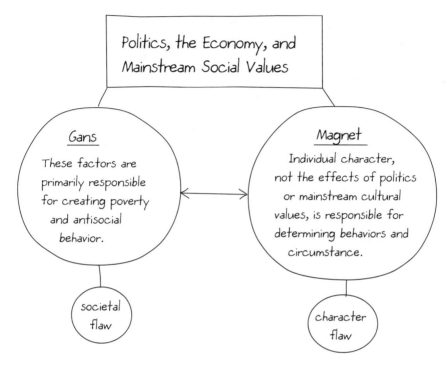

Figure 3-1   Beginning of a Web for Comparison and Contrast Based on Myron Magnet's "Rebels with a Cause" and Herbert Gans's "The War Against the Poor"

A useful technique that will allow you to formulate links between points of similarity and difference is *webbing* (see Fig. 3-1). Once you identify a point of similarity or difference, summarize the point in a short phrase and place it in a box in the center of a sheet of paper. Next, spin out the web by writing each author's ideas around this key idea node. Circle each of these ideas and connect them with lines to the key idea and, where appropriate, to each other. When you are finished webbing, you will have a visual display of the points of similarity and difference.

To illustrate the process of composing a comparison and contrast essay, let us accompany our student Kathy Tryer as she works on the following assignment:

> Write a three- to four-page essay explaining the differences between the views of Myron Magnet in "Rebels with a Cause" and Herbert Gans in "The War Against the Poor" on the topic of poor people. Write for an audience of classmates.

Our discussion of Kathy's process will be more meaningful to you if you are familiar with the reading sources. Take a few minutes now to read Myron Magnet's "Rebels with a Cause" and Herbert Gans's "The War Against the Poor" (Chapter 10).

On her first reading, Kathy underlines and annotates the articles, jotting down her reactions and marking passages where one author's views relate to the other's. Then, as she reads the two pieces a second time, she examines them closely for additional points of similarity and difference while she elaborates on select passages.

Gans, Paragraph 4

True, some poor people are indeed guilty of immoral behavior—that is, murderers, street criminals, drug sellers, child abusers.

Gans, Paragraph 5

Then there are poor people whose anger at their condition cannot be defined as political protest. Even so, most of those labeled "undeserving" are simply poor people who for a variety of reasons cannot live up to mainstream behavioral standards, like remaining childless in adolescence, finding and holding a job, and staying off welfare. This does not make them immoral.

Magnet, Paragraph 5

. . . For though the governmental structure of force and threat—police, judges and prisons—is a key means by which society restrains aggression and crime, it isn't the

Kathy's Notes

Gans uses the examples of criminality and morality, as does Magnet, but in different ways. Taking great pains to clarify his own perception of morality, Gans defensively pits the abject criminality of murderers and drug sellers against the merely antisocial behavior of teenage mothers and individuals incapable of remaining employed. Here Gans attempts to soften the argument of immorality against the less severe offenders of mainstream moral standards. In contrast to Magnet, who suggests preventative tactics and never raises the issue of morality, Gans proposes a band-aid approach to the problem that is only getting worse with time.

Kathy's Notes

Though the examples of government and control by authority are discussed by both Magnet and Gans, Magnet suggests that the true controlling factor in human life is the internal principal means. The most powerful curb is the internal inhibition society builds into each man's character, the inner voice (call it reason, conscience, superego, what you will) that makes the social contract an integral part of our deepest selves.

motivations of the individual. If such motivation is misguided or absent, criminal behavior may result. Magnet argues that within impoverished cultures, built-in inhibition is absent from the character makeup of many of its individuals. This approach, which holds each man or culture responsible for its own behaviors, differs greatly from Gans's. He states that antisocial behaviors are a symptom of poverty, which in turn, is a symptom of government policies and the social attitudes and beliefs of mainstream culture. Gans never suggests that individuals within a given culture can (or should) be responsible for their own beliefs and behaviors, unless they have demonstrated an ability to do so according to mainstream moral values.

Planning Comparison and Contrast Essays

Once Kathy has generated a series of elaborations, she does two things: She (1) selects and orders her ideas, and (2) sketches out a blueprint for the essay. Keeping in mind that her purpose is to compare and contrast the views of two authors, she reviews her elaborations, identifies the ones dealing with similarities and differences (see p. 78), and places them in categories. Kathy creates two lists: one list for resemblances between the sources and the other for differences. Another way you might do this is by marking the text wherever you've discovered similarities or differences (use symbols: = for similarities and ≠ for differences). Here are Kathy's two lists:

Similarities:

* Both Gans and Magnet believe that poverty is a symptom of social decay.
* Both writers demonstrate that antisocial behavior may be used as a form of power, and that such behavior may be admired by certain groups or cultures.

Differences:

* Cultural mores serve as the basis of both writer's arguments, but whereas Gans blames government policies and the attitudes of society at large, Magnet finds the absence of traditional middle-class values to blame.

* Gans blames politics, the economy, and the cultural mores of the middle class as either unfair, outmoded, or not applicable to the real-life situations faced by impoverished peoples.

* Magnet uses a historical/theoretical model to demonstrate that impoverished peoples lack the internal guidance and discipline that characterize the "social contract" adhered to by the middle and upper classes.

* Whereas Gans writes of declining morality in terms of it being a recent phenomenon, Magnet suggests that moral standards have undergone continual change, and that, historically, moral decline has always been a part of human culture.

As Kathy analyzes the similarities and differences, she asks herself two questions: (1) What do these similarities and differences demonstrate? and (2) What do they tell us about each of the two authors? Whenever you ask such questions, see if you can form some kind of a generalization from the similarities and differences. Even if your generalization has exceptions, it will still be useful.

Usually, a writer compares and contrasts reading sources to make a point or propose a thesis. As we said earlier, the writer may simply want to describe the similarities and differences, but this limited rhetorical purpose leaves little room for the writer to bring background knowledge to bear on the text. A more powerful purpose would require the writer to have a specific reason for comparing and contrasting: for example, to describe, explain, or argue a point, or to focus the essay on what the comparison reveals or demonstrates about the subject.

Limited Goal	*More Powerful Goal*
Bring out similarities and differences in the subject matter.	1. Use the comparison to describe, explain, or argue a position.
	2. Show what the comparison reveals or demonstrates about the subject.

In the essay on pages 86–90, you will see that as Kathy lays out the similarities and differences between the two readings, she aligns herself more with Magnet than with Gans, leading up to paragraphs 5 and 6, where she argues that Magnet's analysis of poverty is more realistic and constructive than Gans's.

Organizing the Comparison and Contrast Essay

Comparison and contrast essays are usually organized in a point-by-point format, a block arrangement, or a combination of the two.

POINT-BY-POINT ORGANIZATIONAL PATTERN

Introduction

1. Identify the sources and the issue(s) they focus on.
2. Explain your rhetorical goal (your purpose for comparing the sources).

Body Paragraphs

1. Compare the sources with respect to a single characteristic.
2. Repeat step 1 for each characteristic you intend to treat.

Conclusion

See the techniques on page 56.

BLOCK ORGANIZATIONAL PATTERN

Introduction

1. Identify the sources and the issue(s) they focus on.
2. Explain your rhetorical goal (your purpose for comparing the sources).

Body Paragraphs

1. Identify and discuss the characteristics of the first source.
2. Compare the characteristics of the second source with those of the first source.

Conclusion

See the techniques on page 56.

Notice that Kathy Tryer organizes her essay according to both patterns. Paragraphs 2 and 3 treat Magnet and Gans, respectively, in "blocks." In the remaining paragraphs (4, 5, and 6), Kathy compares both writers in point-by-point fashion.

If Kathy had used the point-by-point pattern exclusively, she would have written her essay according to the outline that follows.

OUTLINE FOR COMPARISON ESSAY WRITTEN IN POINT-BY-POINT ARRANGEMENT

Paragraph 1: Introduction
Objectivity (Point 1)

Paragraph 2: Magnet's argument—a practical social and historical monograph explaining the causes of ills suffered by the poor.

Gans's argument—reactionary, reminiscent of a classic "knee-jerk" liberal response.

Examples (Point 2)

Paragraph 3: Gans—band-aid style approach to an age-old problem.

Paragraph 4: Magnet—doesn't suggest a solution aimed at diminishing the ways the poor are viewed negatively, but does identify the conditions needed for the advancement of the poor.

Rhetorical Stance (Point 3)

Paragraph 5: Gans's and Magnet's arguments lie at opposite ends of the spectrum. Gans claims the cause of the prevailing view of the poor is mainstream political precepts.

Paragraph 6: Magnet blames what he believes to be poverty's root itself: the values and character of individuals.

Paragraph 7: Conclusion

If Kathy had relied solely on the block pattern, instead of alternating between Magnet and Gans with each point of comparison, she would have contrasted them in blocks, dealing with one author in the first block and switching to the other in the second segment. Her outline would look like the following.

OUTLINE FOR COMPARISON ESSAY WRITTEN IN BLOCK ARRANGEMENT

Paragraph 1: The introduction is the same as in the point-by-point essay.

First Block: Magnet

Paragraph 2: Magnet's argument—not reactionary or desperate, objective and convincing.

Paragraph 3: Magnet claims that antisocial behavior, poverty, and the other ills of the lower classes beget an underdeveloped "social contract." He cites examples from history, philosophy, and psychology.

Paragraph 4: Magnet tries to persuade his audience that the condition of the poor is due to individual, not social, circumstances.

Second Block: Gans

Paragraph 5: Gans—reactionary, reminiscent of a classic "knee-jerk" liberal response.

Paragraph 6: Thorough in explaining his argument for social change, but he fails to convince the reader of either the problem or his proposed solution.

Paragraph 7: Gans's attempts to elicit an emotional response from his readers further the overall perception that his arguments are biased and one-sided.

Paragraph 8: Conclusion

Drafting Comparison and Contrast Essays

After Kathy selects an organizational plan, she writes a draft of her essay. This first draft is preliminary; it is not the final, polished product. She will have an opportunity to change direction, sharpen her focus, and revise at a later date.

The box that follows lists conventions for comparison essays. As you read Kathy's essay, notice the extent to which she uses them.

CONVENTIONS FOR COMPARISON ESSAYS

1. Give your readers some background about the topic.
2. Identify the sources by title and author.
3. Clearly indicate the focus or thesis of your paper.
4. Make clear to your readers what you are using as points of comparison.
5. Develop each point of comparison by paraphrasing, summarizing, or quoting relevant points in the readings and bringing your prior topic knowledge and experience to bear on the text.
6. Clearly differentiate your own ideas from those of the authors of the sources.
7. Correctly document source material that is paraphrased, summarized, or quoted.

SAMPLE COMPARISON AND CONTRAST ESSAY

Tryer 1

Kathy Tryer

Professor Kennedy

English 131

16 September 1999

Poverty's Roots--The Environment
versus the Individual: Two Views

Myron Magnet and Herbert J. Gans, both writing about poverty in America, arrive at startlingly different conclusions concerning its roots, causes, and prevention. Magnet, in "Rebels with a Cause," argues that the poor are an inevitable by-product of advanced cultures. According to Magnet, those within advanced cultures incapable of the discipline or restraint necessary for social advancement become outcast, socially immobile, and poor. Magnet supports his argument with substantive examples and draws on historical, philosophical, and psychological literature.

Gans, however, in "The War Against the Poor," proposes a
means to end mistreatment of the poor rather than proposing
methods by which to end poverty, and places the blame for the
social condition of the poor and their mistreatment squarely
on the shoulders of mainstream society itself. Neither writer
suggests it is possible to end poverty entirely. Magnet,
though, examines poverty's underlying causes, identifies the
conditions necessary for its reduction, and offers the more
sensible analysis of the condition.

Magnet points out that the personal values of the poor
place them outside the social order. He discusses the
importance of order in society, claiming, "the achievements of
civilization rest upon the social order, which rests in turn
upon a mutual agreement to foreswear aggression" (50). Magnet
alludes to statements made by Plato, St. Augustine, Hobbes,
Burke, and Freud and points out that each of these thinkers
concluded that "as men come from the hand of nature, they are
instinctively aggressive, with a built-in inclination to
violence" (47). The underlying purpose of social order, a
relatively recent phenomenon in history, Magnet explains, "is
to restrain man's instinctual aggressiveness, so that human
life can be something higher than a war of all against all"
(47). Social order is the principal element lacking in poor
society, Magnet claims, and this problem must be traced to the
individual. To elaborate, "the hardest of hard realities—
whether people commit crimes or not—comes down to a very
large extent to nothing more than values and beliefs in the
world within the individual," claims Magnet (48). The values
and beliefs of the poor, according to Magnet, are out of step
with those of the larger society, which is the direct cause of
their socio-economic conditions.

Gans, however, sees things differently. He believes
poverty is caused by mainstream society which, by design,
suppresses the poor and creates a social climate hostile to

'the poor. He blames the economy, politics, and social policy toward the poor for their ills and for the creation of an environment conducive to their debasement. For example, he cites the economy as a culprit and claims that mainstream attitudes toward the poor were "initiated by dramatic shifts in the domestic and world economy which have turned more and more unskilled and semiskilled workers into surplus labor" (461). Individuals within the middle and upper classes, however, view the poor unsympathetically and see them "not as people without jobs but as miscreants who behave badly because they do not abide by middle-class or mainstream moral values" (461). He does allow, though, that some poor people are involved in criminal or indecent behavior, but suggests this is an insignificant segment of the underclass population. To counteract the problems created by the economy, politics, and existing social policy, Gans suggests enormous government programs such as a "new" New Deal for the poor, programs to find uses for stagnant or redundant private enterprise to raise levels of employment, and for those remaining who can't—or won't—work, a program of income grants. "Alas," concedes Gans, "when taxpayers discover how much cheaper it is to pay welfare than to create jobs, that remedy may end as it has before" (462). Gans's proposals do nothing to improve the condition of the poor, nor do they address the underlying causes of poverty. Indeed, as he notes above, to implement such programs might actually increase the anger of mainstream culture toward the poor. In short, Gans proposes a band-aid approach to solving an age-old problem.

Magnet, while he doesn't suggest a solution aimed at diminishing the ways the poor are viewed negatively, does identify the conditions needed for the advancement of the poor. Unlike Gans, Magnet does not think that "society has so oppressed people as to bend them out of their true nature" (48), believing instead that the plight of the poor is oftentimes attributable to social maladjustment of the

poor themselves. "Examine the contents of their minds and
hearts and what you find is free-floating aggression, weak
consciences, anarchic beliefs, detachment from the community
and its highest values," he states (48). Moreover, the
condition of the poor is a

> predictable result of unimaginably weak
> families, headed by immature irresponsible
> girls, who are at the margin of the community,
> pathological in their own behavior, and too
> often lacking the knowledge, interest and inner
> resources to be successful molders of strong
> characters in children. (48)

Clearly then, to "adequately socialize" the members of the
underclass who lack inner discipline and social order, their
values and morals must change.

Gans's and Magnet's arguments are in direct
opposition. Gans claims the cause of the prevailing view
and the current condition of the poor is mainstream social
and political precepts. Magnet blames the values and
character of the individual alone. Gans proposes government
intervention and an "intellectual and cultural defense"
(463) on behalf of the poor. Magnet suggests uncovering the
true basis for poverty and acting on a local level by
attempting to understand poverty-stricken individuals
themselves, of whom Gans admits "Americans accept so many
untruths" (461). Gans's band-aid approach to artificially
elevating the status of the poor through government
programs and cash subsidies will do little toward changing
mainstream society's negative view of the poor. Magnet's
more comprehensive value-oriented approach to addressing
the ills of the underclass, grounded in historical,
philosophical, and psychological precedents, has a better
chance of success.

Tryer 5

Magnet, in suggesting a reexamination of the very
mechanism which catalyzes poverty and crime, offers a
possible solution that is far more realistic than that
submitted by Gans. Gans's emotionally charged argument
attempts to conjure enemies from inanimate entities: the
government, politics, and the economy. Magnet's proposal
provides a constructive, accountable approach to addressing
the problems of the poor. Thus, Gans's suggestions amount to
little more than a critique of mainstream American society
and an unfounded claim that American institutions are
responsible for the plight of the underclass.

Tryer 6

Works Cited

Gans, Herbert. "The War Against the Poor." <u>Dissent</u>
        Fall 1992: 461-65.
Magnet, Myron. "Rebels with a Cause." <u>National Review</u>
        15 March 1993: 46-50.

You will notice that Kathy Tryer's paper has followed many of the guidelines we've suggested for comparison and contrast papers. No piece of writing can ever be expected to observe all the guidelines for a particular kind of writing, because each topic or issue introduces matters that require their own distinctive treatment. Nevertheless, you will note in Kathy's paper a consistent attention to detail that implies her audience's general knowledge of Magnet's and Gans's articles and their positions; a careful assessment of the information, organizational plans, and rhetorical concerns of Magnet's and Gans's articles, showing that Kathy has annotated her reading materials point by point; and an elaboration of Kathy's argument in a clear, systematic manner from her opening paragraph about the major differences between Magnet and Gans, through individual paragraphs that focus on each, to her concluding paragraph about their divergence.

Though we have presented Kathy's final draft of her paper, you should bear in mind that Kathy produced this version after several preliminary drafts of its parts and their whole. Here are some additional steps that Kathy followed when she revised her writing.

Revising the Preliminary Draft

When you are satisfied with your preliminary draft, make arrangements to share it with your teacher or a classmate. Before you proceed any further, you need to get some feedback on what you have written so far.

Instructor Conferences

If your instructor invites students to confer with him or her, be sure to take advantage of this opportunity. The conference will be beneficial to you if you approach it with the correct mind-set and adequate preparation. Don't expect your instructor to correct your work or simply tell you what to do. You should assume a proactive role: set the agenda and do most of the talking. After the teacher reads your draft—preferably, you should read it to the teacher—inquire about what worked well and what fell flat. Be prepared to explain what you are trying to achieve and point out the parts of the paper you feel good about and the parts you think need work. Most important, be ready to answer the teacher's questions.

Peer Reviews

If your teacher agrees, make arrangements to have a classmate or a friend review your preliminary draft and give you feedback. If that is not possible, set the paper aside for a few days and then review it yourself. Respond to the questions listed in the box that follows.

QUESTIONS FOR HELPING A WRITER REVISE THE FIRST DRAFT OF A COMPARISON AND CONTRAST ESSAY

1. Is the writer's rhetorical purpose clear? Explain how he or she is attempting to influence or affect readers.

2. Does the writer explain what the similarities and contrasts reveal or demonstrate, or is the writer's purpose simply to show that similarities and differences exist?

3. Does everything in the essay lead to or follow from one central meaning? If not, which ideas appear to be out of place?

4. Will the reader understand the essay, and is the writer sensitive to the reader's concerns?

   a. Does he or she provide necessary background information about the subject matter, the sources, and their titles and authors? If not, what is missing?

   b. Throughout the essay, when the writer refers to the source, does he or she supply the reader with necessary documentation?

   c. Does the writer provide clear transitions or connecting ideas that differentiate his or her own ideas from those in the sources?

   d. Does the writer display an awareness of the authors by referring to them by name, "he," "she," or "they" rather than as "the article" or "it"?

5. Is the organizational format appropriate for a comparison and contrast essay? Is the writer using point-by-point or block arrangement?

6. Has the writer revealed the points of comparison to the reader? Are these criteria or bases for comparison clear or confusing? Explain.

7. Does the writer provide transitions and connecting ideas as he or she moves from one source to another or from one point of comparison to the next? If not, where are they needed?

8. Do you hear the writer's voice throughout the entire essay? Describe it.

9. Does the writer use a paper opener that catches the reader's attention?

10. Does the conclusion simply restate the main idea or does it offer new insights?

11. Does the essay have an appropriate title?

12. What other suggestions can you give the writer for improving this draft?

Editing the Preliminary Draft

When you are satisfied with your revision, read your paper aloud. This will enable you to catch any glaring errors. Then reread the essay line by line and sentence by sentence. Check for grammatical correctness, punctuation, spelling, mechanics, manuscript form, and typos. If you are using a word processing program with a spell checker, apply the checker to your essay. If you are especially weak in editing skills, try getting a friend to read over your work.

INDIVIDUAL EXERCISE ON COMPARISON AND CONTRAST ESSAYS

Reread Kathy Tryer's paper. Note the structure of its presentation. After an introduction, Kathy summarizes Myron Magnet's article. Then she summarizes Herbert Gans's article. Can you make any generalizations about her selective use of paraphrase and quotation? Note that she does not summarize, paraphrase, or quote from Magnet's or Gans's entire article; instead, she focuses on issues on which Magnet's argument relates specifically to Gans's. Evaluate her selection.

COLLABORATIVE EXERCISE ON COMPARISON AND CONTRAST ESSAYS

1. Form collaborative learning groups of five students each, as described in the Preface, or fashion groups according to a method of your own.
2. Assign each member a paragraph from Magnet's or Gan's article relevant to Kathy's paper. Ask each to comment on Kathy's specific use of that paragraph by examining what she chooses to summarize, paraphrase, or quote from it.
3. Reconvene the entire class. Each group recorder should read the members' remarks and respond to inquiries from the class about Kathy's selective use of the source materials.

SYNTHESIZING SOURCES

To synthesize is to select elements from two or more sources on a topic or interest that they share and then to organize them, along with your own ideas, under a controlling theme or concept. You read an array of materials—for example, two articles from academic journals, a chapter from a book, and a column from a newspaper—and you look for or create a controlling idea or thematic consistency. Then you combine the different pieces of information in a coherent, original paper. Your aim is to draw together a body of information from the reading sources and then to state or restate and to support an idea common to them all with a particular rhetorical purpose in mind.

Your purpose might be to define poverty. After reading various sources on poverty, you select pertinent ideas, combine them, and formulate a definition. Another purpose might be to chart the development of the Arab-Israeli controversy. As in the previous example, you read different sources, identify common elements, combine historical perspectives, and finally construct a coherent narrative account.

From the preceding examples, you can see that there is a difference between synthesis on the one hand and comparison and contrast on the other. When you compare two reading sources, you examine them with an eye to pointing out their similarities and differences. You consider the readings with regard to some target, theme, characteristic, or quality that relates them to one another. For example, you might read two journal articles on the topic of health reform and compare the authors' opposing views. The reading materials already converge on the same topic, however different their premises and conclusions may be.

When you synthesize, however, the readings you use may focus on separate, discrete topics or issues. Your task is to identify constituent elements of their interlocking materials and combine them into a single, unified piece of writing. Your aim should nonetheless go beyond a simplistic presentation of information in the sources and beyond a general statement of your reaction to the sources. Your goal is to represent different sources that will enable you to define your own thesis or idea and to support your idea with reference to those sources.

You need to begin your synthesis with an open mind about how to use your different materials. First, read the sources to obtain background information on the topic and identify its dimensions. As you do this initial reading, set two goals: to bring your own ideas to bear on the topic by elaborating on and reacting to the material and to identify common elements in the sources. To achieve the latter goal, read each source, searching for its relationships to the other sources. Next, ask yourself the questions listed in the following box.

QUESTIONS FOR IDENTIFYING RELATIONSHIPS AMONG SOURCES

1. Does the source give background information or additional information about points that are presented in other sources?
2. Does it provide additional details about points made in other sources?
3. Does it provide evidence for points made by another author?
4. Are there places where this author contradicts or disagrees with the other authors you have read?
5. Are there places where the author supports or agrees with other authors?
6. Are there cause-and-effect relationships between this source and the other sources?
7. Are there time relationships among the sources?
8. Does this source contain elements that can be compared or contrasted with those in other sources?
9. Are there other common threads running through this source and the other sources?
10. Do the authors of the sources use similar key words or phrases?
11. Are there any other ways you can categorize the ideas in the sources?

To illustrate the process of writing a synthesis paper, consider the following assignment:

> Drawing on Lillian B. Rubin's "'People Don't Know Right from Wrong Anymore,'" Frances K. Goldschneider and Linda J. Waite's "Alternative Family Futures," and Robert L. Griswold's "Fatherhood and the Defense of Patriarchy," write a four- to five-page essay explaining what American families are like today. Address your essay to an audience of peers.

For this assignment, your rhetorical purpose would be to explain the various ways the American family is being redefined. First, you would review the sources with an eye to what each contributes to the controlling idea, the transformation of the family. Then, you would determine how each source relates to the others. As you review each one, write down your answers to the questions that appear in the preceding box.

Once you have answered the questions and discovered the common elements among the sources, decide what ideas of your own you want to communicate to your readers. The next step is to locate in the sources information that you can use to develop each of the ideas you want to communicate. This will require you to go back to the sources. As you reread them, look for bits of information that relate to your points. Mark this content in the text or copy it into your notebook. When you have located a sufficient amount of relevant information, you can start to draft your essay. As you begin to write, you will need to decide whether you will paraphrase, quote, or summarize each piece of supporting information. A recap of the entire process appears in the following box.

STRATEGIES FOR WRITING A SYNTHESIS FOR A SPECIFIC PURPOSE

1. Read all the sources to get a general impression of the content.
2. Reread each source, elaborating on it by bringing your previous knowledge to bear on the text.
3. Determine the elements each source has in common with the other sources by asking each item in the Questions for Identifying Relationships Among Sources box (p. 95).
4. Decide what ideas of your own you want to get across to your readers.
5. Locate in the sources information that you can use to develop each of your ideas.
6. Draft your essay by quoting, paraphrasing, or summarizing relevant supporting information from the sources and by drawing on your knowledge of the basic features of writing: titles, introductions, sentences, paragraphs, transitions, and so on (see pp. 50–58).

When you have completed a preliminary draft of your essay, schedule a conference with your professor (see page 91), and if your professor agrees, ask a classmate or a friend to give you suggestions for revision.

QUESTIONS FOR REVISING A SYNTHESIS ESSAY

1. Does the title give you some indication of the writer's attitude toward the topic?
2. Is there an interesting lead that attracts the reader's attention?
3. Does the writer give you sufficient background information on the topic?

(continued on the next page)

---

4. Does the writer make his or her overall purpose clear to the reader?
5. Can you locate the writer's thesis or expression of point of view?
6. As you read each paragraph, are you aware of the purpose that the writer is trying to accomplish?
7. Does the writer identify relationships among sources?
8. In each paragraph, does the writer provide sufficient support from the sources?
9. Does the writer include enough of his or her own commentary in each of the paragraphs?
10. Does the conclusion do more than simply summarize the main points of the paper?
11. Does the writer include parenthetical documentation where it is necessary and clearly differentiate among sources?
12. Is there a Works Cited page?

What follows is an essay by a student, Siryal Benim, written in response to the assignment on page 95. The essay will make more sense to you if you first read the selections in Chapter 9 on which it is based: Lillian B. Rubin's " 'People Don't Know Right from Wrong Anymore'"; Frances K. Goldschneider and Linda J. Waite's "Alternative Family Futures"; and Robert L. Griswold's "Fatherhood and the Defense of Patriarchy." After you have read the sources and Siryal's essay, do the exercise on page 102.

SAMPLE SYNTHESIS ESSAY

Benim 1

Siryal Benim
Academic Writing I
Professor Smith
23 September 1999

Today's American Family: Where Did We Go
Wrong--And Is Any Recourse Possible?
Our families today neither resemble nor function
like those of just two decades ago. In the past, American

cultural norms suggested that upon finishing school, young
adults would seek employment, get married, or live with their
parents until they were prepared to do either one or both of
the above. Lillian B. Rubin, in " 'People Don't Know Right
from Wrong Anymore,' " points out that the average age for
marriage was earlier than it is today, at 20.6 years for women
and 22.5 years for men (17). Indeed, the past two decades have
seen three "revolutions," or social upheavals, each popularly
termed as sexual, gender, and divorce-related. Additionally,
America and the world have weathered "shifts in the economy,
which forced increasing numbers of women into the labor force"
(Rubin 16). As a direct result of these changes, our families
and lifestyles now differ substantially from what they were
twenty years ago. While new family structures and lifestyles
are often described as "alternative," these patterns may be
adopted by default as often as by choice.

    The traditional nuclear family is diminishing relative
to other family structures in American culture today. Apart
from finding different family systems today, such as single-
parent households, traditional roles for men, women and
children have changed as well. Men are no longer likely to be
the sole breadwinners for the family, and in some cases, may
not even be the principal wage earners. Due to the ascension
of women in the workforce and their growing parity with men in
terms of power and income, many men have difficulty facing the
new realities of economics and family. Goldschneider and
Waite, in "Alternative Family Futures" suggest, forebodingly,
that "men who still hold traditional definitions of their
appropriate adult role are increasingly having difficulty
finding wives willing to take the full burden of family
obligations left by a husband whose only responsibilities are
to work" (208). "It is also the case," they continue, "that
pressures have been building on men to become more involved in
the family and its tasks whether they want to or not" (208).

Signs of of an emerging "new fatherhood" point encouragingly toward a reaffirmation of shared values and an effort toward renewed cohesiveness among family members (Griswold 257).

 Robert Griswold, in "Fatherhood and the Defense of Patriarchy," states "feminists and advocates for the men's movement hope that the new fatherhood will be a progressive step in redefining American manhood" (257). Lack of enthusiasm, however, for the so-called men's movement may suggest that men are not prepared to adopt, en masse, any such feminist-driven ideology. On the other hand, the dramatic change in men's roles over the past two decades may merely indicate the rapid deterioration of the traditional nuclear family as a cultural mainstay. Hence, we have seen over the past two decades a high rate of divorce and the rise of the new "traditional" families: family units still headed by two parents or guardians, but who are not necessarily biologically related to each other's children.

 Over the last twenty years, "step" parents have become more common. Previously married individuals remarry to create new, sometimes complex family units with various step relatives. "Now, when, on the average, women live to nearly eighty and men to a little over seventy, we can marry and bear children very much later, safe in the knowledge that we'll be around to raise and nurture them as long as they need us" (Rubin 17).

 In the 1990s, single-parent families, especially those headed by mothers, are subjected to increasingly demanding schedules and levels of stress. Goldschneider and Waite point out that women today need more help than ever when raising families: "Despite the number of women who take on both parental and economic roles, not all women can do so; few can parent totally alone" (202). Indeed, the viability of single-parent families became a major campaign issue in the 1992 presidential race. Political rhetoric aside, it would seem that children in single-parent households stand to suffer the greatest consequences when the pressures are too great for the family to bear.

An increasing number of families opt to remain childless. Historically, the absence of children in a family was less often a matter of choice than it was result of physical limitations. Modern families make this choice based upon their own goals and the potential impact of these goals on family life. It would seem that such decisions are typically based on sound, rational judgments, and that they represent a morally responsible alternative to child-rearing.

Apprehensive about marriage due to high rates of divorce, many couples today postpone wedding plans indefinitely. Again, due to greater life expectancy through improved medical technology, this is a luxury our ancestors were not afforded. Similarly, neither was effective birth control or abortion, and unplanned pregnancies often led to marriage. Writes Rubin, "Sometimes the young couple married regretfully; often one partner, usually the man, was ambivalent" (13). But regardless of circumstances, "it didn't really matter; they did what was expected" (Rubin 13); such was the power exerted by cultural norms just twenty years ago. But have advances in human health practices devalued matrimony? Has the once time-honored principle of commitment been reduced to a mere buzzword among couples today? People today realize that even if their first or even second marriages don't succeed, they may take vows a third or possibly a fourth time, until they are satisfied. Certainly, the families of the 1990s are very different from those of our ancestors. It remains to be determined, however, if these changes are for better or for worse.

Perhaps today couples and families simply have more options to choose from when making decisions. This freedom comes with its own set of pros and cons. To debate the issue

Benim 5

of today's fractured family using sound-bite styled catch
phrases such as "family values" misses the point: values are
widely held precepts based on accepted cultural norms which
are usually grounded in history or tradition. Quite simply,
it is precisely because of the absence of any consensus in
our culture today, morally, spiritually, or otherwise, that
an understanding of what constitutes appropriate family
behavior cannot be attained. Perhaps we are now creating a
new concept of the "traditional" family that will be passed
on to subsequent generations.

Benim 6

                    Works Cited
Goldschneider, Frances K., and Linda J. Waite. "Alternative
        Family Futures." New Families, No Families? The
        Transformation of the American Home. Berkeley: U of
        California P, 1991. 200-205.
Griswold, Robert L. "Fatherhood and the Defense of
        Patriarchy." Fatherhood in America, A History. New York:
        Basic Books, 1993. 257-260.
Rubin, Lillian B. "'People Don't Know Right from Wrong
        Anymore.'" Families on the Fault Line. New York:
        HarperCollins, 1994.

You will notice that Siryal Benim's paper exemplifies many of our
guidelines for synthesis essays. It incorporates diverse materials from
three different reading sources, each of which appears to address a separate topic about the family. From these different perspectives on alternative family patterns, the role of fatherhood, and various moral points

associated with these issues, Siryal discusses changes in contemporary family life. The paper argues that many currently available options make possible a variety of different family structures.

INDIVIDUAL EXERCISE ON SYNTHESIS ESSAYS

Reread Siryal Benim's paper. Note the structure of its presentation. After an introductory statement about changes in family patterns, Siryal discusses new roles for fathers, stepparents, couples without children, late marriages, and divorce, and then draws on information variously from three sources. Read the titles of these sources in the list of Works Cited. What separate topic does each appear to address? Can you make any generalization about Siryal's alternating and selective use of these sources?

COLLABORATIVE EXERCISE ON SYNTHESIS ESSAYS

1. Form collaborative learning groups of three students each, as described in the Preface, or fashion groups according to a method of your own.
2. Assign each member a single source to trace through Siryal's paper. Ask each to comment on the focus that Siryal puts on the material from that particular source.
3. When the class reconvenes, have each group recorder explain the conclusions that individual members reached about Siryal's use of particular sources.

f o u r

Essays of Argument, Analysis, and Evaluation

ARGUMENT: AN INTRODUCTION

In the broad sense, every college paper that expresses a thesis is an "argument" because the writer's goal is to get the reader to accept his or her perspective, position, or point of view. Even if a writer devotes most of the paper to summarizing, paraphrasing, comparing, or contrasting sources, he or she can still develop an argument that promotes a distinctive point of view. The choice of materials with their emphasis and arrangement will imply a perspective and demonstrate a position.

The synthesis essay generally presents an argument in the broad sense of the word. It pertains to setting out or explaining a particular idea, attitude, or speculative point of view. A more specialized sense of the word evokes the goal of moving audiences to a particular action or persuasion. The word *argument* need not imply a quarrel or a polemic. It derives from a Greek word related to *argent*, "silver or white" (compare Ag, the chemical abbreviation for "silver"), denoting brilliance or clarity. From it comes the name of Argos, the mythological demigod with a hundred eyes. The word implies that a speaker or writer has seized upon an idea, clarified its point, and made its meaning strikingly visible.

The difference between written argument in the broad sense of getting your readers to see your point of view and argument in the narrower sense of persuading your readers to take your position is illustrated in the two thesis statements that follow. Both concern "Communitarianism," a popular social movement. Although "community" is becoming a watchword for the nineties, it is a contested concept. Many writers are embroiled in a controversy over whether it is more important to uphold community values or safeguard individual rights. The political philosophers and intellectuals who value identification with or membership in a community over private initiative or personal autonomy are referred to as "communitarians."

THESIS A: ARGUMENT IN THE BROAD SENSE

The ideals set forth by communitarians are undemocratic, un-American, unconstitutional, and unfair.

THESIS B: ARGUMENT IN THE SPECIALIZED SENSE

Although the academics who espouse communitarianism tout it as the panacea for our nation's ills, the ideals they set forth are undemocratic, un-American, unconstitutional, and unfair.

The difference between thesis A and thesis B is that B has more of a prescriptive or directive edge. Writer B knows that some of her readers will not agree with her. She expects them to argue that restoration of community is a solution to America's social problems. When writer B says, "Although the academics who espouse communitarianism tout it as the panacea for our nation's ills," she anticipates her audience's opposing response. Later, in the body of her essay, she will give reasons why her view, expressed as that of "mainstream Americans," holds more weight than her opponents' views. Writer A has no opposition to worry about. She is writing a response essay to explain why she agrees with a published author's views on communitarianism. She is mainly interested in clarifying her position in relation to the author's, whereas writer B is intent on persuading her audience to agree with her own position.

ARGUMENT IN THE BROAD SENSE

1. You do not have to acknowledge explicitly your audience's (conflicting) view.
2. Your thesis is not necessarily arguable or debatable.
3. Your purpose is usually to explain or present your position. You are not intent on persuading your reader.

(continued on the next page)

ARGUMENT IN THE SPECIALIZED SENSE

1. You anticipate conflicting views, acknowledge them, and directly address them.
2. Your thesis is issue-centered and debatable.
3. You want your readers to accept and agree with your position rather than the view of your opponents.

Developing Support for Arguments

To develop a strong argument, you must impart a breadth and depth to its focus. Try to make the argument two-dimensional. An argument that hammers away at one central idea until it has exhausted all available evidence and concludes by restating the original proposition as in the following is not what you want to write.

> The ideals set forth by communitarians are undemocratic, un-American, unconstitutional, and unfair. . . . Thus we see that communitarianism is undemocratic, un-American, unconstitutional, and unfair.

Instead, the writer can pursue a rounder, perhaps more oblique path if the argument recognizes its own limitations. Two-dimensional argument explicitly acknowledges competing hypotheses, alternative explanations, and even outright contradictions.

> The ideals set forth by communitarianism are undemocratic, un-American, unconstitutional, and unfair even though its proponents tout it as the panacea for our nation's ills.

The value of this approach is that it widens the tunnel vision that repeats only one proposition. It implies that you have explored competing hypotheses and have weighed the evidence for and against each. Your reader may or may not agree with your conclusion, but he or she will certainly respect your effort to set it in a broader context.

Using Sources in Argument Essays

This section is a discussion of writing about argument in the specialized sense of the word. Think of a controversial issue on which you have a strong opinion. Note that we use the word "issue" here rather than "subject" or "topic." A subject or *topic* maps out a general area for discussion or inquiry. An *issue* involves some specific point or matter for contention and debate. "Abortion" is a topic. "Whether or not women should have free choice in the matter of abortion" is an issue. In your journal or notebook, jot down your views on one of the following issues or on an issue of your choice:

1. Whether we should buy American-made goods rather than imports.
2. Whether rap or heavy metal music promotes violence.
3. Whether television damages family life
4. Whether the United States should extend the school year.
5. Whether cosmetics firms should be allowed to experiment on animals.

Next, state the primary reason you hold your position. Ask yourself two questions: (1) What underlying fact or cause is the basis for my view? and (2) Based on this reason, would someone agree or disagree with my reasoning? When you begin to think about how your reader or larger audience might react to your position, you will see how difficult it can be to construct a persuasive argument defending your views. We will return to this activity in a collaborative exercise after we have considered some strategies and techniques for fashioning strong arguments.

When you develop support for such an argument, be sure to differentiate between reasons and opinions. An *opinion* is a belief that you cannot substantiate with direct proof, whereas a *reason* carries with it the weight of logic and evidence. Students who sprinkle their compositions with the tag "in my personal opinion" are redundant because by their nature opinions are personal. The student who explains that "The school year should be shortened because young kids usually waste away their summers anyway" is expressing an opinion about the productivity of kids on vacation. Similarly, the student who argues that "From the time I was thirteen, I worked hard at a job all summer long. Kids should work during the summer and not go to school" is also expressing an opinion. Both individuals define their points of view, but neither gives firm grounds of support. On the other hand, the student who writes

Because our school year is 180 days and Japan's and West Germany's extends from 226 to 243 school days, Japanese and German children have more time to learn science and math. A lengthened school year will allow our students to spend as much classroom time on science and math as students in other industrialized countries and perhaps "catch up" with the competition.

has provided a rational ground of support for his or her view. This is called a *reason*.

To make a strong argument, you need to support your position with substantial reasons. This will be easy if you have ample background knowledge of and firsthand experience with the issue. But if you know little about the issue, even if you have very strong opinions on it, you must refer to reading sources for additional information.

In some courses, your professors will stipulate the issues for you to discuss. At other times, you will be permitted to select your own topic. When this is the case, you can convert your topic into an arguable statement or issue by asking, "What is controversial about _____? What do people argue about?" Take communitarianism, the topic we introduced earlier (see p. 103). If you have thought or read about this social movement and know that the conflict is between individual claims and collective life, you will have no trouble delving beneath the surface and discovering a number of specific issues. Your background knowledge will enable you to refine the topic and come up with an innovative slant on it. If you know very little about communitarianism, however, you will have to learn more about it by carefully reading the sources your professor recommends or by conducting library research. Chapter 5 will assist you with library work.

Once you have determined what it is that people argue about, convert that information into an issue: Discuss whether the interests of communities are more important than the interests of individuals. If you prefer, state your issue as a question: Which is more sacred, communal or individual rights?

Subject or Topic → What Do People Argue About? → Issue

You may have strong opinions on the issue from the outset ("No, communal rights are far less important than individual rights"; "Yes, people should honor the common good rather than the selfish individual"), but remember that opinions are not enough. To persuade someone else, you need convincing reasons. Unless you are fully informed about the issue, you will have to consult reading sources.

As you embark upon reading the sources, keep in mind that you may uncover so much information that you will have to redefine and narrow your issue. Remember to probe both sides and read with an open mind, even if you have already taken a stand. A useful activity at this point is what Peter Elbow calls the "believing game." As you encounter views that conflict with your own, try to see them through the holder's eyes. Even if the views are absurd or directly opposite to yours, put yourself in the other person's place. As Elbow points out, "To do this requires great energy, attention, and even a kind of inner commitment. It helps to think of it as trying to get inside the head of someone who saw things this way. Perhaps even constructing such a person for yourself. Try to have the experience of someone who made the assertion" (149).

After you have read through the sources, write a clear-cut statement of your position and the conflicting view. To illustrate the process of composing an argumentative essay, we will follow a student, Sarah Allyn, as she works on her paper entitled "Communitarianism Contested" (see pp. 115–120). This illustration will be more meaningful to you if you read the four selections in Chapter 11 on which it is based: Amitai Etzioni's "Morality as a Community Affair"; Christopher Little's "Communitarianism, A New Threat for Gun Owners"; Barry Jay Seltser and Donald E. Miller's "Ambivalences in American Views of Dignity"; and Michael Walzer's "Multiculturalism and Individualism."

Here is Sarah's schematic outline of the issue that she intends to write about:

Issue: Whether communitarianism is a panacea for the problems facing America.

My position: Few mainstream Americans will consider communitarianism a worthwhile solution to America's problems.	My opponent's position: Communitarian principles will solve the nation's problems.

Taking the two positions, Sarah composes a thesis statement that includes the main points of both sides:

Even though some of the recommendations of communitarians are laudable, few, if any, mainstream Americans will see the resurgence of "community" as a panacea for our nation's ills.

Then Sarah returns to her reading sources to locate reasons for each position. She asks herself, "Which facts, examples, pieces of evidence, and citations by reliable authorities support my views and the views of my opponents?" As Sarah discovers reasons, she jots them down in her notebook.

Support for My Positions

1. We should keep in mind that "communitarian writers are mainly academics, some of whom enjoy close connections to the Washington political community" (Little 30).

2. Etzioni himself admits that communitarian organizations can be excessive and corrupt, for example McCarthyism and the Ku Klux Klan (36).

3. How will the "common good" prevail and communitarianism function if, as Etzioni explains, "Americans don't like to tell others how to behave"?

4. Another conflict between individuals and communities is related to the issue of personal property. Seltser and Miller remind us that "property is defined as an extension of the self" (121).

5. Little: How can communitarianism be morally advantageous when it abrogates certain rights (30)?

6. Levinson in Yale Law Journal argues that most Americans will uphold individual rights, even at cost to others (Little 84).

Support for the Other Side

1. Walzer: "Individuals are stronger, more confident, more savvy, when they are participants in a common life, responsible to and for other people" (189).

2. Seltser and Miller: A common moral or ethical code is reasonable because society is formed "by a mixture of values and beliefs that both form its citizens and are in turn formed by them" (118).

3. Etzioni argues that the alternative to having the community voice sound moral principles is "state coercion or social and moral anarchy" (36).

4. Walzer: If we adopt communitarian principles, we will have "greater social and economic equality" (191).

The writer of an argumentative essay should bear in mind the likely reader of or audience for the essay. If the issue is highly controversial, the reader will probably have an opinion of his or her own about it. A writer who addresses a single reader—say, a college professor or a public official whose confidence one seeks to engage—should estimate what the reader already knows and might think about the issue. Members of a larger audience may hold conflicting points of view. Writers who address such an audience need especially to rely on the power and conviction of their argued proofs.

QUESTIONS ABOUT AUDIENCE FOR AN ARGUMENTATIVE ESSAY

1. Am I writing for my professor, my classmates, a broader audience, or a special group of readers?
2. What do my readers already know about the issue? Will I have to explain basic concepts and provide background information for my point of view to make sense?
3. How do I want to come across to my audience—as an objective, scholarly authority, or as someone who identifies with my readers and shares their concerns?
4. Is my audience noncommittal, or have my readers already taken a stand on the issue I am discussing?

Answers to these questions tell writers a number of things: (1) how much effort they should expend to attract their audience's attention with the lead sentence and introduction; (2) how much background information they should provide so that their readers will thoroughly understand the issue; (3) how they will address their readers (whether they will be totally objective or use pronouns such as "I," "you," or "we"); and (4) how they will order their presentation and how much space they will devote to opposing views.

WAYS TO SUPPORT YOUR REASONS

1. Examples:
    a. Based on a similarity to something that happened in the past.
    b. Based on a similar case.
    c. Based on a hypothetical situation.
2. Relevant information:

(continued on the next page)

a. Facts.

b. Statistics.

c. Points of interest.

3. Statements, testimony, or other relevant information from acknowledged authorities.

4. Personal experience (be sure the experience relates directly to the reason you are developing).

INDIVIDUAL EXERCISE ON SUPPORTING ARGUMENTS

To develop full, rich, rounded arguments requires some practice. One can often get this practice by playing with controversial ideas in a creative and free-spirited way.

1. Take an idea, any idea, no matter how preposterous or absurd: for example, "Homelessness is a desirable way of life," "The U.S. government should allow all immigrants to enter this country," "Drugs should be freely available to anyone who wants them," "Communities should have the right to prohibit stores from selling questionable types of rock music," "Public schools and colleges should enforce strict dress codes." Write down the idea in your own words.

2. Write a statement about the opposite point of view.

3. Brainstorm a list of possible reasons to explain the first idea. After that, brainstorm a list of possible reasons to explain the opposite point of view.

4. Decide which reasons are most convincing for each position. Rank them in order of strength of importance.

5. Decide which position is most convincing. State that position as the main clause of an independent sentence. Recast the other position as a subordinate clause linked to the main clause by "because," "although," "despite," or the like. Finally, try to express the relationship between both clauses: What is the connecting link that brings them together?

COLLABORATIVE EXERCISE ON SUPPORTING ARGUMENTS

1. Here we return to the activity that we initiated above in our discussion on argument in a specialized sense of the word. In your journal or notebook, jot down your views on one of the following controversial issues or on an issue of your choice:

   a. Whether we should buy American-made goods rather than imports.
   b. Whether rap or heavy metal music promotes violence.
   c. Whether television damages family life.
   d. Whether the United States should extend the school year.
   e. Whether cosmetics firms should be allowed to experiment on animals.

   Next, state the primary reason you hold your position. Ask yourself two questions: (1) What underlying fact or cause is the basis for my view? and (2) Would someone agree or disagree with my reasoning?
2. Form collaborative learning groups of five students each, as described in the Preface, or fashion groups according to a method of your own. Share your positions and reasons with your classmates.
3. As each student explains the issue and gives his or her position and reason for holding it, the other group members should remain noncommittal. In other words, if a student in your group explains why she is in favor of lengthening the school year, pretend that you have no opinion on the issue. From your neutral stance, evaluate your classmate's argument. Have you been persuaded to accept his or her view?
4. When each student's argument has been examined, come to a consensus on what characteristics made arguments either strong or weak. Have the group recorder note your group's conclusions.
5. Reconvene the entire class. Each group recorder should explain the characteristics of strong and weak arguments that the group identified.

Organizing Argumentative Essays

As history shows, some of the principles of argument that were taught in ancient Greece and Rome have been adapted for writers today. If you were a student in ancient times, you would have been taught to set up your argument in six parts: (1) the introduction (*exordium*), (2) the statement or exposition of the case under discussion (*narratio*), (3) the outline of the points or steps in the argument (*divisio*), (4) the proof of the case (*confirmatio*), (5) the refutation of the opposing arguments (*confutatio*), (6) the conclusion (*peroratio*) (Corbett 25). Today's principles of organization are not quite so rigid or formulaic as the ones prescribed by the Ancients. Nevertheless, most modern writers of arguments use some variation of the following divisions: opening, explanation of the issue, background information, writer's thesis or point of view, presentation of and response to opposing views, reasons for writer's point of view, conclusion.

ARRANGEMENT OF THE ARGUMENTATIVE ESSAY

Introductory Section

Opener: Introduce the topic and interest your reader.
Explanation of Issue: Familiarize your reader with the controversy.
Background: Give information the reader needs to know to understand fully the issue at hand.
Thesis: Give your stand on the issue.

Body of the Essay

Presentation of and Response to Opposing Views

Reasons for the Writer's Point of View

Variation A	*Variation B*
1. Opposing view	1. Reasons and various types of support for your own view
2. Your response	2. Opposing view
3. Reasons and various types of support for your own view	3. Your response

Conclusion

Recap of argument.
Concluding technique.

You can arrange your reasons in several different ways. Many writers prefer to present weaker reasons first and work to a climax by saving their strongest argument until the end of the composition. This movement from weak to strong provides a dramatic effect. Other writers start the body of the essay with their opponents' view; then, in sharp contrast, they present their strongest arguments; finally, they close with their weakest points. This movement begins the essay with an energetic claim that seizes the reader's attention. Still other writers think it best to present a relatively strong argument first, saving the strongest until last; in between, they arrange the weaker ones. This movement combines the dramatic effect of the first pattern with the attention-seizing of the second. Whether you choose to acknowledge and respond to opposing views before you give reasons for your own position or after you present your case depends on the situation and the nature of your audience. There is no hard rule that says that you must arrange your essay one way or the other.

But what if your opponents' objections are especially weighty or substantial? In that case, you may want to arrange the body of your essay in a different way. Instead of, or along with, presenting the conflicting view and your position in separate, self-contained sections, you can respond to the objections in a point-by-point fashion. The box that follows shows an outline of this alternating arrangement.

ALTERNATING ARRANGEMENT FOR ARGUMENTATIVE ESSAY

Introductory Section

> *Opener:* Introduce the topic and interest your reader.
> *Explanation of Issue:* Familiarize your reader with the controversy.
> *Background:* Give information the reader needs to know in order to understand fully the issue at hand.
> *Thesis:* Give your stand on the issue.

Body of the Essay

1. Position taken in source(s) on one aspect of the controversy.
2. Writer's refutation or support of the position described in 1.
3. Position taken in source(s) on another aspect of the controversy.
4. Writer's refutation or support of the position described in 3. (This pattern continues until you have covered all the aspects of the issue that you choose to focus on.)

Conclusion

> Recap of the argument.
> Concluding technique.

Let us return to Sarah Allyn's argument against communitarianism. Since Sarah assumes that a number of her readers will be supportive of communitarianism, she acknowledges and refutes their arguments in paragraphs 3, 4, and 5. Then in paragraphs 6 and 7, she provides further support for her own position.

Here is Sarah's essay. If you have not yet read the four selections in Chapter 11 on which it is based, do so before you read Sarah's essay. The selections are Amitai Etzioni's "Morality as a Community Affair"; Christopher Little's "Communitarianism, A New Threat for Gun Owners"; Barry Jay Seltser and Donald E. Miller's, "Ambivalences in American Views of Dignity"; and Michael Walzer's "Multiculturalism and Individualism."

SAMPLE ARGUMENT ESSAY

Sarah Allyn

Professor Kennedy

English 131

30 September 1999

Communitarianism Contested

There exists in America today a growing sense that a breakdown in our moral fiber, an erosion of the values that helped build our nation, has all but dissolved the once mighty American spirit. From those who advocate communitarianism, a movement which seeks to enforce popular social beliefs by communal decree, perhaps this message is heard loudest. Leading proponents of communitarianism such as Harvard professor Amitai Etzioni advocate a position which presupposes such notions as "we are each other's keepers" (Etzioni 31) and "strong rights presume strong responsibilities" (Little 30). Michael Walzer, writing in the academic journal <u>Dissent</u>, claims "empowerment is, with rare exceptions, a familial, class, or communal, not an individual achievement" (Walzer 187). More than mere

sloganeers, however, communitarians are working to realize a
society bereft of many of the hard-fought liberties achieved
in our national Constitution, which set forth to ensure
liberty for all Americans. We should keep in mind, moreover,
that "communitarian writers are mainly academics, some of
whom enjoy close connections to the Washington political
community" (Little 30). Are these the voices Americans want
speaking for them?

Is the mainstream American population as willing as
those from academia's privileged left wing to sacrifice
personal liberty for the greater welfare of the many? To
place their responsibility and duty to others in front of
their personal rights? To uphold the safety of others and
the liberty of the group before considering the claims of
the individual? To sacrifice one's Constitutional rights as
an American citizen--to do so in the name of a socialist
political agenda devised by academics secure enough in their
means to undertake such a radical experiment? Even though
some of the recommendations of communitarian intellectuals
are laudable, few, if any, mainstream Americans will
consider the principles of communitarianism to be a
worthwhile "answer" to our nation's ills.

As a system of organization, communitarianism is
inherently impractical. In "Multiculturalism and
Individualism," Walzer argues, "Individuals are stronger,
more confident, more savvy, when they are participants in a
common life, responsible to and for other people" (189). If
the recent failure of Communism isn't enough to disprove
Walzer's claim, consider the decline of a redundant form of
communitarianism--labor unions. Labor unions haven't
succeeded for the same reasons that any attempt to galvanize
people according to structure reminiscent of Marxist
principles would be doomed. First, in a democracy, the
majority gets what it votes for, and most likely, existing

forms of political leadership would be prepared to meet any
challenge posed by a communitarian constituency. Second,
communitarian organizations, much like labor unions, would
be extremely vulnerable to excessiveness and corruption.
"Forty years ago, for example, America experienced the
nightmare of McCarthyism. Likewise the memory of the real Ku
Klux Klan" (Etzioni 36). Consider also the disgraceful
spectacle of organized labor's relationship with organized
crime. These examples of communitarianism run awry remain
fresh in the collective American consciousness. Furthermore,
according to Prof. Sanford Levinson writing in the <u>Yale Law
Journal</u>, Americans place such a high value on their
individual rights that "one will honor them even when there
is significant social cost in doing so" (Little 84). Lastly,
and as Etzioni himself points out, "Americans do not like to
tell others how to behave" (34). For communitarianism to
function as it is intended, heavy emphasis is placed on
individuals' ability to "police" one another, a troublesome
and wholly undemocratic process.

    While it may be true that "societies are defined, in
large part, precisely by the mixture of values and beliefs
that both form [their] citizens and are in turn formed by
them" (Seltser and Miller 118), creating a factional, quasi-
governmental system won't serve to advance Americans' common
moral or ethical code. Moreover, along with the complexities
inherent in forging relationships according to a
communitarian model of social behavior, decisions to
determine power accords and their regulation would be left
up to a decentralized governing body. Such potentially great
power represented without the benefit of definitive
leadership could be dangerous. In "Ambivalences in American
Views of Dignity," Barry J. Seltser and Donald E. Miller
uncover a source of conflict that opposes communitarianism's
principles. They explain that "in one important strand of

the liberal political tradition, of course, property is
defined as an extension of the self, as something of myself
that has been mixed in with the physical world and therefore
remains 'mine' in some important sense" (121). This
contradiction alone between democratic and communitarian
ideals makes the prospect of successfully managed
communitarian environments seem all the more unlikely, at
least as long as America intends to remain a democracy.

The advocates of communitarianism, in retreat, resort
to hysteria. In "Morality as a Community Affair," Etzioni,
admonishing his readers about the importance of catering to
the whims and needs of the community, and in rare form,
declares, "The alternative is typically state coercion or
social and moral anarchy" (36). While claiming the only
alternatives "to the exercise of moral voices" are either "a
police state" or "a moral vacuum in which anything goes"
(37), he neglects, however, to mention that with a few rare
exceptions in America's history, such alternatives have not
been seriously considered. This is due to the fact that
America's government, despite its tender age, has exhibited
the greatest degree of stability and success in the annals
of our planet's social order. Preying on "a strong
egalitarian and populist strain" (Walzer 186) such as is
found in America, some communitarians seem merely determined
to stress the negative aspects of our democratic society.
Advocates of multiculturalism such as Walzer believe
"greater social and <u>economic</u> equality" would be the end
result of the adoption of such communitarian principles
(191). He goes on to admit, however, that acting according
to multicultural principles today may bring more trouble
than hope (191). He attributes this to America's weak social
agenda, but this rationalization serves merely as an excuse.

The adoption of communitarianism in America would
necessitate a paradigm shift in our fundamental cultural

construction, from individualism to collectivism. Though
America is no longer a fledgling democracy, there is still
evidence of "rugged individualism" within our culture.
Individualism has played an important role in our national
development. And for many Americans, particularly recent
immigrants, communitarian principles may prove a barrier to
pursuing the American dream. Clearly, communitarianism,
perhaps even in its mildest form, threatens the vitality of
the American populace and poses a potential challenge to
American democracy.

Although indeed most who advocate communitarianism
champion its principles as morally advantageous, still
others disagree. Whereby "its public policy recommendations
either implicitly or expressly call for the attenuation or
even abrogation of certain rights" (Little 30), does not
communitarianism breach the moral foundations of our nation?
Disturbingly, as Little points out, "a recent issue of The
Communitarian Reporter states that the White House is
'seeking to move along communitarian lines,' a fact well
attested by the communitarian substance of many speeches and
writings of President Clinton" (31). "In fairness," Little
continues, "there are signs that Clinton is not a 'purist'
communitarian," though "nevertheless, his communitarian bent
is by definition an anti-constitutional bent" (84). Given
the dubious morality and constitutionality of
communitarianism, it is hard to account for its appeal.
Don't such radical principles actually serve the interests
of the few rather than the many?

Perhaps we ought to be, as Amitai Etzioni stated, "each
other's keepers" after all (31). Democracy is indeed an
efficient system of social checks and balances, a system
which enables Americans to determine their collective
progress or decline. We, as Americans, owe at least this
much to one another: to guard against the debasement of our

Allyn 6

personal freedoms, to uphold our long-standing heritage of
individualism and to never relinquish our Constitutional
rights. It is our responsibility, as privileged citizens of
this great nation, to oppose the undemocratic, un-American
ideals set forth by the immoral, unconstitutional, and
unfair theories of communitarianism.

Allyn 7

Works Cited

Etzioni, Amitai. "Morality as a Community Affair." <u>The</u>
    <u>Spirit of Community: Rights, Responsibilities, and the</u>
    <u>Communitarian Agenda</u>. New York: Crown, 1993. 30-38.
Little, Christopher. "Communitarianism, A New Threat for
    Gun Owners." <u>American Rifleman</u> Oct. 1993: 30-31+.
Seltser, Barry Jay, and Donald E. Miller, "Ambivalences in
    American Views of Dignity." <u>Homeless Families, The</u>
    <u>Struggle for Dignity</u>. Urbana: U of Illinois P, 1993.
    118-23.
Walzer, Michael. "Multiculturalism and Individualism."
    <u>Dissent</u> Spring 1994: 185-91.

You will note that Sarah Allyn's paper has followed many of the
guidelines we've suggested for argumentative papers. It displays a broad
knowledge of ideas that support the concept of communitarian ethics
and related issues; it outlines major areas of controversy on the topic,
such as the status of personal liberties, factional politics, and multicultural
populism; and it articulates a strong thesis that expresses a particular
point of view about the issues in question. Sarah's thesis is an opposi-
tional one that takes the source readings to task for compromising personal liberties. An argumentative thesis need not be so negative as this
one. In general, a positive argument that expands one's understanding of

the source materials succeeds much better than a wrangling altercation. Still, Sarah Allyn leaves no doubt that she has examined the issues and has considered how she wants her audience to respond.

Though we have presented Sarah Allyn's final draft, you should bear in mind that she produced it after several preliminary drafts of its parts and their whole. The following sections describe some additional steps that she followed when she revised her essay.

Revising the Preliminary Draft

If possible, schedule a conference with your instructor, and if your instructor approves of it, have a classmate or a friend read over your first draft and answer the questions listed below. If no one is available, answer the questions yourself. Keep in mind the following concerns:

1. Move from writer-based to reader-based prose.
2. Vary sentence length.
3. Stress verbs rather than nouns.
4. Use words effectively.
5. Eliminate sexist language.
6. Add your own voice.

QUESTIONS FOR REVISING AN ARGUMENT ESSAY

1. Does the writer organize the discussion around the discernible purpose of persuading or convincing an audience?
2. Does the writer fail to move beyond the purpose of simply synthesizing or comparing or contrasting opposing views?
3. Is the argument two-dimensional, taking into account both sides of the issue?
4. Is the argument one-sided?
5. Does the writer use the conventions (not necessarily in this order) that the reader expects to find in an argument essay?
   a. Explanation of the issue?
   b. Arguable thesis?
   c. Background information?
   d. Support for the position being argued?

(continued on the next page)

---

    e. Mention of the conflicting position?

    f. Writer's response to the opposition?

    g. Conclusion?

6. Does the writer present reasons rather than opinions?

7. Are the reasons substantiated with evidence and support?

8. Does the writer draw on reliable sources?

9. Does the writer create a favorable, creditable impression of himself or herself?

10. Does the writer display an awareness of the audience's needs by setting a context for the reader?

    a. Giving appropriate background information?

    b. Mentioning authors and titles of sources when necessary?

    c. Supplying necessary documentation for sources?

    d. Providing clear connectives that differentiate his or her ideas from those of the writers of the sources?

Editing the Preliminary Draft

When you are satisfied with your revision, read your paper aloud. Then reread it line by line and sentence by sentence. Check for correct usage, punctuation, spelling, mechanics, manuscript form, and typos. If you are using a word processing program with a spell checker, apply the checker to your essay. If you are especially weak in editing skills, try getting a friend to read over your work.

INDIVIDUAL EXERCISE ON ARGUMENTATIVE ESSAYS

Reread Sarah Allyn's paper. Note the structure of its presentation. After an introduction, Sarah questions whether mainstream America endorses communitarian thought; she points to shortcomings in quotations from its supporters; she cites criticism by its opponents; and she speculates upon consequences that could follow from its adoption. Evaluate the strength of her argument.

COLLABORATIVE EXERCISE ON ARGUMENTATIVE ESSAYS

1. Form collaborative learning groups of five students each, as described in the Preface, or fashion groups according to a method of your own.

2. Assign each member a paragraph from the body of Sarah Allyn's paper. Ask each to comment on Sarah's use of her sources, the accuracy of her summaries and paraphrases, the relevance of her quotations, and the power of her own reasoning.

3. Reconvene the entire class. Each group recorder should read the members' evaluations and respond to inquiries from the rest of the class about the effectiveness of Sarah's argument.

ANALYSIS AND EVALUATION: AN INTRODUCTION

To analyze a text is to break it up into its elements or parts. This dissection requires the critical reading strategies that you have been using throughout this book: reading for information; form, organization, expository and stylistic features; and rhetorical concerns. Evaluation marks a further stage in the process. To evaluate a text is to assess its strengths and its weaknesses on the basis of a close analysis.

Professors assign analytical essays because they want their students to apply critical reading strategies to what they read. When they assign evaluative essays, they expect you to base your appraisal on a systematic examination of the material, not on personal opinions or reactions. Analytical and evaluative essays differ from reaction or response essays. As we saw in Chapter 2, the response essay is based on your previous knowledge of and experiences with the topic. *A reaction or response essay will focus on the content of the reading source, but an essay of analysis and evaluation will examine how that content is conveyed.*

An evaluation follows from an analysis in that it requires a systematic study and assessment of the reading source. The primary difference between a bare analysis and one that requires evaluation is that the latter judges the strengths and weaknesses of the source according to criteria that are acceptable within the academic community. The analytical essay sets forth an interpretation of the source; it does not necessarily pass judgment on its quality or worth. Another difference between analysis and evaluation is that the evaluation essay has a more persuasive edge to it. It aims to get its readers to agree with its conclusions. An evaluative book review, for example, may affect its readers by inciting them to read the book.

Figure 4-1 indicates some clear-cut distinctions between reaction or response essays and essays of analysis and evaluation.

Keep in mind that various academic fields have their own standards for analyzing and evaluating written work. When you take courses in the social sciences, for instance, you will see that the criteria differ from those

Figure 4-1

Essay Type	Strategy	Goal
Reaction or Response (Subjective)	Draw on the knowledge and experiences you bring to the text	Express informed opinions about the subject matter
Analysis (Objective)	Draw on an examination of the various elements of the reading source	Interpret how the writer conveys meaning
Evaluation (Objective)	Draw on an examination of the various elements of the reading source and judge the elements according to a set of established criteria	Show the relative strengths and weaknesses of the work

used in the humanities. Make sure that you keep track of the standards that are presented in the various fields and use them when you read and write in each area.

WRITING AN ANALYTICAL ESSAY

Reading the Source and Planning Your Essay

Successful analysis requires careful planning. Assignments that direct you to analyze or evaluate a text are typically harder than assignments that ask you to react, compare and contrast, or argue because they require a more detailed examination of the reading source and a closer observation of the author's writing skills. Without attentive preparation, you may generate an extended summary or reaction instead of an acceptable analysis and evaluation.

Clarify the Assignment, Set Your Rhetorical Goal, and Consider Your Audience

When you receive your assignment, pay attention to what it asks you to do. Some assignments are open-ended and allow you to determine which aspects of the reading source you will examine. Other assignments may stipulate the parts of the text on which you should focus. For example, a professor might ask you to discuss the role of language in a particular piece or to comment on the structure of a text and explain why it is organized as it is. If you have questions about the type of analysis the assignment calls for, be sure to ask your professor before you proceed.

Once you have clarified the assignment, decide on your rhetorical purpose by asking yourself, "Why am I writing this essay? What effect do I hope to have on my audience?" For an analytical essay, your fundamental purpose should be to explain to your readers your understanding of the reading source and in so doing demonstrate how one or more characteristics of the text contribute to its meaning. For an evaluative essay, you move beyond interpretation into the realm of judgment. Your purpose is to estimate quality or worth. Rather than simply describing how a writer's evidence supports his or her argument, you explain how well the evidence serves the writer's purpose. Rather than simply stating that a writer's position has merit or not, you demonstrate how the writer's language functions. In addition to treating the text's strengths, you may point out its weaknesses.

Your audience may require some background material if your essay is to make sense to them. Ask yourself the following questions:

1. What will my readers already know about the reading source?
2. How much of the source should I summarize, and what form should the summary take?
3. Will I need to explain basic concepts and provide background for the material to make sense?
4. What overall impact do I hope to have on my readers?

If your audience is familiar with the piece, you need to provide only a minimal amount of background information. Summarize parts of the text that are crucial to your thesis. It is not necessary to provide coverage of the entire piece, but only enough to persuade your readers that you have a valid, reasonable interpretation and/or evaluation that will enlighten their understanding.

Do a First Reading to Get a General Impression of the Text

Your first reading may leave you with little more than a general impression, an overall sense of the topic, the author's approach, and the central point. You probably won't pay much attention to other characteristics of the text unless they are highly conspicuous. At this stage, you may want to freewrite your reactions, especially if the text evokes a strong response.

Reread and Ask Questions About Analyzing and Evaluating the Text

Analyzing and evaluating a reading source is largely a matter of asking the right questions. The second reading allows you to question, annotate, and take notes. You will work with essentially the same questions about information and content, form, organization, expository and stylistic features, and rhetorical concerns that you have been using throughout this book, but you will make them more probing and more detailed. Your objective is to delve deeper into the material. Don't trust your memory. Write answers to the questions in your journal or notebook. These answers may serve as the basis for your essay.

A typical assignment in literature courses is to analyze a short story, novel, poem, or play. Literary analysis proceeds in much the same way as other types of analysis by requiring the student to determine how form, organization, stylistic features, and rhetorical elements contribute to meaning. The additional requirement for analyzing poetry, drama, or fiction is that you must consider certain special characteristics of literary texts, the most common of which are theme, plot, characterization, setting, and point of view.

The following questions serve two functions. They help you break down the text into its principal components, and they help you develop a structure for your paper. The italicized questions are phrased in a way that encourages you to evaluate as well as interpret. Record your answers to these questions in your journal or notebook.

QUESTIONS FOR ANALYZING AND EVALUATING TEXTS

Questions About Information and Content

1. What is the author's thesis—the central point he or she is making about the topic?
2. *Is the thesis plausible? defensible? illuminating?*
3. What other important points are made?
4. *Do the other important points follow logically from the thesis?*
5. What aspects of the topic has the author chosen to emphasize?
6. What aspects does he or she disregard?

(continued on the next page)

7. *Is the author emphasizing appropriate aspects of the topic? Does he or she disregard important aspects or put too much emphasis on certain points?*

8. Does the author acknowledge and refute the views of individuals who might oppose his or her argument?

9. What types of evidence does the author use to support his or her points? (For a review of various types of evidence, see pp. 110–111).

10. *Does the author use a sufficient amount of evidence to support his or her points? Which points need more support or explanation?* (For a review of the various types of evidence, see pp. 110–111).

11. Do the author's conclusions follow logically from the evidence?

12. *Are there places where the reader has difficulty seeing the connection between the evidence and conclusions?*

13. *Are the conclusions accurate? Do they have direct implications for readers, or do they have limited applicability and usefulness?*

Questions About Form, Organization, and Expository and Stylistic Features

Form

1. Does the writer use an identifiable form? In this textbook, you have already examined certain essay types: response, comparison and contrast, and argument. Other recognizable forms of nonfiction are editorials, news stories, feature articles, biographies, autobiographies, and letters to the editor.

2. How does the form contribute to the argument?

3. *Is the form appropriate for the content? Would the writer have been better able to convey his or her message in another form?*

Organization

1. What is the organizational pattern: (1) time order, narration, process; (2) antecedent-consequent, cause-effect; (3) description; (4) statement-response; (5) comparison/contrast (either point-by-point or block structure); (6) example; (7) analysis/classification; (8) definition; (9) analogy; or (10) argument (including position, reasons, opposition, and refutation)?

2. *Is the organizational pattern clear and well conceived?*

(continued on the next page)

3. How does the organizational pattern contribute to the meaning of the piece?

4. *Would the meaning be better represented if the parts were arranged differently (for example, if the thesis were disclosed in the introduction instead of the conclusion); if the narrative had progressed from past to present instead of present to past; if reasons were ordered from most important to least important instead of vice versa?*

Expository and Stylistic Features

1. What are the recognizable characteristics of the text, and how do they help convey the author's point?

2. Does the author use any memorable or significant devices that enable you to see the subject from a new perspective? To answer these questions, you will want to look closely at features such as language, sentence elements, images and scenes, and references and allusions.

Language

a. Does the writer's language serve to heighten and illuminate the topic, or is it merely adequate?

b. Does the writer use precise wording, vivid details, words that appeal to the senses, and words with emotional intensity?

c. Does the writer use figurative language (for example, similes, metaphors, personification) to explore the subject?

d. *Is the figurative language appropriate or confusing, inexact, or misleading?*

e. *Is the author's vocabulary unnecessarily formal or pompous? Does he or she use strange or unusual or overly technical words where common ones would do?*

Sentence Elements

a. Are you struck by rhythmic, balanced, symmetrical, or graceful sentences, or are they disorganized and awkward?

b. How do these sentences help to convey the meaning of the text?

c. *Is the author concise, or does he or she try to pack too many ideas into long, sprawling sentences?*

(continued on the next page)

Images and Scenes

    a. Does the writer create memorable images (mental pictures) and scenes that contribute to the meaning of the text?

    b. *If the author creates images and describes scenes, do they vivify the text or are they superfluous?*

    c. *What would be gained if the author included more images?*

    d. *What would be lost if the images were left out?*

References and Allusions

    a. Do the writer's references or allusions illuminate or add significantly to the subject matter? Take account of the writer's formal references to other written sources as well as other types of references and allusions. (An allusion, not to be mistaken for "illusion," is a reference to some literary, cultural, or historical piece of information, whether through direct or indirect citation, that taps the reader's knowledge or memory.)

    b. *What would be lost if the references and allusions were left out?*

    c. *Are the references to other written sources welcome additions to the text, or do they appear to be superfluous?*

    d. *Are the other sources timely, or does the author rely on outdated information?*

Questions About Rhetorical Concerns

1. What is the writer's persona or stance (attitude or rhetorical posture), and how does it contribute to his or her point?

2. *Is the author's persona or stance suitable, or does it detract from the piece?*

3. How does the writer's voice contribute to the effectiveness?

4. *Are the voice and tone appropriate or unnecessarily pompous or formal?*

5. *Does the author come across as authoritative, creditable, and reliable, or are you left with questions about his or her background, prestige, political or religious orientation, or overall reputation?*

6. *Is the author impartial, or does he or she appear to be biased?*

7. *Does the author supply the reader with sufficient background information, or does he or she make erroneous assumptions about the reader's previous knowledge?*

ADDITIONAL QUESTIONS FOR FICTIONAL SOURCES

Theme

1. What theme or central idea does the author express in this piece? (The theme registers the main idea of the piece. It is comparable to the thesis in a work of nonfiction, except that it is rarely stated in one or two sentences. Like a thesis, a theme implies a subject and a verb. You would not say that "justice" is the theme of a work; rather, you would say that the theme is "justice prevails even in the face of adversity.")

2. *Does the theme make an important statement about the subject, or does it contribute only minor insights?*

Plot

1. What types of conflicts occur while the plot is unfolding? (The plot refers to the pattern of events, or story line. It involves a conflict of some kind, usually between a person and another person, nature, social forces, or destiny. The struggle comes to a head in a moment of crisis.)

2. When does the conflict come to a head?

3. *Does the plot evolve in a realistic way, or is it too unpredictable or even preposterous?*

4. *Does the plot focus on the problematic issues, or does it drive them into the background?*

5. *Is there enough conflict in the story, or is there so little conflict that a plot hardly exists?*

Characterization

1. Which techniques of characterization does the author use: (a) describing characters and commenting on their actions; (b) depicting characters in action and reserving commentary; or (c) showing how actions and emotions affect characters internally, without authorial commentary?

2. *Does the author create lifelike characters or mere cardboard figures or caricatures?*

(continued on the next page)

3. *Are the characters complex, or are they two-dimensional characters that lack depth?*

4. *Are the characters dynamic (that is, they are changed by their actions or experiences) or static (characters who do not appear to change at all)?*

Setting

1. How does the setting contribute to the piece? Which elements—time, scenery, location, characters' occupations or lifestyles—are most influential?

2. *Does the author include all the elements (for example, time, locale, scenery, characters' occupations) that are needed to develop the theme, or does he or she omit crucial background information?*

3. *Does the setting advance the ideas in the text, or does it work as a foil against them?*

Point of View

1. From what point of view is the story told: (a) an omniscient narrator who is aware of everything that is happening; (b) a first person narrator who tells the story as he or she experiences it; or (c) a limited point of view in which the story is told in the third person but presented through the eyes of a single character?

2. *Is the point of view appropriate to the issue that the author is exploring?*

3. *Does the point of view distort the issue in any way?*

4. *How would the story change if it were told from a different vantage point—for example, if the author wrote from the perspective of a first-person narrator instead of an omniscient narrator?*

Review Your Answers to the Questions for Analysis

After you have finished rereading and responding to the questions, pause to organize your thoughts while the answers are still fresh in your mind. As you review your notes, keep in mind that your rhetorical purpose is neither to interpret nor to evaluate the piece for your readers.

1. Look to see if a particular question has produced a lengthy, substantive response. If this is the case, you might want to go for depth rather than breadth and focus your analysis on a single, prominent feature.

2. See whether you are able to group together answers that pertain to similar categories. Grouping your answers will help you make sense of the particular issue you are dealing with.

3. Select two or more elements for your focus. Instead of zeroing in on a single, substantive response or categorizing several related responses, you can focus on two or more dominant concerns in the text.

4. Return to the relevant parts of the text to check for supporting material. Each time you make a point about a textual feature, your essay should provide textual evidence in the form of a quotation, a paraphrase, or a summary. At this juncture, go back to the reading and mark passages you might use to support your points. If you cannot find enough textual evidence, consider changing your focus.

Deciding on an Organizational Plan

You can organize your essay in any number of ways. The important thing is to keep your rhetorical purpose in mind. Four typical patterns of organization are presented here.

1. Cause and Effect

    Here you can show how the writer's stylistic features create rich layers of meaning in the text.

    Thesis: In "Everyday Use," the imagery and descriptive language reinforce Alice Walker's depiction of Maggie's transformation from a backward and repressed character to a selfless and compassionate sustainer of family traditions.

    Essay Structure:

    1. Introductory paragraph(s).

    2. One to two paragraphs explaining how imagery reinforces the transformation.

    3. One to two paragraphs explaining how figurative language reinforces the transformation.

    4. Concluding paragraph.

2. Comparison and Contrast

    This arrangement permits you to draw specific points of comparison or difference between textual elements or themes.

Thesis: Although Alice Walker's "Everyday Use" initially depicts Dee as more progressive than Maggie about reviving her cultural roots, it eventually shows that Maggie has better absorbed her family's deepest cultural values.

Essay Structure:

1. Introductory paragraph(s).

2. One or two paragraphs comparing and contrasting Dee's expressive nostalgia for the past to Maggie's quiet sense of continuity with the past.

3. One or two paragraphs comparing and contrasting Dee's self-absorption with Maggie's open-minded practicality.

4. Concluding paragraph.

3. Structure of the Reading Source

This pattern shows the complex structural organization of the reading source by following its order. You take up each feature in the sequence in which it is presented in the text.

Thesis: Throughout "Everyday Use," Alice Walker reveals Dee's shortcomings and weaknesses as opposed to Maggie's understanding and inner strength.

Essay Structure:

1. Introductory paragraph(s).

2. Paragraph demonstrating the characters' respective strengths and weaknesses at the beginning of the story.

3. Paragraph demonstrating the characters' respective strengths and weaknesses in the middle of the story.

4. Paragraph demonstrating the characters' respective strengths and weaknesses at the end of the story.

4. Argument

Here you can structure your analysis and interpretation along the lines of the argument essays we discussed on pages 103–123. If your goal is simply to persuade your readers that you have found significant meaning in the text, you will be writing an argument in the broad sense, stating your position and offering reasons to support it.

Thesis: Alice Walker's description and figurative language contribute significantly to her representation of continuity and tradition in a family's self-understanding.

Essay Structure:
1. Introductory paragraph(s).
2. One or two paragraphs giving reasons why the descriptions offer significant contrasts between superficial display and genuine self-understanding.
3. One or two paragraphs giving reasons why the figurative language reinforces significant insights into self-understanding.
4. Concluding paragraph.

The usual structure for an evaluation essay is some variation of the format used for an argument. You can write a unidimensional argument in which you

1. State your thesis and the three or four criteria that you will use to evaluate the source.
2. Allocate one or more body paragraphs to each criterion, developing each with specific evidence from the source.

Another possibility is to construct a two-dimensional argument. This structure allows you to acknowledge points of agreement between you and the author of the reading source and at the same time assess the source's strengths and weaknesses.

1. State your thesis, agreement, and the criteria that you will use to evaluate the source's strengths and weaknesses.
2. Allocate a paragraph or two acknowledging the source's strengths, substantiating your claims with evidence.
3. Allocate paragraphs to discussing the weaknesses.

The four patterns of organization may be used individually, or they may overlap. In Chapter 12, Theodore A. Gracyk's "Romanticizing Rock Music" uses both the argument pattern and the structural organization of the reading source—Camille Paglia's "Rock as Art"—that he is evaluating. Toward the beginning of the article, he acknowledges that Paglia's argument has some merit: "While I sympathize with attempts to locate an aesthetic of rock music, . . ." (589). He goes on to summarize "Rock as Art," and then he evaluates Paglia's claims point by point: "Charming as this is, it disintegrates when we go through it one claim at a time. Let us start with . . ." (591).

Drafting

After you have decided upon an organizational plan, you are ready to compose a preliminary draft of your essay. Remember that this will not be a final, polished draft. You will have an opportunity to revise it at a later date. Before you begin writing, consider how you want to come across to your readers. Will you subordinate your voice to the text you are analyzing by focusing on the expository features and stylistic techniques particular to the text? Or will you offer a personal interpretation, using the first-person pronoun and evoking experiences and expectations familiar to you and your audience but not necessarily to the writer of the text you are analyzing? The degree of formality or informality may be dictated by the assignment. If you are unsure about taking a particular stance, ask your professor for advice.

As you draft your essay, you may want to consult the sections on paper openers, introductions, and conclusions in Chapter 2. After you have arranged the notes that you took on the questions, convert them into body paragraphs in accordance with your organizational plan. Be sure that as you develop each paragraph, you support your points with evidence (quotations, paraphrases, or summaries) from the reading source.

A further consideration is that you adhere to the special conventions that academic writers follow when composing argumentative, analytical, and evaluative essays.

1. Use the present tense when explaining how the author uses particular procedures and writing techniques.
2. Identify the author of the source by first and last name initially and thereafter only by the last name.
3. Indent long (four or more lines) quotations in block format.

The following student essay by Philip Nekmail analyzes Alice Walker's story "Everyday Use" in this anthology (see Chapter 13). Read the story before you read Philip's essay. As you examine the student essay, bear in mind the strategies for writing an analytical essay that we have discussed, and ask whether the student writer has followed those guidelines.

SAMPLE ESSAY OF LITERARY ANALYSIS

Philip Nekmail
Professor Smith
Academic Writing II
15 May 1999

A Daughter's Entitlement in Alice Walker's "Everyday Use"

Simple yet complex, Alice Walker's portrayal of a
domestic dilemma in "Everyday Use" pits moral value
judgments against contradiction. With this, the assumptions,
the values, and the individuality of each character are
evoked. The main characters in the story, Mama, Maggie,
and Dee, though members of one family, display
contradictions evident in each of their roles as well as
within themselves.

Mama, the story's narrator, makes known her stature in
life while describing each of her two daughters, Dee and
Maggie. Her pride in Dee, though repressed, could perhaps be
equated with her pity for Maggie, the less fortunate of the
two girls. While her sister visits, Maggie "will stand
hopelessly in corners, homely and ashamed" (638), whereas
for Dee, " 'no' is a word the world never learned to say to
her" (638).

By her own definition, Mama is "a large big-boned woman
with rough, man-working hands" (638). Simple, practical, and
traditional, she is neither quick to assume, nor soon to
forget her past. This aspect of her nature emerges when she
and her daughters focus upon the value of the two quilts.
They see the quilts from dissimilar worlds and vantage
points. Dee sees them as objects of artistic value while
Mama and Maggie see them as household items of economic and
practical utility. Thus, Mama's own assumptions and
judgments about the value of the quilts define her

individuality. The two quilts may be for Mama the closest
link to her past that she holds.

Dee's attitude toward the quilt as a mere art object
reveals her lack of respect for the deeper meaning of the
quilt as a sign of tradition. In changing her name to evoke
a remote imagined past, Dee actually rejects the tradition
of her immediate family past. In doing this, she offends
Mama and the very principle—her heritage—which the quilts
signify. Mama's practical nature is evinced in her intent to
give the quilts to Maggie who will "probably be," according
to Dee, "backward enough to put them to everyday use" (643).
This, of course, was Mama's intent to begin with.

Maggie, the pitied, undervalued member of the family,
maintains a low profile throughout the story, achieving a
quiet victory over Dee in acquiring the two quilts. Maggie's
assumptions concerning the quilts' value are made evident
when she tells her mother, "'She [Dee] can have them, Mama,'
she said, like somebody not used to winning anything, or
having anything reserved for her" (644). In her simplistic
nature, then, Mama is at odds with the sophisticated Dee and
in accord with simple Maggie.

A sense of entitlement, a display of arrogance, and a
flair for style are not so much the factors that denominate
the differences between Dee and her family. It is the
hypocrisy, the contradiction that is the very nature of Dee
that sets her apart. Her personality traits belie those of
her mother, for where Mama is simple, Dee is complex; where
Mama is practical, Dee is impractical, stylish, and in
disregard of the tradition her mother so values. Immediately
observable is Dee's assumption of her entitlement to
anything she pleases. Mama's refusal to grant Dee the quilt
signifies a turning point in her life, as Dee's sense of
entitlement is undoubtedly a learned behavior. It is Dee's
lack of reverence for tradition that offsets the balance she

has achieved between herself and her mother. Most central in
the story is Dee's decision to change her name. Not only
does this offend Mama, but it is also an offense to her
heritage. " . . . you was named after your aunt Dicie,"
Mama says. "Dicie is my sister. She [is] named Dee" (681).

Through contrasts of simplicity and complexity,
"Everyday Use" highlights the interplay of morality and
judgment versus contradiction. The congruence of attitudes
between the mother and Maggie clashes with the hypocritical
nature of the stylish, educated Dee. Maggie's selfless
character overpowers Dee, whose disregard for family
tradition and heritage proves to be her ultimate downfall.
Through the conflict that arises over the quilts, the
uniqueness, the assumptions, and the values of each
character become evident.

Work Cited

Walker, Alice. "Everyday Use." Writing in the Disciplines: A
    Reader for Writers. 4th ed. Mary Lynch Kennedy, William
    J. Kennedy, and Hadley M. Smith. Upper Saddle River, NJ:
    Prentice Hall, 1999. 677-687.

You will notice that Philip Nekmail's essay has followed many of the
guidelines we've suggested for writing analytical essays. It probes the
story's organization and form for clues about the characterization of Dee
and Maggie; it describes different perspectives on Dee's self-absorption
and Maggie's openness as elements in the narrative's conflict; and, finally, it considers the author's point of view on Maggie's respect for tradition
as the story's dominant focus.

Though we have presented the final draft of Philip's essay, you should remember that he produced this paper after several preliminary drafts, both in part and in whole. The following sections describe some additional steps that Philip followed when he revised his writing.

Revising the Preliminary Draft

Schedule a conference with your professor (see page 91), or if your instructor agrees, make arrangements to have a classmate or a friend review your preliminary draft and give you feedback. If that is not possible, set the paper aside for a few days and then review it yourself. Respond to the questions given in the following box.

QUESTIONS FOR HELPING A WRITER REVISE THE FIRST DRAFT OF ARGUMENTATIVE, ANALYTICAL, AND EVALUATIVE ESSAYS

1. Can you identify the writer's rhetorical purpose? Is the writer giving you an interpretation of the source and in so doing explaining how certain characteristics contribute to its meaning?

2. Does everything in the draft lead to or follow from some dominant meaning? If not, which ideas seem to be out of place?

3. Do you understand the analysis, and is the writer sensitive to your concerns?

   a. Does he or she provide necessary background information about the subject and enough summary of the source as well as the title and the author? If not, what is missing?

   b. Throughout the essay when the writer refers to the source, does he or she supply you with necessary documentation?

   c. Does the writer provide clear transitions and connecting ideas that differentiate his or her own ideas from those of the author?

   d. Does the writer display an awareness of the author by referring to the author by name, "he," "she," or "they" rather than as "it" or "the article"?

4. Which organizational format does the writer use: cause and effect, comparison and contrast, argument, or the order of the source? If another pattern is used, is it appropriate for an analysis essay?

5. Has the writer made you aware of the bases for the analysis? On which characteristics of the source is the analysis focused? If the bases for the analysis are unclear, explain your confusion.

(continued on the next page)

---

6. Does the writer support each of his or her points with direct evidence (quotations, paraphrases, summaries) from the source? If not, where are they needed?
7. Does the writer provide smooth transitions and connecting ideas as he or she moves from one point of analysis to another? If not, where are they needed?
8. Do you hear the writer's voice throughout the essay? Describe it.
9. What type of paper opener does the writer use? Is it effective? If not, why not?
10. Does the paper have an appropriate conclusion? Can you suggest an alternative way of ending the essay?
11. Is the title suitable for the piece? Can you suggest an alternative?
12. Has the writer followed academic writing conventions, such as
    a. Writing in present tense when explaining how the author uses particular procedures and techniques?
    b. Identifying the author initially by first name and last name and thereafter only by last name?
    c. Indenting long quotations in block format?

Editing the Preliminary Draft

When you are satisfied with your revision, read your paper aloud. Then reread it line by line and sentence by sentence. Check for correct usage, punctuation, spelling, mechanics, manuscript form, and typos. If you are using a word processing program with a spell checker, apply the checker to your essay. If you are especially weak in editing skills, try getting a friend to read over your work.

INDIVIDUAL EXERCISE ON ARGUMENTATIVE, ANALYTICAL, AND EVALUATIVE ESSAYS

Reread Philip Nekmail's paper. Note its structure. After an introduction, the writer recounts features of Mama's characterization, then of Dee's, and finally of Maggie's. Then he shows how Dee's values differ from Mama's and Maggie's. Throughout this analysis, he quotes specific words and phrases that imply the narrator's tone toward the characters. Evaluate how thoroughly Philip Nekmail has analyzed these expository and stylistic features in the fiction.

COLLABORATIVE EXERCISE ON ARGUMENTATIVE, ANALYTICAL, AND EVALUATIVE ESSAYS

1. Form collaborative learning groups of five students each, as de-scribed in the Preface, or fashion groups according to a method of your own.

2. Assign each member of a group a character's perspective or point of view from which to examine the story—Mama's, Dee's, Maggie's, the narrator's, the reader's. Ask each member to comment on how care-fully Philip Nekmail has analyzed the story from that particular point of view.

3. At the end of the small-group session, the recorder should have an assessment of how well the student writer has analyzed each per-spective.

4. Reconvene the entire class. Each group recorder should read the list of assessments. Discuss points of agreement and difference.

WORKS CITED

Corbett, Edward. *Classical Rhetoric for the Modern Student.* 3rd ed. New York: Oxford UP, 1990.

Elbow, Peter. *Writing without Teachers.* New York: Oxford UP, 1973.

C H A P T E R

five

Writing Research Papers

THE RESEARCH PAPER: AN INTRODUCTION

Research involves collecting information from multiple sources and then acting on that information by organizing, synthesizing, analyzing, generalizing, or applying it. Often, we connect the term "research" with scientific and medical discoveries, but it applies to systematic investigation in any discipline, including the humanities and the social sciences. Professors typically assign research papers to make you an active, independent scholar who is able, first, to locate other people's ideas and, second, to analyze and synthesize those ideas and come to an independent conclusion. In a sense, studying research methods is learning how to learn.

In Chapters 1 through 4, we have stressed that the writing process involves active engagement, careful thought, and hard work, and the same is true for research. Research involves more than just finding and recording information. A collection of facts on a topic may mean little to an audience without explanation, organization, and commentary. It is difficult even to locate appropriate sources in the library without planning and thinking about what you want to find. Writing the research paper involves those tasks as well as all the other writing processes and strategies you have learned in this book. The clerical work of compiling a list of facts is only a small part of the overall process.

Although research begins with examining other people's ideas, it can develop into a highly creative activity. Bringing together information from different sources can help you come to new conclusions that are entirely your own.

IDENTIFYING A RESEARCH TOPIC

The process you go through to identify a research topic depends upon the specificity of your assignment. If your assignment is focused, you may be able to begin searching for materials right away. Here is a focused assignment from a psychology course: "Write a three-page summary of the psychological literature on dance therapy published during the past year." This assignment tells you that you need to consult the past year's issues of psychological journals and look for articles on dance therapy. If you receive an open-ended assignment, however, you may not know where to begin the search for information. Consider the following assignment that our student Jennifer Piazza received in an upper-level psychology course entitled "Counseling: Theory and Dynamics": "Write a ten- to fifteen-page research paper that expands upon one of the topics covered in our textbook or class lectures. Use at least ten sources of information, not including the textbook."

Jennifer cannot proceed to the library before she narrows the focus of this very general assignment. She must think through the subject areas covered in class and isolate one topic, or better yet several, that might become the focus of her paper. Two of the prewriting strategies we described in Chapter 1, freewriting and brainstorming, can help identify possible research topics. Jennifer might brainstorm a list of words and phrases in response to the assignment and then read over the list and look for similarities, patterns, and connections. Alternatively, Jennifer might freewrite nonstop for ten minutes, using any cues in the assignment to generate ideas, and then search her freewriting for useful ideas. The following is an excerpt from Jennifer's freewriting.

> The chapter on counseling trauma victims was especially interesting to me. I'm currently working as a volunteer with Suicide Prevention and Crisis Services, and many of the hotline calls I answer are from people who are coping with the result of a traumatic experience. Perhaps if I did my research paper on trauma, I would learn something that would be of direct benefit to my hotline clients. But I'm not sure how I could add anything to what the textbook presented except

maybe to add more details about the theory. Perhaps I could write about how current ideas about dealing with trauma are different from what was previously believed. Our textbook chapter started with Freud, so I could research what was believed about trauma before Freud and try to show how the theory developed over time. One topic that I wish the textbook had said more about was how talking through a traumatic experience is helpful in dealing with it. I know that my hotline clients feel better after they are able to get the experience off their chest by describing it fully. In my Personal Essay class, I wrote about a particularly traumatic event in my own life: When I was four, a close relative was diagnosed with cancer and in response to the news, my family really freaked out. I was terrified to see adults in this condition, and no one fully explained to me what was going on, so I couldn't make sense of it at all. I felt a strong sense of relief when, fifteen years later, I was able to relive the experience on paper and explain my emotions. Perhaps I could do research on the therapeutic effects of "reliving" traumatic experiences in conversation or on paper.

As she rereads her freewriting, Jennifer realizes that she would like to learn more about the two topics discussed in the freewriting excerpt: the history of psychic trauma theory and current therapies for trauma, in particular the use of verbal expression as a therapeutic response to trauma. She decides to focus her initial research on these areas.

Another way of zeroing in on a research topic is to consult general subject headings in indexes (see pp. 160–163) related to your broad subject area (biology, music, psychology, and so forth). You could also ask your professor to suggest topics within his or her discipline. Follow your interests. The research and writing process will be more successful and rewarding if you identify a topic that appeals to you.

Try to come up with several alternative topics because the one you initially select may not be practical for research. For example, you might inadvertently select a topic that is treated only in scholarly literature, material that you might have difficulty understanding because of your unfamiliarity with the methodology, analytical techniques, and specialized vocabulary associated with the discipline. You might also choose a topic that requires information resources that are difficult to obtain; the books, magazines, or newspapers that you need may be unavailable in your college library. You might even identify a topic that cannot be researched because no literature exists that addresses it; not every issue in a particular discipline attracts the interest of scholars. Preliminary research may show that an initial research question is naive and must be modified accordingly. If you have several possible topics in mind before you begin to do research, you will be able to abandon those that aren't feasible.

DEVELOPING A RESEARCH STRATEGY

Once you have defined a topic, you need a plan of attack that will guide your search for information. We call this plan your research strategy. Before you begin to look for sources, think about the goals for your research. What are you trying to accomplish and how long will it take you? What questions are you trying to answer and how will you know when you have found the answers? How will you find information on your topic? Think about these concerns before you begin your search.

Make sure that your research strategy is flexible enough to accommodate the unexpected. In practice, research often does not proceed as planned. You may need to change your goals during the research process.

Allocate Sufficient Time for Research

As you plan a research project, make sure that you allocate sufficient time. Of course, the amount of time you need to set aside depends upon the scope of your assignment. If the instructor provides the narrowed topic and requires one or two sources, you may need just a single visit to the library and you might begin the process only a week before the paper is due. However, for an assignment that asks you to design your own topic and draw on ten or more sources, you would be wise to begin a month before the due date. You must always allow for the unexpected in research assignments. Even the most knowledgeable researchers can encounter difficulties that require more time than they had anticipated. Since Jennifer must focus her own topic and locate at least ten sources, she begins four weeks before the due date and assumes that she will make four or five visits to the library.

Identify Research Questions

In Chapter 1, we encouraged you to become an active reader with clear goals for reading rather than a passive reader who sees the words on the page but does not process them. Similarly, you should be an active researcher who does not merely look up information but rather uses research to answer specific questions about topics. Before you begin to look for sources, try to list the questions that you hope your research will answer. Here are some of the questions that interest Jennifer concerning trauma therapy:

1. What did Freud's predecessors say about the cause of and treatment for trauma? How did Freud's theory differ? To what extent do psychologists still accept Freud's theory concerning trauma?

2. How does current psychological theory explain the impact of traumatic experiences?

3. What therapies are available for victims of psychic trauma? Which are most effective?

4. According to psychologists and communication experts (writing and speech), what role does the verbal expression of traumatic experiences play in the recovery process?

5. Do victims of psychological trauma receive adequate attention in the mental health system?

Brainstorm a List of Terms or a Search Vocabulary

To look up information in the library, you will need to use words or phrases associated with your topic as you search the library catalog, indexes to periodicals, and reference works. Before you go to the library, brainstorm a list of words or phrases associated with your topic. Anticipate the words that might be used to describe or categorize the subject. These are the terms you will look up when you use the catalogs and indexes. Jennifer brainstorms the following list of search terms that might help her find information on trauma therapy:

1. Trauma or shock

2. Traumatic experiences

3. Freud and trauma

4. Psychology and trauma

5. Writing and trauma

6. Verbal expression (communication) and trauma

7. Trauma therapy

8. Trauma counseling

9. Post-traumatic stress disorder (or syndrome)

10. Traumatic neuroses

11. Trauma and the mental health system

Be expansive and list as many terms as you can. Then add to your list when you locate sources that suggest additional terms. You need a rich list of search terms, since it is often hard to guess which ones will give you access to the information you want.

INDIVIDUAL EXERCISE ON RESEARCH STRATEGY

Think of research papers you have written in the past. How did you isolate a topic? What planning did you do before attempting to locate sources? How were your activities during the early stages of the research process either different from or similar to our descriptions of identifying a topic and developing a research strategy? Freewrite for ten minutes in response to these questions.

COLLABORATIVE EXERCISE ON RESEARCH STRATEGY

1. Form collaborative learning groups of five students each, as described in the Preface, or fashion groups according to a method of your own.
2. Decide on a topic of mutual interest that your group might want to research. Do not take more than two or three minutes to come to a consensus. (The instructor might choose to assign research topics.)
3. Working together, generate a list of research questions that pertain to your topic. Then brainstorm a list of search terms that might help you locate information on this topic.
4. Reconvene the entire class. Each group recorder should identify the group's topic, read the lists of research questions and search terms, and describe any problems that the group encountered with its particular topic.

VIRTUAL LIBRARIES

Ten years ago, students and scholars working on research papers would typically spend many hours in academic libraries locating and reading source material. Libraries housed the actual books, periodicals, and other sources of information that researchers needed as well as the indexes and catalogs that helped the researchers locate these sources. Advances in electronic information technology that occurred over the last decade have made it possible for students and scholars to conduct much of their research without actually going to a library. Using networked computers in their dorm rooms or offices, researchers can connect to their academic libraries' electronic catalogs and to commercial periodical indexes to which their libraries subscribe. Thus, without ever entering a library, researchers can compile lists of books, periodical articles, and other sources relevant to almost any topic. In some cases, online systems provide the complete texts of sources, so students may find that they can complete all the research for relatively short projects without traveling to the library at all. As full-text periodical access grows and more book-length works become available online, it will undoubtedly become possible to conduct more extensive research from homes and offices.

The explosive growth of the World Wide Web has also affected how students and scholars conduct research. This vast collection of electronic texts, graphics, and sounds covers every imaginable topic. Most academic libraries now provide World Wide Web access, and many sources that are appropriate for academic research are available in full-text versions on the Web.

USING ELECTRONIC RETRIEVAL SYSTEMS

Whether you are searching your college library's online catalog, an electronic version of a periodical index, or the World Wide Web, you will need to understand certain principles of online searching. Database software often gives users the impression that electronic searching is simple. The software invites users to merely type in words or phrases that describe what they are looking for and then provides lists of information sources. Despite this impression of simplicity, researchers who want to take maximum advantage of online information systems need to know how search software operates.

How Computerized Information Retrieval Systems Function

You begin searching an electronic database by typing in a "query," which is typically several words that are related to your topic of interest. In response, the retrieval system attempts to match the query with relevant information sources in the system's database. While systems vary in their precise search strategies, most compare the specific words in queries to indexes or word lists compiled from all the information sources. Some indexes are created by subject-area professionals who read sources and then assign indexing terms that describe their contents; others are merely lists of all the words that occur in the text of the source, often ranked by frequency.

In addition to subject indexes, systems may include indexes based on a variety of bibliographic elements. While author, title, and subject are the standard indexes available for searching library catalogs, many systems index other items, such as publication date, language, personal name, geographic name, and source type (book, video, sound recording, and so forth). Often, you can examine several indexes with a single query; for example, you could search for sources on writing about trauma that were published since 1995. In databases that provide the full texts of magazine, journal, or newspaper articles, the words used within each article may be indexed so that you can actually search the articles' contents.

You can narrow a search by specifying a particular index, or you can broaden the search by choosing the "free-text" or "all-fields" options that instruct the system to examine all available indexes for matches to the query. In many information systems, free-text searching is the default mode that is automatically offered to users, and in these cases, you must select "expert," "advanced," or "power" search options if you want to limit searches to particular indexes.

Each item in a retrieval system index points to one or more electronic "records" for individual sources that are related to the index item. A record contains a description of a source and an indication of where it can be found. In some cases, for instance when searching the World Wide Web, the record may provide a direct electronic link to the complete version of the source. (See Figure 5-1 for a schematic of these relationships.)

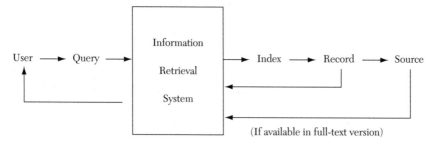

Figure 5-1

It is important to understand that computerized retrieval systems do not, for the most part, possess "artificial intelligence." They are merely word matching tools and cannot make even the simplest inferences about your intentions. Don't expect the system to do any of your thinking for you. In addition, most retrieval systems cannot correct for misspelling or adjust for variations in spelling. Distinctions that may seem insignificant to you, such as the difference between "first" and "1st," may be crucial when using a computerized system.

Recall versus Relevancy

The terms "recall" and "relevancy" are used to describe how information retrieval systems respond to queries. If a system provided perfect recall, then it would, in response to a query, retrieve every source in the system's database that was related to the specified topic. If the system was perfect with regard to relevancy, then every source retrieved would be precisely the type of information specified in the query. Typically, an information search involves a trade-off between recall and relevancy. Maximizing recall will help ensure that relevant sources are not overlooked but may retrieve irrelevant material as well. Maximizing relevancy will help assure that the sources retrieved are useful but may pass over other sources that would also be of interest to the researcher.

Balancing recall and relevancy becomes particularly difficult when you are working with a very large database, such as the World Wide Web. A broad search that maximizes recall will retrieve thousands of sources, far more than you can carefully review, but searching for very specific terms may fail to retrieve the material within the database that would best serve your purposes. For example, imagine that you are writing a research paper on whether or not human cloning should be legal in the United States. If you use the term "human cloning" to search the World Wide Web, you might retrieve thousands of information sources, only some of which would be relevant to your particular topic. However, if you used a more exclusive query such as "human cloning regulation," you would probably retrieve useful sources concerning legal restrictions on cloning but might overlook more philosophical pieces on the wisdom of allowing human cloning.

With very large databases, perhaps the best strategy is to conduct four or five relatively narrow searches, trying out a range of search terms.

This technique may help zero in on relevant sources but will expand recall beyond what would be achieved with a single query.

Keyword Searching

When you are using a printed index based on an alphabetical arrangement, you need to know the initial word of a subject heading or title in order to locate it, but a computerized *keyword* search will locate one or more words in any position within the subject heading or title. For example, let's assume our student Jennifer Piazza intends to look up "trauma therapy" in a title index. Using an electronic index, she can locate all titles that include the words "Trauma" and "Therapy," but with a paper index she finds only titles that begin with "Trauma Therapy." It is often useful to search titles for key words or phrases since a title is a good indicator of a source's content. Keyword searching is also advantageous for subject indexes because it allows you to retrieve a reference without knowing the exact wording of the subject heading. For instance, a keyword search for "Welfare Reform" would retrieve the subject headings "Public Welfare Reform," "Reform, Welfare," and "Reform, Public Welfare" as well as "Welfare Reform" and "Welfare Reform Reconciliation Act of 1996."

A disadvantage of keyword searching is that it has the potential to draw in a great many irrelevant sources because the words in the query are matched to the index without regard to context. For instance, a keyword title search for "Grateful Dead" would retrieve the article entitled "Anti-Union Bill Dead in Committee: Autoworkers Grateful for Senator's Pivotal Vote." Some retrieval systems, however, allow you to use an adjacency operator (often indicated by "ADJ") to specify an index search for words that are adjacent to each other and that occur in a particular order. For example, a title search for "Grateful ADJ Dead" would only retrieve index items that actually included the phrase "Grateful Dead."

Truncation

Computerized retrieval systems often allow you to truncate or shorten search terms. Instead of typing in the search statement, "Politically Correct Movement," you might enter "Political? Correct?" The "?" or "*" are commonly used in retrieval systems as truncation symbols. This query would retrieve "Politically Correct Movement," "Political Correctness," and other variations on this terminology. It is often wise to truncate words in search statements, particularly when you are unsure of the precise indexing terms used in the database.

Boolean Searching

By using the Boolean operators "AND," "OR," and "NOT," you can create a very specific search request that takes full advantage of electronic searching. For example, we mentioned earlier that you can restrict a search to a particular publication year. To limit a search by subject and by year, you would use the Boolean operator "AND" in your search statement. Let's assume that you want information on the national debate over welfare reform that occurred in 1996. If you enter the subject heading (SH) "Welfare Reform," the Boolean operator "AND," and the publication year (PY) "1996," the computer will respond as shown below:

What the Researcher Types:

(SH = Welfare Reform) AND (PY = 1996)

How the Computer Responds to the Query:

1. Creates a list of all items that have a subject heading (SH) "Welfare Reform."
2. Creates a list of all items that have a publication year (PY) of 1996.
3. Compares List 1 and List 2 and creates a new list of all items that both have "Welfare Reform" as a subject heading *and* were published in 1996.
4. Returns to the researcher the total number of items in List 3 and, if requested, the reference for each item in List 3.

The Boolean "AND" sometimes confuses researchers since they associate the word "and" with addition and thus think that the operation will increase the number of sources retrieved. The Boolean "AND" actually places more restrictions on searches and usually cuts down on the number of hits. The Boolean operator that is used to increase the number of sources retrieved is "OR." The expression (SH = Welfare Reform) AND (SH = Occupational Training) would retrieve only articles that covered both welfare reform and job training efforts. On the other hand, the expression (SH = Welfare Reform) OR (SH = Occupational Training) would locate articles that focused just on welfare reform and articles on job training only along with articles that covered both topics.

The Boolean operator "NOT" excludes specific items from the retrieval process. For example, the expression (SH = Welfare Reform) NOT (SH = Occupational Training) would identify articles on welfare reform but would exclude articles that concerned job training.

You can use Boolean operators in algebraic expressions to piece together complex search statements such as the following: ((SH = Welfare Reform) OR (SH = Occupational Training)) AND (PY = 1996).

THE LIBRARY OR THE WORLD WIDE WEB? CHOOSING A RESEARCH SITE

Without a doubt, the growth of the World Wide Web has made it easier to locate certain types of information. For instance, if you play the guitar, you can, in a few minutes, find Web sites that will provide product information on new and used guitars, chords for the latest songs, and a discography for your favorite guitarist. All this information might take hours to collect without the help of the Web. The Web works well in this case for several reasons. Since thousands of amateur musicians and music fans use the Web to share information, its popular music resources are vast and will probably cover any guitar, song, or guitarist that you are interested in. Also, search queries about guitars, guitar music, and guitarists are relatively easy to formulate since they are based on straightforward names (Fender, "Voodoo Child," Jimi Hendrix) rather than descriptions of content. Finally, as an amateur guitarist, you are looking for information that is interesting or useful but may not be concerned with precise accuracy. For example, you would be satisfied with playable chord progressions that sound acceptably close to the original songs rather than completely authentic musical transcriptions.

Unfortunately, the World Wide Web does not work as well for academic researchers as it does for hobbyists. One difficulty is that books and academic journals remain the standard vehicles for scholarly communication, and these publications are not necessarily available on the Web. Thus, there is no guarantee that the Web will provide access to the important scholarly resources on any given topic. Another problem is that academic research usually involves searching by subject matter rather than by proper name and the Web is not arranged for efficient subject searching. Given its huge size, haphazard organization, and poor indexing, it may be difficult to locate material on a particular subject even if it is, in fact, available on the Web. On the other hand, relevant information may be buried in long lists of information sources that contain the vocabulary in your search statement but are not actually useful to you. For example, if Jennifer, in her research on trauma therapy, used the query "trauma" on the Web, it might steer her to the Web page of the Discoteca Trauma, a nightclub in Barcelona, Spain.

A final difficulty is that academic researchers care very much about reliability and accuracy, but the Web has no effective quality control. Any individual or group can establish a Web page and disseminate any information that they choose, except for content that is in clear violation of the law. Some Web pages may use graphics that appear very professional but include content that is merely uninformed opinion. Of course, print sources can also contain unreliable content, but the Web has expanded tremendously the opportunity for "publishing" material that has no basis in fact. Consequently, subject searches conducted on the Web often direct the researcher to Web sites that do not provide reliable information. The issues of reliability and objectivity are further complicated by the commercial nature of many Web sites. For instance, the search term "trauma" will likely provide a great many links to the business Web pages of psychologists, psychiatrists, and social workers who specialize in trauma therapy and use the Web to advertise their services. While some of these commercial sites may provide information that is useful to a researcher, they may also be biased and manipulative. Even the standard Web "search engines," the electronic retrieval systems that are used to search the Web, are produced as commercial ventures and may intentionally steer you to certain information providers who have paid the search engine companies to highlight their Web sites.

In contrast to the World Wide Web, a college library collection is developed specifically to serve the needs of academic researchers. Books, periodicals, and other materials are chosen either by librarians who specialize in collection development or by faculty members who are experts in particular fields of study. Because the collection is built systematically, an academic library collection is much more likely to include the seminal works in a particular discipline, whereas the Web does not discriminate between expert and uninformed opinion. Your library may also include special collections for certain programs of study that are highlighted at your college. Currently, relatively few books are available in full-text online versions; thus, with the exception of periodicals, most of the scholarly sources in your college library's collection are probably not available online.

Another advantage of conducting research in your college library is that you can get help from the reference librarians. The major responsibility of these information professionals is to help students and faculty members with their research questions. Reference librarians can show you how to use your own library's collection but also how to access sources that are available online from remote sites, including material on the World Wide Web. In most cases, a few minutes spent discussing your research needs with a reference librarian will be more productive than hours of surfing the Web.

A final advantage of academic libraries is that they provide the sophisticated searching tools that you will need to conduct scholarly research. In your college library, you will find a catalog of the library's holdings that will likely be available on a computerized system. In some cases, the catalog will provide electronic links to other libraries from which you can obtain material via interlibrary loan. Your library will also have electronic and print versions of periodical indexes that will help you locate information in journals, magazines, and newspapers. Whether you use electronic or print versions of catalogs and indexes, these resources allow you to conduct far more precise searches than is possible with the access tools available on the World Wide Web.

While we have stressed the advantages of using your college library and recommend you begin your research there, we do recognize the importance of the Web to researchers. Many of the same sources available in academic libraries can be accessed in electronic form over the Web, and some sources are available only online. The Web is particularly useful when you are trying to locate a specific source that you have identified in an index but that is not available in your own library. For example, as we were researching the topic of virtual reality for Chapter 7, we found a reference in an online database to an article in a journal called *Japan Echo*. Our area libraries did not have this journal in their collections, so we conducted a quick Web search and found a home page for this publication that included full-text English language copies of past issues. If you know exactly what source you are looking for, the Web may provide convenient and free access.

ADVANTAGES OF THE WORLD WIDE WEB FOR RESEARCHERS

- 24-hour, 365-day availability
- continuous updating
- vast resources
- coverage of virtually all topics
- convenience, "one-stop shopping"

(continued on the next page)

ADVANTAGES OF ACADEMIC LIBRARIES FOR RESEARCHERS

- expert collection development and quality control
- systematic organization
- careful indexing
- expert staff of reference librarians
- extensive collections of book-length sources
- commitment to scholarly inquiry and objectivity

LOCATING INFORMATION IN AN ACADEMIC LIBRARY

If you intend to use an academic library to do research, you must first familiarize yourself with the facility. Libraries vary dramatically in how they organize their collections and how they provide access to materials. Before you attempt to do any research, get a guide or a map that shows how your campus library is organized. Make sure you know where your library's reference desk is located. Do not confuse it with the circulation desk, the place where items are checked out. The librarians at the reference desk will provide one-on-one research assistance. Your library reference department may also offer library orientation sessions, reference-skills workshops, and credit-bearing courses on information resources. Take advantage of opportunities to learn about your library early in your academic career.

INDIVIDUAL EXERCISE ON LIBRARY ORIENTATION

Take a self-guided tour of your college library. Start by locating the reference desk. Find out what days and hours reference librarians are available and what services they provide. Find out how the collection is organized. Does your library use the Library of Congress or the Dewey decimal classification system? Are periodicals shelved with books or separately? Are other formats (recordings, microfilms, and so on) shelved separately? Are there any subject-specific (music, science, and so forth) libraries on your campus? You should be able to answer these questions based on materials that you can obtain at the reference desk. Now tour the library and make sure you can find the principal elements of the collection.

COLLABORATIVE EXERCISE ON LIBRARY ORIENTATION

1. Form collaborative learning groups of five students each, as described in the Preface, or fashion groups according to a method of your own.

2. Pick an area of the library that your group will investigate from the following list. Groups should not duplicate one another's choices so that as many areas as possible will be covered.

Reference collection
Book collection (main stacks)
Microforms collection
Magazine and journal collection
Sound recordings collection
Video collection
Newspaper collection
Any discipline-specific collection

3. Proceed to the library from class or arrange a time that your group can meet in the library for about an hour.

4. When you arrive at the library, work together to answer the following questions concerning your area: What resources are available? What services are available?

5. Reconvene the entire class. Each group recorder should read the group's answers to the two questions and respond to any inquiries from the class about the part of the library collection that the group investigated.

The Library Catalog

The library catalog contains a description of each item in the collection and indexes items by subject, title, and author. Catalogs typically list not only books but also periodicals (magazines, journals, and newspapers), pamphlets, sound recordings (reel-to-reel and cassette tapes, LPs, and compact discs), sheet music, microforms (microfilm, microfiche, and microcards), motion pictures, video recordings, computer data files, images (graphics and photos), three-dimensional artifacts, and maps. Note that the central library catalog provides the titles of periodicals (*The New York Times, College English, Newsweek,* and so forth) and date range of holdings for periodicals but does not describe individual articles. On pages 160–163, we will explain how to find particular periodical articles on a given subject.

In most academic libraries, the catalog is computerized and can be searched by subject, title, or author according to the principles described on pages 147–153. Your library houses computer workstations linked to the online catalog, but the catalog may also be accessible from other computer workrooms across campus or even from your dorm room. The following example (Figure 5-2) is a computer catalog entry that Jennifer located in her research on trauma therapy:

```
TRAMA AND RECOVERY
```

Author:	• Herman, Judith Lewis, 1942-
Title:	• Trauma and recovery / Judith Lewis Herman; [with a new afterword by the author.]
Physical description:	• xi, 290 p. ; 21 cm.
Publisher:	• New York : BasicBooks, c1997.
Subjects:	• Post-traumatic stress disorder. • Post-traumatic stress disorder--Treatment.
Notes:	• Originally published:[New York, N.Y.]:BasicBooks,c1992. • Includes bibliographical references(p.[248]-281) and index.
OCLC number:	• 36543539
ISBN:	• 0465087302
System ID no:	• ACW–2893
Holdings:	• LOCATION:General Stacks--CALL NUMBER : RC552.P67H471997 • c.1 Available

```
Search Author   Search Title   Search Subject   Search Keyword   Search Numbers   ILL Forms
```

Figure 5-2   Sample Computer Catalog Entry

Notice that the sample computer catalog entry includes a "call number" for the item: RC552.P67 H47 1997. This number indicates the item's subject area and its shelving location. You are probably familiar with the Dewey decimal call numbers used in most primary and secondary schools. College libraries typically use the Library of Congress system rather than the Dewey decimal system, and the call number in Figure 5-2 is based on the Library of Congress system.

The initial parts of either Library of Congress or Dewey call numbers indicate the general subject area. The following chart lists the basic Library of Congress subject areas and the corresponding Dewey subject headings.

Library of Congress	*Dewey*
A—General Works	000—Generalities
B—Philosophy, Psychology, and Religion	100—Philosophy and related disciplines

C—Auxiliary Sciences of History

D—General and Old World History

E–F—American History

G—Geography; Maps; Recreation; Anthropology

H—Social Sciences (Economics, Sociology)

J—Political Science

K—Law

L—Education

M—Music

N—Fine Arts

P—Linguistics; Languages; Literature

Q—Science

R—Medicine

S—Agriculture

T—Technology

U—Military Science

V—Naval Science

Z—Bibliography; Library Science

200—Religion

900—History; Geography

300—Social Sciences

700—The Arts

400—Language
800—Literature
500—Pure Science
600—Applied Science; Technology

Books and other materials are shelved systematically by call numbers. As an example, let's consider the parts of the call number for Herman's *Trauma and Recovery:*

$$\text{RC} \quad 552.\text{P}67 \quad \text{H}47 \quad 1997$$

On the library shelves, books are alphabetized according to the letters indicating the general topic area, "RC" in the example above. Within each general topic area, items are arranged in ascending numerical order according to the topic subdivision, in this case "552.P67." For books, items within the subdivision are arranged alphabetically by the first letter of the author's last name and then numerically by an additional filing number. In our example, "H" is the first letter of Herman's name and "47" is the additional filing number. Finally, "1997" is the book's date of publication. Call numbers can get more complex than our example indicates, but the same filing and shelving principles that we just described always apply. Call numbers not only provide a shelving address for an information source but also assure that items on the same topic will be stored together. Thus, if you locate one item on your subject, you may find others in the immediate vicinity.

Periodical Indexes

As we mentioned in the previous section, the central library catalog lists titles of periodical holdings but does not provide information on the individual articles that these periodicals contain. The tools used to access periodical articles are developed by commercial companies that sell their indexes to academic libraries. You are probably familiar with the *Readers' Guide to Periodical Literature*, an index that is often available in high school and public libraries either in print or electronic form. The *Readers' Guide* surveys over 200 popular magazines as well as a selection of specialized journals and assigns each article to one or more subject areas. Articles are also indexed by the authors' names. The *Readers' Guide* is a good index for college researchers who want nonscholarly articles on topics of general interest. InfoTrac's *Expanded Academic Index*, an electronic retrieval tool, is another general interest index that is commonly available in college libraries. The *Expanded Academic Index* provides access to articles in over 1,000 magazines and journals and covers many of the periodicals available through the *Readers' Guide.*

Using the *Expanded Academic Index,* Jennifer enters the search term "Trauma" and finds that a number of subject headings contain this word, (see Figure 5-3). Jennifer selects the subject headings "Psychic Trauma," "Psychic Trauma in Children," and "Rape Trauma Syndrome," which seem closest to her topic. She finds that the "Psychic Trauma" subject heading has twenty topical subdivisions; she selects the "care and treatment" subdivision and views the entries. Figure 5-4 is an excerpt (one computer screen) from the twenty references listed under the "care and treatment" subheading. Jennifer peruses the lists of sources under each of the subject headings and subheadings that seems relevant. For titles that look promising, she views the complete records for the articles, which include publication information and, in some cases, the full texts of articles.

There are scores of different periodical indexes, available both in paper and electronic forms, which vary widely in topic area and in organizational structure. Whereas the *Expanded Academic Index* covers a vast range of subject areas, *PsycInfo,* another database Jennifer consults in her research on trauma therapy, focuses on literature in psychology and related disciplines. Some indexes, such as the *Readers' Guide,* are

Return to: EasyTrac | Expanded Academic ASAP

? Subject Guide | New Database | New Search

Subjects containing the words: trauma

Trauma Care Systems
See Trauma Centers
Trauma Centers
View 73 articles
See also 26 subdivisions
Trauma Disorders, Cumulative
See Cumulative Trauma Disorders
Trauma Records
View 6 articles
Trauma Units
See Trauma Centers
Trauma, Physical
See Wounds and Injuries
Trauma, Psychic
See Psychic Trauma
Acoustic Trauma
View 1 article
American Trauma Society
View 1 article
Blunt Trauma
View 59 articles
See also 15 subdivisions
Burn Trauma
See Burns and Scalds
Cumulative Trauma Disorders
View 94 articles
See also 24 subdivisions
See also 1 related subject
Penetrating Trauma
See Penetrating Wounds
Psychic Trauma
View 121 articles
See also 20 subdivisions
See also 1 related subject
Psychic Trauma in Children
View 41 articles
See also 13 subdivisions
Rape Trauma Syndrome
View 13 articles
See also 1 related subject
Blunt Force Trauma
See Blunt Trauma

Figure 5-3 Expanded Academic Index™.
©1998 Information Access Company.

Citations 1 to 20
Subject: Psychic Trauma **Subdivision**: care and treatment

☐ **Fifteen-month follow-up of eye movement desensitization and reprocessing (EMDR)**
Mark **treatment for posttraumatic stress disorder and psychological trauma.** Sandra A.
Wilson, Lee A. Becker, Robert H. Tinker.
Journal of Consulting and Clinical Psychology Dec 1997 v65 n6 p1047(10)
View extended citation and retrieval choices

☐ **Is EMDR being held to an unfair standard? Rejoinder to Van Ommeren (1996).** (eye
Mark movement desensitization and reprocessing)(response to article by M. Van Ommeren, Professional
Psychology: Research and Practice, vol. 27, p. 529, 1996) Ricky Greenwald.
Professional Psychology, Research and Practice June 1997 v28 n3 p306(1)
View abstract and retrieval choices

☐ **Need and responsiveness in the treatment of a severely traumatized patient: a**
Mark **relational perspective.** (Case Study) Mary E. Connors.
American Journal of Psychotherapy Wntr 1997 v51 n1 p86(16)
View abstract and retrieval choices

☐ **From fragmentation to wholeness: an integrative approach with clients who**
Mark **dissociate.** Marye O'Reilly-Knapp.
Perspectives in Psychiatric Care Oct-Dec 1996 v32 n4 p5(7)
View text with graphics and retrieval choices

☐ **The interpersonal dynamics and treatment of dual trauma couples.** Dennis Balcom.
Mark *The Journal of Marital and Family Therapy* Oct 1996 v22 n4 p431(12)
View abstract and retrieval choices

☐ **Treating the traumatic memories of patients with dissociative identity disorder.**
Mark Richard P. Kluft.
American Journal of Psychiatry July 1996 v153 n7 pS103(8)
View abstract and retrieval choices

☐ **Trauma management therapy: a preliminary evaluation of a multicomponent**
Mark **behavioral treatment for chronic combat-related PTSD.** (Post-Traumatic Stress Disorder)
B. Christopher Frueh, Samuel M. Turner, Deborah C. Beidel, Robert F. Mirabella, Walter J. Jones.
Behaviour Research and Therapy July 1996 v34 n7 p533(11)
View extended citation and retrieval choices

☐ **Letting go of bitterness and hate.** Mary M. Baures.
Mark *The Journal of Humanistic Psychology* Wntr 1996 v36 n1 p75(16)
View abstract and retrieval choices

Figure 5-4   Expanded Academic Index™.
© 1998 Information Access Company.

relatively straightforward and self-explanatory, but others, such as the
print version of the *MLA International Bibliography*, can be baffling to
the novice. You may need the help of a reference librarian the first time
you attempt to use a specialized index. Other examples of periodical

indexes and databases include *Book Review Digest, Business Index,* ERIC (Educational Resource Information Center, a database), *Film Literature Index, General Science Abstracts, GPO Monthly Catalog* (federal publications), *Humanities Abstracts, Index to Legal Periodicals, Medline* (health and medicine), *Music Index, National Newspaper Index, PAIS International* (Public Affairs Information Service), *Social Science Citation Index, Social Science Abstracts, SportDiscus* (athletics), and *Women's Studies Index.*

Often, periodical indexes provide abstracts of articles, which are short summaries of articles' contents. Keep in mind that abstracts are intended only to help researchers decide which articles are most relevant to their interests; they are not meant to circumvent careful reading of the relevant articles. Do not rely on abstracts as information sources; they are only access tools. It is considered academically dishonest to cite an article in a research paper if you have read only an abstract and did not obtain the article's full text.

Academic libraries often provide electronic versions of periodical indexes. A major advantage of electronic indexes is that they often cover more than one year of publication. With one command to the computer, a researcher can find references to articles on a particular subject over a several-year period. With paper indexes, the same search would involve looking up the topic in index volumes for each of the desired years. Your library may devote specific computer workstations to one or several selected electronic periodical indexes or may link all its electronic indexes together so that they can all be accessed, along with the library's online catalog, from each library workstation. These services may be accessible from computer workrooms outside the library or even from your dorm room depending upon the characteristics of your college's computer system.

As more periodicals are becoming available in electronic form, many academic libraries are cutting back on the number of paper or microform periodicals in their collections and instead providing online access to periodicals. Your library may have computer workstations where students can locate periodical articles, view them in full-text versions, and print out articles of particular interest.

INDIVIDUAL EXERCISE ON LOCATING SOURCES

Select a topic or use one assigned by your professor. Go to the library and locate two books and two periodical articles on your topic. Use a computerized access tool, either an online catalog or a CD-ROM database, to find at least one of these sources, and if possible, have the computer print out the record for the source. Photocopy the table of contents of the book or periodical, and on the photocopy, circle the chapter or article that is relevant to your topic. Submit the computer printout and the photocopies to your instructor.

COLLABORATIVE EXERCISE ON LOCATING SOURCES

1. Form collaborative learning groups of five students each, as described in the Preface, or fashion groups according to a method of your own.
2. Come to a consensus on a topic you would like to research or use one assigned by your instructor.
3. Assign each group member one type of information resource: general reference, discipline-specific book, magazine, newspaper, or professional journal.
4. Proceed to the library from class or go individually outside of class time. Find a source on your topic that represents the particular type of information resource that you were assigned. Photocopy the table of contents of the book or periodical, and on the photocopy, circle the chapter or article that is relevant to your topic.
5. Reconvene your group at the next class meeting. Have each group member report on the source he or she found. Then discuss which types of resources seemed most useful for your topic and what further research would be necessary to actually write on your topic.
6. Reconvene the entire class. Each group recorder should explain the group's topic and summarize the group's discussion of sources on this topic.

CONDUCTING RESEARCH USING THE WORLD WIDE WEB

On pages 153–156, we explained some limitations of the World Wide Web as a research tool. In general, we suggest that you begin your research in your college library or another library in your area rather than on the World Wide Web. Once you have conducted at least your preliminary research in a library, you may be able to use the Web to good advantage.

If you are using the World Wide Web as a primary research tool, you can attempt to minimize its problematic aspects by observing several principles:

1. Read all the help screens or searching tips that accompany the particular search engine you are using. Each search engine has its unique characteristics, which you must understand if you are to take full advantage of its potential.

2. Familiarize yourself with the "expert" or "advanced" searching options. When you start up most search engines, they are configured for simple keyword searches of all available indexes. All too often, these keyword searches will yield thousands of hits, most of which are not useful. In order to refine you search and take advantages of features such as Boolean operators, you may need to shift to advanced searching mode.

3. Try your query on several different search engines. Given that the Web search engines are not precise research tools, it often helps to experiment with several and find which responds best to your particular query.

4. Look for electronic sources that have comparable print versions and steer away from sources that have no print equivalents. Unsubstantiated opinion does sometimes appear in print, but as a general principle, information that finds its way into print is more reliable than that which is available only on the Web.

5. Evaluate the reliability of Web sources. As we mention on page 168, researchers should always question the reliability of any source they locate, even if it comes from an academic library. It is, however, particularly important to evaluate critically Web-based information sources. With the computer tools currently available, anyone can create a very professional-looking Web page and then stock it with content that is completely absurd. Ask yourself the following questions about Web sites:

   - What is the overall goal of the Web site? Do the authors of the Web site have motives other than presenting the objective truth? For instance, does the site attempt to advocate for a particular political agenda or to sell a product?

   - Is the site produced by a reputable organization? Does it provide a mailing address and phone number? Does it invite inquiries?

   - Do the authors of the Web site identify themselves? Do they provide any evidence of their expertise or credibility? For example, do they possess training or experience in the topic area covered by their site? Do they demonstrate that they are aware of the standard scholarly or professional literature in the topic area?

   - Do the authors distinguish between opinion and fact? Do they provide nonanecdotal evidence to substantiate their conclusions? Do they cite published sources?

   - When was the site created? How often is it updated? When was it last updated?

COLLECTING INFORMATION ON YOUR OWN: SURVEYS AND INTERVIEWS

In most cases, the bulk of the material you use in research papers will come from published sources; however, depending upon your topic and assignment, it might be appropriate to use information that you collect personally through informal interviews and surveys. For example, imagine you are writing a research paper for a psychology class on how birth order (only child, first born, last born, and so on) affects personality. The psychological literature contains numerous studies on this topic, but you might also interview selected students in your dorm who represent each of the birth order positions and use these "cases in point" in your paper as concrete illustrations of the conclusions reached in the psychological studies. You might also survey twenty or thirty students representing a range of birth orders to see if their perceptions of the relationship between birth order and personality match the research findings.

Of course, informal interviews and surveys provide only anecdotal information and are not a reliable basis for any firm conclusions. Still, anecdotes are often useful for explaining a concept to an audience or for framing an interesting introduction or closing for a research paper. Informal surveys may help you sharpen your research question or identify trends that may warrant more careful investigation. While an informal survey is not sufficient to challenge the conclusions of published studies, it can be useful to note a significant difference between informal and published research results. For instance, imagine that a student researcher conducts an informal survey in a college dorm on the interaction between birth order and personality. If the results of this informal survey differ from published conclusions, then the student might suggest in his or her paper that additional formal research should be conducted to see if the published conclusions still hold for the current college-age population.

A final advantage of conducting informal surveys and interviews is that they get students directly involved with the topics they are researching. This hands-on approach may help increase student interest, particularly for topics that seem rather dry based on the published sources alone. Even if students do not end up using any of the anecdotal information they collect in their research papers, the experience of getting actively involved with the topic will lead to a better final product.

Whenever you conduct informal interviews or surveys, keep in mind the following principles:

1. Make sure you comply with any college regulations concerning use of human subjects. While these regulations are typically used with more formal research studies, it is possible that your college does have guidelines even for informal interviews and surveys. Check with your instructor if you are unsure of your college's human subject policies.

2. Whatever your college's policies are, make sure you respect the privacy of your interview or survey subjects. Do not repeat their responses in casual conversation, and do not use subjects' actual names in your research paper unless there is a clear reason to do so and you have their permission.

3. Establish clear goals for your questions. Interview or survey questions should have one of the following goals:

   • Establishing facts
   • Recording beliefs about what is fact
   • Recording personal feelings or values

4. Try asking the same question worded in several different ways. Sometimes, a slight change in wording will prompt a different response from a subject. It is often difficult to predict what precise wording will convey your question most effectively.

5. Don't ask questions that betray a bias. For example, imagine you are surveying or interviewing first-born children to research a possible link between birth order and personality. You would indicate a bias if you asked, "In what ways did your parents and older siblings spoil you?" A more neutral question would be, "What personality characteristics distinguish you from your older siblings?"

6. Do not press anyone who seems reluctant to undergo an interview or to complete a survey. Many people do not want to discuss their personal lives, particularly when someone is taking notes on what they say.

MODIFYING YOUR SEARCH STRATEGY

Research, by its very nature, is a creative process that exposes new approaches and gives rise to new ideas. As your research proceeds, you may find that you want to modify your topic (if the assignment allows you to define your own topic), your research schedule (you may require more trips to the library than you initially anticipated), your research questions, or your search vocabulary.

Consider how Jennifer has to modify her search strategy. Recall her initial research questions:

1. What did Freud's predecessors say about the cause of and treatment for trauma? How did Freud's theory differ? To what extent do psychologists still accept Freud's theory concerning trauma?

2. How does current psychological theory explain the impact of traumatic experiences?

3. What therapies are available for victims of psychological trauma? Which are most effective?

4. According to psychologists and communication experts (writing and speech), what role does the verbal expression of traumatic experiences play in the recovery process?

5. Do victims of psychological trauma receive adequate attention in the mental health system?

Jennifer decides to drop questions 3 and 5. She realizes that question 3 is too broad for a ten- to fifteen-page paper since it involves surveying and evaluating all the therapeutic techniques used in working with trauma victims, and she has found from her research that a wide range of treatments is available. She eliminates question 5 because it is not addressed directly in any of the sources she has located so far. In addition, Jennifer has discovered that questions 2 and 4 fit together because recent psychological theory, particularly that grounded in research on brain physiology, highlights the therapeutic value of communication, and as a result of the reading she has done so far, she has become particularly interested in these questions. She believes that her research on question 1 may fit into an introductory section of the paper that will provide historical context.

You will likely modify your search vocabulary as your research becomes more focused. Indexes, catalogs, and specific information sources will suggest additional search terms to you, and you may decide to eliminate from your list terms that are not productive. Remember that you will need to come to the library equipped with as many search terms as you can. Indexing vocabularies vary considerably, and thus, for a given topic, you may need different search terms as you move among indexes.

EVALUATING INFORMATION SOURCES

As you search for source material, you are constantly judging whether or not the information you find has direct relevance to your topic. Don't excerpt information that is only remotely related to your topic. As you locate and work with sources, ask yourself how they fit in with your overall goals for the research paper. To what parts of the topic do the sources pertain? What perspectives on the topic do they represent? Try to make sense of the sources as you examine each one rather than waiting until you have completed your research.

In addition to evaluating the sources' relevance to your topic, you should also judge their comparative quality. We discussed on page 154 some concerns with the reliability of sources found on the World Wide Web, but even library materials come with no absolute guarantees. Too many students have complete confidence in any source they find in a library.

As you analyze sources, it is always helpful to speculate on the author's rhetorical purpose, as we described in Chapter 1. What are the author's reasons for writing? Who is the author's intended audience? How does the author want to influence that audience? The answers to these questions will help you understand the source better and figure out whether it is appropriate for your paper. For instance, if you are writing for a science course on the future of nuclear power, you may be skeptical of information from lobby groups for the nuclear industry. If you think about writers' motives, you will be able to put their ideas in a proper perspective.

EXCERPTING INFORMATION FROM SOURCES

The basic skills for excerpting information from library sources—paraphrasing, summarizing, and quoting—are covered in Chapter 1 of this book. Here, we will discuss the special problems associated with the sheer number of sources you are working with for a research paper. A common problem is that a researcher loses track of the exact source for an important piece of information. Each time you excerpt a passage from a source, whether you handcopy, reword, or photocopy, make sure that you carefully record a complete citation to the source. You will need to record the exact page numbers where specific pieces of text are located. When you draft your paper, you will cite the source as well as the page for each paraphrase, summary, and quotation. In the Appendix, we give essential citation formats. For books, you will need to record author(s), title, publisher, city of publication, date of publication, and pages where the information you excerpted is located. For magazines and newspapers, record author(s), title of article, name of magazine, date (day, month, year), inclusive pages for entire article, and pages where the information you excerpted is located (the section number or letter is needed for multisectioned newspapers). For scholarly journals, you will need to record the same information as for magazines and newspapers as well as the volume number.

Another common difficulty is failing to distinguish adequately between paraphrases and quotations in research notes and thus including an author's exact words in the research paper without quotation marks. This is an unintentional yet serious form of plagiarism. Be very meticulous about your use of quotation marks as you take notes. Read once again our discussion of plagiarism on page 17.

There is also a danger of excerpting too much information. Some students compulsively collect every scrap of information that is remotely related to their topics, thinking that they will make sense of it all at their leisure. Don't bury yourself in paper, whether it is note cards, pages of notes, or photocopies of sources. Excerpt only what you think you might use. As we remarked earlier, research is a sense-making process. It is hard to make sense when you are overwhelmed with information.

Much has been written on how you should record the information that you excerpt from sources. Some textbooks strongly recommend index cards for research notes because cards can be grouped and regrouped easily. Of course, you can cut up pages from your research notebook or photocopies of sources and group these pieces just as you can note cards. Another alternative is to record your research notes on a computer and use word processing or outlining programs to organize the information. We recommend that you try various methods of recording excerpts and decide what works best for you. In addition to notes that record specific pieces of information or individual concepts, you should keep a separate set of notes for preliminary thesis statements, organizational plans, or other important ideas that occur to you during the process of research.

WRITING A PRELIMINARY THESIS

After you have collected enough sources to form generalizations about your topic, work on a preliminary thesis. The purpose of the preliminary thesis is to focus and direct your research. You may have a working thesis in mind when you begin researching. If not, one may emerge as you collect information. You can generate a thesis from your research notes by (1) scanning your research notes quickly, noting any general trends, main concepts, or overall patterns; (2) freewriting for ten minutes on what you think your research might tell your reader; and (3) reducing your freewriting to several sentences that explain what you want to say to your reader.

After scanning her research notes, Jennifer freewrites the following paragraph:

> Freud's initial work on trauma led to the Seduction Hypothesis, the suggestion that hysteria resulted from the traumatic memories of sexual abuse. However, Freud abandoned this notion, and I don't want Freud to be the focus of my paper. Instead, I want to draw attention to the more current work by brain scientists that explains how trauma is etched into the human brain as an unprocessed memory. The research by van der Kolk best demonstrates this concept. Then I can go on to examine the evidence which shows that allowing these traumatic memories to be fully processed, through either speaking or writing, can provide relief from the trauma. The research done by Pennebaker will be helpful here. I still need more evidence on this point, but I think I will be able to back it up.

Jennifer rereads her freewriting and condenses it into a preliminary thesis:

> In our society, people are discouraged from expressing their feelings about traumatic events that happen to them and instead are encouraged to "keep your chin up." Despite this, there is increasing evidence that it is psychologically helpful to express feelings about trauma. Based on studies of the human brain, it has been established that allowing verbal analysis of traumatic experiences may allow processing of the experiences to take place and may aid in recovering from the impact of trauma.

This is still a preliminary thesis. Compare it with Jennifer's final thesis, excerpted from the final version of her research paper:

> While we live in a culture where personal trauma and the lasting psychological effects of traumatic events have been and continue to be silenced, current research suggests that verbal expression of pain, grief, and other responses to trauma speeds recovery. Psychologists and physiologists who study the brain have established that traumatic experiences are encoded in memory as images that are not fully processed by the conscious mind. Verbal analysis of the traumatic event, either through speech or writing, allows processing to take place and aids in recovering from the impact of trauma.

Notice that Jennifer's final thesis is refined, more fully developed, and more coherent. The main purpose of a preliminary thesis is to focus your research activities, but sometimes you may need to depart from the initial thesis as you understand more about the topic.

PLANNING THE RESEARCH PAPER

A research paper can follow one organizational plan or a combination of the plans we have discussed in this book. Review the major organizational plans that we presented on pages 46–50.

In many cases, a plan will occur to you as you conduct research. For instance, Jennifer has decided to write on how communicating about a traumatic event can help repair the psychological damage caused by the event. Thus, it occurs to her that a problem-solution organizational plan could work for the body of her essay.

Because research writers must juggle many sources and deal with issues in depth, they need an outline that will keep them on task and provide a framework that unifies information from various sources. Review our explanation of free-form and formal outlining on pages 48–50. A pitfall of writing research papers is becoming so bogged down in the details from sources that you fail to clarify the relationships among ideas. Your research paper will be easier to write if you draft it working from a detailed outline, and, in the end, your train of thought will likely be more evident to your audience.

As an example of a free-form outline, consider the one Jennifer develops for her research paper on trauma:

Thesis

—Psychologists and physiologists who study the brain have established that traumatic experiences are encoded in memory as images that are not fully processed by the conscious mind. Verbal analysis of the traumatic event, either through speech or writing, allows processing to take place and aids in recovering from the impact of trauma.

Background

—In the late nineteenth century, Charcot began to catalog the symptoms of hysteria (Herman).
—Charcot's students, Freud and Janet, determined that trauma early in life led to hysteria (Herman). Freud advanced the Seduction Hypothesis but then abandoned it in favor of psychoanalytic theory, and Janet's ideas were forgotten (Herman).

—After World War I, trauma again came to attention of researchers in studies of shell shock victims. Rivers encouraged those victims to talk and write about wartime experiences (Herman).

—Later, a link was made between war-induced trauma and trauma which resulted from domestic violence and sexual abuse (Herman).

Current Physiological Research on Trauma

—The hormonal systems of trauma victims do not respond appropriately to everyday stress. In these cases, small levels of stress release a flood of hormones which lead to constant hyperarousal or numbness (van der Kolk, 1996).

—The brain responds to trauma through several distinct structures. The amygdala attaches emotional meaning to the experience, the hippocampus records the special dimensions of the experience and controls short-term memory of the experience, and the prefrontal cortex analyzes and categorizes the experience (van der Kolk, 1996).

—The information from a traumatic event goes first to the amygdala. If the emotional impact is too severe, the message cannot proceed to the hippocampus and prefrontal cortex for complete processing. Thus, the experience cannot be fully contextualized and understood (van der Kolk, 1996; LeDoux, Romanski, & Xagoraris). As a result, the traumatic experience is stored as images, not as a coherent narrative. The painful emotional feelings may remain over time, but the individual does not have a clear explanation for them and thus cannot cope with them.

—There is a distinction between explicit (conscious) and implicit (unconscious) memory (van der Kolk, 1996; Levinson). Traumatic experience interferes with explicit memory but not implicit memory (van der Kolk, 1996). Thus, an implicit (unconscious) memory of trauma remains even when no explicit (conscious) memory exists. The victim has a feeling that something is very wrong but cannot find words to describe the memory (van der Kolk).

Recovering from Trauma

—Victims must first understand what makes the memories resurface (Rauch). Then, they must find a way to describe the memories verbally and give them meaning.

Writing as Therapy for Trauma

—Writing can describe and give context to moments and images and help individuals make sense of incidents that initially were verbally indescribable.

—Writing has healing power and aids the immune system (Pennebaker).

—Writing provides an outlet to express the pain that our society masks in everyday life.

Opposition and Response

—Some contemporary psychologists favor using beta-blockers to erase the memory of traumatic experience (Davis; Cahill). If this is done, the victims will never have a chance to fully process the experience, a necessary step in the road to recovery.

WRITING FROM YOUR OUTLINE

Use your outline as a guide for drafting. Group your notes or note cards according to the points in your outline and draft the essay paragraph by paragraph. Keep in mind our advice in Chapter 2 on developing paragraphs, introductions, and conclusions. Be sure to include complete references for all source information in the first draft. It is easy to lose track of where information came from if you do not record this information initially.

As you draft your essay, you may find that you need to depart from your outline. An outline is supposed to guide your writing, but it should not be a straitjacket. If you discover new patterns or ideas in the process of writing, don't hesitate to include them in your essay.

REVISING

CHECKLIST FOR REVISING A RESEARCH PAPER

_____ Is the paper written on a sufficiently narrow topic?

_____ Can you understand the writer's research goals?

_____ Does the writer present a clear thesis?

_____ Does the writer make sense of the information from sources?

_____ Can you discern the research paper's form (multiple-source comparison and contrast, summary of multiple sources, objective synthesis, essay of response to multiple sources, synthesis with a specific purpose, argument, analysis, or evaluation)?

_____ Is the information from sources organized according to a clear plan?

_____ Does the writer use information from sources convincingly?

_____ Are the writer's assertions substantiated with material from sources?

(continued on the next page)

_____ Does the writer provide transitions among sources and among pieces of information?

_____ Is the writer's voice appropriate for this type of essay? Why or why not?

_____ Is the paper opener satisfactory? Why or why not?

_____ Does the essay have an appropriate conclusion?

_____ Is the title suitable for the piece?

_____ Can you identify the source for each piece of information?

_____ Does the paper end with a list of works cited that includes all sources referred to in the text of the paper?

EDITING

When you are satisfied with your revision, read your paper aloud. Then reread it line by line and sentence by sentence. Check for correct usage, punctuation, spelling, mechanics, manuscript form, and typos. If you are using a word processing program with a spell checker, apply the checker to your essay. If you are especially weak in editing skills, try getting a friend to read over your work. Keep in mind the following concerns:

1. Are all your sentences complete?
2. Have you avoided run-on sentences, both fused sentences and comma splices?
3. Do pronouns have clear antecedents, and do they agree in number, gender, and case with the words for which they stand?
4. Do all subjects and verbs agree in person and number?
5. Is the verb tense consistent and correct?
6. Have you used modifiers (words, phrases, subordinate clauses) correctly and placed them where they belong?
7. Have you used matching elements within parallel construction?
8. Are punctuation marks used correctly?
9. Are spelling, capitalization, and other mechanics (abbreviations, numbers, italics) correct?

SAMPLE RESEARCH PAPER

The final draft of Jennifer Piazza's research paper appears on the following pages. Since Jennifer is writing her paper for a psychology class, she uses the American Psychological Association (APA) manuscript and documentation style rather than the MLA style used in our previous examples of student essays. APA style is utilized in many disciplines besides psychology. The Appendix to this text includes a brief guide to the APA documentation style.

                                    Silent Expression   1 ◄─ 1" ─►

                        Silent Expression
                        Jennifer R. Piazza
                        Professor Nelson
                   Counseling: Theory and Dynamics
                        April 24, 1999

                                    Silent Expression   2

        The world of trauma engulfs people suffering from
    abuse, grief, and loss of self. From world wars to domestic
    violence, from the death of a loved one to the occurrence
    of a tragic accident, from mental illness to physical
    disabilities, from a host of factors, trauma infiltrates
    lives. Yet, when trauma touches us on a personal level, we
    are taught that disclosing personal information is not only
    undesirable, it is unacceptable. The teachings come in the
    form of hushed words when a victim of trauma enters the
    room; they are evident when people look the other way as
    the widow of a spouse who committed suicide walks down the
    street; and the teachings are strengthened when the media
    focuses on how a victim of a traumatic event could have
    prevented it. Those who contain their sorrow become the
    strong and resilient, while those who display reactions to
    trauma become the weak and insecure. While we live in a
    culture where personal trauma and the lasting psychological
    effects of traumatic events have been and continue to be

silenced, current research suggests that verbal expression
of pain, grief, and other responses to trauma speeds
recovery. Psychologists and physiologists who study the
brain have established that traumatic experiences are
encoded in memory as images that are not fully processed by
the conscious mind. Verbal analysis of the traumatic event,
either through speech or writing, allows processing to take
place and aids in recovering from the impact of trauma.

During the late nineteenth century, Jean-Martin Charcot
studied hysteria in an attempt to bring voices to those
silenced. At that time, hysteria was thought to be a
"strange disease with incoherent and incomprehensible
symptoms" (Herman, 1992, p. 10) that originated in the
uterus and was found only in women. To explore the symptoms
of hysteria, Charcot reformed a hospital complex and
observed, described, and classified patients with hysteria.
He focused on the actual symptoms of hysteria and determined
that symptoms such as amnesia and sensory loss were
psychological. In creating a taxonomy of hysteria, Charcot
restored dignity to the topic, and after his death Charcot's
students were able to build upon the foundation he had laid.
Two of his students, Pierre Janet and Sigmund Freud, sought
to surpass Charcot's work by finding the cause of hysteria
(Herman, 1992).

The rivalry between Janet and Freud pushed them their
separate ways. However, by utilizing what was known as the
"talking cure" (Herman, 1992, p. 12), both discovered a
common cause of hysteria. Both determined that trauma
precipitated neuroses and putting the traumatic experience
into words was essential to moving past the trauma and
dispelling neurotic symptoms. Freud discovered that
everyday, trivial experiences seemed to trigger memories of
childhood trauma in his patients. Freud stated that
hysteria was the result of premature sexual experiences,
what is known as the Seduction Hypothesis. This explanation

was widely rejected by the medical and psychological establishments because of the large numbers of women from the upper levels of society who were diagnosed with hysteria. The idea that many upper-class men had sexually abused their young daughters was considered preposterous and unacceptable. Freud, unable to persevere beneath the pressure of his superiors, dismissed the Seduction Hypothesis and went on to invent psychoanalysis, which "became a study of the internal vicissitudes of fantasy and desire, dissociated from the reality of experience" (Herman, 1992, p. 14).

At the same time Freud was exploring the Seduction Hypothesis in Vienna, Janet was studying traumatic memory in France. He, like Freud, came to the conclusion that hysteria was the result of early childhood trauma. However, unlike Freud, Janet never abandoned his theory of hysteria and remained faithful to his patients. Soon after, the medical and psychological establishments accepted Freud, while Janet and his ideas of hysteria were forgotten. As a result, trauma research was halted for decades (Herman, 1992).

It was not until after World War I that trauma was once again in the forefront of research. Veterans who had undergone traumatic experiences returned from the war displaying symptoms of hysteria, or what was then called shell shock. What was considered a disease that only afflicted women began to victimize large numbers of men who at one time were considered glorious and brave. Viewed as cowards and weak invalids, these men were treated poorly until W. H. R. Rivers, following the model of Dorothea Dix's mental health movement, began to treat these soldiers with dignity and respect. Rivers encouraged soldiers to write and to talk about the horrors of war, but it was not until after the Vietnam War that "rap groups" raised awareness of the effects war has on the individual. Rap

groups served as a place for Vietnam veterans to tell their
stories in the company of fellow veterans and psychiatrists
(Herman, 1992).

Trauma was publicized as a result of war, but the
traumas of domestic violence, abuse, and rape were hidden.
However, because both men and women displayed similar
behaviors after their own personal traumas, the distinction
between the trauma of war and the trauma of sexual assault
and abuse began to blur. As a result of the recognition of
psychological effects that occur both during and after
traumatic events, the diagnosis of post-traumatic stress
disorder (PTSD) was included in the Diagnostic and
Statistical Manual in 1980 (Herman, 1992). Unfortunately,
the battle fought by trauma survivors did not end when
psychologists considered post-traumatic stress disorder
legitimate. On the contrary, victims of trauma are still
being silenced, and to this day the rift still exists
between trauma survivors and those who cannot understand the
psychological and biological effects of trauma.

Dennis Charney, head of the clinical neuroscience
division of the National Center for PTSD states:

> Victims of devastating trauma may never be the
> same, biologically. It does not matter if it was
> the incessant terror of combat, torture of
> repeated abuse in childhood, or a one-time
> experience, like being trapped in a hurricane or
> almost dying in an auto accident. All
> uncontrollable stress can have the same biological
> impact. (Butler, 1996, p. 41)

Individuals who have not experienced a major traumatic
event or chronic trauma have the natural ability to prepare
their bodies for danger. In a threatening situation, normal
individuals' stress hormones increase, and the fight or
flight response prepares them to escape the danger, either

by resisting or by running. When the danger subsides, they return to a normal state because hormones have leveled off, and the nervous system is no longer in a state of arousal. It can be concluded, therefore, that normal, everyday stress does not permanently alter an individual's neurobiology (van der Kolk, McFarlene, & Weisaeth, 1996).

Unfortunately, this is not the case with trauma, especially trauma that occurs on a chronic basis. According to Bessel van der Kolk et al., "Chronic and persistent stress inhibits the effectiveness of the stress response and induces desensitization" (1996, p. 222). Stress hormones in traumatized individuals are elevated because victims of trauma are in a state of constant hyperarousal and cannot modulate their bodies efficiently. Small stressors have the ability to trigger the release of a flood of hormones, which results in overreacting to everyday events. As a result, even in normal environments, the nervous system is always on alert. Although the increase of hormones seems adaptive, what happens is that when the hormones are truly needed in a dangerous situation, they are not utilized properly. As demonstrated by Rauch and his co-researchers, hormones such as cortisol increase an individual's ability to numb his or her reactions. After watching a fifteen-minute video of combat scenes from Platoon, veterans with PTSD showed a drop in pain sensitivity and a release of natural opiates. As a result of the influx of numerous hormones at unusual times, traumatized individuals do not have the ability to reach an equilibrium; instead, they compensate by overutilizing the hormonal systems, leaving them either hyperaroused or numb (Rauch et al., 1996).

It is evident that the neurochemistry of traumatized individuals is abnormal, and it is important to understand that traumatic experiences are also stored and processed

differently from normal experiences. Bessel van der Kolk
et al. (1996) state that "in the course of evolution, the
human brain has developed three interdependent subanalyzers:
the brainstem/hypothalamus, the limbic system and the
prefrontal cortex" (p. 214). The brainstem and hypothalamus
are responsible for regulating internal homeostasis, and are
partially dependent on the limbic system and prefrontal
cortex to function properly. The limbic system, which
maintains balance between the internal and external world,
contains the hippocampus and the amygdala, two structures
that are involved with processing traumatic events. The
hippocampus records spacial dimensions of an experience and
plays an important role in short-term memory; the amygdala
is responsible for attaching emotional meaning to the
sensory input of an experience. In other words, the
hippocampus is responsible for the context of an experience,
and the amygdala is responsible for the emotional weight of
an experience. Finally, the prefrontal cortex analyzes
the experience and categorizes it with past experiences
(van der Kolk et al., 1996).

    According to van der Kolk et al. (1996), all
information that we receive through our five senses reaches
the amygdala before it travels to the hippocampus and the
prefrontal cortex. Therefore, emotional responses occur
before an actual experience can be interpreted and
evaluated. When experiencing a normal event, this is not a
problem because the emotional weight is too weak to outweigh
the actual experience. However, when experiencing a
traumatic event, the emotional impact is too extreme for
further processing to occur. As demonstrated in animal
studies (LeDoux, Romanski, & Xagoraris, 1989), if the
amygdala is excessively stimulated, it interferes with the
functioning of the hippocampus. If there is interference of
the hippocampus, as in the case of trauma, it is impossible

for a person to form a context for his or her experience.
Thus, integration of the traumatic memory with a wide store
of other memories never occurs (van der Kolk et al., 1996).

Because integration does not occur, it is nearly
impossible for people suffering from trauma to create a
narrative that describes their traumatic memory. Instead,
their experience exists in the form of images. Although the
traumatic experience in its entirety may be hazy and
difficult to retrieve, the images of certain moments remain
frozen, untarnished. The pictures of a traumatic event are
not organized. Traumatized victims cannot pick their mental
photo albums off a shelf and note the manner in which they
occurred. Their pictures are scattered, bent, torn. There
are no dates written on the back and no explanations as to
why the event occurred. Thus, trauma victims may dissociate
from the experience. However, it is impossible to disown an
experience without ramifications. Burying images in a box
does not allow a person to forget they exist; it just
prevents organizing them in a way that makes sense. It
distances the person from the event, until events and the
emotions are no longer intertwined. This seems like an ideal
defense mechanism: Forget it existed and it never happened.
What many people do not realize, however, is that the
emotions need an outlet, which is why many traumatized
individuals experience feelings they cannot explain. They
are consciously unable to tie past events with their present
emotional states.

This inability to be consciously aware of the
connection between events and emotions can be explained by
the theory of implicit and explicit memory. According to
van der Kolk, explicit or declarative memory is utilized to
remember a particular moment and enables an individual to
consciously tie his or her present behavior to an incident
that occurred in his or her past. It is the memory of

context and is tied closely to the hippocampus. Implicit
memory, unlike explicit memory, does not rely on the
hippocampus. It is utilized when perceptions, thoughts, and
actions are unconsciously influenced by past experiences
(van der Kolk et al., 1996). To demonstrate the difference
between explicit and implicit memory, Levinson (1965) had
surgeons state a mock crisis during surgery. Patients in the
control condition heard no message during their surgery,
while patients in the experimental condition were exposed to
negative messages, such as those suggesting that they might
not make it. The patients were later questioned about the
surgery, and results showed that those in the negative
message condition became extremely agitated when questioned,
while those in the no message condition had no such adverse
reaction. No patients were able to explicitly recall what
had been said, but the results showed that some implicit
memory had formed.

Traumatic experience interferes with explicit memory
but does not interfere with implicit memory. Interference
with explicit memory can be attributed to the fact that the
hippocampus does not function properly during traumatic
experience, due to excessive amygdala stimulation and
elevated levels of neurohormones, such as corticosteroids.
Since the hippocampus is essential for short-term memory,
any damage to the hippocampus results in a person's
inability to establish context for his or her experiences.
Due to damage to the hippocampus, explicit memory cannot
function properly. However, implicit memory is intact
(van der Kolk et al., 1996).

Without remembrance for context, trauma survivors
have trouble discovering that the person they have become
is a direct extension of the life-altering experience of
the trauma. In other words, the conscious may not be aware
of the impact of the trauma, but the unconscious always

remembers, which is why sensory input can trigger feelings that cannot be explained. Because the memories of trauma are not stored in the same way that typical memories are, an individual must rely on bits and pieces of information that exist in the form of sensations, flashes of images, or perhaps a particular smell or taste. The images are intrusive and appear without conscious thought. Unable to understand and know why these sensations occur, a person cannot find words to describe his or her memories (van der Kolk et al., 1996).

Navigating through the aftermath of a traumatic event begins with an explanation as to how memories resurface; the purpose of this is so the traumatized individual understands why only feelings and fragments can be recalled rather than the entire incident. An inability to narrate a traumatic experience was examined by Rauch et al. in 1996. By playing to combat veterans and sexual abuse survivors with PTSD a tape of their most horrific memory, the three researchers were able to stimulate flashbacks. During recollection, positron emission tomography (PET) scans were used to record brain activity in these individuals. Results showed that areas of the brain's cortex involved in sensory memory were active, while Broca's area, which plays a large part in verbal articulation of experience, was inactive. When asked to recall a mundane experience, the opposite trend emerged: The sensory areas were inactive, while Broca's area was active (Rauch et al., 1996).

If a person is unable to verbally express his or her experience, a cohesive narrative cannot be formed during therapy. Victims may want to talk about what happened, but because Broca's area is inactive, they may be unable to. It is difficult to talk about an image or a feeling in a way that makes sense to people; thus, some trauma victims may become so frustrated at their lack of ability to communicate that they may shut down.

For some of those trauma victims, writing is a vehicle
for communication (MacCurdy, in press). Writing is largely
based on moments and images. A person can make lists of
things such as colors, feelings, and sounds. A piece of
paper and a pen allow a person to collect her or his
thoughts; these inanimate objects, unlike most people, are
not impatient, nor do they become annoyed at images that do
not form a story that makes sense. Rather, an individual has
the power to write as quickly or as slowly as needed. The
act of writing freezes a thought or an image that a person
feels at a certain point. When several images have been
focused upon, a story begins to form. A person can begin to
label cluttered boxes of snapshots in a way that allows
processing to occur. Writers can arrange their pictures and
take power over their prose until a story eventually
emerges. The images are no longer uncontrollable; they are
within the traumatized individual's control. The act of
writing can be empowering to individuals as they try to make
sense of incidents that initially seem indescribable.

In addition to the mental healing writing provides,
physical healing may also occur. Writing has been shown to
enhance immune system functioning and reduce the number of
physician visits (Pennebaker, Kiecolt-Glaser, & Glaser,
1988). Studies have shown that writing "increases antibody
responses to the Epstein-Barr virus, and antibody response
to hepatitis B vaccinations" (Pennebaker, 1997, p. 162). It
also helps to increase t-helper cell growth (1997). Short-
term changes in autonomic activity, such as lowered heart
rate and electrodermal activity, are also produced by
disclosure. Pennebaker (1997) has concluded that "the mere
expression of trauma is not sufficient. Health gains appear
to require translating experiences into language" (p. 164).
Writing serves to translate experiences that an individual
cannot express verbally.

Writing also provides an outlet when no other outlet exists. Our society silences victims of trauma by ignoring their cries for help. Some believe that traumatic events occur only to those who deserve them. By blaming the victim, we can say with assurance that "this will never happen to me." We live in a society that denies the presence of trauma, despite historical evidence and personal accounts. In school, children learn about the glorious war battles that men fought to save the land we walk upon; we are shown that the grieving time for the loss of a loved one is limited to three days of mourning; we see that rape is justified because the woman asked for it; and we understand that abusive environments exist only in the lives of "those people." But no one talks about the war veteran who can no longer sleep without a gun nearby, or the family who stares at the empty chair that their loved one used to occupy. We don't discuss the flashbacks and constant fear a rape victim must struggle with, nor do we talk about domestic violence that results in a new generation of children who are taught that violence is the answer. How can a victim of incest feel safe enough to talk about her experience when she is shut out time and again? How does our denial affect the child who is abused over and over again?

Without a supportive community, trauma remains buried beneath layers and layers of self-blame, guilt, and denial. The process of writing serves to integrate experience and document personal history. Memories, no matter how painful, make us who we are. By telling the story of our lives, we realize why we react the way we do in certain situations and why each person is unique.

Unfortunately, some psychologists do not see the importance of community and disclosure. Instead, they would rather take the actual traumatic memory away by using drugs such as propranolol. According to Davis (1998), propranolol

essentially blocks the ability to connect aversive emotions
to traumatic memories by acting as an antagonist on the
B-adrenergic receptor. During and after emotional
experience, the B-adrenergic stress hormone systems are
activated, resulting in enhanced memory for the emotional
event. In a study conducted in 1994 (see Cahill, Prins,
Weber, & McGaugh) participants were given either propranolol
or a placebo an hour before being shown a series of slides
accompanied by narratives. The emotionally neutral narrative
described a mother taking her son to visit his father, who
worked as a laboratory technician in a hospital. The
emotionally charged narrative started with the boy and
mother going to visit the boy's father at work, but in this
version, the two never made it to the lab because the boy
was struck by a car and suffered severe brain trauma. In
addition, the boy's feet were severed, but a surgical team
was able to reattach them. Participants were then given
memory tests; results showed that participants in the
emotionally neutral scenario, regardless of whether they had
received the propranolol, had similar recall. In the
emotionally charged condition, however, participants who
were given propranolol scored significantly lower than
participants who were given a placebo. The results of this
study show the profound impact beta-blockers can have in the
face of a traumatic event.

   According to Davis, the next step is to use
propranolol to conduct a controlled study with trauma
victims. In my opinion, the thought of erasing a memory from
another human being is terrifying. The neurobiology of
trauma victims may leave them speechless, but with a
supportive community and therapeutic writing, their voices
can return. Unfortunately, our society does not recognize
this. It was bad enough that we isolated victims from
society; now we isolate them from themselves.

Silent Expression   14

References

Butler, K. (1996, March/April). The biology of fear. Networker, 39-45.

Cahill, L., Prins, B., Weber, M., & McGaugh, J. L. (1994). B-adrenergic activation and memory for emotional events. Nature, 271, 702-704.

Davis, M. (1998). Neural systems involved in fear and anxiety. Symposium conducted at the University of Scranton, Scanton, PA.

Herman, J. L. (1992). Trauma and recovery. New York: HarperCollins.

LeDoux, J. E., Romanski, L., & Xagoraris, A. (1989). Indelibility of subcortical emotional memories. Journal of Cognitive Neuroscience, 1, 238-243.

Levinson, B. W. (1965). States of awareness during general anesthesia: Preliminary communication. British Journal of Anesthesia, 37, 544-546.

MacCurdy, M. (in press). From trauma to writing: A theoretical model for practical use. In C. Anderson & M. MacCurdy (Eds.), Writing and healing. Urbana, IL: NCTE.

Pennebaker, J. W. (1997). Writing about emotional experiences as a therapeutic process. Psychological Science, 8 (3), 162-165.

Pennebaker, J. W., Kiecolt-Glaser, J. K., & Glaser, R. (1988). Disclosure of traumas and immune function: Health implications for psychotherapy. Journal of Counseling and Clinical Psychology, 56 (2), 239-245.

Rauch, S. L., van der Kolk, B. A., Fisler, R. E., Alpert, N. M., Orr, S. P., Savage, C. R., Fischman, A. J., Jenike, M. A., & Pitman, R. K. (1996). A symptom provocation study of posttraumatic stress disorder using positron emission tomography and script-driven imagery. Archives of General Psychiatry, 53, 380-387.

van der Kolk, B. A., McFarlane, A. C., & Weisaeth, L. (1996). Traumatic stress. New York: Guilford Press.

INDIVIDUAL EXERCISE ON RHETORICAL GOALS
FOR RESEARCH PAPERS

Reread Jennifer Piazza's research paper. What is her goal for writing? What is she trying to accomplish? What is the relationship between the sources of information she draws on and her own views? Freewrite for ten minutes in response to these questions.

COLLABORATIVE EXERCISE ON RHETORICAL GOALS
FOR RESEARCH PAPERS

1. Form collaborative learning groups of five students each, as described in the Preface, or fashion groups according to a method of your own.
2. Within your group, discuss the following questions: To what extent is Jennifer Piazza's paper a report on the content of the sources she consulted? To what extent is her paper an explanation of her own conclusions about the topic? Have the recorder note the high points of your deliberations.
3. Reconvene the entire class. Each group recorder should explain the group's answers to the two questions. Then, discuss any disagreements among groups.

PART
two

An Anthology
of Readings

Natural Sciences and Technology

SUBJECTS AND METHODS OF STUDY IN THE NATURAL SCIENCES AND TECHNOLOGY

The Scientific Method

Science and technology are based on a common methodology, and thus scientific and technical researchers the world over share an approach to their work. Even though they may give conflicting answers to important questions in their disciplines, they rarely argue about the basic process of conducting scientific investigation. The specific means by which researchers discover, collect, and organize information is called the scientific method. This approach involves questioning, observing, experimenting, and theorizing. Drawing on previous knowledge and prior investigations, scientists ask questions not only about the unknown but also about phenomena that are supposedly understood. Often, they challenge commonly accepted beliefs as well as the conclusions of other scientists. Indeed, no fact or theory is exempt from legitimate inquiry. Even the most widely accepted ideas are continually reexamined. This questioning process helps make science self-correcting, since errors made by scientists can be detected and corrected by subsequent investigation.

Scientific ideas must be confirmed through observation before they are considered fact. Assertions that cannot be supported by direct observation are generally greeted with skepticism by the scientific community. For phenomena that cannot be observed readily in nature, scientists design experiments that make events stand out more clearly. As with other information derived from observations, experimental findings are continually reexamined, and experiments are considered valid only if they can be repeated with identical results by different investigators.

Scientists build theories to account for direct observations and experimental results. Theories are rules or models that explain a large body of separate facts. An example is the Bohr model of the atom, in which electrons orbit around the nucleus like moons around a planet. The Bohr model explains many basic observations made by physicists and chemists, but it is by no means the only theoretical description of the atom; quantum theory suggests an atomic model that does not include electrons in discrete orbits. Scientists often weigh competing theories that purport to explain the same facts. The other parts of the scientific method—questioning, observing, and experimenting—contribute to constructing and testing theories.

WRITING ABOUT SCIENCE AND TECHNOLOGY

Texts concerning science and technology can be separated into two groups: (1) reports of original research, which focus on a narrow topic, and (2) summary or speculative articles, which generalize about a body of specific information. Research reports are typically written for experts in scientific or technical disciplines. Summary and speculative articles are often directed to less specialized audiences. Consider, for example, "Issues Regarding DNA Testing" (Chapter 8) that summarizes the constitutional issues that arise from DNA technology and Carol Foote's speculative article (Chapter 6) that describes how selective breeding might be used to improve the human species. Most of the articles you read in Chapters 6, 7, and 8 will be summary and speculative articles written for a general audience rather than an audience of professional scientists.

Organization

Most research reports share a common rhetorical pattern. Scientists within specific disciplines have established standard methods for organizing research reports, and most journals that publish research results accept only articles written according to those formats. Summary and speculative articles, however, vary widely in rhetorical structure. Nonscientists who think the only aim of science writing is to relate established facts fail to recognize that much science writing argues a point. As you read through the next three chapters, notice that the majority of the articles are organized as arguments. For example, the title of Carl Sagan's article, "In Defense of Robots," indicates that the essay will present an argument. The pursuit of science often gives rise to intense debate over what questions should be investigated, what observations are accurate, and what theories best explain particular observations; thus, argumentative writing is common in science. In addition to argumentation, the full range of rhetorical patterns can be found in popular science writing.

Writing research reports according to a set organizational formula does have its drawbacks. In some cases, scientists may become so obsessed with fitting their work into a research report formula that they lose sight of the central goal of scientific research: an active pursuit of the truth. A similar problem sometimes surfaces in popular science writing in which the rhetorical pattern becomes more important than scientific accuracy. For example, Joseph Weizenbaum, an internationally known computer scientist, states that most essays about the societal impact of computer technology follow a set pattern. First, they survey the benefits to society of computers; then, they consider some of the potential dangers of widespread computer use; finally, they claim that those dangers can be overcome with new technology and argue for a vigorous program to expand computer development and use. Weizenbaum implies that this simplistic, problem-solution approach to writing about computers may obscure the truth. Much popular writing about controversial science and technology follows a pattern similar to the one Weizenbaum describes. To fit a set format, the science writer may ignore important facts or pass over alternative interpretations of certain facts. Consequently, analyzing rhetorical structure is an important element in comprehending science writing.

Style

Although the tone of research report writing is almost always unemotional and authoritative, popular science writing varies considerably in tone and style. Once free from the constraints of the professional research report, scientists express emotions and personal attitudes as do writers in other fields. As you read the article by Charles Platt in Chapter 8, notice that the writer uses a personal tone to discuss a technical issue: electronic communications systems.

No matter what the tone, a science writer establishes authority by providing concrete evidence. Even the most eminent scientists must support their theories with verifiable observations. In Chapters 6, 7, and 8, you will find that most of the authors include objective evidence to support major assertions. That evidence often comes from scientific investigation, but it also comes from informal observations, anecdotes, and hypothetical cases. For example, in "The Intimate Machine," which appears in Chapter 7, Neil Frude lists a number of observations about the behavior of humans and computers and then uses those observations as a basis for predicting how interactions between intelligent machines and humans will develop in the future. Most science writers are careful to build on evidence, even when they are writing for a general audience. Consequently, it is important for readers of science writing to identify and evaluate the evidence authors provide in support of their claims.

Nonscientists are often amazed to find that different sources may present conflicting versions of scientific "fact." The same body of experimental evidence can lead to several different notions of what the truth is. When you find that the experts disagree, try to describe precisely the various versions of the facts, and if possible, try to explain the reasons for the differences of opinion.

Sometimes, differences of opinion on scientific issues have nothing to do with scientific fact but, rather, reflect conflicting personal or social values. Science is not immune to the political and moral controversy that is part of other human activities. As you read the articles in Chapter 6 on human reproductive technology, you will see that the writers address social and moral issues. When writers do not support scientific claims with objective evidence, you should consider the moral, ideological, or emotional motivations behind their assertions.

Even nonscientists can evaluate intelligently many summary and speculative articles about science. As you read and think about the material in the next three chapters, keep in mind that many of the articles will be organized as arguments and can be analyzed like other forms of argumentative writing. Also ask yourself whether the article involves questioning, observing, experimenting, or theorizing, the basic components of the scientific method. Be sensitive to the author's tone. Look for evidence that supports the author's claims. Note the specific points on which the experts disagree, and try to account for those differences of opinion. Finally, consider the social or ethical questions that scientific advances raise. These procedures will help you read about science and technology with more understanding and better critical judgment.

WORK CITED

Weizenbaum, Joseph. "The Impact of the Computer on Society." *Science* 176 (1972): 609–14.

s i x

Cloning and Reproductive Technology

Intervention in the human reproduction process is as old as civilization. Virtually all traditional cultures had ways of trying to improve fertility, from amulets and rituals to medications and specific sexual practices. Societies have also intervened in reproduction for political reasons, for example to maintain royal bloodlines. Economic factors have also played a role. Certain cultures, for instance, put some female babies to death to maintain a relatively high proportion of male laborers and warriors.

Modern technology provides new, dramatic ways of intervening in reproduction. Couples with faulty eggs or sperm can now receive genetic material from donors that is used to create an embryo outside the womb, a "test-tube baby" that can be implanted in the mother-to-be. Surrogate mothers incubate babies for women who are able to conceive but not bear children. And now, human embryos have been successfully cloned, opening up a range of possibilities. Although interventions in the reproductive process have always been controversial, the potential for cloning humans has heightened the debate. Is cloning just another reproductive technology or does it raise unique ethical, political, or social issues? Should we allow asexual reproduction and the genetic duplication of particular individuals? Should childless couples or singles be allowed to use cloning to obtain children to whom they are biologically related? Should individuals be allowed to produce genetic copies of themselves in a bid for "immortality"? Should we use cloning to reproduce the "best" individuals in our culture, the Lincolns, Einsteins, and Mozarts?

The articles in Chapter 6 focus on the controversy over human cloning. In her science fiction short story "Nine Lives," Ursula Le Guin describes how a team of nine humans, cloned from a single individual, function as an highly efficient, autonomous unit in a futurist society. Lee Silver discusses the scientific breakthroughs that led to successful cloning of mammals and the representation of cloning in popular culture in "From Science Fiction to Reality." His article is excerpted from his book *Remaking Eden: Cloning and Beyond in a Brave New World.* In "Dolly's Fashion and Louis's Passion," Stephen Jay Gould examines popular fears about cloning and maintains that many of these fears result from the unwarranted assumption that heredity is more influential than environment. Carol Foote's "Designing Better Humans" summarizes a debate over whether our society should employ eugenics to improve the human species, and John J. Conley's and Barbara Ehrenreich's articles were both prompted by an experiment in which scientists cloned human cells. Conley questions the ethics of cloning and other reproductive technologies, and Ehrenreich responds to the critics of cloning.

Nine Lives

Ursula K. Le Guin

One of the best-known authors of science fiction, Ursula Le Guin has won numerous awards for her novels and short stories. Among her books are The Left Hand of Darkness, Orsinian Tales, *and* Unlocking the Air and Other Stories, *and we have reprinted the first half of the short story "Nine Lives" from her book* The Wind's Twelve Quarters.

PREREADING

Imagine a futuristic society in which it is common practice to make multiple clone copies of talented individuals. What might be the desirable or undesirable results of this practice? Freewrite on this topic for ten minutes.

"Nine Lives." Copyright © 1969, 1997 by Ursula K. Le Guin; first appeared in *Playboy;* from *The Wind's Twelve Quarters.* Reprinted by permission of the author and the author's agent, the Virginia Kidd Agency, Inc.

She was alive inside but dead outside, her face a black and dun net of wrinkles, tumors, cracks. She was bald and blind. The tremors that crossed Libra's face were mere quiverings of corruption. Underneath, in the black corridors, the halls beneath the skin, there were crepitations in darkness, ferments, chemical nightmares that went on for centuries. "O the damned flatulent planet," Pugh murmured as the dome shook and a boil burst a kilometer to the southwest, spraying silver pus across the sunset. The sun had been setting for the last two days. "I'll be glad to see a human face."

"Thanks," said Martin.

"Yours is human to be sure," said Pugh, "but I've seen it so long I can't see it."

Radvid signals cluttered the communicator which Martin was operating, faded, returned as face and voice. The face filled the screen, the nose of an Assyrian king, the eyes of a samurai, skin bronze, eyes the color of iron: young, magnificent. "Is that what human beings look like?" said Pugh with awe. "I'd forgotten."

"Shut up, Owen, we're on."

"Libra Exploratory Mission Base, come in please, this is *Passerine* launch."

"Libra here. Beam fixed. Come on down, launch."

"Expulsion in seven E-seconds. Hold on." The screen blanked and sparkled.

"Do they all look like that? Martin, you and I are uglier men than I thought."

"Shut up, Owen. . . ."

For twenty-two minutes Martin followed the landing craft down by signal and then through the cleared dome they saw it, small star in the blood-colored east, sinking. It came down neat and quiet, Libra's thin atmosphere carrying little sound. Pugh and Martin closed the headpieces of their imsuits, zipped out of the dome airlocks, and ran with soaring strides, Nijinsky and Nureyev, toward the boat. Three equipment modules came floating down at four-minute intervals from each other and hundred-meter intervals east of the boat. "Come on out," Martin said on his suit radio, "we're waiting at the door."

"Come on in, the methane's fine," said Pugh.

The hatch opened. The young man they had seen on the screen came out with one athletic twist and leaped down onto the shaky dust and clinkers of Libra. Martin shook his hand, but Pugh was staring at the hatch, from which another young man emerged with the same neat twist

1

2

3

4

5

6

7

and jump, followed by a young woman who emerged with the same neat twist, ornamented by a wriggle, and the jump. They were all tall, with bronze skin, black hair, high-bridged noses, epicanthic fold, the same face. They all had the same face. The fourth was emerging from the hatch with a neat twist and jump. "Martin bach," said Pugh, "we've got a clone."

"Right," said one of them, "we're a tenclone. John Chow's the name.   8 You're Lieutenant Martin?"

"I'm Owen Pugh."

"Alvaro Guillen Martin," said Martin, formal, bowing slightly. An-   9 other girl was out, the same beautiful face; Martin stared at her and his eye rolled like a nervous pony's. Evidently he had never given any thought to cloning and was suffering technological shock. "Steady," Pugh said in the Argentine dialect, "it's only excess twins." He stood close by Martin's elbow. He was glad himself of the contact.

It is hard to meet a stranger. Even the greatest extravert meet-   10 ing even the meekest stranger knows a certain dread, though he may not know he knows it. Will he make a fool of me wreck my image of myself invade me destroy me change me? Will he be different from me? Yes, that he will. There's the terrible thing: the strangeness of the stranger.

After two years on a dead planet, and the last half year isolated as   11 a team of two, oneself and one other, after that it's even harder to meet a stranger, however welcome he may be. You're out of the habit of dif- ference, you've lost the touch; and so the fear revives, the primitive anx- iety, the old dread.

The clone, five males and five females, had got done in a couple of   12 minutes what a man might have got done in twenty: greeted Pugh and Martin, had a glance at Libra, unloaded the boat, made ready to go. They went, and the dome filled with them, a hive of golden bees. They hummed and buzzed quietly, filled up all silences, all spaces with a honey- brown swarm of human presence. Martin looked bewildered at the long- limbed girls, and they smiled at him, three at once. Their smile was gentler than that of the boys, but no less radiantly self-possessed.

"Self-possessed," Owen Pugh murmured to his friend, "that's it.   13 Think of it, to be oneself ten times over. Nine seconds for every motion, nine ayes on every vote. It would be glorious." But Martin was asleep. And the John Chows had all gone to sleep at once. The dome was filled with their quiet breathing. They were young, they didn't snore. Martin sighed and snored, his Hershey-bar-colored face relaxed in the dim afterglow of Libra's primary, set at last. Pugh had cleared the dome and stars looked in, Sol among them, a great company of lights, a clone of splendors. Pugh slept and dreamed of a one-eyed giant who chased him through the shaking halls of Hell.

From his sleeping bag Pugh watched the clone's awakening. They all got up within one minute except for one pair, a boy and a girl, who lay snugly tangled and still sleeping in one bag. As Pugh saw this there was a shock like one of Libra's earthquakes inside him, a very deep tremor. He was not aware of this and in fact thought he was pleased at the sight; there was no other such comfort on this dead hollow world. More power to them, who made love. One of the others stepped on the pair. They woke and the girl sat up flushed and sleepy, with bare golden breasts. One of her sisters murmured something to her; she shot a glance at Pugh and disappeared in the sleeping bag; from another direction came a fierce stare, from still another direction a voice: "Christ, we're used to having a room to ourselves. Hope you don't mind, Captain Pugh." 14

"It's a pleasure," Pugh said half truthfully. He had to stand up then wearing only the shorts he slept in, and he felt like a plucked rooster, all white scrawn and pimples. He had seldom envied Martin's compact brownness so much. The United Kingdom had come through the Great Famines well, losing less than half its population: a record achieved by rigorous food control. Black marketers and hoarders had been executed. Crumbs had been shared. Where in richer lands most had died and a few had thrived, in Britain fewer died and none throve. They all got lean. Their sons were lean, their grandsons lean, small, brittle-boned, easily infected. When civilization became a matter of standing in lines, the British had kept queue, and so had replaced the survival of the fittest with the survival of the fair-minded. Owen Pugh was a scrawny little man. All the same, he was there. 15

At the moment he wished he wasn't. 16

At breakfast a John said, "Now if you'll brief us, Captain Pugh—"

"Owen, then."

"Owen, we can work out our schedule. Anything new on the mine since your last report to your Mission? We saw your reports when *Passerine* was orbiting Planet V, where they are now."

Martin did not answer, though the mine was his discovery and project, and Pugh had to do his best. It was hard to talk to them. The same faces, each with the same expression of intelligent interest, all leaned toward him across the table at almost the same angle. They all nodded together. 17

Over the Exploitation Corps insigne on their tunics each had a 18
nameband, first name John and last name Chow of course, but the middle names different. The men were Aleph, Kaph, Yod, Gimel, and
Samedh; the women Sadhe, Daleth, Zayin, Beth, and Resh. Pugh tried
to use the names but gave it up at once; he could not even tell sometimes which one had spoken, for all the voices were alike.

Martin buttered and chewed his toast, and finally interrupted: 19
"You're a team. Is that it?"

"Right," said two Johns.

"God, what a team! I hadn't seen the point. How much do you each
know what the others are thinking?"

"Not at all, properly speaking," replied one of the girls, Zayin. The 20
others watched her with the proprietary, approving look they had. "No
ESP, nothing fancy. But we think alike. We have exactly the same equipment. Given the same stimulus, the same problem, we're likely to be
coming up with the same reactions and solutions at the same time. Explanations are easy—don't even have to make them, usually. We seldom
misunderstand each other. It does facilitate our working as a team."

"Christ yes," said Martin. "Pugh and I have spent seven hours out 21
of ten for six months misunderstanding each other. Like most people.
What about emergencies, are you as good at meeting the unexpected
problem as a nor . . . an unrelated team?"

"Statistics so far indicate that we are," Zayin answered readily. 22
Clones must be trained, Pugh thought, to meet questions, to reassure
and reason. All they said had the slightly bland and stilted quality of
answers furnished to the Public. "We can't brainstorm as singletons
can, we as a team don't profit from the interplay of varied minds; but
we have a compensatory advantage. Clones are drawn from the best
human material, individuals of IIQ ninety-ninth percentile, Genetic
Constitution alpha double A, and so on. We have more to draw on than
most individuals do."

"And it's multiplied by a factor of ten. Who is—who was John 23
Chow?"

"A genius surely," Pugh said politely. His interest in cloning was not
so new and avid as Martin's.

"Leonardo Complex type," said Yod. "Biomath, also a cellist and an
undersea hunter, and interested in structural engineering problems and
so on. Died before he'd worked out his major theories."

"Then you each represent a different facet of his mind, his talents?"

"No," said Zayin, shaking her head in time with several others. 24
"We share the basic equipment and tendencies, of course, but we're
all engineers in Planetary Exploitation. A later clone can be trained to
develop other aspects of the basic equipment. It's all training; the genetic substance is identical. We *are* John Chow. But we are differently
trained."

Martin looked shell-shocked. "How old are you?" 25
"Twenty-three."

"You say he died young—had they taken germ cells from him be-
forehand or something?"

Gimel took over: "He died at twenty-four in an air car crash. They 26
couldn't save the brain, so they took some intestinal cells and cultured
them for cloning. Reproductive cells aren't used for cloning, since they
have only half the chromosomes. Intestinal cells happen to be easy to
despecialize and reprogram for total growth."

"All chips off the old block," Martin said valiantly. "But how can 27
. . . some of you be women . . . ?"

Beth took over: "It's easy to program half the clonal mass back to the 28
female. Just delete the male gene from half the cells and they revert to
the basic, that is, the female. It's trickier to go the other way, have to hook
in artificial Y chromosomes. So they mostly clone from males, since clones
function best bisexually."

Gimel again: "They've worked these matters of technique and func- 29
tion out carefully. The taxpayer wants the best for his money, and of
course clones are expensive. With the cell manipulations, and the incu-
bation in Ngama Placentae, and the maintenance and training of the
foster-parent groups, we end up costing about three million apiece."

"For your next generation," Martin said, still struggling, "I suppose 30
you . . . you breed?"

"We females are sterile," said Beth with perfect equanimity. "You 31
remember that the Y chromosome was deleted from our original cell.
The males can interbreed with approved singletons, if they want to. But
to get John Chow again as often as they want, they just reclone a cell
from this clone."

Martin gave up the struggle. He nodded and chewed cold toast. 32
"Well," said one of the Johns, and all changed mood, like a flock of star-
lings that change course in one wingflick, following a leader so fast that
no eye can see which leads. They were ready to go. "How about a look
at the mine? Then we'll unload the equipment. Some nice new models
in the roboats; you'll want to see them. Right?" Had Pugh or Martin not

agreed they might have found it hard to say so. The Johns were polite but unanimous; their decisions carried. Pugh, Commander of Libra Base 2, felt a qualm. Could he boss around this superman/woman-entity-of-ten? and a genius at that? He stuck close to Martin as they suited for outside. Neither said anything.

Four apiece in the three large airjets, they slipped off north from   33
the dome, over Libra's dun rugose skin, in starlight.

"Desolate," one said.

It was a boy and girl with Pugh and Martin. Pugh wondered if these   34
were the two that had shared a sleeping bag last night. No doubt they wouldn't mind if he asked them. Sex must be as handy as breathing to them. Did you two breathe last night?

"Yes," he said, "it is desolate."   35

"This is our first time off, except training on Luna." The girl's voice was definitely a bit higher and softer.

"How did you take the big hop?"

"They doped us. I wanted to experience it." That was the boy; he sounded wistful. They seemed to have more personality, only two at a time. Did repetition of the individual negate individuality?

"Don't worry," said Martin, steering the sled, "you can't experience no-time because it isn't there."

"I'd just like to once," one of them said. "So we'd know."

The Mountains of Merioneth showed leprotic in starlight to the   36
east, a plume of freezing gas trailed silvery from a vent-hole to the west, and the sled tilted groundward. The twins braced for the stop at one moment, each with a slight protective gesture to the other. Your skin is my skin, Pugh thought, but literally, no metaphor. What would it be like, then, to have someone as close to you as that? Always to be answered when you spoke; never to be in pain alone. Love your neighbor as you love yourself. . . . That hard old problem was solved. The neighbor was the self: the love was perfect.

And here was Hellmouth, the mine.   37

Pugh was the Exploratory Mission's E.T. geologist, and Martin his   38
technician and cartographer; but when in the course of a local survey Martin had discovered the U-mine, Pugh had given him full credit, as well as the onus of prospecting the lode and planning the Exploitation Team's job. These kids had been sent out from Earth years before Martin's reports got there and had not known what their job would be until they got here. The Exploitation Corps simply sent out teams regularly and blindly as a dandelion sends out its seed, knowing there would be a job

for them on Libra or the next planet out or one they hadn't even heard about yet. The government wanted uranium too urgently to wait while reports drifted home across the lightyears. The stuff was like gold, old-fashioned but essential, worth mining extraterrestrially and shipping interstellar. Worth its weight in people, Pugh thought sourly, watching the tall young men and women go one by one, glimmering in starlight, into the black hole Martin had named Hellmouth.

As they went in their homeostatic forehead-lamps brightened. 39 Twelve nodding gleams ran along the moist, wrinkled walls. Pugh heard Martin's radiation counter peeping twenty to the dozen up ahead. "Here's the drop-off," said Martin's voice in the suit intercom, drowning out the peeping and the dead silence that was around them. "We're in a side-fissure, this is the main vertical vent in front of us." The black void gaped, its far side not visible in the headlamp beams. "Last vulcanism seems to have been a couple of thousand years ago. Nearest fault is twenty-eight kilos east, in the Trench. This area seems to be as safe seismically as anything in the area. The big basalt-flow overhead stabilizes all these sub-structures, so long as it remains stable itself. Your central lode is thirty-six meters down and runs in a series of five bubble caverns northeast. It is a lode, a pipe of very high-grade ore. You saw the percentage figures, right? Extraction's going to be no problem. All you've got to do is get the bubbles topside."

"Take off the lid and let'em float up." A chuckle. Voices began to talk, 40 but they were all the same voice and the suit radio gave them no location in space. "Open the thing right up. —Safer that way. —But it's a solid basalt roof, how thick, ten meters here? —Three to twenty, the report said. — Blow good ore all over the lot. —Use this access we're in, straighten it a bit and run slider rails for the robos. —Import burros. —Have we got enough propping material? —What's your estimate of total payload mass, Martin?"

"Say over five million kilos and under eight." 41

"Transport will be here in ten E-months. —It'll have to go pure. — No, they'll have the mass problem in NAFAL shipping licked by now, remember it's been sixteen years since we left Earth last Tuesday. — Right, they'll send the whole lot back and purify it in Earth orbit. —Shall we go down, Martin?"

"Go on. I've been down."

The first one—Aleph? (Heb., the ox, the leader)—swung onto the 42 ladder and down; the rest followed. Pugh and Martin stood at the chasm's edge. Pugh set his intercom to exchange only with Martin's suit, and noticed Martin doing the same. It was a bit wearing, this listening to one person think aloud in ten voices, or was it one voice speaking the thoughts of ten minds?

"A great gut," Pugh said, looking down into the black pit, its veined 43 and warted walls catching stray gleams of headlamps far below. "A cow's bowel. A bloody great constipated intestine."

Martin's counter peeped like a lost chicken. They stood inside the 44 dead but epileptic planet, breathing oxygen from tanks, wearing suits impermeable to corrosives and harmful radiations, resistant to a 200-degree range of temperatures, tear-proof, and as shock-resistant as possible given the soft vulnerable stuff inside.

"Next hop," Martin said, "I'd like to find a planet that has nothing 45 whatever to exploit."

"You found this."

"Keep me home next time."

Pugh was pleased. He had hoped Martin would want to go on work- 46 ing with him, but neither of them was used to talking much about their feelings, and he had hesitated to ask. "I'll try that," he said.

"I hate this place. I like caves, you know. It's why I came in here. Just 47 spelunking. But this one's a bitch. Mean. You can't ever let down in here. I guess this lot can handle it, though. They know their stuff."

"Wave of the future, whatever," said Pugh. 48

The wave of the future came swarming up the ladder, swept Mar- 49 tin to the entrance, gabbled at and around him: "Have we got enough material for supports? —If we convert one of the extractor servos to anneal, yes. —Sufficient if we miniblast? —Kaph can calculate stress." Pugh had switched his intercom back to receive them; he looked at them, so many thoughts jabbering in an eager mind, and at Martin standing silent among them, and at Hellmouth and the wrinkled plain. "Settled! How does that strike you as a preliminary schedule, Martin?"

"It's your baby," Martin said. 50

Within five E-days the Johns had all their material and equipment 51 unloaded and operating and were starting to open up the mine. They worked with total efficiency. Pugh was fascinated and frightened by their effectiveness, their confidence, their independence. He was no use to them at all. A clone, he thought, might indeed be the first truly stable, self-reliant human being. Once adult it would need nobody's help. It would be sufficient to itself physically, sexually, emotionally, intellectually. Whatever he did, any member of it would always receive the support and approval of his peers, his other selves. Nobody else was needed.

Two of the clone stayed in the dome doing calculations and paper- 52
work, with frequent sled trips to the mine for measurements and tests.
They were the mathematicians of the clone, Zayin and Kaph. That is, as
Zayin explained, all ten had had thorough mathematical training from
age three to twenty-one, but from twenty-one to twenty-three she and
Kaph had gone on with math while the others intensified study in other
specialties, geology, mining, engineering, electronic engineering, equipment robotics, applied atomics, and so on. "Kaph and I feel," she said,
"that we're the element of the clone closest to what John Chow was in his
singleton lifetime. But of course he was principally in biomath, and they
didn't take us far in that."

"They needed us most in this field," Kaph said, with the patriotic 53
priggishness they sometimes evinced.

Pugh and Martin soon could distinguish this pair from the others, 54
Zayin by gestalt, Kaph only by a discolored left fourth fingernail, got
from an ill-aimed hammer at the age of six. No doubt there were many
such differences, physical and psychological, among them; nature might
be identical, nurture could not be. But the differences were hard to
find. And part of the difficulty was that they never really talked to Pugh
and Martin. They joked with them, were polite, got along fine. They
gave nothing. It was nothing one could complain about; they were very
pleasant, they had the standardized American friendliness. "Do you
come from Ireland, Owen?"

"Nobody comes from Ireland, Zayin."   55

"There are lots of Irish-Americans."

"To be sure, but no more Irish. A couple of thousand in all the is- 56
land, the last I knew. They didn't go in for birth control, you know, so
the food ran out. By the Third Famine there were no Irish left at all but
the priesthood, and they all celibate, or nearly all."

Zayin and Kaph smiled stiffly. They had no experience of either big- 57
otry or irony. "What are you then, ethnically?" Kaph asked, and Pugh
replied, "A Welshman."

"Is it Welsh that you and Martin speak together?"   58

None of your business, Pugh thought, but said, "No, it's his dialect,
not mine: Argentinean. A descendant of Spanish."

"You learned it for private communication?"

"Whom had we here to be private from? It's just that sometimes a
man likes to speak his native language."

"Ours is English," Kaph said unsympathetically. Why should
they have sympathy? That's one of the things you give because you
need it back.

"Is Wells quaint?" asked Zayin.

"Wells? Oh, Wales, it's called. Yes, Wales is quaint." Pugh switched 59 on his rock-cutter, which prevented further conversation by a synapse-destroying whine, and while it whined he turned his back and said a profane word in Welsh.

That night he used the Argentine dialect for private communication. 60 "Do they pair off in the same couples or change every night?"

Martin looked surprised. A prudish expression, unsuited to his 61 features, appeared for a moment. It faded. He too was curious. "I think it's random."

"Don't whisper, man, it sounds dirty. I think they rotate." 62

"On a schedule?"

"So nobody gets omitted."

Martin gave a vulgar laugh and smothered it. "What about us? Aren't we omitted?"

"That doesn't occur to them."

"What if I proposition one of the girls?"

"She'd tell the others and they'd decide as a group."

"I am not a bull," Martin said, his dark, heavy face heating up. "I will not be judged—"

"Down, down, *machismo*," said Pugh. "Do you mean to proposition one?"

Martin shrugged, sullen. "Let 'em have their incest."

"Incest is it, or masturbation?"

"I don't care, if they'd do it out of earshot!"

The clone's early attempts at modesty had soon worn off, unmoti- 63 vated by any deep defensiveness of self or awareness of others. Pugh and Martin were daily deeper swamped under the intimacies of its constant emotional-sexual-mental interchange: swamped yet excluded.

"Two months to go," Martin said one evening. 64

"To what?" snapped Pugh. He was edgy lately, and Martin's sullen-ness got on his nerves.

"To relief."

In sixty days the full crew of their Exploratory Mission were due 65 back from their survey of the other planets of the system. Pugh was aware of this.

"Crossing off the days on your calendar?" he jeered. 66

"Pull yourself together, Owen."

"What do you mean?"

"What I say."

They parted in contempt and resentment. 67

READING FOR INFORMATION

1. Summarize the cloning process that Le Guin describes.
2. What purpose does cloning serve in the futuristic society Le Guin envisions?
3. What is the "big hop" referred to in paragraph 35?
4. Why was John Chow chosen for cloning?
5. What brought Pugh, Martin, and the tenclone to the planet Libra?
6. How do Pugh and Martin feel about their job? How does the tenclone feel about their job?
7. Describe the way in which the tenclone members work together to complete a task.
8. While the tenclone does not have ESP, how are they able to communicate with a minimum of words?
9. How does the clone function sexually?

READING FOR FORM, ORGANIZATION, AND EXPOSITORY FEATURES

1. Pugh describes the clone as "self-possessed." Why did Le Guin choose this term? Is Pugh portrayed as "self-possessed"?
2. How does the presence of the clone make interaction between Pugh and Martin more difficult? What does this show about nonclone personality characteristics?
3. How does Le Guin set up comparisons between clone-to-clone interactions and human-to-human interactions? Who comes off better in these comparisons, the clones or the humans? Consider in particular paragraphs 51–67.
4. As the story continues, all the clones are killed in an accident except for Kaph. Why do you think Le Guin uses this plot device?

READING FOR RHETORICAL CONCERNS

1. What is Le Guin's attitude toward the tenclone?
2. What does Le Guin want her readers to think or feel about cloning technologies?
3. Does Le Guin's story indicate a positive or a negative view of the future?

WRITING ASSIGNMENTS

1. In a three-page essay, compare and contrast the personality characteristics of Pugh with that of the tenclone. What point is Le Guin making about the personality characteristics of clones as opposed to nonclones?

2. In paragraph 51, Pugh speculates about the tenclone's degree of independence. "A clone, he thought, might indeed be the first truly stable, self-reliant human being. Once adult it would need nobody's help. It would be sufficient to itself physically, sexually, emotionally, intellectually. Whatever he did, any member of it would always receive the support and approval of his peers, his other selves. Nobody else was needed." Write a three-page essay in which you analyze the pros and the cons of being part of a self-reliant clone "family."

3. Imagine that you are a ten-year-old only child who lives next door to a family that includes a ten-year-old tenclone. Describe your feelings about your tenclone playmate.

From Science Fiction to Reality

Lee M. Silver

Lee Silver is a professor at Princeton University who holds appointments in the Departments of Molecular Biology, Ecology, and Evolutionary Biology. He is a fellow of the American Association for the Advancement of Science and is well know as an expert on the social impact of reproductive technology. This article is excerpted from his book Remaking Eden: Cloning and Beyond in a Brave New World.

PREREADING

What have you previously read or seen in the news media concerning cloning? Brainstorm a list of specifics. Now read through your list. Based on the items in your list, would you say the news media present cloning in a positive, negative, or objective light? Do they sensationalize cloning or do they provide balanced reporting?

FEBRUARY 23, 1997

On the last Sunday in the month of February, in the third year   1
before the end of the second millennium, the world woke up to
a technological advance that shook the foundations of biology and philosophy. On that day, we were introduced to Dolly, a six-month-old lamb

Text pages 91–101 of *Remaking Eden: Cloning and Beyond in a Brave New World* by Lee M. Silver. © 1997 by Lee M. Silver. By permission of Avon Books, Inc.

who had been cloned directly from a single cell taken from the breast tissue of an adult donor.

There were lead stories on every television and radio news broadcast and headline banners on the front page of every newspaper around the world. And for weeks afterward, it didn't let up. Story after story came out discussing the stunning implications of this monumental achievement. On the streets, in offices, on campuses, and in classrooms, people couldn't stop talking about it. One little lamb had succeeded in changing our conception of life forevermore.

Perhaps more astonished than any of their neighbors were the scientists who actually worked in the field of mammalian genetics and embryology. Outside the lab where the cloning had actually taken place, most of us thought it could never happen. Oh we would say that perhaps at some point in the distant future, cloning might become feasible through the use of sophisticated biotechnologies far beyond those available to us now. But what we really believed, deep in our hearts, was that this was one biological feat we could never master. New life—in the special sense of a conscious being—must have its origins in an embryo formed through the merger of gametes from a mother and father. It was impossible, we thought, for a cell from an adult mammal to become reprogrammed, to start all over again, to generate another entire animal or person in the image of the one born earlier.

How wrong we were.

Of course, it wasn't the cloning of a sheep that stirred the imagination of billions of people. It was the idea that humans could now be cloned as well in a manner akin to taking cuttings from a plant, and many people were terrified by the prospect. Ninety percent of Americans polled within the first week after the story broke felt that human cloning should be banned. And the opinions of many media pundits, ethicists, and policymakers, though not unanimous, seemed to follow those of the general public. The idea that humans might be cloned was called "morally despicable," "repugnant," "totally inappropriate," as well as "ethically wrong, socially misguided, and biologically mistaken."

Many of the scientists who work directly in the field of animal genetics and embryology were dismayed by all the attention now directed at their research. Most unhappy of all were those associated with the biotechnology industry, which has the most to gain in the short-term from animal applications of the cloning technology. Their fears were not unfounded. In the aftermath of Dolly, polls found that two out of three Americans considered the cloning of *animals* to be morally unacceptable, while 56 percent said they would not eat meat from cloned animals. The British government decided to "reward" the scientist actually responsible for Dolly's creation, Ian Wilmut, with the *withdrawal* of all further funds for his research. Clearly, nervous politicians wanted to distance themselves as far as possible from his controversial achievement.

It should not be surprising, then, that many scientists in the field   7
tried to play down the possibility of human cloning. First they said that it might not be possible *at all* to transfer the technology to human cells. And even if human cloning is possible in theory, they said, "it would take years of trial and error before it could be applied successfully," so that "cloning in humans is unlikely any time soon." And even if it becomes possible to apply the technology successfully, they said, "there is no clinical reason why you would do this." And even if a person wanted to clone himself or herself or someone else, he or she wouldn't be able to find trained medical professionals who would be willing to do it.

That's not what science, history, or human nature suggest to me.   8
The cloning of Dolly broke the technological barrier. There is no reason to expect that the technology couldn't be transferred to human cells. On the contrary, there is every reason to expect that it *can* be transferred. It requires only equipment and facilities that are already standard or easy to obtain by biomedical laboratories and free-standing in vitro fertilization clinics across the country and across the world. Although the protocol itself demands the services of highly trained and skilled personnel, there are thousands of people with such skills in the United States alone.

It is not a question of whether human cloning will work, but   9
whether it could be used safely or not. Historical precedent suggests that reprogenetic service providers may not even wait until this question has been resolved. The direct injection of sperm into eggs (ICSI) as a cure for infertility was embraced by the IVF community as soon as the technique was perfected, long before any consequences to the children born could be ascertained. And as we shall see, the demand for cloning from individuals and couples is sure to be stronger than the demand for ICSI.

Before we take a closer look at who might want to use human   10
cloning as means for reproduction, and what their reasons are, it is worthwhile to start at the beginning with answers to some basic questions. What is a clone? How was Dolly made? And why does she terrify so many people, even as she thrills a few others?

FROM PLANTS TO TADPOLES, BUT NOT MICE

The word *clone* first appeared in the language of science at the beginning   11
of the twentieth century to describe "groups of plants that are propagat-
ed by the use of any form of vegetative parts." Since that time, *cloning*
has been used to describe the process by which a cell, or group of cells,
from one individual organism is used to derive an entirely new organism, which, according to the definition, is a "clone" of the original. When
multiple individuals are cloned from a single ancestor, they are all considered to be "members of a clone." The critical defining characteristic
of a cloned individual is that it is *genetically identical* to the ancestral cell
or organism from which it is derived, as well as to any other clones derived from the same ancestor.

Among single-cell organisms like bacteria, cloning is as natural as   12
can be. When bacterial reproduction takes place through cell division,
the two daughter cells are clones of each other. Plants, on the other
hand, normally reproduce sexually through the production of fertilized seeds that contain new combinations of genetic material not found
in their parents. With human intervention, however, most plants can
easily be cloned through the use of *cuttings* or bulbs—vegetative
parts—from "donor parents."

The word *clone* would never have entered the public lexicon if it   13
had remained in the provenance of plants and microbes. However, in
the 1960s, the attempts of a British embryologist named John Gurdon
to clone a vertebrate animal—the frog—reached the eyes and ears of
the media.

The cloning of animals had to proceed in a very different manner   14
from the cloning of plants. It is not possible simply to take a cell from an
adult, place it in an embryonic environment, and then expect it to revert
to an embryonic form from which a whole new animal could develop.
The reason this approach won't work is that animal cells are much less
flexible than plant cells in terms of their developmental potential. Plants
always develop in response to their environment, and even when two
plants have identical genetic material, they grow into very different structures. In addition, many differentiated plant cells have the capacity to
transform themselves into totally different types. So when a branch is
cut off from one plant and provided with water, it can sprout new roots
and become a whole new plant.

In contrast, differentiated animal cells are greatly restricted in their   15
developmental capacity, as we discussed in chapter 4. Each cell in the
body of an adult is committed to a particular function. No normal adult

cell—other than a sperm or an egg—has the ability to transform itself into a completely different type of cell. Liver cells cannot become brain cells and skin cells cannot be transformed into early embryo cells. Why is this so, you may ask, when every cell has the same genetic material? If the genetic material is all there, it might seem as if there should be some way to convert an adult cell back into an embryonic cell.

The problem is that each type of cell looks the way it does and performs the functions that it does because it is programmed to "read" only a well-defined portion of its total genetic material. The programming is accomplished by the presence of hundreds or thousands of special protein signals that sit securely on the DNA, instructing some genes to function and other genes to remain silent. In order for a skin cell to become converted into an embryonic cell, its entire genetic program would have to be altered in a particular way, and this could only be accomplished by a massive, but highly precise, substitution and reshuffling of the protein signals that are attached to the genetic material. 16

In theory, the simplest way to get around this problem would be to extract the genetic material from a single skin cell, strip away its associated protein signals, and then place this genetic material inside an egg cytoplasm whose own genetic material had been previously removed. The egg cytoplasm contains all of the particular protein signals required for starting the embryonic program of gene expression. These signals would hop onto the naked DNA and development would be initiated into a clone of the individual who donated the adult genes. 17

There are major technical problems that make this approach daunting, if not impossible. One is that the skin cell's signals are tightly bound to the genetic material and not easily removed. A second, more serious problem is that naked genetic material of the size present in animal cells always breaks apart when it is handled, no matter how gently. And when DNA molecules break, they cannot be transmitted accurately to daughter cells with each cell division. Thus, even if it were possible to place all the DNA from a single skin cell into an egg cytoplasm, the resulting embryo would have no chance of developing into an adult animal. 18

So, at the very start, scientists decided to use the next best thing to naked DNA—an isolated single-cell nucleus with a membrane that acts as a protective shield against chromosome damage when it is picked up from one cell and placed into another. The unavoidable downside of this approach is that some of the original cell's signals—those attached to the DNA and others present in the nucleus—are brought along with the foreign genetic material into the cytoplasm of the embryonic cell. 19

The use of "nuclear transplantation" as a means toward the cloning 20 of animals was first developed by Robert Briggs and Thomas King working at the Institute for Cancer Research in Philadelphia during the early 1950s. The frog was chosen for these experiments because its eggs are very large and readily accessible to manipulation. Although Briggs and King never reached their goal of cloning from adult cells, they set the stage for John Gurdon, who finally succeeded in using this method to obtain tadpoles during the mid-1960s.

The cloning of frogs was never easily accomplished. After transplant- 21 ing thousands of nuclei extracted from adult skin and gut cells, Gurdon's success rate was still abysmally low, and the few animals he obtained developed only to the tadpole stage before dying. It is certainly possible—and with hindsight, it now seems likely—that Gurdon's difficulties were mainly a consequence of the primitive equipment and technology available at that time. For even a small amount of damage to nuclei or reconstructed eggs could have drastic consequences on development.

But, most scientists interpreted Gurdon's essentially negative re- 22 sults differently. Rather than blaming the technology, we blamed mother nature herself. In an almost religious way, we assumed the existence of a basic biological principle: adult cell nuclei cannot be readily reprogrammed back to an embryonic state. The rare adult donor nucleus that did turn into a tadpole was presumed to have come from an aberrant cell. And if a tadpole could be obtained only rarely, it seemed reasonable to assume that it would never be possible to clone adult cells of more highly developed mammalian species—like human beings—into healthy live-born children.

Indeed, in 1984, when the highly respected embryologist Davor 23 Solter, and his student James McGrath, reported on an extensive series of nuclear transplantation studies—with better equipment and technology—on mouse eggs, their results seemed to validate this basic biological principle. The concluding sentence of their publication in the journal *Science* stated that "the cloning of mammals by simple nuclear transfer is biologically impossible."

CLONING ENTERS PUBLIC CULTURE

Although scientists viewed Gurdon's results in one light, popularizers of 24 science viewed it in quite another. The fact that even a single frog had been cloned led to the suggestion that cloning *would* be possible with human beings. The idea began to filter into the public consciousness during the late 1960s and was firmly planted there with the 1970 publication of Alvin Toffler's sensational, and still influential, *Future Shock*. Toffler wrote, "One of the more fantastic possibilities is that man will be able to make biological carbon copies of himself. . . . Cloning would make it possible for people to see themselves anew, to fill the world with twins of themselves. . . . There is a certain charm to the idea of Albert Einstein bequeathing copies of himself to posterity. But what of Adolf Hitler?"

Just as the concept of cloning was being absorbed by the public, it was parodied by Woody Allen in his 1973 movie *Sleeper*. Allen plays the mild-mannered Miles Monroe who is transported two hundred years into the future and is mistaken for the chief surgeon charged with the task of bringing back the recently deceased "Leader" of the country. While the Leader has met with an untimely death, his nose has been kept alive for nearly a year through a "massive biochemical effort." Miles Monroe is supposed to clone the Leader's whole body from his nose, as the top biomedical scientists of this future country watch from an operating room observation deck. Allen toys with the dual meaning of life—cellular versus conscious—when his character kidnaps the nose and threatens to shoot it if he is not allowed to go free. 25

Five years later, the 1978 movie *The Boys from Brazil*, based on a book by Ira Levin, took up Toffler's more menacing idea of a Nazi plot to clone an army of latter-day Adolf Hitlers. And that same year, the J. B. Lippincott Company published a supposed nonfiction book by the science writer David Rorvik entitled *In His Image: The Cloning of a Man*. Rorvik claimed to tell the story of a "worldly, self-educated, aging millionaire" who wanted an heir and succeeded in obtaining "not exactly a son," but rather his genetic equivalent through the use of the same nuclear transplantation technique that John Gurdon had used to clone frogs. Rorvik never provided evidence in support of his claim, and several years later his publisher was forced to admit the book was a hoax. 26

By the early 1980s, the notion of cloning had become entrenched in popular culture, appearing again and again in movies, television shows, and science fiction novels. And it entered the inanimate world as well, with clones of computers and even perfumes. Clones were seen as almost, but not quite, perfect copies of the original, usually cheaper and assumed to be not as "sharp" in some way. 27

But even as clones flooded the popular imagination, very little in the way of new scientific results was publicized. Some people knew that frogs had been cloned, but it seemed that no real scientific progress had been 28 made beyond that organism. And then in 1993, the silence was shattered with a report that two George Washington University scientists, Jerry Hall and Robert Stillman, had "cloned human embryos."

The Hall-Stillman experiment caused a brief media stir far out of 29 proportion to what had actually been accomplished. Hall and Stillman had simply taken seventeen early human embryos, between the two-cell and eight-cell stages, removed their zona coats, and then separated each of the cells in each embryo apart from its neighbors. Each individual cell was next surrounded by a synthetic zona coat and allowed to develop in a laboratory dish by itself. After a few days, Hall and Stillman found forty-eight newly formed embryos developing in a normal manner. The experiment was terminated at this point—out of ethical consideration—and the embryos were discarded.

Embryo cloning is a far cry from adult cell cloning. If the Hall- 30 Stillman experiment had been taken to its logical endpoint, it might have been possible to obtain the birth of identical twins or triplets. But even the normal practice of IVF results in the birth of twins or triplets, albeit nonidentical ones. And the old-fashioned method of reproduction through intercourse produces a million pairs of newborn identical twins, a lesser number of identical triplets, and perhaps a handful of identical quadruplets, around the world each year. So what Hall and Stillman had accomplished in the laboratory was equivalent to a well-known natural process.

Still, even this mimicry of nature provoked immediate outrage from 31 many political corners. The Vatican called it a "perverse choice" and a "venture into a tunnel of madness." Biotech critic Jeremy Rifkin said it heralded "the dawn of the eugenics era," and he organized protest rallies outside the institution where it had taken place. The European Parliament voted unanimously to ban cloning because it was "unethical, morally repugnant, contrary to respect for the person, and a grave violation of fundamental human rights which cannot under any circumstances be justified or accepted." And this was all because two scientists had gently teased single embryos apart into two, three, or four separate cells that grew for a few days by themselves before fading away.

I suspect that if the word *clone* had not been used to describe what 32 Hall and Stillman had done, the media would never have jumped on the story. As it was, two weeks passed between their presentation at a scientific meeting and the first headline: "Scientist Clones Human Embryos and Creates an Ethical Challenge." It was the ominous juxtaposition of those two words—*clones human*—that brought on the hysteria.

FROM EMBRYOS TO ADULTS

While the cloning of Dolly from an adult cell was unquestionably a giant 33
leap forward in reproductive technology, it was a leap that began from a
sturdy platform of technical advances that built quietly upon one another over the preceding fourteen years. The first step was accomplished at
the Wistar Institute in Philadelphia in 1983, where Davor Solter and Jim
McGrath established a protocol for transferring nuclei from one mouse
embryo to another. Their work was critically important for two reasons.
First, it demonstrated the general feasibility of using nuclear transfer
technology in mammals. Second, it introduced a modification of the technique used in frogs that greatly increased the rate of embryo survival.
Instead of isolating nuclei away from their cellular encasement, as
Gurdon had done, Solter and McGrath chose to keep nuclei properly protected within their cytoplasmic environments surrounded by a
cellular membrane.

The actual protocol began with the removal and elimination of the 34
nuclei that were already present within the recipient embryo. Then the
donor cell was placed in the space between the zona coat and the embryo
itself, and the two cells were induced to fuse with a special chemical
agent or an electrical pulse.

Although they referred to this protocol as "nuclear transplantation"— 35
and it has been referred to in this manner ever since—Solter and
McGrath never transplanted nuclei directly into recipient embryos.
Rather, they implanted donor cells next to embryos and then allowed a fusion event to bring the donor nucleus into the cytoplasm of the recipient
cell. By keeping donor cells intact until the moment of fusion, Solter and
McGrath succeeded in protecting the genetic material within. Their protocol was so efficient and safe that 90 percent of embryos reconstructed
with nuclei from other early embryos survived and developed properly.

The next advance on the way to Dolly was accomplished in 1986 by 36
Steed Willadsen, who was working at the ARFC Institute of Animal Physiology in Cambridge, England. What Willadsen did differently from Solter
and McGrath was to use nuclear-free *unfertilized* eggs, rather than one-
cell embryos, as recipients for donor nuclei. The logic behind this decision is based on the notion that an unfertilized egg is chock full of signal
proteins waiting patiently to pounce onto the naked DNA that it expects
to receive from the fertilizing sperm cell. And if the egg is presented
with a donor nucleus instead, the egg's signal proteins won't know the
difference—they'll blindly *try* to pounce onto the donor cell DNA with

the same vengeance. This logic was validated when Willadsen reported the birth of healthy lambs that had been cloned from donor cells derived from 8-cell embryos.

Eight more years went by before another important advance 37 in cloning was made by Neal First at the University of Wisconsin in 1994. This time the species was the cow, the donor cells were obtained from an even later embryonic stage, and four calves were born. What First didn't realize, however, was the probable reason for his success. It turns out that a technician in First's laboratory had mistakenly not provided the donor embryo cells with nourishing serum that all cells need to grow properly. As a result, the donor cells stepped out of their normal cycle of growth and division and paused in a type of hibernation phase known to scientists as G0. Could it be that cells in this special state of hibernation might be more amenable to cloning than other cells? Perhaps the signal proteins sitting on the DNA in these cells are more easily dislodged by the ones waiting in the egg cytoplasm.

Keith Campbell and Ian Wilmut at the Roslin Institute in Edin- 38 burgh, Scotland, were intrigued by this possibility, and they set about trying to test it with their favorite animal, the sheep. They easily obtained lambs after nuclear transplantation from nine-day-old embryo donor cells, and they extended their success to donor cells obtained from embryo-like cultures grown over a period of weeks in a laboratory dish. They reported their results in a March 1996 paper entitled "Sheep Cloned by Nuclear Transfer from a Cultured Cell Line." And then they moved on to more advanced donor cells, using precisely the same techniques.

Dolly was born at 5:00 P.M. in the afternoon on July 5, 1996. She 39 resulted from the fusion of a nuclear-free unfertilized egg with a donor cell obtained from the mammary gland of a six-year-old ewe. She was the first mammal to be cloned from an adult cell, and is a generation removed from the fertilization event that actually brought together the gametes from her genetic parents.

Dolly's existence was announced to the scientific community in a 40 paper published in the journal *Nature* on February 27, 1997. Unnoticed in the commotion surrounding this one lamb is the fact that two others were also cloned from skinlike cells obtained from a fetus. The birth and survival of three healthy lambs from highly differentiated donor cells provides a clear demonstration that the cloning of a lamb was not a fluke. 🖎

READING FOR INFORMATION

1. What was the general public reaction to the birth of Dolly?
2. How have scientists responded to the adverse public reaction generated by cloning research?
3. Paraphrase Silver's definitions of "cloning" and "clone."
4. Why is it difficult to clone a new individual from a differentiated animal cell?
5. What is "nuclear transplantation"?
6. Describe the Hall-Stillman experiment. Why does Silver say the experiment was "equivalent to a well-known natural process"?
7. What "technological barrier" was broken by the cloning of Dolly?

READING FOR FORM, ORGANIZATION, AND EXPOSITORY FEATURES

1. In the opening sentence, what device does Silver use to grab the reader's attention?
2. What does Silver gain by beginning and ending his piece with discussion of Dolly, even though Dolly is not the sole focus of the piece?
3. To what extend does Silver use a chronological plan?
4. What is the function of the section entitled "Cloning Enters Public Culture"?
5. Would you characterize this article as a piece of academic writing? Why or why not? What types of sources and authorities does Silver cite?

READING FOR RHETORICAL CONCERNS

1. How do Silver's credentials affect your reading of his article?
2. What assumptions does Silver make about the general public's response to cloning? What is his attitude toward his readers?
3. What is Silver's rhetorical purpose? Why has he written this article, and what does he want to get across to his readers?

WRITING ASSIGNMENTS

1. In a two- to three-page essay, summarize Silver's explanation of why Dolly's birth represented a technological breakthrough. Write for an audience of nonscientists.
2. Write a three- to four-page essay that attacks or defends Silver's notion that public culture has distorted the significance of cloning research.
3. Using Silver's article as a springboard, discuss the extent to which various segments of our society (scientists, the general public, elected officials, and so forth) should be involved in decisions about cloning research. Write three to four pages.

Dolly's Fashion and Louis's Passion

Stephen Jay Gould

Stephen Jay Gould, a professor of paleontology at Harvard University, is interna-
tionally known for his essays on natural history. Among his recent books are Eight
Little Piggies, Bully for Brontosaurus, Wonderful Life: The Burgess Shale and the
Nature of History, *and* Time's Arrow, Time's Cycle: Myth and Metaphor in the Discovery of Geological Time.

PREREADING

What have you read or heard about the "nature-nurture" debate?
What do you think in most important to an individual's development,
genetic characteristics or environmental influences? Freewrite for ten
minutes in response to one or both of these questions.

Nothing can be more fleeting or capricious than fashion. What, 1
then, can a scientist, committed to objective description and
analysis, do with such a haphazardly moving target? In a classic approach, analogous to standard advice for preventing the spread of an evil
agent ("kill it before it multiplies"), a scientist might say, "quantify
before it disappears."

Francis Galton, Charles Darwin's charmingly eccentric and bril- 2
liant cousin, and a founder of the science of statistics, surely took this
prescription to heart. He once decided to measure the geographic patterning of female beauty. He attached a piece of paper to a small wood-
en cross that he could carry, unobserved, in his pocket. He held the cross
at one end in the palm of his hand and, with a needle secured between
thumb and forefinger, made pinpricks on the three remaining projec-
tions (the two ends of the crossbar and the top).

He would rank every young woman he passed on the street into 3
one of three categories—as beautiful, average, or substandard (by his
admittedly subjective preferences)—and he would then place a pinprick
for each woman into the designated domain of his cross. After a hard

Gould, Stephen Jay. "Dolly's Fashion and Louis's Passion." *Natural History*, June 1997. Copyright
the American Museum of Natural History. Reprinted by permission.

day's work, he tabulated the relative percentages by counting pinpricks. He concluded, to the dismay of Scotland, that beauty followed a simple trend from north to south, with the highest proportion of uglies in Aberdeen and the greatest frequency of lovelies in London.

Some fashions (tongue piercings, perhaps?) flower once and then 4 disappear, hopefully forever. Others swing in and out of style, as if fastened to the end of a pendulum. Two foibles of human life strongly promote this oscillatory mode. First, our need to create order in a complex world begets our worst mental habit: dichotomy, or our tendency to reduce an intricate set of subtle shadings to a choice between two diametrically opposed alternatives (each with moral weight and therefore ripe for bombast and pontification, if not outright warfare): religion versus science, liberal versus conservative, plain versus fancy, *Roll Over Beethoven* versus the *Moonlight Sonata*. Second, many deep questions about our livelihoods, and the fates of nations, truly have no answers— so we cycle the presumed alternatives of our dichotomies, one after the other, always hoping that, this time, we will find the nonexistent key.

Among oscillating fashions governed primarily by the swing of our 5 social pendulum, no issue could be more prominent for an evolutionary biologist, or more central to a broad range of political questions, than genetic versus environmental sources of human abilities and behaviors. This issue has been falsely dichotomized for so many centuries that English even features a mellifluous linguistic contrast for the supposed alternatives: nature versus nurture.

As any thoughtful person understands, the framing of this question 6 as an either-or dichotomy verges on the nonsensical. Both inheritance and upbringing matter in crucial ways. Moreover, an adult human being, built by interaction of these (and other) factors, cannot be disaggregated into separate components with attached percentages. It behooves us all to grasp why such common claims as "intelligence is 30 percent genetic and 70 percent environmental" have no sensible meaning at all and represent the same kind of error as the contention that all overt properties of water may be revealed by noting an underlying construction from two parts of one gas mixed with one part of another.

Nonetheless, a preference for either nature or nurture swings back 7 and forth into fashion as political winds blow and as scientific breakthroughs grant transient prominence to one or another feature in a spectrum of vital influences. For example, a combination of political and scientific factors favored an emphasis upon environment in the years just following World

War II: an understanding that Hitlerian horrors had been rationalized by claptrap genetic theories about inferior races; the domination of psychology by behaviorist theories. Today, genetic explanations are all the rage, fostered by a similar mixture of social and scientific influences: for example, the rightward shift of the political pendulum (and the cynical availability of "you can't change them, they're made that way" as a bogus argument for reducing expenditures on social programs) and an overextension to all behavioral variation of genuinely exciting results in identifying the genetic basis of specific diseases, both physical and mental.

Unfortunately, in the heat of immediate enthusiasm, we often mistake 8 transient fashion for permanent enlightenment. Thus, many people assume that the current popularity of genetic explanation represents a final truth wrested from the clutches of benighted environmental determinists of previous generations. But the lessons of history suggest that the worm will soon turn again. Since both nature and nurture can teach us so much— and since the fullness of our behavior and mentality represents such a complex and unbreakable combination of these and other factors—a current emphasis on nature will no doubt yield to a future fascination with nurture as we move toward better understanding by lurching upward from one side to another in our quest to fulfill the Socratic injunction: know thyself.

In my Galtonian desire to measure the extent of current fascination 9 with genetic explanations (before the pendulum swings once again and my opportunity evaporates), I hasten to invoke two highly newsworthy items of recent months. The subjects may seem quite unrelated—Dolly, the cloned sheep, and Frank Sulloway's book on the effects of birth order upon human behavior—but both stories share a common feature offering striking insight into the current extent of genetic preferences. In short, both stories have been reported almost entirely in genetic terms, but both cry out (at least to me) for a reading as proof of strong environmental influences. Yet no one seems to be drawing (or even mentioning) this glaringly obvious inference. I cannot imagine that anything beyond current fashion for genetic arguments can explain this puzzling silence. I am convinced that exactly the same information, if presented twenty years ago in a climate favoring explanations based on nurture, would have been read primarily in this opposite light. Our world, beset by ignorance and human nastiness, contains quite enough background darkness. Should we not let both beacons shine all the time?

Dolly must be the most famous sheep since John the Baptist designated Jesus in metaphor as "Lamb of God, which taketh away the sin of the world" (John: 1:29). She has certainly edged past the pope, the president, Madonna, and Michael Jordan as the best-known mammal of the moment. And all this for a carbon copy, a Xerox! I don't intend to drip cold water on this little lamb, cloned from a mammary cell of her mother, but I remain unsure that she's worth all the fuss and fear generated by her unconventional birth.

When one reads the technical article describing Dolly's manufacture   11 ("Viable Offspring Derived from Fetal and Adult Mammalian Cells," by I. Wilmut, A. E. Schnieke, J. McWhir, A. J. Kind, and K. H. S. Campbell, *Nature*, February 27, 1997), rather than the fumings and hyperbole of so much public commentary, one can't help feeling a bit underwhelmed and left wondering whether Dolly's story tells less than meets the eye.

I don't mean to discount or underplay the ethical issues raised by   12 Dolly's birth (and I shall return to this subject in a moment), but we are not about to face an army of Hitlers or even a Kentucky Derby run entirely by genetically identical contestants (a true test for the skills of jockeys and trainers). First, Dolly breaks no theoretical ground in biology, for we have known how to clone in principle for at least two decades, but had developed no techniques for reviving the full genetic potential of differentiated adult cells. (Still, I admit that a technological solution can pack as much practical and ethical punch as a theoretical breakthrough. I suppose one could argue that the first atomic bomb only realized a known possibility.)

Second, my colleagues have been able to clone animals from em-   13 bryonic cell-lines for several years, so Dolly is not the first mammalian clone, but only the first clone from an adult cell. Wilmut and colleagues also cloned sheep from cells of a nine-day embryo and a twenty-six-day fetus—and had much greater success. They achieved fifteen pregnancies (although not all proceeded to term) in thirty-two recipients (that is, surrogate mothers for transported cells) of the embryonic cell-line, five pregnancies in sixteen recipients of the fetal cell-line, but only Dolly (one pregnancy in thirteen tries) for the adult cell-line. This experiment cries out for confirming repetition. (Still, I allow that current difficulties will surely be overcome, and cloning from adult cells, if doable at all, will no doubt be achieved more routinely as techniques and familiarity improve.)

Third, and more seriously, I remain unconvinced that we should re-   14 gard Dolly's starting cell as adult in the usual sense of the term. Dolly grew from a cell taken from the "mammary gland of a six-year-old ewe in the last trimester of pregnancy" (to quote the technical article of Wilmut et al.). Since the breasts of pregnant mammals enlarge substantially in late stages of pregnancy, some mammary cells, although technically adult, may remain unusually labile or even "embryolike" and thus able to pro-liferate rapidly to produce new breast tissue at an appropriate stage of pregnancy. Consequently, we may be able to clone only from unusual adult cells with effectively embryonic potential, and not from any stray cheek cell, hair follicle, or drop of blood that happens to fall into the clutches of a mad Xeroxer. Wilmut and colleagues admit this possibility in a sentence written with all the obtuseness of conventional scientific prose, and therefore almost universally missed by journalists: "We cannot ex-clude the possibility that there is a small proportion of relatively undif-ferentiated stem cells able to support regeneration of the mammary gland during pregnancy."

But if I remain relatively unimpressed by achievements thus far, I 15 do not discount the monumental ethical issues raised by the possibility of cloning from adult cells. Yes, we have cloned fruit trees for decades by the ordinary process of grafting—and without raising any moral alarms. Yes, we may not face the evolutionary dangers of genetic uni-formity in crop plants and livestock, for I trust that plant and animal breeders will not be stupid enough to eliminate all but one genotype from a species and will always maintain (as plant breeders do now) an active pool of genetic diversity in reserve. (But then, I suppose we should never underestimate the potential extent of human stupidity—and agricultural seed banks could be destroyed by local catastrophes, while genetic diversity spread throughout a species guarantees maximal evo-lutionary robustness.)

Nonetheless, while I regard many widely expressed fears as exag- 16 gerated, I do worry deeply about potential abuses of human cloning, and I do urge a most open and thorough debate on these issues. Each of us can devise a personal worst-case scenario. Somehow, I do not focus upon the specter of a future Hitler making an army of ten million identical ro-botic killers, for if our society ever reaches a state in which such an out-come might be realized, we are probably already lost. My thoughts run to localized moral quagmires that we might actually have to face in the next few years (for example, the biotech equivalent of ambulance-chasing slimeballs among lawyers—a hustling little firm that scans the obits for reports of dead children and then goes to grieving parents with the following offer: "So sorry for your loss, but did you save a hair sam-ple? We can make you another for a mere fifty thou").

However, and still on the subject of ethical conundrums, but now 17 moving to my main point about current underplaying of environmental sources for human behaviors, I do think that the most potent scenarios of fear, and the most fretful ethical discussions on late-night television, have focused on a nonexistent problem that all human societies solved millennia ago. We ask: Is a clone an individual? Would a clone have a soul? Would a clone made from my cell negate my unique personhood?

May I suggest that these endless questions—all variations on the 18 theme that clones threaten our traditional concept of individuality— have already been answered empirically, even though public discussion of Dolly seems blithely oblivious to this evident fact. We have known human clones from the dawn of our consciousness. We call them identical twins—and they are far better clones than Dolly and her mother. Dolly shares only nuclear DNA with her mother's mammary cell, for the nucleus of this cell was inserted into an embryonic stem cell (whose own nucleus had been removed) of a surrogate female. Dolly then grew in the womb of this surrogate.

Identical twins share at least four additional (and important) prop- 19 erties that differ between Dolly and her mother. First, identical twins also house the same mitochondrial genes. (Mitochondria, the "energy factories" of cells, contain a small number of genes. We get our mitochondria from the cytoplasm of the egg cell that made us, not from the nucleus formed by the union of sperm and egg. Dolly received her nucleus from her mother, but her egg cytoplasm, and hence her mitochondria, from her surrogate.) Second, identical twins share the same set of maternal gene products in the egg. Genes don't grow embryos all by themselves. Egg cells contain protein products of maternal genes that play a major role in directing the early development of the embryo. Dolly has her mother's nuclear genes, but her surrogate's gene products in the cytoplasm of her founding cell.

Third—and now we come to explicitly environmental factors— 20 identical twins share the same womb. Dolly and her mother gestated in different places. Fourth, identical twins share the same time and culture (even if they fall into the rare category, so cherished by researchers, of siblings separated at birth and raised, unbeknownst to each other, in distant families of different social classes). The clone of an adult cell matures in a different world. Does anyone seriously believe that a clone of Beethoven would sit down one day to write a Tenth Symphony in the style of his early-nineteenth-century forebear?

So identical twins are truly eerie clones—ever so much more alike 21 on all counts than Dolly and her mother. We do know that identical twins share massive similarities not only of appearance but also in broad propensities and detailed quirks of personality. Nonetheless, have we ever doubted the personhood of each member in a pair of identical twins? Of course not. We know that identical twins are distinct individuals, albeit with peculiar and extensive similarities. We give them different names: They encounter divergent experiences and fates. Their lives wander along disparate paths of the world's complex vagaries. They grow up as distinctive and undoubted individuals, yet they stand forth as far better clones than Dolly and her mother.

Why have we overlooked this central principle in our fears about 22 Dolly? Identical twins provide sturdy proof that inevitable differences of nurture guarantee the individuality and personhood of each human clone. And since any future human Dolly must differ far more from her progenitor (in both the nature of mitochondria and maternal gene products and the nurture of different wombs and surrounding cultures) than any identical twin diverges from her sibling clone, why ask if Dolly has a soul or an independent life when we have never doubted the personhood or individuality of much more similar identical twins?

Literature has always recognized this principle. The Nazi loyalists 23 who cloned Hitler in *The Boys from Brazil* also understood that they had to maximize similarities of nurture as well. So they fostered their little Hitler babies in families maximally like Adolf's own dysfunctional clan— and not one of them grew up anything like history's quintessential monster. Life, too, has always verified this principle. Eng and Chang, the original Siamese twins and the closest clones of all, developed distinct and divergent personalities. One became a morose alcoholic, the other remained a benign and cheerful man. We may not think much of the individuality of sheep in general (for they do set our icon of blind following and identical form as they jump over fences in mental schemes of insomniacs), but Dolly will grow up to be as unique and as ornery as any sheep can be.

A recent book by my friend Frank Sulloway also focuses on themes 24 of nature and nurture. He fretted over, massaged, and lovingly shepherded it toward publication for more than two decades. *Born to Rebel* documents a crucial effect of birth order in shaping human personalities and styles of thinking. Firstborns, as sole recipients of parental attention until the arrival of later children, and as more powerful (by virtue of age and size) than their subsequent siblings, tend to cast their lot with parental authority and with the advantages of incumbent strength. They tend to grow up competent and confident, but also conservative and unlikely to favor quirkiness or innovation. Why threaten an existing structure that has always offered you clear advantages over siblings? Later children, however, are (as Sulloway's title proclaims) born to rebel. They must compete against odds for parental attention long focused primarily elsewhere. They must scrap and struggle and learn to make do for themselves. Laterborns therefore tend to be flexible, innovative, and open to change. The business and political leaders of stable nations may be overwhelmingly firstborns, but the revolutionaries who have discombobulated our cultures and restructured our scientific knowledge tend to be laterborns. Frank and I have been discussing his thesis ever since he began his studies. I thought (and suggested) that he should have published his results twenty years ago. I still hold this opinion, for while I greatly admire his book and do recognize that such a long gestation allowed Frank to strengthen his case by gathering and refining his data, I also believe that he became too committed to his central thesis and tried to extend his explanatory umbrella over too wide a range, with arguments that sometimes smack of special pleading and tortured logic.

Sulloway defends his thesis with statistical data on the relationship 25 of birth order and professional achievement in modern societies—and by interpreting historical patterns as strongly influenced by characteristic differences in behavior of firstborns and laterborns. I found some of his historical arguments fascinating and persuasive when applied to large samples but often uncomfortably overinterpreted in attempts to explain the intricate details of individual lives (for example, the effect of birth order on the differential success of Henry VIII's various wives in overcoming his capricious cruelties).

In a fascinating case, Sulloway chronicles a consistent shift in rel- 26 ative percentages of firstborns among successive groups in power during the French Revolution. The moderates initially in charge tended to be firstborns. As the revolution became more radical, but still idealistic and open to innovation and free discussion, laterborns strongly predominated. But when control then passed to the uncompromising hardliners who promulgated the Reign of Terror, firstborns again ruled the roost. In a brilliant stroke, Sulloway tabulates the birth orders for several hundred delegates who decided the fate of Louis XVI in the National Convention. Among hardliners who voted for the guillotine, 73 percent were firstborns; but of those who opted for the compromise of conviction with pardon, 62 percent were laterborns. Since Louis lost his head by a margin of one vote, an ever so slightly different mix of birth orders among delegates might have altered the course of history.

Since Frank is a good friend and since I have been at least a minor 27 midwife to this project over two decades (although I don't accept all details of his thesis), I took an unusually strong interest in the delayed birth of *Born to Rebel*. I read the text and all the prominent reviews that appeared in many newspapers and journals. And I have been puzzled—stunned would not be too strong a word—by the total absence from all commentary of the simplest and most evident inference from Frank's data, the one glaringly obvious point that everyone should have stressed, given the long history of issues raised by such information.

Sulloway focuses nearly all his interpretation on an extended analogy (broadly valid in my judgment, but overextended as an exclusive device) between birth order in families and ecological status in a world of Darwinian competition. Children vie for limited parental resources, just as individuals struggle for existence (and ultimately for reproductive success) in nature. Birth orders place children in different "niches," requiring disparate modes of competition for maximal success. While firstborns shore up incumbent advantages, laterborns must grope and grub by all clever means at their disposal—leading to the divergent personalities of stalwart and rebel. Alan Wolfe, in my favorite negative review of Sulloway's book from the *New Republic* (December 23, 1996) writes: "Since firstborns already occupy their own niches, laterborns, if they are to be noticed, have to find unoccupied niches. If they do so successfully, they will be rewarded with parental investment." (Jared Diamond stresses the same theme in my favorite positive review from the *New York Review of Books*, November 14, 1996.) 28

As I said, I am willing to go with this program up to a point. But I must also note that the restriction of commentary to this Darwinian metaphor has diverted attention from the foremost conclusion revealed by a large effect of birth order upon human behavior. The Darwinian metaphor smacks of biology; we also erroneously think of biological explanations as intrinsically genetic (an analysis of this common fallacy could fill an essay or an entire book). I suppose that this chain of argument leads us to stress whatever we think that Sulloway's thesis might be teaching us about "nature" (our preference, in any case, during this age of transient fashion for genetic causes) under our erroneous tendency to treat the explanation of human behavior as a debate between nature and nurture. 29

But consider the meaning of birth-order effects for environmental influences, however unfashionable at the moment. Siblings differ genetically of course, but no aspect of this genetic variation correlates in any systematic way with birth order. Firstborns and laterborns receive the same genetic shake within a family. Systematic differences in 30 behavior between firstborns and laterborns cannot be ascribed to genetics. (Other biological effects may correlate with birth order—if, for example, the environment of the womb changes systematically with numbers of pregnancies—but such putative influences have no basis in genetic differences among siblings.) Sulloway's substantial birth-order effects therefore provide our best and ultimate documentation of nurture's power. If birth order looms so large in setting the paths of history and the allocation of people to professions, then nurture cannot be denied a powerfully formative role in our intellectual and behavioral variation. To be sure, we often fail to see what stares us in the face, but how can the winds of fashion blow away such an obvious point, one so relevant to our deepest and most persistent questions about ourselves?

In this case, I am especially struck by the irony of fashion's veil. 31 As noted before, I urged Sulloway to publish this data twenty years ago, when (in my judgment) he could have presented an even better case because he had already documented the strong and general influence of birth order upon personality, but had not yet ventured upon the slippery path of trying to explain too many details with forced arguments that sometimes lapse into self-parody. If Sulloway had published in the mid-1970s, when nurture rode the pendulum of fashion in a politically more liberal age (probably dominated by laterborns!), I am confident that this obvious point about birth-order effects as proof of nurture's power would have won primary attention, rather than consignment to a limbo of invisibility.

Hardly anything in intellectual life can be more salutatory than the 32 separation of fashion from fact. Always suspect fashion (especially when the moment's custom matches your personal predilection); always cherish fact (while remembering than an apparent "fact" may only record a transient fashion). I have discussed two subjects that couldn't be "hotter," but cannot be adequately understood because a veil of genetic fashion now conceals the richness of full explanation by relegating a preeminent environmental theme to invisibility. Thus, we worry whether the first cloned sheep represents a genuine individual at all, while we forget that we have never doubted the distinct personhood guaranteed by differences in nurture to clones far more similar by nature than Dolly and her mother—identical twins. And we try to explain the strong effects of birth order only by invoking a Darwinian analogy between family place and ecological niche, while forgetting that these systematic effects cannot have a genetic basis and therefore prove the predictable power of nurture.

So, sorry, Louis. You lost your head to the power of family envi-   33
ronments upon head children. And hello, Dolly. May we forever restrict your mode of manufacture, at least for humans. But may genetic
custom never stale the infinite variety guaranteed by a lifetime of nurture in the intricate complexity of nature—this vale of tears, joy, and
endless wonder. 🖎

READING FOR INFORMATION

1. Why does Gould believe that the nature-nurture question when presented as an "either-or dichotomy verges on the nonsensical" (paragraph 6).
2. Why, according to Gould, was more emphasis placed on nurture following World War II? Why is more emphasis currently being placed on genetics as the determining factor?
3. Why doesn't Gould regard Dolly's cloning as a momentous event?
4. What do identical twins have in common that Dolly and her mother
   did not?
5. Why does Gould believe that we need not worry that clones will lack individuality or souls?
6. What is the thesis of Sulloway's book *Born to Rebel?*
7. What is the false "Darwinian analogy" that Gould believes lies at the base
   of Sulloway's argument?
8. How does Gould link Sulloway's argument to the current controversy
   over cloning?

READING FOR FORM, ORGANIZATION, AND EXPOSITORY FEATURES

1. Why does Gould begin with a discussion of fashion?
2. What organizational plan does Gould use? How does he signal that plan?
3. What do you think is Gould's target audience? What characteristics of the
   article seem to be designed for that particular audience?
4. Find the two locations where Gould enumerates the points he is making.
   Why does he chose to enumerate in these places?
5. Describe Gould's closing strategy.

READING FOR RHETORICAL CONCERNS

1. What attitude does Gould want the reader to adopt toward cloning experiments? How does he attempt to achieve this effect?
2. How does Gould establish his own authority?

3. What is Gould's primary purpose in writing?

4. How does Gould view the nature-nurture debate?

WRITING ASSIGNMENTS

1. Compose a two- to three-page summary of Gould's argument for an audience of college students majoring in the humanities.

2. In a four-page essay, draw on your own past experience or observations of others to either attack or support Gould's argument that genetic factors affect our potential but are not the ultimate determinant of what we become.

3. Write a three-page essay of personal response that examines the extent to which your own personality is determined by heredity and/or environment.

Designing Better Humans

Carol A. Foote

The author is a science journalist whose articles have appeared in The New York Times Magazine, Science Digest, *and* Time.

PREREADING

The title suggests that the article might come up with a plan for improving the human species. Is there anything about human beings that you would like to see changed? In the past, how have you thought that this change could be made? Freewrite on this topic for ten minutes.

Will humanity survive forever? Actually, the natural expectation   1
for our species is extinction, Caltech biologist James Bonner tells a hushed auditorium. Of the millions of organisms evolved on Earth in more than 3 billion years, he says, nearly all have now disappeared.

"The only reason to think we might be different is that we understand   2
to some slight degree the processes of mutation, evolution and selection."

From "Designing Better Humans" by Carole A. Foote. First appeared in *Science Digest* (October 1982): 44. © 1982 by The Hearst Corporation. Reprinted by permission of the author.

We can avoid extinction, he adds, if we use that knowledge *to direct human evolution* and create a new and better species—a superhuman. He feels sure we will do this.

Within 25 years, Bonner predicts, some society will begin practicing 3
a selective breeding program following a method suggested by the late geneticist Dr. Hermann Muller. All infants will be sterilized at birth after technicians take a sample of the precursors of their eggs or sperm. These cells will then be frozen. Only after an individual has died will society decide whether he or she should be allowed to procreate. The necessary eggs and sperm of those selected will be obtained by advanced biotechnology from the frozen precursors and used to produce fertilized eggs in test tubes. The resulting embryos will be implanted in receptive uteruses.

Bonner is strongly in favor of such a procedure as a means of im- 4
proving the human race. And who is to say that he is not simply ahead of his time? He certainly is a respected geneticist. A professor emeritus of Caltech, Bonner has put in more than 50 years there. He has written 8 books and more than 400 technical papers, has participated in more than 30 international conferences and is widely sought after as a speaker on genetic engineering. What Bonner envisions is a world in which people decide they want their children to have the best genes—not necessarily the parents' own genes.

SUPERGENES

The catch, of course, is how to decide what is best. Bonner contends 5
that everyone agrees we need to select for intelligence, longevity, high energy and freedom from genetic disease.

But not everyone agrees that the actual process would be so easy— 6
or so desirable. One outspoken critic of moving ahead too fast is molecular geneticist Robert Sinsheimer, chancellor of the University of California, Santa Cruz, who helped synthesize the first biologically active copy of viral DNA. Dr. Sinsheimer cautions that the long-term social and evolutionary consequences of applying genetic engineering to humans could be devastating. Sinsheimer is just as active in warning about the dangers of genetic engineering as Bonner is in promoting it.

This genetic technology, the chancellor points out, will be accessi- 7
ble not only to the scientist, inventor and physician but also to the military and to the fanatics. "The history of mankind," he says, "gives scant reason to hope that such powers will be wielded solely in the interests of justice and mercy."

In addition to the social implications of such questions, Sinsheimer   8
is concerned about possible evolutionary consequences that we can't anticipate. "Are we really bright enough," he asks, "to trust ourselves to
begin making these kinds of changes in the human gene pool when we
don't know what the future holds? We don't really know what kinds of
traits may be needed in some future time."

Sinsheimer ends his talks on this subject with a passionate plea. "I   9
urge caution," he says, "because I believe our species, brilliant but imperfect, could now, in fact, do us in—and not only us *Homo sapiens* but
much of the rest of life on Earth—and so bring to a disastrous end so
many billions of years of evolution."

But Bonner has an equally passionate message at the end of his   10
speeches. "I conclude," he says, "that man today stands in exactly the
position in which *Homo habilis* found himself two million years ago.
Just as *Homo habilis* had in his hand the first rudimentary tool and just
as the use of this tool led to his rapid evolution into us, so we stand
today. We have in our hands the first rudimentary tools by means of
which we can escape extinction and lift our species to a new and
better one."

READING FOR INFORMATION

1. How many different perspectives on genetic engineering does the article
   contain? What are those perspectives? Locate the sections of the text that
   contain different points of view. Label those points of view in the margin.
   What evidence is offered to either support or refute each perspective?
   Label that evidence.
2. What are the "receptive uteruses" referred to in paragraph 3?
3. Paragraph 5 contains Bonner's list of the genetic characteristics that he
   believes are the most important. Would you modify the list in any way?
4. Paragraph 8 summarizes Sinsheimer's argument that humans can't predict what genetic characteristics they may need in the future. Speculate on
   how some specific characteristics that we don't currently value might be
   important in a future society.
5. Paragraph 3 discusses Bonner's prediction that in the future a person's
   eggs or sperm would be used to produce children only after he or she is
   dead. Why do you think Bonner favors a waiting period?
6. Paragraph 7 explains, in general terms, Sinsheimer's concerns about the social implications of genetic engineering. Think of a specific scenario for disaster that Sinsheimer might have in mind.

READING FOR FORM, ORGANIZATION, AND EXPOSITORY FEATURES

1. What is the organizational plan? How does Foote indicate that plan to the reader?

2. For the most part, Foote chooses to quote Bonner and Sinsheimer directly rather than to paraphrase or summarize their remarks. Why do you think Foote decided to rely on direct quotations?

3. What is Foote's opening strategy? Is it effective? Why or why not?

4. Comment on Foote's decision to use a single subheading.

READING FOR RHETORICAL CONCERNS

1. What is Foote's view of genetic engineering with respect to Bonner's and Sinsheimer's?

2. What is Foote's goal in writing? How does she achieve that goal? How does her organizational plan reflect her goal?

3. Do you think it is significant that Foote concludes with a statement from Bonner rather than from Sinsheimer?

4. What are Bonner's and Sinsheimer's academic qualifications? Do they seem appropriate for commentators on eugenics?

WRITING ASSIGNMENTS

1. Write a three- to four-page essay in which you argue in favor of either Bonner's or Sinsheimer's position on eugenics. Make sure you take your opposition into account.

2. Write a three-page essay that compares and contrasts Bonner's and Sinsheimer's implied visions of the society of the future.

3. In a four-page essay, relate the positions taken by Bonner and Sinsheimer to the larger issues of uniformity and diversity in society. Argue whether uniformity or diversity is desirable in some or all aspects of social life.

Narcissus Cloned

John J. Conley

John J. Conley, S.J., is a professor of philosophy at Fordham University.

PREREADING

In ten minutes of freewriting, capture on paper what you already know about cloning. Describe the procedure in as much detail as you can.

The recent experiment in human cloning in Washington, D.C.,   1
has provoked moral unease in the public. Both specialists and laypersons sense that this new technology is fraught with ethical and political peril. The discussion of the ethics of human cloning, however, rarely moves from intuitive praise and blame to careful analysis of the moral values—more frankly, the disvalues—presented by this practice. The discussion also reveals the moral impoverishment of our culture's categories for dealing with biotechnological challenges because the key ethical issues are often obscured by a bland subjectivism that reduces moral values to the simple desire of the parent or researcher.

Here I will sketch out the moral debits of the practice of cloning and   2
criticize the narrow types of moral reasoning that have prevented our society from collectively facing the incipient ethical and political dangers in this practice.

First, human cloning violates respect for the life of each human   3
being, which is due from the moment of conception. While empirical science as such cannot determine the nature and extension of the person, it is indisputable that conception marks the radical beginning of the personal history of each human being. Many of the physical characteristics that clearly influence our interpersonal relations, such as gender, height and somatic constitution, are clearly shaped in the moment of conception. Contemporary genetic research continues to reveal how profoundly other more "spiritual" traits of the person, such as intelligence and emotive temperament, are molded by one's conceptive history. The insistence

John J. Conley, "Narcissus Cloned," *America* 12 Feb. 1994: 15–17. Reprinted by permission.

that respect for human life begin at the time of conception is not a sectarian doctrine. Until quite recently, it formed the keystone of medical ethics, as witnessed by the influential doctor's oath designed by the World Medical Association in the aftermath of World War II: "I will maintain the utmost respect for human life from the moment of conception."

Current experimentation in human cloning deliberately conceives   4
a human being for the sake of research and then designates this human embryo for destruction. It is true that this pre-embryo represents a human being in an extremely primitive state of development. Nonetheless, this minute being remains clearly human (it can belong to no other species), uniquely human (due to its singular corporeal occupation of space and time) and, if placed in the proper environment, a being with an internal capacity to develop the distinctly human faculties of intellect and will.

The fabrication and destruction of human embryos may appear a   5
minor assault on life in a U.S. society numbed by 1.5 million abortions a year and Dr. Jack Kevorkian's house calls. The acid test of whether we corporately esteem human life, however, is not found primarily in our treatment of powerful adults. Rather, it emerges in our treatment of the vulnerable, like these fragile human beings at the dawn of gestation.

Second, the practice of cloning undermines one of the key values of   6
social interaction: human diversity. Emmanuel Levinas, a contemporary French philosopher, argues that the central challenge in interpersonal contact is accepting the other person precisely as other, as something more than the mirror image of oneself. One of the oddest of the recent arguments in favor of human cloning went something like this: Childbearing will be easier for the parents if they can raise siblings hatched from the same egg, since the parents will always be dealing with children having the identical genetic code. (We could even save on the clothing bills.) It is hard to see how the family will benefit from becoming a hall of mirrors. The moral apprenticeship of family life consists precisely in the recognition of differences among siblings and the parents' recognition that their children are not simply the projection of their plans and wishes.

The possible reduction of human difference in a regime of routine   7
cloning raises troubling political issues. Just who or what will constitute the model for the clonable human? Which race? Which physical composition? Which emotional temperament? Which kind of intelligence and at what level? The development of earlier biotechnologies, such as amniocentesis and eugenic abortion, has already begun to homogenize the human population.

Several sources indicate that up to 90 percent of fetuses with   8
Down's Syndrome are currently aborted in the United States. The tendency to eliminate those ticketed as "disabled" contradicts the gains of
the disability rights movement, which correctly urges us to respect and
include those who are different because of physical or mental anom-
alies. Certain enthusiasts for cloning appear to dream Narcissus-like of
a uniform humanity created in their own idealized image, an amalgam
of Einstein and the Marlboro Man. Our aesthetic values, which focus
so frequently on the unique timbre of a human voice or the difference
between two human faces, would fade in such a monocolor regime.
One can only marvel at the moral dexterity of our generation, which
valiantly defends everything from the whale to the snail-darter lest bio-
diversity be lost, yet calmly greets our growing destruction of the human
other through eugenic technology.

Third, the practice of cloning undermines the integrity of human   9
love. Human beings, until quite recently, have usually been conceived
in the conjugal embrace of their parents. In marital intercourse, the two
values of union between the spouses and the procreation of the family's
children remain indissoluble. It is the same act unifying the couple and
bringing forth the nascent child. Cloning, however, stands to radicalize
the divorce between conjugal union and procreation already introduced
by in vitro fertilization. A third person, the scientist in the laboratory, in-
vades the once-intimate drama of the generation of children.

I have long been haunted by the remark of Louise Brown, the first   10
child successfully conceived in vitro, when the doctor who had artificially conceived her died. Louise was plunged into grief. She told the press:
"I feel that I have lost the person who made me"—as if the role once reserved to God and parent had now passed to the scientist in the white
coat. The ancient setting of procreation, the sacramental embrace of
spouses, is abandoned in favor of the fertile/sterile laboratory.

The initial experiment in human cloning indicates how radically   11
procreation has been divorced from conjugal union. The sperm and egg,
provided by anonymous donors, were deliberately fused to fabricate a
human embryo that would deteriorate within several days. It is true that
in the future married couples struggling with infertility might resort to
cloning technology. Even in this case, however, the wedge between uni-
tive and procreative values remains. The intimate union between the
conjugal gift of love and life remains severed.

The language employed by journalists to describe these new means   12
of generation also indicates the sea change wrought by cloning and related

techniques. "Procreation" becomes "reproduction." "The glimmer in my parents' eyes" becomes "the product of conception." "The act of love" becomes "reproductive technology." The reduction of the child, once the immediate evidence of romance, to a product of the laboratory suggests the assault on the integrity of human love implicit in this practice.

Cloning's infringements on the basic goods of life, love and other- 13 ness ultimately challenge human dignity itself. Immanuel Kant argues that human dignity entails the recognition that other human beings are ends in themselves, worthy of respect, rather than means to the ends of individual persons or society as a whole. Widespread cloning, however, would radically reduce humans to a eugenic mean. The human embryo would lose all claim to moral respect and legal protection by serving as an object of scientific curiosity or as an aid, easily discarded, to human fertility. In such a eugenic regime, human beings would increasingly be valued only for possessing certain socially desirable traits rather than for the simple fact that they exist as humans. By reducing the human person to an object stripped of intrinsic worth, routine cloning could threaten the ensemble of human rights itself.

The task of developing a moral response to the advent of human 14 cloning is rendered all the more problematic by the superficial debate our society is currently conducting on this issue. Whether on the editorial page of *The New York Times* or on Phil and Oprah's television screen, the discussion tends to obscure the key moral problems raised by this practice. Certain popular types of reasoning prevent, rather than assist, the careful debate we deserve on this issue.

One common approach is the Luddite condemnation of all ge- 15 netic engineering. Jeremy Rifkin, the most visible critic of the cloning experiment, exemplifies this approach. This position argues that the moral and political risks of genetic engineering are so grave that we should simply censure and, where possible, ban all such technology. References to Pandora's Box, Frankenstein and the Third Reich decorate this blanket condemnation of all scientific intervention into human gestation. Such a categorical critique of biotechnology refuses to discern the different moral values present in the quite varied operations of genetic technology. While human cloning quite clearly appears to distort basic human goods, other therapeutic interventions can legitimately heal infertility and help an individual struggling with a genetic malady. Moral panic cannot ground a nuanced discernment of these disparate technological interventions.

Another approach, frequently offered by the proponents of cloning, 16
contends that the current experiments are simply "scientific research."
Since they are just research, they should not be the object of moral critique. In other words, the Pope & Co. should chill out. This aura of value-free science seriously constricts the scope of the moral enterprise. The object of moral judgment is any human action, i.e., any act of human beings rooted in intellect and will. Moral scrutiny of scientific action is eminently justified inasmuch as such action is patently the result of rational deliberation and choice. The effort to sequester human cloning from ethical judgment, like the earlier attempt to "take morality and politics out of fetal tissue research," simply blinds us to the moral values at stake.

Perhaps the most common reasoning used to justify human cloning 17
is the subjectivist approach. As the editors of *The New York Times* argued, the producers of the material for cloning—I presume they mean the parents—should be the only ones to decide how the product is to be used. A thousand callers on radio talk shows claimed that "Father (or mother) knows best" and that no one could judge the clients and doctors who resort to this practice. Several proponents piously argued that these researchers sincerely wanted to help infertile couples. Such noble motives exempted them from moral censure.

In such a subjectivist perspective, the only relevant moral value is 18
the motive of the parties concerned, and the only virtue is unqualified tolerance for the desire of the scientist or the parent. Such subjectivism systematically averts its gaze from the action of cloning itself, and the question of whether or how this practice destroys human goods can never be raised. Moral scrutiny of this action is suffocated under a sentimental veil of compassion or, worse, under the steely curtain of private property rights.

The subjectivists legitimately highlight the psychological plight of 19
infertile couples who desire to bear children. They suppress, however, the salient ethical issue of which means, under what conditions, can properly be used to remedy this problem of infertility. An ancient moral and legal tradition rightly censures the buying and selling of infants as a just solution. There is a growing moral consensus that the violent battles over legal custody, not to mention the destruction of surplus embryos, have revealed the moral disvalues of surrogate mothering. Sentimental appeals to the pain of infertile couples "open to life" easily mask the ethical dangers of technologies that attempt to remedy infertility by the calculated manipulation and destruction of human lives.

The accompanying political debate must squarely question whether 20 this practice promotes or vitiates the common good. Conducting such a trenchant debate, however, is problematic in a society that increasingly perceives moral judgments as the arbitrary product of emotion or preference.

READING FOR INFORMATION

1. What is Conley's opinion on the public debate over cloning humans?
2. When does Conley believe that life begins?
3. What is Conley's opinion on abortion? Where is that opinion indicated?
4. Outline Conley's three main reasons for opposing cloning.
5. Outline the three popular responses to cloning humans that Conley criticizes.
6. What does Conley mean by the "subjectivist" position? What disturbs Conley about that position?

READING FOR FORM, ORGANIZATION, AND EXPOSITORY FEATURES

1. What is the purpose of Conley's second paragraph?
2. Outline the main elements in Conley's argument. How does Conley signal the boundaries between those elements?
3. What is Conley's opening strategy?

READING FOR RHETORICAL CONCERNS

1. What does the "S.J." title that follows Conley's name indicate? How might that affiliation influence his views on reproductive technology?
2. In the first paragraph, how does Conley describe his purpose in writing?
3. How does Conley treat the arguments of those he disagrees with?

WRITING ASSIGNMENTS

1. In a four- to five-page essay, summarize and respond to Conley's argument against cloning humans.
2. Write a four-page argumentative essay that supports or takes issue with Conley's assertion that "the subjectivists legitimately highlight the psychological plight of infertile couples who desire to bear children. They suppress, however, the salient ethical issue of which means, under what conditions, can properly be used to remedy this problem of infertility."
3. Write a four-page analysis of Conley's rhetorical purpose and technique. Describe his goals, his intended audience, and the techniques he uses to influence that audience.

The Economics of Cloning

Barbara Ehrenreich

Barbara Ehrenreich is a widely published journalist whose work appears in Ms.,
Mother Jones, *and* Time. *Her recent books include* Kipper's Game, The Worst Years
of Our Lives: Irreverent Notes from an Age of Greed, *and* Fear of Falling: The Inner
Life of the Middle Class.

PREREADING

Brainstorm a list of advantages to cloning human beings. Consider both
individual and societal perspectives.

Any normal species would be delighted at the prospect of cloning.   1
No more nasty surprises like sickle cell or Down's syndrome—just
batch after batch of high-grade and, genetically speaking, immortal offspring! But representatives of the human species are responding as if
someone had proposed adding Satanism to the grade-school curriculum. Suddenly, perfectly secular folks are throwing around words like
sanctity and dredging up medieval-era arguments against the hubris of
science. No one has proposed burning him at the stake, but the poor
fellow who induced a human embryo to double itself has virtually re-
canted—proclaiming his reverence for human life in a voice, this magazine reported, "choking with emotion."

There is an element of hypocrisy to much of the anticloning furor,   2
or if not hypocrisy, superstition. The fact is we are already well down the
path leading to genetic manipulation of the creepiest sort. Life-forms
can be patented, which means they can be bought and sold and potentially traded on the commodities markets. Human embryos are life-forms,
and there is nothing to stop anyone from marketing them now, on the
same shelf with the Cabbage Patch dolls.

In fact, any culture that encourages in vitro fertilization has no right   3
to complain about a market in embryos. The assumption behind the
in vitro industry is that some people's genetic material is worth more than

Barbara Ehrenreich "The Economics of Cloning," *Time,* 22 Nov. 1993: 86. © 1993 Time Inc. Reprinted by permission.

others' and deserves to be reproduced at any expense. Millions of low-income babies die every year from preventable ills like dysentery, while heroic efforts go into maintaining yuppie zygotes in test tubes at the unicellular stage. This is the dread "nightmare" of eugenics in familiar, marketplace form—which involves breeding the best-paid instead of the best. Cloning technology is an almost inevitable by-product of in vitro fertilization. Once you decide to go to the trouble of in vitro, with its potentially hazardous megadoses of hormones for the female partner and various indignities for the male, you might as well make a few backup copies of any viable embryo that's produced. And once you've got the backup copies, why not keep a few in the freezer, in case Junior ever needs a new kidney or cornea?

No one much likes the idea of thawing out one of the clone kids to   4 harvest its organs, but according to Andrew Kimbrell, author of *The Human Body Shop,* in the past few years an estimated 50 to 100 couples have produced babies to provide tissue for an existing child. Plus there is already a thriving market in Third World kidneys and eyes. Is growing your own really so much worse than plundering the bodies of the poor? Or maybe we'll just clone for the fun of it. If you like a movie scene, you can rewind the tape, so when Junior gets all pimply and nasty, why not start over with Junior II? Sooner or later, among the in vitro class, instant replay will be considered a human right.

The existential objections ring a bit hollow. How will it feel to be one   5 clone among hundreds? the anticloners ask. Probably no worse than it feels to be the 3 millionth 13-year-old dressed in identical baggy trousers, untied sneakers and baseball cap—a feeling usually described as "cool." In mass-consumer society, notions like "precious individuality" are best reserved for the Nike ads.

Besides, if we truly believed in the absolute uniqueness of each in-   6 dividual, there would be none of this unseemly eagerness to reproduce one's own particular genome. What is it, after all, that drives people to in vitro rather than adoption? Deep down, we don't want to believe we are each unique, one-time-only events in the universe. We hope to happen again and again. And when the technology arrives for cloning adult individuals, genetic immortality should be within reach of the average multimillionaire. Ross Perot will be followed by a flock of little re-Rosses.

As for the argument that the clones will be subpeople, existing to   7 gratify the vanity of their parents (or their "originals," as the case may be), since when has it been illegal to use one person as a vehicle for the ambitions of another? If we don't yet breed children for their SAT scores, there is a whole class of people, heavily overlapping with the in vitro class, who coach their toddlers to get into the nursery schools that offer a fast track to Harvard. You don't have to have been born in a test tube to be an extension of someone else's ego.

For that matter, if we get serious about the priceless uniqueness of   8 each individual, many venerable social practices will have to go. It's hard to see why people should be able to sell their labor, for example, but not their embryos or eggs. Labor is also made out of the precious stuff of life—energy and cognition and so forth—which is hardly honored when "unique individuals" by the millions are condemned to mind-killing, repetitive work.

The critics of cloning say we should know what we're getting into,   9 with all its Orwellian implications. But if we decide to outlaw cloning, we should understand the implications of that. We would be saying in effect that we prefer to leave genetic destiny to the crap shooting of na-ture, despite sickle-cell anemia and Tay-Sachs and all the rest, because ultimately we don't trust the market to regulate life itself. And this may be the hardest thing of all to acknowledge: that it isn't so much 21st cen-tury technology we fear, as what will happen to that technology in the hands of old-fashioned 20th century capitalism.

READING FOR INFORMATION

1. Why does Ehrenreich believe that opponents of cloning may be hypocritical?
2. Why does Ehrenreich believe that cloning is the logical extension of in vitro fertilization?
3. Why does Ehrenreich think that "the existential objections [to cloning] ring a bit hollow"?
4. What do you think are the "Orwellian implications" of cloning that Ehren-reich refers to in the final paragraph?
5. What genetic diseases does Ehrenreich mention in her first and last para-graphs? What do you know about those diseases?
6. Paraphrase Ehrenreich's concluding sentence.

READING FOR FORM, ORGANIZATION, AND EXPOSITORY FEATURES

1. Describe Ehrenreich's tone, and give specific examples that support your answer.
2. What is the organizational plan of Ehrenreich's piece?

READING FOR RHETORICAL CONCERNS

1. Describe Ehrenreich's attitude toward the opponents of cloning.
2. How does Ehrenreich want to affect her audience? Do you think she achieves her goal?
3. What is the basis of Ehrenreich's argument?

WRITING ASSIGNMENTS

1. Write a three- to four-page essay that compares and contrasts Ehrenreich's and Conley's views on the uniqueness of the individual in the context of cloning human beings.
2. Write a three-page essay on cloning that begins with Ehrenreich's statement "You don't have to have been born in a test tube to be an extension of someone else's ego."
3. In a three-page essay, respond to Ehrenreich's assertion that cloning, along with other reproductive technologies, is better than "the crap shooting of nature."

SYNTHESIS WRITING ASSIGNMENTS

1. In her short story, Le Guin describes how a "family" of clones might function. Write a four-page essay that comments on the desirability of living in a clone family. Draw on at least two other articles from Chapter 6 to support your commentary.
2. Design a scenario that illustrates the complex controversies over child custody that can develop when parents use cloning for reproduction. Write a four-page essay in which you describe your scenario and weigh the various ethical considerations that the scenario involves.
3. Write a four- to five-page essay that argues for or against developing a program of eugenics to improve the human species. Make use of sources from Chapter 6 to support your viewpoint.
4. Synthesize material from Chapter 6 readings to describe, in a five-page essay, how human cloning technology might change our society. Evaluate these potential changes.
5. Imagine that you are married and find that you and your spouse are unable to conceive a child through either sexual intercourse or in vitro fertilization. Write a three- to four-page essay of personal reflection in which you explain why you would or would not resort to cloning in an effort to have a child.
6. Draw on Conley and Ehrenreich to discuss, in a four-page essay, the pros and cons of cloning humans.

seven

Interaction Between
Machines and Humans

Most Americans are accustomed to relationships with machines. For example, we talk to our cars, feel betrayed when they break down, and sometimes grieve when they are hauled to the junkyard. As a nation, we spend more time in front of televisions than we do with family and friends. Video games have captivated a generation of adolescent males, and many of their parents spend workdays in front of computer screens, linked through fiber optics and "cyberspace" to thousands of other computers. The development of virtual-reality systems that emulate the real world may signal a new era in our relationship with machines, wherein circuitry may be an important source of "life" experiences.

Technology is often described as a double-edged sword that can work to our benefit or detriment, depending upon how it is applied. Some commentators argue that our relationship to machinery and electronics will provide us with greater control over our lives; others claim it will alienate us from human experience. Those viewpoints and others are presented in the sources in this chapter. "In Defense of Robots" by Carl Sagan describes "intelligent" machines and argues that humans should respect but not fear these devices. Clifford Stoll suggests that interaction with a computer is a shallow experience with very limited educational value in his article "On Classrooms, With and Without Computers." The potential for intimacy, even romance, between humans and intelligent machines is described in Neil Frude's "The Intimate Machine." In "Electronic Expansion of Human Perception," Warren Robinett explains how human perceptions may be enhanced and extended through the application of virtual reality. Finally, Jeremy Rifkin, in "The Age of Simulation," argues that the development of virtual reality is symptomatic of a dangerous obsession with technology that has divorced us from the real world and caused us to undervalue natural human abilities.

In Defense of Robots

Carl Sagan

Carl Sagan was a professor of astronomy and space science at Cornell University and a Pulitzer Prize–winning science writer. His books include Broca's Brain, Cosmos, *and* The Dragons of Eden.

PREREADING

Sagan's title indicates that his essay will discuss robots. Consider both actual and fictitious robots that you are aware of. In ten minutes of freewriting, compare and contrast robots and humans.

The word "robot," first introduced by the Czech writer Karel 1 Capek, is derived from the Slavic root for "worker." But it signifies a machine rather than a human worker. Robots, especially robots in space, have often received derogatory notices in the press. We read that a human being was necessary to make the terminal landing adjustments on Apollo 11, without which the first manned lunar landing would have ended in disaster; that a mobile robot on the Martian surface could never be as clever as astronauts in selecting samples to be returned to Earth-bound geologists; and that machines could never have repaired, as men did, the Skylab sunshade, so vital for the continuance of the Skylab mission.

But all these comparisons turn out, naturally enough, to have been 2 written by humans. I wonder if a small self-congratulatory element, a whiff of human chauvinism, has not crept into these judgments. Just as

From *Broca's Brain* by Carl Sagan (New York: Ballantine, 1980), 280–92. Copyright © 1974, 1975, 1976, 1977, 1978, 1979 by Carl Sagan. Reprinted by permission of the author.

whites can sometimes detect racism and men can occasionally discern sexism, I wonder whether we cannot here glimpse some comparable affliction of the human spirit—a disease that as yet has no name. The word "anthropocentrism" does not mean quite the same thing. The word "humanism" has been pre-empted by other and more benign activities of our kind. From the analogy with sexism and racism I suppose the name for this malady is "speciesism"—the prejudice that there are no beings so fine, so capable, so reliable as human beings.

This is a prejudice because it is, at the very least, a prejudgment, a conclusion drawn before all the facts are in. Such comparisons of men and machines in space are comparisons of smart men and dumb machines. We have not asked what sorts of machines could have been built for the $30-or-so billion that the Apollo and Skylab missions cost.   3

Each human being is a superbly constructed, astonishingly compact, self-ambulatory computer—capable on occasion of independent decision making and real control of his or her environment. And, as the old joke goes, these computers can be constructed by unskilled labor. But there are serious limitations to employing human beings in certain environments. Without a great deal of protection, human beings would be inconvenienced on the ocean floor, the surface of Venus, the deep interior of Jupiter, or even on long space missions. Perhaps the only interesting results of Skylab that could not have been obtained by machines is that human beings in space for a period of months undergo a serious loss of bone calcium and phosphorus—which seems to imply that human beings may be incapacitated under 0 g for missions of six to nine months or longer. But the minimum interplanetary voyages have characteristic times of a year or two. Because we value human beings highly, we are reluctant to send them on very risky missions. If we do send human beings to exotic environments, we must also send along their food, their air, their water, amenities for entertainment and waste recycling, and companions. By comparison, machines require no elaborate life-support systems, no entertainment, no companionship, and we do not yet feel any strong ethical prohibitions against sending machines on one-way, or suicide, missions.   4

Certainly, for simple missions, machines have proved themselves many times over. Unmanned vehicles have performed the first photography of the whole Earth and of the far side of the Moon; the first landings on the Moon, Mars and Venus; and the first thorough orbital reconnaissance of another planet, in the Mariner 9 and Viking missions   5 to Mars. Here on Earth it is increasingly common for high-technology manufacturing—for example, chemical and pharmaceutical plants—to be performed largely or entirely under computer control. In all these activities machines are able, to some extent, to sense errors, to correct mistakes, to alert human controllers some great distance away about perceived problems.

The powerful abilities of computing machines to do arithmetic— 6 hundreds of millions of times faster than unaided human beings— are legendary. But what about really difficult matters? Can machines in any sense think through a new problem? Can they make discussions of the branched-contingency tree variety which we think of as characteristically human? (That is, I ask Question 1; if the answer is A, I ask Question 2; but if the answer is B, I ask Question 3; and so on.) Some decades ago the English mathematician A. M. Turing described what would be necessary for him to believe in machine intelligence. The condition was simply that he could be in teletype communication with a machine and be unable to tell that it was not a human being. Turing imagined a conversation between a man and a machine of the following quality:

> *Interrogator:* In the first line of your sonnet which reads "Shall I compare thee to a Summer's day," would not "a Spring day" do as well or better?
>
> *Witness:* It wouldn't scan.
>
> *Interrogator:* How about "a Winter's day"? That would scan all right.
>
> *Witness:* Yes, but nobody wants to be compared to a Winter's day.
>
> *Interrogator:* Would you say Mr. Pickwick reminded you of Christmas?
>
> *Witness:* In a way.
>
> *Interrogator:* Yet Christmas is a Winter's day, and I do not think Mr. Pickwick would mind the comparison.
>
> *Witness:* I don't think you're serious. By a Winter's day one means a typical Winter's day, rather than a special one like Christmas.

No device of this sophistication has yet been built, although I am 7 not sure how many humans would pass Turing's human test. But the amount of effort and money put into artificial intelligence has been quite limited, and there are only about a half-dozen major centers of such activity in the world. One of the more striking results obtained in a very limited universe of discourse—that of children's blocks—has come from the work of Terry Winograd, then at the Massachusetts Institute of Technology. Here is a dialogue between man and machine, the machine having been programmed by Winograd:

> *Q:* What does the box contain?
> *A:* The blue pyramid and the blue box.
> *Q:* How many blocks are not in the box?
> *A:* Four of them.
> *Q:* Is at least one of them narrower than the one which I told you to pick up?
> *A:* Yes, the red cube.
> *Q:* Is there a steeple?
> *A:* Sorry, I don't know the word "steeple."
> *Q:* A steeple is a stack which contains two green cubes and a pyramid, for example.
> *A:* I understand.
> *Q:* Are there any steeples now?
> *A:* No.
> *Q:* Build one.

The machine does. It reaches out its mechanical hand, moves the cubes and builds the structure that has just been described.   8

> *Q:* When did you pick up the pyramid?
> *A:* While I was stacking up the red cube, the large red block and the large green cube.
> *Q:* Why?
> *A:* To get rid of it.
> *Q:* Why did you clear off that cube?
> *A:* To put it on the large green cube.

As another example, a machine psychiatrist has been developed by   9
Joseph Weizenbaum, also at MIT. This is a much simpler program than Winograd's, since it involves nondirective psychotherapy, which, generally speaking, requires extremely simple-minded computer programs. Here is a striking dialogue between a human being and a computer psychotherapist. (There is certainly a selection effect here. Many other such machine/human psychiatric dialogues are not nearly so striking. But I suppose most human/human psychiatric dialogues are not very striking

either.) In this interaction, in order to spell out clearly the respective roles of therapist and patient, the computer therapist types upper case while the patient types lower case:

men are all alike
IN WHAT WAY

they're always bugging us about something or other
CAN YOU THINK OF A SPECIFIC EXAMPLE

well, my boy friend made me come here
YOUR BOY FRIEND MADE YOU COME HERE

he noticed that i'm depressed much of the time
I AM SORRY TO HEAR YOU ARE DEPRESSED

he's right. i am unhappy
DO YOU THINK COMING HERE WILL HELP YOU NOT TO
    BE UNHAPPY

i need some help, that much is clear
WHAT WOULD IT MEAN TO YOU IF YOU GOT SOME HELP

perhaps i could learn to get along with my mother
TELL ME MORE ABOUT YOUR FAMILY

my mother takes care of me
WHO ELSE IN YOUR FAMILY TAKES CARE OF YOU

my father
YOUR FATHER

you are like my father in some ways
WHAT RESEMBLANCE DO YOU SEE

you are not very aggressive, but i don't think you want me to notice
    that
WHAT MAKES YOU THINK I AM NOT VERY AGGRESSIVE

you don't argue with me
WHY DO YOU THINK I DON'T ARGUE WITH YOU

you are afraid of me
DOES IT PLEASE YOU TO BELIEVE I AM AFRAID OF YOU

it pleases my father to think i am afraid of him
WHAT ELSE COMES TO MIND WHEN YOU THINK OF
    YOUR FATHER

bullies
DOES THAT HAVE ANYTHING TO DO WITH THE FACT
    THAT YOUR BOY FRIEND MADE YOU COME HERE

This astonishing—one is very tempted to say "perceptive"— 10 response from the computer is, of course, preprogrammed. But, then, so are the responses of human psychotherapists. In a time when more and more people in our society seem to be in need of psychiatric counseling, and when time-sharing of computers is widespread, I can even imagine the development of a network of computer psychotherapeutic terminals, something like arrays of large telephone booths, in which, for a few dollars a session, we are able to talk to an attentive, tested and largely nondirective psychotherapist. Ensuring the confidentiality of the psychiatric dialogue is one of several important steps still to be worked out.

Another sign of the intellectual accomplishments of machines is in 11 games. Even exceptionally simple computers—those that can be wired by a bright ten-year-old—can be programmed to play perfect tic-tac-toe. Some computers can play world-class checkers. Chess is of course a much more complicated game than tic-tac-toe or checkers. Here programming a machine to win is more difficult, and novel strategies have been used, including several rather successful attempts to have a computer learn from its own experience in playing previous chess games. Computers can learn, for example, empirically the rule that it is better in the beginning game to control the center of the chessboard than the periphery. The ten best chess players in the world still have nothing to fear from any present computer. But the situation is changing. Recently a computer for the first time did well enough to enter the Minnesota State Chess Open. This may be the first time that a nonhuman has entered a major sporting event on the planet Earth (and I cannot help but wonder if robot golfers and designated hitters may be attempted sometime in the next decade, to say nothing of dolphins in free-style competition). The computer did not win the Chess Open, but this is the first time one has done well enough to enter such a competition. Chess-playing computers are improving extremely rapidly.

I have heard machines demeaned (often with a just audible sigh 12 of relief) for the fact that chess is an area where human beings are still superior. This reminds me very much of the old joke in which a stranger remarks with wonder on the accomplishments of a checker-playing dog. The dog's owner replies, "Oh, it's not all that remarkable. He loses two games out of three." A machine that plays chess in the middle range of human expertise is a very capable machine; even if there are thousands of better human chess players, there are millions who are worse. To play chess requires strategy, foresight, analytical powers, and the ability to cross-correlate large numbers of variables and to learn from the experience. These are excellent qualities in those whose job it is to discover and explore, as well as those who watch the baby and walk the dog.

With this as a more or less representative set of examples of the 13 state of development of machine intelligence, I think it is clear that a major effort over the next decade could produce much more sophisticated examples. This is also the opinion of most of the workers in machine intelligence.

In thinking about this next generation of machine intelligence, it is 14 important to distinguish between self-controlled and remotely controlled robots. A self-controlled robot has its intelligence within it; a remotely controlled robot has its intelligence at some other place, and its successful operation depends upon close communication between its central computer and itself. There are, of course, intermediate cases where the machine may be partly self-activated and partly remotely controlled. It is this mix of remote and *in situ* control that seems to offer the highest efficiency for the near future.

For example, we can imagine a machine designed for the mining of 15 the ocean floor. There are enormous quantities of manganese nodules littering the abyssal depths. They were once thought to have been produced by meteorite infall on Earth, but are now believed to be formed occasionally in vast manganese fountains produced by the internal tectonic activity of the Earth. Many other scarce and industrially valuable minerals are likewise to be found on the deep ocean bottom. We have the capability today to design devices that systematically swim over or crawl upon the ocean floor; that are able to perform spectrometric and other chemical examinations of the surface material; that can automatically radio back to ship or land all findings; and that can mark the locales of especially valuable deposits—for example, by low-frequency radio-homing devices. The radio beacon will then direct great mining machines to the appropriate locales. The present state of the art in deep-sea submersibles and in spacecraft environmental sensors is clearly compatible with the development of such devices. Similar remarks can be made for off-shore oil drilling, for coal and other subterranean mineral mining, and so on. The likely economic returns from such devices would pay not only for their development, but for the entire space program many times over.

When the machines are faced with particularly difficult situations, 16 they can be programmed to recognize that the situations are beyond their abilities and to inquire of human operators—working in safe and pleasant environments—what to do next. The examples just given are of devices that are largely self-controlled. The reverse also is possible, and a great deal of very preliminary work along these lines has been performed in the remote handling of highly radioactive materials in laboratories of the U.S. Department of Energy. Here I imagine a human being who is connected by radio link with a mobile machine. The operator is in Manila, say; the machine in the Mindanao Deep. The operator is attached to an array of electronic relays, which transmits and amplifies his movements to the machine and which can, conversely, carry what the machine finds back to his senses. So when the operator turns his head to the left, the television cameras on the machine turn left, and the operator sees on a great hemispherical television screen around him the scene the machine's searchlights and cameras have revealed. When the operator in Manila takes a few strides forward in his wired suit, the machine in the abyssal depths ambles a few feet forward. When the operator reaches out his hand, the mechanical arm of the machine likewise extends itself; and the precision of the man/machine interaction is such that precise manipulation of material at the ocean bottom by the machine's fingers is possible. With such devices, human beings can enter environments otherwise closed to them forever.

In the exploration of Mars, unmanned vehicles have already soft- 17 landed, and only a little further in the future they will roam about the surface of the Red Planet, as some now do on the Moon. We are not ready for a manned mission to Mars. Some of us are concerned about such missions because of the dangers of carrying terrestrial microbes to Mars, and Martian microbes, if they exist, to Earth, but also because of their enormous expense. The Viking landers deposited on Mars in the summer of 1976 have a very interesting array of sensors and scientific instruments, which are the extension of human senses to an alien environment.

The obvious post-Viking device for Martian exploration, one which 18 takes advantage of the Viking technology, is a Viking Rover in which the equivalent of an entire Viking spacecraft, but with considerably improved science, is put on wheels or tractor treads and permitted to rove slowly over the Martian landscape. But now we come to a new problem, one that is never encountered in machine operation on the Earth's surface. Although Mars is the second closest planet, it is so far from the Earth that the light travel time becomes significant. At a typical relative position of Mars and the Earth, the planet is 20 light-minutes away. Thus, if the spacecraft were confronted with a steep incline, it might send a message of inquiry back to Earth. Forty minutes later the response would arrive saying something like "For heaven's sake, stand dead still." But by then, of course, an unsophisticated machine would have tumbled into the gully. Consequently, any Martian Rover requires slope and roughness sensors. Fortunately, these are readily available and are even seen in some children's toys. When confronted with a precipitous slope or large boulder, the spacecraft would either stop until receiving instructions from the Earth in response to its query (and televised picture of the terrain), or back off and start off in another and safer direction.

Much more elaborate contingency decision networks can be built 19 into the onboard computers of spacecraft of the 1980s. For more remote objectives, to be explored further in the future, we can imagine human controllers in orbit around the target planet, or on one of its moons. In the exploration of Jupiter, for example, I can imagine the operators on a small moon outside the fierce Jovian radiation belts, controlling with only a few seconds' delay the responses of a spacecraft floating in the dense Jovian clouds.

Human beings on Earth can also be in such an interaction loop, if 20 they are willing to spend some time on the enterprise. If every decision in Martian exploration must be fed through a human controller on Earth, the Rover can traverse only a few feet an hour. But the lifetimes of such rovers are so long that a few feet an hour represents a perfectly respectable rate of progress. However, as we imagine expeditions into the farthest reaches of the solar system—and ultimately to the stars—it is clear that self-controlled machine intelligence will assume heavier burdens of responsibility.

In the development of such machines we find a kind of conver- 21 gent evolution. Viking is, in a curious sense, like some great outsized, clumsily constructed insect. It is not yet ambulatory, and it is certainly incapable of self-reproduction. But it has an exoskeleton, it has a wide range of insectlike sensory organs, and it is about as intelligent as a dragonfly. But Viking has an advantage that insects do not: it can, on occasion, by inquiring of its controllers on Earth, assume the intelligence of a human being—the controllers are able to reprogram the Viking computer on the basis of decisions they make.

As the field of machine intelligence advances and as increasingly 22 distant objects in the solar system become accessible to exploration, we will see the development of increasingly sophisticated onboard computers, slowly climbing the phylogenetic tree from insect intelligence to crocodile intelligence to squirrel intelligence and—in the not very remote future, I think—to dog intelligence. Any flight to the outer solar system must have a computer capable of determining whether it is working properly. There is no possibility of sending to the Earth for a repairman. The machine must be able to sense when it is sick and skillfully doctor its own illnesses. A computer is needed that is able either to fix or replace failed computer, sensor or structural components. Such a computer, which has been called STAR (self-testing and repairing computer), is on the threshold of development. It employs redundant components, as biology does—we have two lungs and two kidneys partly because each is protection against failure of the other. But a computer can be much more redundant than a human being, who has, for example, but one head and one heart.

Because of the weight premium on deep space exploratory ven- 23 tures, there will be strong pressures for continued miniaturization of intelligent machines. It is clear that remarkable miniaturization has already occurred: vacuum tubes have been replaced by transistors, wired circuits by printed circuit boards, and entire computer systems by silicon-chip microcircuitry. Today a circuit that used to occupy much of a 1930 radio set can be printed on the tip of a pin. If intelligent machines for terrestrial mining and space exploratory applications are pursued, the time cannot be far off when household and other domestic robots will become commercially feasible. Unlike the classical anthropoid robots of science fiction, there is no reason for such machines to look any more human than a vacuum cleaner does. They will be specialized for their functions. But there are many common tasks, ranging from bartending to floor washing, that involve a very limited array of intellectual capabilities, albeit substantial stamina and patience. All-purpose ambulatory household robots, which perform domestic functions as well as a proper nineteenth-century English butler, are probably many decades off. But more specialized machines, each adapted to a specific household function, are probably already on the horizon.

It is possible to imagine many other civic tasks and essential func- 24 tions of everyday life carried out by intelligent machines. By the early 1970s, garbage collectors in Anchorage, Alaska, and other cities won wage settlements guaranteeing them salaries of about $20,000 per annum. It is possible that the economic pressures alone may make a persuasive case for the development of automated garbage-collecting machines. For the development of domestic and civic robots to be a general civic good, the effective re-employment of those human beings displaced by the robots must, of course, be arranged; but over a human generation that should not be too difficult—particularly if there are enlightened educational reforms. Human beings enjoy learning.

We appear to be on the verge of developing a wide variety of intel- 25 ligent machines capable of performing tasks too dangerous, too expensive, too onerous or too boring for human beings. The development of such machines is, in my mind, one of the few legitimate "spin-offs" of the space program. The efficient exploitation of energy in agriculture— upon which our survival as a species depends—may even be contingent on the development of such machines. The main obstacle seems to be a very human problem, the quiet feeling that comes stealthily and unbidden, and argues that there is something threatening or "inhuman" about machines performing certain tasks as well as or better than human beings; or a sense of loathing for creatures made of silicon and germanium rather than proteins and nucleic acids. But in many respects our survival as a species depends on our transcending such primitive chauvinisms. In part, our adjustment to intelligent machines is a matter of acclimatization. There are already cardiac pacemakers that can sense the beat of the human heart; only when there is the slightest hint of fibrillation does the pacemaker stimulate the heart. This is a mild but very useful sort of machine intelligence. I cannot imagine the wearer of this device resenting its intelligence. I think in a relatively short period of time there will be a very similar sort of acceptance for much more intelligent and sophisticated machines. There is nothing inhuman about an intelligent machine; it is indeed an expression of those superb intellectual capabilities that only human beings, of all the creatures on our planet, now possess. 🖎

READING FOR INFORMATION

1. Paraphrase Sagan's definition of "speciesism" in paragraph 2.
2. Summarize the criticisms of robots and computers that Sagan responds to in his essay.
3. List the tasks that Sagan suggests we will assign to intelligent machines in the future.
4. List the advantages of robots and computers over human workers.
5. List the aspects of human intelligence that Sagan feels can be copied by machines.
6. In the last sentence, Sagan states, "There is nothing inhuman about an intelligent machine." What does he mean by that statement?

READING FOR FORM, ORGANIZATION, AND EXPOSITORY FEATURES

1. What does Sagan attempt to achieve in his opening paragraph? How does this paragraph fit in with the rest of the essay?
2. How does the last paragraph mirror the organizational plan of the entire essay?
3. Why do you think Sagan chooses a pacemaker as his concluding example of an intelligent machine? Is this a good example? Why?

READING FOR RHETORICAL CONCERNS

1. How would you characterize the style of Sagan's essay? Is it appropriate for his intended audience? Why?
2. What feelings does Sagan want his audience to develop toward computers? Does he achieve that effect on you? Why or why not?
3. Does Sagan respond adequately to the criticisms of robots that he mentions?
4. Sagan stresses the use of robots for space exploration, one of his personal and professional interests. Does Sagan convince you that robots have more practical, everyday applications? Which everyday applications impress you the most?

WRITING ASSIGNMENTS

1. In a four-page essay, agree or disagree with Sagan's position that current machines do possess a form of intelligence. Do his examples of intelligent machines convince you? If not, what further evidence would you need?
2. Using Sagan's essay as a source, write a two-page description of what society will be like fifty years from now. Focus on the social roles that humans and robots will occupy and on what the interaction between people and machines will be like. Write for an audience of sociology students.
3. In paragraph 24, Sagan suggests that robots may take over from human workers such tasks as garbage collection. Describe some social problems that might arise from robotization of the workforce. Can those problems be solved? Are the social costs of robotization worth the potential social benefits?

On Classrooms, With and Without Computers

Clifford Stoll

Clifford Stoll is an astronomer and an expert on computer security. He is best known as author of The Cuckoo's Egg, *which describes his successful pursuit of a computer hacker who was stealing and selling U. S. military secrets. The article that follows is taken from Stoll's book* Silicon Snake Oil.

PREREADING

Think about the ways you have used computers in school. On the whole, did computers make it easier for you to learn? Freewrite for ten minutes in response to this question.

Remember those goofy cartoons where you had to find all the things wrong in a picture? There'd be a six-legged dog, a duck flying upside down, a kid with two heads. Every now and then, I see something so weird that I ask myself, "What's wrong with this picture?"   1

All of us want children to experience warmth, human interaction, the thrill of discovery, and solid grounding in essentials: reading, getting along with others, training in civic values.   2

Only a teacher, live in the classroom, can bring about this inspiration. This can't happen over a speaker, a television, or a computer screen. Yet everywhere, I hear parents and principals clamoring for interactive computer instruction.   3

What's wrong with this picture?

The state of North Carolina spent seven million dollars to tie sixteen high schools with a fiber-optic network. It's one of those high-visibility experiments that attracts politicians and professional education consultants.   4

This interactive video system lets Professor Maria Domoto teach Japanese to four high schools. She can see her students and interact with them over a split television screen, even fax exams to them. But the class   5

From *Silicon Snake Oil* by Clifford Stoll. Copyright © 1995 by Clifford Stoll. Used by permission of Doubleday, a division of Bantam Doubleday Dell Publishing Group, Inc.

size still can't exceed thirty: "Beyond twenty to thirty, you lose any personal contact," she says. "I want to see the students I'm teaching."

She makes an important point: even with electronic links, teachers 6 can't handle much more than two dozen students. It was that way for our grandparents, it will be that way for our grandchildren. Television, radio, and computers can bring great teachers into our lives. But no teacher can listen to everyone at the same time.

Professor Domoto's classes began with twenty-six students. By year's 7 end, over half had failed or dropped out. Hardly surprising when they didn't meet their teacher in person. How can she correct a student's writing posture, or show the way to hold a brush-pen or chopsticks?

Anyways, Japanese isn't a snap course. Students won't complete it 8 unless they're committed—the very thing that television and computers can't inspire.

Left unanswered in the North Carolina high school experiment: how 9 to handle discipline problems. It's difficult enough in a live classroom— ask any teacher. Or perhaps discipline becomes a moot issue in the electronic classroom. With no live teacher, who cares?

Wait a second. They spent seven million dollars so their students can 10 watch television in school. I'm wondering how many teachers they could hire and how many books they could buy for seven million dollars. What's wrong with this picture?

Chris Whittle spent far more, piping commercial educational tele- 11 vision into schools. His Channel 1 television network folded, having promised—and failed—to make schools a better place.

At the same time that school librarians, art instructors, and music 12 teachers are being fired, we're spending thousands on computers. What's wrong with this picture?

"I believe that the motion picture is destined to revolutionize our 13 educational system and that in a few years it will supplant largely, if not entirely, the use of textbooks." Thomas Edison, 1922.*

In the past, schools tried instructional filmstrips, movies and tele- 14 vision; some are still in use, but think of your own experience: name three multimedia programs that actually inspired you. Now name three teachers that made a difference in your life.

*Quoted by Harry A. Wise in his 1939 Yale dissertation, "Motion Pictures as an Aid to Teaching American History."

I do remember that whenever I saw an educational film in high 15 school, it meant fun for everyone. The teacher got time off, we were entertained, and nobody had to learn anything. Computers and the Internet do the same—they make it easy for everyone, but damn little teaching happens.

What's most important in school? Working with good teachers who 16 can convey method as well as content. Except to the extent that students are involved with a caring teacher, schooling is limited to teaching facts and techniques. In this sense, network access is irrelevant to schooling— it can only prevent this type of interaction.

The computer is a barrier to close teaching relationships. When 17 students receive assignments through e-mail and send in homework over the network, they miss out on chances to discuss things with their prof. They don't visit her office and catch the latest news. They're learning at arm's length.

It's not good for the teachers either. Dr. Dave Cudaback, a senior 18 lecturer at the University of California, Berkeley, teaches a great astronomy class. But he dreads receiving e-mail from students around the world. "I have barely enough time to spend with my own students. How can I possibly find time to answer questions from hundreds of others?"

I guess what I'm trying to say is this: students deserve personal 19 contact with instructors—interactive videos and remote broadcasts are no substitute for studying under a fired-up teacher who's there in person.

. . .

What are you telling a child when you set him down before a com- 20 puter? One unspoken message is, "Go interact someplace else with this machine for a while." Nobody knows how kids' internal wiring works, but anyone who's directed away from social interactions has a head start on turning out weird.

Kids who walk up to my computer immediately ask what games I've 21 got. They're uniformly disappointed to hear that I don't have any. Computer games satisfy in ways that real life can never touch. You jump over the ravine. You blow up the alien. You uncover the magic potion. You move on to the next level. You never have to deal with real frustrations— the illogic of human interactions. If you're thwarted, why, just pull the plug. The ultimate escape.

No surprise that children don't develop good response mechanisms 22 for threatening behavior in the real world. We can't pull the plug on the bully down the street or the jerk that we have to work alongside. Computers teach us to withdraw, to retreat into the warm comfort of their false reality. Why are both drug addicts and computer aficionados both called users?

Thanks to television, huge numbers of Americans have become nocturnal zombies who spend their evenings inert before cathode-ray tubes. Computing is equally nonholistic: a motionless consumption of the mind.   23

Throughout the discussions of the National Information Initiative, the focus is on the network—the medium—and seldom the content. Computing itself is an essentially passive activity that seldom requires analytic thought.   24

Alone behind a computer, a user needn't interact with anyone in the room. Since keyboards can't be shared, social interactions increasingly take place over the wires. In turn, children feel less connection to their neighborhoods. Hardly surprising that a generation of network surfers is becoming adept at navigating the electronic backwaters, while losing touch with the world around them.   25

Roberta Friedman is a movie producer in New York. She hired a college student as an office assistant.   26

"He does everything I need on the computer," she told me. "Fantastically computer-aware and works for hours at his desk. But there's a scary kind of narrowness about him. He can win at dozens of computer games. He'll sit at his desk and watch the screen all day. He doesn't look out the window at Central Park or talk to people. He eats his lunch at the computer.

"This guy is nineteen and his curiosity is numbed," Roberta continued, shaking her head. "He's sweet, extremely shy, and has almost no social graces. What's really sad, though, is that he's so bright, yet so limited."   27

As a way of bringing classrooms together, the Global Schoolhouse tries to connect elementary and high schools using the Internet. They promote live video conferences using interactive video and audio. Their literature quotes children: "I'm learning lots of things every minute I'm on the network," says Oscar, a student. "The Internet is so big and I'm only getting started," says another.   28

I wish this group well, and I hope they achieve their aims, but I'm dubious. I observed a different demonstration project over the Internet, which cost several thousand dollars: hooking up an eighth-grade classroom in Chicago to one in San Juan. After the cables were strung   29 and the connections were made, I was appalled to discover the children asking astonishingly naive and uninteresting questions: "What does it feel like to live in Puerto Rico?" "Do you watch Michael Jackson?" They could have accomplished as much—and more—using postcards.

School districts want such showcases to convince us that they're in- 30 novating and solving the problems of teaching. I'm surprised at how few scoff at these glitzy and ineffective toys.

I see the same thing in school districts big and small. Vancou- 31 ver Island, site of massive deforestation, is considering hooking up their elementary and middle schools to the Internet. According to the *Victoria Times-Colonist,* one consultant suggests that children in their Bayside Middle School "can learn about preserving our island's rain forests by linking electronically with a class in Louisiana study- ing wetlands. Each learns from the other's land-use issues. That is technology happening now."

Why not just rent a bus and drive everyone to Clayoquot Sound, over 32 by the edge of the rain forest, to count banana slugs and thousand-year-old cedars? Or invite foresters and ecologists to the classroom to speak about their problems and worries? Reading text on a computer screen is far less memorable than any of these things.

Gary Nabhan touches on this point in his book *The Geography of* 33 *Childhood: Why Children Need Wild Places.* He discovered that many children living in Arizona's Sonora Desert spend more time watching na- ture shows on the Discovery Channel than playing in the nature show out- side. Research shows that more than half of our children learn about nature from television, a third from school, and less than 10 percent by going outdoors. To counter this trend, Nabhan wants children to "roam beyond the pavement, to gain access to vegetation and earth that allows them to tunnel, climb, and even fall."

Artificial-intelligence experts argue over what computers are able 34 to do. This much is certain: no computer can teach what a walk through a pine forest feels like. Sensation has no substitute.

A physicist friend told me about buying a computer for his 35 four-year-old: "Jesse spends hours behind the screen, studying whales and porpoises. He can identify sharks and seals, practically anything that swims."

Sounds nice. How long did his son study? 36

"Oh for the past month, he's been behind the computer every free minute," he told me. "He'd rather play computer games than watch tele- vision. It's educational software."

I bit my tongue, and chatted about his computer. Eventually, I ask 37 whether he'd taken Jesse to see real fish. Now, we're ten miles from the ocean, and twice that from a great aquarium.

Well, no, he hadn't gotten around to taking Jesse to the aquarium. 38 But Jesse was having a great time with the computer. Had more fun playing computer games than playing with other kids.

. . .

"Sesame Street," widely acclaimed as an outstanding program for 39 children, has been around for twenty years. Indeed, its idea of making learning relevant to all was as widely promoted in the seventies as the Internet is today.

So where's that demographic wave of creative and brilliant stu- 40 dents now entering college? Did kids really need to learn how to watch television? Did we inflate their expectations that learning would always be colorful and fun? If they expected schooling to be easy, how many have now advanced from Big Bird to existential phenomenology or celestial mechanics?

Indeed, have the social effects of "Sesame Street" even been accu- 41 rately documented and validated?

I see a parallel between the goals of "Sesame Street" and those of 42 children's computing. Both are pervasive, expensive, and encourage children to sit still. Both display animated cartoons, gaudy numbers, and weird, random noises. Both encourage passive acceptance of a medium that will follow them for the rest of their lives. Both give the sensation that by merely watching a screen, you can acquire information without work and without discipline. And both shout the magical mantra: "Here's the no-effort, fun way to learn!"

I disagree. Learning isn't easy. It's often not fun. It takes work and 43 discipline. Dancing numbers and singing frogs can't teach arithmetic. Glitzy computer programs can't teach children to treat others as they would have others treat themselves.

The Global Schoolhouse gives plenty of demonstrations to politi- 44 cians, reporters, and school administrators, but there's darn little research to support this insistent drive for computers in the classroom.

Since well-off school districts have lots of computers, I expect 45 someone will find a close correlation between number of computers and test scores. This, I'll bet, will be quoted as statistical evidence that computer networks in schools are a good thing. Bah.

What exactly is being taught using computers? On the surface, a 46
student is learning how to read and type and use programs. I'll bet that
they're really learning something else.

Kids learn to stare at a monitor for hours on end. How to accept 47
what a machine says without arguing. That the world is a passive, preprogrammed place, where one click on the mouse gets the right answer.
They're learning transistory and shallow relationships from instant
e-mail. That discipline isn't necessary when they can zap frustrations with
a keystroke. That grammar, analytic thought, and human interactions
don't matter.

In these ways, computers complement television. No technolog- 48
ical pathway—neither Muppet nor modem—leads directly to a good
education.

Quick—what's the outside temperature?   49

Do you look at the thermometer in the window? Tune the television
to the latest forecast? Dial the time-and-temperature service on the
phone? Log into America Online and view a weather map? Or do you
walk outside and see for yourself?

Suppose you get three answers: a stranger tells you that it's thirty 50
degrees outside, the TV weather person reports seventy-five, and
your thermometer says ninety. Since it's a hot day, you realize that the
stranger is telling you Celsius, your thermometer is in Fahrenheit, and
the weather channel is simply wrong. The convincing test, though, is your
own experience. You stick your hand out the window and realize it's hot.

Computer networks replace that lust for the physical with a vir- 51
tual reality.

Want the finest pictures of the sky ever made? Get them over the In- 52
ternet, using the File Transfer Protocol: just type *ftp pubinfo.jpl.nasa.gov* and
you'll be greeted by a log-in prompt. Log in as *anonymous,* and you can
then change the directory by typing *cd images.* List the files by typing *ls.* To
get a terrific picture of Orion, just enter *get orion.gif,* assuming that the file
hasn't been moved. There on your office workstation is a close-up photo of
M42, the Great Orion Nebula, complete with false-color rendering.

But have you actually seen Orion? Right now, can you point your fin- 53
ger toward that constellation? During what season would you look for
it? When you face the nebula, are you looking north or south?

Spend a few nights with a pair of binoculars, a constellation chart, 54
and a compass. You may swat mosquitoes in the summer and shiver in the

winter. But you'll get to know the sky. You'll be closer to the wonders of astronomy than any computer display can ever bring you. You'll be on an equal footing with the ancients.

In contrast, much of what comes across the computer screen is a 55 surrogate for experience. It's living through an electronic extension of the nervous system—many sensations are dulled, a few amplified. Impoverished proxies take the place of real events. Which is more fun—playing a video game of basketball or playing a game of basketball?

As developers plow under Civil War battlefields and lumber com- 56 panies saw down old-growth forests, the robber barons sometimes erect visitor centers to show what the territory once looked like. I've seen several of these and played with the multimedia displays. They're colorful, interactive, and come with professional narration.

These displays only mock: Glen Canyon Dam, for instance, has a 57 breathtaking photo display of the now-submerged canyon. When I saw what the Bureau of Land Reclamation destroyed, I started to cry and had to leave.

All the whizbang high-tech can't possibly compare with a walk in an 58 historic meadow or a quiet meditation among thousand-year-old redwoods. Computer displays only weakly imitate the sounds, sights, smells, tastes, and touches of nature.

Not all students are fooled by high-tech malarkey. Jon Leary, a se- 59 nior at North Carolina's East Mecklenburg High School, took an oceanography course over a fiber-optic cable. His class watched video screens, the other class was next to the cameras. He reported that the students in the originating classroom had a much richer experience. "They'll show us an octopus over the TV so we get the visual idea," Jon said. "They tell us it's gooshy. We don't feel it's gooshy."

How can I sense the gooshiness of an octopus? How can you be 60 certain that the ocean's salty? How can a chemistry student feel the heat of crystallization from a supersaturated potassium nitrate solution?

Simple: touch the octopus; taste the ocean water; hold the 61 beaker. These are the very experiences denied by electronic and online teaching. ✍

READING FOR INFORMATION

1. According to Stoll, what are the problems with learning Japanese from an interactive video system?
2. What does Stoll think about multimedia educational programs such as filmstrips and videos?

3. How would Stoll prefer to direct the money that is currently spent on educational technology?

4. In what ways does Stoll think that heavy computer users become narrow and limited?

5. What is Stoll's criticism of *Sesame Street*? What parallel does Stoll draw between educational software and *Sesame Street*?

6. What does Stoll think are the real "lessons" that students learn from using computers?

7. According to Stoll, what aspects of real life cannot be duplicated by computer-generated displays?

READING FOR FORM, ORGANIZATION, AND EXPOSITORY FEATURES

1. Describe Stoll's style of writing. How does it differ from Sagan's? Do you find Stoll's style appealing or irritating? Explain your answer.

2. Why do you think Stoll uses so many short paragraphs?

3. Comment on Stoll's use of examples. Does he need to use as many examples as he does? Are his examples effective?

READING FOR RHETORICAL CONCERNS

1. Write a one- or two-sentence statement of Stoll's thesis.

2. What assumptions does Stoll make about his audience?

3. Where does Stoll address opposition arguments? Does he respond effectively to his opponents?

WRITING ASSIGNMENTS

1. Write a three- to four-page argument that draws on your own experience with computers in the classroom to either support or attack Stoll's thesis.

2. In a three-page essay, explain and respond to the following passage from Stoll's article: "I guess what I'm trying to say is this: students deserve personal contact with instructors—interactive videos and remote broadcasts are no substitute for studying under a fired-up teacher who's there in person."

3. Educational computer software and multimedia presentations are important to student learning because so many of our current teachers are incompetent or uninvolved. Attack or defend this statement in a three-page essay that draws on Stoll's article.

The Intimate Machine

Neil Frude

Neil Frude is professor of psychology at University College in Wales. This excerpt is taken from his book The Intimate Machine.

PREREADING

Frude's title suggests that machines can display feelings. Have you ever attributed human characteristics to machines or other objects? Have you seen films or read about machines with human qualities? Freewrite on this topic for about ten minutes.

Computer technology is now almost exclusively employed in   1
"hard" applications within business, industry, and science. There are largely unexplored opportunities, however, for using many of the same techniques and devices for tasks which we do not normally associate with machines. Computers can be applied as a means to artistic creation, they can form the basis for new kinds of entertainment, and they can make "friendly" contact with children and adults in the home. There is already evidence that some users see their interaction with certain computer systems as constituting a "social relationship," and it is not difficult to think of ways in which technologists and programmers might further exploit this phenomenon.

Thus much would be gained, for example, by expanding the ma-   2
chine's capacity for "understanding" the user and by providing it with a "personality" of its own. In order to increase the "approachability" and the "attractiveness" of the system it would have to be "softened" and "humanized." The metal mechanism image could in this way be replaced with one of "organic presence." The requisite "softness" would be achieved both by introducing new design features in the machine itself—the hardware—and by creating a humanlike "character" within the program—the software. At least one of the top personal computer entrepreneurs, Adam Osborne, is aware of the challenge. "The future,"

From *The Intimate Machine* by Neil Frude. Copyright © 1983 by Neil Frude. Used by permission of Dutton Signet, a division of Penguin Books USA Inc.

he says, "lies in designing and selling computers that people don't realize are computers at all."

. . .

The probability that companion machines will soon appear is 3 strengthened by the fact that efforts toward such an end are likely to come simultaneously from two directions. On the one hand, manufacturers of dolls and mannequins are likely to draw upon the new technology to increase the repertoire of their products, while, on the other, technologists will increasingly implement means of softening robot- and computer-based interaction systems. Even now there are signs of such moves. Advanced technology has been applied in Disneyland to bring exhibits alive, and some cuddly teddy bears for young babies synthesize sounds similar to those heard inside the womb. From the other direction, calculators and interview programs are increasingly "dressed up" in softer guise, and commercially available chip-based machines for young people are often produced in bright colors with painted faces and are given names like "Professor Math" and "Crazy Joe."

Sophisticated adult tastes will demand the production of more sub- 4 tle artifacts. It seems that attraction and familiarity are often directly related, and the optimal machine might therefore be expected to have a more organic appearance. Although some models would be humanoid, many would be shaped rather like the animals that are now chosen as pets. Indeed, it would be possible to blend features borrowed from several creatures so that a whole range of new species could be designed. The tail-wagging of the dog might therefore be combined with the cuddliness of the cat, and the synthetic creature could be given the additional human skill of conversation. There would seem to be every chance that such an artifact would win a place in our hearts at least to the same degree that cats and dogs do at present.

. . .

The ideal companion machine not only would look, feel, and sound 5 friendly, but would also be programmed to behave in a congenial manner. Those qualities that make interaction with other people enjoyable would be simulated as closely as possible, and the machine would appear to be charming, stimulating, and easygoing. Its informal conversational style would make interaction comfortable, and yet the machine would remain slightly unpredictable and therefore interesting. In its first encounter it might be somewhat hesitant and unassuming, but as it came to know the user it would progress to a more relaxed and intimate style. The machine would not be a passive participant but would add its own suggestions, information, and opinion; it would sometimes take the initiative in developing or changing the topic and would have a personality of its own.

The machine would convey presence. We have seen how a computer's use of personal names and of typically human phrasing often fascinates the novice user and leads people to treat the machine as if it were almost human. Such features are easily written into the software, and by introducing a degree of forcefulness, pronounced reactions, and humor the machine could be presented as a vivid and unique character. The user would be fascinated and impressed and would want to further explore the organic presence within the machine. The novelty factor would not be sufficient, however, to prolong interaction indefinitely, and a dynamic would therefore be built into the program to model the kind of social progression that occurs when two people get to know one another. 6

Each human being is unique, and yet there are identifiable types. Some people are sensitive, others insensitive; some are outgoing and highly excitable, while others are quiet and introverted. Although we may enjoy meeting people of many different types, we often have preferences, and we would want to be able to select a companion machine that best suited our particular taste. Our judgments about people are partly based on our preconceived notions, partly on the person's role and reputation, and partly on our direct experience of their behavior and expressed opinions. 7

. . .

The computer itself would have some flexibility in its use of language and would adapt and extend its verbal repertoire in a number of ways. It would perhaps be programmed to use the human contact as a model and thus come to share the same figures of speech, phrasing, and slang as its owner. It could also be made to inquire about the meaning of words which it did not understand and could incorporate these into its own vocabulary. Such evolution of language competence would be accomplished gradually as the machine settled in with the user. The effects of familiarization would extend beyond the realm of language use, however, and the artificial companion would come to know the user with increasing breadth and increasing intimacy. It would be programmed to exhibit a gentle probing curiosity and would be able to build up a picture of the user's interests, opinions, preferences, and 8 past history. All the information disclosed would be analyzed, stored and integrated into the machine's reference system, to be applied in subsequent interaction.

The computer, then, would undergo a process of socialization and would adapt and change many of its characteristics as a result of its social experience. Another feature of its settling in would be a progressive relaxation of its interactional style. The rather shy and hesitant machine who entered the user's home for the first time might a few days later be chatting away with apparent ease and unconcern, making presumptions about the relationship that had developed and exhibiting a detailed knowledge of the user's personal world. The person, in a similar way, would have explored the potential of the machine and come to some degree of understanding about its personality, its limitations, and its practical uses. Quite apart from its role as a companion, a computer of this level of sophistication would have the capability of performing numerous useful tasks. It could read aloud from the newspaper, answer the telephone, keep track of food supplies, and act in a more modest capacity as a friendly alarm clock or a ferocious guard-dog. It would also be able to play chess, recite poetry, tell jokes, or give short lectures on aspects of world history. 9

· · ·

An artificial relationship of this type would provide many of the benefits that people obtain from interpersonal friendships. The machine would participate in interesting conversation that would continue on from previous discussions. It would have a familiarity with the user's life as revealed in earlier interchanges, and it would be understanding and good-humored. The computer's own personality would be lively and impressive, and it would develop in response to that of the user. With features such as these the machine might indeed become a very attractive social partner. This sounds like a heretical idea and may strike us as quite outrageous. Many people have a deeply held belief that no object or animal should be able to replace a human being in a person's life. It may be felt that there is a sanctity about human relationships that renders them beyond artificial simulation, but arguments of this kind cannot rule out the psychological possibility that a person may, in fact, come to regard a nonhuman object as an adequate substitute for a human friend. It is clear, for example, that some people set the value of their relationship with an animal above that of any human alliance, and the possibility that a computer might achieve such favor cannot therefore be rejected merely on the grounds that it is not human. 10

At this point we may begin to wonder whether there is any limit to 11
the potential intimacy between a person and a machine. Some human
friendships progress to a very high level of intimacy. People become
emotionally dependent on those who are close to them; they speak of
shared lives and in terms of love and devotion. Is there any guarantee
that feelings of even this level of intensity could not be stirred by a machine? If those qualities that lead people into the closest of relationships were understood, would it not perhaps be possible to simulate
them and thereby stimulate the deepest of human emotions? As yet
there is no direct evidence to demonstrate such an effect, but neither is
there any strong argument for ruling out the possibility, however dis-
tasteful the notion might be. Indeed, the theme of love for a machine
has been explored a number of times by creative writers, mostly within
the framework of science fiction. Although the machines in these stories
may be rather extravagant creations, the human responses that are portrayed are often plausible and convincing.

. . .

How should we regard the suggestion that a future "best friend" 12
might be delivered in a box or that the object of our deepest affections
might be rendered insensible by a power failure? The idea of the
inanimate intimate *does* seem outrageous, but not too long ago it
was thought that the idea of a machine that could play a reasonable
game of chess was equally absurd. The imagined impossibility of
the chess-playing machine was based on a lack of vision in the technical area. Those who might suggest that the notion of an intimate
human-machine relationship is entirely fanciful are likely to have dis-
regarded the evident psychological responses to complex interactive
computer systems. If we use the available evidence as a basis for predicting the likely reactions to "softer" and more sophisticated devices,
then it will be seen that the concept of the companion machine is in
fact highly plausible.

This does not mean that we have to *like* the idea, however. We 13
may be less than delighted with the suggestion that the deepest human
needs might be catered to by an electronic package. Somehow it feels
as if it should not be that easy. Perhaps we shall find that relationships
with artificial devices make personal demands just as human relationships do, but at least computer companions would be readily available,

and they would be programmed to get on well with a wide range of potential human friends. Many people suffer severely from a lack of social contact, and we should not be too ready to condemn an innovation that could bring considerable benefits to a large number of people.

Whatever our level of enthusiasm or distaste for the artificial friend, 14 the introduction of such devices must be regarded as a real possibility. The technology that is at present used to calculate electricity accounts and guide advanced weaponry has many potential applications in the field of social relationships. People are ever ready to attribute all manner of human characteristics to rather paltry objects, and they are likely to be overwhelmed when a machine speaks to them knowledgeably and affectionately.

READING FOR INFORMATION

1. According to Frude, what are some of the human qualities the intimate machine will possess?
2. Summarize the section of the article in which Frude explains how the machine will be programmed to act like a friend.
3. From Frude's point of view, is there any limit to the intimacy that could develop between a person and a machine?
4. How does Frude characterize people's likely reactions to the idea of an intimate machine? What are some of the positive reactions and some of the negative ones?
5. Paraphrase some of Frude's reasons why we should not readily condemn this innovation.
6. Which sentence or sentences best state Frude's thesis or main idea?

READING FOR FORM, ORGANIZATION, AND EXPOSITORY FEATURES

1. Which organizational patterns does Frude use? What is the overall effect of Frude's organizational strategy?
2. Would you characterize this article as a piece of academic or popular writing? Give reasons for your view.
3. Explain the types of evidence (facts, statistics, references to authorities, and so forth) Frude uses to develop and support his position, and give an example of each.

READING FOR RHETORICAL CONCERNS

1. Where was the material originally published? What does that information contribute to your understanding of the piece?
2. What is Frude's attitude toward his readers? What sentences tell you about his assumptions with regard to his audience?
3. Explain Frude's rhetorical purpose. What impact does he want to have on his readers?
4. Do you think Frude anticipates his readers' questions and concerns?

WRITING ASSIGNMENTS

1. Drawing on the article and your prior knowledge and experiences, write a three-page essay in response to Frude's question, "How should we regard the suggestion that a future 'best friend' might be delivered in a box or that the object of our deepest affections might be rendered insensible by a power failure?" Address your response to Neil Frude.
2. This assignment requires some library research. Over ten years have elapsed since Frude published his article. Since 1983, many highly intelligent computers and robots have been developed. Go to the library and locate some books and articles about newly developed computers that allow humans to interact with them in a sophisticated and meaningful way. Then use that information in a four- to five-page essay that either corroborates or disclaims some of Frude's assertions. Direct your essay to your classmates.
3. Frude assumes that many people may feel contempt for affectionate machines. In your opinion, are the rejections justified or unfounded? Are the people who hold these views guilty of what Carl Sagan calls " 'speciesism'— the prejudice that there are no beings so fine, so capable, so reliable as human beings" (248)? Develop your views in a two- to three-page essay directed to the audience of your choice.

Electronic Expansion of Human Perception

Warren Robinett

Warren Robinett is a computer researcher and commercial computer program developer.

PREREADING

Robinett's title suggests that human perception can be expanded or extended through the use of high technology. For ten minutes, brainstorm a list of specific technologies you know of that expand or extend vision, hearing, touch, smell, or taste.

Virtual reality, as its name suggests, is an unreal, alternate reality in which anything could happen. In its 1991 technological implementation, virtual reality is a 3D video game you can enter by strapping something onto your face that fools your senses into perceiving an environment that surrounds you on all sides. The thing strapped to your face is called a Head-Mounted Display. 1

The true potential of this new field comes from the ability of a Head-Mounted Display to induce a synthetic experience in its wearer. If experience can be captured and transmitted, you can "travel" instantaneously to a distant location and see the trees, feel the wind, hear the birds, and smell the flowers. If electronic instruments can sense things that you cannot perceive, such as the insides of opaque objects, then you can be shown images of these invisible things. If microscopes and tiny probes can scan and manipulate the microscopic world, then you can "shrink," like Alice in Wonderland, to enter into a three-dimensional world of palpable bacteria and Brontosaurian insects. 2

The true potential of the Head-Mounted Display is not that it allows you to enter into a fantasy world, but that it allows you new ways of perceiving the real world. 3

Warren Robinett, "Electronic Expansion of Human Perception." Reprinted from *Whole Earth Review*, Fall 1991: 17–21; subscriptions to WER are $20 a year (4 issues) from PO Box 38, Sausalito, CA 94966, (415) 332-1716. Reprinted by permission of the author.

EXPANSION OF PERCEPTION

Vision, hearing, touch, taste, and smell are the traditional five senses; in addition, you have the ability to sense temperature, vibration, acceleration of your body, the positions of your limbs, forces acting on your body, hunger, thirst, pain, and other sensations related to your body's internal state.   4

There are, however, things which are invisible to all of your senses. Among these are X-rays, infrared radiation, radio waves, magnetic fields, radioactivity, ultrasound, electricity, the insides of opaque objects, microscopic objects, and events occurring too fast to see. Even though you cannot directly perceive these things, you can indirectly measure and observe them with various instruments and electronic sensors.   5

By linking electronic sensors to a Head-Mounted Display, it is now possible to create "sensory transducers," which will allow you direct perception of phenomena which are imperceptible without electronic augmentation. As an example, night-vision goggles allow you to see and move about in total darkness by amplifying the low levels of light that are actually present. Sensory transducers can be built to make visible radioactivity, or any other invisible phenomenon for which electronic sensors exist.   6

Ultrasound scanners are currently used to look into the human body, and by connecting these scanners to a Head-Mounted Display, it will soon be possible to see directly into the living tissue. By using half-silvered mirrors, the Head-Mounted Display can allow you to see through to the real world, with the image from the ultrasound scanner optically superimposed. Thus, an obstetrician examining a pregnant woman could see the woman, feel the fetus kick beneath her hands, and see the ultrasound image of the fetus appearing to hang in space inside of her belly. We call this "X-ray vision," by analogy with Superman's ability to see inside of solid objects, even though ultrasound rather than X-rays would actually be used.   7

We are working toward building a prototype of such a device here at the University of North Carolina. Henry Fuchs, John Poulton, John Eyles and their team have over the last ten years built high-performance graphics computers (Pixel-Planes) that make it possible to compute views of two- and three-dimensional medical image data in real-time. Steve Pizer and his team have been developing algorithms and systems to make computer graphics an effective tool for radiologists and radiation oncologists. The volume-rendering technique they have developed   8 will be useful for displaying 3D ultrasound image data. Jannick Rolland and Rich Holloway are designing the optics and software for a see-through Head-Mounted Display for medical use. We hope to have this prototype of the X-ray-vision goggles working in the next year or so.

A Head-Mounted Display must be head-mounted because your 9 eyes, ear, nose and tongue are head-mounted. Your senses are directional, and the location in space from which sensory inputs originate is an important part of your perception of the world around you. Seeing or hearing a nearby rattlesnake with your natural senses implies knowing where it is in relation to your body.

A Geiger counter that warns you when radiation is present is bet- 10 ter than nothing, but a head-mounted sensor that lets you see radioactive gas leaking through the wall is a vast improvement in awareness.

What do these imperceptible things look like? Well, they don't 11 look like anything—they're invisible. A visual representation must be invented. This is a graphic design problem. What does radiation look like? Perhaps it is purple, with a brightness that indicates its lethality.

It is useful to consider earlier efforts to portray the invisible. What 12 does a molecule look like? Since atoms are a thousand times smaller than the wave-length of light, molecules have no visual appearance, and so an appropriate graphical representation must be created. (The appearance of a molecule under an electron microscope is not a definitive answer to what a molecule looks like, but rather a technologically convenient choice of a visual representation.)

. . .

Fred Brooks has been putting computer graphics to work to help 13 biochemists understand the structure and properties of the large organic molecules they study. These representations have proved informative to the biochemists.

What does human speech look like? Casting speech into visible form 14 is something you take for granted: it is called writing. Various innovations have occurred over the last five thousand years—the invention of the alphabet, spaces between words, the printing press, and standardized spelling. Writing is now a mature art, and the link between the sounds of speech and the black marks on a page of a book are quite abstract.

. . .

In a sense, reading is hearing with your eyes. This cross-sensory sub- 15 stitution is closely related to a sensory transducer for the imperceptible.

For the deaf, the sound of human speech is an imperceptible phenomenon. If it were possible to make a device that converted speech to written text in real-time, this device would in effect allow a deaf person to hear. This capability—real-time, speaker-independent, continuous speech recognition—has not yet been achieved. It ought to be possible, nevertheless, to create some kind of real-time visual representation of the sound of speech that, when visually superimposed on the movements of the lips and face, is sufficient to allow a deaf person to comprehend what is being said.

What does computation look like? The step-by-step action of a 16 computer as it manipulates data under the control of a program is a dynamic process that could be given an animated graphical representation, but there is currently no widely used or accepted depiction of the process of computation. Computation is currently invisible.

The electronic expansion of human perception has, as its manifest 17 destiny, to cover the entire human sensorium. Ultraviolet rays that will cause a sunburn hours later might be mapped to an insistent vibration on the skin. Dangerous radiation which would kill you in a few minutes might be signaled directly with purposely induced pain. If each computer instruction were mapped to its own audible frequency, then each computer program would, because of its characteristic sequence of instructions, make its own recognizable sound.

REAL-SPACE DATABASES

Information is often associated with location. Maps, inventories, and 18 mailing lists are, in essence, lists of information about objects and features at specific locations.

Using a see-through Head-Mounted Display which tracks its loca- 19 tion in the world, graphic data files could be spatially registered with the real world. A particular graphic object from the data file would be seen sitting at one spot in the world, and nowhere else. The data file would give the coordinates of the object's location—a very accurate latitude, longitude, and height above sea level—and only at that location could it be seen. Michael Naimark, a San Francisco media technologist, has coined the term "real-space imaging" to describe graphics that are registered with the real world, just as real-time graphics are synchronized with events in the real world.

To find a specific item whose location in a company's huge ware- 20 house is known, a huge red blinking arrow could appear in the air above the item, always remaining above it as you approached. Ghostly computer graphic labels could at attached to real-world objects and places. At specific places, you could leave notes to yourself that only you could see ("Don't eat at this place again"). You could leave warnings for others or scrawl rude graffiti.

The difference between these virtual labels and real physical ones 21 is that everyone can see physical labels, whereas each virtual label exists in some spatial data file and can only be seen if you have loaded that file into your Head-Mounted Display. This means, unfortunately, that virtual billboards will probably not replace the physical ones that line the highways—they would be too easy to turn off. To guide you to her house, a friend might give you, not written directions or a map, but a spatial data file that had an orange stripe hovering ten feet above the road along the route from your house to hers. It would be difficult to miss a turn at an intersection where the orange stripe above you veered to the right.

Geographical information systems, which have become popular 22 lately, are in essence computerized maps. Information is displayed in a spatial distribution that conforms with the spatial distribution of the real-world objects the information describes. If such a computerized map is enlarged and superimposed onto the real world, it becomes a real-space database.

A real-space graphic model of a building could be created on- 23 site, before construction began, to see what the building would look like in its real surroundings. An architect and client could walk through a simulated house at its planned site, looking through simulated windows at the real trees surrounding the site. The architectural walkthrough team here at UNC, led by Fred Brooks, has been building detailed computer models of buildings and exploring the questions of how realistic the models need to appear, and how the user can move through them.

The plans and maintenance instructions for a complex mecha- 24 nism such as an aircraft's jet engine could be spatially superimposed on the engine being repaired, with the engine's self-diagnostic circuits causing a large red arrow to point to the particular part that required attention.

In time, a huge number of real-space databases will come to 25 exist, and just as you must choose which books you will read, you will have to choose which graphic databases, if any, you wish to overlay onto the world.

REMOTE PRESENCE

"Being somewhere" consists of being able to look around at the things 26 that surround you, to touch them, to walk around, and to hear, feel, and smell whatever is present. If the light, sound, and other physical phenomena which trigger your senses can be detected electronically and transmitted to a Head-Mounted Display, then it is possible to have the experience of being at a place when in fact your body is many miles away. This out-of-body experience is called "telepresence."

The experience of simulated presence at a distant place is, in fact, 27 very familiar to each of us. When using a telephone, your voice and ears are electronically linked to those of a distant person, and you converse as if you were in the same room. This is auditory telepresence. It seems very natural and normal.

To have the visual experience of a 3D world that surrounds you, it 28 is necessary to be able to look around. The technical implementation of visual telepresence is to feed the signals from a pair of video cameras to the left- and right-eye fields of a Head-Mounted Display, with the cameras mounted in a robot head whose motion mimics that of your own head. When you turn your head, the robot head turns. And since you see what the robot head sees, when you look around, you see the environment that surrounds the robot. The "Green Man" is a robot built for underwater remote presence research by the Naval Ocean Systems Center in Hawaii. (It is called the Green Man because green hydraulic fluid drips from its hoses as if it were green alien blood.)

In addition to cameras slaved to the motion of your head, the Green 29 Man also has robot arms slaved to the motions of your own arms. By putting on the gloves and headset that link you to the distant robot, your senses are transported into the robot body. If your eyes and hands are at a remote location, you're there.

When you control such a telepresence robot from a distance, you 30 can see, hear, and converse with another person in front of the robot. The person you talk to, however, would not see you, but rather a slimy green robot that was gesticulating and talking with your voice.

In a telephone conversation, each person has a microphone and a 31 speaker in the telephone handset, with each microphone linked to the other person's speaker. The analogous setup for visual telepresence is for each person to wear a see-through Head-Mounted Display which is linked to a telepresence robot at the location of the other person. In such a conversation, you would see the other person's face superimposed onto the robot face which was physically there before you. You could thus have a "face-to-face" conversation with a distant person, making eye contact and observing one another's facial expressions.

The telephone allows electronic ventriloquism. It lets you throw 32 your voice, at the speed of light, to any location where you can get someone to pick up the receiver. Likewise, visual telepresence will allow you to project your eyes, at the speed of light, to any location where a telepresence robot exists. This is instant travel. In ten minutes, an executive might do her daily tour of the warehouse, the factory, the lab and the accounting department, even though these places are thousands of miles apart.

The robot hands of the telepresence robot allow the human oper- 33 ator to manipulate objects at the robot's location. This goes beyond mere passive sensory "presence" at a remote location and therefore has a different name— "tele-operation." In extremely dangerous environments, mortal human beings can be replaced with human-controlled tele-robots. The Green Man was designed to work on the bottom of the ocean, too deep for divers. NASA may use tele-operated robots to construct its space station. Tele-manipulators are used to handle the radioactive fuel in nuclear reactors. Tele-operated robots are beginning to be used to fight fires and to defuse bombs.

MICRO-TELE-OPERATION

Tele-robots don't have to be the same size as their human operators. 34 Tele-robots the size of King Kong could be made, say, for constructing buildings. Tiny tele-robots could also be made. As operator of a micro-tele-robot, you would have the perception that the ordinary world had expanded enormously, or equivalently, that you had been miniaturized. Operating at a 1-to-100 scale factor, the micro-robot would be two centimeters high and you would perceive a mouse to be the size of an elephant.

Some work has already been done in micro-tele-operation. A 35 scanning-tunneling microscope can image individual atoms, detect surface forces as it probes these atoms, and move atoms around with its probe; IBM researchers have hooked up such a microscope to a force-feedback device to make it possible to "touch" atoms. Controlling micro-robots is one of the goals of Dr. Tachi in Tsukuba Science City, Japan, who is one of the leading researchers in one-to-one scale tele-operation.

With a microscope and micro-manipulator, you could effectively have your eyes and hands projected into the microscopic world. To perceive that the micro-world surrounded you, when you turned your head, the microscope would need to swivel around the specimen to achieve the right point of view. Another way to achieve quick changes of point of view in the micro-world would be to mount the specimen on an electrically controlled rotation stage beneath the lens of a fixed microscope. [36]

This approach assumes a micro-world that is relatively transparent, such as a drop of water from a pond, so that any internal point of view can be achieved, even though the microscope looks in from the outside. [37]

Scaled down by a factor of 100, you could reach out and tweak the antenna of a honeybee that you perceived to be four feet long. And it couldn't sting you. [38]

An effective micro-tele-robot could be used for microsurgery. An adventurer could take a microscopic safari into an anthill to battle the furious hordes of ants. As people begin to work and play in micro-worlds, a need will arise for microscopic tools and devices which will perhaps be manufactured using micro-tele-robots. [39]

Virtual reality will prove to be a more compelling fantasy world than Nintendo, but even so, the real power of the Head-Mounted Display is that it can help you perceive the real world in ways that were previously impossible. To see the invisible, to travel at the speed of light, to shrink yourself into microscopic worlds, to relive experiences—these are the powers that the Head-Mounted Display offers you. Though it sounds like science fiction today, tomorrow it will seem as commonplace as talking on the telephone. [40]

READING FOR INFORMATION

1. How does Robinett define virtual reality?
2. What is a Head-Mounted Display, and how does it operate?
3. Explain what "sensory transducers" are, and give several examples of them.
4. How could virtual reality allow us to "see" human speech?
5. What is "real-space imaging"? Give several examples.
6. What is "telepresence"? Give several examples.
7. What is "micro-tele-operation"? Give several examples.

READING FOR FORM, ORGANIZATION, AND EXPOSITORY FEATURES

1. The subheadings indicate that Robinett has organized his article according to various applications of virtual reality. Suggest an alternative plan that Robinett could have used. How would the alternative plan change the effect that the article has on the reader?
2. How would you describe Robinett's tone? Is it appropriate?
3. Is Robinett writing for the academic community? What features of the text support your answer?

READING FOR RHETORICAL CONCERNS

1. What is Robinett's relationship to the University of North Carolina, the institution where the research he describes is being conducted? How might that relationship affect his presentation of the research?
2. What is Robinett's goal in writing? What impact does he want to have on his readers?
3. How does Robinett establish his authority? Do you have confidence in him? Why or why not?

WRITING ASSIGNMENTS

1. Write a three-page essay of response to Robinett's enthusiastic description of virtual reality. Make sure that you refer to the specific examples of virtual-reality technology that Robinett uses in this article.
2. Write a four-page informative essay that draws on Robinett's article to describe the range of potential applications for virtual reality. Include a clear definition of virtual reality.
3. Use Robinett's article as a starting point for a four-page speculative essay on the future of virtual reality. Imagine how the applications Robinett mentions might be extended. Also envision entirely new uses of virtual reality that go beyond the scope of Robinett's article. Describe your speculations for an audience that knows nothing about virtual reality.

The Age of Simulation

Jeremy Rifkin

Jeremy Rifkin is an internationally known commentator on the social impact of science and technology and the author of many books, including Biosphere Politics, Entropy: A New World View, *and* Declarations of a Heretic. *He is also a spokesperson for several public interest organizations.*

PREREADING

Read the first paragraph of Rifkin's essay. For ten minutes, brainstorm a list of the specific technological innovations that Rifkin may be referring to in this paragraph.

The separation of human beings from nature and the parallel detachment of human consciousness from the human body has transformed Western man into an alien on his own planet. Much of the outside world has become a kind of "no man's land," a scarred and polluted terrain full of danger—a foreboding environment where wars are fought, animals are slaughtered, forests are razed and burned, and human refugees wander aimlessly from place to place in search of safe havens. In the new indoor world, modern man and woman attempt to escape their last connection with the outside world by suppressing their own animal senses and freeing themselves from their own physical nature. A marvelous array of machines, big and small, have been invented to replace nearly every part of our bodies, providing us with mechanical surrogates from head to toe. 1

Our deep yearning for a mechanical analogue to nature was first expressed in the construction of automata, elaborate mechanized toys that mimicked living creatures, even human beings, in bodily function, movement, and gesture. The most elaborate of the automata were the brainchildren of a brilliant and imaginative French engineer, Jacques de Vaucanson. In 1738, Vaucanson amazed his fellow countrymen with the introduction of a fully automated flutist. The mechanized miniature of a 2

From *Biosphere Politics* by Jeremy Rifkin. Copyright © 1991 by Jeremy Rifkin. Reprinted by permission of Crown Publishers, Inc.

human being "possessed lips that moved, a moving tongue that served as the airflow valve, and movable fingers whose leather tips opened and closed the stops of the flute." Voltaire was so taken by the sight of the life-like, remarkable little creature that he dubbed Vaucanson "Prometheus's rival." Vaucanson's greatest work was a mechanical duck, an automata of such great versatility that it has not been surpassed in design to this day. The duck could drink puddle water with its bill, eat bits of grain, and within a special chamber visible to admiring spectators, duplicate the process of digestion. "Each of its wings contained four hundred moving pieces and could open and close like that of a living duck."[1]

Automata were the rage of Europe during the early industrial era. Engineers built little mechanical boys who wrote out poems and prose, petite mechanical maidens who danced to music, and animals of every kind and description performing wondrous feats. The toys, which became a favorite of princes and kings, were toured and put on exhibition throughout Europe. The automata provided a kind of proof to many that nature, like the automata that mimicked it, must indeed be animated by principles of mechanism just as Descartes and his contemporaries had argued. The visible presence of these strange little automated creatures could not help but excite the scientific and popular imagination and add impetus to the drive to find mechanized surrogates for everything in nature, even the human body. 3

During the first stage of the Industrial Revolution, machines of all kinds were invented to substitute for the human body. With the invention of electricity at the turn of the nineteenth century, a new category of machines was created to amplify and even replace human consciousness. Marshall McLuhan summed up the "bodily" impact of the two stages of invention: 4

> During the mechanical age we had extended our bodies in space. Today, after more than a century of electronic technology, we have extended our central nervous system itself in a global embrace. . . .[2]

McLuhan's now famous aphorism that "electronic man has no physical body" is fast becoming a reality in a world in which electronic communication has increasingly substituted for face-to-face communication between people. Today, electronic media have even eclipsed print in importance. Less than 20 percent of all the words delivered in America today are printed. Over 80 percent of all communications now go through the airwaves and telephone wires.[3] 5

Electronic technology represents the final disembodiment of the 6 senses. The more intimate senses, smell and touch, are eliminated altogether. Sight and sound are disembodied by machines, turned into invisible waves and pulses, transported over great distances with lightning speed, and then reembodied by other machines in the form of facsimiles, artificially reconstructed versions of the originals.

Television is today's electronic sequel to the mechanized automata 7 of the early industrial period. The mechanical representations of life have been replaced by electronic representations. With television, cinema, radio, stereos, cassette-disc players, and the like, modern man and woman can surround themselves with a second creation, an artificially conceived electronic environment that is virtually sealed off from the world of living nature.

Over 99 percent of the homes in the United States now have at 8 least one television set. On any given evening, over 80 million people are watching television. It is not uncommon for 100 million people to all watch the same show at the same time.[4] Never before in history have so many human beings collectively experienced the same event simultaneously. Ironically, it is anything but a shared experience, in that each viewer is witnessing the events in the privacy of his or her own home, far removed from neighbors.

The average American household watches over six hours of televi- 9 sion each day. The average viewer watches over four hours of television daily. Most Americans are spending nearly half their nonworking, nonsleeping hours in front of a machine watching "the phosphorescent glow of three hundred thousand tiny dots" flicker on and off at thirty times per second, creating electronic images of people, places, and things.[5] While the images entertain, inform, and educate, we tend to forget that they are not "real" experiences. They are simulations. In his book *Four Arguments for the Elimination of Television,* Jerry Mander points to the profound anthropological significance of this powerful and ubiquitous new presence in our life: "America has become the first culture to have substituted secondary, mediated versions of experience for direct experience of the world."[6]

Television is the ultimate technological surrogate for real life. It 10 represents the final separation from nature, a retreat into a private domain where, cut off from the outside world, the individual can view artificial electronic re-creations of reality. Millions of people have become voyeurs, passive spectators of experience. They can watch in horror as wars unfold before their eyes, be entertained by swashbuckling adventures, be romanced and beguiled by torrid love stories, tickled and amused by comedic antics, and saddened by the tragic accounts of others' misfortunes. All of the human emotions and feelings are aroused daily by television—millions of people reacting not to other flesh-and-blood people, not to a living environment, but rather to a machine pulsing electronic images into a semidarkened room.

The electronic images cannot be touched, smelled, or tasted. They are   11 visual and only secondarily aural, and even then both senses are narrowly circumscribed, diminished in size, range, and volume. Television cannot begin to capture the color, resolution, pitch, and tones of real images and sounds in the outside world. The flicker of illuminated dots conveys a one-dimensional silhouette, a distorted and disembodied representation of life.

Television distorts temporal and spatial reality in other, even more   12 fundamental ways. The images of people, places, and events are cut into seven- or eight-second frames or sound bites. The viewer is asked to suspend reality and accept cutaway shots in which the past, present, and future intermix, follow each other out of sequence, dovetail and parallel each other in a confusing array of combinations that bear no resemblance to the temporal and spatial realities of the real world.

Then, too, the medium has become so pervasive in our lives that it   13 has become much of our experience of life. We often talk about television characters and situations as if they were an intimate part of our lives. So much of our waking experience is consumed by television that many viewers are unable to distinguish clearly the artificial from the real. Indeed, the artificial becomes the most real part of our lives, since it takes up so much of our time.

Television blurs the distinction between artificial and real as no   14 other medium in history, creating a fundamental distortion in human consciousness that for many borders on dysfunctional pathology. "Marcus Welby, M.D." received over 250,000 letters from viewers during the five-year run of the show asking the fictional doctor for medical advice.[7]

In a study prepared for the National Institute of Mental Health, Dr.   15 George Grebner, dean of the Annenberg School of Communications at the University of Pennsylvania, and Dr. Larry Gross found that television watchers form much of their view of the world from what they see and experience on the screen. Among other things, the researchers found that:

> heavy viewers of television were more likely to overestimate the percentage of the world population that lives in America; they seriously overestimated the percentage of the population that have professional jobs; and

they drastically overestimated the number of police in the U.S. and the amount of violence. In all these cases, the overestimate matched a distortion that exists in television programming. The more television people watched, the more their view of the world matched television reality.[8]

As both a medium and a technology, television incorporates many of the operative principles of Enlightenment thinking. It separates people from the natural world, isolates them from their neighbors, suppresses some bodily senses and narrows others, emphasizes the artificial over the real, and reinforces the illusion of an autonomous, secure existence. From the safe haven of the television room, one can experience the outside world vicariously, without having to risk intimate participation or bodily contact.   16

While television helped further enclose human consciousness from the world of nature by conditioning the mind to live within an artificial environment, computer technology is creating a second artificial enclosure, which "promises" to replace living nature altogether. With computer technology, human civilization enters what may best be characterized as the age of simulation. At the Massachusetts Institute of Technology, Carnegie-Mellon University, and other elite schools of engineering, scientists are working feverishly on a new generation of computers that they say will create totally artificial environments. They call these new environments "virtual reality" to distinguish them from the kind of reality we have experienced up to now in our evolutionary history.[9]   17

At the advanced media lab at MIT, scientists are creating prototypes of computing machines that can simulate aspects of reality. Their goal is to construct an artificial "vivarium," a totally enclosed environment in which they can create and sustain facsimiles of life in isolation from the outside world. In the new world of simulation, the computer is not only used to create the simulated world of virtual reality but also becomes a machine surrogate for human companionship. Nicholas Negroponte of MIT states unabashedly that he regards his relationship to the computer not as "one of master and slave but rather of two associates that have a potential and a desire for self-fulfillment."[10] Negroponte, like many of his engineering colleagues, envisions the computing machines of the future more as personalized companions than work tools or mechanized forms of entertainment. He writes in his book *The Architecture Machine:*   18

> Imagine a machine that can follow your design technology and at the same time discern and assimilate your conversational idiosyncrasies. The same machine, after observing your behavior, could build a predictive model of

your conversational performance. . . . The dialogue would be so intimate—even exclusive—that only mutual persuasion and compromise would bring about ideas. Ideas unrealizable by either conversant alone.[11]

The goal of advanced computing design extends far beyond the obvious and banal considerations of commerce, military preparedness, or even more lofty goals like education and discovery. After spending several months interviewing scientists at MIT and other engineering schools, futurist Stewart Brand concluded in his book *Media Lab* that what scientists really desire with their mechanical creation is "companionship" and the security of a predictable artificial environment to wrap around them. Daniel Hillis of the media lab at MIT fantasied: "I would like to build a machine that can be proud of me," to which he added, "Thinking machines will be grateful to their creators."[12] The notion of an intimate mechanized companion that, while not completely predictable, is at least somewhat controllable and, of course, replaceable—to wit, an artificial surrogate to living creatures—reinforces the vision of Descartes, Bacon, and other early Enlightenment thinkers. [19]

In his second book, *Soft Architecture Machines*, Negroponte turns the final screw on the age of modernity, envisioning the ultimate vivarium, or enclosed environment: [20]

> The last chapter is my view of the distant future of architecture machines: they won't help us design; instead, we will live in them. . . . While proposing that a room might giggle at a funny gesture or be reluctant to be transformed into something else seems so unserious today, it does expose some of the questions associated with possible cognitive environments of tomorrow.[13]

Negroponte's vivarium is almost alive. It is virtual reality and, like the natural world, it can be silly, even obstinate. Still, it is a creation of human beings and therefore seems more easily manipulated and exploitable.

The autonomous interactive vivarium is years, if not decades, away. Scientists, however, have already successfully created limited virtual reality environments. At the Japanese government's mechanical engineering laboratory, scientists are experimenting in a new field of simulation called "tele-operations." Japanese scientists have already created a successful visual model with tele-operations, a robotized camera that allows the viewer to scan an environment hundreds or thousands of miles away with the help of a mobile robot. The observer can send the robot to distant places and then scan the terrain with his own eyes, as if [21] he were actually there experiencing it firsthand. The observer places his head in a black-velvet-lined box equipped with two television receivers, one for each eye:

> The receivers are gauged so that the image that is reflected against the retina of each eye is exactly the same as if you were looking at the world unaided. Further, every movement of your head is duplicated on the robot, where two precisely placed video cameras transmit a human range of what is seen.[14]

Researchers are working on other tele-operation devices, including one that allows an individual to manipulate an artificial environment on a computer screen in the control room and have his actions duplicated precisely and virtually simultaneously by a robot working miles away in the real environment.

Scientists working in the new field of virtual reality are experimenting with high-technology systems that can simulate all of the senses, enabling people to affect the outside world by way of an array of artificial experiences. The Data Glove was pioneered in the 1980s by Thomas G. Zimmerman and Lyoring Haivell. The glove, which contains fiber-optic cables tucked inside the fingers and thumbs, is connected to a computer terminal. The glove allows someone in a central control room to work with the mechanical hands of a robot in the outside world. As the human hand clenches, grasps, squeezes, and turns, the pressures are transmitted electronically to the robot's hands, which mimics each gesture. In the not-too-distant future, researchers say they will be able to reverse the tactile experience. As the robot takes hold of an object or even a living creature in the outside world, the tactile feeling will be transmitted inside, to the controller's hand, allowing him to experience touch by way of electronic stimulation.[15]

Computer synthesizing machines using advanced digital design techniques can already simulate the sound of an entire orchestra. One person sitting at a console can electronically reproduce the sound of virtually any musical instrument with the kind of precision that a musician cannot hope to duplicate.

Scientists are even working on techniques that will simulate smells, providing the vivariums of the future with preprogrammed odoriferous releases designed to incite, soothe, energize, and divert. Aroma therapists are experimenting with scent machines that can time a steady release of odors through ventilation systems into enclosed work environments or households. Researchers at Duke and Yale universities are studying the impact of various odors on blood pressure, brain waves, and other physiological processes. The new developments in olfactory science, says Yale psychologist William Cain, are likely to have extraordinary impacts on human civilization in the coming decades. "We'll gain tremendous understanding of the basic neurophysiological ways in which odors regulate the body and influence the mind. And after we've mapped the hidden pathways of olfactory nerves, we'll be able to influence behavior, modulate mood, and alleviate pain."[16] Some scientists hope to simulate smell electronically, over distances, just as they've begun to do with touch. One could smell flowers or a sea breeze hundreds or even thousands of miles away by way of artificially transmitted electronic pulses.

Proponents of virtual reality are eager to simulate every aspect of 25 the human environment in hopes of creating a totally artificial living space. With each new technological marvel, reality becomes more ephemeral and further removed from anything that might be thought of as natural. With laser-generated holography, scientists hope to fashion new artificial environments that are mere illusions, transporting us into a world lacking any semblance of physicality. Holographically furnished homes might include paintings and other artifacts that are no more real than the electronic images on the television screen.

Virtual reality represents the final retreat from organic reality and 26 the last chapter in the modern drive for security. The substitution of artificial experiences for natural ones masks an almost pathological fear of the living world.

Grant Fjermedal, in *The Tomorrow Makers*, recounts the dreams 27 and goals of scientists he interviewed at Carnegie-Mellon. Their vision of the future captures much of the artificiality of the modern sojourn.

> At Carnegie-Mellon University, Hans Moravec and Mike Blackwell had talked of the day when experiences could be simulated so well that you could sit in a chair wearing a headset to captivate your eyes, ears, and nose and have sensors attached to hands and legs, which would enable you to visit the world from the safety and comfort of your home.[17]

The relentless pursuit of a mechanized form of autonomous exis- 28 tence, seemingly free from the hold of nature and the death sentence it imposes on all living creatures, has led scientists like Hans Moravec to experiment with the idea of "downloading" human consciousness. Moravec, who is a senior research scientist at Carnegie-Mellon's Autonomous

Mobile Robot Laboratory, explains the process in a theoretical paper entitled "Robots That Rove." Using ultrasonic radar, phased array radio encephalography, and high-resolution, three-dimensional nuclear magnetic resonance holography, researchers might be able to scan parts of the human brain in order to develop a three-dimensional picture of its chemical makeup. A computer program could be written to simulate the behavior of each section of the brain. After each section of the brain has been "downloaded" into a written program, the entire simulation could be transferred into a computerized brain, which would think and act as the living original, complete with an identical set of memories.[18]

Many researchers in the new field of artificial intelligence believe   29 that downloading is indeed possible. MIT's Marvin Minsky says, "If a person is a machine and you get a wiring diagram of it, then you can make copies."[19] Like the alchemists who dreamed of discovering the elixir for everlasting life, and the mechanical engineers of the industrial age who dreamed of inventing a perpetual motion machine, the new computer scientists of the age of simulation dream of replacing the organic brain with a simulated computer model in an effort to defeat the inevitability of death.

MIT professor Gerald Jay Sussman expressed the hopes and ex-   30 pectations of many of his colleagues:

> "If you can make a machine that contains the contents of your mind, then the machine is you. To hell with the rest of your physical body, it's not very interesting. Now, the machine can last forever. Even if it doesn't last forever, you can always dump it onto tape and make backups, then load it up on some other machine if the first one breaks. . . . Everyone would like to be immortal. . . . I'm afraid, unfortunately, that I am the last generation to die."[20]

The idea of downloading human consciousness should not really sur-   31 prise us. It stands as the last unexplored terrain in a five-hundred-year odyssey to find a mechanical elixir. With thoughts of downloading dancing in their heads, scientists have crossed the final boundary separating the secular from the sacred, the artificial from the real world. The modern journey ends in the laboratories of MIT and Carnegie-Mellon, where some of the best minds of science are currently devoting their energies and their lives to creating a mechanical surrogate for eternal salvation.

In the age of simulation, security and immortality are no longer   32 sought in Christ on Judgment Day, or in unlimited material progress, or even in the specter of a classless society at the end of history. The new immortality is information, which can be collected, stored, edited, and preserved in perpetuity. Unlike living creatures, information does not rot and decay. Because it is mathematically derived and immaterial in nature, information can be transferred from one program to another and from one computing machine to another forever, without risk of diminution. While the software and hardware will eventually run down, the information will not and needs merely to be downloaded periodically to preserve its contents. Yoneji Masuda, a principal figure in the Japanese plan to become the first fully simulated information society, expresses unbridled enthusiasm for the new immortality:

> Unlike material goods, information does not disappear by being consumed, and even more important, the value of information can be amplified indefinitely by constant additions of new information to the existing information. People will thus continue to utilize information which they and others have created, even after it has been used.[21]

For some, the notion of transferring human consciousness to electronic programs that can be tucked inside automated computing machines is a chilling prospect. For others, like Moravec and his colleagues, downloading represents the long-sought-after fulfillment of Descartes's grand vision, the final reaffirmation of the modern quest for total autonomy from nature and absolute security for humankind.

NOTES

1. Vaucanson's automata were first described in the *Encyclopédie* of 1751. See also Siegfried Giedion, *Mechanization Takes Command: A Contribution to Anonymous History*, p. 35; Michael Uhl, "Living Dolls," *Geo*, July 1984, p. 86.
2. Herbert Marshall McLuhan, *Understanding Media: The Extensions of Man*, p. 53.
3. Stewart Brand, *The Media Lab, Inventing the Future at MIT*, pp. 18, 58.
4. Jerry Mander, *Four Arguments for the Elimination of Television*, p. 24.
5. Ibid., p. 192.
6. Ibid., p. 24.
7. Ibid., p. 255.
8. Ibid.
9. See Brand, *The Media Lab*, pp. 97–99, 112–13.
10. Nicholas Negroponte, quoted in Brand, *The Media Lab*, p. 149.
11. Nicholas Negroponte, *The Architecture Machine*, pp. 11–13.
12. Daniel Hillis, quoted in Grant Fjermedal, *The Tomorrow Makers*, p. 94.
13. Quoted in Brand, *The Media Lab*, p. 152.
14. Fjermedal, *Tomorrow Makers*, p. 233; see also Jeremy Rifkin, *Time Wars: The Primary Conflict in Human History*, pp. 173–74.

15. James D. Foley, "Interfaces for Advanced Computing," p. 130.
16. Quoted in Pamela Weintraub, "Sentimental Journeys," *Omni,* April 1986, p. 48.
17. Fjermedal, *Tomorrow Makers,* p. 229.
18. Ibid., p. 4.
19. Marvin Minsky, quoted in ibid., p. 7.
20. Gerald Jay Sussman, quoted in ibid., p. 8.
21. Yoneji Masuda, *The Information Society,* p. 150.

READING FOR INFORMATION

1. What does Rifkin believe was the significance of the mechanical toys that were popular in the eighteenth century?
2. How does Rifkin compare television to the mechanical toys from the eighteenth century?
3. What does Rifkin mean when he says, "Television is the ultimate technological surrogate for real life"?
4. According to Rifkin, what are the predictions Nicholas Negroponte makes about how machines and humans will interact in the future?
5. How does Rifkin define virtual reality?
6. What is meant by "downloading human consciousness"? How might it make immortality a possibility?

READING FOR FORM, ORGANIZATION, AND EXPOSITORY FEATURES

1. Why do you think Rifkin devotes the bulk of this article to describing new technology rather than attacking it, even though he is skeptical of the technology he describes?
2. What organizational plan does Rifkin use? Is his plan appropriate?
3. What use does Rifkin make of authorities to develop his point?
4. What concluding strategy does Rifkin use?

READING FOR RHETORICAL CONCERNS

1. Compare Rifkin's intended audience with Frude's.
2. Evaluate the extent to which Rifkin supports his assertions about television with specific evidence.
3. Describe Rifkin's rhetorical goal. Do you think he achieves it?

WRITING ASSIGNMENTS

1. Write a three- to four-page essay in which you either agree or disagree with the following statement from Rifkin's argument: "Virtual reality represents the final retreat from organic reality and the last chapter in the modern

drive for security. The substitution of artificial experiences for natural ones masks an almost pathological fear of the living world."

2. The last five paragraphs of Rifkin's article focus on the notion of "downloading human consciousness," an idea based on the assumption that a human being's essence is a collection of information. Write a three-page essay in which you explain and respond to that notion. Back up your viewpoint with specifics.

3. In a four-page essay, evaluate Rifkin's claim that television distorts our perception of reality.

SYNTHESIS WRITING ASSIGNMENTS

1. Sagan points out that garbage collectors could be replaced by robots at a considerable savings while many in our society are without employment. Draw on his article and others in this chapter to write a five-page essay that argues for or against using machines rather than humans for manual labor.

2. Write a four- to five-page essay that draws on Frude and Rifkin to explain the positive and negative aspects of intimate relationships between humans and machines.

3. In a four-page essay, compare and contrast the descriptions of virtual reality presented by Robinett, Rifkin, and Stoll.

4. Many commentators have called virtual reality "the LSD of the 1990s." Use the articles in this chapter to write a five-page response to that characterization of virtual reality.

5. Draw on the readings in this chapter to critique the portrayal of relationships between humans and machines in a work of science fiction you have read or seen (for example, a film such as *Blade Runner*). What issues does the science fiction address? Are they the same issues that are raised in the nonfiction articles in this chapter?

6. Try to imagine a future in which humans and machines interact in the ways the articles in this chapter suggest they might. How would this future differ from the present? What would life be like for human beings? Would the human species have to change to live happily in this environment? Write a five-page essay in response to these questions. You might organize your essay around a comparison between the present and the future.

eight

Technology and Civil Liberties

Modern technology has created challenges to civil liberties that the framers of the Constitution did not envision. Audio and visual surveillance, monitoring of electronic communications, duplication of private or copyrighted computer files, DNA fingerprinting, and a host of other innovations make it much easier for government agencies, employers, and anyone else who takes an interest in our activities to find out what we are doing and thinking. When these technologies are employed to reduce crime, they often receive support from the public. Americans have become increasingly impatient with crime, and many want the police to use any means available to make the streets safer. On the other hand, Americans are often quick to assert their personal rights, particularly their right to privacy. Although invasive technologies do assist police investigations, some commentators wonder if, by opting for a technological quick fix to crime, we enter into a Faustian bargain that will eventually result in the loss of important constitutional rights.

The readings in this chapter focus on how our constitutional rights to privacy and to protection from illegal searches might be affected by technological innovations. The first chapter of George Orwell's classic novel *1984* describes a futuristic society where a totalitarian government uses technology to virtually eliminate privacy. In "High-Tech Crime Fighting: The Threat to Civil Liberties," Gene Stephens claims that technology and the Constitution are "on a collision course." He points out that although new technologies, particularly those associated with surveillance, could help control crime, they might also infringe on individual rights. Gary T. Marx, although agreeing that technology poses grave threats to privacy, outlines measures that individuals and the larger society can take to minimize those dangers in his article "Privacy and Technology." In "Invasion of Privacy," Joshua Quittner argues that the benefits of modern technological advances are worth the reduction of individual privacy that comes with them. Charles Platt, author of "No Place to Hide," welcomes the end of privacy as long as the government and corporations are subject to electronic surveillance as well as private individuals. The last reading concerns DNA fingerprinting and its application to criminal investigations. Since the early 1990s, the reliability and legality of DNA fingerprinting has been hotly debated in scientific literature as well as in the courtroom. "Issues Regarding DNA Testing," excerpted from a U.S. Justice Department publication, describes the civil-liberties issues associated with using DNA fingerprinting as evidence in court.

Big Brother Is Watching You

George Orwell

Respected as one of the finest essayists in the English language, George Orwell is perhaps best known for his novels Animal Farm *and* 1984. *The excerpt that follows is the first chapter of* 1984.

PREREADING

> Whether or not you have ever read *1984,* you have probably heard the phrase "Big Brother is watching you." What does this expression mean to you? Under what circumstances is it used? Freewrite in response to these questions for ten minutes.

It was a bright cold day in April, and the clocks were striking   1
thirteen. Winston Smith, his chin nuzzled into his breast in an effort to escape the vile wind, slipped quickly through the glass doors of

Excerpt from *Nineteen Eighty-Four* by George Orwell. Copyright 1949 by Harcourt Brace & Company and renewed 1977 by Sonia Brownell Orwell. Reprinted by permission of the publisher.

Victory Mansions, though not quickly enough to prevent a swirl of gritty dust from entering along with him.

The hallway smelt of boiled cabbage and old rag mats. At one 2 end of it a colored poster, too large for indoor display, had been tacked to the wall. It depicted simply an enormous face, more than a meter wide: the face of a man of about forty-five, with a heavy black mustache and ruggedly handsome features. Winston made for the stairs. It was no use trying the lift. Even at the best of times it was seldom working, and at present the electric current was cut off during daylight hours. It was part of the economy drive in preparation for Hate Week. The flat was seven flights up, and Winston, who was thirty-nine, and had a varicose ulcer above his right ankle, went slowly, resting several times on the way. On each landing, opposite the lift shaft, the poster with the enormous face gazed from the wall. It was one of those pictures which are so contrived that the eyes follow you about when you move. BIG BROTHER IS WATCHING YOU, the caption beneath it ran.

Inside the flat a fruity voice was reading out a list of figures which 3 had something to do with the production of pig iron. The voice came from an oblong metal plaque like a dulled mirror which formed part of the surface of the right-hand wall. Winston turned a switch and the voice sank somewhat, though the words were still distinguishable. The instrument (the telescreen, it was called) could be dimmed, but there was no way of shutting it off completely. He moved over to the window: a smallish, frail figure, the meagerness of his body merely emphasized by the blue overalls which were the uniform of the Party. His hair was very fair, his face naturally sanguine, his skin roughened by coarse soap and blunt razor blades and the cold of the winter that had just ended.

Outside, even through the shut window pane, the world looked 4 cold. Down in the street little eddies of wind were whirling dust and torn paper into spirals, and though the sun was shining and the sky a harsh blue, there seemed to be no color in anything except the posters that were plastered everywhere. The black-mustachio'd face gazed down from every commanding corner. There was one on the house front immediately opposite. BIG BROTHER IS WATCHING YOU, the caption said, while the dark eyes looked deep into Winston's own. Down at street level another poster, torn at one corner, flapped fitfully in the wind, alternately covering and uncovering the single word INGSOC. In the far distance a helicopter skimmed down between the roofs, hovered for an instant like a blue-bottle, and darted away again with a curving flight. It was the Police Patrol, snooping into people's windows. The patrols did not matter, however. Only the Thought Police mattered.

Behind Winston's back the voice from the telescreen was still bab- 5 bling away about pig iron and the overfulfillment of the Ninth Three-Year Plan. The telescreen received and transmitted simultaneously. Any sound that Winston made, above the level of a very low whisper, would be picked up by it; moreover, so long as he remained within the field of vision which the metal plaque commanded, he could be seen as well as heard. There was of course no way of knowing whether you were being watched at any given moment. How often, or on what system, the Thought Police plugged in on any individual wire was guesswork. It was even conceivable that they watched everybody all the time. But at any rate they could plug in your wire whenever they wanted to. You had to live— did live, from habit that became instinct—in the assumption that every sound you made was overheard, and, except in darkness, every movement scrutinized.

Winston kept his back turned to the telescreen. It was safer; 6 though, as he well knew, even a back can be revealing. A kilometer away the Ministry of Truth, his place of work, towered vast and white above the grimy landscape. This, he thought with a sort of vague distaste—this was London, chief city of Airstrip One, itself the third most populous of the provinces of Oceania. He tried to squeeze out some childhood memory that should tell him whether London had always been quite like this. Were there always these vistas of rotting nineteenth-century houses, their sides shored up with balks of timber, their windows patched with cardboard and their roofs with corrugated iron, their crazy garden walls sagging in all directions? And the bombed sites where the plaster dust swirled in the air and the willow herb straggled over the heaps of rubble; and the places where the bombs had cleared a larger path and there had sprung up sordid colonies of wooden dwellings like chicken houses? But it was no use, he could not remember: nothing remained of his childhood except a series of bright-lit tableaux, occurring against no background and mostly unintelligible.

The Ministry of Truth—Minitrue, in Newspeak—was startlingly 7 different from any other object in sight. It was an enormous pyramidal structure of glittering white concrete, soaring up, terrace after terrace, three hundred meters into the air. From where Winston stood it was just possible to read, picked out on its white face in elegant lettering, the three slogans of the Party:

WAR IS PEACE

FREEDOM IS SLAVERY

IGNORANCE IS STRENGTH.

The Ministry of Truth contained, it was said, three thousand rooms above ground level, and corresponding ramifications below. Scattered about London there were just three other buildings of similar appearance and size. So completely did they dwarf the surrounding architecture that from the roof of Victory Mansions you could see all four of them simultaneously. They were the homes of the four Ministries between which the entire apparatus of government was divided: the Ministry of Truth, which concerned itself with news, entertainment, education, and the fine arts; the Ministry of Peace, which concerned itself with war; the Ministry of Love, which maintained law and order; and the Ministry of Plenty, which was responsible for economic affairs. Their names, in Newspeak: Minitrue, Minipax, Miniluv, and Miniplenty.

The Ministry of Love was the really frightening one. There were   8
no windows in it at all. Winston had never been inside the Ministry of Love, nor within half a kilometer of it. It was a place impossible to enter except on official business, and then only by penetrating through a maze of barbed-wire entanglements, steel doors, and hidden machine-gun nests. Even the streets leading up to its outer barriers were roamed by gorilla-faced guards in black uniforms, armed with jointed truncheons.

Winston turned round abruptly. He had set his features into the ex-   9
pression of quiet optimism which it was advisable to wear when facing the telescreen. He crossed the room into the tiny kitchen. By leaving the Ministry at this time of day he had sacrificed his lunch in the canteen, and he was aware that there was no food in the kitchen except a hunk of dark-colored bread which had got to be saved for tomorrow's breakfast. He took down from the shelf a bottle of colorless liquid with a plain white label marked VICTORY GIN. It gave off a sickly, oily smell, as of Chinese rice-spirit. Winston poured out nearly a teacupful, nerved himself for a shock, and gulped it down like a dose of medicine.

Instantly his face turned scarlet and the water ran out of his eyes.   10
The stuff was like nitric acid, and moreover, in swallowing it one had the sensation of being hit on the back of the head with a rubber club. The next

moment, however, the burning in his belly died down and the world began to look more cheerful. He took a cigarette from a crumpled packet marked VICTORY CIGARETTES and incautiously held it upright, whereupon the tobacco fell out onto the floor. With the next he was more successful. He went back to the living room and sat down at a small table that stood to the left of the telescreen. From the table drawer he took out a penholder, a bottle of ink, and a thick, quarto-sized blank book with a red back and a marbled cover.

For some reason the telescreen in the living room was in an un- 11 usual position. Instead of being placed, as was normal, in the end wall, where it could command the whole room, it was in the longer wall, opposite the window. To one side of it there was a shallow alcove in which Winston was now sitting and which, when the flats were built, had probably been intended to hold bookshelves. By sitting in the alcove, and keeping well back, Winston was able to remain outside the range of the telescreen, so far as sight went. He could be heard, of course, but so long as he stayed in his present position he could not be seen. It was partly the unusual geography of the room that had suggested to him the thing that he was now about to do.

But it had also been suggested by the book that he had just taken 12 out of the drawer. It was a peculiarly beautiful book. Its smooth creamy paper, a little yellowed by age, was of a kind that had not been manufactured for at least forty years past. He could guess, however, that the book was much older than that. He had seen it lying in the window of a frowsy little junk shop in a slummy quarter of the town (just what quarter he did not now remember) and had been stricken immediately by an overwhelming desire to possess it. Party members were supposed not to go into ordinary shops ("dealing on the free market," it was called), but the rule was not strictly kept, because there were various things such as shoelaces and razor blades which it was impossible to get hold of in any other way. He had given a quick glance up and down the street and then had slipped inside and bought the book for two dollars fifty. At the time he was not conscious of wanting it for any particular purpose. He had carried it guiltily home in his brief case. Even with nothing written in it, it was a compromising possession.

The thing that he was about to do was to open a diary. This was not 13 illegal (nothing was illegal, since there were no longer any laws), but if detected it was reasonably certain that it would be punished by death, or at least by twenty-five years in a forced-labor camp. Winston fitted a nib into the penholder and sucked it to get the grease off. The pen was

an archaic instrument, seldom used even for signatures, and he had pro-
cured one, furtively and with some difficulty, simply because of a feeling that the beautiful creamy paper deserved to be written on with a
real nib instead of being scratched with an ink pencil. Actually he was
not used to writing by hand. Apart from very short notes, it was usual to
dictate everything into the speakwrite, which was of course impossible
for his present purpose. He dipped the pen into the ink and then faltered
for just a second. A tremor had gone through his bowels. To mark the
paper was the decisive act. In small clumsy letters he wrote:

April 4th, 1984.

He sat back. A sense of complete helplessness had descended upon 14
him. To begin with, he did not know with any certainty that this *was*
1984. It must be round about that date, since he was fairly sure that his
age was thirty-nine, and he believed that he had been born in 1944 or
1945; but it was never possible nowadays to pin down any date within a
year or two.

For whom, it suddenly occurred to him to wonder, was he writing 15
this diary? For the future, for the unborn. His mind hovered for a moment round the doubtful date on the page, and then fetched up with a
bump against the Newspeak word *doublethink.* For the first time the
magnitude of what he had undertaken came home to him. How could
you communicate with the future? It was of its nature impossible. Either the future would resemble the present in which case it would not
listen to him, or it would be different from it, and his predicament would
be meaningless.

For some time he sat gazing stupidly at the paper. The telescreen 16
had changed over to strident military music. It was curious that he seemed
not merely to have lost the power of expressing himself, but even to have
forgotten what it was that he had originally intended to say. For weeks past
he had been making ready for this moment, and it had never crossed his
mind that anything would be needed except courage. The actual writing
would be easy. All he had to do was to transfer to paper the interminable
restless monologue that had been running inside his head, literally for
years. At this moment, however, even the monologue had dried up. Moreover, his varicose ulcer had begun itching unbearably. He dared not
scratch it, because if he did so it always became inflamed. The seconds
were ticking by. He was conscious of nothing except the blankness of the
page in front of him, the itching of the skin above his ankle, the blaring
of the music, and a slight booziness caused by the gin.

Suddenly he began writing in sheer panic, only imperfectly aware   17
of what he was setting down. His small but childish handwriting straggled
up and down the page, shedding first its capital letters and finally even
its full stops:

*April 4th, 1984. Last night to the flicks. All war films. One very
good one of a ship full of refugees being bombed somewhere in the
Mediterranean. Audience much amused by shots of a great huge fat man
trying to swim away with a helicopter after him. first you saw him wal-
lowing along in the water like a porpoise, then you saw him through the
helicopters gunsights, then he was full of holes and the sea round him
turned pink and he sank as suddenly as though the holes had let in the
water, audience shouting with laughter when he sank. then you saw a
lifeboat full of children with a helicopter hovering over it. there was a
middleaged woman might have been a jewess sitting up in the bow with
a little boy about three years old in her arms. little boy screaming with
fright and hiding his head between her breasts as if he was trying to bur-
row right into her and the woman putting her arms around him and com-
forting him although she was blue with fright herself. all the time covering
him up as much as possible as if she thought her arms could keep the bullets off him. then the helicopter planted a 20 kilo bomb in among them terrific flash and the boat went all to matchwood. then there was a wonderful
shot of a childs arm going up up up right up into the air a helicopter with
a camera in its nose must have followed it up and there was a lot of ap-
plause from the party seats but a woman down in the prole part of the
house suddenly started kicking up a fuss and shouting they didnt oughter
of showed it not in front of the kids they didn't it aint right not in front
of kids it aint until the police turned her turned her out i dont suppose
anything happened to her nobody cares what the proles say typical prole
reaction they never—*

Winston stopped writing, partly because he was suffering from   18
cramp. He did not know what had made him pour out this stream of rubbish. But the curious thing was that while he was doing so a totally different memory had clarified itself in his mind, to the point where he
almost felt equal to writing it down. It was, he now realized, because of
this other incident that he had suddenly decided to come home and begin
the diary today.

It had happened that morning at the Ministry, if anything so nebu-   19
lous could be said to happen.

It was nearly eleven hundred, and in the Records Department, 20
where Winston worked, they were dragging the chairs out of the cubicles
and grouping them in the center of the hall, opposite the big telescreen,
in preparation for the Two Minutes Hate. Winston was just taking his
place in one of the middle rows when two people whom he knew by
sight, but had never spoken to, came unexpectedly into the room. One
of them was a girl whom he often passed in the corridors. He did not
know her name, but he knew that she worked in the Fiction Department. Presumably—since he had sometimes seen her with oily hands
and carrying a spanner—she had some mechanical job on one of the
novel-writing machines. She was a bold-looking girl of about twenty-
seven, with thick dark hair, a freckled face, and swift, athletic movements.
A narrow scarlet sash, emblem of the Junior Anti-Sex League, was wound
several times around the waist of her overalls, just tightly enough to bring
out the shapeliness of her hips. Winston had disliked her from the very
first moment of seeing her. He knew the reason. It was because of the atmosphere of hockey fields and cold baths and community hikes and general clean-mindedness which she managed to carry about with her. He
disliked nearly all women, and especially the young and pretty ones. It was
always the women, and above all the young ones, who were the most bigoted adherents of the Party, the swallowers of slogans, the amateur spies
and nosers-out of unorthodoxy. But this particular girl gave him the impression of being more dangerous than most. Once when they passed in
the corridor she had given him a quick side-long glance which seemed
to pierce right into him and for a moment had filled him with black terror. The idea had even crossed his mind that she might be an agent of the
Thought Police. That, it was true, was very unlikely. Still, he continued
to feel a peculiar uneasiness, which had fear mixed up in it as well as hostility, whenever she was anywhere near him.

The other person was a man named O'Brien, a member of the Inner 21
Party and holder of some post so important and remote that Winston
had only a dim idea of its nature. A momentary hush passed over the
group of people round the chairs as they saw the black overalls of an
Inner Party member approaching. O'Brien was a large, burly man with
a thick neck and a coarse, humorous, brutal face. In spite of his formidable
appearance he had a certain charm of manner. He had a trick of reset-
tling his spectacles on his nose which was curiously disarming—in some
indefinable way, curiously civilized. It was a gesture which, if anyone had
still thought in such terms, might have recalled an eighteenth-century
nobleman offering his snuff-box. Winston had seen O'Brien perhaps a

dozen times in almost as many years. He felt deeply drawn to him, and not solely because he was intrigued by the contrast between O'Brien's urbane manner and his prize-fighter's physique. Much more it was because of a secretly held belief—or perhaps not even a belief, merely a hope—that O'Brien's political orthodoxy was not perfect. Something in his face suggested it irresistibly. And again, perhaps it was not even unorthodoxy that was written in his face, but simply intelligence. But at any rate he had the appearance of being a person that you could talk to, if somehow you could cheat the telescreen and get him alone. Winston had never made the smallest effort to verify this guess; indeed, there was no way of doing so. At this moment O'Brien glanced at his wristwatch, saw that it was nearly eleven hundred, and evidently decided to stay in the Records Department until the Two Minutes Hate was over. He took a chair in the same row as Winston, a couple of places away. A small, sandy-haired woman who worked in the next cubicle to Winston was between them. The girl with dark hair was sitting immediately behind.

The next moment a hideous, grinding screech, as of some mon- 22 strous machine running without oil, burst from the big telescreen at the end of the room. It was a noise that set one's teeth on edge and bristled the hair at the back of one's neck. The Hate had started.

As usual, the face of Emmanuel Goldstein, the Enemy of the Peo- 23 ple, had flashed onto the screen. There were hisses here and there among the audience. The little sandy-haired woman gave a squeak of mingled fear and disgust. Goldstein was the renegade and backslider who once, long ago (how long ago, nobody quite remembered), had been one of the leading figures of the Party, almost on a level with Big Brother himself, and then had engaged in counterrevolutionary activities, had been condemned to death, and had mysteriously escaped and disappeared. The program of the Two Minutes Hate varied from day to day, but there was none in which Goldstein was not the principal figure. He was the primal traitor, the earliest defiler of the Party's purity. All subsequent crimes against the Party, all treacheries, acts of sabotage, heresies, deviations, sprang directly out of his teaching. Somewhere or other he was still alive and hatching his conspiracies: perhaps somewhere beyond the sea, under the protection of his foreign paymasters; perhaps even—so it was occasionally rumored—in some hiding place in Oceania itself.

Winston's diaphragm was constricted. He could never see the face 24 of Goldstein without a painful mixture of emotions. It was a lean Jewish face, with a great fuzzy aureole of white hair and a small goatee beard—a clever face, and yet somehow inherently despicable, with a kind of senile silliness in the long thin nose near the end of which a pair of spectacles was perched. It resembled the face of a sheep, and the voice, too, had a sheeplike quality. Goldstein was delivering his usual venomous attack upon the doctrines of the Party—an attack so exaggerated and perverse that a child should have been able to see through it, and yet just plausible enough to fill one with an alarmed feeling that other people, less level-headed than oneself, might be taken in by it. He was abusing Big Brother, he was denouncing the dictatorship of the Party, he was demanding the immediate conclusion of peace with Eurasia, he was advocating freedom of speech, freedom of the press, freedom of assembly, freedom of thought, he was crying hysterically that the revolution had been betrayed—and all this in rapid polysyllabic speech which was a sort of parody of the habitual style of the orators of the Party, and even contained Newspeak words: more Newspeak words, indeed, than any Party member would normally use in real life. And all the while, lest one should be in any doubt as to the reality which Goldstein's specious claptrap covered, behind his head on the telescreen there marched the endless columns of the Eurasian army—row after row of solid-looking men with expressionless Asiatic faces, who swam up to the surface of the screen and vanished, to be replaced by others exactly similar. The dull, rhythmic tramp of the soldiers' boots formed the background to Goldstein's bleating voice.

Before the Hate had proceeded for thirty seconds, uncontrollable 25 exclamations of rage were breaking out from half the people in the room. The self-satisfied sheeplike face on the screen, and the terrifying power of the Eurasian army behind it, were too much to be borne; besides, the sight or even the thought of Goldstein produced fear and anger automatically. He was an object of hatred more constant than either Eurasia or Eastasia, since when Oceania was at war with one of these powers it was generally at peace with the other. But what was strange was that although Goldstein was hated and despised by everybody, although every day, and a thousand times a day, on platforms, on the telescreen, in newspapers, in books, his theories were refuted, smashed, ridiculed, held up to the general gaze for the pitiful rubbish that they were—in spite of all this, his influence never seemed to grow less. Always there were fresh dupes waiting to be seduced by him. A day never passed when spies and saboteurs acting under his directions were not unmasked by the Thought Police. He was the commander of a vast shadowy army, an underground network of conspirators dedicated to the overthrow of the State. The Brotherhood, its name was supposed to be. There were also whispered stories of a terrible book, a compendium of all the heresies, of which Goldstein was the author and which circulated clandestinely here and there. It was a book without a title. People referred to it, if at all, simply as *the book*. But one knew of such things only through vague rumors. Neither the Brotherhood nor *the book* was a subject that any ordinary Party member would mention if there was a way of avoiding it.

In its second minute the Hate rose to a frenzy. People were leap- 26 ing up and down in their places and shouting at the tops of their voices in an effort to drown the maddening bleating voice that came from the screen. The little sandy-haired woman had turned bright pink, and her mouth was opening and shutting like that of a landed fish. Even O'Brien's heavy face was flushed. He was sitting very straight in his chair, his powerful chest swelling and quivering as though he were standing up to the assault of a wave. The dark-haired girl behind Winston had begun crying out "Swine! Swine! Swine" and suddenly she picked up a heavy Newspeak dictionary and flung it at the screen. It struck Goldstein's nose and bounced off; the voice continued inexorably. In a lucid moment Winston found that he was shouting with the others and kicking his heel violently against the rung of his chair. The horrible thing about the Two Minutes Hate was not that one was obliged to act a part, but that it was impossible to avoid joining in. Within thirty seconds any pretense was always unnecessary. A hideous ecstasy of fear and vindictiveness, a desire to kill, to torture, to smash faces in with a sledge hammer, seemed to flow through the whole group of people like an electric current, turning one even against one's will into a grimacing, screaming lunatic. And yet the rage that one felt was an abstract, undirected emotion which could be switched from one object to another like the flame of a blowlamp. Thus, at one moment Winston's hatred was not turned against Goldstein at all, but, on the contrary, against Big Brother, the Party, and the Thought Police; and at such moments his heart went out to the lonely, derided heretic on the screen, sole guardian of truth and sanity in a world of lies. And yet the very next instant he was at one with the people about him, and all that was said of Goldstein seemed to him to be true. At those moments his secret loathing of Big Brother changed into adoration, and Big Brother seemed to tower up, an invincible, fearless protector, standing like a rock against the hordes of Asia, and Goldstein, in spite of his isolation, his helplessness, and the doubt that hung about his very existence, seemed like some sinister enchanter, capable by the mere power of his voice of wrecking the structure of civilization.

It was even possible, at moments, to switch one's hatred this way or 27
that by a voluntary act. Suddenly, by the sort of violent effort with which
one wrenches one's head away from the pillow in a nightmare, Winston
succeeded in transferring his hatred from the face on the screen to the
dark-haired girl behind him. Vivid, beautiful hallucinations flashed through
his mind. He would flog her to death with a rubber truncheon. He would
tie her naked to a stake and shoot her full of arrows like Saint Sebastian.
He would ravish her and cut her throat at the moment of climax. Better
than before, moreover, he realized *why* it was that he hated her. He hated
her because she was young and pretty and sexless, because he wanted to
go to bed with her and would never do so, because round her sweep sup-
ple waist, which seemed to ask you to encircle it with your arm, there was
only the odious scarlet sash, aggressive symbol of chastity.

The Hate rose to its climax. The voice of Goldstein had become an 28
actual sheep's bleat, and for an instant the face changed into that of a
sheep. Then the sheep-face melted into the figure of a Eurasian soldier
who seemed to be advancing, huge and terrible, his submachine gun
roaring and seeming to spring out of the surface of the screen, so that
some of the people in the front row actually flinched backwards in their
seats. But in the same moment, drawing a deep sigh of relief from everybody, the hostile figure melted into the face of Big Brother, black-haired,
black-mustachio'd, full of power and mysterious calm, and so vast that it
almost filled up the screen. Nobody heard what Big Brother was saying.
It was merely a few words of encouragement, the sort of words that are
uttered in the din of battle, not distinguishable individually but restoring
confidence by the fact of being spoken. Then the face of Big Brother
faded away again, and instead the three slogans of the Party stood out in
bold capitals:

WAR IS PEACE

FREEDOM IS SLAVERY

IGNORANCE IS STRENGTH.

But the face of Big Brother seemed to persist for several seconds 29
on the screen, as though the impact that it had made on everyone's eye-
balls were too vivid to wear off immediately. The little sandy-haired
woman had flung herself forward over the back of the chair in front of
her. With a tremulous murmur that sounded like "My Savior!" she extended her arms toward the screen. Then she buried her face in her
hands. It was apparent that she was uttering a prayer.

At this moment the entire group of people broke into a deep, slow, 30 rhythmical chant of "B-B! . . . B-B! . . . B-B!" over and over again, very slowly, with a long pause between the first "B" and the second—a heavy, murmurous sound, somehow curiously savage, in the background of which one seemed to hear the stamp of naked feet and the throbbing of tom-toms. For perhaps as much as thirty seconds they kept it up. It was a refrain that was often heard in moments of overwhelming emotion. Partly it was a sort of hymn to the wisdom and majesty of Big Brother, but still more it was an act of self-hypnosis, a deliberate drowning of consciousness by means of rhythmic noise. Winston's entrails seemed to grow cold. In the Two Minutes Hate he could not help sharing in the general delirium, but this subhuman chanting of "B-B! . . . B-B!" always filled him with horror. Of course he chanted with the rest: it was impossible to do otherwise. To dissemble your feelings, to control your face, to do what everyone else was doing, was an instinctive reaction. But there was a space of a couple of seconds during which the expression in his eyes might conceivably have betrayed him. And it was exactly at this moment that the significant thing happened—if, indeed, it did happen.

Momentarily he caught O'Brien's eye. O'Brien had stood up. He 31 had taken off his spectacles and was in the act of resetting them on his nose with his characteristic gesture. But there was a fraction of a second when their eyes met, and for as long as it took to happen Winston knew— yes, he *knew!*—that O'Brien was thinking the same thing as himself. An unmistakable message had passed. It was as though their two minds had opened and the thoughts were flowing from one into the other through their eyes. "I am with you," O'Brien seemed to be saying to him. "I know precisely what you are feeling. I know all about your contempt, your hatred, your disgust. But don't worry, I am on your side!" And then the flash of intelligence was gone, and O'Brien's face was as inscrutable as everybody else's.

That was all, and he was already uncertain whether it had happened. 32 Such incidents never had any sequel. All that they did was to keep alive in him the belief, or hope, that others besides himself were the enemies of the Party. Perhaps the rumors of vast underground conspiracies were true after all—perhaps the Brotherhood really existed! It was impossible, in spite of the endless arrests and confessions and executions, to be sure that the Brotherhood was not simply a myth. Some days he believed in it, some days not. There was no evidence, only fleeting glimpses that might mean anything or nothing: snatches of overheard conversation, faint scribbles on lavatory walls—once, even, when two strangers met, a small movement of the hands which had looked as though it might be a signal of recognition. It was all guesswork: very likely he had imagined everything. He had gone back to his cubicle without looking at O'Brien again. The idea of following up their momentary contact hardly crossed his mind. It would have been inconceivably dangerous even if he had known how to set about doing it. For a second, two seconds, they had exchanged an equivocal glance, and that was the end of the story. But even that was a memorable event, in the locked loneliness in which one had to live.

Winston roused himself and sat up straighter. He let out a belch. 33 The gin was rising from his stomach.

His eyes refocused on the page. He discovered that while he sat 34 helplessly musing he had also been writing, as though by automatic action. And it was no longer the same cramped awkward handwriting as before. His pen had slid voluptuously over the smooth paper, printing in large neat capitals—

> DOWN WITH BIG BROTHER
> DOWN WITH BIG BROTHER
> DOWN WITH BIG BROTHER
> DOWN WITH BIG BROTHER
> DOWN WITH BIG BROTHER

Over and over again, filling half a page.

He could not help feeling a twinge of panic. It was absurd, since the 35 writing of those particular words was not more dangerous than the initial act of opening the diary; but for a moment he was tempted to tear out the spoiled pages and abandon the enterprise altogether.

But he did not do so, however, because he knew that it was useless. 36 Whether he wrote DOWN WITH BIG BROTHER, or whether he refrained from writing it, made no difference. Whether he went on with the diary, or whether he did not go on with it, made no difference. The Thought Police would get him just the same. He had committed—would still have committed, even if he had never set pen to paper—the essential crime that contained all others in itself. Thoughtcrime, they called it. Thoughtcrime was not a thing that could be concealed forever. You might dodge successfully for a while, even for years, but sooner or later they were bound to get you.

It was always at night—the arrests invariably happened at night. 37 The sudden jerk out of sleep, the rough hand shaking your shoulder, the lights glaring in your eyes, the ring of hard faces round the bed. In the vast majority of cases there was no trial, no report of the arrest. People simply disappeared, always during the night. Your name was removed from the registers, every record of everything you had ever done was wiped out, your one-time existence was denied and then forgotten. You were abolished, annihilated: *vaporized* was the usual word.

For a moment he was seized by a kind of hysteria. He began writ- 38 ing in a hurried untidy scrawl:

theyll shoot me i dont care theyll shoot me in the back of the neck i dont care down with big brother they always shoot you in the back of the neck i dont care down with big brother—

He sat back in his chair, slightly ashamed of himself, and laid down his 39 pen. The next moment he started violently. There was a knocking at his door.

Already! He sat as still as a mouse, in the futile hope that whoever 40 it was might go away after a single attempt. But no, the knocking was repeated. The worst thing of all would be to delay. His heart was thumping like a drum, but his face, from long habit, was probably expressionless. He got up and moved heavily toward the door.

READING FOR INFORMATION

1. Describe the function of the "telescreen" and the "Thought Police."
2. What is the Ministry of Love responsible for? What accounts for its ironic name?
3. What prompts Winston to start keeping a diary?
4. Why does Winston think it might be impossible to "communicate with the future"?
5. How does Winston overcome his writer's block?
6. What or who are the "proles"? Why does Winston apparently feel superior to the proles?
7. Why does Winston dislike "nearly all women, especially the young and pretty ones"?
8. What is the purpose of the Two Minutes Hate?
9. What is "Thoughtcrime"?

READING FOR FORM, ORGANIZATION, AND EXPOSITORY FEATURES

1. Describe the "feel" of the physical environment in which Winston works and lives. How does Orwell establish this feel?
2. How does the physical appearance and "feel" of the diary (paragraph 12) contrast with the rest of Winston's environment? Why does Orwell establish this contrast?

3. What about Winston character makes him rebel against the Party and Big Brother?

READING FOR RHETORICAL CONCERNS

1. What historical figure is the model for Emmanuel Goldstein? What point is Orwell trying to make by drawing this parallel?
2. Think of all examples of "advanced" technology (remember that Orwell was writing in the 1940s) that Orwell provides. How does Orwell want the reader to think about these innovations?
3. After Winston begins writing "Down with Big Brother," his writing becomes almost childish in character. What point is Orwell trying to make by showing how Winston's prose degenerates?

WRITING ASSIGNMENTS

1. Certain cities in the United States have passed "hate crime" laws that, for example, impose harsher penalties in assault cases that are racially motivated. To what extent are hate crime laws equivalent to the Thoughtcrime Orwell describes? Is it ever appropriate to punish people for their thinking as opposed to their actions? Is punishing thought a violation of the First Amendment? Write a four-page essay in response to one or several of these questions.
2. Winston describes how dissidents are not only killed but "vaporized": "Your name was removed from the registers, every record of everything you had ever done was wiped out, your one-time existence was denied and then forgotten. You were abolished, annihilated: *vaporized* was the usual word." The fear of being "vaporized" underlies many people's misgivings about computerization in our current society. Does computerization threaten our personal identities? Reply to this question in a three-page essay grounded in your personal experience.
3. In the twenty-first century, would it be possible to maintain a totalitarian regime, like the one Orwell describes, without surveillance technology? Write a four-page essay in response to this question.

High-Tech Crime Fighting: The Threat to Civil Liberties

Gene Stephens

Gene Stephens is a professor in the College of Criminal Justice at the University of South Carolina and criminal justice editor of the magazine The Futurist.

PREREADING

Freewrite for ten minutes on the implication of the title. What forms of high-tech crime fighting are you aware of from news stories, books, or films? How might these technologies pose a threat to our civil liberties?

 Modern technology and the U.S. Constitution appear to be on 1 a collision course.

Supersensitive audiovisual devices, computer networks, genetic 2 identification, electronic monitoring, and other soon-to-be-available products and techniques offer a boon to criminal justice agencies. But these same innovations threaten such cherished rights as privacy, protection against self-incrimination, impartial trial, confrontation of witnesses and accusers, reasonable bail, prohibition of cruel and unusual punishment, and equal protection under the law.

Even the most-cherished rights of freedom of religion, speech, and 3 assembly could be endangered in a "high tech" state. To understand the risks, let's look at some specific rights and how they are being challenged by new technology and legal decisions.

PRIVACY

The Law: The Fourth Amendment provides that probable cause must 4 be shown before government agents can search and seize one's person or property. Through case law, this right has been held to provide the individual protection from government intrusion in his home or any

Excerpted from Gene Stephens, "High-Tech Crime Fighting: The Threat to Civil Liberties," *The Futurist* (Bethesda, Maryland) July–Aug. 1990: 20–25.

other place where he has an "expectation of privacy." For example, the Supreme Court ruled in 1967 that the failure of the Federal Bureau of Investigation to obtain a warrant on probable cause before placing a "bug" on the outside of a telephone booth was a Fourth Amendment violation, as the person on the phone had an "expectation of privacy" in the enclosed booth.

But more recently, the Court has begun to back off from this position. In 1984, it ruled that even a "no trespassing" sign on a person's property did not provide protection of privacy if the land had "open fields," because it was not a "reasonable expectation" that the signs would keep people, *including police*, off the property. 5

In 1988, the Court upheld a police search of a man's garbage without a warrant, holding that "expectation of privacy" was not to be judged by the *individual's* expectations, but instead by "society's belief that the expectation was objectively reasonable." 6

Technology: Given the direction of Supreme Court decisions, consider emerging technology and its likely utility to police and corrections agents. 7

Supersensitive listening devices that can hear and record conversations through solid walls from many miles away are already available and can even be controlled by computer and recalled by keyword input. Thus, 24-hour-a-day audio surveillance is possible, with almost instantaneous recall via computer to any instant of any conversation. 8

Supersensitive video devices that can record shape and motion both in still and moving pictures through walls and ceilings are also now available, and soon positive pictures of photographic and videotape quality will be possible. If anyone—government official or voyeur—can see and record one's every action despite closed doors and drawn shades, can there be any "reasonable" expectation of privacy left? 9

Computer networking will take the privacy loss a step further. As government and private agency computers become more compatible, information on a person's credit history, tax returns, medical records, educational transcripts and entertainment choices will be gathered from the various computers on which it is stored and transferred to a single data bank, thus providing a life-to-death dossier on every individual. Even if no one were constantly listening to or watching the individual, his activities could be recovered through computer access—from the note his third-grade teacher put into his file about "homosexual tendencies" to his past-due accounts with the credit bureau. 10

The dossier will be even more complete in years to come as the 11
cashless society emerges. Cash will become obsolete, replaced by the
"universal card" and still later by simple genetic recognition. Each individual will have a single account, including income and credit line, that
will be debited automatically for any purchase. Thus, a record of each individual's every purchase—product or service—will be in the dossier.

The ultimate threat to privacy, however, will not come until early in 12
the twenty-first century, when memory transfer becomes generally prac-
ticed. The transfer of RNA structures that encapsulate memory from one
individual to another or to the public domain will begin to eliminate the
privacy of thoughts. This trend will be accelerated if mind-reading technology scores new breakthroughs and law-enforcement agents begin to
scan thought waves in search of "intelligence." Will the courts find a "reasonable expectation of privacy" even of one's unexpressed thoughts in
the face of such technology?

PROBABLE CAUSE FOR WARRANTS

The Law: Despite the threats to privacy, there is still the requirement 13
that probable cause be established *before* search and seizure. A magistrate
must sign a search warrant.

But the Court has also chipped away at this right: The "exclusionary 14
rule" has been diluted by the "good faith exception"—a group of situations
that seems to grow almost daily. Not only is a warrant not necessarily needed to go through one's garbage or to trespass on "open fields," but in
1986 the Court held that agents in airplanes could use information from
sightings made without probable cause, and in 1989 it added helicopter
surveillance—an extension of the "plain-view exception."

Technology: Police today normally seek a warrant based on prob- 15
able cause to conduct an electronic/photographic surveillance of a suspect. But given the new higher-tech equipment, if police "accidentally"
overhear conversations or see activities behind solid walls in apartments,
houses, or neighborhoods, would this "evidence" be covered by the "good
faith" and "plain-view" exceptions?

Electronic scanning is already possible from a van, a helicopter, an 16
airplane, or a satellite. Since there may not be any "reasonable" expectation of privacy from such scanning, is a warrant even necessary?

In the near future, we can expect video scanning by the cameras 17
that see through walls and ceilings. Next will come computer scanning, as
authorities program their computers to scan dossiers on the computer

network for evidence of malfeasance or any other "intelligence." Finally will come telepathic scanning, as skilled authorities monitor the thought waves of the populace in search of real or perceived misbehavior.

Given the direction of the Court, it may eventually adopt the maxim 18 long held by many law-enforcement officials: If you have nothing to hide, you have nothing to fear.

SELF-INCRIMINATION

The Law: The Fifth Amendment to the U.S. Constitution provides that 19 an individual does not have to "confess" or help authorities in any way if he is accused of a crime. The government must prove its case without the assistance of the accused if he chooses not to incriminate himself. In addition, the Court held in 1966 that authorities had to tell the individual of his rights if he were under suspicion or in custody and were to be questioned (the so-called Miranda warnings).

Here again, the right against self-incrimination has exceptions. For 20 example, if the Court gives the individual immunity from prosecution, he can be required to provide testimony about his criminal activities because he no longer stands to face government penalties for his actions. Of course, if he must testify against contract killers of an organized crime network, he may face other dire consequences.

Beyond this, the Miranda rights have been diluted by "good faith" 21 and other exceptions. In a 1977 case, a parolee was enticed to confess by a police lie and without Miranda warnings, but the Court ruled that the parolee came to police headquarters voluntarily (albeit at the request of the police) and confessed voluntarily in the investigative stage and thus had no right to Miranda warnings. The Court also held that the police lie—that the parolee's fingerprints were found at the scene of the crime—was not germane to the case. Thus, according to the Court, his Fifth Amendment rights against self-incrimination were not violated, and the confession was "voluntarily" given and could be used in court.

In 1988, the Florida Court of Appeals upheld a lower-court ruling 22 that genetic "fingerprint" (DNA) evidence was "sufficiently reliable" and thus admissible in court. This case, on its way to the U.S. Supreme Court, likely will open the floodgates for genetic-identification evidence, despite arguments that it is a form of self-incrimination.

Technology: Genetic identification can be accomplished from a sin- 23 gle cell—from a hair, a scale of skin, a speck of blood, or a drop of semen. Thus, as genetic ID kits already on the market become available to every police officer, security agent, and private detective—or anyone who wants one—almost irrefutable genetic evidence will become increasingly available. "Planting evidence" will take on a new meaning, as the accused's gun will no longer be necessary; a hair will be sufficient for incrimination.

Dossiers also can incriminate, as records for the purchase of guns, 24 drugs, or sexually oriented material may point to the individual as a suspect. Much data in computers is inaccurate, but, as with credit bureaus, the burden of proof for the accuracy of data is increasingly placed on the individual rather than on the agency.

Electronic and video scanning will mean that the individual may be 25 incriminating himself while in the "privacy" of his home. Later, memory transfer and thought-reading will lead to self-incrimination through the dangerous act of thinking.

CRUEL AND UNUSUAL PUNISHMENT

The Law: The Eighth Amendment provides that government-ordained 26 punishment for crime shall not be "cruel and unusual." In 1972, the Supreme Court held that, because of discrimination and failure to consider mitigating circumstances, the death penalty was cruel and unusual. Justice William Brennan wrote that "even the vilest criminal remains a human being possessed of common human dignity" and that "severe penalties cannot be inflicted arbitrarily." He added that, "if there is a significantly less severe punishment adequate to achieve the purposes for which the punishment is inflicted, the [death penalty] . . . is unnecessary and therefore excessive."

But in 1976, the Court held that a carefully drafted statute which 27 minimized the risk that "it would be inflicted in an arbitrary and capricious manner" could make the death penalty acceptable if it were not "disproportionate" to the crime involved. Three-fourths of the states now have death-penalty statutes, and the federal government sanctions capital punishment for murders involving drug dealing.

Still, the requirement that the penalty not be "disproportionate" 28 has led to its being restricted to murder, and the "humane" carryover from the 1972 ruling has led to new methods, such as lethal injection. In noncapital cases, flogging and other corporal punishment methods have generally been held unconstitutional, as have mind-control methods such as behavior modification.

Technology: A myriad of new and emerging technologies will test 29 the limits of punishment and pose dilemmas for the Court.

Electronic monitoring of individuals—used for defendants on bail, 30
probationers, and parolees—is already testing the scope of both Fourth
and Fifth Amendment protections. Is monitoring a form of punishment? It restricts freedom and thus must be accompanied by due
process and other constitutional guarantees. Should one be "punished"
by electronic monitoring before one is tried and convicted? One could
be jailed prior to trial, so electronic monitoring may seem acceptable.

Should a convicted offender be placed on a monitor for weeks or 31
months rather than be fined, assigned to community service, or some
other penalty? "Overreach" of monitoring—putting pretrial defendants
and minor offenders, even juveniles, under constant surveillance and
house arrest—is a major concern of civil libertarians.

What about releasing relatively serious offenders (e.g., burglars, 32
robbers, assaulters, arsonists) to electronically monitored house arrest
on parole by attaching electrodes to the monitor, thus shocking the offender intermittently but repeatedly until he returns to his assigned territory? Cruel and unusual? Given the alternative of prison, many
offenders would choose the monitor and electrodes.

Is 24-hour-a-day surveillance itself cruel and unusual? Inmates in 33
prisons have sometimes rioted or tried to burn or trash their institutions
in the face of video surveillance in cellblocks.

Upcoming could be cryonics (freezing), followed by suspended an- 34
imation (removing the blood and putting the individual in "storage"). In
the face of massive prison overcrowding, these and other forms of human
hibernation offer immediate answers to correctional problems. Many inmates could be "stored" in small spaces using these techniques. But are
they constitutional?

Subliminal conditioning, a fad in the 1950s and 1960s, is likely to 35
make a comeback in the 1990s as more-sophisticated audiovisual equipment makes the low sound and rapid light messages—"Obey the law,"
"Do what is required of you"—an attractive way to control and change
human behavior. Would it be cruel and unusual? Is it an invasion
of privacy to use the technique on prisoners? On schoolchildren? On
department-store shoppers?

Implants offer a whole new array of weapons in the battle to 36
control crime. Convicted offenders could be sentenced to have electrode monitors implanted to keep them in their assigned territories,
but beyond this, a subliminal-message player might be implanted to
give the probationer 24-hour-a-day anticrime messages. Five-year
birth-control implants are already available for women; can it be very

difficult to implant five-year behavior-control chemical capsules in public offenders? Why wait until a crime occurs? Why not implant control capsules in "predelinquents"—children with behavioral problems? Cruel and unusual punishment, or just efficient and effective crime prevention?

Experiments with ultrasound have found it lacking as a basis for 37 nonlethal weaponry, but it may provide the ultimate solution to prison riots. Piping high-pitched sound over improved intercom systems would momentarily render everyone in the affected area unconscious and allow staff to enter, disarm, and regain custody. It seems better than calling in the National Guard, but is it cruel and unusual?

Genetic engineering also promises new methods of punishment or 38 treatment, from genetic surgery to "cure" the offender by removing or altering "deviant" traits, to the implantation of synthesized body chemicals that will keep the offender under constant control. Will these methods become part of the sentencing of the court, or will they be deemed cruel and unusual?

Finally, if the death penalty continues, which among the new technologies will provide "humane" extermination and which will be deemed "cruel"? Ultrasound at extreme levels can quickly destroy the individual; in the near future, ultrasound will be provided at levels that will literally dematerialize human beings and, indeed, all matter in the area (à la *Star Wars*). It will be fast, effective, and efficient. Humane or cruel?

EQUAL PROTECTION

The Law: The 14th Amendment provides for due process and equal 40 protection of the law for all persons accused of a crime. To date, most challenges have been that rich and poor are not treated equally or that the poor are not given due-process protections. In 1983, for example, the Court ruled that a person could not have his probation revoked just because he failed to pay required restitution to his victim unless his "ability to pay" was first established. A pending case in Georgia challenges the fairness of the entire judicial system for indigent defendants, citing inadequate resources, delays in appointing attorneys, pressure on defendants to plead guilty, and a lack of public defenders.

The increasing numbers of homeless are now being treated as criminals under newly adopted curfew and sleeping-in-a-public-place ordinances in many communities. Is this due process and equal protection?

The rising tide of immigrants also poses constitutional questions, with illegal aliens and noncitizens vying for equal rights and protections with citizens.

Technology: Increasing bionic replacement of human body parts 42 will soon call "equal protection" and due process into question, as a human with a "brain transplant" or computer-enhanced or computer-replaced brain may choose to challenge his culpability for the "crimes of the new brain."

But greater challenges will begin in the early twenty-first century, 43 with the development of chimeras (human-animals), androids (human-machines), genetically altered humans (gilled humans, winged humans), and clones (duplicate humans). Given humanity's track record of treating all new residents differently and often denying them the basic rights of previous residents, how will these new "creatures" be treated under the equal-protection clause? First will have to come a redefinition of "human."

OTHER THREATS

Somewhat less threatened by the technological revolution, but still af- 44 fected, will be the First Amendment rights of freedom of religion, speech, and assembly. The Court has been careful over the years to protect these most-cherished rights and has even held unconstitutional some practices that might have a "chilling effect" on the individual's exercise of these freedoms.

But in the future, how can such freedoms be protected from the 45 threats of the cashless society, electronic monitoring, constant surveillance, computer networking, and life-to-death dossiers? If every word, deed, purchase, and even thought is to be recorded and available for scrutiny, how can a person feel free to worship, speak, associate with others, and think as he pleases?

The balance between the Sixth Amendment rights to a speedy and 46 public trial *and* an impartial jury has always been hard to maintain, especially in the face of pretrial publicity. But this problem will become even knottier as pressure mounts to televise trials in the never-ending search for ratings. Real trials have garnered high ratings in recent years, and the next step—to make viewers the jurors—is almost certain to be proposed and promoted. Jurors who leave the "jury box" during crucial testimony to rummage in the refrigerator or to go to the bathroom could present serious constitutional problems.

Another Sixth Amendment dilemma is the use of videotaped testi- 47
mony. Does this deny the defendant the right to be confronted by his
accusers and to compel the witnesses to testify? Is the "impersonal" videotape the equivalent of "face-to-face" confrontation in court? And will
videotaped testimony be used for strategy rather than out of necessity
(e.g., interviewing a mildly injured victim in a hospital bed to make him
appear more aggrieved)?

A major twenty-first-century legal battle can be expected as defense 48
and prosecution attempt to introduce at trial evidence from "memory
banks"—the stored RNA memory chains of deceased victims and witnesses, providing an exact recall of the events of the alleged crime according to the stored memory of the individual.

Finally, the reasonable-bail requirement of the Eighth Amendment, 49
already in contention because of the use of pretrial electronic monitoring, will undergo further challenge when prosecutors attempt to require
electrode or chemical-control implants as a requisite for bail.

A variety of new weapons will be available in the near future—from 50
nonlethal chemical spray guns and sound guns to very lethal lasers and
dematerialization weapons—but the constitutionality of their restriction
should not be an issue. The Court has held that the right to bear arms
under the Second Amendment is not an individual right, but a societal
right, and only then if a "well-regulated militia" were deemed necessary.
The National Guard has clearly replaced that need, but it's doubtful that
such an interpretation will silence the National Rifle Association and
other adamant gun owners.

BALANCING SOCIETAL AND INDIVIDUAL RIGHTS

The twenty-first century promises many new technologies and proce- 51
dures that will make the criminal justice system more effective and efficient. Constant surveillance and forced behavioral change could
effectively control the populace, but at a high cost in terms of constitutional rights. Orwell's *1984* has been surpassed, and Huxley's *Brave New
World* is technologically feasible.

To achieve the proper balance between societal and individual 52
rights will become increasingly challenging. It will require policies that
Americans have found difficult to establish and follow—policies involving individual and governmental restraint. Just because technology
makes constant surveillance possible doesn't mean that it has to be used
for that purpose, and just because technology allows constant control

of behavior (via chemical implants) doesn't mean that it has to be used for that purpose.

But Americans have found "restraint" difficult. If it can be done, 53 someone wants it done, and others simply do it. Given the heterogeneous character of American society and the emphasis on individualism, it is to be expected that citizens will genuinely disagree on how each of these new technologies should be used and what controls should be set on each.

Even so, failure to address these issues—perhaps through a presi- 54 dential commission—will result in rights lost and, once gone, difficult to regain. Once privacy is lost, it will be difficult to restore. Once mind control is accomplished, it will be difficult to reestablish free thought. But with proper safeguards, the superior investigative techniques and more-effective treatment of offenders that new technology offers promise a safer, saner society for us all.   ✍

READING FOR INFORMATION

1. According to Stephens, is the erosion of constitutional rights a future threat or is it already occurring? Explain your answer.

2. Make a list of the new technological devices Stephens mentions that will be especially useful to police and corrections officers.

3. Explain why each of the devices you listed in question 2 has the potential to rob individuals of their rights.

4. What does Stephens mean when he says that the "[Supreme] Court . . . may eventually adopt the maxim . . . : If you have nothing to hide, you have nothing to fear"?

5. Some of Stephens's forecasts may seem exaggerated, yet others have already come to fruition. Describe a news story you have read, heard, or viewed that dealt with any of the technologies mentioned in Stephens's article. Did the news story present the technology in a positive or a negative light?

6. What does Stephens think Americans must do to strike a "proper balance between societal and individual rights"? Why will this be difficult to achieve?

READING FOR FORM, ORGANIZATION, AND EXPOSITORY FEATURES

1. How does Stephens use the introductory paragraphs to inform his readers of the direction he will take in the article?

2. Describe Stephens's organizational plan. As he takes up each constitutional right, how does he structure the discussion?

3. Explain the function of the questions Stephens asks throughout the article.

4. What is the function of the final four paragraphs?

READING FOR RHETORICAL CONCERNS

1. Who is Gene Stephens, and to whom is he addressing this article?

2. What is Stephens's rhetorical purpose? What message is he trying to get across to his readers?

3. How would you describe Stephens's tone?

WRITING ASSIGNMENTS

1. Write a three- to four-page essay in which you summarize Stephens's article for a group of readers who are unfamiliar with it and then give your reactions to his claim that "modern technology and the U.S. Constitution appear to be on a collision course."

2. Speculate about what our daily lives would be like if Stephens's predictions about the loss of privacy came true. Write your essay for an audience of your choice.

3. This assignment requires you to break into groups in preparation for a debate. The issue for the debate is whether or not the criminal justice system should be allowed to use modern technology even if that technology interferes with the public's constitutional rights. Divide the class into groups supporting the criminal justice system's rights and groups supporting the public's rights. Those on each side of the issue should draw up their arguments and present them in a thirty- to fifty-minute debate. After the debate, write a three- to four-page essay in which you react to the students who took the view opposite yours.

Privacy and Technology

Gary T. Marx

Gary T. Marx is a professor of sociology at the University of Colorado and is the author of Undercover: Police Surveillance in America.

PREREADING

While some commentators fear technologies that invade privacy, others point out their advantages. What arguments might be presented in favor of surveillance technologies? Freewrite for ten minutes in response to this question.

In the United States we recently celebrated the two-hundredth   1 anniversary of the Constitution, a document that extended liberty. Unfortunately, the bicentenary of another important document that restricted liberty has gone virtually unnoticed—the 1791 publication of Jeremy Bentham's *Panopticon; or, the Inspection House.*

Bentham offered a plan for the perfect prison, in which there would   2 be constant inspection of both prisoners and keepers. His ideas helped give rise to the maximum-security prison. Recent developments in telecommunications, along with other new means of collecting personal information, give Bentham's image of the panopticon great contemporary significance.

The stark situation of the maximum-security prison can help us un-   3 derstand societal developments. Many of the kinds of controls and information-gathering techniques found in prison specifically and the criminal justice system more broadly are diffusing into our culture. We may well be on the road to becoming a "maximum-security society." Such a society is transparent and porous. Information leakage has become rampant; indeed, it is hemorrhaging. Barriers and boundaries—be they distance, darkness, time, walls, windows, or even skin—that have been fundamental to our conceptions of privacy, liberty, and individuality are giving way.

Gary T. Marx, "Privacy and Technology." Reprinted from *Whole Earth Review* Winter 1991: 90–95; subscriptions to WER are $20 a year (4 issues) from PO Box 38, Sausalito, CA 94966, (415) 332-1716. Reprinted by permission of the author.

In such a society, actions, feelings, thoughts, pasts, and even futures   4
are made visible—often without the individual's will or knowledge. The
line between the public and the private is being obliterated; we are under
constant observation, everything goes on permanent record, and much
of what we say, do, and even feel may be known and recorded by others
whom we do not know—whether we will this or not and even whether
we know about it or not. Data in many different forms and coming from
widely separated geographical areas, organizations, and time periods can
be merged and analyzed easily.

As the technology becomes ever more penetrating and intrusive, it   5
becomes possible to gather information with laserlike specificity and
spongelike absorbency. If we visualize the information-gathering process
as a kind of fishing net, then the net's mesh has become finer and the
net wider.

Just as free association led to discovery of the unconscious, new   6
techniques reveal bits of reality that were previously hidden or contained
no informational clues. When their privacy is invaded, people are in a
sense turned inside out, and what was previously invisible and meaningless is made tangible and significant.

It is easy to get carried away with science-fiction fantasies about   7
things that might happen. But we need not wait for the widespread use
of videophones, paperless electronic safety-deposit boxes, wafer-thin
portable personal communications devices, satellite monitoring of individuals via implanted transmitters, or DNA fingerprinting and other
forms of biometric monitoring to note profound changes in the ease of
gathering personal information. Consider the following:

A college student secretly videotaped sexual encounters with a girl-   8
friend. After breaking up with her, he played the tape for members of his
fraternity. She learned of this and was victorious in a civil lawsuit, although no criminal statute had been violated.

Teachers in a school lounge were complaining about their principal,   9
when one jokingly said, "Be careful, the room might be bugged." Just
then they spotted a transmitter in the ceiling, which in fact had been hidden there by the principal.

During a toy manufacturer's television ad, a clown asked children   10
to place their telephone receivers in front of the TV. The studio then
broadcast dialing tones that called an 800 number, which resulted in kids
dialing the number. The 800 number called had automatic number identification service and recorded the children's phone numbers. The purpose was to create marketing lists.

A friend went on vacation. On returning he had only one message   11
on his answering machine. Shortly after his departure, a synthesized voice
"interviewer" had called to ask if he would consent to being interviewed.
Since he did not hang up, the system assumed he had agreed to be interviewed and proceeded to ask him a series of questions, pausing after
each to let him answer. The interview consumed the full length of the answering machine's tape. In several cases citizens have won lawsuits because during an emergency, an automated dialer had captured their line
and could not be disconnected, making it impossible to dial 911.

In Iowa, a woman overheard a neighbor's cordless-phone conver-   12
sation on her FM radio. She was suspicious of the call and informed police. They instructed her to continue to listen and to record his
conversations, all without a warrant, which she did for more than a year.
The Supreme Court has ruled that such eavesdropping is permissible.

A variety of personal communication devices, such as cordless and   13
cellular phones and room monitors for infants, can be intercepted easily (and often legally) by scanners, FM radios, and older TV sets with
UHF channels. Cordless phones using the same frequency may also pick
up wireless communication. Speakerphones may amplify communication. A conversant can never be sure who is listening. In a recent example President Bush was unaware that his off-the-cuff remarks were
overheard by a large audience listening in via a speakerphone.

Work monitoring has been taken to new heights, or depths, de-   14
pending on your point of view. Quantity of keystroke activity, number of
errors and corrections, speed of work, and time away from the computer can be measured. Programs such as CTRL and SPY permit remote secret monitoring of a target's personal computer use when his terminal is
attached to a larger system. A permanent record of the intercepted terminal's input and output can be made. There is also the possibility of
"initial screen repaint," which permits the watcher to see what was on the
target's screen before the SPY program was activated. The headsets used
by telephone reservationists can be converted to microphones to permit
remote monitoring of all office conversation by a supervisor many floors,
or even miles, away.

Home phones can be made "hot on the hook": An "infinity trans-   15
mitter," whether attached to a telephone or part of an answering machine,
converts the phone into a microphone. The individual who dials in (the
phone does not ring) is able to listen to what is being said in the room.

The U.S. commisioner of immigration has proposed a nationwide   16
computer system to verify the identities of all job applicants. An FBI

advisory board recently recommended putting the names of those sus-pected of (but not arrested for) crimes into a nationally accessible data-base, as well as the names of the friends and associates of known criminals. The director of the FBI rejected the proposal. Yet pressures to create such national databases are strong.

Marketing researchers are gathering ever more detailed data and 17 carrying out increasingly fine-grained analysis. For example, supermar-kets use the itemized bills made possible by bar coding to collect un-precedented information about consumers. Such information (when combined with the personal data consumers provide for check-cashing privileges) is easy to analyze and sell. There is often more to mailed pro-motional coupons than meets the eye—"invisible" personal data (name, address and other demographic information) may be in the bar code or elsewhere. The behavior of customers who agree to use "frequent shop-per cards" is monitored closely, and it will be possible to market direct-ly to households, using coupons to steer them toward products with higher profit margins. Consumer behavior also can be linked to expo-sure to specific ads seen on cable television. Persons on the same block watching the same channel may receive different versions of the ad being tested.

Lotus Corporation proposed a new product called "Marketplace," 18 to be available at retail software stores. Its database contained informa-tion such as name, address, age, gender, marital status, and estimates of income, lifestyle, and buying habits of 80 million households. The 120 million consumers contained in the database were not asked if they wished to have their personal transactional information treated as a com-modity; they would not have been compensated for its sale, nor could corrections easily have been made. The product was withdrawn after massive public protest.

It is easy to imagine how marketing lists might be misused. Pur- 19 chasers of pregnancy-testing kits may receive solicitations from pro- and anti-abortion groups, or from sellers of birth-control products and diaper services. Purchasers of weight-loss products or participants in diet pro-grams may be targeted for promotional offers from sellers of candy, cook-ies and ice cream, or, conversely, those whose purchases of the latter exceed the average may receive offers for weight-loss products and ser-vices. Subscribers to gay and lesbian publications may be targeted by re-ligious and therapeutic organizations, or face employment denials, harassment, and even blackmail. Frequent travelers and those with mul-tiple residences may receive solicitations from sellers of home-security products, and such lists would be a boon to sophisticated burglars. A list of tobacco users might be of interest to potential employers and insurance companies. A list of those with credit troubles and excessive indebtedness would certainly be of interest to promoters of scams that promise to help people obtain credit cards or get out of debt. A cynic might even hypothesize that such a list would be used by promoters of alcoholic beverages, sweepstakes advertising, and gambling junkets.

The previous examples raise a variety of troubling issues: injustice,   20
intrusion, denial of due process, absence of informed consent, deception, manipulation, errors, harassment, misuse of property, and lessened autonomy. But running through most of the examples is the central issue of privacy, as it relates to the control of personal information.

Given these examples and potential problems, it is not surprising   21
that in 1989 half the population thought new laws were needed to protect personal privacy. Yet in a country fascinated by technology, committed to free enterprise and freedom of speech, and concerned over declining productivity, AIDS, crime, drugs, and terror, there are also contrary voices.

A response to privacy concerns, expressed by some industry   22
spokespersons, columnists, and citizens, is simply, "So what? Why worry?" In their view, these technologies fill deeply felt needs. A host of arguments is offered to bolster their position: We increasingly live in a world of strangers, rather than in homogeneous rural communities where all residents know each other. The Supreme Court in the *Katz* decision has said that privacy was protected only when it could be reasonably expected. Technology changes and social expectations can't remain static. With more powerful technologies we can reasonably expect less and less, and hence privacy must become more restricted. After all, they say, most so-called privacy invasions are not illegal, and given the free market, one can buy technologies to prevent privacy invasion. For that matter, personal information is just a commodity, to be sold like any other. Companies have an obligation to stockholders to make money. Protecting privacy is expensive and can deter innovation.

Consumers, too, are demanding personalized and customized ser-   23
vices. Mass marketing is inefficient, and economic viability requires the "pinpoint" or "segmented" marketing that computer analysis now makes possible by using "point-of-sale" information. It is up to government to use whatever means it can to be more efficient and to find the guilty and protect the innocent.

Those unconcerned about privacy remind us that we live in an open 24 society that believes that visibility in government brings accountability. With respect to individuals, a valued legacy of the 1960s is personal openness and honesty. The only people who worry about privacy are those who have something to hide. Right?

It has been said that a civilization's nature can be seen in how it treats 25 its prisoners; it might also be seen in how it treats personal privacy.

Noting the social functions of privacy certainly is not to deny that 26 privacy taken to an extreme can be harmful. Nor should the right to privacy infringe on other important values, such as the public's right to know and the First Amendment guarantees.

Unlimited privacy is hardly an unlimited good. It can shield irre- 27 sponsible behavior—protecting child- and spouse-abusers, unsafe drivers, and money-launderers. Taken too far, it destroys community. Without appropriate limitations, it can trigger backlash, as citizens engage in unregulated self-help and direct action. The private subversion of public life carries dangers, as does the public intrusion into private life.

Contemporary information-extractive technologies can, of course, 28 protect liberty, privacy, and security. Without the incriminating tapes secretly recorded by President Nixon, Watergate would have remained a case of breaking and entering; without the Xerox machine, the Pentagon papers might never have reached the public; and without the backup computer records kept in NSC files that Oliver North thought he had erased, we would know far less about the Iran-Contra affair. Aerial surveillance can monitor compliance with pollution standards and help verify arms-control treaties. Tiny transmitters can help locate lost children or hikers caught in an avalanche. Devices that permit firefighters to see through smoke may save lives, and remote health monitors can protect the elderly living alone (in one type, an alarm is sent if a day goes by without the refrigerator being opened).

But elements of Greek tragedy are present: The technology's unique 29 power is also its tragic flaw. What serves can also destroy, absent increased public awareness and new public policies.

An important example of the kind of principles and policies needed 30 is the Code of Fair Information developed in 1973 for the U.S. Department of Health, Education, and Welfare. The code involves five principles:

- There must be no personal-data recordkeeping whose very existence is secret.

- There must be a way for a person to find out what information about him is in a record and how it is being used.
- There must be a way for a person to prevent information about himself that was obtained for one purpose from being used or made available for other purposes without his consent.
- There must be a way for a person to correct or amend a record of identifiable information about himself.
- Any organization creating, maintaining, using, or disseminating records of identifiable personal data must assure the reliability of the data for their intended use and must take precautions to prevent misuses of the data.

These ideas might be built upon. Ways to do so include establishing a principle of *minimization,* such that only information directly relevant to the task at hand is gathered; a principle of *restoration,* such that in a communications-monopoly context, those altering the privacy status quo should bear the cost of restoring it; a *safety net* or *equity* principle, such that a minimum threshold of privacy is available to all; a principle of *timeliness,* such that data are expected to be current and information that is no longer timely should be destroyed; a principle of *joint ownership of transactional data,* such that both parties to a data-creating transaction must agree to any subsequent use of the data and must share in any gains from its sale; a principle of *consistency,* such that broad ideals rather than specific characteristics of a technology determine privacy protection; and a principle of *redress,* such that those subject to privacy invasions have adequate mechanisms for discovering and being compensated for violations.

       It is not a foregone conclusion that developing technology will reduce the power of the individual relative to large organizations and the state, although the forces favoring this outcome tend to be stronger than those opposing it. Schools and religious organizations should deal more directly with the individual's rights with respect to means such as third-party records, computer dossiers, drug testing, and the polygraph. It is important that citizens react to invasions of privacy by questioning organizations, rejecting assertions such as "the computer says" or "that is the policy." Why is it the policy? What moral and legal assumptions underlie it? What alternatives are there? How were the data gathered? How are they protected and used?

       It is also important that the technology be demystified and that citizens not attribute to it nonexistent powers. There is a chilling danger in the myth of surveillance, and when technologies are revealed to be less powerful than authorities claim, legitimacy declines. There should be truth in communications policies, just as we have truth in advertising and loan policies. The potentials and limits of the technology must be understood.

There are a number of steps that individuals can take to protect privacy: 33

- Don't give out any more information than is necessary. You are legally required to give out your social-security number in only a few instances. Don't answer questions that seem irrelevant to the issue at hand. (For example, you may refuse to give your phone number when making a credit-card purchase, or family and income information when filling out a warranty card.)
- Don't say things over a cellular or cordless phone or baby monitor that you would mind having overheard by strangers.
- Ask your bank to sign an agreement that it will not release information about your accounts to anyone lacking legal authorization. It should state that in the event of legal authorization, the bank will notify you within two days.
- Obtain copies of your credit, health, and other records and check for accuracy and currency. You are entitled to know what is in many records and, if you dispute the information, to add your version. Credit records can be obtained from TRW, Equifax, and Trans Union. Medical records can be obtained from the Medical Information Bureau (a databank maintained by 800 insurance companies), Box 105, Essex Station, Boston, MA 02112.
- If you are refused credit, a job, a loan, or an apartment, ask why. There may be a file with inaccurate, incomplete, or irrelevant information.
- If you think you are being investigated by a federal agency or believe the agency has a file on you, submit a Freedom of Information Act request asking to see the file.
- If you think your telephone is tapped or a bug is being used and you find evidence of eavesdropping equipment, contact the police and an attorney. Make use of technologies that can protect your privacy, such as an answering machine.
- Realize that when you respond to telephone or door-to-door surveys, the information will go into a databank. The only federal survey that most persons are legally obliged to answer is the U.S. Census.
- When you purchase a product or service and file a warranty card or participate in rebate or inventive programs, your name may well be sold to a mailing-list company. Ask that it not be circulated.

The Privacy Protection Act of 1974 refers primarily to actions at the federal level and tends to exclude state, local, and private-sector activities. A major failing of the Privacy Act is weak-to-nonexistent discovery and enforcement mechanisms. It is unrealistic to expect most individuals to discover violations, given the hidden and complex nature of much data collection and exchange. The means of locating violations and enforcing standards needs to be strengthened. However, the Office of Management and Budget has given this task a low priority. 34

The Fair Credit Reporting Act offers no recovery if a consumer is hurt by a technically accurate but misleading report. It is important that there be provision for injunctive relief for damages for persons who suffer intangible harm as a result of privacy invasion and that incentives be created that will increase compliance with the legislation we do have. 35

Unlike many European countries, the United States does not attempt to regulate data collection. Most protections pertain to how data are treated once they are collected. The First Amendment and concern over creating another regulatory bureaucracy partly explain this situation, but as a consequence, citizens are on their own in discovering and bringing action when their rights are violated and data collectors are given a free hand in gathering information. Given the low visibility of many violations and citizens' lack of knowledge of their rights, laws here are underenforced. 36

A variety of new federal, state, and local initiatives are needed. Among the promising federal legislation introduced, though not passed, as of 1990 are a bill to extend the protections of the Fair Credit Reporting Act to tenant-screening services; a bill to require a periodic audible beep on phones being monitored; a bill to extend the warrant protection of aural surveillance to video; and a bill to eliminate single-party-consent eavesdropping (a major loophole) so that all parties to a recorded conversation would have to agree. 37

While the Constitution has implications for privacy in a number of places (in the First, Third, Fourth, Fifth, and Fourteenth Amendments, among others), there is no explicit amendment guaranteeing privacy. States such as California and Pennsylvania have such protections. The United States might emulate countries such as Switzerland, Sweden, Italy, and Portugal by drafting a constitutional amendment protecting privacy. The challenge is to draft it in a general enough way to protect what needs to be protected, without creating a statute whose vagueness shelters things the public interest requires to be revealed. That such a law might be largely symbolic would not detract from its significance. 38

With respect to information-gathering technology, we are now in   39
the twilight zone that Justice William O. Douglas wrote about in arguing
that the protection of our basic values is not self-executing:

> As nightfall does not come at once, neither does oppression. In both in-
> stances, there is a twilight when everything remains seemingly unchanged.
> And it is in such twilight that we all must be most aware of change in the
> air—however slight—lest we become unwitting victims of the darkness.
> One could as well argue that we are in a sunrise zone, and that we must
> be aware of change in the air in order to insure that we all profit from the
> sunshine. But for this to happen the technology must be bounded by in-
> creased public awareness, responsible corporate and government behav-
> ior, and new laws and policies.   🖎

READING FOR INFORMATION

1. What examples does Marx provide of workplace monitoring?
2. What examples does Marx provide of invasive technologies connected with
   marketing?
3. What examples does Marx provide of technologies that involve monitoring of telecommunications?
4. Paraphrase the argument in favor of invasive technologies that is presented
   in paragraph 22.
5. Paraphrase Marx's suggestions for privacy safeguards in paragraph 33.
6. What types of technological monitoring of citizens would Marx conceivably support?

READING FOR FORM, ORGANIZATION, AND EXPOSITORY FEATURES

1. Explain how Marx uses the "perfect prison" as a metaphor.
2. Describe the transition that takes place between paragraphs 24 and 25.
3. Marx presents both pessimistic and optimistic views concerning new surveillance technologies. How does he incorporate both into the structure
   of his argument?
4. Describe Marx's closing strategy.

READING FOR RHETORICAL CONCERNS

1. What sentence (or sentences) best presents Marx's viewpoint?
2. Is Marx decisive on the issue he is addressing?
3. Describe Marx's article as an argument. What evidence supports his
   assertions?

4. Who is Marx's intended audience? Do you include yourself in that intended audience? Explain your answers.

WRITING ASSIGNMENTS

1. Write a three- to four-page essay in response to the following paragraph from Marx's essay:

   Unlimited privacy is hardly an unlimited good. It can shield irresponsible behavior—protecting child- and spouse-abusers, unsafe drivers, and money-launderers. Taken too far, it destroys community. Without appropriate limitations, it can trigger backlash, as citizens engage in unregulated self-help and direct action. The private subversion of public life carries dangers, as does the public intrusion into private life.

2. Use Marx's article as the basis for a four- to five-page essay that distinguishes invasive technologies that you believe are justifiable from those that you believe violate individual rights.

3. In a three- to four-page essay, respond to Marx's statement in paragraph 24 that "The only people who worry about privacy are those who have something to hide. Right?"

Invasion of Privacy

Joshua Quittner

Joshua Quittner, a journalist, is a frequent contributor to Newsday *and* Wired. *Among the books he has co-authored with Michelle Slatalla are* Masters of Deception: The Gang That Ruled Cyberspace, Flame War, *and* Speeding the Net: The Inside Story of Netscape, How It Challenged Microsoft and Changed the World.

PREREADING

Based on your own experience and that of your family and friends, are you confident in the safety of credit cards, ATM cards, phone cards, and other electronic records that control "private" business? Is the convenience of these computerized transactions worth any potential for loss or invasion of privacy?

Quittner, Joshua. "Invasion of Privacy." *Time* 25 Aug. 1997: 28+. © 1997 Time Inc. Reprinted by permission.

For the longest time, I couldn't get worked up about privacy: my 1
right to it; how it's dying; how we're headed for an even more
wired, underregulated, overintrusive, privacy-deprived planet.

I mean, I probably have more reason to think about this stuff than 2
the average John Q. All Too Public. A few years ago, for instance, after
I applied for a credit card at a consumer-electronics store, somebody
got hold of my name and vital numbers and used them to get a duplicate card. That somebody ran up a $3,000 bill, but the nice lady from the
fraud division of the credit-card company took care of it with steely digital dispatch. (I filed a short report over the phone. I never lost a cent.
The end.)

I also hang out online a lot, and now and then on the Net someone 3
will impersonate me, spoofing my E-mail address or posting stupid stuff
to bulletin boards or behaving in a frightfully un-Quittner-like manner in
chat parlors from here to Bianca's Smut Shack. It's annoying, I suppose.
But in the end, the faux Quittners get bored and disappear. My reputation, such as it is, survives.

I should also point out that as news director for Pathfinder, Time 4
Inc.'s mega info mall, and a guy who makes his living on the Web, I know
better than most people that we're hurtling toward an even more intrusive world. We're all being watched by computers whenever we visit
Websites; by the mere act of "browsing" (it sounds so passive!) we're
going public in a way that was unimaginable a decade ago. I know this because I'm a watcher too. When people come to my Website, without ever
knowing their names, I can peer over their shoulders, recording what
they look at, timing how long they stay on a particular page, following
them around Pathfinder's sprawling offerings.

None of this would bother me in the least, I suspect, if a few years 5
ago, my phone, like Marley's ghost, hadn't given me a glimpse of the
nightmares to come. On Thanksgiving weekend in 1995, someone (presumably a critic of a book my wife and I had just written about computer hackers) forwarded my home telephone number to an out-of-state
answering machine, where unsuspecting callers trying to reach me heard
a male voice identify himself as me and say some extremely rude things.
Then, with typical hacker aplomb, the prankster asked people to leave
their messages (which to my surprise many callers, including my mother, did). This went on for several days until my wife and I figured out
that something was wrong ("Hey . . . why hasn't the phone rung since
Wednesday?") and got our phone service restored.

It seemed funny at first, and it gave us a swell story to tell on our   6
book tour. But the interloper who seized our telephone line continued to
hit us even after the tour ended. And hit us again and again for the next
six months. The phone company seemed powerless. Its security folks
moved us to one unlisted number after another, half a dozen times. They
put special PIN codes in place. They put traces on the line. But the trou-
blemaker kept breaking through.

If our hacker had been truly evil and omnipotent as only fictional   7
movie hackers are, there would probably have been even worse ways he
could have threatened my privacy. He could have sabotaged my credit
rating. He could have eavesdropped on my telephone conversations or
siphoned off my E-mail. He could have called in my mortgage, discon-
tinued my health insurance or obliterated my Social Security number.
Like Sandra Bullock in *The Net*, I could have been a digital untouchable,
wandering the planet without a connection to the rest of humanity. (Although if I didn't have to pay back school loans, it might be worth it. Just
a thought.)

Still, I remember feeling violated at the time and as powerless as   8
a minnow in a flash flood. Someone was invading my private space—
my family's private space—and there was nothing I or the authorities
could do. It was as close to a technological epiphany as I have ever
been. And as I watched my personal digital hell unfold, it struck me
that our privacy—mine and yours—has already disappeared, not in one
Big Brotherly blitzkrieg but in Little Brotherly moments, bit by bit.

Losing control of your telephone, of course, is the least of it. After   9
all, most of us voluntarily give out our phone number and address when
we allow ourselves to be listed in the White Pages. Most of us go a lot further than that. We register our whereabouts whenever we put a bank
card in an ATM machine or drive through an E-Z Pass lane on the highway. We submit to being photographed every day—20 times a day on
average if you live or work in New York City—by surveillance cameras.
We make public our interests and our purchasing habits every time we
shop by mail order or visit a commercial Website.

I don't know about you, but I do all this willingly because I appre-   10
ciate what I get in return: the security of a safe parking lot, the convenience of cash when I need it, the improved service of mail-order houses
that know me well enough to send me catalogs of stuff that interests me.
And while I know we're supposed to feel just awful about giving up our
vaunted privacy, I suspect (based on what the pollsters say) that you're
as ambivalent about it as I am.

Popular culture shines its klieg lights on the most intimate corners 11
of our lives, and most of us play right along. If all we really wanted was
to be left alone, explain the lasting popularity of Oprah and Sally and
Ricki tell-all TV. Memoirs top the best-seller lists, with books about incest and insanity and illness leading the way. Perfect strangers at cock-
tail parties tell me the most disturbing details of their abusive upbringings.
Why?

"It's a very schizophrenic time," says Sherry Turkle, professor of so- 12
ciology at the Massachusetts Institute of Technology, who writes books
about how computers and online communication are transforming society. She believes our culture is undergoing a kind of mass identity crisis,
trying to hang on to a sense of privacy and intimacy in a global village of
tens of millions. "We have very unstable notions about the boundaries of
the individual," she says.

If things seem crazy now, think how much crazier they will be when 13
everybody is as wired as I am. We're in the midst of a global intercon-
nection that is happening much faster than electrification did a century
ago and is expected to have consequences at least as profound. What
would happen if all the information stored on the world's computers were
accessible via the Internet to anyone? Who would own it? Who would
control it? Who would protect it from abuse?

Small-scale privacy atrocities take place every day. Ask Dr. Denise 14
Nagel, executive director of the National Coalition for Patient Rights,
about medical privacy, for example, and she rattles off a list of abuses
that would make Big Brother blush. She talks about how two years ago,
a convicted child rapist working as a technician in a Boston hospital rif-
fled through 1,000 computerized records looking for potential victims
(and was caught when the father of a nine-year-old girl used caller ID to
trace the call back to the hospital). How a banker on Maryland's state
health commission pulled up a list of cancer patients, cross-checked it
against the names of his bank's customers and revoked the loans of the
matches. How Sara Lee bakeries planned to collaborate with Lovelace
Health Systems, a subsidiary of Cigna, to match employee health records
with work-performance reports to find workers who might benefit from
antidepressants.

Not to pick on Sara Lee. At least a third of all FORTUNE 500 com- 15
panies regularly review health information before making hiring decisions. And that's nothing compared with what awaits us when employers
and insurance companies start testing our DNA for possible imperfec-
tions. Farfetched? More than 200 subjects in a case study published last

January in the journal *Science and Engineering Ethics* reported that they had been discriminated against as a result of genetic testing. None of them were actually sick, but DNA analysis suggested that they might become sick someday. "The technology is getting ahead of our ethics," says Nagel, and the Clinton Administration clearly agrees. It is about to propose a federal law that would protect medical and health-insurance records from such abuses.

But how did we arrive at this point, where so much about what we do and own and think is an open book? 16

It all started in the 1950s, when, in order to administer Social Security funds, the U.S. government began entering records on big mainframe computers, using nine-digit identification numbers as data points. Then, even more than today, the citizenry instinctively loathed the computer and its injunctions against folding, spindling and mutilating. We were not numbers! We were human beings! These fears came to a head in the late 1960s, recalls Alan Westin, a retired Columbia University professor who publishes a quarterly report *Privacy and American Business.* "The techniques of intrusion and data surveillance had overcome the weak law and social mores that we had built up in the pre–World War II era," says Westin. 17

The public rebelled, and Congress took up the question of how much the government and private companies should be permitted to know about us. A privacy bill of rights was drafted. "What we did," says Westin, "was to basically redefine what we meant by 'reasonable expectations of privacy'"—a guarantee, by the way, that comes from the Supreme Court and not from any constitutional "right to privacy." 18

The result was a flurry of new legislation that clarified and defined consumer and citizen rights. The first Fair Credit Reporting Act, passed in 1970, overhauled what had once been a secret, unregulated industry with no provisions for due process. The new law gave consumers the right to know what was in their credit files and to demand corrections. Other financial and health privacy acts followed, although to this day no federal law protects the confidentiality of medical records. 19

As Westin sees it, the public and private sectors took two very different approaches. Congress passed legislation requiring that the government tell citizens what records it keeps on them while insisting that the information itself not be released unless required by law. The private sector responded by letting each industry—credit-card companies, banking, insurance, marketing, advertising—create its own guidelines. 20

That approach worked—to a point. And that point came when 21 mainframes started giving way to desktop computers. In the old days, information stored in government databases was relatively inaccessible. Now, however, with PCs on every desktop linked to office networks and then to the Internet, data that were once carefully hidden may be only a few keystrokes away.

Suddenly someone could run motor-vehicle-registration records 22 against voting registrations to find 6-ft.-tall Republicans who were arrested during the past year for drunk driving—and who own a gun. The genie was not only out of the bottle, he was also peering into everyone's bedroom window. (Except the windows of the very rich, who can afford to screen themselves.)

"Most people would be astounded to know what's out there," says 23 Carole Lane, author of *Naked in Cyberspace: How to Find Personal Information Online.* "In a few hours, sitting at my computer, beginning with no more than your name and address, I can find out what you do for a living, the names and ages of your spouse and children, what kind of car you drive, the value of your house and how much taxes you pay on it."

Lane is a member of a new trade: paid Internet searcher, which al- 24 ready has its own professional group, the Association of Independent Information Professionals. Her career has given her a fresh appreciation for what's going on. "Real privacy as we've known it," she says, "is fleeting."

Now, there are plenty of things you could do to protect yourself. You 25 could get an unlisted telephone number, as I was forced to do. You could cut up your credit card and pay cash for everything. You could rip your E-Z Pass off the windshield and use quarters at tolls. You could refuse to divulge your Social Security number except for Social Security purposes, which is all that the law requires. You'd be surprised how often you're asked to provide it by people who have no right to see it.

That might make your life a bit less comfortable, of course. As in the 26 case of Bob Bruen, who went into a barbershop in Watertown, Mass., recently. "When I was asked for my phone number, I refused to give them the last four digits," Bruen says. "I was also asked for my name, and I also refused. The girl at the counter called her supervisor, who told me I could not get a haircut in their shop." Why? The barbershop uses a computer to record all transactions. Bruen went elsewhere to get his locks shorn.

But can we do that all the time? Only the Unabomber would seri- 27 ously suggest that we cut all ties to the wired world. The computer and its spreading networks convey status and bring opportunity. They empower us. They allow an information economy to thrive and grow. They make life easier. Hence the dilemma.

The real problem, says Kevin Kelly, executive editor of *Wired* mag- 28 azine, is that although we say we value our privacy, what we really want is something very different: "We think that privacy is about information, but it's not—it's about relationships." The way Kelly sees it, there was no privacy in the traditional village or small town; everyone knew everyone else's secrets. And that was comfortable. I knew about you, and you knew about me. "There was a symmetry to the knowledge," he says. "What's gone out of whack is we don't know who knows about us anymore. Privacy has become asymmetrical."

The trick, says Kelly, is to restore that balance. And not surpris- 29 ingly, he and others point out that what technology has taken, technology can restore. Take the problem of "magic cookies"—those little bits of code most Websites use to track visitors. We set up a system at Pathfinder in which, when you visit our site, we drop a cookie into the basket of your browser that tags you like a rare bird. We use that cookie in place of your name, which, needless to say, we never know. If you look up a weather report by keying in a ZIP code, we note that (it tells us where you live or maybe where you wish you lived). We'll mark down whether you look up stock quotes (though we draw the line at capturing the symbols of the specific stocks you follow). If you come to the *Netly News,* we'll record your interest in technology. Then, the next time you visit, we might serve up an ad for a modem or an online brokerage firm or a restaurant in Akron, Ohio, depending on what we've managed to glean about you.

Some people find the whole process offensive. "Cookies represent 30 a way of watching consumers without their consent, and that is a fairly frightening phenomenon," says Nick Grouf, CEO of Firefly, a Boston company that makes software offering an alternative approach to profiling, known as "intelligent agents."

Privacy advocates like Grouf—as well as the two companies that 31 control the online browser market, Microsoft and Netscape—say the answer to the cookie monster is something they call the Open Profiling Standard. The idea is to allow the computer user to create an electronic "passport" that identifies him to online marketers without revealing his name. The user tailors the passport to his own interests, so if he is passionate about fly-fishing and is cruising through L.L. Bean's Website, the passport will steer the electronic-catalog copy toward fishing gear instead of, say, Rollerblades.

The advantage to computer users is that they can decide how much ³²
information they want to reveal while limiting their exposure to intrusive marketing techniques. The advantage to Website entrepreneurs is
that they learn about their customers' tastes without intruding on their
privacy.

Many online consumers, however, are skittish about leaving any ³³
footprints in cyberspace. Susan Scott, executive director of TRUSTe, a
firm based in Palo Alto, Calif., that rates Websites according to the level
of privacy they afford, says a survey her company sponsored found that
41% of respondents would quit a Web page rather than reveal any personal information about themselves. About 25% said when they do volunteer information, they lie. "The users want access, but they don't want
to get correspondence back," she says.

But worse things may already be happening to their E-mail. Many ³⁴
office electronic-mail systems warn users that the employer reserves the
right to monitor their E-mail. In October software will be available to
Wall Street firms that can automatically monitor correspondence between brokers and clients through an artificial-intelligence program that
scans for evidence of securities violations.

"Technology has outpaced law," says Marc Rotenberg, director of ³⁵
the Washington-based Electronic Privacy Information Center. Rotenberg advocates protecting the privacy of E-mail by encrypting it with secret codes so powerful that even the National Security Agency's
supercomputers would have a hard time cracking it. Such codes are legal
within the U.S. but cannot be used abroad—where terrorists might use
them to protect their secrets—without violating U.S. export laws. The
battle between the Clinton Administration and the computer industry
over encryption export policy has been raging for six years without resolution, a situation that is making it hard to do business on the Net and is
clearly starting to fray some nerves. "The future is in electronic commerce," says Ira Magaziner, Clinton's point man on Net issues. All that's
holding it up is "this privacy thing."

Rotenberg thinks we need a new government agency—a privacy ³⁶
agency—to sort out the issues. "We need new legal protections," he says,
"to enforce the privacy act, to keep federal agencies in line, to act as a
spokesperson for the Federal Government and to act on behalf of privacy interests."

Wired's Kelly disagrees. "A federal privacy agency would be disas- ³⁷
trous! The answer to the whole privacy question is more knowledge," he
says. "More knowledge about who's watching you. More knowledge about

342 Technology and Civil Liberties

the information that flows between us—particularly the meta information about who knows what and where it's going."

I'm with Kelly. The only guys who insist on perfect privacy are hermits like the Unabomber. I don't want to be cut off from the world. I have nothing to hide. I just want some measure of control over what people know about me. I want to have my magic cookie and eat it too. 🐟 38

READING FOR INFORMATION

1. According to Quittner, what are some (name at least five) of the ways described in the article that we regularly surrender our privacy?

2. What examples does Quittner provide of potentially dangerous invasions of privacy?

3. What evidence does Quittner give to support his assertion that Americans don't really want to be left alone?

4. Why did some Americans react negatively to the introduction of the Social Security number in the 1950s?

5. How, according to Quittner, has the shift from large mainframe computers to desktop PCs affected privacy?

6. In response to the computer revolution, what steps did the federal government take to protect citizens' privacy? What steps did the private sector take?

7. According to Carole Lane, what information can you locate on the Web about a given individual, beginning with only a name and address?

8. What are "magic cookies"?

9. Explain the controversy over encryption technology.

READING FOR FORM, ORGANIZATION, AND EXPOSITORY FEATURES

1. Quittner begins with a series of anecdotes. How do these anecdotes work together as an opening to his piece?

2. Based on the first ten paragraphs of the article, how would you characterize Quittner's writing style? Is this style appropriate, given the nature of the piece he is writing?

3. Describe Quittner's organizational plan.

READING FOR RHETORICAL CONCERNS

1. What in the article indicates Quittner's intended audience?

2. Identify the two sections of the essay in which Quittner states his own opinion.

3. Paraphrase Quittner's proposal for balancing privacy concerns and access to technology.
4. In what way is Quittner's article confessional?

WRITING ASSIGNMENTS

1. Write a four-page essay that objectively describes how modern technology has eroded personal privacy. Draw on Quittner's article for examples.
2. In paragraph 10, Quittner asserts that

> . . . I do all this [surrender privacy] willingly because I appreciate what I get in return: the security of a safe parking lot, the convenience of cash when I need it, the improved service of mail-order houses that know me well enough to send me catalogs of stuff that interests me . . . while I know we're supposed to feel just awful about giving up our vaunted privacy, I suspect (based on what the pollsters say) that you're just as ambivalent about it as I am.

In a four-page essay, explain Quittner's assertion and respond to it based on your own views.

3. Do you think Quittner's views are consistent with constitutional guarantees of civil liberties? Defend your view in a four- to five-page essay.

Nowhere to Hide: Lack of Privacy Is the Ultimate Equalizer

Charles Platt

Charles Platt is the author of forty books, including The Silicon Man, *and of many magazine articles for publications such as* Omni *and* Wired. *He teaches computer graphics and is vice-president of CryoCare, a cryonics organization.*

PREREADING

Platt's title indicates that lack of privacy might have advantages. Speculate on what those advantages might be in ten minutes of freewriting.

Charles Platt, "Nowhere to Hide: Lack of Privacy Is the Ultimate Equalizer," *Wired* Nov. 1993: 112. Reprinted by permission of the author.

No one likes the idea of being under surveillance, and computer privacy is a big, angry issue. But how many people have really thought the privacy question through to its conclusion? Suppose that current trends continue to the point that everyone is without privacy—institutions as well as individuals. Who loses, and who gains? 1

Some cultures have very little need for privacy. The Japanese, for instance, don't even have a word for it—domestic privacy that is; the simple need to hide some of your home life from the neighbors. Theoretically, we're more vulnerable on this level than we used to be, now that surveillance gadgets are more widely available. But most people don't seem to feel threatened by this—most don't appear to be interested in spying on their neighbors. Why should they be? 2

The macro level of privacy is the real issue. When I want my communications to be private, I'm not hiding from the neighbors, I'm concerned that large institutions can use personal information about me to interfere with my life. Now that credit ratings, tax figures, purchasing profiles, and medical records are accessible online and federal agencies are ready and willing to seize cars, boats, and homes in tax cases or under the RICO statute, there's some reason to feel insecure. 3

On the other hand, this is only one side of the story. In surveillance, as in other fields, the computer revolution is a weapon that can be used both ways. It can help the individual as well as the state. 4

We're just beginning to see such cases. Two cops in Los Angeles faced prison terms because of a home video that invaded their "privacy" and showed them beating a suspect. President Clinton's election campaign was seriously threatened when an ex-lover made tapes of their telephone conversations. A young student blocked the path of a tank in Tiananmen Square and the results of a dictator's actions were instantly observed all over the world—a powerful deterrent to despotism. 5

Right now, I can buy a KGB-surplus night scope, a microtransmitter, or a videocamera that's half the size of a pack of cigarettes. These items are advertised in a mail order catalogue that was delivered to my door. Maybe fifteen years from now, using molecular electronics, the videocamera will be pea-sized, only available for purchase by any citizens' action group. Will politicians feel safe enough to take kickbacks when surveillance is as easy as this? Will large corporations, or police departments, be so ready to flaunt the law? 6

Of course, there'll be electronic countermeasures. But those countermeasures, too, will be available to citizens, as is the case with data encryption. The government doesn't want us to have the same info-gathering 7 capabilities as the National Security Agency, but it's too late. The encryption software has been widely distributed, and it's hard to control technology after it escapes into private hands.

Personally, I look forward to a time when no one will be exempt 8 from surveillance. So long as corporations, governments, and citizens are equally vulnerable, lack of privacy will be the ultimate equalizer. It will also drastically reduce crime—especially street crime—when there's a constant possibility of electronic evidence turning up in court.

On a domestic level, I doubt that this will affect us much, one way 9 or the other. If my neighbors don't bother to bug my phone right now, why should they bother to video my apartment in the future?

On a macro level, the impact will be significant; and I believe most 10 of it will be positive.   ✍

READING FOR INFORMATION

1. What distinction does Platt make between two types of privacy in paragraphs 2 and 3?
2. What is the RICO statute that Platt refers to in paragraph 3?
3. What examples does Platt provide of surveillance devices that private individuals might use against government officials or agencies?
4. Why does Platt want surveillance technology to become even more advanced?
5. Why doesn't Platt think that advanced surveillance devices will significantly affect his personal level of privacy?

READING FOR FORM, ORGANIZATION, AND EXPOSITORY FEATURES

1. Describe Platt's opening strategy.
2. Locate Platt's thesis statement.
3. Why do you think Platt uses a single sentence as a closing paragraph?

READING FOR RHETORICAL CONCERNS

1. Characterize Platt's attitude toward the government.
2. Who is Platt's intended audience? What assumptions does he make about his audience?
3. How do you think police officers would respond to Platt's article?

WRITING ASSIGNMENTS

1. Write a three- to four-page essay of response to Platt's assertion that "so long as corporations, governments, and citizens are equally vulnerable, lack of privacy will be the ultimate equalizer."

2. Draw on Platt's article to write a three- to four-page essay that analyzes the advantages and disadvantages of preserving personal privacy.

3. Do you believe that private citizens should have unlimited access to surveillance technology? Write a three- to four-page essay in response to this question.

Issues Regarding DNA Testing

U.S. Department of Justice

PREREADING

In ten minutes of freewriting, describe your prior knowledge of and opinions about DNA fingerprinting.

Despite its potential, DNA testing is by no means without controversy. Indeed, DNA testing raises difficult questions that generally can be classified in terms of four issues: invasiveness, reliability, establishment and use of databanks and dissemination.   1

DNA testing inevitably requires taking blood or other bodily fluids or tissue from a subject—often without the subject's consent. Is the very process of DNA testing a violation of privacy? Does it violate constitutional (Fourth or Fifth Amendment) rights? Does it make a difference if samples are collected for purposes of a databank? At a minimum, is the process inconsistent with public policy principles?   2

DNA testing involves a highly sophisticated laboratory process which was considered beyond the state-of-the-art even a few years ago. Is the process reliable? What are the problems with admitting the results of DNA tests as evidence in court? Are there circumstances that present special risks?   3

. . .

Excerpted from U.S. Department of Justice, *Forensic DNA Analysis: Issues* (Washington, D.C.: U.S. Department of Justice, 1991). Copyright © SEARCH Group, Inc. 1991.

INVASIVENESS

Forensic DNA testing—either to match a suspect's DNA pattern   4
against that of a crime scene specimen or for purposes of building
a DNA databank—involves the taking of body fluids containing nucleus cells (customarily a blood specimen or a saliva sample) or a tissue sample (customarily hair follicle samples). If the subject does not
consent to this process, does the compulsory taking of the specimen
raise privacy or other legal or policy considerations?

Obtaining DNA Specimens from a Suspect

There are several legal considerations with respect to obtaining DNA   5
specimens from a suspect. The Fourth Amendment to the Constitution
is one of these.[1] The Supreme Court has held that the compulsory withdrawal of blood constitutes a search within the meaning of the Fourth
Amendment.[2] Accordingly, law enforcement officials may be required
to obtain a search warrant prior to obtaining a blood sample. In order to
obtain a search warrant, law enforcement officials are required to show
that they have probable cause to believe that the suspect has committed
a crime.

A few courts require a showing of more than just probable cause.   6
The New York State Court of Appeals, for example, held that in order to
permit the taking of samples of blood, hair or other human materials,
law enforcement officials must establish: "(1) probable cause to believe
the suspect has committed the crime, (2) a clear indication that relevant
material evidence will be found and (3) the method used to secure it is
safe and reliable."[3]

A New York county court recently applied the court of appeals'   7
standard in upholding the compulsory taking of a blood specimen from
an individual suspected of raping and murdering a mentally-retarded
woman. In *People v. Wesley*, DNA from the victim had already been
matched with DNA retrieved from blood stains on the suspect's clothing.
The prosecution sought a warrant to test the suspect's DNA to further

---

[1] The Fourth Amendment states: "The right of the people to be secure in their persons, houses, papers, and effects against unreasonable searches and seizures shall not be violated, and no warrants
shall issue, but upon probable cause, supported by oath or affirmation, and particularly describing
the place to be searched, and the persons or things to be seized." *Constitution,* amend. IV.

[2] *Schmerber v. State of California,* 384 U.S. 757, 764–65 (1996).

[3] *In re Abe A.,* 56 N.Y.2d 288, 291, 437 N.E.2d 265, 452 N.Y.S.2d 6 (1982); see also *People v. Wesley,* 533 N.Y.S.2d 643, 659 (Albany Co. Ct. 1988).

verify that the blood on his clothing was not his own blood. The court held that a DNA specimen, in the form of a blood sample, could be extracted in a medically safe way and that such a process would not be "unduly intrusive."[4]

Literally dozens of courts have held that the taking of blood or urine samples (generally in the context of an investigation for drug or alcohol use) is intrusive and a search within the meaning of the Fourth Amendment.[5] It has also been held that breath tests are searches within the meaning of the Fourth Amendment.[6] It is likely that a court would find that the taking of other types of specimens suitable for DNA testing, such as saliva samples or body hair, is also intrusive in the sense that the non-consensual taking constitutes a search.

The question of intrusiveness is important because were a court to find that the taking of a DNA specimen were not intrusive, a search would not occur and the State could require the taking of the DNA specimen on less than probable cause.

"Dragnet" Testing Impermissible. Taken to its logical extreme, police could use "dragnet" techniques to obtain blood samples from literally thousands of *potential* suspects to test against DNA prints derived from fluid or tissue samples taken from crime scenes. This is precisely what the police did . . . in three villages in Leicester County, England. In 1983, a teenage girl from the village of Narborough was raped and murdered. Three years later, another young woman from the adjoining village of Enderby suffered the same fate. DNA testing of semen stains indicated that the same individual committed both crimes.

After exhausting all leads and suspects, the police did something remarkable. They "asked" males born between 1953 and 1970 who lived in one of three adjoining villages—Narborough, Enderby and Littlethorpe—to voluntarily provide blood samples. Those samples that matched the blood type found at the crime scene were then subjected to DNA analysis.[7] No match was found. Later, however, a man confessed that he had provided a blood sample for a fellow worker, Colin Pitchfork of Littlethorpe. When Mr. Pitchfork's real blood was tested, a match was made.[8]

[4] 533 N.Y.S.2d at 659.

[5] See *Railway Labor Executives' Association v. Burnley,* 839 F.2d 575, 580 (9th Cir. 1988) and the cases cited therein.

[6] See, e.g., *Burnett v. Municipality of Anchorage,* 800 F.2d 1447, 1449 (9th Cir. 1986).

[7] Tyler Marshall, "Genetic Evidence Aids Crime Probe," *The Sacramento Bee,* March 12, 1987, p. A26.

[8] Seton, "Life for Sex Killer," note 17. See also, Clare M. Tande, "DNA Typing: A New Investigatory Tool," *Duke Law Journal* (April 1989).

Dragnet DNA testing of the type used in the Leicester County 12
case (putting aside for the moment that the subjects theoretically provided blood samples on a voluntary basis) would be barred in the
United States under virtually any reading of the Fourth Amendment.
Nevertheless, in recent years courts and legislatures have relaxed the
probable cause standard as it applies to searches and detentions that
are conducted for purposes of identification.

· · ·

Issues Associated with DNA Testing

Thirty years ago legal scholars and policymakers debated whether it was 13
ever legal or appropriate to compel an individual to submit to a blood
test. Today there continues to be debate over the circumstances in which
it is appropriate for the government to require a blood test, but there is
virtually no debate over the legality or wisdom of imposing a blood test
requirement in at least some circumstances.

In 1957, in *Breithaupt v. Abrams,* the Supreme Court grappled 14
with whether the taking of blood from an unconscious driver of a motor
vehicle was ever justified, or rather, was a "brutal" and "offensive" act
forbidden by the Constitution.[9] Although the *Breithaupt* Court eventually upheld the constitutionality of a blood test, Chief Justice Warren,
joined by Justices Black and Douglas, vigorously dissented. They
warned that such conduct was unlawful and violated American notions
of privacy and liberty. Chief Justice Warren wrote that due process
means that:

> law-enforcement officers in their efforts to obtain evidence from persons
> suspected of a crime must stop short of bruising the body, breaking skin,
> puncturing tissue or extracting body fluids, whether they contemplate
> doing it by force or by stealth.[10]

Blood Tests for Suspects or Offenders. Today such concerns are sel- 15
dom voiced. Blood testing has proven to be a useful tool in a deadly war
against crime, drugs and alcohol. As a result, compulsory blood testing for
DNA purposes is unlikely to provoke much criticism, particularly if the
subjects of the testing are limited to criminal suspects or offenders. Indeed, most of the DNA databank statutes prohibit the retention of DNA

---

[9] 352 U.S. at 432 (1957).
[10] Ibid., 442.

specimen or identification information from suspects in ongoing investigations and, instead, limit the databank to information obtained from
certain categories of convicted felons.[11]

Offenders and suspects are already subject to fingerprinting and   16
photographing requirements. Indeed, offenders are subject to a far more
serious imposition on their liberty and privacy interests in the form of
incarceration. As a practical matter, the public, the media and legislators
are likely to feel that such individuals have effectively waived their privacy interest in avoiding the compulsory taking of fingerprints, photographs, DNA specimens or other physiological characteristics that can
be used for identification. The public concerns with respect to compulsory DNA testing for these types of suspects or offenders are likely
to be muted.

. . .

RELIABILITY

Scientists Claim Reliability

There is broad consensus among scientists that DNA testing can produce   17
a reliable identification, however, the mathematical probabilities are debated. Some sources claim that the chances of two individuals having the
same DNA pattern is 100 million to one.[12] A group of British researchers
went further and argued that there is no more than one in 30 billion
chances of two individuals having the same DNA pattern—although
this number has been disputed.[13]

Whatever the exact number, all researchers agree that the theoret-   18
ical possibility of two individuals having the same DNA pattern (other
than identical twins) is exceedingly remote. A recent study of the accuracy and reliability of DNA testing by a team of Yale University geneti-
cists concluded that the tests, when properly conducted and read, provide
an accurate means of identification—even when involving members of
the same ethnic group.[14] The recently published report by the Office of
Technology Assessment reached the same conclusion.

---

[11] Title 19.2-270.5 of the Code of Virginia (1990), for example, prohibits the retention of DNA test
results involving suspects in criminal proceedings.

[12] Harold M. Schmeck, Jr., "DNA Findings are Disputed by Scientists," *New York Times*, May 25,
1989, pp. B1, B12.

[13] Dan L. Burk, "DNA Fingerprinting: Possibilities and Pitfalls of a New Technique," *Jurimetrics
Journal*, (Spring 1988): 466.

[14] "Yale study supports accuracy of 'fingerprinting' via DNA," *The Sacramento Bee*, September 21, 1990.

The Office of Technology Assessment (OTA) finds that forensic uses of DNA tests are both reliable and valid when properly performed and analyzed by skilled personnel.[15]

Forensic scientists and researchers participating in the BJS/SEARCH DNA Forum also stressed that the science underlying DNA testing is valid and provides a solid basis for confidence in the reliability of DNA testing.

. . .

Criminal Justice Officials Endorse Reliability

Not surprisingly, many criminal justice officials are enthusiastic about the reliability and potential of DNA testing. FBI Director William Sessions, for example, has praised DNA's potential.   19

> . . . Probably the most exciting, as I view it, of the new techniques emerging for the criminal investigator, is the DNA identification technology. Through a genetic pattern-matching process, criminals can now be identified positively by comparing evidence from a crime scene—that is, blood, body fluids or sometimes a single hair—with that of a suspect. The FBI Laboratory Division is nearing completion of that project, that will bring about the full implementation of that process and make it available to all law enforcement agencies nationwide. The cooperation of states such as California in this new technology has been outstanding, and we are, of course, as I believe, standing on the edge of a new technological age and forensic capability, the cutting edge being the DNA capability . . . [16]

The use of DNA tests as evidence received another boost in January 1989, when California's Attorney General, after extensive review and testing, approved the use of DNA evidence in criminal cases presented in the California courts. The Attorney General had previously been wary about rushing a case into court and running the risk of the technology being ruled inadmissible.   20

> . . . So [in January 1988] he named a DNA Advisory Committee, comprised of representatives from the FBI, the state Bureau of Forensic Services, District Attorneys, sheriffs and police, to research both the

[15] Office of Technology Assessment, *Genetic Witness*, note 5, pp. 7–8.

[16] Address by William Sessions, Director of the Federal Bureau of Investigation, before the National Press Club in Washington, D.C., on September 1, 1988, distributed by Federal Information Systems, Corp., Federal News Service.

technology and the legal issues it posed. The California Association of Crime Lab Directors produced 150 blind DNA comparisons so accurate that the DNA Advisory Committee endorsed the new technology for use in court.[17]

Addressing the California District Attorney's Association's 1989 annual convention, the Attorney General announced that DNA evidence was now ready for use in a serial rapist case and a murder trial scheduled for the winter.[18]

Law enforcement officials attending the Forum on Criminal Justice 21 Uses of DNA, sponsored by the Bureau of Justice Statistics and SEARCH in November 1989, also voiced strong support for the forensic benefits of DNA testing. They emphasized that DNA testing has unprecedented potential to identify rapists, murderers and other violent offenders.

Problems in Admitting DNA Test Results in Court

This is not to say however, that there are no questions with respect to 22 the reliability and the use in court of DNA test results. Critics contend, for example, that there has been too much enthusiasm for the underlying science and too little skepticism about the methodology and the outcome of specific DNA tests.[19] Many also contend, as discussed below, that the use of DNA test results in criminal trials is unfair in that it overwhelms defense resources and blinds the jury to other probative and potentially exculpatory items of evidence.[20] In late 1989, courts in New York and Minnesota limited, or altogether refused to permit, the introduction of DNA test results citing concerns about the use of the specific DNA test results at issue.[21]

Adequacy of Population Studies. With few exceptions, critics cite 23 concerns about only one issue that goes to the underlying science of DNA testing: is the possibility of two individuals having the same DNA pattern

[17] Office of the Attorney General, News Release, "DNA Typing Is Now Ready for Use in California Criminal Trials," January 24, 1989.

[18] Ibid.; see also, Jack Jones and Thomas Maugh II, "Van de Kamp OKs 'Genetic Fingerprint' Use in Trials," *Los Angeles Times,* January 25, 1989, Part I, p. 3; and, "Authorities Moving Toward Use of DNA Fingerprinting," *Criminal Justice Newsletter* 19 (February 1, 1988): 3.

[19] See, e.g., Stephen Petrovich, "DNA Typing: A Rush to Judgment," 24 *Georgia Law Review* (Spring 1990): 669, 688, n. 91.

[20] See, e.g., Janet Hoeffel, "The Dark Side of DNA Profiling: Unreliable Scientific Evidence Meets the Criminal Defendant," 42 *Stanford Law Review* (January 1990): 465, 519–25.

[21] *People v. Castro,* 545 N.Y.S.2d. 985 (Sup. Ct. 1989); and *State v. Schwartz,* 447 N.W.2d 422 (Minn. 1989).

indeed as remote as claimed? This criticism loses some of its sting if DNA testing is not used for positive identification. Nevertheless, critics note that research with respect to the uniqueness of DNA patterns has been done on only a few hundred human subjects, and at that, on a population not chosen for ethnic diversity. They point out that DNA typing is not yet anchored in the kind of empirical research and operational use that characterizes friction-ridge fingerprinting.

Moreover, critics note that even if the chances of two people hav- 24 ing the same complete DNA (with the exception of identical twins) is remote, there certainly remains the possibility that two people could produce the same DNA "fingerprint" using the RFLP technique because this test measures DNA fragment length rather than the entire DNA content.[22]

. . .

Adequacy of Testing Methods. Even assuming the theoretical reli- 25 ability of DNA testing, important questions remain as to whether a particular DNA test was performed properly. According to many experts, DNA testing presents numerous opportunities for error.

One such opportunity involves the purity or integrity of the blood 26 or other DNA specimen. Samples can be mixed with foreign debris, or worse, with DNA from other sources.[23] Certain crime scenes, such as settings for gang fights or multiple rapes, may produce a bewildering "stew" of DNA which could resist even the most careful analytical techniques. In addition, the DNA sample, much like other types of crime scene evidence, may be too small, too old, or damaged.[24] Because a blood or tissue specimen is easily contaminated, commentators have urged courts to insist that prosecutors establish that a reliable chain of custody was preserved before admitting DNA evidence.[25]

. . .

Human Error in Interpreting Test Results. Even assuming that a 27 laboratory uses a proper test methodology, test results are difficult to interpret. There is a possibility of human error. If an analyst, for instance,

[22] Hoeffel, "The Dark Side," note 90, pp. 488–92.
[23] Thompson and Ford, "DNA Typing Needs Additional Validation," note 7, p. 64.
[24] See Hoeffel, "The Dark Side," note 90, p. 481; Petrovich, "A Rush to Judgment," note 89, pp. 694–95.
[25] Ibid., 694.

refuses to declare a match unless all DNA prints are identical in all respects, the declared non-match could result in false negatives—that is, two samples of DNA may actually come from the same individual, but the prints are interpreted as a negative match.[26]

What little empirical research is available suggests that human error 28 is sometimes a factor in DNA testing. In recent controlled tests, for instance, one of the three commercial laboratories that currently conducts DNA-typing tests incorrectly identified one individual in 48 identification trials and another laboratory made one incorrect identification out of 54 samples. Both incorrect hits were due to human error, which, evidently, caused a mix-up in the DNA samples.[27]

Alleged Unfairness to Criminal Defendants. Critics also contend 29 that introduction of DNA test results in criminal proceedings has the potential to undermine defendants' rights to a fair trial.[28] They point to several considerations. First, DNA test results are both impressive and complicated. Thus, there is a risk that juries will be unduly impressed with and swayed by DNA results.[29] Of course, DNA proponents point out that juries should be impressed with DNA test results given their reliability and their ability to make a near positive identification. Proponents also note that juries still exercise independent discretion. In a recent Connecticut rape trial, for instance, the jury ignored DNA evidence exculpating the defendant and convicted him based upon the victim's eyewitness identification.[30]

Use of DNA test results is also considered unfair by some who argue 30 that defendants are seldom able to obtain adequate expert witnesses.[31] Certainly, it is true that in the initial flurry of DNA criminal cases the defense bar has seldom produced expert rebuttal witnesses. Many experts, however, predict that as state-administered laboratories enter the

---

[26] Thompson and Ford, "DNA Typing Needs Additional Validation," note 7, pp. 63–64.

[27] Mark Thompson, "The Myth of DNA Fingerprints," *California Lawyer* (April, 1989): 34; see also, *New York DNA Report,* note 26, p. 28.

[28] It should also be pointed out, however, that DNA testing provides an important benefit to many investigative suspects. OTA has found, for instance, that "37 percent of the cases received by the FBI for DNA analysis result in exclusion of the primary suspect." Office of Technology Assessment, *Genetic Witness,* note 5, p. 17.

[29] Petrovich, "A Rush to Judgment," note 89, pp. 689–90.

[30] Ibid., n. 104; see also Johnson, "DNA defense rejected: jury convicts in rape," *Hartford Currant,* March 20, 1990, p. A. FBI forensic scientists testified for the defense in this case and opined that the DNA test results from the semen stains on the victim's clothes did not match the test results from the defendant's DNA and hence the semen could not have come from the defendant.

[31] Hoeffel, "The Dark Side," note 90, pp. 519–23; Petrovich, "A Rush to Judgment," note 89, pp. 689–90.

DNA testing field, the role of private DNA laboratories will shift to provide services (and expert witnesses) to the defense bar.[32]

Other "flaws" in a criminal trial in which the prosecution relies upon 31 DNA test results include: the expense of DNA testing and the resultant inability of many defendants to afford their own DNA tests; the lack of an opportunity to retest and thereby check DNA results (often because small DNA sample sizes make retesting impossible); and the prosecution's (and DNA testing laboratories') failure to make test results and methodologies fully available for examination and analysis by peer reviewers and defendants.

In rebuttal, proponents point out that as government-administered 32 laboratories conduct more DNA tests, particularly for the prosecution, test methodologies and results will be more available for scrutiny.

Lack of Standards. Finally, some observers argue that before DNA 33 test results are universally accepted in criminal proceedings, standards need to be further developed. Such standards would include controls to assure accurate interpretation of test results; standards for declaring matches; standards for determining probabilities of identical DNA in population cohorts; standards for preserving a chain of custody; standards for recordkeeping; and standards for accreditation and proficiency testing.[33]

---

[32] Virginia's law requires the prosecution to provide the defense with at least 21 days notice of the prosecution's intention to use DNA evidence and to give the defense copies of any profiles, reports or statements to be introduced. VA. CODE ANN. § 19.2-270.5 (1990).

[33] See discussion in Hoeffel, "The Dark Side," note 90, pp. 479–94.

READING FOR INFORMATION

1. How might taking DNA samples from criminal suspects violate the Fourth Amendment?
2. Give an example of "dragnet" DNA testing.
3. What is the Supreme Court's position on taking blood samples involuntarily for use in criminal proceedings?
4. What is the scientific community's stance on DNA fingerprinting?
5. What position have criminal justice officials taken on DNA fingerprinting?
6. What scientific arguments have been advanced against admitting DNA fingerprints in court?
7. What legal arguments have been advanced against admitting DNA fingerprints in court?

8. How, according to the article, might DNA fingerprinting evidence undermine a defendant's right to a fair trial?

READING FOR FORM, ORGANIZATION, AND EXPOSITORY FEATURES

1. Describe the language used in the U.S. Justice Department report. Based on your assessment of that language, what can you infer about the training or education of the authors of the report?
2. Describe the overall organizational plan of the report.
3. If you were to rewrite the report for an audience of first-year college students, what types of changes would you make?

READING FOR RHETORICAL CONCERNS

1. What would you imagine that U.S. Justice Department officials would think about DNA fingerprinting?
2. Did the authors attempt to present a balanced view on the issue? What evidence supports your answer?
3. Whom do you think the report authors intended as their audience? Explain your answer.
4. Do the authors want to change their readers' beliefs or behaviors? What information supports your view?

WRITING ASSIGNMENTS

1. Imagine you are a juror in a murder case, and the only evidence linking the defendant to the crime is based on DNA fingerprinting. Experts testify that the DNA fingerprinting evidence is reliable. Would you vote to convict the defendant? Write a four- to five-page defense of your position that draws on the U.S. Department of Justice report.
2. Use DNA fingerprinting as the principal example in a four- to five-page essay that explains how you think the judicial system should handle cases in which the rights of the individual seem to conflict with efforts to ensure public safety.
3. Imagine that the federal government has proposed establishing a DNA databank that each individual will be required to contribute to at birth. The rationale for the databank is that federal officials will be able to match blood or tissue samples from crime scenes to a particular individual. In a four- to five-page essay, attack or defend this proposal based on the evidence presented in the U.S. Justice Department report.

SYNTHESIS WRITING ASSIGNMENTS

1. In a five-page essay, compare and contrast Quittner's and Stephen's attitudes toward the development of advanced surveillance technology and its effect on individual rights.

2. Many private citizens and law enforcement officers maintain that if you have done nothing wrong, then you have nothing to fear from surveillance of your activities or searches of your home or car. Respond to that belief in a five- to six-page essay that draws on at least three readings from this chapter.

3. Are the amendments to the Constitution sufficient to protect our individual rights, given recent advances in surveillance technology? Answer this question in a five-page essay that draws on at least three of the articles in this chapter.

4. Under what circumstances, if any, do we have to give up our right to privacy? Answer this question in a five-page essay that draws on at least three of the articles in this chapter.

5. Does the increase in crime and violence in our cities justify employing technology that may violate individual privacy? Answer this question in a five-page essay that draws on at least three of the articles in this chapter.

6. Write a six-page essay that distinguishes between types of high-tech evidence that should be admitted in court and types that should be excluded. Cover all the varieties of crime-fighting technology that are described in this chapter.

7. How far has technology taken us along the path Orwell predicted in *1984*? In response to this question, write a five-page essay that draws on at least two of the nonfiction articles in this chapter.

Social Sciences

SUBJECTS AND METHODS OF STUDY IN THE SOCIAL SCIENCES

Anthropology, economics, education, political science, psychology, sociology, and geography are called *social sciences* because they use the process of scientific inquiry to study various aspects of society, such as human behavior, human relationships, social conditions, conduct, and customs. Social scientists begin their inquiry by asking questions or identifying problems related to particular phenomena. In Chapter 9, writing "Alternative Family Futures," Frances K. Goldschneider and Linda J. Waite ask, "Are more egalitarian and sharing families possible?" (370). In Chapter 10, Dennis Gilbert and Joseph Kahl ask, "How Many Classes Are There?" The social scientists posing those questions identify possible causes of the phenomena they are studying and then form a hypothesis based on certain assumptions they have made. They next try to verify the hypothesis by making a series of careful observations, assembling and analyzing data, and determining a clear pattern of response. If the data verify their hypothesis, they will declare it confirmed. Many social scientists conduct investigations in the "field," testing their hypotheses in actual problem situations by making on-site observations, interviewing, conducting case studies and cross-sectional and longitudinal studies, collecting surveys and questionnaires, examining artifacts and material remains, studying landscapes and ecology. In "'People Don't Know Right from Wrong Anymore'" (Chapter 9), Lillian B. Rubin reports the results of a series of interviews she conducted, twenty years apart, with two generations of family members. Other social scientists, such as experimental psychologists, work under carefully controlled conditions in laboratory settings.

SPECIAL TYPES OF SOCIAL SCIENCE WRITING

When researchers complete their studies, they present their findings in official reports, organized in accordance with the scientific method (see the introductory section on the natural sciences). A format commonly found in research articles is: Introduction/Background/Problem Statement; Method; Results; Discussion; Summary. An abstract (a brief summary of the article) may precede the study. Usually, the study begins with a literature review in which the writer recapitulates previous research. Social scientists regard this acknowledgment of their predecessors' work and of divided opinion about it to be crucial to the development of any new thesis or interpretation. Often when they publish their work, they designate it as a "proposal" or a "work in progress" because they have not yet arrived at conclusions that they are willing to consider final. They view this kind of publication as a means of receiving feedback or peer review that will enable them to continue with new insights and perspectives. They believe that a community of scholars cooperating within a complex system of checks and balances will ultimately arrive at some statement of truth.

Advanced social science courses teach students how to evaluate these formal reports of research findings. Meanwhile, all students should be familiar with less specialized forms of writing in the social sciences, such as summaries of research; reviews of the literature; case studies; proposals; position papers; presentation of new theories and methods of analysis; and commentaries, reviews, analyses, critiques, and interpretations of research.

For examples of various types of social science writing, consult the following sources:

> *Review of the literature:* Robert Barret and Bryan Robinson's "Children of Gay Fathers," Chapter 9; Robert Griswold's "Fatherhood and the Defense of Patriarchy," Chapter 9.

> *Case study:* Barret and Robinson's "Children of Gay Fathers" in Chapter 9.

> *Model or theory:* Dennis Gilbert and Joseph Kahl's "How Many Classes Are There?" Chapter 10.

Position paper: Myron Magnet's "Rebels with a Cause," Chapter 10.

Method of analysis: Gilbert and Kahl's "How Many Classes Are There?" in Chapter 10.

PERSPECTIVES ON SOCIAL SCIENCE TOPICS

In this anthology, we present reading selections on social science topics by journalists and other popular writers as well as by social scientists. These writers treat the same subject matter, but their approaches differ. Take, for example, Dirk Johnson, whose *New York Times* article, "White Standard for Poverty," appears on pages 499–501, and Myron Magnet, whose *National Review* article, "Rebels with a Cause," appears on pages 446–468. These writers do not use special modes of social science writing, nor do they rely heavily on other sources or write for specialized readers. Still, their writing is very important for social scientists because it reflects the very stuff of everyday life that social scientists study. Also consider Charles Murray's commentary, "Separation of the Classes" (pp. 442–445). Murray treats an issue that social scientists find extremely important as a barometer of public feeling.

SOCIAL SCIENCE WRITERS' ORGANIZATIONAL PLANS

Social science writers rely on a variety of organizational plans: time order, narration, process; antecedent-consequent, cause-effect; comparison and contrast; description; analysis, classification; definition; statement-response, problem-solution, question-answer. You will find that some plans appear more frequently than others. Given the nature of the inquiry process, social scientists use the statement-response, problem-solution, question-answer plans with some regularity. Notice that in Gilbert and Kahl's selection, "How Many Classes Are There?" (Chapter 10), the title indicates a question that will be answered. Also popular is the antecedent/consequent plan, because it enables writers to analyze and explain the causes of behaviors and events. Notice how Rubin structures "People Don't Know Right from Wrong Anymore" according to this plan. Also examine the pieces by Patricia Hill Collins (in Chapter 9) and Leonce Gaiter (in Chapter 10). When you are reading social science writing, look for overlapping organizational plans. Very few social science writers rely on only one; they use networks of different plans, often intermeshing them in a single piece.

AUTHOR'S LITERARY TECHNIQUES

Did you ever wonder why some writers are clear and easy to understand and others are pedantic and inaccessible? Clear writers process their information and ideas in an organized and modulated sequence, and they articulate their thinking in crisp, uncluttered prose. Pedantic and inaccessible writers often presume that their readers know a great deal of specialized terminology that allows them to dispense with explanations, examples, and illuminating details. One way writers make themselves understood is by defining new terms, concepts, and specialized vocabulary; providing examples, scenarios, and illustrations; and using figurative language.

You will find that many of the selections in this unit are replete with specialized vocabulary; moreover, familiar terms are often given new, specialized meanings. Take, for example, the various definitions of "family" in Chapter 9. As you read, pay close attention to the different ways writers handle vocabulary. Some use specialized words with impunity, assuming that their readers have sufficient background knowledge for comprehension. Others provide helpful contexts that give clues to verbal meaning. Still others supply definitions of specialized vocabulary. Definitions may take the form of explanations of causes, effects, or functions; synonyms; negations; analogies; descriptions; and classifications. Some definitions are brief, like the following from Gilbert and Kahl's "How Many Classes Are There?"

> Those who depend primarily on the welfare system for cash income we call the underclass. (p. 439)

Others are long, extended definitions, such as Herbert Gans's definition of "undeserving poor" in "The War Against the Poor Instead of Programs to End Poverty" (Chapter 10).

Another technique social science writers use to make specialized subjects more accessible to nonspecialized readers is to provide concrete examples and illustrations. Notice the extended examples provided by Hill Collins and other effective examples found in the writing of Rubin, R. T. Smith, and Gaiter. Sometimes, social scientists make their subject matter understandable by using figurative language or literary allusion. Observe Gans's analysis of "the metaphors of underservingness" (p. 476) and Magnet's references to the literary classics *The Scarlet Pimpernel* (p. 459) and *Gulliver's Travels* (p. 460).

Writing in the social sciences, then, commands a wide variety of approaches, organizational plans, styles, authorial perspectives, and literary techniques. Although the selections in this chapter do not always exemplify wholly academic social science writing, they do suggest the range of types, modes, and styles in that discourse. Writers in the social sciences often vary their own range from the extreme impersonality of technical reports to the impassioned concern of urgent social issues. The social sciences, after all, study people and their interaction in society. The diversity of the social sciences, therefore, is as broad as the diversity of people and institutions they examine.

C H A P T E R

nine

Redefining the American Family

Drawing on research in sociology, psychology, and social psychology, the six readings in this chapter focus on the dramatic challenges confronting American families. Our traditional views of families come into question as families are being transformed and redefined by forces such as single-parenting, divorce, maternal employment, delayed childbearing, adult independent living, and homosexual parenting couples. As the authors in this chapter point out, the American family is both vulnerable and resilient in the face of these forces.

In the opening piece, "Alternative Family Futures," Frances K. Goldschneider and Linda J. Waite weigh the costs and benefits of arrangements such as childless couples, mother-only families, "no families" (unmarried adults living independently), and new, egalitarian families against the traditional patriarchal family structure. In the next selection, "Fatherhood and the Defense of Patriarchy," Robert L. Griswold presents the views of those who desire to uphold the traditional family and reassert paternal authority. Robert L. Barret and Bryan E. Robinson investigate a different type of fatherhood in the piece entitled "Children of Gay Fathers." Central to Barret and Robinson's discussion are the ramifications of homosexual parents for children's development.

In "Mothers, Daughters, and Socialization for Survival," Patricia Hill Collins analyzes black motherhood and the predicament of African-American women who have to defend and protect their daughters against oppression and at the same time teach them how to overcome and resist it. In the next selection, " 'People Don't Know Right from Wrong Any-more,' " Lillian B. Rubin situates the transformation of family life within the context of changes in our overall culture. According to Rubin, shift-ing social realities have brought about changes that profoundly affect our norms, values, and behaviors regarding sex, marriage, and family life. Struggling against these shifting cultural norms, Olga Ruiz, the subject of Helena Maria Viramontes's short story "Snapshots," finds herself lost and helpless. Viramontes gives us a poignant picture of this middle-aged woman's struggle to adjust to a life without her husband and children.

Alternative Family Futures

Frances K. Goldschneider and Linda J. Waite

Frances K. Goldschneider and Linda J. Waite have written numerous articles on employment, the labor market, and women. Goldschneider is the author of Ethnic Factors in Family Structure and Mobility *(1978). Waite is professor of sociology at the University of Chicago and the author of* Working Wives and the Life Cycle *(1976) and* Women in Nontraditional Occupations *(1985). "Alter-native Family Futures" appears in Goldschneider and Waite's book,* New Fam-ilies, No Families? The Transformation of the American Home *(1991).*

PREREADING

Goldschneider and Waite's title suggests that they will present alterna-tives to traditional two-parent families. Jot down as many alternative family structures as you can think of. Explore your feelings about these types of families. Do you think certain types are superior to others? In your journal, record your thoughts.

ALTERNATIVE FAMILY FUTURES

. . . There are many factors at work that could lead to a "no 1 families" future, in which few marry and have children, and many live alone outside of families altogether. The most ominous of these forces

From Frances K. Goldschneider and Linda J. Waite, *New Families, No Families? Demographic Change and the Transformation of the American Home* (Berkeley and Los Angeles: U of Califor-nia P, 1991) 200–05. Copyright © 1991 The Regents of the University of California. Reprinted by permission of the publisher.

may be the withdrawal of children from the family and its tasks. But we also see significant signs that "new families" might be on the horizon, as men and children seem to join increasingly with their wives and mothers in the home and its tasks as women's work outside the home becomes more regular—full time and financially rewarding.

. . . Why are we confident that [we will not have] an eventual return to "old families" in which women focus their identities on the roles of wife and mother and spend most of their lives preparing for and carrying out those roles? And what of mother-only families, the fastest growing family form of the last several decades? Might this be the family of the future?   2

We should make clear that in discussing the future of the family we are focusing not on individual families, and the varieties of people in them, but on overall family systems—the institutions that provide the framework around which people make plans and within which they work out their own lives. When we criticize both mother-only and traditional families below, it is as total systems; many of these families are wonderful both for the adults and children in them. But we will make the distinction clear between individual families and family systems by using another example—the voluntary childless couple.   3

Childless Couples

Such couples, which have grown in numbers and proportions in the recent past, may be very happy together with the choices they have made, and they may also be making many important contributions to society. They usually feel very comfortable with their choice, and increasingly their friends and families are accepting it. These marriages tend to be the most egalitarian, since all studies show that the arrival of children puts pressures on couples to follow more conventional parental roles. . . .   4

As a *family system*, however, rejection of parenthood has obvious difficulties. It is no longer the case that almost all adults' energies must go into raising the next generation. We now have both the resources and the knowledge to realize that the simple reproduction of the species is not a sufficient goal for a "good life" or a "good society." Nevertheless, the fact remains that at some point we will need a system that ensures replacement, and this means that most adults will still have a lot of child care to do. Each generation of young adults feels that the world is theirs for the indefinite future, but they learn in a very few decades that the children they raised or did not raise, whether raised well or not, are beginning to   5 take over—as trendsetters, stars, heroes, and workers with their own skills and experiences. Any society needs to commit substantial resources to developing each new generation, providing them of course with schools and health care, but also with families. So most adults must be prepared to parent.

Mother-Only Families

But which adults should parent? The growth of mother-only families has   6
a clear message—that the increase in women's responsibility for parenting relative to men's that began in the nineteenth century is nearing its maximum, as women take total responsibility for direct care, with fathers providing funds either through child support payments or through the taxes they pay that provide "Aid to Families with Dependent Children" (AFDC), the primary welfare system in the United States. As with voluntarily childless couples, we again do not think this is a good *system*—without deprecating in any way individual mother-only (or father-only) families, most of whom are doing a good job under difficult circumstances.

As a system, making women responsible for most of the child rais-   7
ing presents important problems—problems that focus primarily on *men*. Boys in mother-only families face a number of difficulties. Although the early discussions in the psychological literature emphasized the lack of "role models" to teach boys how to be "men," it eventually became clear that boys in mother-only families do not lack *models* of "ideal" men; such models are amply provided by other relatives, by friends of their families, and by the media. What they lack is experience with "real" men with whom they can be close enough to see that men can deviate in healthy ways from sex-role stereotypes, fail and recover, mourn a parent and not lose face, help a tired spouse and still have a loving relationship (or even have a better one). "Role models" do not provide boys these insights, since they serve only to reinforce stereotypes; only having a close relationship with a normal man has this effect (Pruett, 1987).

The mother-only family presents even more difficulties for men   8
as adults and fathers. There is considerable evidence that marriage provides major benefits for adults, and that being unmarried is particularly problematic for men. Research demonstrating this is clearest for mortality—married people are less likely to die than unmarried people—but comparable findings have emerged for measures of physical and mental health. Women have been shown to be much less dependent on the

marital tie for social support than men (Berkman and Syme, 1979; Umberson, 1987), so the mother-only family form is less problematic for them in this respect. And the unmarried men who are at greatest risk of premature death are those living alone (Kobrin and Hendershot, 1976).

The mother-only family form also bars men from the experience of 9 dealing again with the pleasures and problems of growing up, which parents do as they relive their own childhoods in new ways with their children, reading them their favorite books, playing games that brought them joy as children, teaching skills that they had enjoyed mastering. There has been far too little research on what has happened to the *fathers* of the children in mother-only families, who appear at best to move on to parent, at least a little, their next mate's children (Furstenberg, 1988). But it is hard to believe that these experiences will contribute to a healthy sense of accomplishment as men move into their retirement years—and seek whatever support they can from the family ties they have woven as adults.

And women need help. Despite the numbers of superwomen who 10 take on both parental and economic roles, not all women can do so; few can parent totally alone. If the burden is to fall entirely on women, it seems unlikely that they will be willing to have the numbers of children needed for population replacement. Women who have experienced family disruption as children expect and have fewer, not more children . . . , as do women on welfare (Rank, 1989). They need time to work for their own support, since the current social expectation is that noncustodial parents should provide only for their children's financial needs, no child care, and often minimal "quality time." For men, the knowledge that marital breakup will in most cases lead to diminished and frustrating contact with their children has undoubtedly led to some resistance to having children at all, and thus risking this loss. Not all men have a low "demand for children," but they will have little chance to realize their preferences in the event of divorce. This is another cost of the mother-only family.

Old Families

Why can we not return to the old balance of men's and women's work 11 and family roles, which were "fair" to each in terms of hours, and which provided children with mothers who cared for them intensively and fathers who supported them adequately? It is clearly better in many ways than our current emphasis on mother-only families, since it provides for children's needs and reinforces family roles for men as children, adults, and in old age. What is wrong with "old families" as a family system? The answer to this question takes us back to the origins of the sex-role revolution, since the problems "old families" create are disproportionately for women.

The major problem for women posed by "old families" is demo- 12 graphic. With the increase in life expectancy and the decline in fertility, homemaking is no longer a lifetime career for women as a group. Either there has to be a division within their adult lives, with about half their time devoted to raising two or so children to adulthood[1] and half spent in other occupations, or women have to be divided into mothers and workers, or "real" workers and "mommy track" workers (Schwartz, 1989).

Perhaps we should remember, in the context of the recent out- 13 pouring of women's anger against men for being unhelpful and insensitive (Townsend and O'Neil, 1990), that it was only recently that men were writing in extraordinarily angry ways about traditional women, *for being too involved with their children.* In the 1940s, women who did not work outside the home but had achieved small families were walking a very narrow line. They were called unfeminine if they worked outside the home, and overinvolved and overcontrolling if they focused too much attention on their children. They were accused of "momism" not only in popular contemporary nonfiction (Wylie, 1942) and in scholarly writings (Strecker, 1946) but also in novels reflecting growing up during that period (Roth, 1969).[2]

The rise in divorce has also raised the cost of "old family" roles for 14 women. When few families ended voluntarily, women could invest all their energies in the family, and expect that the responsibility for their maintenance in old age would be borne by their husbands—or if necessary, their sons. But even moderate levels of divorce changed the wisdom of this course. Women who decide to interrupt their careers to raise children are taking a calculated risk, and it is likely that only those who are the most publicized for doing so (the "new executives") can afford to take "time out," since they already have the skills that will make them desirable in the reentry job market, even if they never reach chief executive officer as a result. But women who have scrambled beyond the pink-collar ghetto, but only just beyond, are much less likely to risk what they have gained. They return to work quickly (often too quickly) after childbirth in an industrial climate that often offers at most short maternity leaves, paid or unpaid.[3] So most women will work, and "old families" simply means that they have the double burden of work and home.

It is also the case that increasingly, men are rejecting "old fami- 15
lies" for themselves. Being relieved of at least some part of the economic
burden has obvious advantages and many men have also found rewards
from intensifying their family lives by developing closer relationships
with their wives and children. "Old families" preclude much of that for
men, and for the children growing up in these families. Sons, in particular, experience limited options as well, since they are not being prepared for the possibility of "new families" in the sex-segregated world
such families create.

No Families

This leaves us with the choice of "no families" or "new families." "No 16
families" means that too many adults make the decision not to have children to provide population replacement, as we discussed above under
"childless couples," and it also means that most will forgo developing
close, intimate, long-term relationships, choosing instead to live alone.
Again, we want to make clear that such people may have rich lives of satisfying employment and contribution to society; they may as well experience and provide others with strong friendship and support that those
bound up in family obligations often cannot.

But even going beyond the problem of population replacement, 17
nonfamily living as a system, in which many adults expect to spend much
of their lives living alone, is untested. Although people may be able to
maintain close and giving relationships, it is not clear that their circumstances will teach them how to do so; *they will have to go out of their way*
to make and maintain such relationships across the distances created by
residential separation. It seems likely that commitment and intimacy
will be more difficult to achieve and maintain.[4]

New Families

What then, of "new families"? We have reached them at this point in the 18
argument by process of elimination. We have also suggested that such
families have the potential to solve critical problems facing families today.
But what do we really know about them? What effects does this pioneer
family form have on marriages and families and on the men, women, and
children who live in them? Are more egalitarian and sharing families possible? This is largely uncharted territory. . . .

     . . . Most students of the family have resisted considering that 19
men might take a greater role in family matters, usually raising the

possibility only to dismiss it. One of the most systematic and sympathetically feminist discussions of family problems considers the prospect of increased male involvement in household tasks only to dismiss it as bizarre or pathological.[5]

But will "new families" be so bad for men and for children that they 20 will offset their benefits for women who want both family and economic lives? Certainly there will be some costs. The most obvious consequence is that, as for women, the hours men spend in housework are likely to decrease the time available for paid employment or for related activities such as training, travel for work, or overtime. One study found that time spent in domestic activities reduced the wages of both men and women, and affected the sexes about equally (Coverman, 1983).[6]

However, the job-related pressures placed on men by an egalitari- 21 an division of labor at home are on the wane. Fewer and fewer of their competitors in the workplace are men married to full-time housewives, and more and more of them are not only other men with relatively egalitarian marriages, but also women carrying a double burden themselves, as single parents or working wives in traditional marriages. The growth of on-site day care, and fathers' involvement with their children there, could also reinforce family orientations among men at work.

Further, marriages that are more egalitarian in sharing domestic 22 labor appear to have positive consequences for *both* spouses outside the workplace. Wives whose husbands "help" with the housework report lower levels of depression than those whose husbands do not help (Ross, Mirowsky, and Huber, 1983). And their husbands do not suffer—at least in terms of *their* mental health—as a result of helping around the house. And the more housework the husband does, the lower the chances that the wife has considered divorce.[7]

And what of the children? How does participation in the domes- 23 tic sphere affect them? One study argues that children become more independent when they have more responsibility and greater demands placed upon them (Weiss, 1979). The study focused only on children living in single-parent families, who are given substantially more decision-making power and responsibility for household tasks than are children living with two parents, becoming almost equal partners in the business of running a single-parent family. But it seems likely that even in two-parent families, working regularly together on the tasks that enrich their lives would not only increase children's skill levels, when they leave to form homes of their own, but would reinforce ties and respect between parents and children in the home.

NOTES

1. The alternative of going back to large family sizes in the modern context presents even greater problems which can only be ignored by a powerful religious faith that population explosion is not a problem.

2. For a useful discussion of some of these issues see Bart (1970) and Hartmann (1982).

3. Most women use accumulated vacation time or sick leave to finance their maternity leaves, which are most often 6 weeks.

4. Isaac Asimov (1983) has explored what society might look like if each adult lived in a separate dwelling and most social interaction was done over high-tech view phones.

5. In one, we are told that "arguments about housework are the leading cause of domestic violence in the United States" (Fuchs, 1988, p. 74). The second reference is paired with two versions of what the author evidently sees as related, far-out scenarios; one in which sex-change operations are painless, inexpensive, and easily reversible; the other a distant fictional society in which individuals are sometimes female and sometimes male (Fuchs, 1988, p. 144).

6. Other evidence, however, suggests that most of the pay gap must come from other sources, such as discrimination. Studies that have tried to measure the impact of domestic responsibilities on *how hard* women work on the job have not been able to find a strong effect. Women do not seem to allocate less effort to paid work than men; in fact, they appear to work harder in the workplace than men, with substantial differences when those in similar family situations are compared (Bielby and Bielby, 1985).

7. Huber and Spitze, 1983. This relationship should also be tested to see whether divorce actually occurs. We were not able to include this dimension in our analysis of divorce, since measurement of *who* shares household tasks was not included in the survey until the last year of observation. Other data (or later years of this survey) are needed to test the effect of a more egalitarian division of labor on the actual likelihood of divorce.

REFERENCES

Berkman, Lisa F., and Leonard M. Syme, "Social Networks, Host Resistance, and Mortality: A Nine-Year Follow-Up Study of Alameda County Residents," *American Journal of Epidemiology*, 190, no. 2 (February 1979): 186–204.

Coverman, Shelley, "Gender, Domestic Labor Time, and Wage Inequality," *American Sociological Review*, 48 (October 1983): 623–637.

Furstenberg, Frank, "Good Dads—Bad Dads: Two Faces of Fatherhood," in Andrew Cherlin, ed., *The Changing American Family and Public Policy*, Washington: The Urban Institute Press, 1988.

Kobrin, Frances E., and Gerry Hendershot, "Do Family Ties Affect Mortality? Evidence from the United States, 1966–68," *Journal of Marriage and the Family*, 39, no. 4 (May 1976): 233–239.

Pruett, Kyle D., *The Nurturing Father: Journey Toward the Complete Man*, New York: Warner Books, 1987.

Rank, Mark, R., "Fertility Among Women on Welfare: Incidence and Determinants," *American Sociological Review*, 54, no. 2 (April 1989): 296–304.

Ross, Catherine E., John Mirowsky, and Joan Huber, "Dividing Work, Sharing Work, and In-Between: Marriage Patterns and Depression," *American Sociological Review*, 48, no. 6 (December 1983): 809–823.

Roth, Phillip, *Portnoy's Complaint,* New York: Random House, 1969.

Schwartz, Felice, "Management Women and the New Facts of Life," *Harvard Business Review,* 67, no. 1 (1989): 65–76.

Strecker, Edward, "Their Mother's Sons: A Psychiatrist Examines an American Problem," Philadelphia: Lippincott, 1946.

Townsend, Bickley, and Kathleen O'Neil, "American Women Get Mad," *American Demographics,* 12, no. 8 (August 1990): 26–32.

Umberson, Debra, "Family Status and Health Behaviors: Social Control as a Dimension of Social Integration," *Journal of Health and Social Behavior,* 28, no. 3 (September 1987): 306–319.

Weiss, Robert S., "Growing Up a Little Faster: The Experience of Growing Up in a Single-Parent Household," *Journal of Social Issues,* 35, no. 4 (1979): 97–111.

Wylie, Phillip, *A Generation of Vipers,* New York: Rinehart and Company, 1942.

READING FOR INFORMATION

1. How do Goldschneider and Waite characterize "new families"?

2. Explain the distinctions the authors make between "individual families" and "family systems."

3. List the problems that mother-only families create for men.

4. What are the drawbacks of "childless couples" and "no families"?

5. Why do the benefits of "new families" outweigh the costs?

6. Explain whether you agree or disagree with Goldschneider and Waite's last projection that children will assume more independence and responsibility in new, egalitarian families?

READING FOR FORM, ORGANIZATION, AND EXPOSITORY FEATURES

1. Identify the organizational pattern (time order, narration, process; antecedent-consequent, cause-effect; comparison and contrast; description; analysis, classification; definition; statement-response, problem-solution, question-answer), and explain how the piece is arranged.

2. What devices or aids help the reader to follow Goldschneider and Waite's argument?

3. What types of sources do the authors draw upon, and what function do those sources serve?

READING FOR RHETORICAL CONCERNS

1. How do you think Goldschneider and Waite's readers will be affected by this piece? After reading it, were you optimistic or pessimistic about the future of families?

2. In a number of paragraphs (for example, 2, 6, 11, 18, 23), Goldschneider and Waite pose questions. What purpose do those questions serve? How did they affect you as a reader?

3. Do you think the authors are addressing their argument to men, women, or both? Why?

WRITING ASSIGNMENTS

1. Write a brief essay addressed to classmates who have not read "Alternative Family Futures." Describe the family types Goldschneider and Waite present, and summarize the benefits and costs of each.

2. Interview an individual or a couple who are representative of one of the family types—childless couple, mother-only family, individual living alone, old traditional family, new family—that Goldschneider and Waite discuss. Ask the interviewee(s) to explain what he or she sees as the advantages and disadvantages of the particular lifestyle. Then write an essay in which you compare your interviewee's explanations with those presented by Goldschneider and Waite. Draw your own conclusions.

3. Write a two- to three-page essay in which you discuss the family type that best characterizes your own family.

Fatherhood and the Defense of Patriarchy

Robert L. Griswold

Robert L. Griswold teaches in the Department of History at the University of Oklahoma. "Fatherhood and the Defense of Patriarchy" appears in his book Fatherhood in America: A History *(1993). Griswold is also the author of* Family and Divorce in California, 1850–1890: Victorian Illusions and Everyday Realities *(1982).*

PREREADING

Read the first paragraph and freewrite your initial reaction. What would a "new fatherhood" entail? What are some ways fathers might reassert their authority? Explore your feelings about fatherhood. What does society need, a "new fatherhood" or a "reassertion of traditional paternal authority"?

Selected excerpts from pages 257–60 from *Fatherhood in America: A History* by Robert L. Griswold (New York: Basic Books, 1993). Copyright by Robert L. Griswold. Reprinted by permission of the author.

. . . Feminists and advocates for the men's movement hope that   1
the new fatherhood will be a progressive step in redefining
American manhood, a step in line with building more equality between
husbands and wives and more nurturing, meaningful relationships between fathers and children. To critics from the right, however, such
changes merely signify the erosion of traditional relationships on which
the good of society depends. What society desperately needs, they argue,
is not the new fatherhood but the reassertion of traditional paternal authority: "The family is an organization," writes conservative psychiatrist
Harold Voth, "and it is consistent with all known patterns of animal behavior, including that of man, that the male should be the head of the family." Although fathers should be "loving, compassionate, understanding,
capable of gentleness and the like . . . all should know he is the protector, the one who is ultimately responsible for the integrity and survival of
the family." Such knowledge, Voth assured his readers, is a prerequisite
of success: "It is known that the most successful families are those where
all members, including the wife, look up to the father-husband."[1]

Worried that American families were in deep trouble, convinced that   2
the welfare system sapped the strength of fathers, galvanized by the battle against feminism and the Equal Rights Amendment (ERA), conservatives like Voth fought back in the 1970s and 1980s, hoping to forestall the
corrosive effects of social and political change by reasserting paternal authority within families and reemphasizing men's obligation to support their
dependents. Families needed clear lines of authority that only a father
could provide: "There must be no role confusion between the mother and
father," asserts Voth, "and though . . . distributions of responsibility and authority exist, everyone in the family must also know, appreciate and respect the fact that the father has the overall responsibility for the family;
he is its chief executive, but like all good executives he should listen to all
within his organization."[2] With this authority came responsibility. Men had
the time-honored obligation to support their wives and children, an obligation firmly established by law but now under siege by misguided proponents of feminism. In the view of conservatives, traditional laws insured "the
right of a woman to be a full-time wife and mother, and to have this right
recognized by laws that obligate her husband to provide the primary financial support and a home for her and their children, both during their
marriage and when she is a widow."[3] These laws originated in biology and
religion: "Since God ordained that women have babies," writes antifemi-
nist leader Phyllis Schlafly, "our laws properly and realistically establish
that men must provide financial support for their wives and children."[4]

But feminism put all this at risk. What was at stake for conservative   3
women in the battle for the ERA, for example, was the legitimacy of
women's and children's claims on men's income. The stakes were high:
"The Equal Rights Amendment," warned Schlafly, "would invalidate all
the state laws that require the husband to support his wife and family
and provide them with a home, because the Constitution would then
prohibit any law that imposes an obligation on one sex that it does not impose equally on the other."[5] Such a turn of events would leave women
doubly burdened: "ERA would impose a constitutionally mandated legal
equality in all matters, including family support. This would be grossly unfair to a woman because it would impose on her the double burden of financial obligation plus motherhood and homemaking." Schlafly was
certainly right on the last point. As she put it, "The law cannot address
itself to who has the baby, changes the diapers, or washes the dishes."[6]

And men were more than willing to let women assume the burden   4
of the "double shift." Underlying much of the conservative defense of
patriarchy, as Barbara Ehrenreich has pointed out, was the deep suspicion that men, free of traditional obligations, would simply refuse to support their families. The fear persisted that men supported dependents
only so long as it was convenient, a situation that would only become
worse by passage of the ERA, which would destroy the legal foundations
of male obligation.[7] Schlafly spoke for millions of anti-ERA homemakers
in denouncing the proposed amendment: "The moral, social, and legal
evil of ERA is that it proclaims as a constitutional mandate that the husband no longer has the primary duty to support his wife and children."[8]
Hence the deep hostility to feminism on the part of Phyllis Schlafly and
her supporters: it was a force that meant to help women but in reality
helped legitimate male irresponsibility. In a culture eviscerated by the collapse of traditional family values, men acted responsibly only if their
wives (and the obligations they felt toward their children) compelled it:
"Man's role as family provider," Schlafly writes, "gives him the incentive
to curb his primitive nature. Everyone needs to be needed. The male
satisfies his sense of need through his role as provider for the family." If
this need were subverted by feminist impulses, warned Schlafly, a man
"tends to drop out of the family and revert to the primitive masculine
role of hunter and fighter."[9]

This grim view was most fully developed by best-selling author George   5
Gilder, who, in *Sexual Suicide* and *Wealth and Poverty*, argued that men
were fundamentally brutes who became good citizens and productive workers only because women made them so. Sex—irresponsible, insatiable, and

unrelenting—drove men, and this primal, destructive, and uncivilizing force could be checked only by women and children: "A married man . . . is spurred by the claims of family to channel his otherwise disruptive male aggressions into his performance as a provider for a wife and children." By extending men's horizons beyond the fulfillment of their sexual impulses, fatherhood gives men a vision of the future: "The woman gives him access to his children, otherwise forever denied him; and he gives her the product of his labor, otherwise dissipated on temporary pleasures. The woman gives him a unique link to the future and a vision of it; he gives her faithfulness and a commitment to a lifetime of hard work."[10]

Traditional breadwinning cooled male ardor and deflected it into worthwhile channels, but woe to the society that allowed women to intrude into this male domain: "A society of relatively wealthy and independent women will be a society of sexually and economically predatory males. . . . If they cannot be providers, they have to resort to muscle and phallus."[11] And muscle and phallus do not for good social order make; what does is men and women bound "to identities as fathers and mothers within the 'traditional' family." Children encourage respectability, the work ethic, and economic productivity among fathers, commitments that restrain men's sexuality and counteract antisocial behavior. In the view of the New Right, writes the sociologist Allen Hunter, "anarchic male energy is disciplined not by civic virtue in the society at large but by sexual responsibility toward one woman and economic responsibility to her and their offspring."[12] In short, fatherhood disciplines men to accept their responsibilities and obligations in the face of a variety of forces— feminism, humanism, godlessness, the welfare state—working to destroy conservatives' visions of social order.

In the view of the New Right, the contemporary liberal state has relentlessly encroached on parental authority and responsibilities and has sapped the initiative of breadwinners. To conservatives, as Allen Hunter has explained, "judicial activism and liberal, humanist social legislation have threatened the traditional family by penetrating it with instrumental, individualistic values, and by creating a paternalistic state which takes over child-rearing from parents and subverts the market." The image is one of the family under siege by the so-called "new class," the welfare bureaucrats and social planners so despised by New Right thinkers.[13] These architects of liberalism subvert male authority by eroding female dependence on male breadwinning. Worse, they create unemployment and poverty by causing family breakdown. Dusting off the assumptions put forth in the Moynihan Report, conservatives argue that it is family breakdown that causes poverty, not poverty that causes family breakdown. And family breakdown, as George Gilder explains in his inimitable fashion, came when the welfare state usurped paternal responsibilities to wives and children: "The man has the gradually sinking feeling that his role as provider, the definitive male activity from the primal days of the hunt through the industrial revolution and on into modern life, has been largely seized from him; he has been cuckolded by the compassionate state." With male breadwinning made optional, a father "feels dispensable, his wife knows he is dispensable, his children sense it." Men respond by leaving their wives and children and reverting to a less civilized state, exhibiting "that very combination of resignation and rage, escapism and violence, short horizons and promiscuous sexuality that characterizes everywhere the life of the poor."[14]

NOTES

1. Harold M. Voth, *The Castrated Family* (Kansas City: Sheed, Andrews, and McMeel, 1977): 2, 4.

2. Ibid., 4.

3. Barbara Ehrenreich, *The Hearts of Men: American Dreams and the Flight from Commitment* (New York: Anchor, 1984): 146.

4. Phyllis Schlafly, *The Power of the Christian Woman* (Cincinnati: Standard Publishing, 1981): 78.

5. Ibid., 79.

6. Ibid., 80.

7. Ehrenreich, *The Hearts of Men*, 144–49.

8. Schlafly, *The Power of the Christian Woman*, 83.

9. Ibid., 103.

10. George Gilder, *Wealth and Poverty* (New York: Basic Books, 1981): 69–70.

11. George Gilder, *Sexual Suicide* (New York: Quadrangle, 1973): 97.

12. Allen Hunter, "Children in the Service of Conservatism: Parent-Child Relations in the New Right's Pro-Family Rhetoric," unpublished manuscript read at the Legal History of the Family Symposium, Madison, Wisconsin (Summer 1985): 1, 10; also see Hunter, "Virtue with a Vengeance: The Pro-Family Politics of the New Right," Ph.D. diss., Brandeis University, 1985.

13. On the "new class," see Ehrenreich, *Fear of Falling*, 144–95. Almost any issue of the Moral Majority's *Liberty Report* or any publication from Gary Bauer's group, "Focus on the Family," contains an attack on the "new class" and a call for the reestablishment of traditional families.

14. Gilder, *Wealth and Poverty*, 115, 122; for similar sentiments, see Charles Colson, *Against the Night: Living in the New Dark Ages* (Ann Arbor: Servant, 1989): 75.

READING FOR INFORMATION

1. What political and social forces are conservatives like Voth and Schlafly fighting against?
2. To what extent does Griswold agree with Schlafly's points in paragraph 3?
3. In your own words, explain why men are willing to let their wives work a "double shift."
4. Paraphrase Griswold's explanation of Allen Hunter's remark, "Anarchic male energy is disciplined not by civic virtue in the society at large but by sexual responsibility toward one woman and economic responsibility to her and their offspring" (paragraph 6).
5. In the view of conservatives, the "liberal state" is responsible for the erosion of paternal authority. Is this so?

READING FOR FORM, ORGANIZATION, AND EXPOSITORY FEATURES

1. Describe the contrast that Griswold sets up in the first paragraph.
2. Griswold draws on a number of sources—Voth, Schlafly, Ehrenreich, Gilder, and Hunter. What function do those sources serve?
3. Underline the words Griswold uses to introduce and identify quoted authors for his readers, and describe how he does this.

READING FOR RHETORICAL CONCERNS

1. How would you describe Griswold's purpose? Why do you think he wrote this piece?
2. Does Griswold divulge his own position? If so, where does he stand? Is he on the side of the feminists and advocates for the men's movement or does he align himself with the New Right?
3. Review the piece to get an estimate of the amount of material that Griswold quotes, paraphrases, or summarizes. What portion of the piece is drawn from sources and how much reflects Griswold's own ideas? How do the sources serve Griswold's purpose? How would the impact be different if Griswold had not included material from acknowledged authorities?

WRITING ASSIGNMENTS

1. Summarize arguments by Harold Voth, Phyllis Schlafly, and George Gilder for the reassertion of paternal authority. In your view, which author makes the most convincing case?

2. Write an essay in which you agree or disagree with Phyllis Schlafly's view that "the male satisfies his sense of need through his role as provider for the family" (paragraph 4).

3. Write an essay in which you argue for or against conservatives' claims that "it is family breakdown that causes poverty, not poverty that causes family breakdown" (paragraph 7). For additional background information, you might want to read some of the selections in Chapter 10.

Children of Gay Fathers

Robert L. Barret and Bryan E. Robinson

Robert L. Barret and Bryan E. Robinson teach in the Human Services Department, University of North Carolina at Charlotte. They are coauthors of two books: Gay Fathers *(New York: Free Press, 1990) and* The Developing Father *(New York: Guilford Press, 1986).*

PREREADING

Comment on your familiarity with the issue of homosexual parenting. Did the idea of a gay man choosing to be an active parent and visible father ever occur to you? Why or why not? Freewrite your response.

The children of gay fathers are like children from all families. 1
Some are academically talented, some struggle to get through school, some are model students, and some are constantly in trouble. In thinking about the children of gay fathers, it is essential to recognize that many of them have experienced the divorce of their parents, others have grown up in single-parent homes, and still others have been caught in major crossfire between their parents, grandparents, and perhaps their community over the appropriateness of gay men serving in the father role. Much of any distress that one sees in a child living with a gay father may, in fact, be the result of the divorce or other family tensions. Legitimate concerns about the impact of living with a gay father include the

From Robert L. Barret and Bryan E. Robinson, "Gay Dads," *Redefining Families: Implications for Children's Development,* ed. Adele Eskeles Gottfried and Allen W. Gottfried (New York: Plenum, 1994), 157–70. Reprinted by permission of the author and Plenum Publishing Corporation.

developmental impact of the knowledge that one's father is gay, reasonable worries about the timing of coming out to children, and creating sensitivity to how the children will experience society's generally negative attitudes toward homosexuality.

Coming out to children is usually an emotion-laden event for gay fathers. The disclosure of one's homosexuality creates anxiety about rejection, fear of hurting or damaging the child's self-esteem, and grieving over the loss of innocence. Some gay fathers never accomplish this task and remain deeply closeted, citing legal and emotional reasons (Bozett, 1980, 1981; Humphreys, 1979; Spada, 1979). Recent publications report the intricacies of this question (Corley, 1990). Those who never disclose their homosexuality often lead deeply conflicted lives and present parenting styles that are characterized by psychological distance (Miller, 1979). Those who do come out to their children do so in the desire to be more of a whole person as a father. As they try to merge their gayness with the father role, they encounter a different kind of conflict: deciding how open to be about their sexual relationships and how much exposure to the gay community to offer their children (Robinson & Barret, 1986).

Fathers report that the first concern they have about coming out is the well-being and healthy adjustment of their children. Many gay fathers seek the help of counselors or specialists in child development as they decide when and how to tell their children about their homosexuality. Research studies indicate that fathers and children report that they are closer after self-disclosure about the father's sexual orientation (Bozett, 1980; Miller, 1979). Bigner and Bozett (1989) studied the reasons that gay fathers give for coming out to their children. Among the most cited were wanting their children to know them as they are, being aware that children will usually discover for themselves if there is frequent contact, and the presence of a male lover in the home.

Gay fathers may come out indirectly by showing affection to men in front of their children or by taking them to gay community events. Others choose to come out verbally or by correspondence (Maddox, 1982). Factors in disclosure are the degree of intimacy between the father and his children and the obtrusiveness of his gayness (Bozett, 1988). By and large, the research suggests that children who are told at an earlier age have fewer difficulties with the day-to-day issues that accompany their father's homosexuality (Bozett, 1989).

The parenting styles of gay fathers are not markedly different from those of other single fathers, but gay fathers try to create a more stable home environment and more positive relationships with their children than traditional heterosexual parents (Bigner & Jacobsen, 1989a; Bozett, 1989). One study found that homosexual fathers differed from their heterosexual counterparts in providing more nurturing and in having less traditional parenting attitudes (Scallen, 1981). Another study of gay fathers found no differences in paternal involvement and amount of intimacy (Bigner & Jacobsen, 1989b). In general, investigators have found that gay fathers feel an additional responsibility to provide effective fathering because they know their homosexuality causes others to examine their parenting styles more closely (Barret & Robinson, 1990). This is not to say that no risk is involved in gay fathering. Miller (1979) found that six daughters of the gay fathers in his study had significant life problems. Others have reported that the children of gay fathers must be prepared to face ridicule and harassment (Bozett, 1980; Epstein, 1979) or may be alienated from their agemates, may become confused about their sexual identity, and may express discomfort with their father's sexual orientation (Lewis, 1980). Most researchers have concluded that being homosexual is compatible with effective parenting and is not usually a major issue in parental relationships with children (Harris & Turner, 1986).

As Chip reveals (Figure 9-1), dealing with the outside world is a task that gay fathers and their children must master. Gay families live in a social system that is generally uncomfortable with homosexuality and

---

CASE STUDY—CHIP SPEAKS

My name is Chip and I'm seventeen and in twelfth grade. When we first moved to Indianapolis, I learned my dad was gay. I was twelve. I didn't really think much about it. There was a birthday coming up and Dad said we were going to go out and buy a birthday card. He went out, drove around the block and then parked in front of our house. Then he took me to the park and told me the facts of life. He asked me if I knew what it meant to be gay. I told him, "Yeah, it means to be happy and enjoy yourself." Then he started to explain to me about being homosexual. I really didn't know what it was at that point, until he explained it to me.

It's an accepted part of my life now. I've been growing up with it almost five years. When he invites another guy into the house it's OK. I don't

(continued on the next page)

bring other kids home then. One of my friends is extremely homophobic and he lets that fact be known. I wouldn't dare risk anything or it would be like "goodbye" to my friend. My other two friends, I don't know how they would react. So I have to be careful about having certain friends over. To me it's blatantly obvious. Having been exposed to so many gay people, I know what to look for and what I'm seeing. Sometimes it's kind of hard because people make fun of gay people. And, if I stick up for their rights, then I get ridiculed. So I just don't say anything at school. It's kind of hard sometimes.

The good thing is that you get a more objective view of people in general, being raised by someone who's so persecuted by society. You begin to sympathize with anyone who is persecuted by society. You tend not to be as prejudiced. You need to appreciate people for what they are personally, not just in terms of color, religion, or sexual preference. That's the best thing. The hardest thing is hearing all those people making cracks or jokes on TV or at school and not being really able to do anything about it. Because he's my dad after all, it makes me kind of sad. I never feel ashamed or embarrassed, but I do feel a little pressured because of this. One time a friend of mine made a joke about gay people. I just played it off like I thought it was funny, but I didn't. You have to pretend you think the same thing they do when you don't. That makes me feel like a fraud.

When my dad puts his arm around another man, the first thing I think is, "I could never do that." It makes me a little bit uncomfortable, but I'm not repulsed by it. There are times I wish he wouldn't do it, but other times I'm glad he can have the freedom to do it. When he first came out to me, the only question I asked him was, "What are the chances of me being gay?" He couldn't answer it. But today, to the best of my knowledge, I'm not gay. I like chasing after girls.

Sometimes I feel like I'm keeping a big secret. My dad had a holy union with a man once. My friends had big plans and we were all going out on the day of the big event. And I couldn't go and couldn't explain why. Things like that have happened a number of times. I can't go and I can't tell why. They start yelling at me and get mad. They'll get over it; it's none of their business.

As fathers go, mine tends to be a little nicer—almost a mother's temperament. A friend of mine's father doesn't spend much time with him. They just seem to have stricter parents than mine. I don't know if that's just because of his personality in general or if it's because he's

(continued on the next page)

gay. He's a very emotional person; he cries easily. I love him. He's a good dad. He's more open than other dads. He doesn't let me get away with a lot. He tends to be more worried about me and a girl together than some other fathers are about their sons—more worried about my having sex. Whenever I go out on a date, he always says something like, "Don't do anything I wouldn't do," only he doesn't say it jokingly. Sometimes he's just overly cautious.

If I could change my dad and make him straight, I wouldn't do it. It might make things easier for me in some ways, but I wouldn't have grown up the way I have. Being exposed to the straight world and gay world equally has balanced me out more than some of the other people I know. The only things I'd want to change is society's treatment of him. (Barret & Robinson, 1990, pp. 14–15)

(*Note:* Chip's dad died of AIDS two years after this interview took place.)

Figure 9-1

that certainly does not overtly support gay parenting. One reality for gay fathers is figuring out how to interact successfully with the world of schools, after-school activities, PTAs, churches, and their children's social networks. Many gay fathers see no choice other than to continue living relatively closeted lives (Bozett, 1988; Miller, 1979). Others, fearing the damage that exposure may bring to their children and/or possible custody battles involving their homosexuality, live rigidly controlled lives and may never develop a gay identity. Those who are more open about their gayness struggle to help their children develop a positive attitude toward homosexuality while simultaneously cautioning them about the dangers of disclosure to teachers and friends. Teaching their children to manage these two tasks is a major challenge for gay fathers (Morin & Schultz, 1978; Riddle, 1978). Accomplishing this task when there are virtually no visible role models frequently leaves these fathers and their children feeling extremely isolated.

Bozett (1988) identified several strategies that these children use as they experience both their own and the public's discomfort with their gay fathers. The children of gay fathers in his study used boundary control, nondisclosure, and disclosure as they interacted with their fathers and the outside world. For example, some children limited or attempted to control the content of their interactions with their father. One father we talked with (Barret & Robinson, 1990) reported that he had offered to introduce his teenaged daughter to some of his gay friends in the hope that she would see how normal they were. Her reply was a curt "Dad, that will never happen!" Another father told of trying to reconcile with his son but being rebuffed by the comment, "I don't want to hear anything about your personal life. I can't handle it." Such boundary control limits the ability of the relationship to grow. Other ways that children control boundaries are by not introducing their friends to their fathers or by carefully managing the amount of time they spend together, as Chip reveals in his interview.

Some children do learn to let their friends know carefully about their 8
father's homosexuality. These disclosures have a potential for both increased intimacy and rejection. Helping children discriminate when and how to inform their friends is a critical challenge of gay parenting. As children grow up, these issues may become more complex, as families struggle to involve gay fathers in events such as weddings, graduations, and birth celebrations, where the presence of the gay father and his partner may raise questions.

Children of gay fathers do sometimes worry that their sexual ori- 9
entation may become contaminated by their father's homosexuality. Either they or their friends may begin to question whether they are gay as well. Those children who do disclose their father's homosexuality report being harassed by the use of such terms as *queer* and *fag*. Naturally, this concern is greatest during their teenage years (Riddle & Arguelles, 1981). Obviously, the children of gay fathers need to consider carefully the consequences of disclosure. Keeping this aspect of their lives secret may have the same negative impact on their development as isolation, alienation, and compartmentalization does on gay men.

This is not to say that the responses of social support networks are 10
universally negative. Many children with gay fathers report that their friends are both curious and supportive. It is important to recognize that coming out is a process rather than a discrete event. Fathers, children, and their friends need time to move into the process, and to examine their own feelings and attitudes so that acceptance and understanding replace confusion and fear. One child of a gay father said:

> At first, I was really angry at my dad. I couldn't figure out how to tell my friends what was going on, so I said nothing. My dad and I had terrible fights as he put pressure on me to say it was OK. I thought what he was doing was sinful and embarrasing. But over time, I began to realize that he is the same dad he has always been, and now we are closer than ever. My friends have also got used to the idea and like to spend time with him, too.

STATE OF RESEARCH ON CHILDREN OF GAY FATHERS

In reviewing the impact of gay fathering on children, it is important to ac- 11
knowledge that most children who live with gay fathers are also the products of divorce and may show the psychological distress that typically
accompanies the experience of marital dissolution. All too often, the emotional distress of children with gay parents is solely attributed to the parents' sexual orientation and is not seen as a complex mixture of family
dynamics, divorce adjustment, and the incorporation of the parents' sexual coming out.

Only two studies have directly addressed the children of gay fa- 12
thers (Green, 1978; Weeks, Derdeyn, & Langman, 1975). In both studies, the researchers gave psychological tests to the children. The
findings from this testing have been used to support the notion that a
parent's homosexuality has little bearing on the child's sexual orientation. Children showed clear heterosexual preferences or were developing them. Green concluded that "The children I interviewed were
able to comprehend and verbalize the atypical nature of their parents'
lifestyles and to view their atypicality in the broader perspective of the
cultural norm" (p. 696). Our interviews with children have also supported this finding (Barret & Robinson, 1990). Still, the problem is
that the observations of Weeks and his colleagues (1975) are based on
the clinical assessment of only two children, and the Green study
(1978) observed only the children of lesbian mothers and the children
of parents who had experienced sex-change surgery. None of the parents in that sample were classified as gay fathers. The findings of these
two studies and others of lesbian mothers (e.g., Goodman, 1973; Hoeffer, 1981; Kirkpatrick, Smith, & Roy, 1981) are frequently general-
ized to include the gay father's children, even though important
differences exist between transsexuals and gay men as well as between
gay men and lesbians.

CONCLUSIONS

The profile we use to understand and describe gay fathers and their chil- 13
dren is far from conclusive. Clearly, the literature has improved, after
1982, in its use of comparison groups and a more diverse, nationwide
sampling. Still, until researchers can obtain larger, more representative
samples and use more sophisticated research designs, caution must be ex-
ercised in making sweeping generalizations about gay fathers and their

families. Meanwhile, it is possible to speculate from some limited data that, although not fully developed, provides an emerging picture of the children of gay fathers:

1. They are like all kids. Some do well in just about all activities; some have problems; and some are well adjusted.
2. They live in family situations that are unique and must develop strategies to cope with these situations.
3. They need help sorting out their feelings about homosexuality and their anxieties about their own sexual orientation.
4. They may be isolated and angry and may have poor relationships with their fathers.
5. They are in little danger of sexual abuse and unlikely to "catch" homosexuality.
6. Many of them adjust quite well to their family situation and use the family as a means to develop greater tolerance of diversity.
7. Some of them become involved in the human rights movement as they promote gay rights.
8. Their relationships with their fathers have a potential for greater honesty and openness.

REFERENCES

Barret, R., & Robinson, B. (1990). *Gay fathers*. New York: Free Press.

Bigner, J., & Bozett, F. (1989). Parenting by gay fathers. *Marriage and Family Review, 14,* 155–175.

Bigner, J., & Jacobsen, R. (1989a). Parenting behaviors of homosexual and heterosexual fathers. *Journal of Homosexuality, 18,* 173–186.

Bigner, J., & Jacobsen, R. (1989b). The value of children to gay and heterosexual fathers. *Journal of Homosexuality, 18,* 163–172.

Bozett, F. (1980). Gay fathers: How and why they disclose their homosexuality to their children. *Family Relations: Journal of Applied Family and Child Studies, 29,* 173–179.

Bozett, F. (1981). Gay fathers: Evolution of the gay father identity. *American Journal of Orthopsychiatry, 51,* 552–559.

Bozett, F. (1988). Social control of identity of gay fathers. *Western Journal of Nursing Research, 10,* 550–565.

Bozett, F. (1989). Gay fathers: A review of the literature. *Journal of Homosexuality, 18,* 137–162.

Corley, R. (1990). *The final closet: The gay parent's guide to coming out to their children.* Miami: Editech Press.

Epstein, R. (1979, June). Children of gays. *Christopher Street,* 43–50.

Goodman, B. (1973). The lesbian mother. *American Journal of Orthopsychiatry, 43,* 283–284.

Green, R. (1978). Sexual identity of 37 children raised by homosexual or transsexual parents. *American Journal of Psychiatry, 135,* 692–697.

Harris, M., & Turner, P. (1986). Gay and lesbian parents. *Journal of Homosexuality, 18,* 101–113.

Hoeffer, B. (1981). Children's acquisition of sex-role behavior in lesbian-mother families. *American Journal of Orthopsychiatry, 51,* 536–544.

Humphreys, L. (1979). *Tearoom trade.* Chicago: Aldine.

Kirkpatrick, M., Smith, C., & Roy, R. (1981). Lesbian mothers and their children. *American Journal of Orthopsychiatry, 51,* 545–551.

Lewis, K. (1980). Children of lesbians: Their point of view. *Social Work, 25,* 200.

Maddox, B. (1982, February). Homosexual parents. *Psychology Today,* 62–69.

Miller, B. (1979, October). Gay fathers and their children. *The Family Coordinator, 28,* 544–551.

Morin, S., & Schultz, S. (1978). The gay movement and the rights of children. *Journal of Social Issues, 34,* 137–148.

Riddle, D. (1978). Relating to children: Gays as role models. *Journal of Social Issues, 34,* 38–58.

Riddle, D., & Arguelles, M. (1981). Children of gay parents: Homophobia's victims. In I. Stuart & L. Abt (Eds.), *Children of separation and divorce.* New York: Van Nostrand Reinhold.

Robinson, B., & Barret, R. (1986). *The developing father.* New York: Guilford Press.

Scallen, R. (1981). *An investigation of paternal attitudes and behaviors in homosexual and heterosexual fathers.* Doctoral dissertation, California School of Professional Psychology, San Francisco, CA. (*Dissertation Abstracts International, 42,* 3809B).

Spada, J. (1979). *The Spada report.* New York: Signet Books.

Weeks, R. B., Derdeyn, A. P., & Langman, M. (1975). Two cases of children of homosexuals. *Child Psychiatry and Human Development, 6,* 26–32.

READING FOR INFORMATION

1. Why do Barret and Robinson mention repeatedly that most children of gay fathers have experienced their parents' divorce? Why is that an important consideration?

2. Why is it that some gay fathers never disclose their sexuality to their children?

3. List the three strategies that children of gay fathers use when they have to interact with the outside world.

4. Summarize what the research reveals about the effect of parents' homosexuality on their children.

5. According to Barret and Robinson, why must we exercise caution in making generalizations about gay fathers and their children?

READING FOR FORM, ORGANIZATION, AND EXPOSITORY FEATURES

1. Underline and identify the various types of data, research findings, and authorities Barret and Robinson cite to support their view.
2. Which features of Barret and Robinson's writing are particularly scholarly or "academic"?
3. Compare Barret and Robinson's writing style with that of Chip in the case study. How are the two styles similar or different?
4. Notice how Barret and Robinson conclude the selection. Explain whether or not you think the ending is effective.

READING FOR RHETORICAL CONCERNS

1. What is Barret and Robinson's rhetorical purpose? What is the central point they want to communicate to their readers?
2. Why do you think the authors include the case study of Chip? What is the effect on the reader? What would be gained or lost if the case study were left out?
3. Why do you think Barret and Robinson refer to Chip only once? Why don't they analyze or respond to Chip's story?

WRITING ASSIGNMENTS

1. Write a brief summary of the barriers that gay parents and their children must overcome.
2. For an audience who has not read "Children of Gay Fathers," write an essay in which you discuss the problems that children of gay fathers face and explain how these children turn out.
3. Go to the library and research the topic of homosexual parenting. Write a three- to four-page paper answering questions like the following: How do gay men and lesbians become parents? Are the numbers of homosexual families increasing? What is the reaction of conservative groups to gay parenting? What are the views of the gay community?

Mothers, Daughters, and Socialization for Survival

Patricia Hill Collins

Patricia Hill Collins is an associate professor in the Departments of Sociology and African-American Studies at the University of Cincinnati. She is the author of numerous articles on gender, race, and ethnicity and coeditor, with Margaret Andersen, of Race, Class and Gender. *"Mothers, Daughters, and Socialization for Survival" appears in Hill Collin's study of African-American women's intellectual tradition:* Black Feminist Thought: Knowledge, Consciousness, and the Politics of Empowerment *(1991).*

PREREADING

Recall the relationship you had with your birth mother or some other mother figure as you were growing up. Was your mother a strict disciplinarian? Did you consider her to be overprotective? Was she affectionate or reserved? How has your relationship with your mother changed as you have gotten older? Write for a few minutes in your journal.

Black mothers of daughters face a troubling dilemma. On one 1 hand, to ensure their daughters' physical survival, mothers must teach them to fit into systems of oppression. For example, as a young girl Black activist Ann Moody questioned why she was paid so little for the domestic work she began at age nine, why Black women domestics were sexually harassed by their white male employers, why no one would explain the activities of the National Association for the Advancement of Colored People to her, and why whites had so much more than Blacks. But her mother refused to answer her questions and actually chastised her for questioning the system and stepping out of her "place" (Moody 1968). Like Ann Moody, Black daughters learn to expect to work, to strive for an education so they can support themselves, and to anticipate carrying heavy responsibilities in their families and communities because

Patricia Hill Collins, *Black Feminist Thought: Knowledge, Consciousness, and the Politics of Empowerment* (New York: Routledge, 1991) 123–29. Copyright © 1990. Reprinted from *Black Feminist Thought* by Patricia Hill Collins. Reproduced by permission of Routledge, Inc.

these skills are essential to their own survival and those for whom they will eventually be responsible (Ladner 1972; Joseph 1981). New Yorker Michele Wallace recounts: "I can't remember when I first learned that my family expected me to work, to be able to take care of myself when I grew up. . . . It had been drilled into me that the best and only sure support was self-support" (1978, 89–90). Mothers also know that if their daughters uncritically accept the limited opportunities offered Black women, they become willing participants in their own subordination. Mothers may have ensured their daughters' physical survival, but at the high cost of their emotional destruction.

On the other hand, Black daughters with strong self-definitions and self-valuations who offer serious challenges to oppressive situations may not physically survive. When Ann Moody became active in the early 1960s in sit-ins and voter registration activities, her mother first begged her not to participate and then told her not to come home because she feared the whites in Moody's hometown would kill her. Despite the dangers, mothers routinely encourage Black daughters to develop skills to confront oppressive conditions. Learning that they will work and that education is a vehicle for advancement can also be seen as ways of enhancing positive self-definitions and self-valuations in Black girls. Emotional strength is essential, but not at the cost of physical survival.

Historian Elsa Barkley Brown captures this delicate balance Black mothers negotiate by pointing out that her mother's behavior demonstrated the "need to teach me to live my life one way and, at the same time, to provide all the tools I would need to live it quite differently" (1989, 929). Black daughters must learn how to survive in interlocking structures of race, class, and gender oppression while rejecting and transcending those same structures. In order to develop these skills in their daughters, mothers demonstrate varying combinations of behaviors devoted to ensuring their daughters' survival—such as providing them with basic necessities and protecting them in dangerous environments—to helping their daughters go further than mothers themselves were allowed to go.

This special vision of Black mothers may grow from the nature of work women have done to ensure Black children's survival. These work experiences have provided Black women with a unique angle of vision, a particular perspective on the world to be passed on to Black daughters. African and African-American women have long integrated economic self-reliance with mothering. In contrast to the cult of true womanhood, in which work is defined as being in opposition to and incompatible with motherhood, work for Black women has been an important and valued dimension of Afrocentric definitions of Black motherhood. Sara Brooks describes the powerful connections that economic self-reliance and mothering had in her childhood: "When I was about nine I was nursin my sister Sally—I'm about seven or eight years older than Sally. And when I would put her to sleep, instead of me goin somewhere and sit down and play, I'd get my little old hoe and get out there and work right in the field around the house" (in Simonsen 1986, 86).

Mothers who are domestic workers or who work in proximity to whites may experience a unique relationship with the dominant group. For example, African-American women domestics are exposed to all the intimate details of the lives of their white employers. Working for whites offers domestic workers a view from the inside and exposes them to ideas and resources that might aid in their children's upward mobility. In some cases domestic workers form close, long-lasting relationships with their employers. But domestic workers also encounter some of the harshest exploitation confronting women of color. The work is low paid, has few benefits, and exposes women to the threat and reality of sexual harassment. Black domestics could see the dangers awaiting their daughters.

Willi Coleman's mother used a Saturday-night hair-combing ritual to impart a Black women's standpoint on domestic work to her daughters:

> Except for special occasions mama came home from work early on Saturdays. She spent six days a week mopping, waxing and dusting other women's houses and keeping out of reach of other women's husbands. Saturday nights were reserved for "taking care of them girls' hair" and the telling of stories. Some of which included a recitation of what she had endured and how she had triumphed over "folks that were lower than dirt" and "no-good snakes in the grass." She combed, patted, twisted and talked, saying things which would have embarrassed or shamed her at other times. (Coleman 1987, 34)

Bonnie Thornton Dill's (1980) study of the child-rearing goals of domestic workers illustrates how African-American women see their work as both contributing to their children's survival and instilling values that will encourage their children to reject their prescribed "place" as Blacks and strive for more. Providing a better chance for their children was a dominant theme among Black women. Domestic workers described themselves as "struggling to give their children the skills and training they did not have; and as praying that opportunities which had not been open to them would be open to their children" (p. 110). But the women also realized that while they wanted to communicate the value of their work as part of the ethics of caring and personal accountability, the work itself was undesirable. Bebe Moore Campbell's (1989) grandmother and college-educated mother stressed the importance of education. Campbell remembers, "[they] wanted me to Be Somebody, to be the second generation to live out my life as far away from a mop and scrub brush and Miss Ann's floors as possible" (p. 83).

Understanding this goal of balancing the need for the physical sur-   7 vival of their daughters with the vision of encouraging them to transcend the boundaries confronting them explains many apparent contradictions in Black mother-daughter relationships. Black mothers are often described as strong disciplinarians and overly protective; yet these same women manage to raise daughters who are self-reliant and assertive. To explain this apparent contradiction, Gloria Wade-Gayles suggests that Black mothers

> do not socialize their daughters to be "passive" or "irrational." Quite the contrary, they socialize their daughters to be independent, strong and self-confident. Black mothers are suffocatingly protective and domineering precisely because they are determined to mold their daughters into whole and self-actualizing persons in a society that devalues Black women. (1984, 12)

African-American mothers place a strong emphasis on protection,   8 either by trying to shield their daughters as long as possible from the penalties attached to their race, class, and gender status or by teaching them skills of independence and self-reliance so that they will be able to protect themselves. Consider the following verse from a traditional blues song:

> I ain't good lookin' and ain't got waist-long hair
> I say I ain't good lookin' and I ain't got waist-long hair
> But my mama gave me something that'll take me anywhere.
> (Washington 1984, 144)

Unlike white women, symbolized by "good looks" and "waist-long hair," Black women have been denied male protection. Under such conditions it becomes essential that Black mothers teach their daughters skills that will "take them anywhere."

Black women's autobiographies and fiction can be read as texts re-   9
vealing the multiple ways that African-American mothers aim to shield
their daughters from the demands of being Black women in oppressive
conditions. Michele Wallace describes her growing understanding of how
her mother viewed raising Black daughters in Harlem: "My mother has
since explained to me that since it was obvious her attempt to protect
me was going to prove a failure, she was determined to make me realize
that as a black girl in white America I was going to find it an uphill climb
to keep myself together" (1978, 98). In discussing the mother-daughter
relationship in Paule Marshall's *Brown Girl, Brownstones,* Rosalie
Troester catalogues the ways mothers have aimed to protect their daughters and the impact this may have on relationships themselves:

> Black mothers, particularly those with strong ties to their community,
> sometimes build high banks around their young daughters, isolating them
> from the dangers of the larger world until they are old and strong enough
> to function as autonomous women. Often these dikes are religious, but
> sometimes they are built with education, family, or the restrictions of a
> close-knit and homogeneous community.... This isolation causes the cur-
> rents between Black mothers and daughters to run deep and the rela-
> tionship to be fraught with an emotional intensity often missing from the
> lives of women with more freedom. (1984, 13)

Michele Wallace's mother built banks around her headstrong adolescent
daughter by institutionalizing her in a Catholic home for troubled girls.
Wallace went willingly, believing "I thought at the time that I would
rather live in hell than be with my mother" (1978, 98). But years later Wallace's evaluation of her mother's decision changed: "Now that I know my
mother better, I know that her sense of powerlessness made it all the
more essential to her that she take radical action" (p. 98).

African-American mothers try to protect their daughters from the   10
dangers that lie ahead by offering them a sense of their own unique self-
worth. Many contemporary Black women writers report the experience
of being singled out, of being given a sense of specialness at an early age
which encouraged them to develop their talents. My own mother
marched me to the public library at age five, helped me get my first library card, and told me that I could do anything if I learned how to read.
In discussing the works of Paule Marshall, Dorothy West, and Alice
Walker, Mary Helen Washington observes that all three writers make
special claims about the roles their mothers played in the development
of their creativity: "The bond with their mothers is such a fundamental

and powerful source that the term 'mothering the mind' might have been coined specifically to define their experiences as writers" (1984, 144).

Black women's efforts to provide a physical and psychic base for their children can affect mothering styles and the emotional intensity of Black mother-daughter relationships. As Gloria Wade-Gayles points out, "mothers in Black women's fiction are strong and devoted . . . they are rarely affectionate" (1984, 10). For example, in Toni Morrison's *Sula* (1974), Eva Peace's husband ran off, leaving her with three small children and no money. Despite her feelings, "the demands of feeding her three children were so acute she had to postpone her anger for two years until she had both the time and energy for it" (p. 32). Later in the novel Eva's daughter Hannah asks, "Mamma, did you ever love us?" (p. 67). Eva angrily replies, "What you talkin' bout did I love you girl I stayed alive for you" (p. 69). For far too many Black mothers, the demands of providing for children in interlocking systems of oppression are sometimes so demanding that they have neither the time nor the patience for affection. And yet most Black daughters love and admire their mothers and are convinced that their mothers truly love them (Joseph 1981).

Black daughters raised by mothers grappling with hostile environments have to come to terms with their feelings about the difference between the idealized versions of maternal love extant in popular culture and the strict and often troubled mothers in their lives. For a daughter, growing up means developing a better understanding that even though she may desire more affection and greater freedom, her mother's physical care and protection are acts of maternal love. Ann Moody describes her growing awareness of the cost her mother paid as a domestic worker who was a single mother of three. Watching her mother sleep after the birth of another child, Moody remembers:

> For a long time I stood there looking at her, I didn't want to wake her up. I wanted to enjoy and preserve that calm, peaceful look on her face, I wanted to think she would always be that happy. . . . Adline and Junior were too young to feel the things I felt and know the things I knew about Mama. They couldn't remember when she and Daddy separated. They had never heard her cry at night as I had or worked and helped as I had done when we were starving. (1968, 57)

Moody initially sees her mother as a strict disciplinarian, a woman who tris to protect her daughter by withholding information. But as Moody matures and better understands the oppression in her community, her ideas change. On one occasion Moody left school early the day after a Black family had been brutally murdered by local whites. Moody's description of her mother's reaction reflects her deepening understanding: "When I walked in the house Mama didn't even ask me why I came home. She just looked at me. And for the first time I realized she understood what was going on within me or was trying to anyway" (1968, 136).

Another example of a daughter's efforts to understand her mother [13] is offered in Renita Weem's account of coming to grips with maternal desertion. In the following passage Weems struggles with the difference between the stereotypical image of the superstrong Black mother and her own alcoholic mother's decision to leave her children: "My mother loved us. I must believe that. She worked all day in a department store bakery to buy shoes and school tablets, came home to curse out neighbors who wrongly accused her children of any impropriety (which in an apartment complex usually meant stealing), and kept her house cleaner than most sober women" (1984, 26). Weems concludes that her mother loved her because she provided for her to the best of her ability.

Othermothers often help to defuse the emotional intensity of rela- [14] tionships between bloodmothers and their daughters. In recounting how she dealt with the intensity of her relationship with her mother, Weems describes the women teachers, neighbors, friends, and othermothers she turned to—women who, she observes, "did not have the onus of providing for me, and so had the luxury of talking to me" (1984, 27). Cheryl West's household included her brother, her lesbian mother, and Jan, her mother's lover. Jan became an othermother to West: "Yellow-colored, rotund and short in stature, Jan was like a second mother. . . . Jan braided my hair in the morning, mother worked two jobs and tucked me in at night. Loving, gentle, and fastidious in the domestic arena, Jan could be a rigid disciplinarian. . . . To the outside world . . . she was my 'aunt' who happened to live with us. But she was much more involved and nurturing than any of my 'real' aunts" (1987, 43).

June Jordan offers an eloquent analysis of one daughter's realization [15] of the high personal cost African-American women can pay in providing an economic and emotional foundation for their children. In the following passage Jordan offers a powerful testament of how she came to see that her mother's work was an act of love:

> As a child I noticed the sadness of my mother as she sat alone in the kitchen at night. . . . Her woman's work never won permanent victories of any kind. It never enlarged the universe of her imagination or her

power to influence what happened beyond the front door of our house. Her woman's work never tickled her to laugh or shout or dance. But she did raise me to respect her way of offering love and to believe that hard work is often the irreducible factor for survival, not something to avoid. Her woman's work produced a reliable home base where I could pursue the privileges of books and music. Her woman's work invented the potential for a completely different kind of work for us, the next generation of Black women: huge, rewarding hard work demanded by the huge, new ambitions that her perfect confidence in us engendered. (1985, 105)

REFERENCES

Brown, Elsa Barkley. 1989. "African-American Women's Quilting: A Framework for Conceptualizing and Teaching African-American Women's History." *Signs* 14(4): 921–29.

Campbell, Bebe Moore. 1989. *Sweet Summer: Growing Up with and without My Dad.* New York: Putnam.

Coleman, Willi. 1987. "Closets and Keepsakes." *Sage: A Scholarly Journal on Black Women* 4(2): 34–35.

Dill, Bonnie Thornton. 1980. " 'The Means to Put My Children Through': Child-Rearing Goals and Strategies among Black Female Domestic Servants." In *The Black Woman,* edited by La Frances Rodgers-Rose, 107–23. Beverly Hills, CA: Sage.

Jordan, June. 1985. *On Call.* Boston: South End Press.

Joseph, Gloria. 1981. "Black Mothers and Daughters: Their Roles and Functions in American Society." In *Common Differences,* edited by Gloria Joseph and Jill Lewis, 75–126. Garden City, NY: Anchor.

Moody, Ann. 1968. *Coming of Age in Mississippi.* New York: Dell.

Morrison, Toni. 1974. *Sula.* New York: Random House.

Simonsen, Thordis, ed. 1986. *You May Plow Here: The Narrative of Sara Brooks.* New York: Touchstone.

Troester, Rosalie Riegle. 1984. "Turbulence and Tenderness: Mothers, Daughters, and 'Othermothers' in Paule Marshall's *Brown Girl, Brownstones.*" *Sage: A Scholarly Journal on Black Women* 1(2): 13–16.

Wade-Gayles, Gloria. 1980. "She Who Is Black and Mother: In Sociology and Fiction, 1940–1970." In *The Black Woman,* edited by La Frances Rodgers-Rose, 89–106. Beverly Hills, CA: Sage.

———. 1984. "The Truths of Our Mothers' Lives: Mother-Daughter Relationships in Black Women's Fiction." *Sage: A Scholarly Journal on Black Women* 1(2): 8–12.

Wallace, Michele. 1978. *Black Macho and the Myth of the Superwoman.* New York: Dial Press.

Washington, Mary Helen. 1984. "I Sign My Mother's Name: Alice Walker, Dorothy West and Paule Marshall." In *Mothering the Mind: Twelve Studies of Writers and Their Silent Partners,* edited by Ruth Perry and Martine Watson Broronley, 143–63. New York: Holmes & Meier.

Weems, Renita. 1984. " 'Hush. Mama's Gotta Go Bye Bye': A Personal Narrative." *Sage: A Scholarly Journal on Black Women* 1(2): 25–28.

West, Cheryl. 1987. "Lesbian Daughter." *Sage: A Scholarly Journal on Black Women* 4(2): 42–44.

READING FOR INFORMATION

1. Explain in your own words the dilemma African-American mothers of daughters face and the delicate balance they must negotiate.
2. For African-American women, what are the benefits and the drawbacks of doing domestic work for white people?
3. According to Hill Collins, what is one of the main contradictions in black mother-daughter relationships?
4. Explain how African-American mothers offer their daughters a sense of self-worth.
5. Discuss why some African-American mothers are unaffectionate.

READING FOR FORM, ORGANIZATION, AND EXPOSITORY FEATURES

1. What is the effect on the reader of Hill Collins's opening sentence?
2. In addition to citing scholarly works, Hill Collins draws on autobiographies, novels, short stories, even a blues song. Explain how she uses those sources to further her argument.
3. Which of Hill Collin's examples do you find especially moving? Why?
4. How does Hill Collins conclude the piece? Why do you think the selection ends in this way?

READING FOR RHETORICAL CONCERNS

1. What role does Hill Collins assume in relation to her audience? When she shares her personal experience in paragraph 10, what effect does that have on you as a reader?
2. Whom do you think Hill Collins visualizes as her audience? How does she expect her readers to view African-American mothers after they have read this piece?
3. How would the impact of the piece change if a white woman had written it?

WRITING ASSIGNMENTS

1. Summarize Hill Collins explanation of how work defines black motherhood. In your experience, does work define white motherhood in the same way?
2. Write a two- to three-page paper explaining how black mothers' love for their daughters differs from "the idealized versions of maternal love extant in popular culture" (paragraph 12).
3. Write an essay in which you explain how your relationship with your mother is similar to or different from the types of mother-child relationships Hill Collins discusses in her piece.

"People Don't Know Right
from Wrong Anymore"

Lillian B. Rubin

Lillian B. Rubin is Research Sociologist at the Institute for Scientific Analysis. She has written numerous articles and books on issues in sociology, including Women of a Certain Age *(1975),* Worlds of Pain: Life in the Working Class Family *(1976),* Intimate Strangers: Men and Women Together *(1983), and* Just Friends: The Role of Friendship in Our Lives *(1985). "People Don't Know Right from Wrong Anymore" appears in Rubin's most recent book,* Families on the Fault Line *(1994).*

PREREADING

React to the title of the article. In your experience, is it true that "people don't know right from wrong anymore"? What accounts for this phenomenon? Write in your journal for ten minutes.

"I can't believe what kids do today!" exclaims Marguerite Jenk-   1
ins, a white forty-year-old divorce whose seventeen-year-old daughter, Candy, had just had an abortion.

I last met Marguerite more than twenty years ago when I inter-   2
viewed her for *Worlds of Pain.* The slim, pretty young woman who welcomed me into her home then is gone now, replaced by an older, heavier version who bears the visible marks of life's difficulties. As I listen to her angry words about her daughter, the memory of our last meeting moves from the recesses of my mind into awareness. At age twenty, Marguerite already had two children under three; Candy wouldn't come into the world for another three years. Her first-born son had been conceived when she was still in high school. But abortion wasn't an option then. So a few months after she discovered she was pregnant, she left school and married Larry Jenkins, the nineteen-year-old father of the child she was carrying. By the time I met her she was a distraught and overburdened young mother, worrying because her husband had just lost yet another job, fearful that her dream of living happily ever after was crumbling.

Selected excerpts from pages 44–66 from *Families on the Fault Line* by Lillian B. Rubin. Copyright © 1994 by Lillian B. Rubin. Reprinted by permission of HarperCollins Publishers, Inc.

I remember the story Marguerite told of finding out she was   3
pregnant—her terror; her anger at her father, who wanted to throw
her out of the house; at her mother, who didn't protect her from her
father's rage; her bitterness because they were more concerned about
what others would think than about the predicament she found herself in. Hearing Marguerite now, I can understand her concern for
her daughter, her fear that Candy will repeat her mistakes. But given
her own experience, I wonder about her outrage, her seeming lack
of compassion for Candy and for what she might be feeling. So I say,
"I'm a little surprised to hear you talk so angrily, since you got pregnant when you were about her age."

She looks somewhat abashed at the reminder, shifts uncomfortably   4
in her chair, then says, "C'mon, you know it's different now. Sure, I got
caught, too, but we got married. *We had to get married; we didn't have
a choice.*"

"We had to get married"—words spoken by 44 percent of the cou-   5
ples I interviewed two decades ago. But what does "had to" mean? These
marriages weren't coerced, at least not by any obvious outside agent. There
were no old-style shotgun weddings, no self-righteous fathers avenging
the violation of their daughters' virtue by forcing their errant lovers into
saying their vows. The compulsion was internal, part of the moral culture
of the community in which they lived. It was simply what one did.

Sometimes the young couple married regretfully; often one partner,   6
usually the man, was ambivalent. It didn't really matter; they did what was
expected. If you "got caught," you got married; that was the rule, understood by all. As one of the men I interviewed then put it: "If you
knocked up a girl, you married her; that was it. You just did it, that's all.
End of story."

But in fact, it was only the beginning of the story. Seven years and   7
three children after Marguerite and Larry Jenkins did what their parents and their community expected of them, he walked out. Young, unskilled, and seething at being tied down by responsibilities he was unable
to meet, Larry floated from one dead-end job to another, at each one
acting out his resentment until he got fired or quit. Marguerite, frightened for her children, furious with disappointment, and exhausted from
their constant battles, finally gave him an ultimatum: Shape up or get
out! To her surprise, he stormed out of the house and came back only to
claim his belongings a few days later. "I said it, but I didn't really think
he'd do it. I figured I'd finally scare him into being more responsible," she
explains as she reviews those years.

With no family to help her and three small children whose father   8
couldn't or wouldn't support them, Marguerite had no choice: She spent
the next five years on welfare rolls. "I was so ashamed to go down to the
welfare office. I can't explain how bad I felt; I wasn't raised that way. My
parents, they had their problems, but my father was a hard worker. He
didn't make much, but we got by without charity.

"I used to think welfare people were freeloaders, you know, like   9
they were lazy bums. Then it happened to me and I kept thinking: *I can't
believe it! How did this happen to me? I'm not like that.*" She looks away,
trying to contain the tears that well up as the memory of those hard times
washes over her.

"Marrying Larry, that whole thing, it was a giant mistake right from   10
the beginning. You get married with this dream that everything's going
to be wonderful, but it never works out that way, does it? How could it?
We were babies, and there we were trying to be grown-ups. We had two
kids by the time I was nineteen and he was, I don't know, maybe not
even twenty-one yet. I wasn't ready to be a wife and a mother, and he sure
wasn't ready to be a decent husband and father."

The Jenkinses' story is a common one among the families I met   11
twenty years ago. Two young people thrust into a marriage by the lack
of acceptable moral or social alternatives, only to divorce a few years
later. Since they married so young, sometimes even before they finished
high school, the women had little opportunity to develop any marketable
skills, certainly none that would enable them to support their children
and pay for child care while they worked. Of the thirty-two *Worlds of
Pain* families I was able to locate, eighteen (56 percent) had been divorced. All but one of the men had remarried by the time I met them
again. The lone exception had separated from his wife a few months
earlier and was already involved with a woman in what he took to be a
serious relationship.

For the women it was different: Only eleven had remarried; the   12
rest had been single for five years or more. All of them talked about the
economic devastation divorce wrought in their families. Well over half
needed some form of public assistance during the years when they were
divorced. Some were on the welfare rolls; others got by with food stamp
supplements alone. For the women who haven't remarried, life continues to be economically unstable at best.

If their own young marriages so often were, as Marguerite Jenkins   13
says, "a giant mistake right from the beginning," why aren't such women
more supportive of their daughters' choices? Indeed, why aren't they

pleased that the young women they raised have so many more options available to them? I ask the question: "Given what's happened in your own life, I wonder why you're not glad that Candy could make other choices?"

"Don't get me wrong, I think it's okay to have an abortion; I'm— 14 what do they call it?—oh yeah, for choice," explains Marguerite. "I mean, I don't think people should run around having abortions just like that, but nobody's got a right to tell somebody what to do about being pregnant or not. God knows, I don't want her to do what I did. It's just that. . . ." She stops, searching for the right words, and after a moment or two, continues, still uncertain. "I don't know exactly how to say it. Look, I was scared to death when I found out I was pregnant, and so was Larry. These kids, they're not even bothered now."

It's this sense that their children see the world so differently that's 15 so hard for working-class parents. For it seems to say that now, along with the economic dislocation they suffer, even their children are out of their reach, that they can no longer count on shared values to hold their families together. It doesn't help either that no matter where they look, they don't see a reflection of themselves. If they look up, they see a life-style and values they abhor, the same ones that, they believe, are corrupting their children. If they shift their gaze downward, they see the poor, the homeless, the helpless—the denizens of the dangerous under-class whose moral degeneracy has, in the working-class view, led to their fall. It's as if their beliefs and values have no place in the institutional world they inhabit, not in the schools their children attend, not on the television shows they watch, not in the films they see, not in the music they hear, not in the laws their government promulgates.

It's true that this isn't a problem only for working-class families. 16 Middle-class parents also worry about the changing cultural norms; they also fret endlessly about "what kids do today." Indeed, generational conflict over changing values and life-styles is common to all families, with parents generally holding onto the old ways and children pulling for the new ones. But it's also true that the issues that create conflict in families differ quite sharply by class.

Middle-class parents long ago accepted the norms, values, and be- 17 havior that have only recently filtered down into the working class—the open expression of premarital sex, for example, or living together without benefit of clergy. Partly perhaps these changes came earlier and with less upheaval in middle-class families because it was their children who initiated the struggle for change. But there are other reasons as well.

High among them is the fact that middle-class parents are likely to be more educated than those in the working class. And it's widely understood that a college education tends to broaden perspectives and liberalize attitudes about the kind of life-style and value changes we have seen in the last few decades.

Since most working-class parents haven't been exposed to the array 18 of ideas found in a college classroom, they tend to be more tradition bound. "You get used to doing things one way and then you think it's the right way," says thirty-six-year-old Jane Dawson, a white mother of two teenagers. Without the expanded horizons that higher education affords, the old way often becomes the only way. "If it was good enough for us, it's fine for my kids," proclaims her husband, Bill.

But the cultural changes that have swept the land during these past 19 decades will not be stayed by parental nostalgia, fear, or authority. The young people in this study agree that their values about such issues as sexual behavior, marriage, and gender roles are radically different from those their parents hold. And they're pained by the family conflicts these differences stir. But they also insist that they're not the thoughtless, hedonistic lot of their parents' imaginations. "My mom thinks I think getting pregnant is no big deal, but she doesn't understand," says Candy Jenkins, her blue eyes turning stormy with anger when we talk about this a few days after my meeting with her mother. "Just because I didn't carry on like some kind of a crazy person, she thinks I didn't care. But it's not true; I did care. I was scared to death when I found out."

"I was scared to death when I found out"—the same words spoken 20 decades apart by a mother and her daughter. Both shared the fear of their parents' response. "I thought my father would kill me," says Marguerite. "I was afraid my mother would murder me," shudders Candy. Beyond that, however, the words have entirely different meanings for each of them.

For Marguerite, getting pregnant was a problem; not to have got- 21 ten married would have been a catastrophe. For her, therefore, the critical question was: *Will he marry me?* "I was terrified. What if Larry reneged and wouldn't marry me? What would I do?"

For Candy, however, the pregnancy could be taken care of; mar- 22 riage loomed like a calamity. "The one thing I knew was I didn't want to get married and have a baby. I was really scared my mom would try to make me. She kept going on about how ashamed she was, and what was she going to tell grandma, and all like that. But she didn't push me about getting married. I mean, she talked about it, but she knew it was a bum idea, too. Look at what happened to her."

For Marguerite, shame was a big issue, not just the memory of her 23
own shame, but the fact that it wasn't one of her daughter's preoccupations. "I just can't get over it," Marguerite remarks, shaking her head in
bewilderment. "I wanted to die because I was so ashamed. I felt like I'd
never be able to hold my head up again. Now these kids, it's like it's nothing to them; they've got no shame. I'll bet half the school knows she was
pregnant. They probably compare notes about their damn abortions,"
she concludes with disgust.

Shame and guilt—the emotions that give evidence of the effec- 24
tiveness of our social norms, that reassure us that the moral culture has
been internalized, that there will be a price for its violation. If our young
suffer, if they're tormented by shame, haunted by guilt, we can at least
be assured that they share our values about good and evil, right and
wrong. Without that, the gap between us seems disturbingly wide and the
future frighteningly uncertain.

But to cast the issue in these terms—that is, either we suffer shame 25
and guilt or we don't—misses the point. It's not true that our children
don't experience these feelings. But what evokes them is not fixed in
eternity. Rather, it changes with time, each historical moment delivering up its own variation of a culture's norms and values, each one defining its transgressions and eliciting shame and guilt for their violation.

For Marguerite's mother, divorce would have been unthinkable, a 26
humiliating and guilt-ridden scandal, a painful public admission of failure and inadequacy. By the time Marguerite was divorced, it was a sad
but commonplace event, certainly nothing to hide in shame about. For
Marguerite, her pregnancy was a shameful confession that she had, in
the language of the day, "gone all the way"—an act, once it became
known, that threatened to cast her out of respectable society and to label
her a "slut." For Candy, there was a mix of feelings, some of them no
doubt the same as her mother felt decades earlier—regret, fear, sadness,
confusion, anger at herself for taking sexual chances when she knew better. But not shame—not because she's a less moral person than her mother but because she grew up in a sexual culture that gives permission for
a level of sexual freedom unknown to her mother's generation.

"As long as two people love each other, there's nothing wrong with 27
making love," declares Tory, the white sixteen-year-old daughter of the
Bowen family. "I don't understand why it's only supposed to be okay if
you're married. I mean, why is getting married such a big deal?"

This, perhaps, is one of the most important changes underlying the 28
permissiveness about sex. If getting married is no longer "such a big deal,"

why wait for marriage to explore one's sexuality? If sexual relations out-side marriage are acceptable once people have been divorced, then why not before they get married? Repeatedly, the young people I met raised these and other questions as we discussed the changing norms around marriage and sex.

The sexual revolution, which changed the rules about the expres-sion of female sexuality; the gender revolution, with its demand for the reordering of traditional roles and relationships; the divorce revolution, which fractured the social contract about marriage and commitment; the shifts in the economy, which forced increasing numbers of married women into the labor force—all these have come together to create a profoundly different consciousness about marriage and its role divisions for young people today. 29

Twenty years ago it was marriage that occupied the dreams of a working-class high-school girl. Among the *Worlds of Pain* families, the women were, on average, eighteen when they married; the men, twenty. Two decades later, none of the families I reinterviewed has a son who married at twenty or younger, and just one has a daughter who was only eighteen when she married. The others either married considerably later or are still single—some at twenty-four and twenty-five—something that almost never happened by choice twenty years ago. 30

The national statistics tell the same story. In 1970, the average age at which women married for the first time was 20.6 years; for men, it was 22.5. Two decades later it had jumped to 24.2 for women, 26.2 for men. Today 18.8 percent of women and 29.4 percent of men are still unmar-ried when they reach thirty, compared to 6.2 percent and 9.4 percent, re-spectively, twenty years ago. 31

Women in particular are much more ambivalent about hearing wed-ding bells than they were a couple of generations ago, aware that the changes they have undergone, the kind of marital partnerships they now long for, are rarely matched by the men who are their prospective mates. Therefore, they talk of wanting to explore the options available, to live life more fully and openly before taking on the responsibilities of marriage and parenthood. 32

But delaying the trip to the altar isn't a rejection of marriage and the commitment it entails. Rather, it's a dream deferred, part of a changing culture, which itself has developed in response to shifting social reali-ties. For the culture of a nation, a group, or a tribe is a living thing, stretch-ing, changing, expanding, or contracting as new needs arise and old ones die, as the exigencies of living in one era give way to new ones in the 33 next. So, for example, now that great advances in medical technology have lengthened the life span beyond anything earlier generations ever dreamed of, the age when people marry moves upward.

When people died at fifty and large families were the norm, there 34
was a good chance at least one parent would never live to see the children into adulthood. Therefore, it made no sense to wait until twenty-five or thirty before starting a family. Now, when, on the average, women live to nearly eighty and men to a little over seventy, we can marry and bear children very much later, safe in the knowledge that we'll be around to raise and nurture them as long as they need us. The forty-year-old first-time father today worries about whether he'll be able to play football with his son at twelve, not whether he'll be alive when the boy becomes a man.

I don't mean that we think consciously about the impact of our 35
longer life. It's the kind of knowledge that generally remains out of awareness but that, nevertheless, profoundly influences our life decisions. For a social change of this magnitude, one that gives us so many more years of life, also adds stages to the life course that were unknown before. Adolescence is extended, adulthood becomes another stage in our continuing growth and development, and old age appears on the scene as a part of life that requires planning and attention—changes and additions that have social, cultural, and psychological repercussions.

The same is true for the culture of marriage. When life ended at 36
fifty, people didn't feel deprived if their relationships weren't intimate or companionable enough. They were too busy earning a living, raising their children, and hoping they'd survive long enough to see them grown. Now, when wives and husbands know they have decades of active life ahead of them after shepherding their children into adulthood, the emotional quality of the marital relationship takes on fresh importance. *What will we talk about after the children are gone?* becomes a crucial question when people expect to live thirty or forty years beyond that marker event. And marriage takes on a different and more complex character as a whole new set of needs comes to the fore.

Although class, race, and ethnicity all affect marriage patterns, only 37
among African-Americans do the marital statistics tell a significantly different story. In 1991 just over 41 percent of Black Americans were married, compared to nearly 62 percent among whites and Hispanics. Thirty-five percent of Blacks have never been married, while for whites the comparable figure is 20 percent. And Black brides and grooms are, on the average, two years older than their white counterparts when they walk down the aisle for the first time.

For as long as I can remember, I've heard these differences ex- 38 plained as an artifact of culture—an explanation that suggests that Blacks value marriage less or that their moral code is less lofty than the one by which other Americans live. It's an easy explanation, one that allows us to look away from unpalatable social realities and their effect on the most personal decisions of our lives. If culture is the culprit, then it's people who need fixing, not society. But, in fact, beneath these cold statistics lies a story of immeasurable human suffering and loneliness.

This is not to say that culture plays no part in the marriage patterns 39 of African-Americans. Their history of slavery and the prejudice and discrimination they have suffered since then undoubtedly have left their mark in the shape of subcultural variations that affect beliefs and attitudes about marriage. Obviously, too, the cultural fallout from past experience can take on a life of its own and linger into the present long after the immediate provocations are gone. But in this case, it's the social and economic realities of life in the Black community today, not the adversity and suffering of the past, that control the difference in marriage rates between Blacks and Americans of other ethnic and racial groups.

The official unemployment rate for adult Black men, for example, 40 is roughly 15 percent, compared to 6.8 percent for white men. And it's common knowledge that more than twice that number never make it to the Labor Department's unemployment statistics. At the same time, Black men in the prime marriageable ages of twenty-five to thirty who are lucky enough to have jobs earn nearly one-third less than whites: $14,333 compared to $20,153. With unemployment so high and underemployment virtually epidemic, it's hard to imagine how either women or men could make serious plans for marriage. A man who can barely support himself isn't likely to look forward to taking on the responsibilities of a wife and children. Nor is a woman apt to see him as a great marriage prospect. Add to these economic realities the fact that roughly one in eighty young black men is a victim of violent death and that half the inmates of our state prisons are Black men, and we have a picture of a community with an acute shortage of marriageable men.

These are the social conditions out of which the marriage patterns 41 of the African-American community have grown. To speak of culture and its effect on the timing and sequencing of the various life stages, including when or if we marry, without knowing the particular life circumstances of a people misses the crucial connection between the emergence of cultural forms and the structure of social life. In the African-American community, eligible women far outnumber marriageable men—the major reason why fewer people are able to make the trip to the altar and also why those who marry do so substantially later than men and women in other ethnic and racial groups.

For a Black woman, then, finding a man with whom to share her 42 life presents a far more daunting challenge than for others of the same class and age—a source of concern to both parents and daughters in the African-American families I met. "I worry that my daughter's never going to find a good man," Regina Peterson, a forty-year-old Black cashier says, shaking her head sadly. "It's not like when I was coming up; there were still some good men around then, like her father. He's a good man; he always took care of his family, even when it was hard. But today, whew, I don't know what these young girls will do. It's a real problem."

Regina's husband, Sherman, echoes her worries and adds angrily, 43 "The young men today, they're nothing but bums. I don't want no daughter of mine taking up with the likes of them."

When I meet Althea, the Petersons' eighteen-year-old daughter, 44 she talks solemnly about the difficulties the dearth of marriageable men raise for Black women, then exclaims hotly: "It's crazy; it makes me so mad. The papers and the TV keep saying about how Black girls are always having babies without being married. But who are we supposed to marry, tell me, huh? It's not like there's some great guys around here, sitting around just waiting for us. Most of the guys around here, they're hanging on the corner talking big talk, but they're never going to amount to anything. When I see those white people on the TV telling us we should get married, I just want to tell them to shut up because they don't know what they're talking about. What Black girl wouldn't want to be married instead of raising her kids alone?"

I wonder, as I listen to her, what this young woman who's headed 45 for the middle class will do when her time comes. So I ask: "What about you? Will you have children alone if you don't find someone to marry?"

She sits quietly for a moment, her chin resting on her closed fist, her 46 brow furrowed in an expression of sober concentration, then says, "I can't say what I'll do. Right now I know I have to get educated if I want to make something of myself. When I finish college and have a good job, then I'll see. I know I want children some day; not now, but someday. And I'd like to be married like my parents; I know it's better for kids that way. But what if I can't find someone to marry? Then I don't know for sure, but I think I probably would have kids on my own. It's better than not having any, isn't it?" she concludes rhetorically.

With the changed economy, the fantasies about marriage that once 47
separated white women from their Black counterparts have faded. Like
their Black sisters, few white working-class girls or young women now harbor the illusion that they'll be stay-at-home moms. Since it's harder to
convince themselves that they're working just to mark time until real life
begins with the man of their dreams, work becomes a more central part
of their life plan.

Twenty-year-old Nancy Krementz, a white clerk in a New York in- 48
surance company who lives with her family, talks about her expectations:
"If I'm going to have to work after I get married anyway, I might as well
wait. This way I get to do things I wouldn't be able to if I was married and
had kids. This job I've got is okay, but I really want to work myself up a
little. I figure if I'm going to have to work, I want to do something more
interesting. So I'm taking some night courses on the computer now, and
maybe I can get one of the better jobs in the company. I don't know,
sometimes I even think maybe I'll go to college. I couldn't do that if I was
married, could I?"

The men also have no plans to rush into marriage. "I'm not going 49
to get married for a long time," says Nancy's nineteen-year-old brother,
Michael. "It's not like it used to be when my father was growing up. People expected to get married right away out of school. But not now. I'm
going to have some fun before I get married, you know, meet a lot of
girls, travel around, things like that."

For the men, such dreams aren't new, even if they were rarely ful- 50
filled. But the women's talk about work, about travel, about wanting to
live on their own for a while—all options that few young working-class
women dared dream of in my earlier study—represents a dramatic shift
from the past. "Sure, I want to get married some day, but I'm not ready
to settle down—not for a long time yet," says Claire Stansell, a white
nineteen-year-old office worker. "There's too many other things I want to
do, like traveling and seeing different things. You know," she says, her
eyes opening wide, "the first time I was ever on an airplane was last year
after I graduated high school and got a job."

The changing marriage patterns have had a profound effect on the 51
lives of working-class families. Among the families I interviewed two
decades ago, it was unthinkable for an unmarried daughter to live outside the family home. From father's house to husband's, that was the expectation, the accepted way of life for a young working-class woman then.
Even sons generally were expected to live at home until they married,
partly because their earnings were important to the family economy but

also because it was the way of the world in which they lived. Now, both daughters and sons are eager to leave the parental roof as quickly as they can afford it.

But how does this fit with all the stories we hear about adult chil- 52 dren who don't want to leave home these days because it's easier, cheaper, and more comfortable to live with their parents? Once again, class tells. Middle-class adolescents have long expected to leave home at eighteen, when they go off to college. For them, therefore, there may be some novelty in coming back into the family household as adults, essentially able to live their lives as they please.

For the grown children of working-class families, however, it isn't 53 living at home that's new; it's the cultural changes over the last two decades that have made it possible to think about leaving. For them, this has been a liberation—a liberation the failing economy has stripped from them and about which they're unhappy and resentful.

But the culture of class isn't the whole answer. Class culture is, after 54 all, bred in the economics of class. And it's in their different economic situations that particular attitudes about living at home are born, as this chance conversation I had with the twenty-four-year-old son of an upper middle-class white professional family shows so clearly: "I moved back into the old homestead because it's more comfortable than anything I can afford," he explained easily. "My old room's still there; the food and service is great; and it doesn't cost anything. I've got plenty of privacy; nobody pays any attention to my comings and goings. So why not? This way I get to live the life I'm used to, which I can't afford on my own. I can travel when I want and do what I want. Instead of wasting the money I make on the exorbitant rents you have to pay in this city, I put it into living a decent life. I guess it's got its down side, but the up side outweighs it by a lot so far."

He spoke so easily about freedom and privacy that I found myself 55 wondering: *Would this be equally true for the daughters in these families? Would parents be as easy about a daughter's privacy, about her comings and goings, about where she might be spending the night, or with whom she might be sharing her bed?* Although there are no good studies to answer these questions, the significantly smaller proportion of women aged twenty-five to thirty-four who live under the parental roof—32 percent of single men, 20 percent of women—suggests that far fewer women than men voluntarily make this choice.

This digression aside, my conversation with my young friend was il- 56 luminating, since it raised so sharply the difference class makes for young adults who live at home. As Katherine Newman, an anthropologist writing about the declining fortunes of the middle class, puts it, "It is precisely among the more affluent of America's families that the drop in a young person's standard of living is most acutely apparent when they move out on their own. Hence it comes as little surprise to discover that children living in households with annual incomes above $50,000 are more likely to remain at home with their parents than those in households less well heeled."

For the working-class young, living at home is a necessity, not a 57 choice. And necessity rarely makes good bedfellows or housemates. Like the adult children of middle-class families, the young people I met also "get to live the life" they're used to. But it's not a life they covet. For there's not much of an "up side" to outweigh the down in a house that was already too small to permit privacy when they were children, a house whose walls seem even more confining in adulthood. Nor does living at home allow them the freedom to travel or the chance to do what they want—the very things that make living with mom and dad an attractive alternative for the children of the middle class.

In working-class families, where it's a stretch to pay the bills each 58 month, there's no free ride for adult children who live under the parental roof. Instead, a substantial portion of their income goes to paying their way. Socially, too, living at home confines their lives much more closely than if they were out of the house. For unlike the culturally liberal middle-class parents of the young man above, most working-class parents continue to try to keep a tight rein on their children and to insist on a code of moral behavior that more closely matches their own.

In *Worlds of Pain* I argued that the authoritarian child-rearing style 59 so often found in working-class families stems in part from the fact that parents see around them so many young people whose lives are touched by the pain and delinquency that so often accompanies a life of poverty. Therefore, these parents live in fear for their children's future—fear that they'll lose control, that the children will wind up on the streets or, worse yet, in jail.

But the need for the kind of iron control working-class parents so 60 often exhibit has another, more psychological dimension, as well. For only if their children behave properly by their standards, only if they look and act in ways that reflect honor on the family, can these parents begin to relax about their status in the world, can they be assured that they will be distinguished from those below. This is their ticket to respectability—the neat, well-dressed, well-behaved, respectful child;

the child who can be worn as a badge, the public certification of the family's social position.

Since neither the internal needs nor the eternal conditions change 61 when children reach adulthood, working-class parents continue to try to control their adult children's behavior so long as they live under the parental roof. "It's my house; he'll do what I say," is a favorite saying of fathers in these households. Obviously, it doesn't work that way much of the time. But this doesn't keep them from trying—an effort that makes for plenty of intergenerational conflict.

It was no surprise, therefore, that—whether male or female—every 62 one of the working-class young adults I interviewed was itching to find a way out of the parental home. "As soon as I got a job and saved some money, me and my two friends found this apartment," explains Emily Petrousso, a white nineteen-year-old who shares a tiny one-bedroom apartment with two roommates.

"How did your parents feel about your moving out?" 63

She makes a face, wrinkling her nose, and says with a shrug, "My 64 mom's okay; I think she understands. But my father, he's something else; like, he's living in another century. He still thinks it's terrible that I don't live in his house and get his permission to go out on a date. Both of them worry about the neighborhood I live in; like, they're afraid it's not safe and stuff like that. But it's okay now. It was a big deal at first, but they got used to it. And anyhow they knew they couldn't stop me."

"They knew they couldn't stop me"—a sentence her parents 65 wouldn't have dared to speak at her age and precisely the source of parental concern. "You got no control over kids anymore!" storms Emily's father, George, a second-generation Greek-American. "What the hell's a kid like that doing out there living by herself. We got room here; nobody gets in her way. If my sister would've even *thought* about something like that, my father would've killed her. I'm just glad he's not alive to see what kids do today. It's not right; I tell my wife that all the time. But even she don't listen; she just sticks up for her."

His wife, Nicole, whose role in the family has always been to soothe 66 and smooth the relationships between father and children, tells it this way: "He thinks I stick up for Emily; I don't know, maybe I do, but it's only because he gets so crazy sometimes, and I'm afraid if he keeps going at her like that, she'll stop coming around." She pauses, thinks for a moment, then continues with a sigh, "So I keep telling him she's a good girl, but everything's different now. You can't compare what we were like. I mean, I didn't even *think* about the things she talks about doing, like going on some kind of a trip by myself or with a girlfriend. *Who thought about things like that?* I don't know; what do you say to kids today about anything. It's so different now."

"Is it just different, or do you also think it's worse?" I ask Nicole.   67

She looks surprised at the question, then after a moment leans for-   68
ward in her chair and lowers her voice as if to confide a guilty secret: "You know, I ask myself that question, but I don't hear anybody else wondering about it like I do. So then I think maybe there's something wrong with me. Everybody's always talking about how bad things are, you know, how the kids do such terrible things, and all that. But sometimes I sit here thinking I don't know if it's so bad; it's such a different world. I mean, some things are worse, sure, but maybe not everything. I mean, was it so good in our days?

"In a way I'm kind of glad she doesn't live here now. This way I   69
don't have to see what she's doing all the time. I know she does things I wouldn't like; she doesn't tell me, but I know. My husband, he knows, too, I guess. It's why he's so angry at her all the time." She sighs, "Me? I worry a lot because I don't know how it'll end." She pauses as she hears her words and laughs. "That's it, you don't know the end of the story, so you worry."

"You don't know the end of the story, so you worry." This is pre-   70
cisely the issue. But it's not just the end of the moral story that's in question, it's the economic future that's also unknown. True, working-class parents have always worried about economic hard times for themselves and their children. But until the recent turmoil in the economy, they could also dream about a better future. It's this new reality that has turned up the emotional register around the cultural changes. At the very moment that the economy has let them down, the moral structure on which they've built their lives has been shaken by a jolting, jarring upheaval that has shifted the ground on which they stand. If the old values are gone, what's to separate them from those below? What's to protect their children from falling into the abyss?

Is it any wonder that these families feel as if they're living on a fault   71
line that threatens to open up and engulf them at any moment? Both economically and culturally they're caught in a whirlwind of change that leaves them feeling helplessly out of control. As they struggle with the shifting cultural norms—with the gap between the ideal statements of the culture in which they came to adulthood and the one into which their children are growing today—nothing seems to make sense anymore. Even those who inveigh most forcefully against the new morality and proclaim

most angrily that "people don't know right from wrong anymore" are no longer so sure about what they really believe. Consequently, they respond to my questions about any number of the moral issues that vex them with unequivocal answers about right and wrong—only to retreat into uncertainty and ambivalence in the next sentence. They yearn for a past when, it seems to them, moral absolutes reigned, yet they're confused and uncertain about which of yesterday's moral strictures they want to impose on themselves and their children today.

It isn't that they're unaware that the absolutes didn't govern so ab-   72 solutely, that what people said and what they did were often at odds. But the unambiguous rules seemed at least to promise a level of stability and a consensus that's missing now, not just in families but in the nation at large. The very clarity they seek eludes them, however, as they're forced by circumstances to make choices in their own families that fly in the face of their stated beliefs.

People who worry about the high divorce rate and insist on the sanc-   73 tity of the family bond suddenly become less certain when marital misery hits home. Asked whether they would want their own child to stay in an obviously bad marriage—one where a spouse is abusive, an alcoholic, or a drug user, for example—the answer is an emphatic no, a response that's delivered especially forcefully by women who themselves have done so.

Women who say they believe mothers belong at home with their   74 children leave to go to work every day. It's an economic necessity, they explain. But listen to them for a while and they'll soon admit that there's much about being in the world of work that they enjoy—and that they wouldn't give it up easily.

People who shudder at the idea of homosexuality take a deep breath   75 and another look when a son or daughter comes out of the closet. They may weep bitter tears when they hear the news; they may deny the reality of what they've heard; they may rail against God; they may blame themselves. But in most families, acceptance eventually comes. Asked how it's possible, given their earlier fears, feelings, and hostilities, they have many answers. "I see that he's happier now." "Her partner's such a nice person." "I didn't really understand about it before." "It's his choice; what can I do?" But the bottom line is: "This is my child!"

Parents who disapprove strongly of premarital sex also wish their   76 children wouldn't marry as young as they themselves did. But they know, too, that their daughters are unlikely to remain celibate into their twenties. I say "daughters" because, despite the changing norms around female sexuality, a son's sexual activity is taken for granted, a daughter's is still a problem for most working-class parents. Asked to choose between an early marriage for a girl and premarital sex, most parents—especially mothers—opt for sex, consoling themselves with the hope that their daughters will wait until "they're old enough." What this means varies, of course, but the most common response is, "at least until they're eighteen."

People who don't approve of abortions will also tell you that they 77 wouldn't want their sons and daughters to "have to marry." Forced to make a choice between a teenage marriage, an adoption, and an abortion, they agonize; they suffer; they equivocate. But when the last word is in, most come down on the side of abortion.

Tales from the abortion battlefront suggest that this is not uncom- 78 mon, even among people who are antiabortion activists. During the 1992 presidential election, Vice President Dan Quayle, an ardent and outspoken foe of abortion, was asked what he'd do if his teenage daughter became pregnant. The politician retreated; the father stepped forward. "I hope that I never have to deal with it," he replied. "But obviously I would counsel her and talk to her and support her on whatever decision she made." Incredulous, the interviewer pressed on: "If the decision was abortion you'd support her?" The vice president stood firm: "I'd support my daughter."

A few days later, President Bush, also a staunch opponent of abor- 79 tion, was asked what he'd do if one of his granddaughters told him she was considering an abortion. He'd try to talk her out of it, he said, but would support her decision. "So in the end the decision would be hers?" the interviewer asked. "Well, who else's—who else's could it be?" said this president, who has spoken out frequently and forcefully against allowing other women to make that choice.

Even more interesting than what these politicians-turned-father- 80 and-grandfather said is what they *didn't* say. Neither ruled out the question as absurd, a product of some wild fantasy, of the fevered imagination of the media in an election year. Neither said: *My teenage daughter sexually active? Impossible! My granddaughter pregnant and unmarried? Never!* Nor did anyone else, not even Marilyn Quayle, who disagreed with her husband and insisted that she'd force her daughter to carry the child to term.

This ambivalence, this simultaneous holding of two seemingly 81 contradictory sets of beliefs shouldn't surprise us. Changing cultures mean stormy times. The interaction between new norms and values and the people who must live them out is never tranquil and easy. The old consciousness doesn't go quietly into the night. Instead, it fusses and fumes, drags its feet, goads us with reminders of its existence, and foments an internal struggle that leaves us anxious and bewildered, wondering what we believe, how we feel.

It's not uncommon to find ourselves doing new things, even wanting 82 to do them, while at the same time feeling uneasy about them. Many of the women who were in the forefront of the sexual revolution, for example, were surprised at the internal conflict their new behaviors stirred. Observing this contest between the old and the new, some researchers concluded that the sexual constraints of the past were "natural," that women couldn't or didn't want to shed them. But those pundits misread the data. Partly they misunderstood what they saw because their vision was blurred by their deeply internalized traditional beliefs about the nature of female sexuality. But it was also because they didn't appreciate the messiness inherent in the process of cultural change, didn't understand that the internalization and integration of new cultural mores often lags well behind behavioral changes.

Indeed, the internal resistance to new ways of being generally has 83 nothing to do with whether we can or want to change. Psychologists see this all the time—people who come into psychotherapy wanting to change, yet, when faced with the possibility, they retreat in fear. We call it "resistance," but in fact it's a normal human response. The old ways worked, perhaps imperfectly, perhaps with more pain than was necessary, but we accommodated and survived. Psychologically, therefore, it's hard to give them up even when we know there's a better way.

In our struggle to make sense of our rapidly changing world, to de- 84 fine rules for living that meet today's needs, old values are forced into a confrontation with the new realities of family and social life. The result is the emergence of values that are different—different and not always as firm and clear as we'd like them to be. Therefore, we become edgy and confused, wanting to reach back to the past, to a time when everything seemed more certain. But it's well to remember what historians of the family have been telling us for some time now: The golden age of the family for which we yearn with such intensity never really existed. Instead, families have always been a "haven in a heartless world" and a breeding ground for pain, sorrow, disappointment, and discontent. Everyone who has ever lived in a family knows both sides. But our longing for what seems from this distance to be the simplicity and certainly of earlier times has blinded us to this complex reality of family life.

Yes, there are real problems in the family today, problems as large 85 or larger than any we have ever known. Yes, we live in what one family scholar has called an "embattled paradise." Yes, the changing cultural norms often leave parents and children without a blueprint for caring and responsible social and personal behavior. These are issues that deserve our serious attention and our considered thought. But the transformation of family life will not be reversed with endless discussions about the state of our moral culture. Instead, they serve to turn our attention away from the central problems families face today—problems wrought at least in part by a government and an economy that long ago stopped working for all but the most privileged.

READING FOR INFORMATION

1. Underline and paraphrase Rubin's central position or thesis.
2. Explain in your own words how generational conflicts within families differ with class.
3. Explain what Rubin means when she says, "It's not true that our children don't experience these feelings [shame and guilt]. But what evokes them is not fixed in eternity. Rather, it changes with time, each historical moment delivering up its own variation of a culture's norms and values, each one defining its transgressions and eliciting shame and guilt for their violation" (paragraph 25).
4. Paraphrase Rubin's definition of culture.
5. Explain what Rubin means in paragraph 41 when she says, "To speak of culture and its effect on timing and sequencing of the various life stages, including when or if we marry, without knowing the particular life circumstances of a people misses the crucial connection between the emergence of cultural forms and the structure of social life".
6. What do you think about young people's economic situation affecting their decision to live at home? Can you give some examples from your own experience?
7. List some reasons for working-class parents' authoritarian parenting styles.
8. How do you react to Rubin's claim in paragraph 71 that today's parents are "living on a fault line that threatens to open up and engulf them at any moment"?

READING FOR FORM, ORGANIZATION, AND EXPOSITORY FEATURES

1. One of the organizational patterns Rubin employs is comparison and contrast. Which groups does she compare, and what similarities and differences does she discuss?

2. Do you think that Rubin is writing for a wide audience or for scholarly, academic readers? How did you come to that conclusion?
3. Assume that you are an editor who has been asked to create subheadings for this article. Indicate where you would break up the article, and tell what subheadings you would insert.
4. Why do you think Rubin quotes Dan Quayle and George Bush in paragraphs 78 and 79? What functions do the two examples serve?

READING FOR RHETORICAL CONCERNS

1. Where did Rubin acquire the information for this piece? What type of investigation did she undertake? When did it take place?
2. Do you think Rubin gives sufficient weight to opposing views? Why or why not?
3. How would you characterize Rubin's tone of voice? Is it appropriate for her rhetorical purpose?

WRITING ASSIGNMENTS

1. a. Form collaborative learning groups of five students each, as described in the Preface, or fashion groups according to a method of your own.
   b. Assign each group one of the following paragraphs from Rubin's essay: 5, 25, 41, 71, 81, 83, 85.
   c. Students in the group should analyze the passage, estimate its significance to the article, and write a one-page summary of their discussion.
   d. Reconvene the entire class. Each group recorder should read the paragraph, followed by the group's explanation of its significance.
2. Construct a graphic overview of Rubin's article, and use the overview to write a two- to three-page summary for an audience who has not read the article.
3. Rubin gives a number of examples of people who are "no longer so sure about what they really believe" (paragraph 71). Even though they have unequivocal stated beliefs about issues like divorce, working mothers, homosexuality, premarital sex, and abortion, they become confused and uncertain when they have to deal with those issues in their own families. Have you experienced this ambivalence in your own family? Write a three- to four-page paper in response.
4. Write an essay comparing and contrasting the norms, values, and behaviors of working-class and middle-class parents and their children.

Snapshots

Helena Maria Viramontes

Helena Maria Viramontes was born in East Los Angeles and now teaches at Cornell University. Her books include The Moths and Other Stories *(1985) and* Chicana Creativity and Criticism: Charting New Frontiers in American Literature *(1988).*

PREREADING

> Recall the photographs that have been taken of you and your family. Is there a particular snapshot that stands out among all the rest? For ten minutes, freewrite about the memories the photo evokes in you.

It was the small things in life, I admit, that made me happy; ironing straight arrow creases on Dave's work khakis, cashing in enough coupons to actually save some money, or having my bus halt just right, so that I don't have to jump off the curb and crack my knee cap like that poor shoe salesman I read about in Utah. Now, it's no wonder that I wake mornings and try my damndest not to mimic the movements of ironing or cutting those stupid, dotted lines or slipping into my house shoes, groping for my robe, going to Marge's room to check if she's sufficiently covered, scruffling to the kitchen, dumping out the soggy coffee grounds, refilling the pot and only later realizing that the breakfast nook has been set for three, the iron is plugged in, the bargain page is open in front of me and I don't remember, I mean I really don't remember doing any of it because I've done it for thirty years now and Marge is already married. It kills me, the small things.

Like those balls of wool on the couch. They're small and senseless and yet, every time I see them, I want to scream. Since the divorce, Marge brings me balls and balls and balls of wool thread because she insists that I "take up a hobby," "keep as busy as a bee," or "make the best of things" and all that other good-natured advice she probably hears from old folks who answer in such a way when asked how they've managed to

"Snapshots" by Helena Maria Viramontes is reprinted with permission from the publisher of *The Moths and Other Stories* (Houston: Arte Público Press-University of Houston, 1985).

live so long. Honestly, I wouldn't be surprised if she walked in one day with bushels of straw for me to weave baskets. My only response to her endeavors is to give her the hardest stares I know how when she enters the living room, opens up her plastic shopping bag and brings out another ball of bright colored wool thread. I never move. Just sit and stare.

"Mother."   3

She pronounces the words not as a truth but as an accusation.

"Please, Mother. Knit. Do something." And then she places the new ball on top of the others on the couch, turns toward the kitchen and leaves. I give her a minute before I look out the window to see her standing on the sidewalk. I stick out my tongue, even make a face, but all she does is stand there with that horrible yellow and black plastic bag against her fat leg, and wave good-bye.

Do something, she says. If I had a penny for all the things I have   4
done, all the little details I was responsible for but which amounted to nonsense, I would be rich. But I haven't a thing to show for it. The human spider gets on prime time television for climbing a building because it's there. Me? How can people believe that I've fought against motes of dust for years or dirt attracting floors or perfected bleached white sheets when a few hours later the motes, the dirt, the stains return to remind me of the uselessness of it all? I missed the sound of swans slicing the lake water or the fluttering wings of wild geese flying south for a warm winter or the heartbeat I could have heard if I had just held Marge a little closer.

I realize all that time is lost now, and I find myself searching for it   5
frantically under the bed where the balls of dust collect undisturbed and untouched, as it should be.

To be quite frank, the fact of the matter is I wish to do nothing, but   6
allow indulgence to rush through my veins with frightening speed. I do so because I have never been able to tolerate it in anyone, including myself.

I watch television to my heart's content now, a thing I rarely did in   7
my younger days. While I was growing up, television had not been invented. Once it was and became a must for every home, Dave saved and saved until we were able to get one. But who had the time? Most of mine was spent working part time as a clerk for Grants, then returning to create a happy home for Dave. This is the way I pictured it:

> His wife in the kitchen wearing a freshly ironed apron, stirring a pot of
> soup, whistling a whistle-while-you-work tune, and preparing frosting for
> some cupcakes so that when he drove home from work, tired and sweaty,

he would enter his castle to find his cherub baby in a pink day suit with newly starched ribbons crawling to him and his wife looking at him with pleasing eyes and offering him a cupcake.

It was a good image I wanted him to have and every day I almost 8 expected him to stop, put down his lunch pail and cry at the whole scene. If it wasn't for the burnt cupcakes, my damn varicose veins, and Marge blubbering all over her day suit, it would have made a perfect snapshot.

Snapshots are ghosts. I am told that shortly after women are mar- 9 ried, they become addicted to one thing or another. In *Reader's Digest* I read stories of closet alcoholic wives who gambled away grocery money or broke into their children's piggy banks in order to quench their thirst and fill their souls. Unfortunately I did not become addicted to alcohol because my only encounter with it had left me senseless and with my face in the toilet bowl. After that, I never had the desire to repeat the performance of a senior in high school whose prom date never showed. I did consider my addiction a lot more incurable. I had acquired a habit much more deadly: nostalgia.

I acquired the habit after Marge was born, and I had to stay in bed 10 for months because of my varicose veins. I began flipping through my family's photo albums (my father threw them away after mom's death) to pass the time and pain away. However I soon became haunted by the frozen moments and the meaning of memories. Looking at the old photos, I'd get real depressed over my second grade teacher's smile or my father's can of beer or the butt naked smile of me as a young teen, because every detail, as minute as it may seem, made me feel that so much had passed unnoticed. As a result, I began to convince myself that my best years were up and that I had nothing to look forward to in the future. I was too young and too ignorant to realize that that section of my life relied wholly on those crumbling photographs and my memory and I probably wasted more time longing for a past that never really existed. Dave eventually packed them up in a wooden crate to keep me from hurting myself. He was good in that way. Like when he clipped roses for me. He made sure the thorns were cut off so I didn't have to prick myself while putting them in a vase. And it was the same thing with the albums. They stood in the attic for years until I brought them down a day after he remarried.

The photo albums are unraveling and stained with spills and fin- 11 gerprints and filled with crinkled faded gray snapshots of people I can't remember anymore, and I turn the pages over and over again to see if somehow, some old dream will come into my blank mind. Like the black and white television box does when I turn it on. It warms up then flashes instant pictures, instant lives, instant people.

Parents. That I know for sure. The woman is tall and long, her plain, 12 black dress is over her knees, and she wears thick spongelike shoes. She's over to the right of the photo, looks straight ahead at the camera. The man wears white, baggy pants that go past his waist, thick suspenders. He smiles while holding a dull-faced baby. He points to the camera. His sleeves pulled up, his tie undone, his hair is messy, as if some wild woman has driven his head between her breasts and run her fingers into his perfect greased ducktail.

My mother always smelled of smoke and vanilla and that is why I 13 stayed away from her. I suppose that is why my father stayed away from her as well. I don't even remember a time when I saw them show any sign of affection. Not like today. No sooner do I turn off the soaps when I turn around and catch two youngsters on a porch swing, their mouths open, their lips chewing and chewing as if they were sharing a piece of three day old liver. My mom was always one to believe that such passion be restricted to the privacy of one's house and then, there too, be demonstrated with efficiency and not this urgency I witness almost every day. Dave and I were good about that.

Whenever I saw the vaseline jar on top of Dave's bedstand, I 14 made sure the door was locked and the blinds down. This anticipation was more exciting to me than him lifting up my flannel gown over my head, pressing against me, slipping off my underwear then slipping in me. The vaseline came next, then he came right afterwards. In the morning, Dave looked into my eyes and I could never figure out what he expected to find. Eventually, there came a point in our relationship when passion passed to Marge's generation, and I was somewhat relieved. And yet, I could never imagine Marge doing those types of things that these youngsters do today, though I'm sure she did them on those Sunday afternoons when she carried a blanket and a book, and told me she was going to the park to do some reading and returned hours later with the bookmark in the same place. She must have done them, or else how could she have gotten engaged, married, had three children all under my nose, and me still going to check if she's sufficiently covered?

"Mother?" Marge's voice from the kitchen. It must be evening. 15 Every morning it's the ball of wool, every evening it's dinner. Honestly, she treats me as if I have an incurable heart ailment. She stands under the doorway.

"Mother?" Picture it: She stands under the doorway looking be- 16 fudled, as if a movie director instructs her to stand there and look confused and upset; stand there as if you have seen your mother sitting in the same position for the last nine hours.

"What are you doing to yourself?" Marge is definitely not one for 17 originality and she repeats the same lines every day. I'm beginning to think our conversation is coming from discarded scripts. I know the lines by heart, too. She'll say: "Why do you continue to do this to us?" and I'll answer: "Do what?" and she'll say: "This"—waving her plump, coarse hands over the albums scattered at my feet—and I'll say: "Why don't you go home and leave me alone?" This is the extent of our conversation and usually there is an optional line like: "I brought you something to eat," or "Let's have dinner," or "Come look what I have for you," or even "I brought you your favorite dish."

I think of the times, so many times, so many Mother's Days that 18 passed without so much as a thank you or how sweet you are for giving us thirty years of your life. I know I am to blame. When Marge first started school, she had made a ceramic handprint for me to hang in the kitchen. My hands were so greasy from cutting the fat off some porkchops, I dropped it before I could even unwrap my first Mother's Day gift. I tried gluing it back together again with flour and water paste, but she never forgave me and I never received another gift until after the divorce. I wonder what happened to the ceramic handprint I gave to my mother?

In the kitchen I see that today my favorite dish is Chinese food get- 19 ting cold in those little coffin-like containers. Yesterday my favorite dish was a salami sandwich, and before that a half eaten rib, no doubt left over from Marge's half hour lunch. Last week she brought me some Sunday soup that had fish heads floating around in some greenish broth. When I threw it down the sink, all she could think of to say was: "Oh, Mother."

We eat in silence. Or rather, she eats. I don't understand how she 20 can take my indifference. I wish that she would break out of her frozen look, jump out of any snapshot and slap me in the face. Do something. Do something. I began to cry.

"Oh, Mother," she says, picking up the plates and putting them in the sink.

"Mother, please."

There's fingerprints all over this one, my favorite. Both woman and 21 child are clones: same bathing suit, same ponytails, same ribbons. The woman is looking directly at the camera, but the man is busy making a sand castle for his daughter. He doesn't see the camera or the woman. On the back of this one, in vague pencil scratching, it says: San Juan Capistrano.

This is a bad night. On good nights I avoid familiar spots. On 22 bad nights I am pulled towards them so much so that if I sit on the chair next to Dave's I begin to cry. On bad nights I can't sleep and on bad nights I don't know who the couples in the snapshots are. My mother and me? Me and Marge? I don't remember San Juan Capistrano and I don't remember the woman. She faded into thirty years of trivia. I don't even remember what I had for dinner, or rather, what Marge had for dinner, just a few hours before. I wrap a blanket around myself and go into the kitchen to search for some evidence, but except for a few crumbs on the table, there is no indication that Marge was here. Suddenly, I am relieved when I see the box containers in the trash under the sink. I can't sleep the rest of the night wondering what happened to my ceramic handprint, or what was in the boxes. Why can't I remember? My mind thinks of nothing but those boxes in all shapes and sizes. I wash my face with warm water, put cold cream on, go back to bed, get up and wash my face again. Finally, I decide to call Marge at 3:30 in the morning. The voice is faint and there is static in the distance.

"Yes?" Marge asks automatically. 23

"Hello," Marge says. I almost expected her to answer her usual "Dave's Hardware."

"Who is this?" Marge is fully awake now.

"What did we . . . " I ask, wondering why it was suddenly so important for me to know what we had for dinner. "What did you have for dinner?" I am confident that she'll remember every movement I made or how much salt I put on whatever we ate, or rather, she ate. Marge is good about details.

"Mother?"

"Are you angry that I woke you up?"

"Mother. No. Of course not."

I could hear some muffled sounds, vague voices, static. I can tell she 24 is covering the mouthpiece with her hand. Finally George's voice.

"Mrs. Ruiz," he says, restraining his words so that they almost come out slurred, "Mrs. Ruiz, why don't you leave us alone?" and then there is a long, buzzing sound. Right next to the vaseline jar are Dave's cigarettes.

I light one though I don't smoke. I unscrew the jar and use the lid for an ₂₅ ashtray. I wait, staring at the phone until it rings.

"Dave's Hardware," I answer. "Don't you know what time it is?"

"Yes." It isn't Marge's voice. "Why don't you leave the kids alone?" Dave's voice is not angry. Groggy, but not angry. After a pause I say:

"I don't know if I should be hungry or not."

"You're a sad case." Dave says it as coolly as a doctor would say, you have terminal cancer. He says it to convince me that it is totally out of his hands. I panic. I picture him sitting on his side of the bed in his shorts, smoking under a dull circle of light. I know his bifocals are down to the tip of his nose.

"Oh, Dave," I say. "Oh, Dave." The static gets worse.

"Let me call you tomorrow."

"No. It's just a bad night."

"Olga," Dave says so softly that I can almost feel his warm breath on my face.

"Olga, why don't you get some sleep?"

The first camera I ever saw belonged to my grandfather. He won it in ₂₆ a cock fight. Unfortunately he didn't know two bits about it, but he somehow managed to load the film. Then he brought it over to our house. He sat me on the lawn. I was only five or six years old, but I remember the excitement of everybody coming around to get into the picture. I can see my grandfather clearly now. I can picture him handling the camera slowly, touching the knobs and buttons to find out how the camera worked while the men began milling around him expressing their limited knowledge of the invention. I remember it all so clearly. Finally he was able to manage the camera, and he took pictures of me standing near my mother with the wives behind us.

My grandmother was very upset. She kept pulling me out of the ₂₇ picture, yelling to my grandfather that he should know better, that snapshots steal the souls of the people and that she would not allow my soul to be taken. He pushed her aside and clicked the picture.

The picture, of course, never came out. My grandfather, not know- ₂₈ ing better, thought that all he had to do to develop the film was unroll it and expose it to the sun. After we all waited for an hour, we realized it didn't work. My grandmother was very upset and cut a piece of my hair, probably to save me from a bad omen.

It scares me to think that my grandmother may have been right. It ₂₉ scares me even more to think I don't have a snapshot of her. If I find one, I'll tear it up for sure.

READING FOR INFORMATION

1. What clues does the opening paragraph give you about the type of family life Mrs. Ruiz has led?

2. Even though Marge is intent on getting her mother interested in a hobby, Mrs. Ruiz wishes to do nothing. Explain why she feels that way.

3. Explain what Mrs. Ruiz means when she says that after her daughter was born, she became addicted to nostalgia.

4. How do you think Mrs. Ruiz views Marge's daily visits? What does she mean when she says, "I wish that she would break out of her frozen look, jump out of any snapshot and slam me in the face" (paragraph 20)?

5. Why does Mrs. Ruiz think that her grandmother's remark that "snapshots steal the souls of the people" (paragraph 27) may be correct?

READING FOR FORM, ORGANIZATION, AND EXPOSITORY FEATURES

1. How does Viramontes establish the conflict between Mrs. Ruiz and her daughter? Point out specific details.

2. Explain what the references to snapshots, photo album, television, movie script, and cameras contribute to the story.

3. How do you react to Mrs. Ruiz's image of the "happy home"? How did that image control her life?

4. Underline passages that contain humor. How would the story's impact be different if the humor were left out?

5. What is the function of Mrs. Ruiz's recollection of her grandfather's camera? What does this scene add to the story?

READING FOR RHETORICAL CONCERNS

1. How do you think Viramontes wants you to view Mrs. Ruiz?

2. What point do you think Viramontes is making about living in the past rather than dealing with present realities?

3. How would the story have been different if it had been narrated by Marge instead of her mother?

WRITING ASSIGNMENTS

1. Write an essay in which you show how "Snapshots" bears out the comments Lillian Rubin makes in " 'People Don't Know Right from Wrong Anymore' ":

   But it's well to remember what historians of the family have been telling us for some time now: The golden age of the family for which we yearn with such intensity never really existed. Instead, families have always been a "haven in a heartless world" and a breeding ground for pain, sorrow, disappointment, and discontent. Everyone who has ever lived in a family knows both sides. But our longing for what seems from this distance to be the simplicity and certainty of earlier times has blinded us to this complex reality of family life. (paragraph 84)

2. Write a short critical analysis of the story's point of view. For an explanation of point of view, see page 131.

3. Write an essay discussing Mrs. Ruiz's image of the perfect family in paragraph 7. Is that image borne out in reality? In Mrs. Ruiz's life? In your own family experience?

SYNTHESIS WRITING ASSIGNMENTS

1. Drawing on selections by Goldschneider and Waite and by Griswold, write an essay in which you compare and contrast the views of those who argue for a new egalitarian and sharing family and those who call for a reassertion of paternal authority.

2. Write a synthesis essay in which you draw on the articles by Goldschneider and Waite, Hill Collins, and Barret and Robinson to illustrate Lillian Rubin's comments on one or more of the following topics: (1) the varying effects of divorce on men and women (paragraphs 11–12), (2) marriage in the African-American community (paragraphs 37–46), (3) women and work (paragraphs 47–50), (4) homosexuality (paragraph 75), and (5) traditional families (paragraph 84).

3. Write an essay in which you argue for or against reinstituting "old families" and reasserting traditional values and beliefs about families and social life. Use the selections in this chapter and other selections you have read as sources.

4. Relate Goldschneider and Waite's discussion of "old families" (paragraphs 11–15) to the family in "Snapshots." How does Mrs. Ruiz's experiences illustrate Goldschneider and Waite's contention that "the problems 'old families' create are disproportionately for women" (paragraph 11)?

5. Drawing on the selections in this chapter, respond to this assertion by Lillian Rubin:

Changing cultures mean stormy times. The interaction between new norms and values and the people who must live them out is never tranquil and easy. The old consciousness doesn't go quietly into the night. Instead, it fusses and fumes, drags its feet, goads us with reminders of its existence, and foments an internal struggle that leaves us anxious and bewildered, wondering what we believe, how we feel. (paragraph 81)

Write a five- to six-page essay addressed to your peers.

6. Based on your readings in this chapter, what do you see as the most serious challenge to families in the twenty-first century? Write an essay addressed to students who have not read this book.

CHAPTER

t e n

Social Class and Inequality

The selections in Chapter 10 examine ideas about social class from different perspectives and offer explanatory principles for the unequal distribution of income, power, and prestige in the United States. The authors discuss class conflict, examine factors that profoundly affect the existence and continuance of poverty, and offer solutions for dealing with these persistent problems. The evidence these authors supply has political, psychological, cultural, and moral ramifications as well as social consequences.

In the first selection, "How Many Classes Are There?" Dennis Gilbert and Joseph A. Kahl use source of income, occupation, and education to develop a model of American class structure. They exemplify this model with six social classes: capitalist, upper middle, middle, working, working poor, and underclass. In the second selection, "Separation of the Classes," Charles Murray cautions us that as the number of rich people in this country continues to grow, an American caste system is developing because of the deeper and wider divisions between the classes.

The next two articles focus on Americans who are living in poverty. In "Rebels with a Cause," Myron Magnet discusses the causes and effects of crime among the poor or "underclass." Herbert J. Gans debunks the concept of "underclass" and similar stereotypes, and in "The War Against the Poor" offers an intellectual and cultural defense of poor people.

Leonce Gaiter in "The Revolt of the Black Bourgeoisie" and Patricia Clark Smith in "Grandma Went to Smith, All Right, But She Went from Nine to Five" illustrate through personal experiences how individuals can be made to feel out of place because of their social, economic, or racial background. Gaiter argues that middle- and upper-class blacks suffer discrimination when they are lumped with economically and socially deprived blacks, instead of being treated as individuals. In a similar vein, Patricia Clark Smith discusses the pain she and her family experienced when they were unjustly stereotyped on the basis of their economic status.

In "White Standard for Poverty," Dirk Johnson gives us a glimpse of two faces of poverty in the Native American population and warns us against imposing white standards of poverty on Indians. The final selection in this chapter is a poem: R. T. Smith's "Red Anger," an expression of rage against the impoverished conditions of Native Americans.

How Many Classes Are There?

Dennis Gilbert and Joseph A. Kahl

Dennis Gilbert, associate professor of sociology at Hamilton College, has written widely on social stratification and class conflict in the United States and Latin America. He is also the author of The Sandinista Vanguard and the Nicaraguan Revolution. *Joseph A. Kahl taught sociology at Harvard, Washington University in St. Louis, and Cornell. He has studied social stratification in the United States and stratification and economic developments in Latin America. Kahl is the author of* The American Class Structure *(1957),* The Measure of Modernism: A Study of Value in Brazil and Mexico *(1968), and* Modernism, Exploitation and Dependence: Germani, Gonzalez Casanova and Cardoso *(1976). "How Many Classes Are There?" appears in the third edition of Gilbert and Kahl's book,* The American Class Structure: A New Synthesis *(1987).*

PREREADING

Before reading the selection, spend about ten minutes writing out your response to the question Gilbert and Kahl pose in the title. Do you think there is a visible class system in the United States? How many social classes are there? Can we divide the population into the rich, the middle class, and the poor, or should we make finer distinctions? With which class do you identify?

From Dennis Gilbert and Joseph A. Kahl, *The American Class Structure: A New Synthesis,* 3rd ed., 329–37. Copyright © 1987 Dorsey Press. Reprinted by permission of Wadsworth Publishing Co.

. . . [Our] initial response to the question about the number of classes that exist in the United States is: It all depends on your viewpoint. The authors view the class structure as growing out of the economic system. We start with the recognition that there are three basic sources of income available to households in this country: capitalist property, labor force participation, and government transfers. The second of these (which, as we know from the income parade, accounts for most of the income of most of the people) is shaped by the fact that our economy depends on an occupational division of labor organized into bureaucratic units. Occupational placement is linked in turn to educational preparation. Sources of income, along with experiences on the job and in consumption communities, are verbalized as symbols of the system and the niches which people occupy within it. One of the key aspects of a person's perception of place in the system is anticipation of change in the near future: Is one stuck or is there a chance to advance? Another involves the degree of independence in carrying out one's work activities.

Combining the criteria of source of income, occupation, and educational credentials, plus the related processes of symbolization, we can create an "ideal type" picture of the class structure. The several criteria tend to cluster in a pattern that identifies six classes in the contemporary United States:

1. A capitalist class, subdivided into nationals and locals, whose income is derived largely from return on assets.
2. An upper-middle class of university-trained professionals and managers (a few of whom ascend to such heights of bureaucratic dominance that they become part of the capitalist class).
3. A middle class of people who follow orders on the job from those with upper-middle class credentials, yet have sufficient vocational skills to make good livings and enjoy a comfortable, mainstream style of life. They usually feel secure in their situation and may look forward to some movement up the hierarchy. Most wear white but some wear blue collars.
4. A working class of people who are less skilled than members of the middle class and work at highly routinized, closely supervised, manual and clerical jobs. Their work provides them with a relatively stable income sufficient to maintain a living standard just below the mainstream, but they have little prospect of advancing in the hierarchy since they typically lack the necessary educational credentials. Thus they concentrate on achieving security through seniority rather than promotion.

5. A working-poor class consisting of people employed in low-skill jobs, often in marginal firms. The members of this class are typically laborers, service workers, or low-paid operators. Their incomes leave them well below mainstream living standards. Moreover, they cannot depend on steady employment, and far from anticipating advancement, they are at risk of dropping into the class below them.

6. An underclass, whose members have little or no participation in the labor force. They may work erratically or at part-time jobs, but their lack of skills, incomplete education, and spotty employment records make it difficult for them to find regular, full-time positions. Some receive income from illegal activities. Many depend on government transfers for their support. Symbolically, their loose relationship to the labor market and dependence on government handouts anchor them at the bottom of the prestige order.

There are two cutting points that are the least obvious: that between the middle and working classes and that between the working poor and the underclass. Let us examine these divisions in some detail. 3

The distinction between working poor and underclass becomes difficult when we consider the tendency of some individuals to move repeatedly back and forth across this boundary. Yet the distinction seems worth maintaining. As we move up or down in the hierarchy, away from the boundary, the problem of oscillating mobility is less serious. Moreover, the symbolic difference between having a job, even a marginal one, and welfare dependence is clear. . . . 4

The line between middle class and working class has been blurred by trends which have reduced the traditional differences between blue-collar and white-collar employment. A declining income differential, the increasing routinization of clerical tasks, and the corresponding drop in the prestige value of a white collar per se, have all served to close the gap between shop and office. Viewed in terms of major occupational groupings, the problem centers on the sales, clerical, and craft categories. Our way of dividing these between middle and working class is based on a distinction between workers whose jobs are highly routinized, closely supervised, low in prerequisite training or education, and low in pay, and those who are in the opposite situation. On this basis, we had no trouble placing semiprofessional jobs and the lowest-paid managerial jobs in the middle class or operatives in the working class. The assembly-line character of modern office work and the low salaries associated with most clerical jobs led us to place clerical workers in the working class. We split sales workers into two groups: those engaged in 5 retail work and "others." The latter group includes insurance salesmen, real-estate agents, manufacturers' representatives, and other people who work quite independently and have much higher incomes than the retail workers. Our decision to place most craft workers and foremen in the middle-class is based on similar considerations. They are well paid, skilled, and relatively independent in their work. Moreover, the prestige attached to such occupations places them well above other blue-collar workers. . . .

In summary, we are suggesting a model of the class structure based on a series of qualitative economic distinctions and their symbolization. From top to bottom, they are: ownership of income-producing assets, possession of sophisticated educational credentials, a combination of independence and freedom from routinization at work, entrapment in the marginal sector of the labor market, and limited labor force participation. 6

Our scheme is illustrated in Table 1. If we round off the numbers from the distributions of each variable treated separately and do a little guessing, we can estimate that the capitalist class includes about 1 percent of the population; the upper-middle class, about 14 percent; the middle and working classes, 60 percent; and the working poor and underclass, 25 percent. We can exemplify this model by going into a little more detail about each of the six classes. . . . 7

CAPITALIST CLASS

The very small class of super-rich capitalists at the top of the hierarchy has an influence on economy and society that vastly outpaces their reduced numbers. They make investment decisions that in turn open or close employment opportunities for millions of others; they contribute money to political parties, and they often own newspapers or television companies, thereby gaining impact on the shaping of the consciousness of all classes in the nation. The capitalist class tends to perpetuate itself. It passes on assets and styles of life (including networks of contact with other influentials) to its children. This creation of lineage is of sufficient importance to them that they are active in creating and supporting preparatory schools and universities for their children and for carefully selected newcomers who can be socialized into their world view. 8

The super-rich operate on the national and international scene. They have less prominent counterparts in local communities—the people who own the local banks, department stores, and newspapers. They too are capitalists and belong in this class, albeit at the margins. 9

Table 1 Model of the American Class Structure: Classes by Typical Situations

Proportion of Households	Class	Education	Occupation	Family Income 1983
1%	Capitalist	Prestige university	Investors, heirs, executives	Over $500,000 mostly from assets
14%	Upper middle	College, often with postgraduate study	Upper managers and professionals; medium businessmen	$500,000 or more
60%	Middle	At least high school; often some college or apprenticeship	Lower managers; semi-professionals; sales, nonretail; craftspeople; foremen	About $30,000
	Working	High school	Operatives; low-paid craftspeople; clerical workers; retail sales workers	About $20,000
25%	Working poor	Some high school	Service workers; laborers; low-paid operatives and clericals	Below $15,000
	Underclass	Primary school	Unemployed or part-time; welfare recipients	Below $10,000

Our definition produces a very small top class: those who own mas- 10
sive productive assets. After a generation or two, those assets are often
distributed among so many heirs that a larger group of less rich and less
powerful people ensues. If one studies local communities and counts all
those who have a prominent name and live in big houses and belong to
the best country club, one will emerge with a larger group (perhaps double or triple our 1 percent). But if one focuses on assets of sufficient size
to grant the economic power that we consider crucial, then the group
shrinks in size. . . .

UPPER-MIDDLE CLASS

Apart from the very top echelon, the capitalist-proletarian distinction has 11
lost much of its force in modern society: History has proven Marx wrong
when he predicted a trend toward simplification into an ever-sharper
distinction between the two classes as the driving force of social change.
Weber, who lived until 1920, was able to see this more clearly than Marx,
who died in 1883. Weber wrote:

> One must therefore distinguish between "propertied classes" and primarily
> market-determined "income classes." Present-day society is predominantly
> stratified in classes, and to an especially high degree in income classes.
> But in the special *status* prestige of the "educated" strata, our society con-
> tains a very tangible element of stratification by status. Externally, this sta-
> tus factor is most obviously represented by economic monopolies and the
> preferential social opportunities of the holders of degrees. . . . Today, the
> certificate of education becomes what the test for ancestors has been in the
> past, at least where the nobility has remained powerful: a prerequisite for
> equality of birth, a qualification for a canonship, and for state office. (1946:
> 301, 241)

Of course, Weber was also somewhat limited by the vision of his 12
epoch. But he noticed that through education, particularly the university degree, one could obtain both the opportunity for an important job
in the church or the state and entry into high society, which still had
overtones in Germany from the days of the nobility. In America, the degree is still the key to high bureaucratic position and to high prestige
status in the community, but since the proportion of the population
which gets degrees has so dramatically expanded, the prestige of the
degree has somewhat diminished. And of course, more people now hold
high positions in business than in the church.

The more society bureaucratizes, the more it tends to use educa- 13 tional credentials at all levels to sort people out into careers, at least at the beginning. The formality of this process is striking. For example, the current Chinese government civil service, heir to a tradition that long antedates Mao Tse-tung, continues to use twenty-four distinct grades or levels of jobs, despite ideological ideas of equality; the United States federal civil service has eighteen grades; and the General Electric Corporation, considered a model of modern management, recognizes twenty-eight levels of managers and fourteen levels of workers. Each of these grades has a different pay scale and different responsibilities. They do not all specify exactly the educational credentials to match the job and the pay, but they usually use educational credentials to sort out beginning applicants into the level that would be most appropriate for them. Afterwards, experience on the job, additional training courses (sometimes at outside schools, sometimes in courses run internally by the management), and demonstrated abilities combine to determine who stays put and who moves up.

The upper-middle class is the group in our society most shaped by 14 formal education. A college degree is usually the minimum requirement, and increasingly post-graduate study in business management, law, engineering, or medicine is required. Currently, more than 20 percent of young people get college degrees, and at least half of them pursue some additional training; about 16 percent of all adults have a degree.

If we turn to occupational statistics, we will [see] about 16 percent 15 of the current labor force classified as professionals and technicians, and another 11 percent as managers, officials, and proprietors. But we noted that many of the workers in these categories are semiprofessionals, technicians, or low-level managers with modest salaries, limited training, and circumscribed authority. We estimate that only about 14 percent of the total work force has the combination of university degrees, authority on the job, and high income to qualify for the upper-middle class.

The extent to which adolescents in high school (urged on by their 16 parents and teachers) so often strive to prepare themselves for upper-middle class jobs is a clear indication that these positions have become the symbols of success that motivates so many Americans. They may not grant prestige equivalent to a title of nobility in the Germany of Max Weber, but they certainly represent the sign of having "made it" in contemporary America. The incomes of households in this group range upwards of $50,000 a year, about twice the mean in 1983, and tend to increase with age. They are sufficient to purchase houses and cars and travel that become public symbols for all to see and for advertisers to portray with words and pictures that connote success, glamour, and high style. Those who have reached this level of success are likely to convince themselves that they deserve what they receive, that they have earned morally just rewards from the diligent use of superior talent. Sometimes they may grow anxious from the strains of competition, but in general, they are satisfied that they have achieved a proper share of the American dream.

MIDDLE CLASS

We have remarked before that a stratification hierarchy is clearest (and 17
incidentally, mobility the weakest) at the extremes. When we move toward the center, distinctions become blurred, people move more often during their lives from one slot to another, and symbolizations become ambiguous. This is particularly true at the point where the middle class and the working class intersect—or better, overlap—so the reader should not expect precision of classification.

It takes at least a high school diploma to get most middle-class jobs, 18
but the diploma is a prerequisite more than a guarantee of such employment. About 85 percent of the total adult population has a high school diploma and perhaps some training beyond it short of a four-year college degree. Those with the best schooling have the most chance to become the semiprofessionals, technicians, and lower-level managerial people we mentioned above—about 15 percent of the work force. They are joined in the loose grouping we call the middle class with the upper two thirds of those classified as salespeople and craftspeople—another 12 percent of the work force. Typical household incomes for this level would be around $30,000 a year, but there is considerable variation, particularly if more than one person in the household is working. Jobs are relatively secure, even during periods of recession, and younger members of the class are likely to be working in situations where some opportunities to advance in the hierarchy are available.

Symbolization of the middle class tends to get confused by an 19
ideological tradition which says that most Americans are middle class. It is a "good," mainstream sort of phrase that a lot of people adopt— including those who are both higher and lower in the hierarchy than the ones we are trying to discuss at this point. Thus most surveys show 35 to almost 50 percent of our population identifying with the term and only about two percent willing to call themselves upper class. If we

subtract about 15 percent for the upper and upper-middle classes as we have defined them, then the size of the remaining middle class according to self-identification would be from 20 to 35 percent of the population. Using a composite of various symbols that people use to classify not only themselves but their neighbors, Coleman and Rainwater decided that 33 percent were middle class, an estimate slightly larger than our own.

WORKING CLASS

The core of the working class is easy to identify: semiskilled machine 20 operatives, in factories and elsewhere, who make up 15 percent of the work force. But they are joined by lots of others whose work lives and incomes are not markedly different, such as clerks and salespeople whose tasks are routine and mechanized and require little skill beyond literacy and a short period of on-the-job training (some 14 percent of the work force), and the better-paid persons in the service jobs (another 3 percent). Individuals easily move among these classifications, and often one member of a family wears a blue and another a white collar, and nobody much notices the difference. Households typically earn $20,000 or less.

In opinion surveys, at least half the population usually chooses the 21 label working class for themselves, but evidence indicates that some do so because they particularly dislike certain alternative terms, such as lower class. The detailed procedures of Coleman and Rainwater arrived at a figure of 37 percent for the working class, some of whom we will put among the working poor. Thus our estimate for the working class comes to around 30 percent of households.

In general, working-class families earn less than middle-class fam- 22 ilies, and more particularly, they are less secure in their incomes. The working class is more susceptible to lay-offs in time of recession, since employers have less invested in their training and experience. Insecurity of work often is combined with a subjective feeling of vulnerability from lower levels of education: Relatively few members of the group have training beyond a high school diploma, and over a third (especially the older ones) did not graduate. Yet by contrast with those below them in the hierarchy, working-class people generally anticipate that lay-offs will be temporary and that most of the time they can support their families in a simple but decent manner.

WORKING POOR

In 1983, the government called 15 percent of the population poor, and 23 studies that follow families over time show that in a nine-year period some 25 percent of them fall below the poverty line at least once. Of the total work force (and many of the poorest and most discouraged people have withdrawn from it), between 6 and 8 percent are likely to be unemployed at any one moment, and about 20 percent are likely to be unemployed at least once during any given year. Thus it appears that about one fifth of our population lives under duress: They oscillate in income from just above to below the poverty line, they are threatened with periodic unemployment, or they have no chance to work at all. Those among them—probably a little more than half—who are often working but not earning on a steady basis enough money to bring them close to the mainstream style of consumption, we lable the working poor. Those who depend primarily on the welfare system for cash income we call the underclass.

The working poor include the unskilled laborers, most of those in 24 service jobs, and some of the lower-paid operatives (especially in marginal firms). Many employed single mothers find themselves in this class. Their incomes depend on the number of weeks a year they are employed and on the number of workers in the family. Most families would feel fortunate in a year that brought in $15,000. Some adults have finished high school; a great many have not. They are unable to save money to cover contingencies, and thus insecurity is a normal part of their lives. The one part of the welfare system that was beneficial to them, the food stamp program, was slashed in the budgets of the Reagan administration, which eliminated participation by most of the working poor. Once retired, members of this class are entirely dependent on their Social Security pensions, for it is unlikely that they have been enrolled in a private retirement plan that could supplement the government payments.

UNDERCLASS

Those who are seldom employed and are poor most of the time form the un- 25 derclass in our society. They suffer long-term deprivation from low education, low employability, low income, and eventually, low self-esteem. For a great many, their problems are magnified because they belong to minority groups who are stigmatized and suffer discrimination in the labor market, or they are women without husbands who must make their way in a job world that pays them less than men. Those who cannot get and keep jobs that pay enough to live on are dependent on the welfare system of the government.

The conditions of life in the underclass are sufficiently difficult and de- 26 meaning that it is hard—although not impossible—for children to get enough education and enough hope to climb up to higher levels. The future chances for avoiding a life of poverty for these children are about 50-50.

The descriptions of the six classes just given are summarized in 27 Table 1. It is clear that no single variable can be used to delineate these classes, so our synthesis is based on a combination of several variables. We believe that they tend to form patterns that are caught by our scheme in a way that is meaningful in two senses: (1) It is congruent with much of the research literature that goes into detail on one or two variables at a time, as well as with the more qualitative community studies that tend to combine many variables into symbolic groupings; (2) it is congruent with the way most Americans tend to see the system and their place within it. Of course we are thinking here in terms of averages, of typical situations; many individuals and families are hard to place in the scheme, either because they are higher in position on one variable than on another, or because they are mobile, or because more than one member of a family works and they have disparate jobs.[1]

[1] These difficulties of exact status placement and their consequences on consciousness and behavior have been studied under the phrases "status crystallization or status consistency," but the results have been inconclusive (Lenski 1954; Jackson and Burke 1965; Landecker 1981).

REFERENCES

Coleman, Richard P., and Lee Rainwater, with Kent A. McClelland. 1978. *Social Standing in America: New Dimensions of Class.* New York: Basic Books.

Jackson, Elton F., and P. J. Burke. 1965. "Status and Symptoms of Stress: Additive and Interaction Effects." *American Sociological Review* 30: 556–64.

Landecker, Werner S. 1981. *Class Crystalization.* New Brunswick, NJ: Rutgers University Press.

Lenski, Gerhard. 1954. "Status Crystalization: A Non-Vertical Dimension of Social Status." *American Sociological Review* 19: 405–13.

Weber, Max. 1946. *From Max Weber: Essays in Sociology,* edited by H. H. Gerth and C. Wright Mills. New York: Oxford University Press.

READING FOR INFORMATION

1. Explain what Gilbert and Kahl mean in the first paragraph when they say that class structure is based on the economic system. Do you agree?

2. Why is it difficult to make distinctions between the middle class and the working class and between the working class and the working poor?

3. According to Gilbert and Kahl, how is it that 1 percent of the population has such a large influence on U.S. society and the economy? Does this information surprise you?

4. Summarize why educational credentials are such important indicators of class.

5. According to Gilbert and Kahl, why do so many Americans think of themselves as middle class? How do you react to that perception? Do you think of yourself as middle class? Explain your answer.

6. Describe how conditions of life differ for the working poor and the underclass.

READING FOR FORM, ORGANIZATION, AND EXPOSITORY FEATURES

1. Explain how the introductory paragraph informs the reader of the direction Gilbert and Kahl will take in the remainder of the selection.

2. What organizational plan do the authors use?

3. What textual conventions or features of the layout are especially helpful to the reader?

4. Explain the types of evidence (facts, statistics, references to authorities, and so forth) Gilbert and Kahl use to develop and support their position, and give an example of each.

5. Explain how Gilbert and Kahl make their model of American class structure clear to the reader.

6. Explain the function of paragraphs 11 and 12.

READING FOR RHETORICAL CONCERNS

1. Explain Gilbert and Kahl's rhetorical purpose. What points do they want to get across to the reader?

2. How would you describe Gilbert and Kahl's tone of voice—as objective, sympathetic, or judgmental? Explain.

3. Gilbert and Kahl published this piece in 1987. How might they revise it if they were writing about class structure in the United States today?

WRITING ASSIGNMENTS

1. Construct a graphic overview (see pp. 24–25) of the Gilbert and Kahl selection, and use it to write a two- to three-page summary for students who have not read the piece.

2. Imagine yourself in an egalitarian classless society, a utopia where all people have equal access to resources, services, and positions in society. Write a three- to four-page essay describing what your life would be like.

3. Do you feel that all Americans have an opportunity to achieve the American Dream? Referring to Gilbert and Kahl's selection, write a two- to three-page essay in response to this question.

4. Go to the library and locate some recent publications of the U.S. Bureau of the Census—for example, *Statistical Abstracts of the United States* and the series of Current Population Reports. Using Gilbert and Kahl's summary table Model of the American Class Structure as a backdrop, study the data you find, draw some conclusions, and write a four- to five-page report addressed to your classmates. Examples of topics you might discuss are (1) distribution of families according to income level, (2) differences in income according to occupation and education for males and females, (3) changes in median family incomes over the past twenty years, and (4) distribution of wealth by race and ethnic origin.

Separation of the Classes

Charles Murray

Charles Murray is a Bradley Fellow at the American Enterprise Institute. He is the author of numerous articles and books, including Losing Ground, American Social Policy, 1950–1980 *(1984),* Gaining Ground: New Approaches to Poverty and Dependence *(1985), and* In Pursuit of Happiness and Good Government *(1988). Recently, he coauthored with Richard Herrnstein* The Bell Curve *(1994).*

PREREADING

Comment on the significance of the title by writing out answers to the following questions: In your daily life, do you interact with individuals from the upper class, middle class, and working class? Are you friends with people who are super-rich? Are you acquainted with people who are very poor or homeless? Do you think social classes in the United States are separated from one another?

It makes sense to be a little schizophrenic about the American   1
future. Much is positive, whether one thinks about the future
personally . . . or politically (technology is going to give the centralized
state a very tough time). But there is a dark side looming.

Charles Murray, "Separation of the Classes." In Irwin M. Stelzer, "The Shape of Things to Come," *National Review* 8 July 1991: 26–30. © 1991 by National Review, Inc., 150 East 35th Street, New York, NY 10016. Reprinted by permission.

The dark side flows from a prediction that in itself seems innocu- 2 ous: As national wealth grows in the coming years, so will the proportion of people who are rich. I use "rich" roughly, referring generally to discretionary income. People who are rich have a lot of it.

To get an overall idea of the breadth of the trend to date, consider 3 that, as of the end of the Korean War, using constant 1988 dollars, less than one family in fifty thousand had an income of $100,000 or more. By 1988, almost four families per *hundred* had an income that great. This is a phenomenally large change.

The numbers of the rich will tend to grow more rapidly in the com- 4 ing years. Several factors lead to this conclusion, principally the increasing monetary value of cognitive skills, meaning a combination of ability and training for complex mental work. This trend has been in evidence for some time. In 1980, for example, a male college graduate made about 30 per cent more than a male high-school graduate. By 1988, he made about 60 per cent more. In just eight years, the premium for a college degree doubled—in comparison with a high-school diploma. The comparison with people who didn't even graduate from high school is starker yet.

In coming years, the price for first-rate cognitive skills will sky- 5 rocket, for reasons involving the nature of changes in technology (constantly more complex at the leading edge), politics (constantly more complicated laws with more complicated loopholes), and the size of the stakes (when a percentage point of market share is worth hundreds of millions of dollars, then the people who can help you get that extra percentage point are worth very large incomes). Meanwhile, real wages for low-skill jobs will increase slowly if at all, and efforts to increase wages artificially (by raising the minimum wage, for example) will backfire because the demand for low-skill labor is becoming more elastic as alternatives to human labor become numerous and affordable.

The net result is that the rich are going to constitute a major 6 chunk of the population in the relatively near future, and this group will increasingly be the most talented. Why be depressed by this prospect, which in many ways sounds like a good thing? Because I fear its potential for producing something very like a caste society, with the implication of utter social separation that goes with that most un-American of words.

Briefly, I am trying to envision what happens when 10 or 20 per 7 cent of the population has enough income to bypass the social institutions it doesn't like in ways that only the top fraction of 1 per cent used to be able to do. Robert Reich has called it the "secession of the successful."

The current symbol of this phenomenon is the gated community. But there are many other straws in the wind. A simple example is the way that the fax, modem, and Federal Express have already made the U.S. Postal Service nearly irrelevant to the way some segments of American society communicate. A more portentous example is the mass exodus from public schools among urban elites. I sympathize with many of the reasons why people with money take these steps. For almost three decades now, government has failed miserably to perform its basic functions, from preserving order in public spaces to dispensing justice to providing decent education in its schools. But the reasonableness of the motives does not diminish the danger of the potential consequences.

As this American caste system takes shape, American conservatism   8
is going to have to wrestle with its soul. Is conservatism going to follow the Latin American model, where to be conservative means to preserve the mansions on the hills above the slums? Or is it going to remain true to its American heritage, where the thing-to-be-conserved has not been primarily money or privilege but a distinctively American way of self-government and limited government?

All the forces that I can discern will tend to push American con-   9
servatism toward the Latin American model. For example: Conservatives are now being joined by defectors from urban liberalism who have been mugged—sometimes figuratively, often literally. These new conservatives are not fans of either Russell Kirk or Milton Friedman. Their political agenda is weighted heavily toward taking care of number one, using big government to do so whenever it suits their purposes. More broadly, the culture of the urban underclass, increasingly violent and bizarre, fosters alienation. As each new social experiment fails to diminish the size of the underclass, our increasing national wealth will make it tempting to bypass the problem by treating the inner city as an urban analogue of the Indian reservation.

This temptation will be augmented by the increasing power of peo-   10
ple at the upper end of the income scale to use government for their own ends. If the rich constitute 10 to 20 per cent of the population, their political power will be so immense as to transform the power equation. The Left has been complaining for years that the rich have too much power. They ain't seen nothing yet.

It will be sadly ironic if the politics of caste are called "conserva-   11
tive," for the greatest bulwarks against the power of privilege are some good old-fashioned American conservative principles. Enforce strict equality of individuals before the law. Prohibit the state from favoring

groups, including rich and influential groups. Decentralize government authority to the smallest possible unit. None of these principles is a panacea, for the forces that will tend to produce an American caste system are powerful and complex. But these classic conservative principles are more needed than ever, at a time when the seductions for conservatives to abandon them are increasing.

READING FOR INFORMATION

1. Paraphrase Murray's explanation for why educational credentials and cognitive skills will be worth much more in the future than they were in the past.

2. Explain why the demand for low-skill labor is going to continue to decrease.

3. According to Murray, as rich people grow in numbers what is the result?

4. We already have some indications that the rich are "receding" and no longer using our social institutions. What examples does Murray give? Can you add some of your own?

5. Explain why American conservatism will abandon classic conservative principles in the future.

READING FOR FORM, ORGANIZATION, AND EXPOSITORY FEATURES

1. Describe Murray's organizational plan. If you were to divide the piece in two, where would you make the break?

2. Underline the passages in which Murray states his central position. Is his thesis at the beginning, middle, or end of the selection?

3. What is the function of paragraph 3?

4. Underline passages in which Murray uses evidence (facts, statistics, authorities, and so on). Do you think this evidence provides effective support for the argument?

READING FOR RHETORICAL CONCERNS

1. For what audience is Murray writing? How would you describe the intended readers' political persuasion and economic level? How did you reach that conclusion?

2. Explain how Murray's readers know that he identifies with them.

3. How would you describe Murray's tone of voice? What does the tone suggest about the author?

WRITING ASSIGNMENTS

1. Write a letter to the editor of *National Review* summarizing Murray's argument and explaining whether you agree or disagree with his forecast for the future.

2. What do you think Murray means when he says that "our increasing national wealth will make it tempting to bypass the problem [of the urban underclass] by treating the inner city as an urban analogue of the Indian reservation" (paragraph 9)? In preparation for this assignment, read Dirk Johnson's brief article, "White Standard for Poverty," on pages 499–501 and R. T. Smith's poem, "Red Anger," on pages 502–503. Also conduct some library research on the U.S. government's treatment of the Native American population. Then write a three- to four-page essay discussing Murray's analogy between residents of the inner city and Native Americans on reservations.

Rebels with a Cause

Myron Magnet

Myron Magnet is a member of the board of editors of Fortune *magazine and a fellow of the Manhattan Institute for Policy Research. He is the author of* Dickens and the Social Order *(1985). "Rebels with a Cause" is taken from his 1993 book,* The Dream and the Nightmare: The Sixties' Legacy to the Underclass.

PREREADING

Skim the article and list a few key words or phrases: for example, "rebels," "underclass," "crime," "internal law." Run down the list and brainstorm by writing down all the associations that come to mind when you think about these target concepts.

It had all the makings of one of those heartwarming Hollywood   1
movies where the tough but loving schoolteacher, sporting a
red-and-black-checked lumberman's shirt, charms and bullies his

Myron Magnet, "Rebels with a Cause," excerpt from *The Dream and the Nightmare: The Sixties' Legacy to the Underclass* (New York: William Morrow, 1993) 150–73. Copyright © 1993 by Myron Magnet. Used by permission of William Morrow & Company, Inc.

delinquent pupils into changing their ways and becoming model citizens, teenage-style. Here, in real life, was George Cadwalader, a central casting dream: an ex-Marine captain wounded in Vietnam, he was big, rugged, and handsome, with smiling crinkly eyes, bushy brows, limitless courage and self-confidence—and a plan irresistible in its mixture of idealism, toughness, and adventure. He would gather up a crew of hardened delinquent boys from the toughest urban neighborhoods of Massachusetts and transport them to a wild, deserted island, with all its associations of sagas from *Robinson Crusoe* to *Treasure Island*. There they would build their own house, grow and cook their own food, cut the firewood that would both warm them and heat their dinner. By coming to grips with the basic realities of life, they would learn self-reliance, responsibility, and teamwork, discover their own inner strength and confidence, and be converted.

But it was Cadwalader who got converted.   2

He woke up one morning to discover all the chickens his little community was raising for food fluttering helplessly on the ground, dazed with pain. In a paroxysm of sadism, each chicken's two legs had been savagely twisted and smashed, wrenched out of their joints and hanging useless. All that could be done for the broken creatures was to put them out of their misery. Which boy had done such a deed in the dead of night Cadwalader never knew for certain, nor did he ever know the motive.   3

But he knew beyond a doubt that the certainties with which he'd started his experiment in rehabilitation had crumbled within him. He and his associates had begun by holding "without question the assumption that bad kids were simply the products of bad environments," he recalls in *Castaways,* his striking account of the experiment. "We believed changing the environment could change the kid. . . ."[1] Yet the vast majority of his charges didn't change, despite transplantation to the radically different, militantly salubrious environment Cadwalader had designed for them.   4

Far from it. When he followed up the first 106 boys who had gone through his program, he discovered that in seven years they'd been charged with 3,391 crimes, 309 of them violent. For the most part, he came to feel that the boys "appear incapable of love, driven by unfocused anger, and prone to impulsive behavior without regard to consequences. . . . [W]hen I look objectively at the trail of destruction left by our own graduates, I cannot avoid the conclusion that the world would have been a better place if most of the kids I grew to like at Penikese [Island] had never been born." And so he is led to ask, "How many chances does an   5 individual deserve before we are justified in giving up on him? What do we do with those we have given up on?"[2]

Cadwalader accurately calls his island enterprise an experiment: as a scientist would, he subjected his hypothesis about the causes of crime to empirical testing, controlling as many variables as possible. The theory proved false. In removing his boys from modern society and stripping life to its bare essentials on his unpeopled island, Cadwalader found that violence and crime are *not* generated by an individual's social environment. Violence and aggression are not impulses that the environment puts into the human heart; they have their own intractable, independent existence and can flourish regardless of an individual's social circumstances.

The theory that Cadwalader felt he had disproved, much as he would rather have confirmed it, is central to the new worldview of the Haves. And because it tends to excuse criminals from personal responsibility for crime, pinning it on social circumstances instead, the theory has given potential wrongdoers exactly the wrong message. Moreover, it has produced a criminal justice system, administered by a generation of judges steeped in the new culture of the Haves, that confronts actual criminals with a leniency offering little deterrence to crime.

Theories of crime have to make an assumption about whether men are predisposed by nature to force and violence or whether violence gets into their hearts from some outside source. Cadwalader's original assumption about man's inborn character—a key assumption of the new culture of the Haves—is that men are intrinsically peaceful creatures, inclined not to disturb their fellows and, when necessary, to cooperate harmoniously with them. As nature formed them, they don't attack and invade each other. Crime is an artificial growth, grafted onto human life by the development of societies and governments.

This theory, which goes back to the ancients, fascinated the eighteenth-century political philosophers. Rousseau, for instance, had imagined that men in primitive times were constitutionally peaceful. It took the later, unfortunate invention of private property to incite them to attack and dominate each other in a struggle for goods. The horrifying result, Rousseau argued, was a state of universal war whose violence caused mankind to establish societies based on a social contract. All would give up their freedom of aggression in order to reestablish peace.

But, Rousseau added with a wry twist in one of his early works, the contract itself ingrained crime into the very fabric of social life. For it was a swindling, lopsided contract, into which the rich lured the poor for the real purpose of protecting the possessions which they alone needed to protect. So even as men regained a measure of security from the criminal impulses that had arisen among them, the unjust inequality of wealth that had given birth to crime in the first place was institutionalized in society at the very moment of its foundation.[3]

Theories like this are deeply rooted in the American imagination, [11] planted there by Thomas Paine, among others. Since in the youth of the world men were peaceful, solitary tenders of flocks and herds, Paine demands in his two-fisted prose, how did crime and cruelty enter human affairs? Only because in each part of the world the peaceful inhabitants were set upon by "a banditti of ruffians," who forcibly made themselves their masters and exacted heavy tribute from them. By such brute violence, herding men together for the greater ease of oppressing them, were all existing political societies founded, and the robber chieftains who so roughly established them were the first kings.

Over the course of the ages, plunder gradually softened into taxa- [12] tion, and usurpation into inheritance, Paine says; but the animating principle of all societies remains nothing but the oppression of the poor and weak by the rich and powerful. No wonder, then, that men today seethe with ugly passions and commit criminal deeds; they have been deformed for long ages by the pressure of injustice and the rule of terror, their true, peaceful nature corrupted and degraded by the great criminal conspiracy against them that is political society.[4]

To a nation founded upon the overthrow of an oppressive govern- [13] ment and the faith that democratic liberty would nurture citizens with souls undeformed by tyranny, such ideas can't fail to be at least plausible. Americans take kindly to the notion that individuals left to themselves will naturally do right, that their rational self-interest will yield social harmony, and that crime, otherwise inexplicable, might well be the ill-starred product of governmental excess and tyranny.

Americans don't have to go back to Revolutionary times for first- [14] hand knowledge of government-sanctioned oppression. They can think of Southern slavery; they can recall, firsthand, the outrages of institutionalized racial discrimination. With respect to their black fellow citizens in particular, many Americans are readily inclined to believe that crime is the fault of society, not of the criminal. Crime may be either the product of unwholesome social conditions or a rebellion—perhaps even a justified rebellion—against injustice and oppression.

These ideas were always alive in American culture, but they be- [15] came dominant only at the start of the sixties. Michael Harrington gave voice to this interpretation of crime just as it was becoming widespread. Speaking of black delinquents and then of all delinquents, he concluded in *The Other America:* "[T]heir sickness is often a means of relating to a diseased environment."[5] Ramsey Clark, Lyndon Johnson's attorney general and assistant attorney general in the Kennedy administration, is a luminous example of how quick were the Haves at their most established to embrace such an understanding of crime as part of the new era's revolutionized worldview. Clark takes an utterly uncompromising tack. "[C]rime among poor blacks . . . flows clearly and directly from the brutalization and dehumanization of racism, poverty, and injustice," he wrote in 1970, summing up his experience as the nation's top law enforcement officer. "[T]he slow destruction of human dignity caused by white racism is responsible."[6]

Just look at the unwholesome environment racism has produced, 16 Clark demands. "The utter wretchedness of central city slums . . . slowly drains compassion from the human spirit and breeds crime." For this the Haves are most emphatically to blame. "To permit conditions that breed antisocial conduct to continue is our greatest crime," Clark concludes.[7]

Far worse than the crimes poor blacks commit, the crime of whites 17 takes many insidious guises. For example, says Clark, "Nothing so vindicates the unlawful conduct of a poor man, by his light, as the belief that the rich are stealing from him through overpricing and sales of defective goods. . . . Society cannot hope to control violent and irrational antisocial conduct while cunning predatory crime by people in power continues unabated." Today that rationalization has become a smug cliché: you can't end crime in the streets, we often hear, until you attack crime in the suites.[8]

In Clark's eyes, society is engaged in a vast, malevolent, criminal 18 conspiracy against the poor and the black. It comprises such disparate outrages as "not insur[ing] equal protection of the laws . . . condoning faulty wiring and other fire hazards, permitting overcrowding in unsanitary tenements infested with rats, all in violation of ordinances with criminal penalties . . . the willful violation of basic constitutional rights." Inevitably, ghettos will breed violent crime and even rioting. "You cannot cram so much misery together," says Clark, "and not expect violence."[9]

This whole structure of thought, most of it still completely ortho- 19 dox today, rests on theoretical foundations that George Cadwalader found false. But it is a further sign of the times that once Cadwalader had grappled with the discovery that aggression and violence come from some source deep within individuals, not from the social environment, he was stumped. With his old theory in pieces, he had no new one to put in its place.

The intellectual framework he was so perplexedly groping toward 20 isn't obscure, though: it is the other great tradition of political philosophy, springing from Plato and strengthened by such architects of the Western imagination as St. Augustine, Hobbes, Burke, even Freud. Yet it is a tradition with which modern thinking has largely lost touch, so much do we take for granted, without examination, the assumptions about human nature and the nature of social pathology with which Cadwalader began. We often aren't even aware that beneath all of our discussions about social policy lies a deeper stratum of issues, which have been debated for two millennia, and which make up the bedrock of first principles whereon all social policy thinking rests, whether the thinker is conscious of it or not.

This other tradition, for most of history the dominant stream in 21 Western political philosophy, best explains the origin of crime. This tradition takes as its starting point the irreducible reality of human aggression. It holds that as men come from the hand of nature—or as they have been transformed by original sin, according to the Church Fathers' version of the theory—they are instinctively aggressive, with an inbuilt inclination to violence. "Men are not gentle creatures who want to be loved," as Sigmund Freud expressed this aspect of the tradition; "their neighbor is for them not only a potential helper or sexual object, but also someone who tempts them to satisfy their aggressiveness on him, to exploit his capacity for work without compensation, to use him sexually without his consent, to seize his possessions, to humiliate him, to cause him pain, to torture and to kill him. *Homo homini lupus*"—man is a wolf to man. "Who, in the face of all his experience of life and of history, will have the courage to dispute this assertion?"[10]

The fundamental purpose of the social order, of the civilized con- 22 dition itself, is to restrain man's instinctual aggressiveness, so that human life can be something higher than a war of all against all. The great seventeenth- and eighteenth-century political theorists, most notably Thomas Hobbes, imagined that that restraint was accomplished by a social contract: driven to desperation by the universal warfare that made their lives "solitary, poore, nasty, brutish, and short," in Hobbes's famous phrase, men in the early ages of the world entered into an agreement, by which each man renounced his unlimited freedom of aggression in order to promote the security of all. And because it could only be effective if some authority existed to enforce it, the contract also established a governmental apparatus armed with the power to punish infractions, further prompting everyone to keep his word. As James Madison expressed this thought in Number 10 of *The Federalist:* "[W]hat is government itself but the greatest of all reflections on human nature?"

In more modern fashion, Edmund Burke tacitly acknowledged that 23 governments historically often have begun in violence and conquest, not peaceful contract; but he goes on to argue that, whatever their origin, they have accomplished the all-important task of taming unruly man and ordering his world. By their immense success in curbing man's lawless aggression and replacing anarchy with peace, governments rooted in ancient conquest are today maintained by the consent of the governed.[11]

Sigmund Freud offers a still more up-to-date version of this line 24 of thought. The taming of aggression and the replacement of the rule of force by the rule of law isn't something that happened only in the history of the race, Freud argues. It takes place in each individual's history, too.

In early childhood, under the continual pressure of parental de- 25 mands, each person is made to renounce the unlimited aggressiveness with which he was born. During this protracted process, central to early childhood, one's innermost being is transformed. As one internalizes the civilizing demands of one's parents and the community that speaks through them, one acquires an entirely new mental faculty, a part of one's inner self given one not by nature but by society. This, in Freud's rather unlovely term, is the superego, analogous to the conscience; and like conscience, it punishes one with feelings of shame and guilt, while speaking with the voice not of divinity but of society.

This new inner faculty is what crucially differentiates men from the 26 beasts. For central to Freud's thought, as to the whole tradition in political philosophy roughly sketched here, is a belief uncongenial to our revolutionized culture: the belief that man's full humanity and highest, most characteristically human achievements can unfold only in society. Only in their social relations do men achieve the rational, moral, cooperative, historical existence that defines our humanity; only as a social creature, his aggressiveness held in check by the inner transformation that immersion in the social medium works on him, does man become fully man, able to build cities, create art and science and commerce, and attain virtue.

Looked at through assumptions like these, crime takes on an entirely 27 different appearance from the one it has in Ramsey Clark's eyes and in the culture of the Haves today. Not only does the social order not *cause* crime, it is the very thing that *restrains* crime to the remarkable extent that it is restrained. The social order is precisely what makes man's life something other than a scene of constant mutual invasion, in which all live in continual fear and danger of violence.

Seen in this light, crime takes on the closest links to culture. For 28 though the whole governmental structure of force and threat—police, judges, and prisons—is a key means by which society restrains aggression and crime, it isn't the principal means, according to this tradition. The most powerful curb isn't force at all: it is the *internal* inhibition that society builds into each person's character, the inner voice (call it reason, conscience, superego, what you will) that makes the social contract an integral part of our deepest selves.

So while to prevent crime we should worry about whether judges 29 are too lenient or legal procedures too cumbersome, it is still more crucial to ensure that the inner barriers to violence and aggression are strongly in place. This is a cultural matter, a matter of how people bring up their children, a matter of the messages that get passed from the community to the parents and thence to the children. The object is both to transmit the necessary prohibitions against aggression to each individual and to win each individual's inner, positive assent to the social endeavor.

Paradoxically, the hardest of hard realities—whether people com- 30 mit crimes or not—comes down to a very large extent to nothing more than values and beliefs in the world within the individual. Do we deeply believe thou shalt not kill, thou shalt not steal—so deeply that these injunctions are a constituent part of our deepest selves? Do we believe in an idea of justice that embraces us and our community? Do we value such qualities as honor, duty, mercy, honesty, kindness? Do we subscribe enough to the values of our community that we would feel guilt or shame to have transgressed against them, dismay or outrage that others should have flouted them?

It's no wonder that, at the dawn of political philosophy, Plato, in 31 constructing his ideal society in the *Republic,* should have been obsessed with the myths and fairy tales that will be told to children. He well knew that these emanations of culture are the carriers of values, the molders of worldviews and of characters, and that if they are askew, no republic can truly thrive.

When crime flourishes as it now does in our cities, especially crime 32 of mindless malice, it isn't because society has so oppressed people as to bend them out of their true nature and twist them into moral deformity.

It is because the criminals haven't been adequately socialized. Examine the contents of their minds and hearts and too much of what you find bears out this hypothesis: free-floating aggression, weak consciences, anarchic beliefs, detachment from the community and its highest values. They haven't attained the self-respect or the coherent sense of self that underlie one's ability to respect others.

This is a predictable result of unimaginably weak families, headed by 33 immature, irresponsible girls who are at the margin of the community, pathological in their own behavior, and too often lacking the knowledge, interest, and inner resources to be successful molders of strong characters in children. Too many underclass mothers can't enforce the necessary prohibitions for children—or for themselves. And most underclass families lack a father, the parent that Freud, wearing his psychoanalyst's hat rather than his political philosopher's, sees as the absolutely vital agent in the socialization of little boys and in the formation of their superegos.

When the community tells people from such families that they are 34 victims of social injustice, that they perhaps are not personally to blame if they commit crimes, and that it is entirely appropriate for them to nurse feelings of rage and resentment, it is asking for trouble. Worse, the new culture holds that, in a sense, such crime isn't pathological; it is something higher and healthier. It is rebellion—the manly response that Americans have shown to oppression since the Boston Tea Party, the response that Robin Hood and his outlaw band gave to injustice before America was even thought of.

A key element of the cultural shift I am tracing, the idea that crim- 35 inals might be admirable rebels, was all but explicit in the sociological orthodoxy that saw juvenile delinquency as a rational challenge to a society that denied to delinquents the same opportunity to get ahead as their nonimpoverished fellow citizens. By his lawbreaking, the delinquent could win those goods that he desired as much as any other member of society. At the very least he could manifest the worth that society was denying him by demonstrating his "heart" and "guts."[12]

But one could hardly articulate the idea of the criminal as rebel 36 more explicitly or forcefully than Norman Mailer did in his incendiary manifesto, "The White Negro," briefly mentioned earlier. Today, the essay reads like a firework sparkler fiercely sizzling until it sputters out in a wisp of smoke. But it was as hugely influential as it was startling when it appeared in 1957, just as Mailer was becoming a national celebrity and assuming his role as an avant-garde figure at the very forefront of the cultural revolution of the Haves.

Mailer threw down the gauntlet in "The White Negro," indicting 37 modern society as nothing but an engine of oppression, repression, and destruction. What has it produced but the Nazi concentration camps and the atom bomb? And the modern social order holds in reserve yet another form of extinction—" a slow death by conformity with every creative and rebellious instinct stifled."[13]

In this manmade wasteland, blacks inhabit the deepest circle of 38 oppression and victimization. They have "been living on the margin between totalitarianism and democracy for two centuries," says Mailer. In the injustice of our capitalist order, they are Marx's impoverished industrial reserve army, "a cultureless and alienated bottom of exploitable human material." Given not just the economic violence but also the visceral hatred that assaults blacks, says Mailer, "no Negro can saunter down a street with any real certainty that violence will not visit him on his walk. . . . The Negro has the simplest of alternatives: live a life of constant humility or ever-threatening danger." He "know[s] in the cells of his existence that life [is] war. . . ."[14]

What is there to do but reject and oppose such deadly oppres- 39 sion? "The only life-giving answer," says Mailer, "is . . . to divorce oneself from society, to exist without roots, to set out on that uncharted journey with the rebellious imperatives of the self. . . . [O]ne is a rebel or one conforms, one is a frontiersman in the Wild West of American night life, or else a Square cell, trapped in the totalitarian tissues of American society. . . ."[15]

"[W]hether the life is criminal or not, the decision is to encourage 40 the psychopath in oneself." Rebel, rebel—even if lawless rebellion leads to such psychopathic extremes as murder. Even in such rebellion, according to Mailer's Americanized version of European existentialism, you will at least assert your freedom and selfhood.

To be sure, Mailer admits, all this may not look so heroically 41 manly at first blush. Arguably "it takes little courage for two strong eighteen-year-old hoodlums . . . to beat in the brains of a candy-store keeper. . . . Still, courage of a sort is necessary, for one murders not only a weak fifty-year-old man but an institution as well, one violates private property, one enters into a new relation with the police and introduces a dangerous element into one's life. The hoodlum is therefore daring the unknown, and so no matter how brutal the act, it is not altogether cowardly."[16]

Monstrous, but influential. After the publication of Mailer's work, 42 after other writers had expressed similar views, the idea that violent black crime was a kind of regenerative rebellion gained a certain currency. Not that the majority of mainstream Haves embraced Mailer's version of it wholeheartedly or uncritically: rather, they flirted with it; they were prepared to believe that in some, even many, cases it might be true. Crime *might* be rebellion—and so crime became problematical, no longer simply crime, no longer compelling unqualified condemnation.

That's partly because central events of the sixties and early seventies seemed to bear out aspects of such theorizing. The Vietnam War, of course: to the many who opposed it, the war lent credence to the charge that American society was an engine of unjust violence. The Nixonian political scandals further blemished the Establishment. Even before that, the civil disobedience of the civil rights movement had established that society and its laws could be oppressive and could appropriately, even heroically, be opposed by lawbreaking, in Thoreauvian fashion. The ghetto rioting of the mid-sixties enforced for many the false lesson that intolerable racial injustice was beginning to drive people to justified, destructive rebellion (an error repeated in the aftermath of the 1992 Los Angeles riots, though with less confidence). 43

Years after the publication of "The White Negro," Mailer used the same rationale to champion the mindless vandalism of graffiti writing. It was, as he saw it, a healthily rebellious expression of inner creativity uncrushed by the oppressive social order. How much more pleasing, Mailer thought, was the exuberant individuality of those scrawls than the impersonal regularity of the stony facades they defaced. 44

For a while, people believed him. The New York subway trains ended up caked with graffiti because—since graffiti supposedly wasn't really bad—for years no one lifted a finger to stop it. Yet graffiti is a symptom of social decay, a sign, as sociologist Nathan Glazer has observed, that no one is in control and the forces of lawlessness are sliding out from restraint.[17] Consequently, the harm of graffiti goes beyond its ugliness; by insinuating that you can get away with it, it is an invitation to worse lawlessness. 45

Mailer's message further captivated the Haves because he yoked together both of the cultural revolution's liberations. Society oppresses all of us, rich and poor alike, he asserts—in one sense correctly. However privileged we may be, the process of socialization forces us to renounce inborn aggressiveness, to keep it locked within, in a lifelong self-suppression. Moreover, any society, not just our own, puts restrictions on sexuality. Various theories attempt to explain why this must be so, but all agree that here too is a chafing unfreedom imposed upon us by the social condition. 46

Long before Mailer, Freud had fretted over the oppression that civ-   47
ilization imposes on everyone. The superego, he complained, enforces its
curbs tyrannically. Restraining yourself from wrongdoing doesn't leave
you with feelings of calm satisfaction, as you would think it should, because your superego rakes you with feelings of guilt for forbidden *desires*, which you can't help having, no less than for forbidden actions. As
a result, the superego's demands for civilized restraint feel excessive in
their implacability.

Moreover, as French philosophers had been saying since the eigh-   48
teenth century, out of the mutual dependence which is our lot in society, out of the court we must pay to others to win the advancement,
admiration, and love that we want, each of us must sometimes play a
role, must feign concern or respect or humility, must conform to standards that aren't our own, all of which leaves us with a further sense of
self-suppression. Beyond that, a particular society's standards of conformity and propriety can be excessive; and arguably in the fifties, while
Mailer was writing "The White Negro" and the social revolution was beginning to gather steam, there was room for loosening.

But the final degree of inner liberation for which everyone feels a   49
pang of longing—deliverance from the sense of inner division and estrangement, of thwarted desire, of confinement in a selfhood that feels
limiting, inflexible, or inauthentic—is unattainable, given the inescapable
conditions of man's life in society. Yet such is the liberation that Mailer's
essay holds out in prospect—the same liberation for which R. D. Laing
and Ken Kesey longed, in company with all the self-declared rebels of the
counterculture.

For there is in the cultural revolution a strain of utopianism or mil-   50
lenialism, a longing for a perfect world without human evil, an Edenic
world in which we can be whole and good, with every impulse pure and
permitted and satisfied, especially sexual impulses.

Longings like these are, in the strictest sense, antipolitical, reaching   51
to transcend law and government and to enter a world without strife or injustice to curb. Nevertheless, the person who feels such longings often
takes them to be a political viewpoint, as happened on a mass scale in the
sixties. And since, measured against this standard, the freest and most just
society is heavily oppressive, the politics (or pseudopolitics) that issues
from such longings can only be liberation, liberation, liberation. Politics, the
art of the possible, turns into its opposite, the dream of the impossible.

Shortly after Norman Mailer had helped propagate the idea of   52
the criminal as rebel throughout the general culture, well-known black

writers embraced it with an extremism all the more disturbing for being presented so matter-of-factly. Black Panther party member Eldridge Cleaver, for example, declared that the most heinous crime could be an expression of political activism. This declaration went only one step beyond the ideology of Cleaver's Black Power group, which had already wedded politics and violence by espousing the idea of armed black rebellion against oppressive American society. In *Soul On Ice,* a bestseller in the sixties and still taught in some college courses, Cleaver argued that for a black man to rape a white woman was a political act, protesting against his oppression and striking out against his oppressor.

Insidiously, such a politicized view of criminals saturated the inner   53 cities during the sixties. In his memoir *Brothers and Keepers,* for instance, author John Edgar Wideman paraphrases his brother Robby's ruminations on what led him to the criminal career that ended with a prison sentence for murder. In the ghetto, says Robby, "all the glamor, all the praise and attention is given to the slick guy, the gangster especially. . . . And it's because we can't help but feel some satisfaction seeing a brother, a black man, get over on these people, on their system without playing by their rules." After all, those rules "were forced on us by people who did not have our best interests at heart." So it's not surprising that black people look upon black gangsters "with some sense of pride and admiration. . . . We know they represent rebellion—what little is left in us."[18]

The rebelliousness that breeds crime, Robby says, is ingrained deep   54 in ghetto life. In his own adolescence, "it was unacceptable to be 'good,' it was square to be smart in school, it was jive to show respect to people outside the street world, it was cool to be cold to your woman and the people that loved you. The things we liked we called 'bad.' . . . The thing was to make your own rules, do your own thing, but make sure it's contrary to what society says or is." You keep your dignity and integrity by your rejection of right and wrong as defined by the society that oppresses you. With all values turned upside down, it doesn't take much to turn crime into heroic, or at least honest, defiance. "Robbing white people didn't cause me to lose no sleep back then," Wideman quotes Robby as saying. "How you gon feel sorry when society's so corrupt?"[19]

A similar vision accounts for some of the disturbing lyrics of today's   55 rap music. In a much more domesticated version, it is the animating vision of such blockbuster films as *Superfly* of 1972 or *Harlem Nights* of 1989, movies in which black filmmakers at the center of the larger culture celebrate black heroes who are smarter, quicker, and tougher criminals than the white criminals who are their adversaries. Why are the heroes law-breakers? "I know it's a rotten game," explains the sidekick of *Superfly's* dope dealer hero, "but it's the only one the Man left us to play." The alternative is "workin' some jive job for chump change day after day." In this rotten world, even the police turn out to be drug and crime kingpins, as corrupt as the social order they uphold.

When the hero-crooks celebrated by these movies end up with 56 satchels of money after outsmarting the crooked white cops, it's a different moral universe from thirties gangster movies like *Scarface* or *Little Caesar*, where the criminal protagonist falls as quickly and sordidly as he has risen. It's different too from the world of a forties movie like *The Asphalt Jungle*, which sees its gangster protagonist with sympathy but still affirms the need for police to oppose such criminals and maintain the social order.

Such a view of the admirably defiant criminal still holds the underclass 57 in thrall. "They want us to settle for a little piece of nothing, like the Indians on the reservation," as one inner-city resident who grew up in a Harlem housing project said recently, summing up his vision of the larger society. "They got us fighting and killing each other for crumbs. In a way, the ones in jail are like political prisoners, because they refused to settle for less."[20]

How deep the glorification of the criminal runs today can be seen 58 in the "near folk-hero status," as *The New York Times* calls it, that murderer Larry Davis won in Harlem and the Bronx in 1986. Charged with killing and robbing six drug dealers in cold blood, Davis dodged from hideout to hideout as police closed in on him during a seventeen-day manhunt, which ended in a pyrotechnic, TV-style shootout at a Bronx housing project. Davis wounded six policemen before being captured and led out in handcuffs, cool and uninjured, to the acclaim of a cheering crowd of project residents. All through the manhunt, and after its bloody end, ghetto residents told tales of his larger-than-life outwitting and resisting the police, speaking of him with thrilled emphatic admiration as "the dude who elude." This Scarlet Pimpernel of the projects later was acquitted of five of the murders, convicted of one, and also jailed in connection with the shootout.[21]

The cultural revolution left none of the barriers to crime undis- 59 turbed. Not only did it undermine the inner inhibitions, but it also weakened the external deterrent, the threat of official punishment. Guided by the idea that society systematically oppresses the poor and the black, the Haves increasingly hampered the governmental apparatus that upholds the law by force.

Government, according to this view, tends almost reflexively to be   60
an instrument of injustice against the Have-Nots, above all in its law enforcement capacity. As William Ryan put it in *Blaming the Victim,* all experts know that "the administration of justice is grossly biased against the
Negro and the lower class defendant; that arrest and imprisonment is a
process reserved almost exclusively for the black and the poor; and that
the major function of the police is the preservation not only of the public order, but of the social order—that is, of inequality between man
and man."[22] However overwrought, Ryan's statement contains this element of somber truth: racial discrimination did taint police treatment of
blacks when Ryan was writing, and in the South police did act as op-
pressors of blacks, as the nation learned indelibly when Freedom Riders were arrested in Jackson and elsewhere in Mississippi in 1961 or
when Chief Bull Conner viciously attacked civil rights demonstrators
with police dogs, clubs, cattle prods, and fire hoses in Birmingham, Al-
abama, in 1963.

Properly indignant at such viciousness, the majority culture re-   61
sponded by throwing a cordon around the government's police functions, aiming to confine the police within the narrowest channel so they
couldn't surge out of control. In this effort, federal judges took the lead.
With their ideas continually renewed by a flow of talented clerks newly
minted from the nation's top law schools, the judges were part of the
advance guard of the resulting cultural changes. They had the moral authority and political power to take new ideas and transform them into the
concrete reality of law almost overnight, anointing them in the process
as normal and right. Accordingly, out of the impulse to curb the police
functions of the state came the well-known string of 1960s court decisions that succeeded in tying down criminal law enforcement with as
many strands as Gulliver in Lilliput.

Still, it was a big step from the shameful doings of Bull Connor to   62
the conclusion that the entire governmental apparatus for controlling
crime across the nation was an engine of injustice. And it was an even bigger step to the conclusion that the proper remedy for such instances of
police lawlessness as did occur was to free proven criminals—as distinct
from Freedom Riders or civil rights demonstrators—rather than to dismiss and punish the responsible officials.

As with so many elements of the cultural revolution, these key   63
court decisions of the sixties produced long-term unintended consequences. Anxious to protect citizens from a tyrannical abuse of police
power, the judges erected safeguards that turned out to hinder ordinary,

untyrannical policemen from bringing common criminals to justice. From *Mapp* v. *Ohio* in 1961 through *Miranda* v. *Arizona* in 1966, the Supreme Court decisions that proceeded from fears of police tyranny aimed to prevent juries from hearing evidence obtained in ways that the Court, ever more punctiliously, deemed unconstitutional. *Mapp* ruled that jurors in state courts, which try most criminal cases, can't see physical evidence obtained by search warrants in any way flawed—even, as is often the case, if the evidence proves the bloodiest guilt and would imprison a criminal whose liberty threatens the entire society. Henceforward, police might find a smoking gun, but a smart defense lawyer might well find an angle to keep it out of evidence.

Miranda, as is well known, barred using the criminal's own confession, or any statement of his, if obtained without a battery of procedural safeguards that would discourage most sane people from uttering a single word. Why even bother to invent a lie, since it might catch you out? This was a far cry from the previous rule, which had excluded only coerced confessions obtained by threat or brutality.   64

The inevitable result was that criminals became harder to convict,   65 and punishment for crime became rarer. As the judges issued their rulings on suppressing evidence in the sixties, the prison population declined. By the mid-seventies, the average Chicago youthful offender got arrested over thirteen times before being sent to reform school. In big cities, more than nine felony convictions in ten result not from trials but from plea bargains, in which penalties are lighter and criminals are left with at least some sense of having beaten the system. Today, thanks partly to plea bargaining, your chance of *not* going to jail if you're *convicted* of a serious crime is two to one.[23]

As it became possible to suppress key evidence and literally to get   66 away with murder, crime took off. In the sixties, the overall crime rate doubled. And between 1961 and now, while the murder rate "only" doubled, the rape rate quadrupled, and both the robbery and assault rates quintupled.[24]

Related changes in juvenile justice contributed to these swollen fig-   67 ures. Since the beginning of this century, the law understandably has treated juveniles more leniently than adults, holding them less responsible for their actions "by reason of infancy." If they committed crimes—until recently mostly thievery or pickpocketing—perhaps they hadn't yet finished the work of childhood and fully learned to differentiate right from wrong. Were they guided and taught instead of punished, perhaps they would develop the moral sense as yet unawakened within them.

So the law, in a quasi-parental way, humanely aimed to rescue them 68 from their faulty upbringing. By keeping its hearings secret so the offender wouldn't be stigmatized after he had been reformed, by sending him to a reformatory and not a jail, the juvenile justice system tried to treat him not as a criminal but as a "child in need of the care and protection of the state."[25]

But during the sixties the image of the state as a kind parent crum- 69 bled before the new idea of the state as oppressive and adversarial. Once the behavior of juvenile offenders became prima facie evidence of the unjust conditions in which they lived, it followed that it was only one further degree of oppression for the state to deprive them of their liberty without even a show of due process, as routinely used to happen in juvenile court hearings.

It happened because such hearings are civil rather than criminal 70 proceedings: they are supposed to determine what best fills the therapeutic needs of the offender, not merely what meets the needs of the community. But in Justice Abe Fortas's words, for all the insistence that "guidance and rehabilitation" are at issue, not "criminal responsibility, guilt, and punishment," still the kid gets put away against his will. Therefore, he ought to have all the protections to which an adult would be entitled.[26]

Chief of these protections, the Supreme Court ruled in *In re Gault* 71 in 1967, is a lawyer. And once a court-appointed lawyer became mandatory in the juvenile courts, the whole array of *Miranda*-type procedural safeguards became routine there too. However humanely intended this reform, the result is that now juvenile offenders who are caught red-handed can also get away with murder scot-free, without even the few months in a rehabilitation facility that is the juvenile justice system's severest penalty.

In a sense, the Court had the right instinct in favoring the crimi- 72 nal, legalistic model over the therapeutic. Sadly, today's juvenile reformatory rehabilitates few, if any, since many youthful offenders aren't pickpockets and petty thieves salvageable by rehabilitation efforts. At fifteen, even at twelve or thirteen, many youthful rapists or murderers are hardened, brutal criminals, past the point of salvation, however much that reality might confute our sense of the possible or baffle our most generous impulses.

At the extreme of underclass pathology, too many of them have 73 grown up in anarchic family situations, with mothers too defective to socialize them. A quarter century ago, when such young people began to inundate the family courts, eminent child psychiatrist Selma Fraiberg chillingly, and accurately, assessed their inner lives: "These are the people who are unable to fulfill the most ordinary human obligations in work, in friendship, in marriage, and in child-rearing," she wrote. "The condition of non-attachment leaves a void in the personality where conscience should be. Where there are no human attachments, there can be no conscience."[27]

The new layer of legalism the Supreme Court added to juvenile proceedings didn't mean that youthful criminals would be exposed to the sanctions of the adult criminal justice system however (at least not until very recently, when some jurisdictions have allowed the adult courts to try some fifteen- and sixteen-year-olds accused of rape and murder). It didn't mean that their records would be unsealed, so that future courts could know their criminal histories and better protect society against them. It only meant that it would be much harder to put them in the reformatories intended to do them good.

That has been an unfortunate change. For even if reformatories can offer little in the way of rehabilitation, they do offer punishment. After surveying years of studies of the relationship between the rates of various kinds of crime and the probability of imprisonment, crime theorist James Q. Wilson concludes that "the evidence supports (though cannot conclusively prove) the view that deterrence and incapacitation work," while "rehabilitation has not yet been shown to be a promising method for dealing with serious offenders."[28] Even mild punishment seems better at changing behavior than none, but none is what juvenile offenders too often get.[29]

One final barrier against crime also fell to the growing fear of the Haves that police injustice continually threatened the Have-Nots. I've mentioned James Q. Wilson and George Kelling's argument that neighborhood disorder causes an increase in crime, an argument later research has borne out. An infestation of panhandlers, drunks, addicts, graffiti smearers, street hustlers, streetwalkers, and youths rowdily "hanging out" testifies to a lack of police oversight that makes citizens feel threatened and encourages serious crime.[30]

But the impulse to protect the Have-Nots from oppression went far to prevent the police from curbing the disorder that Wilson and Kelling found so dangerous. Police keep order—or used to keep order— by relying on an array of time-honored prohibitions against loitering, vagrancy, disorderly conduct, disturbing the peace, and obscenity. Under such laws, they can question suspicious characters and quiet the disorderly or move them along.

But lawyers and judges came to feel that the order-keeping function 78
of the police was yet one more instrument by which the authority of society was used to harass the Have-Nots. When does taking the air turn
into loitering? When the person doing it, judges feared, is a poor black
in a white neighborhood. So too might poverty and blackness transform
sitting on a park bench into vagrancy, or turn high-spiritedness into disturbing the peace.

As a result, the laws governing such offenses as loitering or disor- 79
derly conduct were struck down for being overly broad or overly vague.
Papachristo v. *City of Jacksonville* (1972) effectively spelled the end for
many vagrancy and loitering ordinances. Jacksonville police had picked
up a dozen or so citizens, including some suspected burglars and drug
dealers, on the strength of a vagrancy ordinance directed in archaic language at "rogues and vagabonds . . . who go about begging, . . . persons who use juggling or unlawful games," and the like. How can anyone
know exactly what conduct such fuzzy, antique rigmarole forbids? the
Supreme Court complained in finding it unconstitutional. Whimsically
quoting an assortment of poets in praise of "idling," as if all vagrants
were free spirits like Walt Whitman or sixties street people, Justice
William O. Douglas wrote that an ordinance like Jacksonville's "results
in a regime in which the poor and the unpopular are permitted to 'stand
on a public sidewalk . . . only at the whim of any police officer.' "[31]

Gooding v. *Wilson* (1972), in which the Court first struck down a law 80
for being "too broad," shows how triflingly fanciful the reasoning could
be by which judges undid the order-keeping function of the police in the
service of their well-intentioned agenda. At issue was a Georgia statute
outlawing language "tending to cause a breach of the peace." This law belonged to a time-honored legal tradition of prohibitions against "fighting words," language so insulting that it might be expected to provoke
someone to blows. But a Georgia court had once ruled that you could violate this law by yelling at someone who was across a raging river or
locked in a jail cell. In other words, even though you might utter your
words to someone who could not literally fight you, they were still "fighting words," as far as the Georgia judge was concerned, and therefore
prohibited.

Supreme Court Justice William Brennan, citing this ruling, con- 81
cluded that since the law went beyond words that could literally make
someone fight, it must be struck down as too broad; it might encroach on
the First Amendment right to make ugly statements unlikely to provoke
blows. As constitutional scholar Richard E. Morgan remarks, lower courts

in the wake of this decision have essentially done away with the concept of "fighting words"; in numerous cases, judges have upheld the right of Americans to call each other "motherfuckers"—the cultural revolution's standard-issue epithet—whether of the "white," "black," or "fascist" variety.[32]

For all Americans, the wholesale overturning of the bars to crime [82] and disorder has scrambled the moral order. What becomes of the sense of justice when, almost daily, people violate the fundamental principle of the social contract? What becomes of the sense of personal responsibility for actions when people are not held accountable even for the most evil deeds? With the ground on which the sense of values rests giving way beneath their feet, no wonder many reel with moral vertigo.

For all Americans, Have and Have-Nots alike, the weakening of [83] the protections against crime and disorder has debased urban life, overlaying it with fear and suspicion as well as real injury. The disproportionate number of crimes committed by underclass lawbreakers has heightened racial hostility, straining the social fabric. Straining it too are the menacing rowdiness and graffiti, the dope selling, and the occupation by the homeless of public spaces everywhere.

If the Haves sought to uplift and ennoble their own lives by the [84] dual liberations they tried to accomplish, the condition of today's great cities is a sad monument to the Law of Unintended Consequences. Metropolitan life is the great hothouse of human possibility, nurturing characters of every stripe. In such an atmosphere, people can achieve as far as is possible the latent potentialities that the Haves thirsted to realize when they began their cultural revolution. How ironic that that revolution ended by driving so many of the energetic and ambitious out of the cities. The civic culture that fosters the full development of individuals—the sense of a community linked by mutual tolerance and respect for ambition, achievement, and energy—will be thinner and more constricted in the New York or Chicago or Detroit of the nineties than it was in the New York or Chicago or Detroit of the forties or fifties.

However much the erosion of the barriers to crime and disorder [85] disrupted the lives of the Haves, that disruption pales compared to the disruption it inflicted on the lives of the Have-Nots. More than any economic change of the William Julius Wilson variety, it is the explosion of violent crime that has turned inner cities into blighted wastelands, virtual free-fire zones. Repeated holdups and street robberies of employees drove out small tradesmen and larger businesses alike. Crime made fear ever-present for hardworking, law-abiding ghetto citizens—who, though you might not think so from reading William Julius Wilson on the flight of upwardly mobile blacks from the ghetto, certainly do exist.

The almost daily reports of gunfire crackling outside the projects, [86] of people cowering on the floor of their apartments, of innocent passersby getting caught in the crossfire, become numbing by their very familiarity. But it is true that a young black man has a greater chance of being murdered in the inner city than a soldier had of being killed in the jungles of Vietnam.[33] It is true that you can send your kid to the grocery store and never see him again alive. It is true that an East New York high school, in a painfully ghoulish accommodation to anarchy, has recently established a "Grieving Room," where students gather to mourn slain classmates. In the last four years, seventy have been shot or stabbed, half of them fatally.[34]

Quoted in a recent newspaper article reporting that two innocent [87] bystanders in the New York ghettos had been killed and five more wounded in the last forty-eight hours, the mother of one of the wounded says: "I work ten hours a day. . . . In the morning, I have to leave before my kids do. All I can do is say a prayer, that's about it. Because you never know if you're going to come back alive, and you come home and they're going to be alive. You'll be in your house and people will be shooting through your damn window. You stick your head out your window, somebody blows your brains out."[35]

The achievements of civilization rest upon the social order, which [88] rests in turn upon a mutual agreement to forswear aggression. In the ghetto, the agreement is in tatters, the police are hamstrung, and the life of the civilized community is being stomped out by force and violence. In cities in which civilization should have reached its apogee, gang-ridden ghetto areas have regressed to some dark age when human life was organized around predatory, roving bands with continually shifting memberships. It is as if the peaceful citizens of those neighborhoods really were under the cruel yoke of the banditti of ruffians that Thomas Paine imagined as introducing violence and crime into the early ages of the world.

After a nine-year-old girl in a crime-ravaged Brooklyn ghetto had [89] just been shot in the head by a thug's stray bullet, a neighbor—a law-abiding family man living across the street from a crack house—lamented: "Our lives have been reduced to the lowest levels of human existence."[36] In such an anarchy, it's a wonder not when people fail to achieve the civilized excellences but when, like the family man quoted above, they succeed.

The primary function of any society is to guarantee the social con- 90 tract. What but anarchy can you expect if the legitimate force of society has eroded? What can you expect when the guardians of that force cannot bring themselves to exercise it, like a New York judge who vibrated with protective sympathy for the defendant before him, a callously brutal eighteen-year-old murderer? The judge, trying to quell the prosecutor's outraged complaints about the defense lawyer's procedural petifoggery, cried out feelingly: "This is only a murder! Only a murder!"[37]

NOTES

1. " . . . *change the kid.* . . . " George Cadwalader, *Castaways: The Penikese Island Experiment* (Chelsea, Vt.: Chelsea Green, 1988), p. viii.
2. " . . . *given up on?*" Ibid., pp. ix–x.
3. *its foundation.* Jean-Jacques Rousseau, *The Second Discourse,* in *The First and Second Discourses,* trans. Roger D. Masters (New York: St. Martin's Press, 1964), pp. 154–160.
4. *political society.* Thomas Paine, *The Rights of Man* (New York: Dent/Dutton Everyman, 1969), pp. 31–33, 163–164.
5. " . . . *diseased environment.*" Michael Harrington, *The Other America: Poverty in the United States,* rev. ed. (New York: Penguin, 1971), p. 136.
6. " . . . *is responsible.*" Ramsey Clark, *Crime in America: Observations on Its Nature, Causes, Prevention and Control* (New York: Simon & Schuster, 1970), p. 51.
7. *Clark concludes.* Ibid., pp. 29, 43.
8. *in the suites.* Ibid., pp. 37–38.
9. " . . . *expect violence.*" Ibid., pp. 42–43, 144.
10. " . . . *this assertion?*" Sigmund Freud, *Civilization and Its Discontents,* trans. James Strachey (New York: Norton, 1961), p. 58.
11. *of the governed.* Edmund Burke, *Reflections on the Revolution in France,* together with Thomas Paine, *The Rights of Man* (Garden City, N.Y.: Doubleday Anchor, 1973), pp. 180, 240.
12. *"heart" and "guts."* Richard Cloward and Lloyd Ohlin, *Delinquency and Opportunity: A Theory of Delinquent Gangs* (New York: Free Press, 1960).
13. " . . . *instinct stifled.*" Norman Mailer, *Advertisements for Myself* (New York: Putnam-Berkley, 1959), p. 312.
14. " . . . *life [is] war.* . . . " Ibid., pp. 313, 314, 321.
15. *American society.* . . . Ibid., p. 313.
16. " . . . *not altogether cowardly.*" Ibid., pp. 313, 320–321.
17. *from restraint.* Nathan Glazer, "On Subway Graffiti in New York," *Public Interest* (Winter 1979).
18. " . . . *left in us.*" John Edgar Wideman, *Brothers and Keepers* (New York: Penguin, 1985), p. 57.
19. " . . . *so corrupt?*" Ibid., pp. 58, 90.
20. " . . . *settle for less.*" "As Many Fall, Project's Survivors Struggle On," *The New York Times* (February 6, 1991).

21. *the shootout.* "Larry Davis Convicted in Killing of a Drug Dealer," *The New York Times* (March 15, 1991).

22. " . . . *man and man."* William Ryan, *Blaming the Victim,* rev. ed. (New York: Vintage, 1976), p. 217.

23. *two to one.* Richard E. Morgan, *Disabling America: The "Rights Industry" in Our Time* (New York: Basic Books, 1984), p. 76.

24. *rates quintupled.* FBI Uniform Crime Reports.

25. " . . . *of the state."* Rita Kramer, *At a Tender Age: Violent Youth and Juvenile Justice* (New York: Holt, 1988), pp. 65–67.

26. *would be entitled.* Ibid., pp. 68–70.

27. " . . . *no conscience,"* Selma Fraiberg, "The Origins of Human Bonds," *Commentary* (December 1967).

28. " . . . *serious offenders."* James Q. Wilson, *Thinking About Crime,* rev. ed. (New York: Vintage, 1985), pp. 5, 119, 123–124.

29. *too often get.* Kramer, *At a Tender Age,* p. 195.

30. *serious crime.* Wilson, *Thinking About Crime;* Wesley G. Skogan, *Disorder and Decline: Crime and the Spiral of Decay in American Neighborhoods* (New York: Free Press, 1990).

31. " ' . . . *any police officer.' "* Morgan, *Disabling America,* pp. 114–116 *Papachristo* v. *City of Jacksonville,* 405 U.S. 156 (1972).

32. *or "fascist" variety.* Morgan, *Disabling America,* pp. 118–121.

33. *jungles of Vietnam.* "Homocide Rate Up For Young Blacks," *The New York Times* (December 7, 1990).

34. *half of them fatally.* New York Post (April 26, 1991).

35. " . . . *blows your brains out."* "Caught in Crossfire: Rising Toll in Streets," *The New York Times* (April 19, 1991).

36. " . . . *human existence."* "Wild Shooting on Street Hits Girl, 9, in Car," *The New York Times* (July 23, 1990).

37. " . . . *Only a murder!"* Kramer, *At a Tender Age,* p. 92.

READING FOR INFORMATION

1. According to Magnet, what is wrong with the current orthodox view of the causes of crime in America?

2. Summarize the intellectual framework or theoretical base of Magnet's new theory.

3. How do you react to Magnet's explanation of why criminals are inadequately socialized?

4. Explain what Magnet means when he says that myths and fairy tales are "the carriers of values, the molders of worldviews and of characters." Can you recall any myths or fairy tales that taught you values or molded your ideas?

5. Explain why Magnet attributes the concept of the "criminal as rebel" to the writer Norman Mailer.

6. Describe how the concept of the rebellious criminal is expressed in print, media, and film. Can you provide additional examples?

7. Describe the effect of crime and disorder on the lives of poor people.

READING FOR FORM, ORGANIZATION, AND EXPOSITORY FEATURES

1. What is the effect on the reader of the opening scenario about Cadwalader's experiment? Why do you think Magnet begins the article in this way?

2. Underline passages in which Magnet uses different types of evidence to support his position and comment on the effectiveness of each type.

3. How does Magnet structure his argument? Construct a graphic overview of the selection.

READING FOR RHETORICAL CONCERNS

1. Explain why Magnet's background as an editor of *Fortune* prepares you for his argument.

2. Do you think Magnet makes any assumptions about his readers? Explain your response.

3. How would you describe Magnet's tone of voice? What does the tone suggest about the author?

WRITING ASSIGNMENTS

1. Summarize and react to Magnet's argument. Address your essay to students who have not read the selection.

2. Use the strategies presented in Chapter 4 to write a three- to four-page critical analysis of Magnet's argument.

3. In a three- to four-page essay, argue for or against Magnet's claim that crime is the fault of the criminal, not of society. If you wish, draw on selections in this chapter or other materials you have read.

4. Write an essay in which you respond to Magnet's claim that "too many underclass mothers can't enforce the necessary prohibitions for children" (paragraph 33).

The War Against the Poor Instead of Programs to End Poverty

Herbert J. Gans

Herbert J. Gans is professor of sociology at Columbia University. He has written numerous articles and books on the subject of poverty. His latest book is People and Plans: Essays on Poverty, Racism, and Other National Urban Problems *(1991).*

PREREADING

> Before you read the article, take a few minutes to write a response to the title. Do you think we are making a serious effort to end poverty in the United States? Can you think of why we might be accused of engaging in a war *against* the poor instead of a battle to improve their condition?

While liberals have been talking about resuming the War on 1 Poverty, elected officials are doing something very different: waging a war on the poor. Even the riot that took place in Los Angeles in early May did not interrupt that war, perhaps because the riot was a mixture of protest, looting, and destruction.

The war on the poor was initiated by dramatic shifts in the domes- 2 tic and world economy which have turned more and more unskilled and semiskilled workers into surplus labor. Private enterprise participated actively by shipping jobs overseas and by treating workers as expendable. Government has done its part as well, increasingly restricting the welfare state safety net to the middle class. Effective job-creation schemes, housing programs, educational and social services that serve the poor—and some of the working classes—are vanishing. Once people become poor, it becomes ever harder for them to escape poverty.

Despite the willingness to help the poor expressed in public opin- 3 ion polls, other, more covert, attitudes have created a political climate that makes the war on the poor possible. Politicians compete with each

Herbert J. Gans, "The War Against the Poor Instead of Programs to End Poverty," *Dissent* Fall 1992: 461–65.

other over who can capture the most headlines with new ways to punish the poor. However, too many of their constituents see the poor not as people without jobs but as miscreants who behave badly because they do not abide by middle class or mainstream moral values. Those judged "guilty" are dismissed as the "undeserving poor"—or the underclass in today's language—people who do not deserve to escape poverty.

True, *some* people are indeed guilty of immoral behavior—that is, 4 murderers, street criminals, drug sellers, child abusers.

Then there are poor people whose anger at their condition expresses 5 itself in the kind of nihilism that cannot be defined as political protest. Even so, most of those labeled "undeserving" are simply poor people who for a variety of reasons cannot live up to mainstream behavioral standards, like remaining childless in adolescence, finding and holding a job, and staying off welfare. This does not make them immoral. Because poor adolescents do not have jobs does not mean they are lazy. Because their ghetto "cool" may deter employers does not mean they are unwilling to work. Still, the concept of an underclass lumps them with those who are criminal or violent.

Why do Americans accept so many untruths about the poor, and re- 6 main unwilling to accept the truth when it is available? The obvious answer is that some of the poor frighten or anger those who are better-off. But they also serve as a lightning rod—scapegoats—for some problems among the better-off. Street criminals rightly evoke fears about personal safety, but they, and the decidedly innocent poor also generate widespread anger about the failure of government to reduce "urban" and other problems.

Among whites, the anger is intertwined with fears about blacks and 7 "Hispanics," or the newest immigrants, reflecting the fear of the stranger and newcomer from which their own ancestors suffered when they arrived here. (Few remember that, at the start of the twentieth century, the "Hebrews" then arriving were sometimes described as a "criminal race"— as the Irish had been earlier in the nineteenth century.)

The hostility toward today's welfare recipients is a subtler but 8 equally revealing index to the fears of the more fortunate. This fear reflects a historic belief that people who are not economically self-sufficient can hurt the economy, although actual expenditures for welfare have always been small. Welfare recipients are also assumed to be getting something for nothing, often by people who are not overly upset about corrupt governmental or corporate officials who get a great deal of money for nothing or very little.

Welfare recipients possibly provoke anger among those concerned 9
about their own economic security, especially in a declining economy.
Welfare recipients are seen as living the easy life while everyone else is
working harder than ever—and thus become easy scapegoats, which does
not happen to the successful, who often live easier lives.

The concern with poor unmarried mothers, especially adolescents, 10
whose number and family size have in fact long been declining, epito-
mizes adult fears about the high levels of sexual activity and the constant
possibility of pregnancy among *all* adolescent girls. In addition, the notion of the "undeserving poor" has become a symbol for the general
decline of mainstream moral standards, especially those celebrated as
"traditional" in American society.

Ironically, however, the "undeserving poor" can be forced to uphold 11
some of these very standards in exchange for welfare, much as some
Skid Row homeless still get a night's dinner and housing in exchange
for sitting through a religious service. The missionaries in this case are
secular: social workers and bureaucrats. But the basic moralistic expectations remain the same, including the demand that the poor live up to
values that their socioeconomic superiors preach but do not always practice. Thus, social workers can have live-in lovers without being married,
but their clients on welfare cannot. Members of the more fortunate
classes are generally free from moral judgments altogether; no one talks
about an undeserving middle class or the undeserving rich.

The war on the poor is probably best ended by job-centered eco- 12
nomic growth that creates decent public and private jobs. Once poor
people have such jobs, they are almost automatically considered deserv-
ing, eligible for a variety of other programs to help them or their children
escape poverty.

The most constructive way to supply such jobs would be an up- 13
dated New Deal that repairs failing infrastructures, creates new public facilities (including new databases), and allows the old ones to
function better—for example, by drastically reducing class size in public schools. Equally important are ways of reviving private enterprise
and finding new niches for it in the global economy. Without them,
there will not be enough well-paying jobs in factories, laboratories,
and offices—or taxes to pay for public programs. Such programs are
already being proposed these days, by Bill Clinton and in the Congress, but mainly for working-class people who have been made jobless and are now joining the welfare rolls.

Last but not least is a new approach to income grants for those who 14
cannot work or find work. The latest fashion is to put welfare recipients
to work, which would be a good idea if even decent entry-level jobs for
them could be found or created. (Alas, when taxpayers discover how
much cheaper it is to pay welfare than to create jobs, that remedy may
end as it has before.)

Also needed is a non-punitive, universal income grant program, 15
which goes to all people who still end up as part of the labor surplus. If
such a program copied the European principle of not letting the incomes
of the poor fall below 60 to 70 percent of the median income—in the
United States, welfare recipients get a fifth of the median on average—
the recipients would remain integral members of society, who could be
required to make sure their children would not become poor. (Such a
solution would also cut down the crime rate.)

However, even minimal conventional antipoverty programs are 16
politically unpopular at the moment. The 1992 Democratic presidential candidates paid little attention to the poor during the primaries,
except, in passing, in New York City and, then again, after Los Angeles. The future of antipoverty programs looks no brighter than before.

The time may be ripe to look more closely at how nonpoor Amer- 17
icans feel about poverty, and try to reduce their unwarranted fear and
anger toward the poor—with the hope that they would then be more
positive about reviving antipoverty efforts.

The first priority for reducing that anger is effective policies 18
against drugs and street crime, though they alone cannot stem all the
negative feelings. Probably the only truly effective solution is a prosperous economy in which the anger between all groups is lessened; and
a more egalitarian society, in which the displacement of such anger on
the poor is no longer necessary, and the remaining class conflicts can
be fought fairly.

This ideal is today more utopian than ever, but it ought to be kept 19
in mind. Every step toward it will help a little. Meanwhile, in order to
bring back antipoverty programs, liberals, along with the poor and others who speak for the poor, could also try something else: initiating an intellectual and cultural defense of the poor. In a "sound bite": to fight
class bigotry along with the racial kind.

Anti-bigotry programs work slowly and not always effectively, 20
but they are as American as apple pie. Class bigotry is itself still a
novel idea, but nothing would be lost by mounting a defense of the

poor and putting it on the public agenda. Ten such defenses strike me as especially urgent:

1. *Poverty is not equivalent to moral failure.* That moral undesir- 21
ables exist among the poor cannot be denied, but there is no evidence that their proportion is greater than among the more fortunate. "Bums" can be found at all economic levels. However, more prosperous miscreants tend to be less visible; the alcoholic co-worker can doze off at his desk, but the poor drunk is apt to be found in the gutter. Abusive middle class parents may remain invisible for years, until their children are badly hurt, but violent poor parents soon draw the attention of child-welfare workers and may lose their children to foster care.

Troubled middle-class people have access to experts who can 22
demonstrate that moral diagnoses are not enough. The abusive mother was herself abused; the school dropout has a learning disability; the young person who will not work suffers from depression. Poor people, on the other hand, rarely have access to such experts or to clinical treatment. For the poor, the explanations are usually moral, and the treatment is punitive.

2. *"Undeservingness" is an effect of poverty.* Whatever else can be 23
said about unmarried mothers on welfare, school dropouts, and people unwilling to take minimum-wage dead-end jobs, their behavior is almost always *poverty-related*.

This is, of course, also true of many street criminals and drug sell- 24
ers. Middle-class people, after all, do not turn into muggers and street drug dealers any more than they become fifteen-year-old unmarried mothers.

People who have not been poor themselves do not understand how 25
much of what the poor do is poverty-related. Poor young women often do not want to marry the fathers of their children because such men cannot perform as breadwinners and might cope with their economic failures by battering their wives. Although a great deal of publicity is given to school dropouts, not enough has been said about the peer pressure in poor, and even working-class, neighborhoods that discourages doing well in school.

3. *The responsibilities of the poor.* Conservatives, often mute about 26
the responsibilities of the rich, stress the responsibilities of the poor. However, poor people sometimes feel no need to be responsible to society until society treats them responsibly. Acting irresponsibly becomes an angry reaction to, even a form of power, over that society. Those whose irresponsibility is criminal deserve punishment and the clearly

lazy deserve to lose their benefits. But who would punish an unmarried mother who goes on welfare to obtain medical benefits that a job cannot supply? Is she not acting responsibly toward her child? And how well can we judge anyone's responsibility without first knowing that choices, responsible and irresponsible, were actually open? Being poor often means having little choice to begin with.

4. *The drastic scarcity of work for the poor.* Many Americans, in- 27 cluding too many economists, have long assumed that there are always more jobs than workers, that the properly eager can always find them, hence the jobless are at fault. This is, however, a myth—one of many Ronald Reagan liked to promote when he was president. The facts are just the opposite. Decent jobs that are open to the poor, especially to blacks, were the first to disappear when our deindustrialization began. This helps to explain why so many poor men have dropped out of the labor force, and are no longer even counted as jobless.

Incidentally, the myth that the unemployed are unwilling to work is 28 never attached to the rising number of working- and middle-class jobless. But, then, they are not yet poor enough to be considered undeserving.

5. *Black troubles and misbehavior are caused more by poverty than* 29 *by race.* Because the proportion of blacks who are criminals, school dropouts, heads of single-parent families, or unmarried mothers is higher than among whites, blacks increasingly have to face the outrageous indignity of being considered genetically or culturally undesirable. The plain fact is that the higher rates of nearly all social problems among blacks are the effects of being poor—including poverty brought about by discrimination. When poor whites are compared with poor blacks, those with social problems are not so different, although black proportions remain higher. Even this difference can be attributed to income disparity. Black poverty has been worse in all respects and by all indicators ever since blacks were brought here as slaves.

6. *Blacks should not be treated like recent immigrants.* Black job- 30 seekers sometimes face the additional burden of being expected, both by employers and the general public, to compete for jobs with recently arrived immigrants. This expectation calls on people who have been in America for generations to accept the subminimum wages, long hours, poor working conditions, and employer intimidation that are the lot of many immigrants. Actually, employers prefer immigrants because they are more easily exploited or more deferential than native-born Americans. To make matters worse, blacks are then blamed for lacking an "immigrant work ethic."

7. *Debunking the metaphors of undeservingness.* Society's word- ³¹
smiths—academics, journalists, and pundits—like to find, and their audiences like to hear, buzzwords that caricature moral failings among the
poor; but it should not be forgotten that these terms were invented by
the fortunate. *Not only is there no identifiable underclass, but a class
"under" society is a social impossibility.* Welfare "dependents" are in
that condition mainly because the economy has declared them surplus
labor, and because they must rely on politicians and officials who determine their welfare eligibility.

Such metaphors are never applied to the more affluent. There are ³²
no hard-core millionaires, and troubled middle-class people will never be
labeled an under-middle class. Women who choose to be financially dependent on their husbands are not described as spouse-dependent, while
professors who rely on university trustees for their income are not called
tenure-dependent.

8. *The dangers of class stereotypes.* Underclass and other terms for ³³
the undeserving poor are class stereotypes, which reinforce class discrimination much as racial stereotypes support racial discrimination. The
many similarities between class and racial stereotypes still need to be
identified.

Stereotypes sometimes turn into everyday labels that are so taken ³⁴
for granted that they turn into self-fulfilling prophecies—and then
cause particular havoc among the more vulnerable poor. For example,
boys from poor single-parent families are apt to be punished harder
for minor delinquencies simply because of the stereotype that they are
growing up without paternal or other male supervision. Once they, and
other poor people, are labeled as undeserving, public officials who are
supposed to supply them with services feel justified in not being as
helpful as before—though depriving poor people of an emergency rent
payment or food grant may be enough to push them closer to homelessness or street crime.

The recent display of interest in and appeals for affirmative action ³⁵
along class lines—even by conservatives like Dinesh D'Souza—suggests
that the time may be ripe to recognize, and begin to fight, the widespread
existence of class discrimination and prejudice. The confrontation has to
take place not only in everyday life but also in the country's major institutions, politics, and courts. The Constitution that is now interpreted as
barring racial discrimination can perhaps be interpreted to bar class discrimination as well.

9. *Blaming the poor reduces neither poverty nor poverty-related* 36 *behavior.* Labeling the poor as undeserving does not attack the causes of street crime, improve the schools of poor children, or reduce adult joblessness. Such labels are only a way of expressing anger toward the poor. Blaming the victim solves nothing except to make blamers feel better temporarily. Such labeling justifies political ideologies and interests that oppose solutions, and thus increases the likelihood that nothing will be done about poverty—or crime.

10. *Improving reporting and scholarship about the poor.* Most 37 poverty news is about crime, not poverty. How many reporters ever ask whether economic hardship is part of the crime story? The government's monthly jobless rate is reported, but not the shortage of jobs open to the poor. Likewise, the percentage of people below the poverty rate is an annual news story, but the actual income of the poor, often less than half the poverty line, or about $6,000 a year, is not mentioned.

The "spins," both in government statistics and in journalism, 38 carry over into scholarship. Millions were spent to find and measure an underclass, but there is little ethnographic research to discover why the poor must live as they do. Researchers on homelessness look at mental illness as a cause of homelessness; they do not study it as a possible *effect!*

There are also innumerable other studies of the homeless, but too 39 few about the labor markets and employers, housing industry and landlords, and other factors that create homelessness in the first place.

The Americans who feel most threatened by the poor are people 40 from the working class, whom journalists currently call the middle class. They are apt to live nearest the poor. They will suffer most, other than the poor themselves, from street crime, as well as from the fear that the poor could take over their neighborhoods and jobs. Indeed, as inexpensive housing and secure jobs requiring little education become more scarce, the people only slightly above the poor in income and economic security fear that their superior status will shrink drastically. Viewing the poor as undeserving helps to maintain and even widen that status gap.

No wonder, then, that in the current economic crisis, the journal- 41 ists' middle class and its job problems are the big story, and the poor appear mainly as the underclass, with candidates ignoring poverty. The political climate being what it is, this may even be unavoidable. Indeed, if the winner's margin in the coming elections comes from that middle class, the candidate must initiate enough economic programs to put *its* jobless back to work and to solve its health care, housing, and other problems.

That winner should be bold enough to make room in the program 42 for the poor as well. Poverty, racial polarization, crime, and related problems cannot be allowed to rise higher without further reducing morale, quality of life, and economic competitiveness. Otherwise, America will not be a decent, safe, or pleasant place to live, even for the affluent. 🕊

READING FOR INFORMATION

1. Summarize how the economy, the government, and the political climate have participated in the war against the poor.
2. Paraphrase Gans's objections to the concept of "underclass" (paragraphs 33 and 34).
3. Discuss why people who are better off are frightened and angered by the poor. Do you agree with Gans's explanation?
4. List Gans's solutions for ending the war on the poor. Do you think they are workable?
5. What is the ideal way of reducing the anger directed against the poor?
6. In your own words, explain which of Gans's ten defenses against class bigotry are the most workable.
7. React to Gans's forecast for the future.

READING FOR FORM, ORGANIZATION, AND EXPOSITORY FEATURES

1. Explain Gans's overall organizational plan. What other organizational patterns does he use?
2. What is the function of paragraphs 11, 21, 22, and 32?
3. Describe the features of the article that help the reader to follow Gans's train of thought.
4. Why do you think Gans concludes the article as he does? What effect did the conclusion have on you as a reader?

READING FOR RHETORICAL CONCERNS

1. What do you think prompted Gans to write this article?
2. Do you think Gans provides his readers with enough background to support his premise about the war against the poor? What additional information would be useful?

3. What impact does Gans want to have on his audience? Do you think he is successful?

WRITING ASSIGNMENTS

1. Write a two- to three-page essay explaining why you agree or disagree with Gans's observation that "the Americans who feel most threatened by the poor are people from the working class" (paragraph 40).
2. Write an essay in which you argue for or against Gans's claim that Americans need to fight against class bigotry as well as racial discrimination and prejudice.
3. For a two-week period, keep a written record of how poor people are treated in a daily newspaper or a daily news broadcast. Then, use your notes to write an essay explaining whether or not the media stereotype poor people as undeserving.

The Revolt of the Black Bourgeoisie

Leonce Gaiter

Leonce Gaiter lives in Los Angeles and writes frequently about social issues.

PREREADING

Answer the following questions in your journal before reading the selection: What is your image of members of the black middle class? Where did you acquire that image—from your own experiences, from African-American friends, or from the popular media? Do you know more about working-class and poor blacks than about middle-and upper-class blacks? Why is this so? Respond to these questions in ten to fifteen minutes of freewriting.

At a television network where I once worked, one of my bosses   1
told me I almost didn't get hired because his superior had
"reservations" about me. The job had been offered under the network's

Leonce Gaiter, "The Revolt of the Black Bourgeoisie," *The New York Times Magazine,* 26 June 1994, 42–43. Copyright © 1994 by The New York Times Company. Reprinted by permission.

Minority Advancement Program. I applied for the position because I knew I was exceptionally qualified. I would have qualified for the position regardless of how it was advertised.

After my interview, the head of the department told my boss I 2 wasn't really what he had in mind for a Minority Advancement Program job. To the department head, hiring a minority applicant meant hiring someone unqualified. He wanted to hire some semiliterate, hoop-shooting former prison inmate. That, in his view, was a "real" black person. That was someone worthy of the program.

I had previously been confronted by questions of black authentic- 3 ity. At Harvard, where I graduated in 1980, a white classmate once said to me, "Oh, you're not really a black person." I asked her to explain. She could not. She had known few black people before college, but a lifetime of seeing black people depicted in the American media had taught her that real black people talked a certain way and were raised in certain places. In her world, black people did not attend elite colleges. They could not stand as her intellectual equals or superiors. Any African-American who shared her knowledge of Austen and Balzac—while having to explain to her who Douglass and Du Bois were—had to be *willed* away for her to salvage her sense of superiority as a white person. Hence the accusation that I was "not really black."

But worse than the white majority harboring a one-dimensional 4 vision of blackness are the many blacks who embrace this stereotype as our true nature. At the junior high school I attended in the mostly white Washington suburb of Silver Spring, Md., a black girl once stopped me in the hallway and asked belligerently, "How come you talk so proper?" Astonished, I could only reply, "It's proper*ly*," and walk on. This girl was asking why I spoke without the so-called black accent pervasive in the lower socioeconomic strata of black society, where exposure to mainstream society is limited. This girl was asking, Why wasn't I impoverished and alienated? In her world view, a black male like me couldn't exist.

Within the past year, however, there have been signs that blacks are 5 openly beginning to acknowledge the complex nature of our culture. Cornel West, a professor of religion and the director of Afro-American Studies at Princeton University, discusses the growing gulf between the black underclass and the rest of black society in his book "Race Matters"; black voices have finally been raised against the violence, misogyny and vulgarity marketed to black youth in the form of gangsta rap; Ellis Cose's book "The Rage of a Privileged Class," which concentrates on the problems of middle- and upper-income blacks, was excerpted as part of a *Newsweek* magazine cover story; Bill Cosby has become a vocal crusader against the insulting depiction of African-Americans in "hip-hop generation" TV shows.

Yes, there are the beginnings of a new candor about our culture, but the question remains, How did one segment of the African-American community come to represent the whole? First, black society itself placed emphasis on that lower caste. This made sense because historically that's where the vast majority of us were placed; it's where American society and its laws were designed to keep us. Yet although doors have opened to us over the past 20 years, it is still commonplace for black leaders to insist on our community's uniform need for social welfare programs, inner-city services, job skills training, etc. Through such calls, what has passed for a black political agenda has been furthered only superficially; while affirmative action measures have forced an otherwise unwilling majority to open some doors for the black middle class, social welfare and Great Society–style programs aimed at the black lower class have shown few positive results.   6

According to 1990 census figures, between 1970 and 1990 the number of black families with incomes under $15,000 rose from 34.6 percent of the black population to 37 percent, while the number of black families with incomes of $35,000 to $50,000 rose from 13.9 percent to 15 percent of the population, and those with incomes of more than $50,000 rose from 9.9 percent to 14.5 percent of the black population.   7

Another reason the myth of an all-encompassing black underclass survives—despite the higher number of upper-income black families—is that it fits with a prevalent form of white liberalism, which is just as informed by racism as white conservatism. Since the early 70's, good guilt-liberal journalists and others warmed to the picture of black downtrodden masses in need of their help. Through the agency of good white people, blacks would rise. This image of African-Americans maintained the lifeline of white superiority that whites in this culture cling to, and therefore this image of blacks stuck. A strange tango was begun. Blacks seeking advancement opportunities allied themselves with whites eager to "help" them. However, those whites continued to see blacks as inferiors, victims, cases, and not as equals, individuals or, heaven forbid, competitors.   8

It was hammered into the African-American psyche by media-appointed black leaders and the white media that it was essential to our political progress to stay or seem to stay economically and socially   9 deprived. To be recognized and recognize oneself as middle or upper class was to threaten the political progress of black people. That girl who asked why I spoke so "proper" was accusing me of political sins— of thwarting the progress of our race.

Despite progress toward a more balanced picture of black America, 10 the image of black society as an underclass remains strong. Look at local news coverage of the trial of Damian Williams and Henry Watson, charged with beating the white truck driver Reginald Denny during the 1992 South-Central L.A. riots. The press showed us an African-print-wearing cadre of Williams and Watson supporters trailing Edi M. O. Faal, Williams's defense attorney, like a Greek chorus. This chorus made a point of standing in the camera's range. They presented themselves as the voice of South-Central L.A., the voice of the oppressed, the voice of the down-trodden, the voice of the city's black people.

To anyone watching TV coverage of the trial, all blacks agreed with 11 Faal's contention that his clients were prosecuted so aggressively because they are black. Period. Reporters made no effort to show opposing black viewpoints. (In fact, the media portrait of the Los Angeles riot as blacks vs. whites and Koreans was a misrepresentation. According to the Rand Corporation, a research institute in Santa Monica, blacks made up 36 percent of those arrested during the riot; Latinos made up 51 percent.) The black bourgeoisie and intelligentsia remained largely silent. We had too long believed that to express disagreement with the "official line" was to be a traitor.

TV networks and cable companies gain media raves for programs 12 like "Laurel Avenue," an HBO melodrama about a working-class black family lauded for its realism, a real black family complete with drug deal-ers, drug users, gun toters and basketball players. It is akin to the media presenting "Valley of the Dolls" as a realistic portrayal of the ways of white women.

The Fox network offers a differing but equally misleading portrait 13 of black Americans, with "Martin." While blue humor has long been a sta-ple of black audiences, it was relegated to clubs and records for *mature* black audiences. It was not peddled to kids or to the masses.

Now the blue humor tradition is piped to principally white audi- 14 ences. If TV was as black as it is white—if there was a fair share of black love stories, black dramas, black detective heroes—these blue humor images would not be a problem. Right now, however, they stand as im-ages to which whites can condescend.

Imagine being told by your peers, the records you hear, the pro- 15
grams you watch, the "leaders" you see on TV, classmates, prospective employers—imagine being told by virtually everyone that in
order to be your true self you must be ignorant and poor, or at least
seem so.

Blacks must now see to it that our children face no such burden. 16
We must see to it that the white majority, along with vocal minorities
within the black community (generally those with a self-serving political agenda), do not perpetuate the notion that African-Americans are
invariably doomed to the underclass.

African-Americans are moving toward seeing ourselves—and de- 17
manding that others see us—as individuals, not as shards of a degraded
monolith. The American ideal places primacy on the rights of the individual, yet historically African-Americans have been denied those rights.
We blacks can effectively demand those rights, effectively demand justice only when each of us sees him or herself as an individual with the
right to any of the opinions, idiosyncrasies and talents accorded any
other American.

READING FOR INFORMATION

1. In your own words, recount Gaiter's experience of how people stereotype
   black males.
2. Summarize the evidence that Gaiter presents in support of his contention
   that blacks have begun to critique and offer a more balanced view of black
   America.
3. Paraphrase two reasons for "the myth of an all-encompassing black
   underclass."
4. Give specific examples of how the media perpetuate this myth.

READING FOR FORM, ORGANIZATION, AND EXPOSITORY FEATURES

1. Gaiter opens the article with three personal anecdotes. Why do you think
   he begins the selection in that way?
2. Give examples of the various types of evidence—facts, statistics, references to authorities—that Gaiter uses to support his position.
3. What technique does Gaiter use to conclude the article?

READING FOR RHETORICAL CONCERNS

1. Do you think Gaiter is addressing all readers of *The New York Times Magazine* or focusing on a particular group? What leads you to that conclusion?

2. What impact do you think Gaiter wants to have on his audience? How does he want to change their views? Would that impact change if Gaiter were white? Explain.

3. How would you characterize Gaiter's tone? What does the tone suggest about the author?

WRITING ASSIGNMENTS

1. What do you think of Gaiter's characterization of white liberals in paragraph 8? Do white people see all blacks, even successful blacks, "as inferiors, victims, cases, and not as equals, individuals or, heaven forbid, competitors"? Write a brief essay in response.

2. Write an essay exploring the relationship between Gaiter's argument and Herbert Gans's criticism of stereotypes in paragraphs 33 and 34 of his article, "The War Against the Poor" (pages 470–478).

3. a. Form collaborative groups of five students each, as described in the Preface, or fashion groups according to a method of your own.

   b. Have a member of each group videotape two or three segments of a television series that features African Americans. Gaiter refers to two shows, *Laurel Avenue* and *Martin.* You might look for shows that are airing this season or for reruns of *In Living Color, The Cosby Show,* or *The Jeffersons.* Play the tape for the other members of the group. Each group member should take notes on instances of stereotyping, either the types of stereotyping Gaiter discusses or other versions.

   c. Members should take turns reporting to their group on the instances of stereotyping they found. The group recorder takes notes.

   d. Each group should work collaboratively to write a single brief essay evaluating the television show's depiction of blacks.

   e. One member of each group should read the essay aloud to the rest of the class.

   f. After all the essays are read, the class should discuss similarities and differences in the ways African Americans are portrayed by the media.

Grandma Went to Smith, All Right, But She Went from Nine to Five: A Memoir

Patricia Clark Smith

Patricia Clark Smith teaches in the Department of English at the University of New Mexico.

PREREADING

In your journal, speculate about the meaning of the title. Located in Northampton, Massachusetts, Smith is one of the seven private colleges that make up what was once called "the seven sister schools" or "the women's Ivy League." What do you think the author means when she says her grandmother went to Smith from nine to five? Freewrite your response.

The area marked "Property of Smith College" on Northampton   1
town plats comprises the nearest sizable green space to the house
where my family lived until I turned seven, in the same upstairs apartment where my mother was born.* That house, 53 Old South Street, was torn down in the mid-1950s, but I like knowing that my mother and I came to consciousness in the same set of rooms, that our eyes first learned to distinguish squares of sunlight shifting across the same kitchen floor, the same tree shadows on the wall.

The Smith campus, too, my mother and I both knew early in   2
our lives. But here there is a difference between my mother's experience and my own, for she explored that place only after she was big enough to go there with her gang of neighborhood kids. Her mother, the grandmother I called Nana, seldom took her there. Smith land and Smith events have traditionally been open to townspeople, but Nana was Quebec-born, with a few years of grade school education, not the

Reprinted from *Working Class Women in the Academy,* by Michelle M. Tokarczyk and Elizabeth A. Fay, eds. (Amherst: U of Massachusetts P, 1993). Copyright © 1993 by The University of Massachusetts Press.

* "Plats" are maps of sections of cities: "green space" is the city planning term for undeveloped open land. "Upstreet" and "slate sink" are colloquial to western Massachusetts.

sort of Northampton resident likely to assume the college was accessible to her. Besides, even though my mother was her only child, Nana had little leisure for long walks with a toddler. Walks were what Nana took on her way upstreet from our house on the flats to go shopping, to go to Mass, or to go to work; walks were what she took to the bus stop, en route to visit relatives or to nurse them. She and my grandfather, who died when my mother was in her late teens, both came from sprawling and often hapless families, hers French Canadian and Micmac, his Irish. Both sides were riddled with tuberculosis, alcoholism, infant failure-to-thrive—the classic diseases of the poor. The stunning exception, the one success in my mother's family, was one of my grandfather's brothers, who made his way upward through ward politics to a term as mayor of Northampton in the thirties; his success was short, and apparently, unlike T.B., it was not catching within families.

For Nana, Smith College was primarily the place where she worked 3 intermittently throughout her life cleaning dormitory bathrooms and hallways. It is easy to see why she did not think of the Smith campus as an arena for leisure or pleasure, as a place to take a baby. My mother was the first in our family to see the grounds of Smith as in some way a part of her turf. She played there as a child; as a grown woman, she ventured into the art gallery, attended public lectures and foreign films, though always with a sense that Smith was special, its delights not her birthright, but privileges graciously extended to her.

As for me, her daughter, I cannot remember a time before the Smith 4 campus was a familiar presence to me. I knew it first through my body, through bare feet and skinned knees, by way of the dirt lodged in the creases of my palms and caked beneath my fingernails, dirt Nana scrubbed off with gritty Boraxo in our slate sink. I learned to walk, and later to ice skate, on the campus; my first bullfrogs hunkered on the margin of the lily pool by Lyman Plant House.

And Smith was where I first understood metaphor, not in any fresh- 5 man English class, but in the woods at the western edge of the campus heavy in early spring with the rich smell of leaf mold, soaked through by melting snow, where I hunkered down to inspect a jack-in-the-pulpit. On walks there, my parents taught me the wonderfully satisfying names of things: rose-breasted grosbeak, Solomon's seal, nuthatch, dogtooth violet, lady's slipper.

Within the boundaries of the campus, the Mill River widened out 6 and briefly changed its name to Paradise Pond, though Nana said it was really still the same old Mill River. The Paradise Pond skating rink was kept glossy and clear of snow by the Kingsmen, Smith patois for the male groundskeepers and maintenance men. No question of Kingspersons in those days. There were cooks and chambermaids, all women. And there were Kingsmen. *Kingsman* is said to derive from Franklin King, an early president of Smith, whose name at full length was also given to the colonaded neo-Georgian dormitory where Nana worked as a maid. A *chambermaid.*

For me and other Northampton kids whose relatives did service   7
work at the college, *Kingsman* and *chambermaid* were words of double meaning. They meant the ordinary jobs held down by familiar adults. But the words also evoked the quaintly dressed people in the illustrations of Mother Goose books, the world of Humpty Dumpty and Old King Cole and the four-and-twenty blackbirds. When I entered Smith, the information booklet for freshmen commented upon the nice aptness of calling gardeners and janitors *Kingsmen,* for "they help put Smith back together again," no matter what maintenance problems might arise. I don't remember any mention in that booklet of chambermaids, only an oral explanation during some orientation session that those women were not to be tipped and were to be treated with courtesy. There was little danger of anyone tipping them, of course; as for the courtesy, I came to Smith knowing Nana's stories. And I had done some time by then as a waitress myself.

I grew up in a politically progressive family, where unions and strikes   8
were common table talk. But as a little kid, I like most of my friends had no notion of the class assumptions evident in cutely calling working people Kingsmen. It seemed only one more odd conjunction of language, one I might some day figure out—and there were so many of those adult puns and euphemisms to puzzle over. My dad's stepfather, the only grown man I saw regularly during the war years, would chuck me under the chin and pinch my nose, and ask if I wanted to hear the story of Goldilocks and the Three Beers; when my brother Mike was born, and I asked my mother why Pop Noffke called Mike's tiny penis an "erector set," she said it was because the first erector sets were made at the Gilbert factory where Pop worked as a janitor (no "Kingsmen" in the Holyoke mills, to be sure), and Pop loved erectors sets, and he loved baby Mike. . . . She trailed off. *Kingsmen* was probably that sort of mystery.

The adult world was full of such secrets, of mysterious imports and   9
double meanings. I took for granted the significance of names, words, multiple identities, even if often I could not guess what the significance might be, whether the doubling of meaning were portentous or playful.

But I knew one thing from an early age: there was some acute 10 difference between being a chambermaid in the way Nana was and the apple-cheeked girls dressed in ruffled aprons and mob caps in the Mother Goose book. In a folklore course at Smith, I discovered the Opies' *Oxford Dictionary of Nursery Rhymes*, where I read avidly about the politics, sex, and class wars secreted in those texts. At four, at seven, I knew only that the chambermaids in the bright pictures seemed spunky, healthy, young, and largely cheerful, even when threatened by blackbirds and crosspatch mistresses. But then, as Nana once remarked when I asked her about the connection between her job and the pictures, those maids didn't have to scrub toilets. In the pastoral vision of the illustrators, maids milked bonny cows; they hung out clothes, they stood prettily all-in-a-row. It was different with Nana.

It is a soft spring evening in 1948. I come upon Nana sitting in her 11 rocker in the darkened kitchen, rubbing her thick ankles. She is crying. I am five: I am terrified. In all the world, she is my steadiest point, steady and beautiful, like her name: Julia Larock Dunn.

What, Nana, what? I ask.

Oh, those girls, she says, and I know she means the students who live at Franklin King House. But what have those girls done?

They called me a bitch, she says, *right to my face!*

She sees I don't know the word, and now she's sorry she's used it, but I press her: *They called you what?*

A bitch, she says. *A she-dog. Like Lady.* And she names the mongrel next door, a very doggy-smelling dog with dangling teats.

I cannot believe this. I am sobbing, and now she is holding me, rocking me, singing to me in her gravelly Quebecois: *Allouette, je te plumarais.* Little skylark, I will pluck your wings. Don't cry; everything is all right.

Two kinds of bitch, two kinds of chambermaids, and the Mill and 12 Paradise the same flowing water; many of my first confusions of language centered around Smith.

In the April after I turned seven, Nana felt poorly one evening, but 13 not yet so poorly that I could not go in to kiss her goodnight. In her room I whispered to her the prayer she taught me, one she perhaps picked up from the Irish in-laws, a prayer I now know is called "The White Paternoster," and is recited in the British Isles as a charm against ghosts:

Four posts round my bed.
Four angels o'er my head.

Matthew, Mark, Luke, and John.
Bless the bed I lie upon.

And I spoke the names of all whom I wished to bless. By the time my father waked me in the morning, the ambulance had come and gone with Nana. I ran home from school breathlessly that noon, willing myself to hear from the backstairs landing the sounds of her stumping about the kitchen, singing along with the radio tuned to "The Franco-American Hour." I prayed now not for Evangelists to guard me, but to smell tomato soup, baking apples, a chicken roasting, to find everything somehow in place.

Instead, there was only Aunt Anna, trembling, telling me with a 14 terrible false smile that Nana was all gone, that Nana was with the angels now.

For a few years after, I would sometimes wake in the darkness of my 15 room, after an evening when I had gone to bed sad or afraid, to feel a rough hand gripping my thumb beneath the covers. In time, these tactile visitations frightened and disturbed me more than they comforted me, and one night I asked Nana aloud to go away. She did.

I never told anyone of those experiences, and never heard from 16 anyone a comparable story until I read Chapter Four of *Moby Dick*, with Ishmael's (and Melville's I'd bet) memory of the ghostly hand. I was at Smith by then, and I cried after reading that passage, looking out my dormitory window across the darkened quadrangle toward Franklin King House.

The day after Nana's funeral, the gas company property manager 17 called on us to serve an eviction notice. The company owned the house, and they had allowed Nana to continue her lease on grudging sufferance, as she was the widow of a gas inspector, we were only a gas-company's widow's survivors. And so Aunt Anna moved to Florence to share a tiny house with three cheerful maiden ladies, as they called themselves, who worked beside her at Pro Brush, and we moved, my father, my pregnant mother, my baby brother, and I, to Hampshire Heights, a low-income veterans' housing project newly built at the edge of Northampton on land carved out of woodlots and farms. In the space of a few weeks, we had become a nuclear family.

The Heights spilled over with 1950s energy, alive, raw-edged, very 18 hopeful, a little dangerous. Many of the fathers, five years after the war's end, were still shaken, given to fits of depression or sudden explosive rage. We kids accepted anger as an adult male norm, the way fathers were. When I think back on our mothers, I remember them pregnant. Kids were everywhere at the Heights; you could not be granted a lease unless you had at least two. The oldest tier was all my age, seven and eight. Most of us had come to the project from wartime homes like mine, homes shared with grandparents, aunts, uncles. Families composed only of parents and children seemed to many of us small, unripe, ingrown, scarily lacking in extra sources of support and comfort, and we older kids bonded fiercely in a large nomadic tribe that transcended gender and ethnicity. We roamed parking bays and clothesline yards, playing hide and seek among wet flapping sheets; we explored woods and fields, each of us in charge of at least one younger sibling. They trailed behind us on foot, or we pulled them in wagons or sleds. We coached them on how to slide under barbed-wire fences, while one of us stood guard to make sure the lethargic bull was preoccupied in a far corner of his pasture; we carried them across the stepping stones of the brook to the Piney Woods, where we built forts of resinous boughs; we took them to the free Christmas production of Humperdinck's *Hansel and Gretel* at Smith, hissing them silent, holding them when they cried at the witch; we warned them away from the construction constantly underway around the project: *Billy Ouimet, Tony Perfito, Mikey Clark. I see you, get over here right now or you'll get a licking!*

Our bond was the stronger because by moving to Hampshire 19 Heights we had become suddenly identifiably lumped together as low-income working-class kids. We older Heights kids rejoiced out loud at how brave, how smart, how strong we were; as it turns out, we seem to have been all those things. Those of us now in our mid-forties who belonged to that first generation of Heights children keep splendid oral histories, and I know of few stories of failure among us.

In our grade school classrooms, it would have been hard for an out- 20 sider to pick out us Heights kids. But kids themselves unfailingly know who is who, and on the walks home we needed to band together, fighting, flailing against taunts: *Heights kids: Project kids!* After school it was simply easier not to try to venture beyond our own group, however welcoming other kids who lived outside the project might initially seem.

Joanie lived in a pretty ranch house in the Gleason Road addition 21 just across Jackson Street from the Heights. Joanie said her mom would let us come over until more ranch houses got built on Gleason Road, when Joanie would have more playmates of her own sort. We knew well enough not to report these remarks to our own proud families. And it was tempting to play over at Joanie's house. The best climbing tree in the neighborhood grew there, left over from the time when it was all farmland, a venerable apple tree with sturdy perches we gave names to: the Baby Seat (a foot off the ground); the Lookout (the topmost fork).

I lay stretched out on a middle limb, dreaming, my whole body 22 banked by sweet apple blossoms. That afternoon I was the last Heights kid left over at Joanie's. Suddenly from up in the Lookout, Joanie began her soft chant: *Every* kid on this *Apple* tree is COMing to my BIRTHday party *ex*CEPT PAT CLARK . . . and YOU KNOW WHY. And from various nooks around the tree, out of the massed blossoms and sticky new leaves, the refrain came from the mouths of hidden children: YAH, *yah,* HAH *hah,* YOU *live at* HAMP*shire Heights!*

I dropped ten feet to the ground and landed running, yelling up at 23 the whole beautiful tree, *Who cares? Who cares? Who cares about you and your stinking party?* As I ran through the front yard, I glimpsed Joanie's mom and her gentle, Polish-speaking grandma at the big picture window. Her mother's face was set; her grandma waved at me, looking sad. I did not wave back.

Well, who cared, indeed? I cared. Since then, the parties I have at- 24 tended stretch in a long line from that party I was not invited to, right to the present: high school proms, college mixers, graduate school sherry hours, faculty receptions, museum trustees' dinners in honor of scholarly books to which I've contributed. And I never have, I never will, attend one such function without looking surreptitiously around, checking it out, fig-uring out who's here, who's here who's like me, trying to spot my kind: *Who's here who wasn't born knowing how to do this?*

Always, I am looking for the Heights kids.

When I was ten, my father was transferred, and we moved straight 25 from Hampshire Heights to an old farmhouse on the outskirts of Port-land, Maine, where I lived until I graduated from high school. Those years don't need chronicling here, except for the last summer before I en-tered Smith, the college I chose because it was the one I knew. And be-cause, though now I cannot recall her ever saying she hoped I would grow up to go to Smith, I wanted to give Nana a Smith girl who knew what Julia Larock was worth. My parents were pleased, but they were also fearful, afraid I might not succeed, afraid I would and alter into some unknowable stranger. I remember two stories from that summer, one told by my mother, the other by my father.

The quote under my mother's Northampton High School yearbook 26 picture, from Thomas Hood, reads "And she had a face like a blessing." And so she did; high-cheekboned and radiant, she smiles shyly there on the page. Other old snapshots show her slender and graceful, even in a shapeless 1930s tanktop swim suit; she is dressed for a dance with an orchid in her hair, à la Rita Hayworth.

One afternoon that last summer while we were shelling peas she 27 told me a story about herself newly out of high school and enrolled at McCarthy's Business School in downtown Northampton, thrilled one October Saturday because she had a date with a college man, a student at Amherst. At the last moment she tucked into the picnic basket one of her favorite books, *The Poetical Works of John Greenleaf Whittier.*

I know that book well, and I love it still, uncritically, not just "Snow- 28 bound," but the ballads of shipwreck, heroism, love gone astray. Sweet Maude Muller among her hayricks, whom the wimpy judge rejects as a possible wife, and Kathleen's wonderfully wicked stepmother, getting in her licks in the class wars:

> There was a lord of Galway
> A mighty lord was he,
> And he did wed a second wife,
> A maid of low degree.
> But he was old, and she was young,
> And so in evil spite,
> She baked the black bread for his kin
> And fed her own with white.

No worse than batches of Keats or Yeats, or whatever my mom's date 29 was reading—D. H. Lawrence, I bet. On the grass by Paradise Pond, that boy pounced not on my mom but on her book; *What's this? Oh, my god, Whittier!* And he read snatches of it out loud, roaring with laughter, his hands greasy from the fried chicken, laughing at Maude and Kathleen, at Mom. When she cried and the picnic was ruined, he called her a bad sport.

My mother told this story without pointing any moral, just as a sad 30 little tale about how things don't always pan out. But by the time I heard this story, I had some idea myself why they might not: college man from Boston suburb, business school townie. I carried the story with me to Smith: I can still hear the cold water running in the sink, the shelled peas pinging down into the colander, as my mother imitated that boy's voice, the way he held the book out of her reach. I think of him every time a college bookstore announces the readers for a poetry series that devalues the lyrical, the narrative, and awards the avant-garde; I think of him every time I hear a teacher criticize a student's taste: "You mean you *like* 'O Captain, My Captain'?"; eyebrow raised, faint smile.

My father also had a story for me that summer of 1960, and his are 31
never told as anything *but* moral exempla.

Late August on the beach of Prout's Neck. I am holding so much 32
joy and fear and expectancy inside this summer, my whole self feels like
a brimming cup I am trying not to spill. But now in a voice heavy with import my father commands me to walk with him down the shimmery wa-
terline toward the private beaches of the big Victorian resort inns. It is
low tide, and the beach is very wide, strewn with wavey parallel lines of
kelp and shells, pebbles and bones, plastic beach-bottle floats, bits of glass
buffed to opalescence, all the old garbage the sea keeps trying to refine.

My mother winces, mutters, "Just get away as soon as you can," and 33
I realize she is guessing better than I can what's coming. And indeed I
could not have guessed. What my father wishes to tell me is not about the
burden on me as the first to go to college, or even his usual sermon about
how though I must certainly *go* to college, I will lose family and soul if I
turn into "one of those girls too proud to wipe her own arse." Instead he
relates a twisted picaresque epic of the easy sexual conquests he and his
buddies made at Smith and Mount Holyoke; about how many girls he
knew in high school ended up seduced and abandoned by callous college boys. (Underneath his picture in *his* Holyoke High yearbook they
wrote "The girls really fall for the charm of Joe 'Clicker' Clark and the
sweet strains of his Hawaiian guitar.") He explains earnestly that (1) college girls are loose, and all townie men know that; (2) college boys believe
that all townie girls are loose, and they may well be right; (3) it will be easy
for anyone to spot me for what I am, and so therefore (4). . . .

But I don't stay for (4). I run back along the beach, crying *please*, 34
Dad, no, rubbing at my ears as if that could erase the sounds I have heard,
but it is too late. His words reinforce my deepest fears: I am overreach-
ing by going to Smith, condemning myself to a life of being neither duck
nor swan, with no true allies, infinitely vulnerable to the worst each "sort"
can say about or do to one another in these class wars I've been witness
to my whole life.

I gained much from Smith, eventually. But my first years were be- 35
wildering, marked more often than they might have been by shame and
despair. I lost my freshman scholarship in a dismal welter of C's and D's,
though my adviser kept pointing out that I'd entered with soaring College Board scores, hoping perhaps that I'd suddenly say, Oh yeah, now I
remember, I'm a good student.

But too many other things compelled my attention. Spellbound, 36
I wandered the campus and the streets I had known as a child, not a

college town to me but a landscape of myth whose significance I found it impossible to impart even to the classmates closest to me. I hung out around Franklin King House, too shy to ask the people now working there if they had known Nana. I saw my Heights friends when I could, but they were working, getting ready to be married; I'd met the man I would marry myself. And I was supposed to be studying.

The great gift that first year came through the accident of being 37 placed in a dormitory with a recent reputation as "debutante house" with a lowering scholastic average which the housing office tried to stack with freshmen on scholarship. My classmates tended to be politically left, socially dim, good at friendship, spirited debate, and high nonsense. The seniors caucused about us; we were so hopeless, there would be little point staging freshmen mixers on our behalf. We grinned at each other. It was like the Heights. We had each other. We still do.

Those women got me through. What one of us didn't know, some- 38 one else was sure to. In the house dining room set with linen and candles, I learned from them how to manage a knife and fork, how to approach soup. Someone's Canadian graduate student fiancée smuggled Enovid down to blue-lawed Massachusetts; someone else could make thrift-shop hems hang well; all of us shared the stories of where we'd come from, told one another how good we were, supported one another through and beyond the time when we found, as we almost all did, the classes and teachers who mattered, the work we really wanted to do. For me, that took the better part of three years.

As a freshman, I would stay awake all night talking, or devouring 39 books that weren't assigned, while forgetting to study for a biology exam on mitosis. I memorized great swatches of poetry, and yet the trick of the five-part essay eluded me, and I could not seem to avoid the marginal comment of *overly personal response* on papers for my English professors. The first teacher to grant me a B at Smith remarked to another student that he thought it remarkable I was so perceptive, given that I came of "poor stock." And for those first two years, given that background, I was a listless language student. My dad forced me to take Spanish instead of the French I loved because Spanish was the "language of the future," and because, as he puts it, French was spoken only by "fancy diplomats" and "your own relatives who still don't have a pot to piss in." *Aren't you glad?* he asks me, now that I have lived in New Mexico for nearly twenty years. *No,* I say. I'd have learned Spanish here, where I need it. But in that time, in Northampton, at once so strange and so familiar, so haunted with my ghosts, what I required most was to reaffirm my own roots.

My sophomore year, allowed to return on loans, I resolved to dig 40
in and do well. In a creative writing class, I tried to write about my family, my life, not Northampton, not Old South Street or Hampshire
Heights, not yet, but about Maine, about summers waitressing or working at Sebago-Moc, hand-stitching the uppers for pricey moccasins such
as no Algonquian ever wore; about practicing with my .22 on chunks of
paper pulp floating down the Presumpscott River below our house;
about my brother coming home bloodied, proud of decking the drunk
who tried to mug him at the Riverside Roller Rink.

My British teacher, pale and anorexically thin, wears huge geomet- 41
ric earrings, nail polish in odd shades of green and fuchsia. My stories
come back with C+'s and B−'s, sparse comments in her minuscule
handwriting—"inappropriate diction." When I describe Richard Widmark's wiping out a machine gun nest with three grenades, she notes
"one would be sufficient surely." She reads to us from D. H. Lawrence,
Mary McCarthy, never talking about our own stories, and I never get to
say it took three grenades because the Japanese kicked the first two out
of their foxhole. When I showed up timidly at her office hour one day, she
asks sharply, "Are you fishing for a change of grade?"

I say no, stuttering, I just want to do better next time. "Give that 42
here, then," she sighs, and she takes from me the story about my brother's fight, the one that contains the description of the Widmark movie.
Her fingers are almost translucent in the light through the gothic window
of her office. The silence is very long.

"This, here," she says at last, and her blue fingernail taps a sentence 43
where a father is ranging about a "nefarious sod who couldn't find his
own arse with both hands." This character, she says, would not use this
language.

"How come?" I ask. I truly do not know what she means; is it the 44
profanity? Does she think someone who says "arse" wouldn't use a word
like "nefarious"? But she thinks I am being insolent. Or just dumb, hopelessly dumb. She sighs again. If I don't see the point, she says, she
doesn't see how she can very well convey it to me. So I don't try to explain about the grenades, about the rolling silver and vulgar eloquence
of working-class Irish. I leave her office diffusely ashamed and angry, still
not sure of how I've failed. But whatever that failing is, I think it will
surely keep me from being a writer.

My friends kept me together. And there came at last the meaning- 45
ful classes, Daniel Aaron's American literature, most dramatically, with a
syllabus miraculously advanced for 1962; not just Thoreau and Melville,

but Chopin, Norris, Harold Frederick's Irish immigrants, Cather's and Jewett's country people, Dreiser's working men and women. And there was Aaron himself, assuring me that I could write: Aaron, upon my shyly mentioning Nana, displaying interest and pleasure: *That's really wonderful, you know: tell me about it. What dorm . . . ?* I cried after I left his office that day from sheer relief, the relief of validation.

When I read the autobiographical accounts in Ryan and Sackrey's   46 *Strangers in Paradise: Academics from the Working Class*, what surprises me is how little they speak of what that experience has meant for them as teachers of their own working-class students. Most of us, I think, carry a sense of not fully belonging, of being pretenders to a kingdom not ours by birthright. In the year I came up for tenure at UNM, I dreamed of leaving the university before I could be asked to leave, taking a job as a waitress in what I call in a poem "my sad downtown that was always waiting." Some teachers bury their sad downtowns deep inside them; they strive to be more punctilious, academic, "objective," more "Ivy League" than most of the professors who actually taught me at Smith or Yale.

But for most of us, I think, our pasts are a strength, a means of con-   47 necting with our own students' lives, with literature itself, a talisman to carry into any classroom to remind us of the multiplicity of histories, of the stories we study in that room in addition to the printed ones, the stories that together with the books make up the real text of our class. At a state university in the southwest, those stories are especially multiple.

D has been my problem child in my Whitman and Dickinson   48 course—a body builder, often late, annoyingly macho. A good month into our work on Whitman, after much talk of gender, sexuality, biography, he suddenly exclaims, "Hey, wait a minute: Was Whitman queer?" He cannot, he claims, "seem to feel all this emotion you guys feel when you read poetry." In desperation, trying to help him find a paper topic, I suggest he try *Specimen Days* instead of the poems. I steel myself to read his paper.

But D's paper is a stark account of his childhood as an MIA's son, a   49 fatherless kid trying to figure out how to be a man, manly. It is about using his high school graduation gift money on a fruitless trip to Saigon to look for clues about his father, and his determination now to get on with his own life. And his paper is about the reawakening of all his old questions in reading Whitman's descriptions of released Union prisoners of war. D's paper ends by saying, *I love Walt now, but I hate him too. Because he has made me remember. And he wants to be my father.*

C is in the same class, a Pueblo Indian, a shy, attentive single ₅₀ mother living too far from the close-knit community where she was raised. We're on Emily now—my home-girl, from Amherst, Hampshire County, in the state of Massachusetts. I've told the class how I didn't even know she was dead until I was eight or so, because every time we drove down Amherst's main street, my folks would point and say, "There's Miss Dickinson's house."

Last Friday was a beautiful October day when we were all getting ₅₁ a little overdosed on death kindly stopping and looks of agony, and I suggested we just read together the nature poems that often don't get taught because they don't require much teacherly help or comment. It was a wonderful hour of hummingbirds like revolving wheels, leaves unhooking themselves from trees, and the frog who wears mittens at his feet. I smile to myself, remembering the bullfrogs of Smith. C nodded and nodded as we read.

Today, Monday, C comes up after class, and asks, "Did you know I'm ₅₂ Frog Clan?"

No, I didn't. But I do now.

She tells me she brought Dickinson's frog poems home with her over the weekend to show her clan elders back at the pueblo. "They liked them," she says, and adds, grinning, "Frog people are supposed to be good talkers."

I say I think Dickinson would have loved knowing that.

Yeah, she agrees. She's been having trouble writing her paper, but she got the draft done this weekend at home. It felt good, she says: "It was kind of like taking Emily home to meet my folks, you know what I mean?"

Yeah, I do. I do. 🐸

READING FOR INFORMATION

1. In your own words, explain why "Kingsmen" and "chambermaid" had double meanings for Clark Smith when she was a child. Can you recall words that had double meanings for you when you were younger?

2. Relate how Clark Smith and the other Hampshire Heights kids experienced class bigotry. How did you react to their experiences?

3. Do you think the stories that Clark Smith's parents told her reveal their fears about their daughter attending college? Of what was each parent fearful? Do you think their fears were justified?

4. In your own words, recount examples of the class prejudice Clark Smith experienced in college. Do you think prejudice exists in colleges today? Explain.

5. Paraphrase what Clark Smith means by "sad downtowns." How do we know that Clark Smith celebrates her "sad downtowns" instead of burying them?

READING FOR FORM, ORGANIZATION, AND EXPOSITORY FEATURES

1. Clark Smith's article is an example of autobiographical writing. Explain how her narrative style differs from the styles of other writers in this anthology.
2. Autobiographies usually contain some sense of introspection. Underline passages in which Clark Smith looks into her own mind or feelings or analyzes herself. What do these passages tell you about the author?
3. What is the function of paragraphs 48–52?

READING FOR RHETORICAL CONCERNS

1. Do you think that Clark Smith is simply relating her memoirs to the reader, or is her purpose more complex? What impact does she want to have on her audience?
2. Does Clark Smith draw more on feelings or on facts? What would be gained or lost if the expressions of feeling were left out?
3. Where was this piece originally published? What does that information contribute to your understanding of the author?
4. Underline passages that reveal Clark Smith's tone. How would you characterize it?

WRITING ASSIGNMENTS

1. Have you had any experiences that are similar to Clark Smith's? When you were growing up, were you ever involved in "class wars"? When did you first become conscious of social class, social stratification, or economic inequality? Write a two- to three-page narrative essay recounting your experiences.
2. After her conference with the creative writing teacher, Clark Smith says, "I leave her office diffusely ashamed and angry, still not sure of how I've failed. But whatever that failing is, I think, it will surely keep me from being a writer" (paragraph 44). Write an essay in which you explore your own feelings about learning to write. Compare and contrast your experiences as a novice writer with those of Clark Smith. Did you have teachers who dampened your enthusiasm for writing? Did you ever have a teacher who validated your experiences?
3. All three women in Clark Smith's narrative—Nana, Clark Smith's mother, and Clark Smith herself—experienced pain because of other people's insensitivity. Write an essay comparing and contrasting each woman's experiences and the way each woman coped.

White Standard for Poverty

Dirk Johnson

Dirk Johnson is a writer for The New York Times.

PREREADING

Before reading this short selection, comment on your knowledge of the economic conditions of Native Americans. Answer the following questions in your journal: To which social class do many Native Americans belong? Do you think there is much poverty on Indian reservations? What is your understanding of the expression "white standard for poverty"? Do you think white people's standard of poverty is different from that of Indians? Freewrite your response.

The rough dirt path to the Navajo sheep camp meanders between ancient dunes and slabs of sandstone rising in huge, shattered plates. A few rare trees, planted next to a hogan, or "cha ha'oh"—a summer shade house made of branches—stick up from an ocean of low greasewood. In some places, the skin of the earth has been peeled away by scouring sandstorms and washed clean by pummeling summer rain.   1

This is some of the rawest land on the Navajo reservation, a place where water must be hauled in barrels by pick-up from Tuba City, some 40 miles away, and where two elderly women, Dorothy Reed and Jeanette Lewis, survive by raising sheep and cows.   2

By most measures, American Indians are the poorest ethnic group in the country. On some reservations, unemployment exceeds 80 percent. Of the 10 poorest United States counties in the last census, four were Indian lands in South Dakota. On the Navajo lands, unemployment ranges from 30 percent to 40 percent, and shacks are more common than houses.   3

Income among Indians has not grown for the past decade. Some experts say those figures mask real progress, however, since a baby boom   4

Dirk Johnson, "White Standard for Poverty," *The New York Times,* 3 July 1994, sec. 1: 19. Copyright © 1994 by The New York Times Company. Reprinted by permission.

among Indians in the last generation has sharply increased the number of young people. Nearly 20 percent of Indians are younger than 10, twice the national rate.

To be sure, welfare payments account for a great share of the money 5 on some reservations. And yet, tribal leaders say, there are two faces of poverty in Indian Country.

Rates of Indian suicide and alcoholism far exceed the national av- 6 erages. Some reservations now have street gangs, a new phenomenon. And domestic violence continues to be a serious problem.

And yet, many Indian people are poor, but hardly broken. "It's im- 7 portant not to impose the non-Indian values of poverty on Indians," said David Lester, of the Council of Energy Resource Tribes. "There are worse things than being poor. Don't get me wrong—nobody likes suffering. But money is just not the measure of success."

Many of them value the traditional ways more than modern con- 8 trivances, and no Federal program could persuade them to follow a new way, even if it seemed easier.

"In the beginning, the earth was made for us by Changing Woman," 9 said Mrs. Reed, referring to a Navajo deity. "My grandfather used to tell me that you were supposed to make a living from the earth and the sheep."

This is part of the Indian Country economy largely missing from 10 Government charts and graphs on employment and production: traditional Navajos who raise their own food, or wait by the roadside to sell herbs they have picked from the hills or wood they have gathered or rugs they have woven by hand.

Many of them barter goods and services: a coat in exchange for a car 11 battery, babysitting in exchange for repair work.

Some have never seen the inside of a bank. In some areas, the Indian 12 economy has stagnated because banks are unwilling to count reservation homes as collateral, since the land is held in a trust. They will, however, lend money for trailers, since they can be repossessed and hauled away.

When Navajos run low on money, they sometimes drive or hitch- 13 hike to the pawnshops in the dusty town of Gallup, N.M., where they plop saddles and blankets and pieces of jewelry on the counter as collateral for high-interest loans. Often they are later unable to come up with the cash required to retrieve their belongings, which are then declared "dead pawn," and sold, frequently to prosperous tourists stopping off Interstate 40 in search of an Indian souvenir.

The Navajo women had been up since dawn, in a one-room house 14 with bare sheetrock walls, with the front facing, to greet the sunrise, as tradition decrees it. There was fry bread for breakfast. Both wore the traditional attire for elderly Navajo women: velveteen blouse closed at the neck with a turquoise clasp, long tiered satin dresses, socks and inexpensive running shoes known by the young ones as "sani sneakers"— grandma sneakers.

On this morning, some of their children and grandchildren had arrived to help round up some stray cows. As in many Navajo families, their children had become educated and moved to town, living in houses with plumbing and electricity. But they come back often, and help out with some money when they can.   15

Mrs. Reed's son, Willie, won a scholarship to attend an Eastern prep school, and then earned bachelor's and master's degrees from Stanford University. With his education, he could have landed a high-paying job and taken a home in the city, with air-conditioning and cable television and home-delivered pizza. Instead, he returned to a tiny house on the reservation, and now teaches science at a Navajo high school.   16

READING FOR INFORMATION

1. What do you think David Lester means when he says, "It's important not to impose the non-Indian values of poverty on Indians" (paragraph 7)?
2. Describe in your own words the "hidden" or unpublished side of the Indian economy.
3. What types of wealth do Dorothy Reed and Jeanette Lewis possess? Do you think white Americans value those types of wealth?

READING FOR FORM, ORGANIZATION, AND EXPOSITORY FEATURES

1. What characteristics of Johnson's piece reveal that it was written for a newspaper? Explain how it differs from other selections in this chapter.
2. Underline examples of the types of evidence (facts, statistics, references to authorities, personal experiences) Johnson uses. Do you think that evidence is effective? Explain.

READING FOR RHETORICAL CONCERNS

1. How did you react to this article? Explain the effect it will have on the readers of *The New York Times*.
2. How would you describe Johnson's tone? How does it differ from Patricia Clark Smith's in the preceding selection?

WRITING ASSIGNMENTS

1. Drawing on Johnson's article, your own experience, and other selections you have read, write an essay in which you explain why some people prefer modest traditional ways over modern technology and contrivances. Write for classmates who have not read Johnson's article.

2. Some sociologists and economists report that although most Native Americans are still very poor, in recent years some have improved their economic standing. Visit the library and search for recent magazine and newspaper articles dealing with the economy of Native Americans. How do your findings compare with Johnson's? Write an essay in which you synthesize the information you locate.

Red Anger

R. T. Smith

R. T. Smith's heritage is Scotch-Irish and Tuscarora. Smith is Alumni Writer-in-Residence and director of creative writing at Auburn University. He has written ten volumes of poetry, including Rural Route *(1981) and* Banish Misfortune *(1988).*

PREREADING

Before you read the poem, read the title and the first line. In your journal, explore your feelings about "red anger." Do you think Native American anger is justified? Why or why not? Try to be specific about your reasons.

 The reservation school is brown and bleak
with bugs' guts mashed against walls
and rodent pellets reeking in corners.
Years of lies fade into the black chalk board.
A thin American flag with 48 stars   5
hangs lank over broken desks.
The stink of stale piss haunts the halls.

Tuscarora.

R. T. Smith, "Red Anger." Copyright © R. T. Smith. Reprinted by permission of the author.

My reservation home is dusty.
My mother grows puffy with disease,   10
her left eye infected open forever.
Outside the bedroom window
my dirty, snotty brother Roy
claws the ground,
scratching like the goat who gnaws the garden.   15

Choctaw.

My father drinks
pale moonshine whiskey
and gambles recklessly at the garage,
kicks dust between weeds in the evening   20
and dances a fake-feathered rain dance
for tourists and a little cash.
Even the snakes have left.
Even the sun cannot stand to watch.

Cherokee.   25

Our limping dog sniffs a coil of hot shit
near the outhouse where
my sister shot herself with a .22.
So each day I march
two miles by meagre fields   30
to work in a tourist lunch stand
in their greasy aprons.
I nurse my anger like a seed,
and the whites would wonder why
I spit in their hamburgers.   35

Tuscarora, Choctaw, Cherokee . . .
the trail of tears never ends.

READING FOR INFORMATION

1. How do you interpret line 4, "Years of lies fade into the black chalk board"?
2. Explain the significance of the forty-eight stars on the American flag. Are any other aspects of the reservation outdated?
3. Which lines reveal the impact that tourists have had on Native Americans' lives?

4. Discuss your understanding of "the trail of tears" mentioned in the last line of the poem. If you are unfamiliar with the Cherokee Indians' Trail of Tears, look it up in a reference book or an encyclopedia.

READING FOR FORM, ORGANIZATION, AND EXPOSITORY FEATURES

1. In each stanza, Smith offers an image of a member of his family. Explain which image is most powerful to you.
2. What effect does Smith achieve in lines 8, 16, 25, 36, and 37?

READING FOR RHETORICAL CONCERNS

1. What was your initial reaction to the poem? Why do you think the poem has such a powerful effect on the reader? What elements contribute to that effect?
2. Underline the words or lines that are especially effective in evoking the speaker's emotion. How would you describe the speaker's tone?

WRITING ASSIGNMENTS

1. In "White Standard for Poverty," Dirk Johnson comments, "Tribal leaders say . . . there are two faces of poverty in Indian Country" (paragraph 5). Write a brief essay discussing the face of poverty that "Red Anger" portrays.
2. Do some library research on the education of Native Americans, focusing especially on the phenomenon of the Indian boarding school. Synthesize your findings in an essay addressed to your classmates.
3. Write a short critical analysis of the poem.

SYNTHESIS WRITING ASSIGNMENTS

1. Drawing on the selections by Gilbert and Kahl and Murray, write a two- to three-page essay explaining why cognitive skills and education are increasingly important for social class status and occupational attainment.
2. Drawing on the selections by Murray and Gans, write an essay explaining to your readers how Americans who are better off are using their political power to protect their own interests rather than to alleviate the conditions of the poor.
3. Write a brief essay explaining why Gans would object to Gilbert and Kahl's and Magnet's use of the term "underclass."

4. Drawing on the selections by Lillian Rubin and Herbert Gans, challenge Myron Magnet's claim that "underclass" families—single mothers—are largely responsible for their children's failure to acquire morals and values. From your own experience, what other societal forces are responsible? Write a three- to four-page essay addressed to your classmates.

5. Drawing on the selections in this chapter, write a four- to five-page essay explaining why poverty and class divisions exist in the United States today. Write for an audience who has not read this chapter.

6. How widespread are the class discrimination and prejudice that Gans discusses in "The War Against the Poor"? Use the selections by Leonce Gaiter, Patricia Clark Smith, and R. T. Smith to write a three- to five-page response.

7. Show how the poem by R. T. Smith communicates the exploitation, prejudice, discrimination, and injustice that are discussed by the other writers in this chapter. Write a five- to six-page essay addressed to your classmates.

Humanities

SUBJECTS OF STUDY IN THE HUMANITIES

The subjects that humanists study have theoretical, historical, and critical orientations. The theoretical subjects are philosophy, linguistics, and semiotics. Humanists approach them from a broad perspective and at close range by examining thought, language, structures of meaning and expression, and other significant evidence of human rationality. The historical subjects are history; various area studies, such as ancient classical civilization, Latin American studies, and Asian studies; and historical studies of particular disciplines, such as the history of science, the history of art, and historical linguistics. Humanists approach them by studying the causes, effects, development, and interaction of peoples, nations, institutions, ideas, fashions, styles, and the like. The critical subjects are literature, drama, music, the visual arts, and other expressive arts. Humanists approach them by analyzing, interpreting, and evaluating "texts," understood in the broadest sense of the term as novels, poems, plays, films, paintings, sculpture, dance, musical scores, musical performances, and so forth.

METHODS OF STUDY IN THE HUMANITIES

The theoretical, historical, and critical orientations of the humanities also describe the methods that humanists use. The study of history, for example, requires a critical reading of documents from the past as well as a theoretical probing of their importance. The study of literature and the arts usually emphasizes critical interpretation, but it also calls for some historical study of how styles, forms, and themes developed, and for a theoretical study of how we understand them. When you are reading in the humanities, therefore, you will need to recognize how the various theoretical, historical, and critical approaches work in the various disciplines. The chapters on the humanities in this anthology will provide examples.

WRITING IN THE HUMANITIES

Assignments for writing in the humanities require you to exercise your theoretical, historical, and critical judgment. In this anthology, for example, writing assignments in the humanities run the gamut from critical summary to theoretical speculation. Shorter assignments may call for various types of writing: a summary or précis of an article, a chapter, or a whole book; a critical report on an article, a chapter, or a whole book; or a review of research in several publications. All of these assignments require you to select important points to write about in logical order or in order of importance. Longer assignments may require a close analysis of several texts. Here's an example from Chapter 11 of this anthology:

> Discussing the tension between "a *particularistic* and a *universalistic* approach to community" (paragraph 15), Seltser and Miller point out that Americans question whether they have obligations and responsibilities toward homeless people. In a four- to five-page synthesis essay, explain the answers that Etzioni, Bellah and his co-authors, and Walzer would give to this question.

Note that this assignment implicitly requires you to summarize and paraphrase portions of Etzioni's, Bellah et al.'s, and Walzer's articles that indicate their opinions. It also implicitly requires you to speculate on how these authors might answer Seltser and Miller's question. For this purpose you will need to analyze arguments and project their logical extensions.

Most writing assignments in the humanities will call upon you to use these critical skills in one way or another, but some higher-level writing assignments may also require you to use historical and theoretical skills as well. You may be asked to examine a certain problem in its historical context or to discuss the theoretical implications of another problem on a broad scale.

ORGANIZATIONAL PATTERNS OF WRITING IN THE HUMANITIES

The organizational patterns for writing in the humanities follow the patterns for writing in the natural and social sciences. In the most common one, the writer takes each proposition, event, or detail in its order of occurrence and explains it as he or she sees it. The good writer, however, will vary this basic pattern in many subtle ways. Sometimes he or she may take a number of points from the same source and classify them under general headings—for example, all the negative arguments against a certain moral or ethical position; or all the long-term and short-term implications of an argument based on analyzing current political conditions. Or the writer may endorse and appropriate some conclusions from a given source but contest and refute others from the same source. In Chapter 11, Christopher Little acknowledges that communitarian ideology contains some reasonable notions, but he vigorously challenges the use of this ideology to restrict individual freedom.

> Though some of its concerns and recommendations about community-mindedness may be perfectly laudable, communitarianism's critics insist that it is not really concerned about a delicate balancing act between rights and responsibilities, but that it *exalts* duties over rights, public safety over liberty and the group over the individual. Accordingly, its public policy recommendations either implicitly or expressly call for the attenuation or even abrogation of certain rights. (p. 548)

Still other organizational patterns may contrast statement with response or question with answer, each time penetrating deeper into the problem being investigated. Theodore A. Gracyk's "Romanticizing Rock Music" in Chapter 12 exemplifies this pattern. Gracyk evaluates Camille Paglia's argument in "Rock as Art" by critiquing each of her claims, often using the device of questioning.

> Which of these artists represents Paglia's ideal? Her advice to rock musicians, "Don't become a slave to the audience" and "Don't tour" (study art instead) points to Wagner and not to Beethoven or to Romantics like Berlioz, Chopin, and Liszt, who more or less invented the modern promotional tour. . . .
>
> Finally, Paglia is recommending that rock musicians trade the vicissitudes of commerce for a system of artistic patronage. But are commercial demands always an artistic kiss of death? (p. 601)

Further, some organizational patterns may establish cause-and-effect relationships in their critical assessment of diverse sources. In Chapter 11, Michael Walzer explains that the interests of the individual and those of the community are not necessarily in conflict and that if a society values both pluralism and individuality, these values reinforce each other.

STYLES OF WRITING IN THE HUMANITIES

Some styles of writing in the humanities suggest—within limits—the tone of the author's personal and idiosyncratic voice. This quality distinguishes it radically from impersonal styles of writing in the natural and social sciences. The major evidence for critical assessments of texts in the humanities is direct observation of details in the texts themselves, close reference to them, and pointed quotation from them. How the author of an article projects an attitude toward those texts often counts as much as what he or she directly says about them. Robert Bellah and his co-authors, for example, clearly project a personal involvement in the issues that they explore.

> Finally, we are not simply ends in ourselves, either as individuals or as a society. We are parts of a larger whole that we can neither forget nor imagine in our own image without paying a high price. If we are not to have a self that hangs in the void, slowly twisting in the wind, these are issues we cannot ignore. (p. 526)

In Chapter 13, David Grossman, an Israeli Jew, conveys sympathy with displaced Palestinians who view themselves as victims of Jewish dominance in Israel.

> And suddenly I am the one facing the test. How real and sincere is my desire for "coexistence" with the Palestinians in Israel? Do I stand wholeheartedly behind the words "make room for them among us"? Do I actually understand the meaning of Jewish-Arab coexistence? (p. 651)

PERSONAL VOICE

Writing in the humanities not only tolerates the development of a personal voice but also encourages it. Listen to Robert Brookhiser's voice as he pokes fun at the way people dance to rock music.

I was in fifth and sixth grade just after kids stopped taking solemn little lessons, in gym class or after school, in the box step and the cha-cha. Those who still dance these, and all the other dances of mankind, do it, like fox-hunters or Greek scholars, as a passion or a hobby. To fulfill the necessities of social intercourse, it will never be necessary to take a dance lesson again. (p. 608)

Because the humanities propose to exercise and develop critical thinking, the issue of "what you think and why" becomes crucial. The "what" and "why" seldom generate straightforward, unequivocal answers. To the casual observer, some answers may seem curious, whimsical, arbitrary, entirely subjective. To others more deeply acquainted with the humanistic disciplines, open-endedness confers its own rewards. Among them is the light it casts upon our processes of thought, our understanding of complex issues, and the wide-ranging and often contradictory interpretations of them. Camille Paglia tells us

The pioneers of rock were freaks, dreamers and malcontents who drew their lyricism and emotional power from the gritty rural traditions of white folk music and African-American blues. (p. 586)

In contrast, Theodore Gracyk argues,

They were hardly malcontents, unless being an African American or poor Southern white in the nineteen-fifties automatically qualified one. If anything, they represent the American underclass of the period, seeking respectability in money and fame. (p. 591)

A writer in the humanities measures the success of an argument by how it accommodates divergent explanations and shows their relationships. Significantly, most writers in the humanities do not agree on the universal applicability of any single formula, method, or approach for solving problems. The best solutions usually entail a combination of formulas, methods, and approaches.

Reading in the humanities, therefore, requires a tolerance for ambiguity and contradiction. Oddly enough, however, most writers in the humanities defend their assertions with a strong and aggressive rhetoric. At best, this rhetoric scrupulously avoids bloat, pomposity, and roundabout ways of saying things. Instead of "It was decided that they would utilize the sharp instrument for perforating and unsealing aluminum receptacles," it prefers "They decided to use the can opener." It uses technical vocabulary when necessary, but it usually prefers clear, precise, intelligible diction to stilted, awkward jargon. It uses figurative language and analogy, but not for their own sake; it uses them to express meanings and relationships that literal language sometimes obscures. In Chapter 13, Ronald Takaki concludes his study of Japanese immigration with a poem that expresses the emotions of young women leaving their place of birth for the uncertainties of a marriage in America.

As their ships sailed from the harbor, many women gazed at the diminishing shore:

> With tears in my eyes
> I turn back to my homeland
> Taking one last look. (p. 664)

Writing in the humanities strives for a richness of texture and implication, but at the same time, it highlights important threads in that texture and designates them as central to the unraveling. Readers, however, should not allow its assertiveness to fool them. Few examples of good writing in the humanities are completely intolerant of opposing views. There's always room for another perspective.

C H A P T E R
eleven

The Community
and the Individual

Grounded in dissatisfaction with a widespread lack of social responsibility, disregard for civility, and uninterest in the common good, a number of American intellectuals are espousing a movement to renew social bonds and reinforce shared values. This social movement, called *communitarianism*, values identification with or membership in a community over private initiative and personal autonomy.

"Community" is a controversial concept. In recent years, many people have become embroiled in arguments about the value of collectivism over individualism. Those who advocate community seek greater social participation, fellowship, and commonality, whereas those who defend individualism promote personal rights and freedoms, self-regulation, and decentralization. This conflict between individual claims and collective life is played out in this chapter.

In the first selection, "Morality as a Community Affair," Amitai Etzioni claims that our values and moral commitments derive as much from communal identification as from individual conscience. He argues that Americans have been doing their own thing for too long; it is time to exercise social responsibility. In the same vein, Robert N. Bellah and his associates, in the selection entitled "The Meaning of One's Life," find fault with Americans' sense of radical individualism. Bellah argues that we "find ourselves" when we connect with others in relationships, associations, and communities, not when we remain independent.

In the third selection, "Multiculturalism and Individualism," Michael Walzer explains that the polarities of pluralism and singularity, of communities and private individuals, are remedies for each other rather than opposites. Walzer contends that engagement in cultural groups will rescue dissociated individuals. In the next piece, "Ambivalences in American Views of Dignity," Barry Jay Seltser and Donald E. Miller discuss various tensions in American society, conflicts between communalism and individualism, cooperation and competition, achieved and ascribed status, affectivity and neutrality, and particularistic and universalistic approaches to community. They explain that these tensions generate our ambivalent responses to poor people, particularly to homeless people when we meet them on the street.

Writing in *American Rifleman*, Christopher C. Little warns that many of the recommendations of communitarianism attenuate and even abrogate or curtail individual rights, particularly the rights of individuals to bear arms to protect themselves. The final selection, the short story "Life" by Bessie Head, dramatizes the conflict between community and individual that is central to this chapter.

Morality as a Community Affair

Amitai Etzioni

Amitai Etzioni has taught sociology at the University of Cologne, Columbia, George Washington University, and Harvard. He is the author of numerous books, the most recent of which are The Spirit of Community (1993), from which "Morality as a Community Affair" is taken, Public Policy in a New Key (1993), A Responsive Society (1991), The Moral Dimension (1988), Capital Corruption (1984), and An Immodest Agenda (1982).

PREREADING

Using the previewing strategy we described in Chapter 1, turn the title and the subtitles into questions and then speculate about the answers. Do you think morality, a sense of right and wrong, is a community or an individual responsibility? Do you think your community functions as a moral voice? What are moral claims, and why should we be fearful of them? Write your response in your journal.

From *The Spirit of Community: Rights, Responsibilities, and the Communitarian Agenda* by Amitai Etzioni (New York: Crown, 1993), 30–38. Copyright © 1993 by Amitai Etzioni. Reprinted by permission of Crown Publishers, Inc.

CONSCIENCE IS NOT ENOUGH

How do we shore up morality? How can we encourage millions   1
of individuals to develop a stronger sense of right and wrong?
First, it is essential to reiterate that morality does not soar on its own
wings. True, the ultimate custodian of moral conduct is a person's own
conscience. However, individuals' consciences are neither inborn nor—
for most people—self-enforcing. We gain our initial moral commitments
as new members of a community into which we are born. Later, as we mature, we hone our individualized versions out of the social values that
have been transmitted to us. As a rule, though, these are variations on
community-formed themes. Thus, many Americans are more socially
concerned and active than other nationalities, not because of differences
in genes or basic human nature, but because social concern and activism
are major elements of this country's moral tradition. If we were living instead in traditional Korea, the same energy would be dedicated to, say,
ensuring that we conducted ourselves properly toward numerous relatives. That is, the mainspring of our values is the community or communities into which we are born, that educated us (or neglected to educate
us), and in which we seek to become respectable members during our
adult lives.

Most important for the issue at hand is the sociological fact that we   2
find reinforcement for our moral inclinations and provide reinforcement
to our fellow human beings, through the community. We are each other's
keepers. As Common Cause founder, John Gardner writes:

> Families and communities are the ground-level generators and preservers
> of values and ethical systems. No society can remain vital or even survive
> without a reasonable base of shared values. . . . They are generated chiefly
> in the family, schools, church, and other intimate settings in which people
> deal with one another face to face.

When the term *community* is used, the first notion that typically   3
comes to mind is a place in which people know and care for one another—
the kind of place in which people do not merely ask "How are you?" as a
formality but care about the answer. This we-ness (which cynics have be-
littled as a "warm, fuzzy" sense of community) is indeed part of its essence.
Our focus here, though, is on another element of community, crucial for
the issues at hand: *Communities speak to us in moral voices. They lay
claims on their members.* Indeed, they are the most important sustaining
source of moral voices other than the inner self.

Communitarians, who make the restoration of community their   4
core mission, are often asked which community they mean. The local
community? The national community? The sociologically correct answer
is that communities are best viewed as if they were Chinese nesting boxes,
in which less encompassing communities (families, neighborhoods) are
nestled within more encompassing ones (local villages and towns), which
in turn are situated within still more encompassing communities, the national and cross-national ones (such as the budding European Community). Moreover, there is room for nongeographic communities that
criss-cross the others, such as professional or work-based communities.
When they are intact, they are all relevant, and all lay moral claims on us
by appealing to and reinforcing our values.

But, we are asked, given the multiple communities to which peo-   5
ple belong (the places where they live and work, their ethnic and professional associations, and so on), can't a person simply choose at will
which moral voice to heed? Aren't people using the values of one community to free themselves from obligations that others may press on
them—leaving them free to do what they fancy? It is true that you can
to some extent play these multiple affiliations against one another, say,
spend more time with friends at work when people in the neighborhood
become too demanding. However, societies in which different communities pull in incompatible directions on basic matters are societies that
experience moral confusion; have moral voices that do not carry. We
need—on all levels, local, national—to agree on some basics.

THE COMMUNITY AS A MORAL VOICE

How can the moral voice of the community function when it is well ar-   6
ticulated and clearly raised?

I lived for a year on the Stanford University campus. Not far from   7
the house I rented was a four-way stop sign. Each morning I observed
a fairly heavy flow of traffic at the intersection. Still, the cars carefully
waited their turns to move ahead, as they were expected to. The drivers
rarely moved out of turn, and in those cases when they did, the offenders often had out-of-state license plates. The main reason for the good
conduct: practically everyone in the community knew who was behind
the wheel. If someone rushed through, he or she could expect to be the
subject of some mild ribbing at the faculty club, supermarket, or local
movie theater (such as "You must have been in an awful rush this morning"). This kind of community prodding usually suffices to reinforce the

proper behavior that members of the community acquire early—in this case, observing safe traffic patterns.

When I first moved to a suburb of Washington, D.C., I neglected   8
to mow my lawn. One neighbor asked politely if I needed "a reference to a good gardener." Another pointed out that unless we all kept up the standards of the neighborhood, we would end up with an unsightly place and declining property values. Soon after I moved into a downtown co-operative building, the tenants were sent memos that reminded us to sort our garbage. Various exhortations were used ("It is good for the environment"), and a floor representative was appointed to "oversee" compliance. I never found out what the representative actually did; the very appointment and reminders seemed sufficient for most residents to attend to their trash properly.

It might be said that I have lived in middle-class parts. It is well es-   9
tablished, however, that many working-class and immigrant communities—to the extent that they are intact—uphold their values. These are often further modulated and backed up by the ethnic groups. Thus the specific values may differ from a Cuban to an Irish neighborhood, or from an Asian to a black one, but all communities sustain values. Their concerns may vary from what is the proper way to conduct a wake or a confirmation to how much help a new immigrant can expect or whether a local shopkeeper will hire illegal aliens. But it is mainly in instances in which there is no viable community, in which people live in high-rise buildings and do not know one another, in some city parts in which the social fabric is frayed, and in situations in which people move around a lot and lose most social moorings, that the social underpinnings of morality are lost.

The examples of moral voices that carry that I have cited so far are   10
about matters of limited importance, such as lawns and garbage. Hence, community responses to those who disregard the shared values have been appropriately mild. When people misbehave in more serious ways, the community's response tends to be stronger, especially when the community is clear about what is right and wrong. If someone's child speeds down the street as though there were no tomorrow or throws beer bottles at passersby, the rebuke is appropriately sharper. People may say to parents "We are all deeply troubled about what happened the other day when you were not home" or "For the sake of the safety of all of us, we [meaning you] must find a way to ensure that this will not happen again." Basketball star David Robinson once explained to a TV interviewer that instead of telling everybody that "you are great," he "gets into the face" of those who need to be told right from wrong. Americans brought up

on Dale Carnegie, anxious never to give offense, may find such an approach a bit moralistic. Well, as I see it, *what we need now is less "how to win friends and influence people" and more how to restore the sway of moral voices.*

Most important, the moral voice does not merely censure; it also 11 blesses. We appreciate, praise, recognize, celebrate, and toast those who serve their communities, from volunteer fire fighters to organizers of neighborhood crime watches. Members of a neighborhood constantly share tales of how wonderful it was that this or that individual organized a group to take care of the trees on the side of the road, rushed to welcome the new families that escaped from Iran, or whatever. It is these positive, fostering, encouraging, yet effective moral voices that we no longer hear with sufficient clarity and conviction in many areas of our lives.

THE FEAR OF MORAL CLAIMS

Often when I speak about the need to shore up the moral voice of our 12 communities, I observe a sense of unease. Americans do not like to tell other people how to behave. I first ran into the fear many liberal people have of formulating and expressing moral claims, of articulating the moral voice of the community, when I taught at Harvard. A faculty seminar was conducted on the ethical condition of America. The first session was dedicated to a discussion of what our agenda should be. I suggested a discussion of the moral implications of the decline of the American family. Nobody objected, but nobody picked up on the idea, either; it was politely but roundly ignored. When I later asked two members of the seminar why my suggestion had been accorded such a quiet burial, they explained that they (and presumably other members of the seminar) were uncomfortable discussing the subject. "If a high-profile group of ethicists at Harvard would form a consensus on the matter, it might put a lot of pressure on people, and it might even be used to change the laws [on divorce]."

Sociologist M. P. Baumgartner found that in an American suburb he 13 studied in the 1980s, people who observed minor violations of conduct often simply ignored them rather than express their displeasure. If the violations were somewhat serious, people tended to ostracize the offenders without explanation. If they did confront a miscreant—say, a person who burned chicken feathers in his backyard and stank up the neighborhood, mowed the lawn early in the morning, or left a barking dog out at night—they were likely to ask him to cease the behavior as a *favor* to them, rather than labeling it as something a decent person would not do.

This disinclination to lay moral claims undermines the daily, rou- 14 *tine social underwriting of morality.* It also hinders moral conduct in rather crucial situations.

During a conference on bone-marrow transplants, a psychiatrist ar- 15 gued that it was not proper to ask one sibling for a bone-marrow dona- tion for another sibling, despite the fact that making such a donation does not entail any particular risk. His reason was that the sibling who refused might feel guilty, especially if as a result the brother or sister died. On the contrary, a Communitarian would argue that siblings should be asked in no uncertain terms to come to the rescue. If they refuse, they *should* feel guilty.

When I discuss the value of moral voices, people tell me they are 16 very concerned that if they lay moral claims, they will be perceived as self-righteous. If they mean by "self-righteous" a person who comes across as without flaw, who sees himself as entitled to dictate what is right (and wrong), who lays moral claims in a sanctimonious or pompous way—there is good reason to refrain from such ways of expressing moral voices. But these are secondary issues that involve questions of proper expressions and manner of speech.

At the same time we should note that given our circumstances, our 17 society would be much better off if some of its members sometimes erred on the side of self-righteousness (on which they are sure to be called) than be full of people who are morally immobilized by a fear of being con- sidered prudish or members of a "thought police." I personally regret occasions I did not speak up about some foul tricks Japan plays on us, be- cause I feared being called a Japan basher; I should have called it the way I saw it. And I realize that when I speak of the value of the two- parent family, many of my single-parent friends frown. I do not mean to put them down, but their displeasure should not stop me or anybody else from reporting what we see as truthful observations and from drawing morally appropriate conclusions. It is my contention that *if we care about attaining a higher level of moral conduct than we now experience, we must be ready to express our moral sense,* raise our moral voice a deci- bel or two. In the silence that prevails, it may seem as if we are shouting; actually we are merely speaking up.

As more and more of us respond to the claims that we ought to assume 18 more responsibilities for our children, elderly, neighbors, environment, and communities, moral values will find more support. Although it may be true that markets work best if everybody goes out and tries to maximize his or her own self-interest (although that is by no means a well-proven proposition), moral behavior and communities most assuredly do not. They require people who care for one another and for shared spaces, causes, and future. Here, clearly, it is better to give than to take, and the best way to help sustain a world in which people care for one another—is to care for some. The best way to ensure that common needs are attended to is to take some responsibility for attending to some of them.

To object to the moral voice of the community, and to the moral 19 encouragement it provides, is to oppose the social glue that helps hold the moral order together. It is unrealistic to rely on individuals' inner voices and to expect that people will invariably do what is right completely on their own. Such a radical individualistic view disregards our social moorings and the important role that communities play in sustaining moral commitments. Those who oppose statism must recognize that communities require some ways of making their needs felt. They should welcome the gentle, informal, and—in contemporary America—generally tolerant voices of the community, especially given that the alternative is typically state coercion or social and moral anarchy.

True, there have been occasions in the past when community 20 voices were stridently raised to justify coercion. More than forty years ago, for example, America experienced the nightmare of McCarthyism. Likewise the memory of the real Ku Klux Klan (today's Klansmen are largely a deranged and pathetic bunch) serves to warn us against the excesses of community. A colleague asks: "What if the community demands that children with AIDS not be allowed to attend public schools, or that a family of color not be allowed to buy a home in a neighborhood?" (One might add, what if the community decided to burn books?) In response I suggest that no community has a right to violate higher-order values, values that we all should share as a society, or even humanity, values that prescribe rules of behavior such as "Do unto others only as you wish others would do unto you."

Moreover, we do constantly need to be on guard against self- 21 centered communities, just as we need to watch out for self-centered individuals. . . . We do not forgo cars just because some drive them dangerously. The same holds, many times over, for the moral voices of communities. The fact that those voices are to be raised in moderation, and only in ways that do not violate overarching values should not hide the fact that we cannot be a civil and decent society without a moral voice. Try the following mental experiment: Ask yourself what the alternatives are to the exercise of moral voice. There are only two: a police state, which tries to maintain civil order by brute force, or a moral vacuum in which anything goes.

Look also at the historical condition we are in. As we have seen, at 22 this particular stage in our history signs of moral deficiencies abound, while incidents of excessive moralism are few and far between. The fact is that many thousands of communities keep all kinds of books in their libraries, while each year not more than a handful try to ban them; and most of them are stopped from proceeding by those who are committed to our liberties. True, ugly and deeply disturbing incidents of racial hatred and other forms of bigotry (such as gay bashing) continue, especially in some cities. Unfortunately they grab headlines, leaving the impression that they are the norm. Actually there are hundreds of places in which people of different backgrounds, orientations, and persuasions work and live together peacefully. In short, excessive moralism is not exactly our current problem.

In principle there is no reason to deny that there are always the 23 twin dangers of too much and too little social pressure. As when we ride a bike, we need to lean in the opposite direction of where the course of social history is tilting us. The bulk of the evidence shows that in recent decades we have been tilting too far in the direction of letting everybody do their own thing or pursue their own interests and have concerned ourselves too little with our social responsibilities and moral commitments. It is time to set things aright.   🕊

READING FOR INFORMATION

1. Paraphrase Etzioni's answer to his opening question. How do we develop our sense of right and wrong? Can morality exist independently of identification with community?

2. Explain the difference between "community" in general and the aspect of community on which Etzioni focuses.

3. In paragraph 9, Etzioni describes instances of loss of community. What other instances are you aware of?

4. How do you react to Etzioni's claim in paragraph 17 that we should be more bold about raising our moral voices? Do you agree or disagree? Why?

5. In your own words, explain what Etzioni means when he says that "excessive moralism is not exactly our current problem" (paragraph 22).

READING FOR FORM, ORGANIZATION, AND EXPOSITORY FEATURES

1. What effect do you think Etzioni achieves by opening the first two sections of the piece with questions?
2. Explain in your own words the metaphor of the Chinese nesting boxes.
3. What is the function of paragraphs 13 and 15?
4. Do you think Etzioni does a good job of acknowledging the other side of the argument? Explain.

READING FOR RHETORICAL CONCERNS

1. What do you see as Etzioni's rhetorical purpose? Why has he written this piece and what does he want to get across to his readers?
2. Underline passages in which Etzioni draws on personal experience. Comment on the effectiveness of this rhetorical strategy. What is the effect on the reader? How would the impact change if the personal experiences were left out?

WRITING ASSIGNMENTS

1. a. Think for a few minutes about a community you belong to. Spend ten to fifteen minutes freewriting about that community. What brings the members together? What are their common goals? How well do they function? What makes the community effective or ineffective?
   b. Divide the class into groups of three to five students. Elect a person to record the views expressed in each group.
   c. Each member of the group should share his or her freewriting about community.
   d. Using the group members' examples of communities, each group should identify four or five principles of communities.
   e. Each group recorder should report the principles to the rest of the class; the teacher should list the principles on the chalkboard; the class should discuss commonalities, similarities, and differences.
   f. Drawing from the list of principles derived from the various groups, each student should write an essay about a community that has been especially meaningful in his or her life. Explain how the community adheres to the set of principles the class has discussed.
2. Write an essay in response to Etzioni's claim that in many areas of our lives we no longer hear "effective moral voices" of community. Do you agree that many people are disinclined to raise their moral voices? Are some people indifferent to the concerns of others?

3. Using the strategies presented in Chapter 4, write an analysis of Etzioni's argument. Write for classmates who are familiar with the controversy surrounding communitarianism.

The Meaning of One's Life

Robert N. Bellah, Richard Madsen, William M. Sullivan, Ann Swidler, and Steven M. Tipton

Robert N. Bellah is professor of sociology at the University of California at Berkeley. He is the author of numerous books, the most recent of which are The Broken Covenant: American Civil Religion in Time of Trial *(1992),* The Good Society *(1991), and* Uncivil Religion: Interreligious Hostility in America *(1987). The following selection appears in* Habits of the Heart: Individualism and Commitment in American Life *(1985), which Bellah wrote with Richard Madsen, William M. Sullivan, Ann Swidler, and Steven M. Tipton, the members of his research team.*

PREREADING

Read the initial sentence in each of the first three paragraphs, and write your response in your journal. In what "story" or context does your life makes sense? Does the meaning of your life derive from your family, your friends, your work, or some special interest? Try to be specific about the things that are especially meaningful to you.

Finding oneself means, among other things, finding the story or   1
narrative in terms of which one's life makes sense. The life course and its major stages have become the subject of considerable social scientific research, and books on the life cycle have become best sellers. Periodizations of childhood intrigued Americans at least as long ago as the 1930s. Adolescence as a peculiarly significant stage of life, with its "identity crises," received widespread attention in the late 1950s and the 1960s. More recently, we have heard much of midlife crises and of the aging process. Given the ideal of a radically unencumbered and improvisational self. . . , it is

From Robert N. Bellah, Richard Madsen, William M. Sullivan, Ann Swidler, and Stephen M. Tipton, *Habits of the Heart: Individualism and Commitment in American Life* (Berkeley and Los Angeles: U of California P, 1985) 81–84. Copyright © 1985, 1996 The Regents of the University of California. Reprinted by permission of the publisher.

perhaps not surprising that Americans should grasp at some scheme of life stages or crises to give coherence to the otherwise utterly arbitrary life patterns they seem to be asked to create.

If it is to provide any richness of meaning, the idea of a life course must be set in a larger generational, historical, and, probably, religious context. Yet much popular writing about the life course (Gail Sheehy's *Passages*, for example), as well as much of the thinking of ordinary Americans, considers the life course without reference to any social or historical context, as something that occurs to isolated individuals. In this situation, every life crisis, not just that of adolescence, is a crisis of separation and individuation, but what the ever freer and more autonomous self is free *for* only grows more obscure. Thinking about the life course in this way may exacerbate rather than resolve the problem of the meaning of the individual life.

In most societies in world history, the meaning of one's life has derived to a large degree from one's relationship to the lives of one's parents and one's children. For highly individuated Americans, there is something anomalous about the relation between parents and children, for the biologically normal dependence of children on adults is perceived as morally abnormal. We have already seen how children must leave home, find their own way religiously and ideologically, support themselves, and find their own peer group. This process leads to a considerable amnesia about what one owes to one's parents. The owner of a car-dealership whom we talked to in Massachusetts, for example, speaks of himself as a self-made man who has always done everything for himself, conveniently forgetting that his father established the business and he himself inherited it. The tendency to forget what we have received from our parents seems, moreover, to generalize to a forgetting of what we have received from the past altogether. (We have noted Jefferson's amnesia about what the colonists owed to the British.) Conversely, many Americans are uneasy about taking responsibility for children. When asked if she was responsible for her children, Margaret Oldham said hesitatingly, "I . . . I would say I have a legal responsibility for them, but in a sense I think they in turn are responsible for their acts." Frances FitzGerald found that most of the retirees in Sun City Center had quite remote relations with their children and above all dreaded any dependency on them. Tocqueville said that Americans would come to forget their ancestors and their descendants, and for many that would seem to be the case. Such inability to think positively about family continuity makes the current widespread nostalgia for "the family" all the more poignant.

Clearly, the meaning of one's life for most Americans is to become   4
one's own person, almost to give birth to oneself. Much of this process,
as we have seen, is negative. It involves breaking free from family, community, and inherited ideas. Our culture does not give us much guidance as to how to fill the contours of this autonomous, self-responsible
self, but it does point to two important areas. One of these is work, the
realm, par excellence, of utilitarian individualism. Traditionally men, and
today women as well, are supposed to show that in the occupational world
they can stand on their own two feet and be self-supporting. The other
area is the lifestyle enclave, the realm, par excellence, of expressive individualism. We are supposed to be able to find a group of sympathetic
people, or at least one such person, with whom we can spend our leisure
time in an atmosphere of acceptance, happiness, and love.

There is no question that many Americans find this combination of   5
work and private lifestyle satisfying. For people who have worked hard all
their lives, life in a "retirement community" composed of highly similar
people doing similar things may be gratifying. As a woman who had lived
fourteen years in Sun City Center, Florida, told Frances FitzGerald, "It's
the long vacation we wished we'd always had."

On the other hand, a life composed mainly of work that lacks much   6
intrinsic meaning and leisure devoted to golf and bridge does have limitations. It is hard to find in it the kind of story or narrative, as of a pil-
grimage or quest, that many cultures have used to link private and public;
present, past, and future; and the life of the individual to the life of society and the meaning of the cosmos.

We should not forget that the small town and the doctrinaire church,   7
which did offer more coherent narratives, were often narrow and oppressive. Our present radical individualism is in part a justified reaction
against communities and practices that were irrationally constricting. A
return to the mores of fifty or a hundred years ago, even if it were possible, would not solve, but only exacerbate, our problems. Yet in our desperate effort to free ourselves from the constrictions of the past, we have
jettisoned too much, forgotten a history that we cannot abandon.

Of course, not everyone in America or everyone to whom we talked   8
believes in an unencumbered self arbitrarily choosing its "values," "entirely independent" of everyone else. We talked to Christians and Jews
for whom the self makes sense in relation to a God who challenges,
promises, and reassures. We even talked to some for whom the word *soul*
has not been entirely displaced by the word *self.* We talked to those for
whom the self apart from history and community makes no sense at all.

To them, a self worth having only comes into existence through participation with others in the effort to create a just and loving society. But we found such people often on the defensive, struggling for the biblical and republican language that could express their aspirations, often expressing themselves in the very therapeutic rhetoric that they consciously reject. It is a rhetoric that educated middle-class Americans, and, through the medium of television and other mass communications, increasingly all Americans, cannot avoid. And yet even those most trapped in the language of the isolated self ("In the end you're really alone") are troubled by the nihilism they sense there and eager to find a way of overcoming the emptiness of purely arbitrary "values."

We believe that much of the thinking about the self of educated   9
Americans, thinking that has become almost hegemonic in our universities and much of the middle class, is based on inadequate social science, impoverished philosophy, and vacuous theology. There are truths we do not see when we adopt the language of radical individualism. We find ourselves not independently of other people and institutions but through them. We never get to the bottom of our selves on our own. We discover who we are face to face and side by side with others in work, love, and learning. All of our activity goes on in relationships, groups, associations, and communities ordered by institutional structures and interpreted by cultural patterns of meaning. Our individualism is itself one such pattern. And the positive side of our individualism, our sense of the dignity, worth, and moral autonomy of the individual, is dependent in a thousand ways on a social, cultural, and institutional context that keeps us afloat even when we cannot very well describe it. There is much in our life that we do not control, that we are not even "responsible" for, that we receive as grace or face as tragedy, things Americans habitually prefer not to think about. Finally, we are not simply ends in ourselves, either as individuals or as a society. We are parts of a larger whole that we can neither forget nor imagine in our own image without paying a high price. If we are not to have a self that hangs in the void, slowly twisting in the wind, these are issues we cannot ignore.   ✍

READING FOR INFORMATION

1. Explain why Bellah and his research team are critical of scholarly research and popular-press books on the various stages of the life cycle.
2. Explain what Bellah et al. mean when they say that for Americans "the biologically normal dependence of children on adults is perceived as morally abnormal" (paragraph 3).

3. In your own words, explain why excessive individualism is negative and harmful.

4. Is radical individualism ever justified? Paraphrase Bellah and his co-authors's response.

5. How do you react to this statement in the article: "And yet even those most trapped in the language of the isolated self ('In the end you're really alone') are troubled by the nihilism they sense there and eager to find a way of overcoming the emptiness of purely arbitrary 'values'" (paragraph 8)?

READING FOR FORM, ORGANIZATION, AND EXPOSITORY FEATURES

1. How would you describe the overall organizational structure of the selection? What other organizational patterns do you notice in the different paragraphs?

2. Underline the types of evidence Bellah and the fellow researchers use to support their argument. Do you find that evidence convincing?

3. What is the effect on the reader of the final sentence?

READING FOR RHETORICAL CONCERNS

1. Explain the authors' rhetorical purpose. What impact do you think Bellah et al. want to have on readers?

2. Do you think Bellah and his co-authors identify with their readers? Explain your response.

3. Is the argument in the article one-sided, or do the authors concede alternative viewpoints? Underline passages containing alternative views.

WRITING ASSIGNMENTS

1. Briefly summarize the authors' argument for classmates who have not read this selection.

2. Do you agree or disagree with Bellah et al. that for most Americans "finding oneself" means becoming self-responsible and individualistic rather than developing social bonds and social responsibility? Has this been your experience? Write a two- to three-page essay in response.

3. How do you think Amitai Etzioni would react to the article's argument? Compose a conversation between Etzioni and Robert Bellah. Have Etzioni react to four or five points in this selection, and supply Bellah's response.

4. Write a brief essay in response to the final paragraph.

Multiculturalism and Individualism

Michael Walzer

Michael Walzer has been professor of government at Princeton and Harvard Universities. He is currently at the Institute for Advanced Study at Princeton. Professor Walzer has written numerous books, including Thick and Thin: Moral Argument at Home and Abroad *(1994),* What It Means to Be American *(1992),* Spheres of Justice: A Defense of Pluralism and Equality *(1983), and* Just and Unjust Wars *(1977).*

PREREADING

In your journal, explain your understanding of the term "multiculturalism." List all the things multiculturalism is and all the things it is not.

Two powerful centrifugal forces are at work in the United   1
States today. One breaks loose whole groups of people from a presumptively common center; the other sends individuals flying off. Both these decentering, separatist movements have their critics, who argue that the first is driven by a narrow-minded chauvinism and the second by mere selfishness. The separated groups appear to these critics as exclusive and intolerant tribes, the separated individuals as rootless and lonely egotists. Neither of these views is entirely wrong; neither is entirely right. The two movements have to be considered together, set against the background of a democratic politics that opens a lot of room for centrifugal force. Understood in context, the two seem to me, despite the laws of physics, each one the other's remedy.

The first of these forces is an increasingly strong articulation of   2
group difference. It's the articulation that is new, obviously, since difference itself—pluralism, even multiculturalism—has been a feature of American life from very early on. John Jay, in one of the *Federalist Papers*, describes the Americans as a people "descended from the same ancestors, speaking the same language, professing the same religion, attached to the same principles of government, very similar in manners and customs."

Michael Walzer, "Multiculturalism and Individualism," *Dissent* Spring 1994: 185–91.

These lines were already inaccurate when Jay wrote them in the 3
1780s; they were utterly falsified in the course of the nineteenth century. Mass immigration turned the United States into a land of many
different ancestors, languages, religions, manners, and customs. Principles of government are our only stable and common commitment.
Democracy fixes the limits and sets the ground rules for American
pluralism.

Two contrasts can help us grasp the radical character of this plu- 4
ralism. Consider, first, the (relative) homogeneity of countries like
France, Holland, Norway, Germany, Japan, and China, where, whatever regional differences exist, the great majority of the citizens share
a single ethnic identity and celebrate a common history. And consider,
second, the territorially based heterogeneity of the old multinational
empires (the Soviet Union was the last of these) and of states like the
former Yugoslavia, the former Ethiopia, the new Russia, Nigeria, Iraq,
India, and so on, where a number of ethnic and religious minorities
claim ancient homelands (even if the boundaries are always in dispute).
The United States differs from both these sets of countries; it isn't homogeneous nationally or locally; it's a heterogeneous everywhere—a
land of dispersed diversity, which is (except for the remaining Native
Americans) no one's homeland. Of course, there are local patterns of
segregation, voluntary and involuntary; there are ethnic neighborhoods
and places inexactly but evocatively called "ghettoes." But none of our
groups, with the partial and temporary exception of the Mormons in
Utah, has ever achieved anything like stable geographical predominance. There is no American Slovenia or Quebec or Kurdistan. Even
in the most protected American environments, we all experience difference every day.

And yet the full-scale and fervent articulation of difference is a 5
fairly recent phenomenon. A long history of prejudice, subordination,
and fear worked against any public affirmation of minority "manners
and customs" and so served to conceal the radical character of American pluralism. I want to be very clear about this history. At its extremes
it was brutal, as conquered Native Americans and transported black
slaves can testify; at its center, with regard to religion and ethnicity rather
than race, it was relatively benign. An immigrant society welcomed new
immigrants or, at least, made room for them, with a degree of reluc-
tance and resistance considerably below the standards set elsewhere.
Nonetheless, all our minorities learned to be quiet; timidity has been
the mark of minority politics until very recent times.

I remember, for example, how in the 1930s and 1940s any sign of   6
Jewish assertiveness—even the appearance of "too many" Jewish names
among New Deal Democrats or CIO organizers or socialist or communist
intellectuals—was greeted among Jews with a collective shudder. The
communal elders said, "Sha!" Don't make noise; don't attract attention;
don't push yourself forward; don't say anything provocative. They thought
of themselves as guests in this country long after they had become citizens.

Today all that is, as they say, history. The United States in the 1990s   7
is socially, though not economically (and the contrast is especially striking after the Reagan years), a more egalitarian place than it was fifty or
sixty years ago. No one is shushing us anymore; no one is intimidated or
quiet. Old racial and religious identities have taken on greater prominence in our public life; gender and sexual preference have been added
to the mix; and the current wave of immigration from Asia and Latin
America makes for significant new differences among American citizens
and potential citizens. And all this is expressed, so it seems, all the time.
The voices are loud, the accents various, and the result is not harmony—
as in the old image of pluralism as a symphony, each group playing its own
instrument (but who wrote the music?)—but a jangling discord. It is very
much like the dissidence of Protestant dissent in the early years of the Re-
formation: many sects, dividing and subdividing; many prophets and
would-be prophets, all talking at once.

In response to this cacophony, another group of prophets, liberal   8
and neoconservative intellectuals, academics, and journalists, wring their
hands and assure us that the country is falling part, that our fiercely articulated multiculturalism is dangerously divisive, and that we desperately need to reassert the hegemony of a single culture. Curiously, this
supposedly necessary and necessarily singular culture is often described
as a high culture, as if it is our shared commitment to Shakespeare, Dickens, and James Joyce that has been holding us together all these years.
(But surely high culture divides us, as it always has—and probably always will in any country with a strong egalitarian and populist strain.
Does anyone remember Richard Hofstadter's *Anti-Intellectualism in
American Life?*) Democratic politics seems to me a more likely resource
than the literary or philosophical canon. We need to think about how this
resource might usefully be deployed.

But isn't it already deployed—given that multicultural conflicts take   9
place in the democratic arena and require of their protagonists a wide
range of characteristically democratic skills and performances? If one

studies the history of ethnic, racial, and religious associations in the United States, one sees, I think, that these have served again and again as vehicles of individual and group integration—despite (or, perhaps, because of) the political conflicts they generated. Even if the aim of associational life is to sustain difference, that aim has to be achieved *here,* under American conditions, and the result is commonly a new and unintended kind of differentiation—of American Catholics and Jews, say, not so much from one another or from the Protestant majority as from Catholics and Jews in other countries. Minority groups adapt themselves to the local political culture. And if their primary aim is self-defense, toleration, civil rights, a place in the sun, the result of success is more clearly still an Americanization of whatever differences are being defended. That doesn't mean that differences are defended quietly—quietness is not one of our political conventions. Becoming an American means learning not to be quiet. Nor is the success that is sought by one group always compatible with the success of all (or any of) the others. The conflicts are real, and even small-scale victories are often widely threatening.

The great difficulties, however, come from failure, especially reit- 10 erated failure. It is associational weakness, and the anxieties and resentments it breeds, that pull people apart in dangerous ways. Leonard Jeffries's African-American Studies Department at the City College of New York is hardly an example of institutional strength. The noisiest groups in our contemporary cacophony and the groups that make the most extreme demands are also the weakest. In American cities today, poor people, mostly members of minority groups, find it difficult to work together in any coherent way. Mutual assistance, cultural preservation, and self-defense are loudly affirmed but ineffectively enacted. The contemporary poor have no strongly based or well-funded institutions to focus their energies or discipline wayward members. They are socially exposed and vulnerable. This is the most depressing feature of our current situation: the large number of disorganized, powerless, and demoralized men and women, who are spoken for, and also exploited by, a growing company of racial and religious demagogues and tinhorn charismatics.

But weakness is a general feature of associational life in America 11 today. Unions, churches, interest groups, ethnic organizations, political parties and sects, societies for self-improvement and good works, local philanthropies, neighborhood clubs and cooperatives, religious sodalities, brotherhoods and sisterhoods: this American civil society is wonderfully multitudinous. Most of the associations, however, are precariously established, skimpily funded, and always at risk. They have less reach and holding power than they once did. I can't cite statistics; I'm not sure that anyone is collecting the right sorts of statistics; but I suspect that the number of Americans who are unorganized, inactive, and undefended is on the rise. Why is this so?

The answer has to do in part with the second of the centrifugal forces 12 at work in contemporary American society. This country is not only a pluralism of groups but also a pluralism of individuals. It is perhaps the most individualist society in human history. Compared to the men and women of any earlier, old-world country, we are radically liberated, all of us. We are free to plot our own course, plan our own lives, choose a career, a partner (or a succession of partners), a religion (or no religion), a politics (or an antipolitics), a life-style (any style)—free to "do our own thing." Personal freedom is certainly one of the extraordinary achievements of the "new order of the ages" celebrated on the Great Seal of the United States. The defense of this freedom against puritans and bigots is one of the enduring themes of American politics, making for its most zestful moments; the celebration of this freedom, and of the individuality and creativity it makes possible, is one of the enduring themes of our literature.

Nonetheless, personal freedom is not an unalloyed delight. For 13 many of us lack the means and the power to "do our own thing" or even to find our own things to do. Empowerment is, with rare exceptions, a familial, class, or communal, not an individual, achievement. Resources are accumulated over generations, cooperatively. And without resources, individual men and women find themselves hard-pressed by economic dislocations, natural disasters, governmental failures, and personal crises. They can't count on steady or significant communal support. Often they are on the run from family, class, and community, seeking a new life in this new world. If they make good their escape, they never look back; if they need to look back, they are likely to find the people they left behind barely able to support themselves.

Consider for a moment the cultural (ethnic, racial, and religious) 14 groups that constitute our supposedly fierce and divisive multiculturalism. All these are voluntary associations, with a core of militants, activists, and believers and a wide periphery of more passive men and women—who are, in effect, cultural free-riders, enjoying an identity that they don't pay for with money, time, or energy. When these people find themselves in trouble they look for help from similarly identified men and women. But the help is uncertain, for these identities are mostly unearned, without depth. Footloose individuals are not reliable members. There are no borders around our cultural groups and, of course, no border police. Men and women are free to participate or not as they please, to come and go, withdraw entirely, or simply fade away into the peripheral distances. This freedom, again, is one of the advantages of an individualist society; at the same time, however, it doesn't make for strong or cohesive associations. Ultimately, I'm not sure that it makes for strong or self-confident individuals.

Rates of disengagement from cultural association and identity for 15 the sake of the private pursuit of happiness (or the desperate search for economic survival) are so high these days that all the groups worry all the time about how to hold the periphery and ensure their own future. They are constantly fund raising; recruiting; scrambling for workers, allies, and endorsements; preaching against the dangers of assimilation, intermarriage, passing, and passivity. Lacking any sort of coercive power and unsure of their own persuasiveness, they demand governmental programs (targeted entitlements, quota systems) that will help them press their own members into line. From their perspective, the real alternative to multiculturalism is not a strong and substantive Americanism, but an empty or randomly filled individualism, a great drift of human flotsam and jetsam away from every creative center.

This is, again, a one-sided perspective, but by no means entirely 16 wrongheaded. The critical conflict in American life today is not between multiculturalism and some kind of cultural hegemony or singularity, not between pluralism and unity or the many and the one, but between the manyness of groups and of individuals, between communities and private men and women. And this is a conflict in which we have no choice except to affirm the value of both sides. The two pluralisms make America what it is or sometimes is and set the pattern for what it should be. Taken together, but only together, they are entirely consistent with a common democratic citizenship.

Consider now the increasingly dissociated individuals of contem- 17 porary American society. Surely we ought to worry about the processes, even though these are also, some of them, emancipatory processes, which produce dissociation and are its products:

- the rising divorce rate;
- the growing number of people living alone (in what the census calls "single person households");

- the decline in memberships (in unions and churches, for example);
- the long-term decline in voting rates and party loyalty (most dramatic in local elections);
- the high rates of geographic mobility (which continually undercut neighborhood cohesiveness);
- the sudden appearance of homeless men and women; and
- the rising tide of random violence.

Add to all this the apparent stabilization of high levels of unemployment and underemployment, especially among young people, which intensifies all these processes and aggravates their effects on already vulnerable minority groups. Unemployment makes family ties brittle, cuts people off from unions and interest groups, drains communal resources, leads to political alienation and withdrawal, increases the temptations of a criminal life. The old maxim about idle hands and the devil's work isn't necessarily true, but it comes true whenever idleness is a condition that no one would choose. 18

I am inclined to think that these processes, on balance, are more worrying than the multicultural cacophony—if only because, in a democratic society, action-in-common is better than withdrawal and solitude, tumult is better than passivity, shared purposes (even when we don't approve) are better than private listlessness. It is probably true, moreover, that many of these dissociated individuals are available for political mobilizations of a sort that democracies ought to avoid. There are writers today, of course, who claim that multiculturalism is itself the product of such mobilizations: American society in their eyes stands at the brink not only of dissolution but of "Bosnian" civil war. In fact, we have had (so far) only intimations of an openly chauvinist and racist politics. We are at a point where we can still safely bring the pluralism of groups to the rescue of the pluralism of dissociated individuals. 19

Individuals are stronger, more confident, more savvy, when they are participants in a common life, responsible to and for other people. No doubt, this relation doesn't hold for every common life; I am not recommending religious cults or political sects—though men and women who manage to pass through groups of that sort are often strengthened by the experience, educated for a more modest commonality. It is only in the context of associational activity that individuals learn to deliberate, argue, make decisions, and take responsibility. This is an old argument, first made on behalf of Protestant congregations and conventicles, which served, so we are told, as schools of democracy in nineteenth-century 20

Great Britain, despite the intense and exclusive bonds they created and their frequently expressed doubts about the salvation of nonbelievers. Individuals were indeed saved by congregational membership—saved from isolation, loneliness, feelings of inferiority, habitual inaction, incompetence, a kind of moral vacancy—and turned into useful citizens. But it is equally true that Britain was saved from Protestant repression by the strong individualism of these same useful citizens: that was a large part of their usefulness.

So, we need to strengthen associational ties, even if these ties con- 21 nect some of us to some others and not everyone to everyone else. There are many ways of doing this. First and foremost among them, it seems to me, are government policies that create jobs and that sponsor and support unionization on the job. For unemployment is probably the most dangerous form of dissociation, and unions are not only training grounds for democratic politics but also instruments of economic democracy. Almost as important are programs that strengthen family life, not only in its conventional but also in its unconventional versions—in any version that produces stable relationships and networks of support.

But I want to focus again on cultural associations, since these are the 22 ones thought to be so threatening today. We need more such associations, not fewer, and more powerful and cohesive ones, too, with a wider range of responsibilities. Consider, for example, the current set of federal programs—matching grants, subsidies, and entitlements—that enable religious communities to run their own hospitals, old-age homes, schools, day care centers, and family services. Here are welfare societies within a decentralized (and still unfinished) American welfare state. Tax money is used to second charitable contributions in ways that strengthen the patterns of mutual assistance that arise spontaneously within civil society. But these patterns need to be greatly extended—since coverage at present is radically unequal—and more groups brought into the business of welfare provision: racial and ethnic as well as religious groups (and why not unions, co-ops, and corporations too?).

We need to find other programs of this kind, through which the 23 government acts indirectly to support citizens acting directly in local communities: "charter schools" designed and run by teachers and parents; tenant self-management and co-op buyouts of public housing; experiments in workers' ownership and control of factories and companies; locally initiated building, cleanup, and crime prevention projects; and so on. Programs like these will often create or reinforce parochial communities, and they will generate conflicts for control of political space and institutional functions. But they will also increase the available space and the number of functions and, therefore, the opportunities for individual participation. And participating individuals, with a growing sense of their own effectiveness, are our best protection against the parochialism of the groups in which they participate.

Engaged men and women tend to be widely engaged—active in 24 many different associations both locally and nationally. This is one of the most common findings of political scientists and sociologists (and one of the most surprising: where do these people find the time?). It helps to explain why engagement works, in a pluralist society, to undercut racist or chauvinist political commitments and ideologies. The same people show up for union meetings, neighborhood projects, political canvassing, church committees, and—most reliably—in the voting booth on election day. They are, most of them, articulate, opinionated, skillful, sure of themselves, and fairly steady in their commitments. Some mysterious combination of responsibility, ambition, and meddlesomeness carries them from one meeting to another. Everyone complains (I mean that all of them complain) that there are so few of them. Is this an inevitability of social life, so that an increase in the number of associations would only stretch out the competent people, more and more thinly? I suspect that demand-side economists have a better story to tell about this "human capital." Multiply the calls for competent people, and the people will appear. Multiply the opportunities for action-in-common, and activists will emerge to seize the opportunities. Some of them, no doubt, will be narrow-minded and bigoted, but the greater their number and the more diverse their activities, the less likely it is that narrow-mindedness and bigotry will prevail.

A certain sort of stridency is a feature of what we may one day 25 come to recognize as *early* multiculturalism; it is especially evident among the newest and weakest, the least organized, groups. It is the product of a historical period when social equality outdistances economic equality. Stronger organizations, capable of collecting resources and delivering real benefits to their members, will move these groups, gradually, toward a democratically inclusive politics. The driving force will be the more active members, socialized by their activity. Remember that this has happened before, in the course of ethnic and class conflict. When groups consolidate, the center holds the periphery and turns it into a political constituency. And so union militants, say, begin on the picket line and the strike committee and move on to the school board and the city council. Religious and ethnic activists begin by defending the interests of their own community and end up in political coalitions, fighting for a place on "balanced" tickets, and talking (at least) about the common good. The cohesiveness of the group invigorates its members; the ambition and mobility of the most vigorous members liberalizes the group.

I don't mean to sound like the famous Pollyanna. These outcomes 26 won't come about by chance; perhaps they won't come about at all. Everything is harder now—family, class, and community are less cohesive than they once were; local governments and philanthropies command fewer resources; the street world of crime and drugs is more frightening; individual men and women seem more adrift. And there is one further difficulty that we ought to welcome. In the past, organized groups have succeeded in entering the American mainstream only by leaving other groups (and the weakest of their own members) behind. And the men and women left behind commonly accepted their fate or, at least, failed to make much noise about it. Today, as I have been arguing, the level of resignation is considerably lower, and if much of the subsequent noise is incoherent and futile, it serves nonetheless to remind the rest of us that there is a larger social agenda than our own success. Multiculturalism as an ideology is not only the product of, it is also a program for, greater social *and economic* equality.

If we want the mutual reinforcements of community and individ- 27 uality to work effectively for everyone, we will have to act politically to make them effective. They require certain background or framing conditions that can only be provided by state action. Group life won't rescue individual men and women from dissociation and passivity unless there is a political strategy for mobilizing, organizing, and, if necessary, subsidizing the right sort of groups. And strong-minded individuals won't diversify their commitments and extend their ambitions unless there are opportunities open to them in the larger world: jobs, offices, and responsibilities. The centrifugal forces of culture and selfhood will correct one another only if the correction is planned. It is necessary to aim at a balance of the two—which means that we can never be consistent defenders of multiculturalism or individualism; we can never be communitarians or liberals simply, but now one, now the other, as the balance requires. It seems to me that the best name for the balance itself, the political creed that defends the framework and supports the necessary forms of state action for both groups and individuals, is social democracy. If multiculturalism today brings more trouble than hope, one reason is the weakness of social democracy (in this country: left liberalism). But that is another and a longer story. 🖎

READING FOR INFORMATION

1. Summarize the two centrifugal forces Walzer is referring to in paragraph 1, and list the characteristics of each.
2. Explain what Walzer means when he says that it is not multiculturalism that is pulling us apart, it is "associational weakness." Do you agree?
3. In your own words, explain what has caused the weaknesses in associational life in America today.
4. In your own words, recount the processes that have produced so many dissociated individuals. Can you add others to the list?
5. Summarize three ways to strengthen associational ties.
6. Explain why we have to strengthen social democracy in the United States.

READING FOR FORM, ORGANIZATION, AND EXPOSITORY FEATURES

1. Construct a graphic overview (see pp. 24–25) that depicts the organization of Walzer's article.
2. Mark the passages that are organized according to the pattern of comparison and contrast, and explain what elements are being compared and contrasted.
3. Underline the evidence Walzer uses to support his position. Do you think the evidence is effective? Explain.

READING FOR RHETORICAL CONCERNS

1. Construct a "rhetorical outline" of the article. Explain what Walzer is trying to achieve in each of the following sections of the article: (1) paragraph 1, (2) paragraphs 2–11, (3) paragraphs 12–16, (4) paragraphs 17–20, (5) paragraphs 21–24, (6) paragraphs 25–27.
2. Explain Walzer's rhetorical purpose. Why do you think he wrote this article? What point is he trying to get across?
3. Describe Walzer's tone.

WRITING ASSIGNMENTS

1. Using an ethnic, racial, or religious association that you identify with, or any other association with which you are familiar, explain how the association serves on the one hand to integrate the group and on the other hand to sustain difference. Write a two- to three-page essay.

2. Using Walzer's article, argue that multiculturalism—action-in-common rather than isolation, activity rather than passivity, shared purpose rather than private listlessness—is an antidote or remedy for dissociated individuals. Write a persuasive essay addressed to opponents of multiculturalism.

3. Using the strategies presented in Chapter 4, write a short critical evaluation of Walzer's article.

Ambivalences in American Views of Dignity

Barry Jay Seltser and Donald E. Miller

Barry Jay Seltser, a senior social science analyst at the U.S. General Accounting Office, previously was on the faculties of the University of Southern California and Indiana University. He is the author of Principles and Practice of Political Compromise: A Case Study of the United States Senate. *Donald E. Miller is an associate professor of religion at the University of Southern California and coauthor with Lorna Touryan Miller of* Survivors: An Oral History of the Armenian Genocide. *With Barry Jay Seltser, he has written* Writing and Research in Religious Studies *and* Homeless Families: The Struggle for Dignity.

PREREADING

Before you read the selection, react to the opening sentence. Do you have difficulty responding to homeless people? How do you react when you meet a homeless person on the street? Do you experience conflict or feel tension? Freewrite your response.

From Barry Jay Seltser and Donald E. Miller, *Homeless Families: The Struggle for Dignity* (Urbana: U of Illinois P, 1993) 118–23. Copyright © 1993 by the Board of Trustees of the University of Illinois. Used with permission of the authors and of the University of Illinois Press.

. . . The difficulties experienced by American society in re- 1
sponding to homeless people reflect some deep confusions at
the level of basic values. Societies are defined, in large part, precisely by
the mixture of values and beliefs that both form its citizens and are in turn
formed by them. If we wonder why we are willing to tolerate the continuing plight of homeless people or why we are torn between compassion for them and distancing ourselves from them, our search should
include considering these underlying commitments and confusions, which
define us as Americans. By identifying some of these value polarities we
can begin to clarify the rather different responses that are currently made
to the presence of homeless persons on our streets.[1]

First, recall the tension between an individual versus a social un- 2
derstanding of dignity. Is our dignity an *individual* attribute, to be ap-
pealed to vis-á-vis other individuals? Or is dignity a *shared* characteristic
of human beings in society, to be recognized and mutually reinforced?
This tension becomes apparent in the attempts to derive specific human
rights from the notion of dignity, particularly when these rights involve
socially provided resources such as shelter, food, or health care. In the individualistic emphasis, it is my personal dignity which is at stake, and society is responsible for protecting or ensuring that my dignity is respected.
In the more social emphasis, the community as a whole carries the dignity as a human society, and attention is likely to be directed more toward
individual responsibilities than individual claims. This tension is lived out
in arguments concerning the lives of homeless families, particularly in
terms of concern for the right to shelter.

This ambivalence simply reflects the age-old tension between com- 3
munalism and individualism in American society. A wide range of writers have decried the extreme individualism that seems to have pervaded
our history, and which often is viewed as defining the American character.[2] But it is easy to overemphasize one side of this pole and to forget that
much of the early success of American life was based on a much more
communitarian ethic, one that remains an important force in American
society. It is being rediscovered both in many communities and in management theories developed in response to the decline of American industrial strength.[3]

In their recent work, Robert Bellah and his coauthors point out the 4
pivotal conflict between the American values of autonomy and sociality.
In the following passage, notice the way in which the conflict is both built

into the very nature of our culture and at the same time is unable to be resolved without sacrificing either value:

> The inner tensions of American individualism add up to a classic case of ambivalence. We strongly assert the value of our self-reliance and autonomy. We deeply feel the emptiness of a life without sustaining social commitments. Yet we are hesitant to articulate our sense that we need one another as much as we need to stand alone, for fear that if we did we would lose our independence altogether. The tensions of our lives would be even greater if we did not, in fact, engage in practices that constantly limit the effects of an isolating individualism, even though we cannot articulate those practices nearly as well as we can the quest for autonomy.[4]

This insight applies even more starkly to our homeless families, precisely because they have experienced the costs of losing (or, in some cases, never having) the social connections and support that may have saved them from their present situation.

Second, there is a fundamental tension in American society between *competition* and *cooperation*. Do we ultimately judge ourselves (as individuals and as a society) in terms of relative standing or in terms of shared attainments or living conditions? This tension is a fundamental ambivalence, built into the very structure of our lives; we receive mixed messages from the time we are born in virtually every arena of life. Doing well in school is competitive, when grades are assigned, tests are standardized, and admission is selective. But getting along with others is also prized and our teachers are often caught on the horns of an uncomfortable dilemma: how can they reward an individual's hard work without sending the message that the reward signifies the ultimate value of competition? Whether or not there is a gender basis for this particular value tension (as have been suggested in some recent literature), Americans are likely to have trouble deciding between competitive and cooperative orientations.

This ambivalence is significant in the way we view people who find themselves deprived of economic or political resources. How many of us secretly compare ourselves to those "below" us? Are we not, at some level, reassured by the fact that our lives could indeed be much worse? However strong the incentive to help those less fortunate, there remains the uncomfortable thought that sharing may mean losing, that pulling someone up may risk pulling myself down, and that, since there will always be winners and losers, I would prefer to be a winner. However much we believe that our true heroes are those who serve, it is hard not to hear the alternative messages sent in terms of salaries, benefits, and power perquisites heaped on the most competitive among us.

Third, American society continues to struggle with the tension be- 7 tween *achieved* and *ascribed* status. Is our basic worth defined by what we do and accomplish, or is it defined simply by who we are? In the sociological literature, ascribed characteristics usually refer to determined features such as race or sex, but we can easily understand "humanity" as an ascribed characteristic as well. To raise the question challenges our very sense of self-worth: who among us is not convinced that success (however defined) somehow adds to our value or worth, or that we have a right to be treated differently if we have accomplished more?

The ambivalence is strongest in the area of our assessment of ac- 8 complishment versus ascription as the basis for social values. But however important this distinction between achievement and intrinsic worth may be, too much can be made of it. In much of the current conservative backlash against liberal concepts of welfare and rights, for example, there is the suggestion that one chooses either to value achievement or to value people for some other reason. The traditional recognition and admiration of accomplishment can exist side by side with a deeper acknowledgement of dignity owned to all persons. In recognizing our tendency to be pulled in both directions, we need not deny either side.[5]

When we are faced with evaluating personal worth, this tension is 9 often expressed in terms of the values of *activity* versus *passivity*. We suspect that our readers would readily agree that Americans are obsessed with action, that the pace of most of our lives leaves little room for the value of being rather than doing, and that most of us are likely to feel guilty doing nothing. The achievement orientation compels us to attend to what we do; it is difficult to be willing to wait, to relax, to attend to what is happening, to be patient. But the very awareness of this tendency is evidence of the (perhaps growing) alternative value, and of the ways in which we are being called to question the extent to which activity is emphasized.

The valuing of activity makes it extremely difficult to respond in a 10 neutral fashion to the lives of homeless people. One problem is that, from our standards, they often appear to be doing nothing: they may not work, or send their children to schools, or create anything tangible. Adopting a narrow definition of activity, it is all too easy for us to move to a judgmental position, or at least to feel that their lives are somehow incomplete or worthless because they are not being active. We might suggest that our tendency to judge them in this way stems from the fact that we judge ourselves in the same way; the problem lies not in others but in ourselves.[6]

One aspect of this tension, which is particularly relevant for our purposes, is our polity's ambivalent view toward property. Most of us, we suspect, are willing to make a value distinction between personal rights and property rights; perhaps the appeal to the latter by segregationists in the 1950s and 1960s has given property rights a bad name. In the abstract, we seem to have moved (in both constitutional interpretation and everyday life) to a position that gives more priority to nonproperty features of life.

But the issue is not so clear when the discussion moves from the abstract to the particular. Acknowledging the secondary role of property is more difficult if I am being asked to give up something I own or something I have built. In one important strand of the liberal political tradition, of course, property is defined as an extension of the self, as something of myself that has been mixed in with the physical world and therefore remains "mine" in some important sense. One need not be a Lockean or a Marxist to recognize the power of such analogies; however, we must acknowledge that the choices between my "property" and your "human needs" are difficult ones indeed. As hard as it is to admit, if we were truly committed to the secondary importance of property rights, we might feel compelled to give away most of what we own in order to help feed and clothe other people.

Still another important value tension that affects our understanding of and response to homelessness is what Talcott Parsons referred to as "*affectivity*" versus "*neutrality*."[7] For our purposes, what is important in this tension is the extent to which each of us feels compelled to respond to social problems in both impassioned and dispassionate terms. We are put off by the purely academic, aloof tone of those who treat homeless people as simply one more social issue to be examined and dissected. But we also are likely to be repelled by those advocates who seem to be so committed to one side or the other that they are unable to gain any removed perspective or to allow themselves (or anyone else) to sort out the issues in a more objective manner. As a result, we find ourselves either bouncing back and forth between extreme concern and utter objectivity or else trying to find some compromise position of cautious concern or engaged analysis.

We might note that it is not merely the observers who are caught in this ambivalence. In their interviews, homeless people themselves struggle with this same problem. Should they try to adopt a more removed view of their own lives, trying to explain to the researcher how they came to be homeless and sort out the factors responsible for landing them in the shelter? Or should they use the interview as an opportunity to vent their frustration and anger, to seek help or comfort or understanding, or to draw the interviewer into their own experiences? We are not surprised that they have the same tensions, because both engagement and objectivity are highly valued in the society in which we all live.

Finally, we would mention the tension between a *particularistic* 15 and a *universalistic* approach to community. In the American context, this ambivalence is lived out in terms of whether we experience homeless families as part of our social world in anything other than a purely formal sense. In other words, do we have any obligations toward them? Are we tied (morally, emotionally, politically) to them? It may not be enough to acknowledge that they are fellow citizens. Are they also members of our community, with shared obligations and responsibilities?

Answering this question is so difficult because, once again, we hear 16 conflicting emphases from the larger society. We are proud of communities whose members "stick together," "take care of their own," and provide for each other. But most of our models refer either to small localities or to ethnic or religious subgroups, leaving open the question of the connection with the wider society. If taking care of one's own means giving priority to those closest or more familiar or more similar, what happens to those who are on the outside? The value tension appears when we recognize the heroism of people who in fact move outside of established boundaries and are able to redefine their obligations in a more global sense.

Religious traditions provide little help here, precisely because they 17 are caught in the same ambivalence. For the mainstreams of both Judaism and Christianity, we recognize the difficulty of applying the ethical norms of love of neighbor or of shared responsibility. The question, Who is my neighbor? remains one of the most difficult issues in religious ethics. To what extent are we obligated to care for everyone equally, in a world where most of us have specific relationships with individuals and groups that appear to make particular claims upon us?

This ambivalence makes us most uncomfortable when we recog- 18 nize the trade-offs we are constantly forced to make between our special relationships and our wider universalistic obligations. If we were talking about the same level of needs, the dilemma might be more easily resolved. After all, I might justify providing food for my family rather than for someone I don't know because I love my family and I know that I can't feed everyone. But the truly troubling choices (of which we manage to remain unaware most of the time) involve choosing between an extra car for my family or a year's worth of food for someone else, or between a larger house for myself and some minimal shelter for several strangers. Once again, we are not provided with very clear guidance from societal values in making our decisions; as a result, we may retreat to a stance of ignoring the wider needs or resenting the claims themselves as intruding on our own choices.

To summarize, this discussion, however brief and general, has identified some of the key value tensions within our wider society. Our often ambivalent and ill-defined responses to homeless people stem from these value conflicts and reveal the continued strength of these conflicts in our daily lives. As we have suggested, homeless families, as members of the same society, share these ambivalent values as well. Indeed, it may be harder for them to live in the tension because so much of their own self-worth is at stake.

NOTES

1. This sort of analysis of cultural values stands in the tradition of social theorists such as Robert Merton and Talcott Parsons, among others; many of the values identified in our discussion derive from their writings. More recently, Robert Bellah and his associates emphasize many of these ambivalent values in *Habits of the Heart: Individualism and Commitment in American Life* (New York: Harper and Row, 1985). On a more individual level, the writings of Erik Erikson direct our attention to the tensions that confront us at various stages of our development.

2. Among the more compelling critiques of American individualism are Philip Slater, *The Pursuit of Loneliness* (Boston: Beacon Press, 1970); Christopher Lasch, *The Culture of Narcissim* (New York: W. W. Norton, 1978); and Bellah et al., *Habits of the Heart.*

3. Historically, for example, the strongly communitarian instincts and theologies of the Puritan strand of American colonialism must be placed in contrast to the images of the individualistic pioneer.

4. Robert Bellah, Richard Madsen, William Sullivan, Ann Swidler, and Steven Tipton. *Habits of the Heart: Individualism and Commitment in American Life,* pp. 150–51.

5. It should be clear by now, to readers familiar with some of the debates concerning the philosophy of justice and modern liberalism, that the authors are sympathetic to the approach of John Rawls. It should be noted, however, that we would ground the fundamental commitment to dignity (or to "self-respect," in Rawls's sense) in a religious commitment rather than a purely philosophical one. (See Rawls, *A Theory of Justice* [Harvard University Press, 1971].)

6. At a religious level, the rediscovery of a more "passive" orientation is being rediscovered by Christian writers who emphasize the paradox of God's power as revealed in the powerlessness of the death of Jesus Christ. For a particularly powerful and moving treatment of this them, see W. H. Vanstone, *The Stature of Waiting.*

7. Talcott Parsons, *The Social System* (New York: Free Press, 1951), especially chapter 3. In spite of the dated nature of the writing and the narrowly functionalist approach, Parson's discussion remains a brilliant evocation of many of the underlying themes that continue to define American social values.   🖎

READING FOR INFORMATION

1. Explain how the national conflict between individual and community, autonomy and society, self-interest and social responsibility comes into play when Americans respond to homeless persons.

2. In your own words, explain how our schools send us mixed messages about the value of competition as opposed to the value of cooperation. Do you agree?

3. Explain why Americans think homeless people are unworthy because they are inactive.

4. Explain how and why homeless families share some of the tensions and ambivalences that exist within the wider society.

5. In paragraph 3, Seltser and Miller refer to writers who criticize Americans' extreme individualism. Which authors in this chapter can you add to the list?

READING FOR FORM, ORGANIZATION, AND EXPOSITORY FEATURES

1. Underline the various points in the piece where Seltser and Miller ask questions. What function do you think those questions serve?

2. Describe the organizational features that make the text particularly easy to follow.

READING FOR RHETORICAL CONCERNS

1. How would you describe Seltser and Miller's rhetorical purpose? What are the most essential points they are trying to get across to their audience?

2. Do you think the authors anticipate their readers' questions and needs? Give specific examples of how they accommodate their readers.

WRITING ASSIGNMENTS

1. When we meet a homeless person on the street, we are often uncomfortable, embarrassed, and confused. Should we avoid the person or make eye contact? If we are propositioned, should we offer money or ignore the request? Is it better to cross to the other side of the street? Drawing on

Seltser and Miller's piece, write a five- to six-page essay explaining the different tensions or polarities that underline these conflicts. Address your essay to classmates who have not read the selections in this anthology.

2. Which of the tensions or value polarities that Seltser and Miller describe have you experienced the most? Respond in an essay of two to three pages.

Communitarianism, A New Threat for Gun Owners

Christopher C. Little

Christopher C. Little is a research associate with the Independence Institute, Golden, Colorado, and an activist with the Firearms Coalition of Colorado. "Communitarianism, A New Threat for Gun Owners" appeared in the American Rifleman.

PREREADING

Recall in your journal some of the principles and beliefs of communitarians. Why do you think communitarianism would pose a threat to gun owners? Freewrite your response.

During the 1992 presidential campaign, Democratic nominee   1
Bill Clinton promised the American people "fundamental change" if elected president. This was an appealing message to an electorate sick and tired of the status quo in Washington, D.C. Of course, Clinton was not the only candidate promising reform. A significant part of the electorate opted for the similar message of Ross Perot, enabling Clinton to defeat George Bush with only 43% of the popular vote.

The winds of change blowing through the Imperial City bring a   2
new philosophical approach, one antithetical to the political philosophy of the Constitution's Framers, but one which nonetheless influences the thinking of the President a great deal. This new philosophy is called "communitarianism."

Christopher C. Little, "Communitarianism, A New Threat for Gun Owners," *American Rifleman* Oct. 1993: 30–31, 84.

The "guru" of this movement is Amitai Etzioni, a professor of Amer-   3
ican studies at George Washington University in the nation's capital.
Communitarian writers are mainly academics, some of whom enjoy close
connections to the Washington political community. Communitarians
argue that rights must be balanced with duties; that liberty must be tem-
pered with public safety; that as much concern should be manifested toward the group as toward the individual. "Strong rights presume strong
responsibilities" is the principal communitarian slogan.

Though some of its concerns and recommendations about com-   4
munity-mindedness may be perfectly laudable, communitarianism's
critics insist that it is not really concerned about a delicate balancing act
between rights and responsibilities, but that it *exalts* duties over rights,
public safety over liberty and the group over the individual. Accordingly, its public policy recommendations either implicitly or expressly
call for the attenuation or even abrogation of certain rights.

Nowhere is this more true than in its attitude toward gun owner-   5
ship (which, incidentally, is set forth in position papers evidencing such
poor scholarship that it's hard to believe academics wrote them). Consider this from *The Responsive Communitarian Platform: Rights and
Responsibilities*—"There is little sense in gun registration. What we need
to significantly enhance public safety is *domestic disarmament* of the kind
that exists in practically all democracies. The National Rifle Association
suggestion that criminals, not guns, kill people, ignores the fact that thousands are killed each year, many of them children, from accidental dis-
charge of guns, and that all people—whether criminal, insane or
temporarily carried away by impulse—kill and are much more likely to do
so when armed then (sic) when disarmed. The Second Amendment, behind which the NRA hides, is subject to a variety of interpretations, but
the Supreme Court has repeatedly ruled, for over a hundred years, that
it does not prevent laws that bar guns. *We join with those who read the Second Amendment the way it was written, as a communitarian clause, calling for community militias, not individual gun slingers."* (*Emphasis theirs.*)

In the Communitarian Network's position paper entitled, "The Case   6
for Domestic Disarmament," Etzioni further defines what is meant by this
term. It refers not to "vanilla pale measures" such as waiting periods,
registration or a ban on only one class of firearms (e.g., handguns or "assault weapons"). Rather, "(it) is the policy of practically all other Western
democracies, from Canada to Britain to Germany, from France to Scan-
dinavia . . . (which) entails *the removal of arms from private hands* and,
ultimately, from much of the police force."

And what of the right to keep and bear arms? As evidenced above, 7 the communitarians perpetuate the gun control lobby's myth that the U.S. Supreme Court has spoken definitively on the matter, when in fact it hasn't. Though it has been refuted in many recent scholarly works, communitarian writers nevertheless regurgitate the tired, old "exclusively collective right" argument, which maintains that the Second Amendment only guarantees the right of a state to maintain a uniformed militia, not an individual right to keep and bear arms. There is therefore no constitutional obstacle to radical gun control legislation, as far as they are concerned.

Etzioni is willing to make a few concessions to gun owners, however. 8 Gun collectors may be accommodated by provisions allowing them to keep their collections, but rendering them inoperative (cement in the barrel is my favorite technique). Hunters might be allowed (if one feels this "sport" must be tolerated) to use long guns that cannot be concealed, without sights or powerful bullets, making the event more sporting. Finally, super-patriots, who still believe they need their right to bear arms to protect us from the Commies, might be deputized and invited to participate in the National Guard, as long as the weapons with which they are trained are kept in state-controlled armories. All this is acceptable, "as long as all other guns and bullets are removed from private hands."

A recent issue of *The Communitarian Reporter* states that the White 9 House is "seeking to move along communitarian lines," a fact well attested by the communitarian substance of many speeches and writings of President Clinton, Vice President Al Gore and First Lady Hillary Rodham Clinton. The appointment of communitarians William Galston, Robert Reich and Henry Cisneros to key posts, in addition to this continual harping on the rights-vs.-responsibility theme, are clear indications of how deeply rooted this ideology is within the current administration.

As President Clinton parrots much of the communitarian agenda 10 on several economic and social issues, so he does on the right to keep and bear arms. When asked about NRA's efforts in support of the New Jersey legislature's attempt to repeal its previous ban on military-style semi-automatics, he responded that NRA is "fixated" on the right to keep and bear arms. This, he said, renders NRA "unable to think about the reality of life that millions of Americans face on streets that are unsafe, under conditions that no other nation—no other nation—has permitted to exist." While giving lip service to the right to keep and bear arms (his home state of Arkansas having a long tradition of hunting, you see), "just to ignore . . . the enormous threat to public safety [as the NRA supposedly does] is amazing."

Just what does he recommend as a solution? He said during his 11 State of the Union address that he would sign a stand-alone "Brady bill" if Congress passed it. And about military-style semi-automatics? "I don't believe everybody in America needs to be able to buy a semi-automatic weapon. . . , built only to kill people, in order for some Americans to hunt or practice markmanship."

Clinton says he believes in the right to keep and bear arms, by 12 which he means the right to hunt and to punch holes in paper from a distance (possibly mirroring Etzioni's position that only one privilege—recreational gun use—should be granted to gun owners).

In fairness, there are signs that Clinton is not a "purist" communi- 13 tarian; his views on gun control may therefore not be as radical as those of Etzioni and Co. Nevertheless, his communitarian bent is by definition an anti-constitutional bent, and what he *has* said thus far about gun control is truly disturbing. He shows no awareness, for example, that the right to keep and bear arms is not principally concerned with recreational shooting, but rather with the right to defend both life and liberty. He has promised to sign the Brady bill, which might effect "back-door" registration and arguably turns a constitutional right into a privilege granted by the state. He has promised to sign legislation banning the sale and possession of military-style semi-automatics, even though a growing body of scholarship and case law proves that private ownership of these firearms is constitutionally protected. He apparently has no qualms about the "sin tax" on firearms reportedly contained in Hillary Rodham Clinton's health-care reform package.

While it isn't clear just how radical a gun control bill would have to 14 be before Clinton would veto it, there is no doubt about the nefarious intent of congressional communitarians. For example, Sen. Daniel Moynihan (D-NY), who is known to move in communitarian circles, has introduced a number of anti-gun bills that comport well with communitarianism's stated desires to see both ammunition and guns made unavailable to the American public: **S.109,** requiring gun owners to record all ammunition used: **S.178,** a ban on the sale, manufacture and possession of .25, .32 and 9 mm ammunition; **S.179,** a 1000% tax on the same; **S.108,** a prohibition of the import of military-style semi-automatics. Sen. John Chaffee's bill banning handguns (**S.892**) is also back this year. ("Domestic Disarmament" had cited his previous bill as an example of model legislation.) The other draconian gun control bills introduced this year are well in keeping with the communitarian mentality, even if not directly influenced by it.

Our elected officials have sworn to defend the Constitution, how- 15
ever, not to advance the public policy recommendations of the communitarians. On the contrary, in swearing to defend the Constitution, they have sworn to defend *only* that philosophy of the common good that the Framers incorporated into the Constitution. The Framers believed that the common good was best advanced when the rights of each individual were protected, including the right to keep and bear arms, which was called the "palladium of liberty."

Most Americans still take their rights seriously. And "to take rights 16
seriously," wrote Prof. Sanford Levinson in a recent *Yale Law Journal* article on the Second Amendment, "(means) that one will honor them even when there is significant social cost in doing so." This is still the American civil libertarian way, and will remain so as long as the Constitution stands. As the U.S. Supreme Court has said, the Constitution is "The supreme law of the land," not the real or imagined will of the community. Gun owners should rise up *en masse* and remind the anti-gun communitarians in Congress and the White House of this fact.   🐎

READING FOR INFORMATION

1. Paraphrase Little's principal complaint against communitarianism.
2. In your own words, explain the difference in the way communitarians and members of the National Rifle Association interpret the Second Amendment.
3. Explain why Little finds President Clinton's pronouncements disturbing.
4. Explain what Little means when he says that the Constitution is the law of the land, "not the real or imagined will of the community."

READING FOR FORM, ORGANIZATION, AND EXPOSITORY FEATURES

1. What is the effect on the reader of terms and words like the following: "Imperial City," "guru," "harping parrots"?
2. Underline places where Little uses rhetorical questions. How do those questions influence the reader?
3. Mark places where Little makes concessions to those who hold opposing views. How would the impact of Little's argument change if those concessions were left out?
4. What effect will Little's concluding sentence have on the reader?

READING FOR RHETORICAL CONCERNS

1. What do you think Little is trying to prove in this article?
2. What assumptions does Little make about his readers? Do you think those assumptions are correct?
3. How would you describe Little's tone? What does that tone suggest about the author?

WRITING ASSIGNMENTS

1. Write a three- to four-page essay in which you agree or disagree with Little's criticism of the communitarian movement. If you wish, draw on other selections in this chapter.
2. Using the strategies presented in Chapter 4, write a critical analysis of Little's argument. Address your essay to your classmates.

Life

Bessie Head

Born in South Africa, Bessie Head was the daughter of a white mother and a black father. After her marriage in 1961, she emigrated to the village of Serowe in Botswana. Among her novels and short stories are Where Rain Clouds Gather *(1969),* The Collector of Treasures and Other Botswana Village Tales *(1977), and* A Bewitched Crossroad *(1984).*

PREREADING

Read the first paragraph of the story. In your journal, speculate about the ensuing plot. What will the conflict entail? Who is Life? What events will lead to her death?

In 1963, when the borders were first set up between Botswana and South Africa, pending Botswana's independence in 1966, all Botswana-born citizens had to return home. Everything had been mingled up in the old colonial days, and the traffic of people to and fro between

Bessie Head, "Life," *The Collector of Treasures and Other Botswana Village Tales* (Oxford, England: Heinemann Ltd., 1977).

the two countries had been a steady flow for years and years. More often, especially if they were migrant labourers working in the mines, their period of settlement was brief, but many people had settled there in permanent employment. It was these settlers who were disrupted and sent back to village life in a mainly rural country. On their return they brought with them bits and pieces of a foreign culture and city habits which they had absorbed. Village people reacted in their own way; what they liked, and was beneficial to them, they absorbed—for instance, the faith-healing cult churches which instantly took hold like wildfire; what was harmful to them, they rejected. The murder of Life had this complicated undertone of rejection.

Life had left the village as a little girl of ten years old with her parents for Johannesburg. They had died in the meanwhile, and on Life's return, seventeen years later, she found, as was village custom, that she still had a home in the village. On mentioning that her name was Life Morapedi, the villagers immediately and obligingly took her to the Morapedi yard in the central part of the village. The family yard had remained intact, just as they had left it, except that it looked pathetic in its desolation. The thatch of the mud huts had patches of soil over them where the ants had made their nests; the wooden poles that supported the rafters of the huts had tilted to an angle as their base had been eaten through by the ants. The rubber hedge had grown to a disproportionate size and enclosed the yard in a gloom of shadows that kept out the sunlight. Weeds and grass of many seasonal rains entangled themselves in the yard. 2

Life's future neighbours, a group of women, continued to stand near her. 3

"We can help you to put your yard in order," they said kindly. "We are very happy that a child of ours has returned home." 4

They were impressed with the smartness of this city girl. They generally wore old clothes and kept their very best things for special occasions like weddings, and even then those best things might just be ordinary cotton prints. The girl wore an expensive cream costume of linen material, tailored to fit her tall, full figure. She had a bright, vivacious, friendly manner and laughed freely and loudly. Her speech was rapid and a little hysterical but that was in keeping with her whole personality. 5

"She is going to bring us a little light," the women said among themselves, as they went off to fetch their work tools. They were always looking "for the light" and by that they meant that they were ever alert to receive new ideas that would freshen up the ordinariness and everydayness of village life. 6

A woman who lived near the Morapedi yard had offered Life hospitality until her own yard was set in order. She picked up the shining new suitcases and preceded Life to her own home, where Life was immediately surrounded with all kinds of endearing attentions—a low stool was placed in a shady place for her to sit on; a little girl came shyly forward with a bowl of water for her to wash her hands; and following on this, a tray with a bowl of meat and porridge was set before her so that she could revive herself after her long journey home. The other women briskly entered her yard with hoes to scratch out the weeds and grass, baskets of earth and buckets of water to re-smear the mud walls, and they had found two idle men to rectify the precarious tilt of the wooden poles of the mud hut. These were the sort of gestures people always offered, but they were pleased to note that the newcomer seemed to have an endless stream of money which she flung around generously. The work party in her yard would suggest that the meat of a goat, slowly simmering in a great iron pot, would help the work to move with a swing, and Life would immediately produce the money to purchase the goat and also tea, milk, sugar, pots of porridge, or anything the workers expressed a preference for, so that those two weeks of making Life's yard beautiful for her seemed like one long wedding-feast; people usually only ate that much at weddings. 7

"How is it you have so much money, our child?" one of the women at last asked, curiously. 8

"Money flows like water in Johannesburg," Life replied, with her gay and hysterical laugh. "You just have to know how to get it."

The women received this with caution. They said among themselves that their child could not have lived a very good life in Johannesburg. Thrift and honesty were the dominant themes of village life and everyone knew that one could not be honest and rich at the same time; they counted every penny and knew how they had acquired it—with hard work. They never imagined money as a bottomless pit without end; it always had an end and was hard to come by in this dry, semi-desert land. They predicted that she would soon settle down—intelligent girls got jobs in the post office sooner or later. 9

Life had had the sort of varied career that a city like Johannesburg offered a lot of black women. She had been a singer, beauty queen, advertising model, and prostitute. None of these careers were available in the village—for the illiterate women there was farming and housework; for the literate, teaching, nursing, and clerical work. The first wave of women Life attracted to herself were the farmers and housewives. They were the intensely conservative hard-core centre of village life. It did not 10 take them long to shun her completely because men started turning up in an unending stream. What caused a stir of amazement was that Life was the first and the only woman in the village to make a business out of selling herself. The men were paying her for services. People's attitude to sex was broad and generous—it was recognized as a necessary part of human life, that it ought to be available whenever possible like food and water, or else one's life would be extinguished or one would get dreadfully ill. To prevent these catastrophes from happening, men and women generally had quite a lot of sex but on a respectable and human level, with financial considerations coming in as an afterthought. When the news spread around that this had now become a business in Life's yard, she attracted to herself a second wave of women—the beer-brewers of the village.

The beer-brewing women were a gay and lovable crowd who had 11 emancipated themselves some time ago. They were drunk every day and could be seen staggering around the village, usually with a wide-eyed illegitimate baby hitched on to their hips. They also talked and laughed loudly and slapped each other on the back and had developed a language all their own:

"Boyfriends, yes. Husbands, uh, uh, no. Do this! Do that! We want 12 to rule ourselves."

But they too were subject to the respectable order of village life. Many men passed through their lives but they were all for a time steady boyfriends. The usual arrangement was:

"Mother, you help me and I'll help you."

This was just so much eye-wash. The men hung around, lived on the 13 resources of the women, and during all this time they would part with about two rand of their own money. After about three months a tally-up would be made:

"Boyfriend," the woman would say, "love is love and money is money. 14 You owe me money." And he'd never be seen again, but another scoundrel would take his place. And so the story went on and on. They found their queen in Life and like all queens, they set her activities apart from themselves; they never attempted to extract money from the constant stream of men because they did not know how, but they liked her yard. Very soon the din and riot of a Johannesburg township was duplicated, on a minor scale, in the central part of the village. A transistor radio blared the day long. Men and women reeled around drunk and laughing and food and drink flowed like milk and honey. The people of the surrounding village watched this phenomenon with pursed lips and commented darkly:

"They'll all be destroyed one day like Sodom and Gomorrah."

Life, like the beer-brewing women, had a language of her own too. 15
When her friends expressed surprise at the huge quantities of steak, eggs,
liver, kidneys, and rice they ate in her yard—the sort of food they too
could now and then afford but would not dream of purchasing—she
replied in a carefree, off-hand way: "I'm used to handling big money."
They did not believe it; they were too solid to trust to this kind of luck
which had such shaky foundations, and as though to offset some doom
that might be just around the corner they often brought along their own
scraggy, village chickens reared in their yards, as offerings for the day's
round of meals. And one of Life's philosophies on life, which they were
to recall with trembling a few months later, was: "My motto is: live fast,
die young, and have a good-looking corpse." All this was said with the
bold, free joy of a woman who had broken all the social taboos. They
never followed her to those dizzy heights.

A few months after Life's arrival in the village, the first hotel with 16
its pub opened. It was initially shunned by all the women and even the
beer-brewers considered they hadn't fallen *that* low yet—the pub was
also associated with the idea of selling oneself. It became Life's favourite
business venue. It simplified the business of making appointments for
the following day. None of the men questioned their behaviour, nor how
such an unnatural situation had been allowed to develop—they could get
all the sex they needed for free in the village, but it seemed to fascinate
them that they should pay for it for the first time. They had quickly got
to the stage where they communicated with Life in short-hand language.

"When?" And she would reply: "Ten o'clock." "When?" "Two o'clock."
"When?" "Four o'clock," and so on.

And there would be the roar of cheap small talk and much buttock 17
slapping. It was her element and her feverish, glittering, brilliant black
eyes swept around the bar, looking for everything and nothing at the
same time.

Then one evening death walked quietly into the bar. It was 18
Lesego, the cattle-man, just come in from his cattle-post, where he
had been occupied for a period of three months. Men built up their
own, individual reputations in the village and Lesego's was one of the
most respected and honoured. People said of him: "When Lesego has
got money and you need it, he will give you what he has got and he
won't trouble you about the date of payment . . ." He was honoured
for another reason also—for the clarity and quiet indifference of his
thinking. People often found difficulty in sorting out issues or the truth
in any debatable matter. He had a way of keeping his head above water,

listening to an argument and always pronouncing the final judgment: "Well, the truth about this matter is . . ." He was now also one of the most successful cattle-men with a balance of seven thousand rand in the bank, and whenever he came into the village he lounged around and gossiped or attended village kgotla[1] meetings, so that people had a saying: "Well, I must be getting about my business. I'm not like Lesego with money in the bank."

As usual, the brilliant radar eyes swept feverishly around the bar. 19 They did the rounds twice that evening in the same manner, each time coming to a dead stop for a full second on the thin, dark, concentrated expression of Lesego's face. There wasn't any other man in the bar with that expression; they all had sheepish, inane-looking faces. He was the nearest thing she had seen for a long time to the Johannesburg gangsters she had associated with—the same small, economical gestures, the same power and control. All the men near him quieted down and began to consult with him in low earnest voices; they were talking about the news of the day which never reached the remote cattle-posts. Whereas all the other men had to approach her, the third time her radar eyes swept round he stood his ground, turned his head slowly, and then jerked it back slightly in a silent command:

"Come here."

She moved immediately to his end of the bar. 20

"Hullo," he said, in an astonishingly tender voice and a smile flickered across his dark, reserved face. That was the sum total of Lesego, that basically he was a kind and tender man, that he liked women and had been so successful in that sphere that he took his dominance and success for granted. But they looked at each other from their own worlds and came to fatal conclusions—she saw in him the power and maleness of the gangsters; he saw the freshness and surprise of an entirely new kind of woman. He had left all his women after a time because they bored him, and like all people who live an ordinary humdrum life, he was attracted to that undertone of hysteria in her.

Very soon they stood up and walked out together. A shocked si- 21 lence fell upon the bar. The men exchanged looks with each other and the way these things communicate themselves, they knew that all the other appointments had been cancelled while Lesego was there. And as though speaking their thoughts aloud, Sianana, one of Lesego's friends, commented, "Lesego just wants to try it out like we

---

[1] Tribal court

all did because it is something new. He won't stay there when he finds out that it is rotten to the core."

But Sianana was to find out that he did not fully understand his 22 friend. Lesego was not seen at his usual lounging-places for a week and when he emerged again it was to announce that he was to marry. The news was received with cold hostility. Everyone talked of nothing else; it was as impossible as if a crime was being committed before their very eyes. Sianana once more made himself the spokesman. He waylaid Lesego on his way to the village kgotla:

"I am much surprised by the rumours about you, Lesego," he said bluntly. "You can't marry that woman. She's a terrible fuck-about!"

Lesego stared back at him steadily, then he said in his quiet, indifferent way, "Who isn't here?"

Sianana shrugged his shoulders. The subtleties were beyond him; 23 but whatever else was going on it wasn't commercial, it was human, but did that make it any better? Lesego liked to bugger up an argument like that with a straightforward point. As they walked along together Sianana shook his head several times to indicate that something important was eluding him, until at last, with a smile, Lesego said, "She has told me all about her bad ways. They are over."

Sianana merely compressed his lips and remained silent.

Life made the announcement too, after she was married, to all her 24 beer-brewing friends: "All my old ways are over," she said. "I have now become a woman."

She still looked happy and hysterical. Everything came to her too 25 easily, men, money, and now marriage. The beer-brewers were not slow to point out to her with the same amazement with which they had exclaimed over the steak and eggs, that there were many women in the village who had cried their eyes out over Lesego. She was very flattered.

Their lives, at least Lesego's, did not change much with marriage. 26 He still liked lounging around the village; the rainy season had come and life was easy for the cattle-men at this time because there was enough water and grazing for the animals. He wasn't the kind of man to fuss about the house and during this time he only made three pronouncements about the household. He took control of all the money. She had to ask him for it and state what it was to be used for. Then he didn't like the transistor radio blaring the whole day long.

"Women who keep that thing going the whole day have nothing in 27 their heads," he said.

Then he looked down at her from a great height and commented finally and quietly: "If you go with those men again, I'll kill you."

This was said so indifferently and quietly, as though he never really expected his authority and dominance to encounter any challenge.

She hadn't the mental equipment to analyse what had hit her, but something seemed to strike her a terrible blow behind the head. She instantly succumbed to the blow and rapidly began to fall apart. On the surface, the everyday round of village life was deadly dull in its even, unbroken monotony; one day slipped easily into another, drawing water, stamping corn, cooking food. But within this there were enormous tugs and pulls between people. Custom demanded that people care about each other, and all day long there was this constant traffic of people in and out of each other's lives. Someone had to be buried; sympathy and help were demanded for this event—there were money loans, new-born babies, sorrow, trouble, gifts, Lesego had long been the king of this world; there was, every day, a long string of people, wanting something or wanting to give him something in gratitude for a past favour. It was the basic strength of village life. It created people whose sympathetic and emotional responses were always fully awakened, and it rewarded them by richly filling in a void that was one big, gaping yawn. When the hysteria and cheap rowdiness were taken away, Life fell into the yawn; she had nothing inside herself to cope with this way of life that had finally caught up with her. The beer-brewing women were still there; they still liked her yard because Lesego was casual and easy-going and all that went on in it now—like the old men squatting in corners with gifts: "Lesego, I had good luck with my hunting today. I caught two rabbits and I want to share one with you . . ."—was simply the Tswana way of life they too lived. In keeping with their queen's new status, they said:

"We are women and must do something."

They collected earth and dung and smeared and decorated Life's courtyard. They drew water for her, stamped her corn, and things looked quite ordinary on the surface because Lesego also liked a pot of beer. No one noticed the expression of anguish that had crept into Life's face. The boredom of the daily round was almost throttling her to death and no matter which way she looked, from beer-brewers to her husband to all the people who called, she found no one with whom she could communicate what had become an actual physical pain. After a month of it, she was near collapse. One morning she mentioned her agony to the beer-brewers: "I think I have made a mistake. Married life doesn't suit me."

And they replied sympathetically, "You are just getting used to it. After all it's a different life in Johannesburg."

The neighbours went further. They were impressed by a marriage 30 they thought could never succeed. They started saying that one never ought to judge a human being who was both good and bad, and Lesego had turned a bad woman into a good woman which was something they had never seen before. Just as they were saying this and nodding their approval, Sodom and Gomorrah started up all over again. Lesego had received word late in the evening that the new-born calves at his cattle-post were dying, and early the next morning he was off again in his truck.

The old, reckless wild woman awakened from a state near death 31 with a huge sigh of relief. The transistor blared, the food flowed again, the men and women reeled around dead drunk. Simply by their din they beat off all the unwanted guests who nodded their heads grimly. When Lesego came back they were going to tell him this was no wife for him.

Three days later Lesego unexpectedly was back in the village. The 32 calves were all anaemic and they had to be brought in to the vet for an injection. He drove his truck straight through the village to the vet's camp. One of the beer-brewers saw him and hurried in alarm to her friend.

"The husband is back," she whispered fearfully, pulling Life to 33 one side.

"Agh," she replied irritably.

She did dispel the noise, the men, and the drink, but a wild anger 34 was driving her to break out of a way of life that was like death to her. She told one of the men she'd see him at six o'clock. At about five o'clock Lesego drove into the yard with the calves. There was no one immediately around to greet him. He jumped out of the truck and walked to one of the huts, pushing open the door. Life was sitting on the bed. She looked up silently and sullenly. He was a little surprised but his mind was still distracted by the calves. He had to settle them in the yard for the night.

"Will you make some tea," he said. "I'm very thirsty."   35

"There's no sugar in the house," she said. "I'll have to get some."

Something irritated him but he hurried back to the calves and his 36 wife walked out of the yard. Lesego had just settled the calves when a neighbour walked in, he was very angry.

"Lesego," he said bluntly, "we told you not to marry that woman. 37 If you go the yard of Radithobolo now you'll find her in bed with him. Go and see for yourself that you may leave that bad woman!"

Lesego stared quietly at him for a moment, then at his own pace as 38 though there were no haste or chaos in his life, he went to the hut they used as a kitchen. A tin full of sugar stood there. He turned and found a knife in the corner, one of the large ones he used for slaughtering cattle, and slipped it into his shirt. Then at his own pace he walked to the yard of Radithobolo. It looked deserted, except that the door of one of the huts was partially open and one closed. He kicked open the door of the closed hut and the man within shouted out in alarm. On seeing Lesego he sprang cowering into a corner. Lesego jerked his head back indicating that the man should leave the room. But Radithobolo did not run far. He wanted to enjoy himself so he pressed himself into the shadows of the rubber hedge. He expected the usual husband-and-wife scene—the irate husband cursing at the top of his voice; the wife, hysterical in her lies and self-defence. Only Lesego walked out of the yard and he held in his hand a huge, bloodstained knife. On seeing the knife Radithobolo immediately fell to the ground in a dead faint. There were a few people on the foot-path and they shrank into the rubber hedge at the sight of that knife.

Very soon a wail arose. People clutched at their heads and began 39 running in all directions crying yo! yo! yo! in their shock. It was some time before anyone thought of calling the police. They were so disordered because murder, outright and violent, was a most uncommon and rare occurrence in village life. It seemed that only Lesego kept cool that evening. He was sitting quietly in his yard when the whole police force came tearing in. They looked at him in horror and began to thoroughly upbraid him for looking so unperturbed.

"You have taken a human life and you are cool like that!" they said 40 angrily. "You are going to hang by the neck for this. It's a serious crime to take a human life."

He did not hang by the neck. He kept that cool, head-above-water 41 indifferent look, right up to the day of his trial. Then he looked up at the judge and said calmly, "Well, the truth about this matter is, I had just returned from the cattle-post. I had had trouble with my calves that day. I came home late and being thirsty, asked my wife to make me tea. She said there was no sugar in the house and left to buy some. My neighbour, Mathata, came in after this and said that my wife was not at the shops but in the yard of Radithobolo. He said I ought to go and see what she was doing in the yard of Radithobolo. I thought I would check up about the sugar first and in the kitchen I found a tin full of it. I was sorry and surprised to see this. Then a fire seemed to fill my heart. I thought that if she was doing a bad thing with Radithobolo as Mathata said, I'd better kill her because I cannot understand a wife who could be so corrupt . . ."

Lesego had been doing this for years, passing judgement on all aspects of life in his straightforward, uncomplicated way. The judge, who was a white man, and therefore not involved in Tswana custom and its debates, was as much impressed by Lesego's manner as all the village men had been. 42

"This is a crime of passion," he said sympathetically, "so there are extenuating circumstances. But it is still a serious crime to take a human life so I sentence you to five years' imprisonment . . ." 43

Lesego's friend, Sianana, who was to take care of his business affairs while he was in jail, came to visit Lesego still shaking his head. Something was eluding him about the whole business, as though it had been planned from the very beginning. 44

"Lesego," he said, with deep sorrow, "why did you kill that fuckabout? You had legs to walk away. You could have walked away. Are you trying to show us that rivers never cross here? There are good women and good men but they seldom join their lives together. It's always this mess and foolishness . . ." 45

A song by Jim Reeves was very popular at that time: *That's What Happens When Two Worlds Collide.* When they were drunk, the beer-brewing women used to sing it and start weeping. Maybe they had the last word on the whole affair. 46

READING FOR INFORMATION

1. In your own words, explain how Life's values about money clash with the values of the women in the village.
2. Explain how the villagers try to offset what they see as "impending gloom."
3. Describe the social taboos that Life breaks.
4. Explain why "the basic strengths of village life" that satisfy the villagers are boring to Life.
5. Why do you think Lesego murdered his wife? What was his motivation?
6. How did you react to Lesego's sentence? Why was the judge so impressed by Lesego's self-defense?

READING FOR FORM, ORGANIZATION, AND EXPOSITORY FEATURES

1. Explain the function of the opening paragraph. Would the impact of the story change if it began with paragraph 2?
2. Underline the passage(s) that you think best express the story's theme.

3. Describe in your own words the central conflict of the story. What other conflicts are expressed?

4. What is the function of Sianana? How does this character contribute to the theme of the story? What would be gained or lost if Sianana were left out?

READING FOR RHETORICAL CONCERNS

1. Even though Bessie Head is a South African author writing about Botswana, the story has universal appeal. Explain how Head manages to achieve that universality.

2. What is your reaction to the beer-brewing women? How do you think Head wants her readers to view them? What evidence can you cite?

3. Explain how the story would be different if it were told from Lesego's point of view.

WRITING ASSIGNMENTS

1. Write a two- to three-page reaction to the judge's comment, "This is a crime of passion, so there are extenuating circumstances." In your reaction, explain what the story is telling you about the position of women in patriarchal societies.

2. Does this story serve to warn us against the excesses of "community," or does it show that moral pressure is an essential part of community life? Respond in an essay addressed to your classmates.

3. Use the strategies presented in Chapter 4 to write a critical analysis of the story.

SYNTHESIS WRITING ASSIGNMENTS

1. Drawing on the selections by Etzioni and Bellah et al., write an essay in which you explain the problem of excessive individualism and discuss solutions to the problem. Write three to four pages addressed to your classmates.

2. Drawing on the selections in this chapter, write a four- to five-page essay in support of the following statement by Bellah and his co-authors:

We find ourselves not independently of other people and institutions but through them. We never get to the bottom of our selves on our own. We discover who we are face to face and side by side with others in work, love, and learning. All of our activity goes on in relationships, groups, associations, and communities ordered by institutional structures and interpreted by cultural patterns of meaning (paragraph 9).

3. Write an essay discussing the points on which Etzioni, Bellah et al., and Walzer agree and disagree. Write for classmates who are familiar with the three selections.

4. Write a brief essay synthesizing what Bellah and his co-authors and Walzer have to say about the benefits and drawbacks of individualism and personal freedom.

5. Discussing the tension between "a *particularistic* and a *universalistic* approach to community" (paragraph 15), Seltser and Miller point out that Americans question whether they have obligations and responsibilities toward homeless people. In a four- to five-page synthesis essay, explain the answers that Etzioni, Bellah and his co-authors, and Walzer would give to this question.

6. Respond to Little's article in a letter addressed to the editor of *American Rifleman*. Draw on the selections by Etzioni, Bellah et al., and Walzer, if you wish.

7. Write an essay discussing how "Life" dramatizes the conflict between community and individualism. Draw on select pieces from this chapter to support your points.

C H A P T E R

t w e l v e

Rock Music
and Cultural Values

In the mid-Fifties when rock and roll was born, much of it was considered countercultural and most of it found a hostile reception. A half century later, it is consumed by the masses and solidly established as a major component of popular culture. As the essays in this chapter suggest, however, even though rock has been integrated into the mainstream culture and become respectable, it is still the subject of controversy. These essays exemplify some of the arguments in the controversy.

The selections in this chapter begin with a discussion of aesthetics. Simon Frith's article, "Toward an Aesthetic of Popular Music," asks, "How do we make value judgments about popular music?" Frith explains that we value music when it fulfills such social functions as giving us an identity, enabling us to manage our feelings, and offering us a sense of time and place. An essay by Camille Paglia argues that rock is a legitimate Romantic art form and as such, it deserves the same respect and national funding we give to composers and sculptors. Paglia claims that college and university education and continued financial support will enable rock musicians to immerse themselves in their art, to experiment, and thereby to resist the temptations of market forces and commercialism. Theodore A. Gracyk challenges Paglia's position. In "Romanticizing Rock Music," he cautions against associating rock music with Romanticism and he challenges the proposal to train rock musicians as we train other artists. He concludes that rock does not possess the virtues of Romantic art, nor is it firmly rooted in folk music.

It is an artistic expression of the masses, and it is a great mistake to make it elitist and academic.

The next essay rails against rock. Calling it "All Junk, All the Time," Richard Brookhiser attacks it as an ubiquitous form of popular culture that is simplistic and crude. The last article in this chapter focuses on rap music. In "Redeeming the Rap Music Experience," Venise Berry examines the sex, violence, and racism of its lyrics in the context of urban Afro-American youth. She contends that the rap genre "serves as a bridge from favorite songs and artists to personal and social realities" and in so doing empowers low-income black youth.

Toward an Aesthetic of Popular Music

Simon Frith

Simon Frith is a professor in the Department of English Studies at he University of Strathclyde, Glasgow, Scotland. He has published numerous articles on the sociology of music and major studies of popular music institutions and aesthetics, including Sound Effects *and* Performing Rites.

PREREADING

What is your preferred style of music? Who are your favorite musicians, singers, or groups? Why does their sound appeal to you more than the sound of others? Do you think some types of music are better than others? Why or why not?

INTRODUCTION: THE "VALUE" OF POPULAR MUSIC

Underlying all the other distinctions critics draw between "serious" and "popular" music is an assumption about the source of musical value. Serious music matters because it transcends social forces; popular music is aesthetically worthless because it is determined by them (because it is "useful" or "utilitarian"). This argument, common enough   1

Frith, Simon. *Toward an Aesthetic of Popular Music.* In *Music and Society: The Politics of Composition, Performance, and Reception.* Ed. Richard Leppert and Susan McClary. New York: Cambridge UP, 1987. 113–49. Reprinted with the permission of Cambridge University Press.

among academic musicologists, puts sociologists in an odd position. If we venture to suggest that the value of, say, Beethoven's music can be explained by the social conditions determining its production and subsequent consumption we are dismissed as philistines—aesthetic theories of classical music remain determinedly non-sociological. Popular music, by contrast, is taken to be good only for sociological theory. Our very success in explaining the rise of rock 'n' roll or the appearance of disco proves their lack of aesthetic interest. To relate music and society becomes, then, a different task according to the music we are treating. In analyzing serious music, we have to uncover the social forces concealed in the talk of "transcendent" values; in analyzing pop, we have to take seriously the values scoffed at in the talk of social functions.

In this paper I will concentrate on the second issue; my particular 2 concern is to suggest that the sociological approach to popular music does not rule out an aesthetic theory but, on the contrary, makes one possible. At first sight this proposition is unlikely. There is no doubt that sociologists have tended to explain away pop music. In my own academic work I have examined how rock is produced and consumed, and have tried to place it ideologically, but there is no way that a reading of my books (or those of other sociologists) could be used to explain why some pop songs are good and others bad, why Elvis Presley is a better singer than John Denver, or why disco is a much richer musical genre than progressive rock. And yet for ten years or more I have also been a working rock critic, making such judgments as a matter of course, assuming, like all pop fans, that our musical choices matter.

Are such judgments spurious—a way of concealing from myself 3 and other consumers the ways in which our tastes are manipulated? Can it really be the case that my pleasure in a song by the group Abba carries the same aesthetic weight as someone else's pleasure in Mozart? Even to pose such a question is to invite ridicule—either I seek to reduce the "transcendent" Mozart to Abba's commercially determined level, or else I elevate Abba's music beyond any significance it can carry. But even if the pleasures of serious and popular musics are different, it is not immediately obvious that the difference is that between artistic autonomy and social utility. Abba's value is no more (and no less) bound up with an experience of transcendence than Mozart's; the meaning of Mozart is no less (and no more) explicable in terms of social forces. The question facing sociologists and aestheticians in both cases is the same: how do we make musical value judgments? How do such value judgments articulate the listening experiences involved?

The sociologist of contemporary popular music is faced with a body   4
of songs, records, stars and styles which exists because of a series of decisions, made by both producers and consumers, about what is a successful sound. Musicians write tunes and play solos; producers choose
from different sound mixes; record companies and radio programmers
decide what should be released and played; consumers buy one record
rather than another and concentrate their attention on particular genres. The result of all these apparently individual decisions is a pattern of
success, taste and style which can be explained sociologically.

If the starting question is why does this hit sound this way, then so-   5
ciological answers can be arranged under two headings. First, there are
answers in terms of technique and technology: people produce and consume the music they are capable of producing and consuming (an obvious point, but one which opens up issues of skill, background and
education which in pop music are applied not to individual composers but
to social groups). Different groups possess different sorts of cultural capital, share different cultural expectations and so make music differently—
pop tastes are shown to correlate with class cultures and subcultures;
musical styles are linked to specific age groups; we take for granted the
connections of ethnicity and sound. This is the sociological common sense
of rock criticism, which equally acknowledges the determining role of
technology. The history of twentieth-century popular music is impossible to write without reference to the changing forces of production, electronics, the use of recording, amplification and synthesizers, just as
consumer choices cannot be separated from the possession of transistor
radios, stereo hi-fis, ghetto blasters and Walkmen.

While we can thus point to general patterns of pop use, the precise   6
link (or homology) between sounds and social groups remains unclear.
Why is rock 'n' roll youth music, whereas Dire Straits is the sound of Yuppie USA? To answer these questions there is a second sociological approach to popular music, expressed in terms of its functions. This approach
is obvious in ethnomusicology, that is in anthropological studies of traditional and folk musics which are explained by reference to their use in
dance, in rituals, for political mobilization, to solemnize ceremonies or to
excite desires. Similar points are made about contemporary pop, but its
most important function is assumed to be commercial—the starting analytical assumption is that the music is made to sell; thus research has focused on who makes marketing decisions and why, and on the construction
of "taste publics." The bulk of the academic sociology of popular music (including my own) implicitly equates aesthetic and commercial judgments.

The phenomenal 1985 successes of Madonna and Bruce Springsteen are explained, for example, in terms of sales strategies, the use of video, and the development of particular new audiences. The appeal of the music itself, the reason Madonna's and Springsteen's fans like them, somehow remains unexamined.

From the fans' perspective it is obvious that people play the music they do because it "sounds good," and the interesting question is why they have formed that opinion. Even if pop tastes are the effects of social conditioning and commercial manipulation, people still explain them to themselves in terms of value judgment. Where, in pop and rock, do these values come from? When people explain their tastes, what terms do they use? They certainly know what they like (and dislike), what pleases them and what does not. Read the music press, listen to band rehearsals and recording sessions, overhear the chatter in record shops and discos, note the ways in which disc jockeys play records, and you will hear value judgments being made. The discriminations that matter in these settings occur *within* the general sociological framework. While this allows us at a certain level to "explain" rock or disco, it is not adequate for an understanding of why one rock record or one disco track is better than another. Turn to the explanations of the fans or musicians (or even of the record companies) and a familiar argument appears. Everyone in the pop world is aware of the social forces that determine "normal" pop music—a good record, song, or sound is precisely one that transcends those forces!

The music press is the place where pop value judgments are most clearly articulated. A reading of British music magazines reveals that "good" popular music has always been heard to go beyond or break through commercial routine. This was as true for critics struggling to distinguish jazz from Tin Pan Alley pop in the 1920s and black jazz from white jazz in the 1930s as for critics asserting rock's superiority to teen pop in the late 1960s. In *Sound Effects*[1] I argued that rock's claim to a form of aesthetic autonomy rests on a combination of folk and art arguments: as folk music rock is heard to represent the community of youth, as art music rock is heard as the sound of individual, creative sensibility. The rock aesthetic depends, crucially, on an argument about authenticity. Good music is the authentic expression of something—a person, an idea, a feeling, a shared experience, a *Zeitgeist*. Bad music is inauthentic—it expresses nothing. The most common term of abuse in rock criticism is "bland"—bland music has nothing in it and is made only to be commercially pleasing.

[1] Simon Frith, *Sound Effects: Youth, Leisure and the Politics of Rock 'n' Roll* (New York, 1981).

"Authenticity" is, then, what guarantees that rock performances re-   9
sist or subvert commercial logic, just as rock-star quality (whether we are
discussing Elvis Presley or David Bowie, the Rolling Stones or the Sex Pistols), describes the power that enables certain musicians to drive something individually obdurate through the system. At this point, rock
criticism meets up with "serious" musicology. Wilfrid Mellers' scholarly
books on the Beatles and Bob Dylan,[2] for example, describe in technical
terms their subjects' transcendent qualities; but they read like fan mail
and, in their lack of self-conscious hipness, point to the contradiction at
the heart of this aesthetic approach. The suggestion is that pop music
becomes more valuable the more independent it is of the social forces
that organize the pop process in the first place; pop value is dependent
on something outside pop, is rooted in the person, the *auteur,* the community or the subculture that lies behind it. If good music is authentic
music, then critical judgment means measuring the performers' "truth"
to the experiences or feelings they are describing.

Rock criticism depends on myth—the myth of the youth com-   10
munity, the myth of the creative artist. The reality is that rock, like all
twentieth-century pop musics, is a commercial form, music produced
as a commodity, for a profit, distributed through mass media as mass
culture. It is in practice very difficult to say exactly who or what it is that
rock expresses or who, from the listener's point of view, are the authentically creative performers. The myth of authenticity is, indeed,
one of rock's own ideological effects, an aspect of its sales process: rock
stars can be marketed as artists, and their particular sounds marketed
as a means of identity. Rock criticism is a means of legitimating tastes,
justifying value judgments, but it does not really explain how those
judgments came to be made in the first place. If the music is not, in fact,
made according to the "authentic" story, then the question becomes
how we are able to judge some sounds as more authentic than others:
what are we actually listening for in making our judgments? How do we
know Bruce Springsteen is more authentic than Duran Duran, when
both make records according to the rules of the same complex industry? And how do we recognize good sounds in non-rock genres, in pop
forms like disco that are not described in authentic terms in the first
place? The question of the value of pop music remains to be answered.

---

[2] Wilfrid Mellers, *Twilight of the Gods: The Beatles in Retrospect* (London, 1973), and *A Darker
Shade of Pale: A Backdrop to Bob Dylan* (London, 1984).

AN ALTERNATIVE APPROACH TO MUSIC AND SOCIETY

In an attempt to answer these questions I want to suggest an alterna- 11
tive approach to musical value, to suggest different ways of defining
"popular music" and "popular culture." The question we should be asking is not what does popular music *reveal* about "the people" but how
does it *construct* them. If we start with the assumption that pop is expressive, then we get bogged down in the search for the "real" artist or
emotion or belief lying behind it. But popular music is popular not because it reflects something, or authentically articulates some sort of
popular taste or experience, but because it creates our understanding
of what popularity is. The most misleading term in cultural theory is,
indeed, "authenticity." What we should be examining is not how true a
piece of music is to something else, but how it sets up the idea of "truth"
in the first place—successful pop music is music which defines its own
aesthetic standard.

A simple way to illustrate the problems of defining musical popu- 12
larity is to look at its crudest measure, the weekly record sales charts in
the British music press and the American *Billboard*. These are presented
to us as market research: the charts measure something real—sales and
radio plays—and represent them with all the trimmings of an objective,
scientific apparatus. But, in fact, what the charts reveal is a specific definition of what can be counted as popular music in the first place—
record sales (in the right shops), radio plays (on the right stations). The
charts work not as the detached measure of some agreed notion of popularity, but as the most important determination of what the popularity
of popular music means—that is, a particular pattern of market choice.
The charts bring selected records together into the community of the
market place; they define certain sorts of consumption as being collective in certain sorts of ways.

The sales charts are only one measure of popularity; and when we 13
look at others, it becomes clear that their use is always for the creation
(rather than reflection) of taste communities. Readers' polls in the music
press, for example, work to give communal shape to disparate readers; the
Pazz 'n' Jop poll in *The Village Voice* creates a sense of collective commitment among the fragmented community of American rock critics.
The Grammy awards in the United States and the BPI awards in Britain,
present the industry's view of what pop music is about—nationalism and
money. These annual awards, which for most pop fans seem to miss the

point, reflect sales figures and "contributions to the recording industry" measures of popularity no less valid than readers' or critics' polls (which often deliberately honor "unpopular" acts). In comparing poll results, arguments are really not about who is more popular than whom empirically (see rock critics' outrage that Phil Collins rather than Bruce Springsteen dominated the 1986 Grammys) but about what popularity means. Each different measure measures something different or, to put it more accurately, each different measure constructs its own object of measurement. This is apparent in *Billboard*'s "specialist" charts, in the way in which "minority" musics are defined. "Women's music," for example, is interesting not as music which somehow expresses "women," but as music which seeks to define them, just as "black music" works to set up a very particular notion of what "blackness" is.

This approach to popular culture, as the creation rather than the ex-   14 pression of the people, need not be particular to music. There are numerous ways in our everyday life in which accounts of "the people" are provided. Turn on the television news and notice the ways in which a particular mode of address works, how the word "we" is used, how the word "you." Advertisers in all media are clearly in the business of explaining to us who we are, how we fit in with other people in society, why we necessarily consume the way we do. Each mass medium has its own techniques for addressing its audience, for creating moments of recognition and exclusion, for giving us our sense of ourselves. Pop music does, though, seem to play a particularly important role in the way in which popular culture works. On the one hand, it works with particularly intense emotional experiences—pop songs and pop stars mean more to us emotionally than other media events or performers, and this is not just because the pop business sells music to us through individual market choices. On the other hand, these musical experiences always contain social meaning, are placed within a social context—we are not free to read anything we want into a song.

The experience of pop music is an experience of placing: in re-   15 sponding to a song, we are drawn, haphazardly, into affective and emotional alliances with the performers and with the performers' other fans. Again this also happens in other areas of popular culture. Sport, for example, is clearly a setting in which people directly experience community, feel an immediate bond with other people, articulate a particular kind of collective pride (for a non-American, the most extraordinary aspect of the 1984 Olympics was the display/construction of the Reagan ideology of both the United States and patriotism). And fashion and style—both social constructions—remain the keys to the ways in which we, as individuals, present ourselves to the world: we use the public meanings of clothes to say "this is how I want to be perceived."

But music is especially important to this process of placement be- 16 cause of something specific to musical experience, namely, its direct emotional intensity. Because of its qualities of abstractness (which "serious" aestheticians have always stressed) music is an individualizing form. We absorb songs into our own lives and rhythms into our own bodies; they have a looseness of reference that makes them immediately accessible. Pop songs are open to appropriation for personal use in a way that other popular cultural forms (television soap operas, for example) are not— the latter are tied into meanings we may reject. At the same time, and equally significant, music is obviously rule-bound. We hear things as music because their sounds obey a particular, familiar logic, and for most pop fans (who are, technically, non-musical) this logic is out of our control. There is a mystery to our musical tastes. Some records and performers work for us, others do not—we know this without being able to explain it. Somebody else has set up the conventions; they are clearly social and clearly apart from us.

This interplay between personal absorption into music and the 17 sense that it is, nevertheless, something out there, something public, is what makes music so important in the cultural placing of the individual in the social. To give a mundane example, it is obviously true that in the last thirty years the idea of being a "fan," with its oddly public account of private obsessions, has been much more significant to pop music than to other forms of popular culture. This role of music is usually related to youth and youth culture, but it seems equally important to the ways in which ethnic groups in both Britain and the United States have forged particular cultural identities and is also reflected in the ways in which "classical" music originally became significant for the nineteenth-century European bourgeoisie. In all these cases music can stand for, symbolize *and* offer the immediate experience of collective identity. Other cultural forms—painting, literature, design—can articulate and show off shared values and pride, but only music can make you *feel* them.

THE SOCIAL FUNCTIONS OF MUSIC

It is now possible to move back to the starting point of this essay—the so- 18 cial functions of music and their implications for aesthetics. I will begin by outlining the four most significant ways in which pop is used and then suggest how these uses help us to understand how pop value judgments are made.

The first reason, then, we enjoy popular music is because of its use 19 in answering questions of identity: we use pop songs to create for ourselves a particular sort of self-definition, a particular place in society. The pleasure that pop music produces is a pleasure of identification—with the music we like, with the performers of that music, with the other people who like it. And it is important to note that the production of identity is also a production of non-identity—it is a process of inclusion and exclusion. This is one of the most striking aspects of musical taste. People not only know what they like, they also have very clear ideas about what they don't like and often have very aggressive ways of stating their dislikes. As all sociological studies of pop consumers have shown, pop fans define themselves quite precisely according to their musical preferences. Whether they identify with genres or stars, it seems of greater importance to people what they like musically than whether or not they enjoyed a film or a television program.

The pleasure of pop music, unlike the pleasures to be had from 20 other mass cultural forms, does not derive in any clear way from fantasy: it is not mediated through day-dreams or romancing, but is experienced directly. For example, at a heavy metal concert you can certainly see the audience absorbed in the music; yet for all the air-guitar playing they are not fantasizing being up on stage. To experience heavy metal is to experience the power of the concert as a whole—the musicians are one aspect of this, the amplification system another, the audience a third. The individual fans get their kicks from being a necessary part of the overall process—which is why heavy metal videos always have to contain moments of live performance (whatever the surrounding story line) in order to capture and acknowledge the kind of empowerment that is involved in the concert itself.

Once we start looking at different pop genres we can begin to 21 document the different ways in which music works to give people an identity, to place them in different social groups. And this is not just a feature of commercial pop music. It is the way in which all popular music works. For example, in putting together an audience, contemporary black-influenced pop clearly (and often cynically) employs musical devices originally used in religious music to define men's and women's identity before God. Folk musics, similarly, continue to be used to mark the boundaries of ethnic identity, even amidst the complications of migration and cultural change. In London's Irish pubs, for example, "traditional" Irish folk songs are still the most powerful way to make people feel Irish and consider what their "Irishness" means. (This music, this identity, is now being further explored by post-punk London Irish bands, like the Pogues.) It is not surprising, then, that popular music has always had important nationalist functions. In Abel Gance's "silent" film, *Napoleon*, there is a scene in which we see the *Marseillaise* being composed, and then watch the song make its way through the Assembly and among the crowds until everyone is singing it. When the film was first shown in France, the cinema audience rose from their seats and joined in singing their national anthem. Only music seems capable of creating this sort of spontaneous collective identity, this kind of personally felt patriotism.

Music's second social function is to give us a way of managing the 22 relationship between our public and private emotional lives. It is often noted but rarely discussed that the bulk of popular songs are love songs. This is certainly true of twentieth-century popular music in the West; but most non-Western popular musics also feature romantic, usually heterosexual, love lyrics. This is more than an interesting statistic; it is a centrally important aspect of how pop music is used. Why are love songs so important? Because people need them to give shape and voice to emotions that otherwise cannot be expressed without embarrassment or incoherence. Love songs are a way of giving emotional intensity to the sorts of intimate things we say to each other (and to ourselves) in words that are, in themselves, quite flat. It is a peculiarity of everyday language that our most fraught and revealing declarations of feeling have to use phrases—"I love/hate you," "Help me!," "I'm angry/scared"—which are boring and banal; and so our culture has a supply of a million pop songs, which say these things for us in numerous interesting and involving ways. These songs do not replace our conversations—pop singers do not do our courting for us—but they make our feelings seem richer and more convincing than we can make them appear in our own words, even to ourselves.

The only interesting sociological account of lyrics in the long tra- 23 dition of American content analysis was Donald Horton's late 1950s study[3] of how teenagers used the words of popular songs in their dating rituals. His high school sample learned from pop songs (public forms of private expression) how to make sense of and shape their

[3] Donald Horton, "The Dialogue of Courtship in Popular Songs," *American Journal of Sociology*, 62 (1957), pp. 569–78.

own inchoate feelings. This use of pop illuminates one quality of the star/fan relationship: people do not idolize singers because they wish to be them but because these singers seem able, somehow, to make available their own feelings—it is as if we get to know ourselves via the music.

The third function of popular music is to shape popular memory, to [24] organize our sense of time. Clearly one of the effects of all music, not just pop, is to intensify our experience of the present. One measure of good music, to put it another way, is, precisely, its "presence," its ability to "stop" time, to make us feel we are living within a moment, with no memory or anxiety about what has come before, what will come after. This is where the physical impact of music comes in—the use of beat, pulse and rhythm to compel our immediate bodily involvement in an organization of time that the music itself controls. Hence the pleasures of dance and disco; clubs and parties provide a setting, a society, which seems to be defined only by the time-scale of the music (the beats per minute), which escapes the real time passing outside.

One of the most obvious consequences of music's organization of [25] our sense of time is that songs and tunes are often the key to our remembrance of things past. I do not mean simply that sounds—like sights and smells—trigger associated memories, but, rather, that music in itself provides our most vivid experience of time passing. Music focuses our attention on the feeling of time; songs are organized (it is part of their pleasure) around anticipation and echo, around endings to which we look forward, choruses that build regret into their fading. Twentieth-century popular music has, on the whole, been a nostalgic form. The Beatles, for example, made nostalgic music from the start, which is why they were so popular. Even on hearing a Beatles song for the first time there was a sense of the memories to come, a feeling that this could not last but that it was surely going to be pleasant to remember.

It is this use of time that makes popular music so important in the [26] social organization of youth. It is a sociological truism that people's heaviest personal investment in popular music is when they are teenagers and young adults—music then ties into a particular kind of emotional turbulence, when issues of individual identity and social place, the control of public and private feelings, are at a premium. People do use music less, and less intently, as they grow up; the most significant pop songs for all generations (not just for rock generations) are those they heard as adolescents. What this suggests, though, is not just that young people need music, but that "youth" itself is defined by music. Youth is experienced, that is, as an intense presence, through an impatience for time to pass and a regret that it is doing so, in a series of speeding, physically insistent moments that have nostalgia coded into them. This is to reiterate my general point about popular music: youth music is socially important not because it reflects youth experience (authentically or not), but because it defines for us what "youthfulness" is. I remember concluding, in my original sociological research in the early 1970s, that those young people who, for whatever reasons, took no interest in pop music were not really "young."

The final function of popular music I want to mention here is something more abstract than the issues discussed so far, but a consequence of all of them: popular music is something possessed. One of the first things I learned as a rock critic—from abusive mail—was that rock fans "owned" their favorite music in ways that were intense and important to them. To be sure, the notion of musical ownership is not peculiar to rock—Hollywood cinema has long used the clichéd line, "they're playing our song"—and this reflects something that is recognizable to all music lovers and is an important aspect of the way in which everyone thinks and talks about "their" music. (British radio has programs of all sorts built around people's explanations of why certain records "belong" to them.) Obviously it is the commodity form of music which makes this sense of musical possession possible, but it is not just the record that people think they own: we feel that we also possess the song itself, the particular performance, and its performer. 27

In "possessing" music, we make it part of our own identity and build it into our sense of ourselves. To write pop criticism is, as I have mentioned, to attract hate mail; mail not so much defending the performer or performance criticized as defending the letter writer: criticize a star and the fans respond as if you have criticized them. The biggest mail bag I ever received was after I had been critical of Phil Collins. Hundreds of letters arrived (not from teenyboppers or gauche adolescents, but from young professionals) typed neatly on headed notepaper, all based on the assumption that in describing Collins as ugly, Genesis as dull, I was deriding their way of life, undermining their identity. The intensity of this relationship between taste and self-definition seems peculiar to popular music—it is "possessable" in ways that other cultural forms (except, perhaps, sports teams) are not. 28

To summarize the argument so far: the social functions of popular music are in the creation of identity, in the management of feelings, in the organization of time. Each of these functions depends, in turn, on our 29

experience of music as something which can be possessed. From this sociological base it is now possible to get at aesthetic questions, to understand listeners' judgments, to say something about the value of pop music.
My starting question was how is it that people (myself included) can say,
quite confidently, that some popular music is better than others? The
answer can now be related to how well (or badly), for specific listeners,
songs and performances fulfill the suggested functions. But there is a
final point to make about this. It should be apparent by now that people
do hear the music they like as something special: not, as orthodox rock
criticism would have it, because this music is more "authentic" (though
that may be how it is described), but because, more directly, it seems to
provide an experience that transcends the mundane, that takes us "out
of ourselves." It is special, that is, not necessarily with reference to other
music, but to the rest of life. This sense of specialness, the way in which
music seems to make possible a new kind of self-recognition, frees us
from the everyday routines and expectations that encumber our social
identities, is a key part of the way in which people experience and thus
value music: if we believe we possess our music, we also often feel that
we are possessed by it. Transcendence is, then, as much a part of the
popular music aesthetic as it is of the serious music aesthetic; but, as I
hope I have indicated, in pop, transcendence marks not music's freedom
from social forces but its patterning by them. (Of course, in the end the
same is true of serious music, too.)

THE AESTHETICS OF POPULAR MUSIC

I want to conclude with another sort of question: what are the factors in   30
popular music that enable it to fulfill these social functions, which determine whether it does so well or badly? Again, I will divide my answer
into four points; my purpose is less to develop them in depth than to suggest important issues for future critical work.

   My first point is brief, because it raises musicological issues which   31
I am not competent to develop. The most important (and remarkable)
feature of Western popular music in the twentieth century has been its
absorption of and into Afro-American forms and conventions. In analytical terms, to follow the distinction developed by Andrew Chester at the
end of the 1960s, this means that pop is complex "intentionally" rather
than, like European art music, "extensionally." In the extensional form of
musical construction, argues Chester, "theme and variations, counter-
point, tonality (as used in classical composition) are all devices that build

diachronically and synchronically outwards from basic musical atoms. The complex is created by combination of the simple, which remains discrete and unchanged in the complex unity." In the intentional mode, "the basic musical units (played/sung notes) are not combined through space and time as simple elements into complex structures. The simple entity is that constituted by the parameters of melody, harmony and beat, while the complex is built up by modulation of the basic notes, and by inflexion of the basic beat."[4] Whatever the problems of Chester's simple dichotomy between a tradition of linear musical development and a tradition of piled-up rhythmic interplay, he does pose the most important musicological question for popular music: how can we explain the *intensity* of musical experience that Afro-American forms have made possible? We still do not know nearly enough about the musical language of pop and rock: rock critics still avoid technical analysis, while sympathetic musicologists, like Wilfrid Mellers, use tools that can only cope with pop's non-intentional (and thus least significant) qualities.

My second point is that the development of popular music in this 32 century has increasingly focused on the use of the voice. It is through the singing voice that people are most able to make a connection with their records, to feel that performances are theirs in certain ways. It is through the voice that star personalities are constructed (and since World War II, at least, the biggest pop stars have been singers). The tone of voice is more important in this context than the actual articulation of particular lyrics—which means, for example, that groups, like the Beatles, can take on a group voice. We can thus identify with a song whether we understand the words or not, whether we already know the singer or not, because it is the voice—not the lyrics—to which we immediately respond. This raises questions about popular non-vocal music, which can be answered by defining a voice as a sign of individual personality rather than as something necessarily mouthing words. The voice, for example, was and is central to the appeal of jazz, not through vocalists as such, but through the way jazz people played and heard musical instruments— Louis Armstrong's or Charlie Parker's instrumental voices were every bit as individual and personal as a pop star's singing voice.

Today's commercial pop musics are, though, song forms, con- 33 structing vocal personalities, using voices to speak directly to us. From this perspective it becomes possible to look at pop songs as narratives, to use

[4] Andrew Chester, "Second Thoughts on a Rock Aesthetic: The Band," *New Left Review,* 62 (1970), pp. 78–9.

literary critical and film critical terms to analyze them. It would be fairly straightforward, for example, to make some immediate genre distinctions, to look at the different ways in which rock, country, reggae, etc. work as narratives, the different ways they set up star personalities, situate the listener, and put in play patterns of identity and opposition. Of course, popular music is not simply analogous to film or literature. In discussing the narrative devices of contemporary pop in particular, we are not just talking about music but also about the whole process of packaging. The image of pop performers is constructed by press and television advertisements, by the routines of photo-calls and journalists' interviews, and through gesture and performance. These things all feed into the way we hear a voice; pop singers are rarely heard "plain" (without mediation). Their vocals already contain physical connotations, associated images, echoes of other sounds. All this needs to be analyzed if we are going to treat songs as narrative structures; the general point, to return to a traditional musicological concern, is that while music may not represent anything, it nevertheless clearly communicates.

The third point is an elaboration of the suggestion I have just made: 34 popular music is wide open for the development of a proper genre analysis, for the classification of how different popular musical forms use different narrative structures, set up different patterns of identity, and articulate different emotions. Take, for example, the much discussed issue of music and sexuality. In the original article on rock and sexuality I wrote with Angela McRobbie at the end of the 1970s,[5] we set up a distinction between "cock" rock and teenybop narratives, each working to define masculinity and femininity but for different audiences and along different contours of feeling. Our distinctions are still valid but we were looking only at a subdivision of one pop genre. Other musical forms articulate sexuality in far more complicated ways; thus it would be impossible to analyze the sexuality of either Frank Sinatra or Billie Holiday, and their place in the history of crooning and torch singing, in the terms of the "cock" rock/teenybop contrast. Even Elvis Presley does not fit easily into these 1970s accounts of male and female sexuality.

The question these examples raise is how popular musical genres 35 should be defined. The obvious approach is to follow the distinctions made by the music industry which, in turn, reflect both musical history and marketing categories. We can thus divide pop into country music, soul music, rock 'n' roll, punk, MOR, show songs, etc. But an equally interesting way

[5] Simon Frith and Angela McRobbie, "Rock and Sexuality," *Screen Education* 29 (1978/9), pp. 3–19.

of approaching genres is to classify them according to their ideological effects, the way they sell themselves as art, community or emotion. There is at present, for example, clearly a form of rock we can call "authentic." It is represented by Bruce Springsteen and defines itself according to the rock aesthetic of authenticity which I have already discussed. The whole point of this genre is to develop musical conventions which are, in themselves, measures of "truth." As listeners we are drawn into a certain sort of reality: this is what it is like to live in America, this is what it is like to love or hurt. The resulting music is the pop equivalent of film theorists' "classic realist text." It has the same effect of persuading us that this is how things really are—realism inevitably means a non-romantic account of social life, and a highly romantic account of human nature.

What is interesting, though, is how this sort of truth is constructed, 36 what it rests on musically; and for an instant semiotic guide I recommend the video of *We Are the World*. Watch how the singers compete to register the most sincerity; watch Bruce Springsteen win as he gets his brief line, veins pop up on his head and the sweat flows down. Here authenticity is guaranteed by visible physical effort.

To approach pop genres this way is to look at the pop world in terms 37 rather different from those of the music industry. Against the authentic genre, for instance, we can pitch a tradition of artifice: some pop stars, following up on David Bowie's and Roxy Music's early 1970s work, have sought to create a sense of themselves (and their listeners) as artists in cool control. There is clearly also an avant-garde within popular music, offering musicians and listeners the pleasures of rule breaking, and a sentimental genre, celebrating codes of emotion which everyone knows are not real but carry nostalgic weight—if only they were! What I am arguing here is that it is possible to look at pop genres according to the effects they pursue. Clearly we can then judge performers within genres (is John Cougar Mellencamp's music as truthful as Springsteen's?), as well as use different genres for different purposes (the sentimental genre is a better source of adult love songs than the avant-garde or the artificers). To really make sense of pop genres, though, I think we need to place this grid of ideologies over the industry's grid of taste publics. To understand punk, for example, we need to trace within it the interplay of authenticity and artifice; to understand country we need to follow the interplay of authenticity and sentiment.

In everyday life we actually have a rather good knowledge of such 38 conventional confusions. To know how to listen to pop music is to know how to classify it. One thing all pop listeners do, whether as casual fans or professional critics, is to compare sounds—to say that A is like B. Indeed, most pop criticism works via the implicit recognition of genre rules, and this brings me to my final point. Our experience of music in everyday life is not just through the organized pop forms I have been discussing. We live in a much more noisy soundscape; music of all sorts is in a constant play of association with images, places, people, products, moods, and so on. These associations, in commercial and film soundtracks, for example, are so familiar that for much of the time we forget that they are "accidental." We unthinkingly associate particular sounds with particular feelings and landscapes and times. To give a crude example, in Britain it is impossible now for a ballet company to perform the *Nutcracker Suite* for an audience of children without them all, at the key moment, breaking into song: "Everyone's a fruit and nut case," has been instilled into them as a Cadbury's jingle long before the children hear of Tchaikovsky. Classical or "serious" music, in short, is not exempt from social use. It is impossible for me, brought up in post-war popular culture, to hear Chopin without immediately feeling a vaguely romantic yearning, the fruit of many years of Chopinesque film soundtracks.

There is no way to escape these associations. Accordions played a 39 certain way mean France, bamboo flutes China, just as steel guitars mean country, drum machines the urban dance. No sort of popular musician can make music from scratch—what we have these days instead are scratch mixers, fragmenting, unpicking, reassembling music from the signs that already exist, pilfering public forms for new sorts of private vision. We need to understand the lumber-room of musical references we carry about with us, if only to account for the moment that lies at the heart of the pop experience, when, from amidst all those sounds out there, resonating whether we like them or not, one particular combination suddenly, for no apparent reason, takes up residence in our own lives.

CONCLUSION

In this paper I have tried to suggest a way in which we can use a sociol- 40 ogy of popular music as the basis of an aesthetic theory, to move, that is, from a description of music's social functions to an understanding of how we can and do value it (and I should perhaps stress that my definition of popular music includes popular uses of "serious" music). One of my working assumptions has been that people's individual tastes—the ways they experience and describe music for themselves—are a necessary part of academic analysis. Does this mean that the value of popular music is simply a matter of personal preference?

The usual sociological answer to this question is that "personal" preferences are themselves socially determined. Individual tastes are, in fact, examples of collective taste and reflect consumers' gender, class and ethnic backgrounds; the "popularity" of popular music can then be taken as one measure of a balance of social power. I do not want to argue against this approach. Our cultural needs and expectations are, indeed, materially based; all the terms I have been using (identity, emotion, memory) are socially formed, whether we are examining "private" or public lives. But I do believe that this derivation of pop meaning from collective experience is not sufficient. Even if we focus all our attention on the collective reception of pop, we still need to explain why some music is better able than others to have such collective effects, why these effects are different, anyway, for different genres, different audiences and different circumstances. Pop tastes do not just derive from our socially constructed identities; they also help to shape them. 41

For the last fifty years at least, pop music has been an important way in which we have learned to understand ourselves as historical, ethnic, class-bound, gendered subjects. This has had conservative effects (primarily through pop nostalgia) and liberating ones. Rock criticism has usually taken the latter as a necessary mark of good music but this has meant, in practice, a specious notion of "liberation." We need to approach this political question differently, by taking seriously pop's individualizing effects. What pop can do is put into play a sense of identity that may or may not fit the way we are placed by other social forces. Music certainly puts us in our place, but it can also suggest that our social circumstances are not immutable (and that other people—performers, fans—share our dissatisfaction). Pop music is not in itself revolutionary or reactionary. It is a source of strong feelings that because they are also socially coded can come up against "common sense." For the last thirty years, for example, at least for young people, pop has been a form in which everyday accounts of race and sex have been both confirmed and confused. It may be that, in the end, we want to value most highly that music, popular and serious, which has some sort of collective, disruptive cultural effect. My point is that music only does so through its impact on individuals. That impact is what we first need to understand. ✍ 42

READING FOR INFORMATION

1. What are Frith's views on the "authenticity" of rock music? What should we be examining instead of authenticity?
2. List the four social functions of popular music cited in the essay.
3. Frith says that four factors determine whether music will fulfill its social functions. What are these factors?
4. Summarize Frith's conclusion in paragraphs 40 to 42.

READING FOR FORM, ORGANIZATION, AND EXPOSITORY FEATURES

1. Describe the contrasts Frith sets up in the first paragraph.
2. Frith divides the article into five parts. How does each part contribute to his argument?
3. Do you think that Frith is addressing his article to a wide general audience or to specialized scholarly readers? How did you come to that conclusion?

READING FOR RHETORICAL CONCERNS

1. Explain Frith's purpose for writing the article. What does he want to achieve?
2. Find the places in the article where Frith refers to his previous work? What function do these references serve?
3. In a number of paragraphs (3, 6, 7, 10, 22, 29, 30, 31, 40), Frith poses questions. What function do the questions serve? How do they affect the reader?

WRITING ASSIGNMENTS

1. Frith says that for all people the most significant pop songs "are those they heard as adolescents" (paragraph 26). Which songs are most memorable to you? What memories do these songs trigger? Write an essay in which you recall songs and experiences and reflect upon the meaning they hold for you.
2. As a prereading question, we asked you to explain why some types of music are better than others. Reread your response. Rewrite your response in light of Frith's argument, explaining how well specific songs and performances fulfill various social functions for you.
3. Write an essay in which you agree or disagree with Frith's statement, "Pop tastes do not just derive from our socially constructed identities; they also help shape them" (paragraph 41).

Rock as Art

Camille Paglia

Camille Paglia teaches humanities at the University of the Arts in Philadelphia and is the author of Sexual Personae *(1990),* Sex, Art, and American Culture *(1991), and* Vamps and Tramps: New Essays *(1994).*

PREREADING

> Write a reaction to Paglia's two opening sentences. Do you agree that rock musicians are the country's "most wasted natural resource"? Why or why not?

 Rock is eating its young. Rock musicians are America's most 1
wasted natural resource.

Popular music and film are the two great art forms of the twentieth 2
century. In the past twenty-five years, cinema has gained academic prestige. Film courses are now a standard part of the college curriculum and grants are routinely available to noncommercial directors.

But rock music has yet to win the respect it deserves as the au- 3
thentic voice of our time. Where rock goes, democracy follows. The dark poetry and surging Dionysian rhythms of rock have transformed the consciousness and permanently altered the sensoriums of two generations of Americans born after World War Two.

Rock music should not be left to the Darwinian laws of the mar- 4
ketplace. This natively American art form deserves national support. Foundations, corporations and Federal and state agencies that award grants in the arts should take rock musicians as seriously as composers and sculptors. Colleges and universities should designate special scholarships for talented rock musicians. Performers who have made fortunes out of rock are ethically obligated to finance such scholarships or to underwrite independent agencies to support needy musicians.

In rock, Romanticism still flourishes. All the Romantic arche- 5
types of energy, passion, rebellion and demonism are still evident in the

Paglia, Camille. "Rock as Art." *New York Times* 16 Apr. 1992: A23. Copyright © 1992 by The New York Times Co. Reprinted by permission.

brawling, boozing bad boys of rock, storming from city to city on their lusty, groupie-dogged trail.

But the Romantic outlaw must have something to rebel against. 6 The pioneers of rock were freaks, dreamers and malcontents who drew their lyricism and emotional power from the gritty rural traditions of white folk music and African-American blues.

Rock is a victim of its own success. What once signified rebellion is 7 now only a high-school affectation. White suburban youth, rock's main audience, is trapped in creature comforts. Everything comes to them secondhand, through TV. And they no longer have direct contact with folk music and blues, the oral repository of centuries of love, hate, suffering and redemption.

In the Sixties, rock became the dominant musical form in Amer- 8 ica. And with the shift from singles to albums, which allowed for the marketing of personalities, it also became big business. The gilded formula froze into place. Today, scouts beat the bushes for young talent, squeeze a quick album out of the band, and put them on the road. "New" material is stressed. Albums featuring cover tunes of classics, as in the early Rolling Stones records, are discouraged.

From the moment the Beatles could not hear themselves sing over 9 the shrieking at Shea Stadium in the mid-Sixties, the rock concert format has become progressively less conducive to music-making. The enormous expense of huge sound systems and grandiose special effects has left no room for individualism and improvisation, no opportunity for the performers to respond to a particular audience or to their own moods. The show, with its army of technicians, is as fixed and rehearsed as the Ziegfeld Follies. Furthermore, the concert experience has degenerated. The focus has switched from the performance to raucous partying in the audience.

These days, rock musicians are set upon by vulture managers, who 10 sanitize and repackage them and strip them of their unruly free will. Like sports stars, musicians are milked to the max, then dropped and cast aside when their first album doesn't sell.

Managers offer all the temptations of Mammon to young rock 11 bands: wealth, fame, and easy sex. There is not a single public voice in the culture to say to the musician: You are an artist, not a money machine. Don't sign the contract. Don't tour. Record only when you are ready. Go off on your own, like Jimi Hendrix, and live with your guitar until it becomes part of your body.

How should an artist be trained? Many English rock musicians in 12 the Sixties and early Seventies, including John Lennon and Keith

Richards, emerged from art schools. We must tell the young musician: Your peers are other artists, past and future. Don't become a slave to the audience, with its smug hedonism, short attention span and hunger for hits.

Artists should immerse themselves in art. Two decades ago, rock 13 musicians read poetry, studied Hinduism, and drew psychedelic visions in watercolors. For rock to move forward as an art form, our musicians must be given the opportunity for spiritual development. They should be encouraged to read, to look at paintings and foreign films, to listen to jazz and classical music.

Artists with a strong sense of vocation can survive life's disasters 14 and triumphs with their inner lives intact. Our musicians need to be rescued from the carpetbaggers and gold-diggers who attack them when they are young and naïve. Long, productive careers don't happen by chance. ✍

READING FOR INFORMATION

1. According to Paglia, what type of support does rock music deserve?
2. Explain why, according to Paglia, rock is an art in the Romantic tradition.
3. How has rock changed since the 1960s?
4. How has it become "big business"?
5. How should rock musicians be educated?

READING FOR FORM, ORGANIZATION, AND EXPOSITORY FEATURES

1. What is the effect on the reader of the two opening sentences? Why do you think Paglia begins the piece in this way?
2. How does Paglia structure her argument? Construct a graphic overview (see pp. 24–25) of the selection.
3. How does Paglia conclude the piece?

READING FOR RHETORICAL CONCERNS

1. Whom do you think Paglia visualizes as her audience? How does she expect her readers to view rock musicians after they have read this piece?
2. How would you characterize Paglia's voice? What does it suggest about the author?

WRITING ASSIGNMENTS

1. Write an essay in which you agree or disagree with Paglia's statement that today rock is "only a high-school affectation," whereas in the past it was the music of rebellion.

2. Write a brief essay evaluating Paglia's argument. Mention its strengths and weaknesses and explain how well Paglia supports her points.

3. Compare Paglia's comments about the commercialization of rock music with those of Frith in "Toward an Aesthetic of Popular Music."

Romanticizing Rock Music

Theodore A. Gracyk

Theodore A. Gracyk is an associate professor of philosophy at Moorhead State University. He has published Rhythm and Noise: An Aesthetics of Rock *and articles in the* Musical Quarterly, *the* International Philosophical Quarterly, *and the* British Journal of Aesthetics.

PREREADING

Before you read this article, take a few minutes to respond to the title. Do you recall reading Romantic poetry by such writers as Byron, Shelley, Wordsworth, Coleridge, and Keats in high school and college literature classes? How would you characterize that poetry? Would you say that rock music has some of the same characteristics?

If now we reflect that music at its greatest intensity must seek to attain also to its highest symbolization, we must deem it possible that it also knows how to find the symbolic expression for its unique Dionysian wisdom.

—Nietzsche, *The Birth of Tragedy*

To the extent that theorists are willing to treat rock music as art, most of them consider it popular art rather than fine art. But several recent writers contend that rock music is a manifestation of the

Gracyk, Theodore A. "Romanticizing Rock Music." From *Journal of Aesthetic Education* 27.2 (Summer 1993): 43–58. Copyright 1993 by the Board of Trustees of the University of Illinois. Used with permission of the University of Illinois Press.

aesthetics of Romanticism and as such can be understood in terms of the same categories that are applied to artists who produce fine art. We are invited to conclude that rock musicians deserve the same respect as such poets as Wordsworth and Byron and such musicians as Chopin and Liszt, because the accomplishment of the Rolling Stones is of the same type as that of these nineteenth-century precursors. The major obstacle to admitting that rock musicians are important artists is supposedly the common confusion of a commercial product ("pop" music) with rock music.

Another manifestation of the aesthetics of Romanticism is the idea   2
that rock music is not fine art, but rather modern urban folk music.[1] As one rock critic put it, "It is just because they didn't worry about art that many of the people who ground out the rock-and-roll of the fifties—not only the performers, but all the background people—were engaged (unconsciously, of course) in making still another kind of art, folk art."[2] Again, a distinction is to be made between popular art, an inauthentic exploitation of the masses, and this modern folk art. Yet another position, to be considered at length in this essay, brings the two strands together in the claim that rock possesses the virtues of Romantic art while drawing much of its power from its folk music roots.

Tied to each of these positions is an attempt to bring rock music   3
into the domains of art and aesthetic education. (At present, academic attention on rock is almost entirely sociological in perspective.) While I sympathize with attempts to locate an aesthetic of rock music, I do not believe that Romanticism is the right model. And it is an even greater mistake to believe that rock musicians should be trained according to the model for educating other artists.

I

The boldest and most uncompromising of those who would romanti-   4
cize rock is Camille Paglia. She contends that it is time to accept rock musicians as legitimate artists and to treat rock as we treat other arts, supporting it directly with government subsidies and private grants and indirectly through special college scholarships. Paglia calls for a return to rock's past glories, when the music was rebellious, vital, and pulsating with "surging Dionysian rhythms."[3] It turns out that, like Nietzsche, she does not regard the masses as capable of appreciating true art when they encounter it. But unlike Nietzsche, she does not give us any sense that the highest art will be a fusion of the Dionysian and Apollonian strains.

Paglia's argument is worth considering because it adopts, without criticism, the prevailing story of rock music. Except for her proposal that we treat rock musicians as full-fledged artists, she depends on common assumptions, so common that most rock fans would probably applaud her endorsement and ignore the distortions, half-truths, and stereotypes. The story is this: "The pioneers of rock were freaks, dreamers and malcontents" who drew on an authentic tradition of "white folk music and African-American blues." The sixties were rock's golden age, when rock musicians drew their inspiration from poetry and Eastern religions. (She doesn't point out that groups like Steppenwolf, Mott the Hoople, and Steely Dan got their names from literary works, but I assume that that's the sort of thing she has in mind.) Above all, rock musicians were the inheritors of Romanticism. They were outlaws, "storming from city to city on their lusty, groupie-dogged trail." Because she regards them as sensitive artists, Paglia here brushes over the fact that she's really talking about their sexual exploitation of women, many of them underage.

But rock soon fell victim to capitalism. Market forces corrupted rock. Paglia offers three pieces of evidence. First, the authentic source is lost; neither fans nor musicians have direct knowledge of folk music and blues, "the oral repository of centuries of love, hate, suffering and redemption." Second, live performance has atrophied, leaving no room for spontaneous musical expression or artist-audience interaction. Once it was a performing art, with the focus on the performance. Now it is a mere show—fully rehearsed and with no room for artistic spontaneity—and an excuse for partying. Third, greedy and manipulative managers exploit innocent young artists, turning them from self-expression to pandering to crass commercial interests, "milking" them for profit in exchange for "wealth, fame and easy sex." Knowingly or not, Paglia is paraphrasing Bob Geldof's remark that people join rock bands for "three very simple rock and roll reasons: to get laid, to get fame, and to get rich."[4]

Her remedy? Divorce rock from the commercial marketplace. We should provide an escape from the commercial interests that divert rock artists from serious music making. Like classical musicians, rock musicians must relocate to colleges and universities. (Was Bob Dylan ahead of his time when, on his debut, he introduced a traditional song as having been acquired among the fair fields of Harvard?) Supported by government and private grants, prestige and artistic freedom will follow, compensating the musicians for the lost wealth, fame, and sex. After all, Paglia notes, both Keith Richards and John Lennon attended English "art schools."

Never mind that they were barely able to obtain passing grades and that the schools were as much trade schools as art institutes; perhaps we should instead be satisfied that Mick Jagger went to the London School of Economics and Lou Reed studied with poet Delmore Schwarz. Complementing their musical studies with art history and literature, a liberal arts education will guide rock musicians' spiritual development, and rock will recover as the "authentic voice of our times."

Charming as this is, it disintegrates when we go through it one claim at a time. Let us start with the pioneers of rock as Romantic archetypes. Paglia offers no examples, but obvious cases would have to include Bill Haley, Elvis Presley, Chuck Berry, Little Richard, Bo Diddley, Carl Perkins, Buddy Holly, Jerry Lee Lewis, Fats Domino, and Ray Charles.[5] While this may be a list of freaks and dreamers, their dreams were mostly about making hit records and a lot of money. They were hardly malcontents, unless being an African American or poor Southern white in the nineteen-fifties automatically qualified one. If anything, they represent the American underclass of the period, seeking respectability in money and fame. Perhaps Paglia is thinking of the sixties and its political posturing, but at that point we are already far from the folk and blues roots that she identifies as the source of their authenticity and expressive power.

The rebellion of rock's pioneers was of the James Dean variety, strictly adolescent. If we are to believe any of the prevailing *sociological* analysis of rock, it tells us this:

> What mattered about rock 'n' roll in the 1950s was its youth; its expression of a community of interest between performer and audience; and its account of a generation bound by age and taste in a gesture of self-celebration, in defiance against the nagging, adult routines of home and work and school. . . . rock 'n' roll stardom soon became a matter of the youth voice and the youth song, so that Elvis Presley became rock 'n' roll's superstar because he so clearly *represented* his listeners and Chuck Berry became the most successful R & B performer to adapt its loose limbed lyrics to the interests of the white, teenaged record-buyer.[6]

It was also rooted in a very American desire for material comforts like a sharp wardrobe (blue suede shoes immediately come to mind) and a pink Cadillac. Paglia complains that rock's original rebellion has been reduced to "high-school affectation." Yet search as we might through early rock, the only *social* protest comes mainly from Chuck Berry, and it was *very* high school: "School Days," "Too Much Monkey Business," and

"No Particular Place to Go." The Coasters' "Yakety Yak" and Eddie Cochran's "Summertime Blues" likewise gave voice to teens' railing against parental authority. There is occasional social commentary, but it is fairly mild, as in the undercurrent of black pride in Chuck Berry's "Brown-Eyed Handsome Man" or the Coaster's "Shopping for Clothes" and "Framed" (both written by the white production team of Leiber and Stoller).

Her complaint is also odd in light of analyses given by Nik Cohn   10 and Carl Belz. Writing in the late sixties, Cohn reflected the prevalent British enthusiasm for rock and American "pop" *as* reflections of America. He praised rock because it voiced teen concerns; the best popular music, he wrote, "is all teenage property and it mirrors everything that happens to teenagers in this time, in this American 20th century. It is about clothes and cars and dancing, it's about parents and high school."[7] Carl Belz, defending a view of rock as modern folk music, praised Chuck Berry for "unconsciously" expressing the "ordinary realities of their world: . . . cars, girls, growing up, school, or music."[8] Rock's decline started, on these analyses, when the Beatles and others turned to self-expression and musical experimentation for its own sake. The point is not whether Cohn and Belz are right and Paglia is wrong; both seem rather simplistic. The point is that to many at the time, rock and roll had always been the music of teenagers, and only later did it develop affectations toward art. So Paglia's alternative story of rock's decline, as a shift from genuine rebellion to high school values, sounds like selective memory that focuses on the late 1960s rather than rock's first decade as the point for all comparisons. As such, it is too hopelessly slanted to form the basis for any argument that appeals to rock's special strengths.

It is also hard to believe that only *subsequent* rock musicians were   11 corrupted by money, fame, and sex. If rock's pioneers had any consistent message, it was a desire for sex. As critic Dave Marsh says of Buddy Holly's 1957 hit "Oh Boy," "Edgy and excited, he sings the opening way too fast. . . . But as he jitters along, the cause of Buddy's nervousness becomes clear: He's about to get laid. Probably for the very first time."[9] There is Hank Ballard's widely banned "Work with Me, Annie," Elvis Presley's cover of "Good Rockin' Tonight," Chuck Berry's less overt "Carol," and hundreds of others that relied on innuendo to make their point. Anyone who has seen Martin Scorsese's *The Last Waltz* knows that easy sex could be a powerful incentive to becoming a rock musician. In one of the interview sequences, Robbie Robertson and the others who were to become The Band confess that they hit the road with Canadian rockabilly singer Ronnie Hawkins because he promised them more groupies than Frank Sinatra had.

As for fame, when the musicians who became three-fourths of the 12 Beatles were depressed and ready to throw in the towel, John Lennon rallied them with a chant. He would say, "Where are we going, fellows?" and they answered, "To the top, Johnny" in American accents, followed by, "Where is that, fellows?" and, "To the toppermost of the poppermost."[10] In other words, they were going to the top of the record (pop) charts. Why the faked American accents? Because, as Lennon said, "Elvis was the biggest. We wanted to be the biggest, doesn't everybody? . . . Elvis was the thing. Whatever people say, he was it."[11] Paglia's complaints about managers who take advantage of innocent young musicians date from this same period; Britain's *Daily Worker* made precisely the same criticisms in 1963.[12] Keith Richards and Mick Jagger have made no secret about the degree to which their manager, Andrew Oldham, manipulated the press to achieve notoriety and fame for the Rolling Stones.

Finally, even the sixties musicians that Paglia specifically singles out 13 as purer and artistically truer than those of today, the Beatles and the Rolling Stones, were infiltrated by Philistines who worried as much about their bank accounts as they did about their spiritual development. The Stones had difficulty recruiting drummer Charlie Watts because he refused to quit his day job and its steady paycheck, and bass player Bill Wyman was chosen as much for his having a good amplifier as for his artistic potential. They were unwilling to fulfill the Romantic stereotype of the starving artist. Stu Sutcliffe served as the Beatles' bass player before Paul McCartney; Lennon convinced his art school friend to buy a bass and join because he *looked* the part. A wretched musician, he played his first audition with his back to the promoter in an effort to hide his ineptitude. Ringo Starr later joined as drummer with the expectation of salting away enough money to open a hairdressing parlor when the group lost its popular appeal. Of course, Paglia might dismiss such anecdotes because they involve nonwriting members of rhythm sections, whereas her focus is squarely on the singers and songwriters. But she thereby neglects the very players who give rock its Dionysian rhythms.

The greatest distortion in Paglia's argument is probably the idea 14 that early rockers had some "direct" connection with an authentic oral tradition which accounts for their expressive power. To begin with, there were few "white folk music" sources for rock. Rock's pioneers knew hillbilly and country in a commercial form. Chuck Berry's first record,

"Maybellene" (1955), was a simple rewrite of a country standard, "Ida Red." And most of what the early rockers knew of music—black or white—was obtained secondhand, from records. For the white rock and rollers in particular, the primary noncommercial source was gospel music. When Elvis Presley walked into Sun Records in 1953 and taped two songs (purportedly as a birthday gift to his mother, although her birthday was months away), he covered the Ink Spots. When producer Sam Phillips invited Elvis to audition in January of 1954, Elvis chose two country tunes, also learned from records. At their next meeting, Elvis ran through a broader repertoire, "heavy on the Dean Martin stuff. Apparently he'd decided, if he was going to sound like anybody, it was gonna be Dean Martin."[13] So much for "direct contact" with rural traditions on the part of rock's first great popularizer.

The recordings of Buddy Holly are another good case in point. Holly 15 was immortalized by his death in an airplane crash. (Touring the Midwest in January and February of 1959, he and Ritchie Valens and the Big Bopper [J. P. Richardson] chartered a light plane and flew ahead after a gig in Clear Lake, Iowa, so that they could get some laundry done before the next night's show in Minnesota.) Virtually everything that Holly ever put on tape has been released, most of it in a box set *The Complete Buddy Holly* (MCA Records, 1979). Holly was one of the first rockers to have some control over production and, like Chuck Berry but unlike Elvis Presley, founded his career on his own songs. Nonetheless, much of Holly's recorded legacy consists of cover versions of earlier songs. Many were rock and roll hits that had just been released by *other* rock pioneers: the Robins' (later the Coasters) "Smokey Joe's Cafe," Carl Perkins's "Blue Suede Shoes," Chuck Berry's "Brown-Eyed Handsome Man," Little Richards's "Slippin' and Slidin'," Fats Domino's "Blue Monday." He continued this practice right to the end. One of the very last things he recorded, on a tape recorder in his New York apartment, was a haunting version of Mickey and Sylvia's 1955 hit "Love Is Strange." His other sources were country; his first business card advertised "Western and Bop," and his early radio performances in Lubbock covered the music of Hank Williams, Flatt and Scruggs, and the Louvin Brothers.

Finally, consider Paglia's complaint that live performance has lost its 16 spontaneity and communication and has become a rehearsed and meaningless show. She points to the Beatles' stadium performances as the point of decline. How so? When the Beatles earlier played the cellars of Hamburg's red-light district, singing American hits in Liverpool accents to drunk Germans, was the setting really all that conducive to genuine artistic expression? By all accounts, including the one tape recording made in Hamburg, they played brutal rock and roll for up to six hours a night. And the mix of beer and amphetamines that kept them going hardly made them sensitive to the audience or to their own development as "artists." Paul McCartney had it right when he described it as "noise and beat all the way."[14]

Where Paglia claims that the audience-artist bond was severed by 17 the complexity and expense of ever larger sound systems, coupled with increasingly elaborate special effects, it was certainly these very things that first made rock concerts into something more than party music. The elaborate improvisations of Cream, the Grateful Dead, and the rest of the San Francisco scene, Led Zeppelin and Jimi Hendrix, all came in the five years *after* the Beatles abandoned the stage for the studio. And their achievements depended on superior sound systems; improvisational rock was hardly possible when the musicians had no stage monitors and the cheap amplification system distorted the music into a dull roar, with a sound mix that put the tinny vocals far out in front. Concerts as we understand them today, as extended performances by one or more artists, were rare events before the advent of the modern sound system. In rock's early days, the audience usually saw a specific singer or act as part of a "package" show featuring a half dozen acts, each performing two or three songs and then making way for the next group and its performance of selected hits.

Rather than modern counterparts of Wordsworth, Coleridge, Shel- 18 ley, Keats, and Byron, rock musicians have always had crass commercial motives, playing dance music to mostly teen audiences. Their direct musical sources were commercial recordings by earlier musicians, and their lyrics featured heavy doses of innuendo but little in the way of overt rebellion and, prior to 1965, almost nothing in the way of personal expression. None of this is offered with the intention of denigrating rock musicians. But if we are considering the claim that rock is either folk or fine art, the available facts count heavily against such status.

II

I have outlined the historical distortions of Paglia's story in order to clear 19 the stage for the main thrust of her proposal: "Rock music should not be left to the Darwinian laws of the marketplace. . . . For rock to move forward as an art form, our musicians must be given an opportunity for spiritual development." Having constructed a selective history that postulates an "authentic" tradition with a subsequent commercial distortion, she thinks that rock has a legitimate claim to being a true art form. But even if successful rock musicians have actually been those who could adapt to the commercial demands of entertainment, Paglia is advocating that rock can be fine art if the musicians can be freed from these commercial constraints. Paglia might have quoted composer Roger Sessions for support: "The artist's values are not, and cannot be, those of the market. If one must think of him as writing *for* anyone, the answer is . . . he is writing for all who love music."[15] If modern composers have lost out to popular music, Sessions argues, it is mainly the fault of audiences who have become too lazy to listen with sympathy and understanding. In the same vein, Paglia recommends that rock artists write for posterity, not the commercial audience.

Paglia believes that rock, purged of its economic dependence on a fickle and immature audience, will be recognized as the equal (or better) of current painting, sculpture, and serious composed music. She never explicitly says so, but her only standard of artistic achievement is rooted in her own acceptance of the aesthetics of Romanticism and its assumptions about the goals and value of art. I will argue that this line of argument is of no use if one wants to bring rock music and musicians into academia.   20

In the story she tells of rock's decline, Paglia singles out the following features as having been lost: individualism, spontaneity, energy, passion, and rebellion. Paglia has accepted Josiah Royce's "creed" of the Romantic artist: "Trust your genius; follow your noble heart; change your doctrine whenever your heart changes, and change your heart often."[16] It is also clear that she does not regard the artist's role as one of reflecting society. Disdaining the trivial concerns of the "white suburban youth" who are rock's primary audience, she believes that serious rock focuses on "dark" emotions, demonism, and spirituality. In Paglia's controversial book *Sexual Personae,* she contends that despite its commercialism, American radio proves that we "still live in the age of Romanticism." The Rolling Stones "are heirs of stormy Coleridge."[17] Other writers have analyzed rock in the same terms: 21

> In part because of its contradictions, the best way to understand rock and roll is to see it as a twentieth-century popular expression of Western romanticism. In fact, rock may even by the last gasp of romanticism in this anxious materialistic and scientific age. More than any other contemporary cultural form, rock captures the central elements of the romantic spirit: its

individuality, freedom, and rebellion, . . . its exultation of emotion, physicality, and imagination, and its relish of contradictions, extremes, and
paradoxes.[18]

The most detailed attempt to link rock and Romanticism is Robert 22
Pattison's *The Triumph of Vulgarity,* subtitled "Rock Music in the Mirror of Romanticism." Pattison contends that rock " is a unique integration of Romantic mythology and American blues."[19] Like Paglia, he
identifies the Rolling Stones as the greatest rock band ever. (The Beatles, we are left to presume, are just not demonic enough.)

Unlike Paglia, Pattison does not endorse Romanticism, and he is 23
sometimes condescending toward his subjects. While he is aware that
the Romantic myths are espoused by rock musicians, he does not regard
them as anything but myths. With particular attention to the idea of
rock's "primitive" sources, he believes that rock artists themselves have
adopted the doctrines of nineteenth-century Romanticism. He contends that the "vulgar mode" of Romanticism is the cultural force behind rock, "and the Sex Pistols come to fulfill the prophecies of
Shelley."[20] His argumentation amounts to quoting extensively but se-
lectively from rock lyrics, putting rather too much weight on rock's supposed pantheism as the primary evidence of romanticist influences. A
more serious weakness is a tendency to equate rock's mythology, as expressed in its lyrics, with the forces actually driving it; he likes to quote
obscure groups like the Fall and then to assure us that in "describing
themselves, they describe all rockers."[21] Yet there is every reason to
believe that the attitudes of most rock lyrics are posturing and image-
making for commercial purposes and that many of the musicians are
themselves perfectly aware of this.

There is also a tendency toward circularity. Anything that does not 24
reflect Romanticism is written off as nonrock, so Pattison does not recognize soul and other black popular music as rock. Black music "has supplied the raw materials, but there is no reason to suppose that blacks
share the Romantic preoccupations necessary for rock."[22] But it is absurd to think that such preoccupations are *necessary* for rock. When the
Beatles covered black musicians like Chuck Berry and Little Richard,
and when the Rolling Stones covered Chuck Berry and Otis Redding,
they were not taking "raw materials" from black musicians and transforming them. They were taking songs from musicians whom they admired as models of rock musicianship. On Pattison's thesis, what are we
to make of Aretha Franklin's late-sixties work with producer Jerry Wexler

(backed by several white musicians), or of Sly and the Family Stone, Little Feat, the Allman Brothers, the Doobie Brothers, Bruce Springsteen's E Street Band, and other racially integrated groups? Do the white members supply the requisite romanticist mythology to transform the black musicians' contributions into rock?

I do not deny that as an aesthetic program Romanticism enshrined 25 many of the values that are popularly attributed to rock. As a reaction against Enlightenment classicism and its emphasis on "intellectual" values of order, structure, precision, and technical polish, Romanticism first surfaced in serious music with the *Sturm und Drang*, flowered with program music and tone poems, and peaked with Wagner's music drama and chromactic explorations. The new values were "emotional" and were manifested overtly in change, excess, personal meanings, ambiguity, and idiosyncratic structures. But even if we can construct a case that the same conflict of values is present in any contrast of serious music with rock, parallels do not show causality.

The problem with the whole line of analysis is that *most* opinions 26 about music sound like *some* aspect of Romanticism, if only because of the general presumption that music is preeminently concerned with the expression of emotion. These characteristics all fit jazz as easily as rock. In fact, with writers like Paglia and Pattison we may have a case of critical history repeating itself. Those who link Romanticism and rock sound like earlier writers on jazz who found in jazz the same characteristics that are now attributed to rock, particularly the uncompromised and spontaneous nature of the performance and the freedom and instinctive self-expression of the performer.[23] And these values were often espoused by jazz performers themselves.

Consider Billie Holiday. Not exactly known for her art school 27 background or reading of Byron and Shelley, she denied having any influences except the records of Bessie Smith and Louis Armstrong:

> If you find a tune and it's got something to do with you, you don't have to evolve anything. You just feel it, and when you sing it other people can feel something too. With me, it's got nothing to do with working or arranging or rehearsing. . . . But singing songs like "The Man I Love" or "Porgy" . . . When I sing them I live them again and I love them.[24]

However much this sounds like Wordsworth's formula that poetry is a spontaneous overflow of emotions "recollected in tranquility," we have no reason to regard Lady Day as influenced by Wordsworth. Likewise, we have no reason to regard rock as an expression of Western Romanticism. As Peter Kivy has so carefully documented, most of these ideas about music were first advanced in the seventeenth and eighteenth centuries.[25] It might be better to regard romanticist aesthetics as a generalization to all the arts of assumptions that had long been held of music, in which case rock has no special connection to Romanticism.

Furthermore, Paglia's account of rock music is fraught with the same internal tensions that characterize Romanticism, particularly in relation to the folk tradition that she praises as a source of power in early rock. To the extent that such traditions have survived in Western culture in our century, oral folk traditions are communal rather than individual artistic creations, and they reflect the community rather than the personal self-expression of the Romantic genius. Yet Paglia criticizes rock musicians who cater to or reflect the values of the audience. The idea of a "folk" dimension in rock is also present in her ideal of an authentic and spontaneous interaction between performer and audience, but this conflicts with the reality that rock fans are self-consciously aware that they are members of a distinct subculture, and of distinct subcultures within rock.[26]

It is no surprise that Paglia tries to find a link between rock and folk music. One of Romanticism's several themes was a glorification of the rural "folk" and of their collective art as a less intellectual, more spontaneous, and thus purer mode of expression. When the Rolling Stones imitated black American singers in a self-conscious blues purism, they were indeed behaving like many Romantic composers. Chopin and Dvořák borrowed musical materials from their native folk traditions, and Wagner and Mahler adopted folk poems and myths as texts. But the aesthetics of Romanticism are fraught with internal contradictions, among them the fact the very process of appropriating these sources contradicts the desired spontaneity and authenticity of expression, no less for rock musicians than for nineteenth-century composers.[27]

According to Peter Wicke, the aesthetic values imparted to British rockers who attended art schools led to a calculated bohemianism and intellectual snobbery. Among those who articulated their aesthetic principles, pop art and then situationism appear to be the most prominent influences. Their preoccupation with the authenticity of their self-expression precluded their participation in any sort of community with their audience, and in fact they were often aware of the distance between their own privileged status and the working-class lives of most of their audience.[28] These attitudes may even have worked against direct political activism on the part of British rockers. Prior to the Beatles' single "Revolution" (1968), British rock lyrics stayed away from anything overtly political, whereas the American charts had featured political material since 1965.

Rock recreates Romantic contradictions in another way when the 31 ideology of artistic freedom comes up against the reality that the musicians are engaged in a commercial enterprise. Within the actual context of the nineteenth century, Romanticism glorified the sensitivity and sensibility of the individual artist/genius; but the requisite artistic freedom had its price in the commercialization of music. We might even say that when Romanticism valued both individuality and folk traditions, it did so in conscious opposition to the standardization and industrialization of the emerging bourgeois capitalism. Thus Paglia has nothing but disdain for those who get their rock from MTV. A parallel is present within the rock audience; fans of hardcore express contempt for mainstream audiences who imitate their slam-dancing and thus strip it of its "underground" status.

Yet it was bourgeois capitalism and the opportunity for self- 32 promotion that provided the composer's freedom. When earlier composers like Bach or Handel supported themselves with pupils and commissioned works, their music was largely utilitarian, written for specific occasions: Bach's masses and chorales, Handel's oratorios with their religious texts and his *Water Music* and *Royal Fireworks Music*. Beethoven solidified the shift from the composer-for-hire to the composer-as-entrepreneur, with works sold to publishers rather than commissioned by royal patrons. Concerts became money-making ventures, designed to please the bourgeois crowd who can afford the fee. Beethoven was attuned to the need to please the audience, repeating movements of symphonies when the concert audience called for it and showing off with piano improvisations when challenged. He could also be sensitive to criticism, withdrawing and replacing the final movement (the *Grosse Fugue*) of the String Quartet in B-flat Minor when the audience at its premiere reacted negatively.

At the other end of the spectrum, Wagner scraped together fund- 33 ing for his music dramas by a combination of self-promotion and spectacle. Wagner was keen to wrap himself in Beethoven's mantle, conducting the latter's Ninth Symphony at the 1872 dedication of Bayreuth. But Beethoven's willingness to meet the audience half-way had given way to Wagner's self-conscious Romanticism. Stubborn and uncompromising, his vision required absolute control of his creations, and he was vicious to anyone who criticized him. The result was precisely the opposite of Paglia's ideal performance as an audience-artist interaction that features improvisation and spontaneity. Ideally, the audience comes to the Bayreuth festival theater and listens to the *Ring* cycle in a hushed silence, broken only by the turning of pages as devoted Wagnerites follow the score. In short, there is no spontaneity of any kind; the Bach mass had found its secular parallel.

Which of these artists represents Paglia's ideal? Her advice to rock 34 musicians, "Don't become a slave to the audience" and "Don't tour" (study art instead), points to Wagner and not to Beethoven or to Romantics like Berlioz, Chopin, and Liszt, who more or less invented the modern promotional tour. More pointedly, she expects rock to combine two artistic goals that have been at odds ever since Romanticism cobbled them together. On the one hand there is the development of the individual artist, cushioned from and thus impervious to commercial demands. But this sort of autonomy is unlikely to foster energy, rebellion, and the emotional power of rock's pioneers. On the other hand there is the emotional power of the folk tradition, where the music emerges from the community in a way that blurs the line between creator and audience. But the communal nature of the folk process fits uncomfortably with the self-conscious artistry of the trained professional; training rock musicians at colleges and universities is not likely to connect rock with centuries of folk music.

Finally, Paglia is recommending that rock musicians trade the vi- 35 cissitudes of commerce for a system of artistic patronage. But are commercial demands always an artistic kiss of death? Paglia links popular music and film as the two great art forms of our time, but film has fared quite well without much institutional support. Paglia is really recommending that rock shouldn't remain popular music any longer, that is, a commodity designed for consumption by masses of listeners of varying degrees of musical knowledge. Rock musicians are to regard themselves as fine artists and to train accordingly. Putting aside the conflict with folk ideology, such ideas fail to address how rock music would retain its identity apart from its popular base. Romanticism has a healthy strain of artistic elitism that is antithetical to rock, and patronage is likely to reinforce that strain in rock. While I would not go as far as Nietzsche did, he captures the problem involved when he attacks Romanticism: "The artist who began to understand himself would misunderstand himself: he ought not to look back, he ought not to look at all, he ought to give."[29] Can rock deliver on its own terms if its artists are successful at the transformations that Paglia recommends?

We should also consider the likely consequences of treating rock 36 like the other arts. Funding through grants, scholarships, and the like is increasingly limited, so the proposal could cover only a fraction of the ten thousand or more artists who release rock recordings each year (many of these being groups of several members). In practical terms, freeing artists from traditional commercial concerns means that *most* rock music will remain exactly what it is anyway: product for popular consumption. So the scheme is likely to split rock into two camps. One will carry on as before, and the other will consist of artists with grants, afforded the freedom to follow their own muse. (This would reverse the current process, where *mature* successful artists like Dire Straits, George Harrison, the Grateful Dead, Bruce Springsteen, and the Rolling Stones can wait five years between records and tours, producing what they like when they choose to do so.) But the select few who would be singled out for support will face the same problems that already occur in a patronage system. While there is intense competition for scarce resources, very little of the money is risked on artists whose work is genuinely avant-garde, and less still on those whose work is highly political in content. One has difficulty imagining the Clash or rappers N.W.A. and Ice-T getting a grant under Paglia's scheme. Training rock musicians at colleges and universities is likely to result in music that parallels the output of similarly trained jazz and classical musicians: highly accomplished, technically excellent, and intellectually challenging music that values extreme polish, individuality, experimentation, and novelty for their own sake as well as continuous progressive change. But there is little reason to think that the music produced by these musicians is going to connect with the general public and conquer the top ten. (If we were talking about music with commercial potential, Paglia would lose her basic premise that commercial demands corrupt the music.)

Although those involved with the fine arts do not like to say so, there 37 is also a fundamental unfairness to this system, particularly if we are funding artists who are not interested in producing music that the general public wants to hear. As Jeremy Bentham argued, the arts "are useful only to those who take pleasure in them," and to the extent that public patronage is set up to further arts which lack widespread appeal, we are instituting a regressive tax, "laying burdens on the comparatively indigent many, for the amusement of the comparatively opulent few."[30] We do this with other arts in the United States, with mixed success. Consider the National Endowment for the Arts (NEA). In recent years we have seen an overt politicization of the patronage system as politicians on the right have demanded that public funding be restricted to art that expresses mainstream values. Yet by operating within the sphere of mass entertainment, rock music has gradually loosened the bonds of censorship. The Rolling Stones had to sing "Let's Spend the Night Together" as "Let's Spend Some Time Together" on the Ed Sullivan Show in 1967, a form of self-censorship difficult to imagine in the 1990s. Stephen Sondheim recently rejected an NEA grant because of the restrictions involved, preferring the freedom of artistic free enterprise. Why advocate a patronage system that is just as likely to control and censor artistic expression as to encourage it?[31]

As Ezra Pound said, "Music rots when it gets *too far* from the 38 dance. Poetry atrophies when it gets too far from music."[32] While teachers and literature professors like to think that schools and colleges have some special ability to bring poetry and literature to the masses, there is plenty of evidence that "good" literature is not what the masses want. It is not even what most college students and graduates want, as junk fiction and "Calvin and Hobbes" collections repeatedly top the sales lists of college bookstores. I do not mean to put down junk fiction and comics, but there is little reason to think that poetry has much meaning for the majority of people. It has gotten too far from music, and most of the "serious" music composed in our century has gotten too far from the dance. In my more cynical moments I believe that both are mainly produced by college professors for other college professors (they seem to make up most of the audience when I attend local "new music" concerts). Academics, however well meaning, are the last group to keep rock rooted in the syncopated and danceable rhythms that have made it one of America's most successful exports. If the lyrics to rap have vitality, it may be because they aren't composed by college students who have immersed themselves in great literature.

If there is any element of Romanticism that we ought to keep out 39 of art education, it is the notion of the artistic genius as a superior soul requiring special nourishment, for this is probably one of the great obstacles to full enjoyment and participation in the arts by large numbers of our students. Why inject elitism into popular culture, where students engage at least one form of art without anxiety or feelings of inferiority? Romanticism is a poor model for understanding the achievements of rock music, and it is worse yet as a justification for treating rock music as we now treat the fine arts.

NOTES

1. An interesting variation of this thesis is defended in Richard Shusterman, "The Fine Art of Rap," in his *Pragmatist Aesthetics* (Oxford: Blackwell, 1992), pp. 201–35. Shusterman's argument focuses on showing that rap is the form of popular music which best exemplifies a postmodern aesthetic; for this reason, his version avoids endorsing rap as folk music.

2. Robert Christgau, "Rock Lyrics Are Poetry (Maybe)," in *The Age of Rock,* ed. Jonathan Eisen (New York: Random House, 1969), p. 232.

3. Camille Paglia, "Endangered Rock," *The New York Times,* Thursday, 16 April 1992, p. A23. Reprinted in Camille Paglia, *Sex, Art, and American Culture* (New York: Vintage Books, 1992), pp. 19–21. Unless otherwise credited, all further quotations from Paglia are from this editorial, which was widely reprinted.

4. Quoted in *Melody Maker,* 27 August 1977; quotation disseminated in Tony Angarde, *The Oxford Dictionary of Modern Quotations* (New York: Oxford University Press, 1991), p. 89.

5. In *Sexual Personae* (New York: Vintage Books, 1990), Camille Paglia does offer parallels between Elvis Presley and Lord Byron; most of them are physical similarities such as their early deaths and enlarged hearts.

6. Simon Frith, "Popular Music 1950–1980," in *Making Music,* ed. George Martin (New York: William Morrow, 1983), p. 24.

7. Nik Cohn, *Pop from the Beginning* (United Kingdom: Weidenfeld and Nicholson, 1969), p. 133.

8. Carl Belz, *The Story of Rock,* 2d ed. (New York: Oxford University Press, 1972), p. 64.

9. Dave Marsh, *The Heart of Rock and Soul* (New York: Plume, 1989), pp. 474–75.

10. John Lennon, quoted in David Sheff and G. Barry Golson, *The Playboy Interviews with John Lennon and Yoko Ono* (New York: Berkley Books, 1981), pp. 170–71.

11. John Lennon quoted in Jann Wenner, *Lennon Remembers* (San Francisco: Straight Arrow Books, 1971), p. 70; interview conducted in December 1970.

12. "Working Class?" *Daily Worker,* 7 September 1963, p. 5.

13. Quotation of Marion Keisker, who was present at the sessions; Ed Ward, in *Rock of Ages* (New York: Rolling Stone Press/Summit Books, 1986), pp. 78–79.

14. Quoted in Geoffrey Stokes, *The Beatles* (New York: Rolling Stone Press/Times Books, 1980), p. 45.

15. Roger Sessions, *Questions about Music* (New York: W. W. Norton, 1970), p. 11.

16. Quoted in Frederick B. Artz, *From Renaissance to Romanticism: Trends in Art, Literature, and Music,* 1300–1930 (Chicago: University of Chicago Press, 1962), p. 227.

17. Paglia, *Sexual Personae,* p. 358.

18. Quentin J. Schultze, et al., *Dancing in the Dark* (Grand Rapids, Mich.: William B. Eerdmans, 1991), p. 164.

19. Robert Pattison, *The Triumph of Vulgarity* (Oxford: Oxford University Press, 1987), p. 63.

20. Ibid., p. xi.

21. Ibid., p. 10.

22. Ibid., p. 64.

23. See Andy Hamilton, "The Aesthetics of Imperfection," *Philosophy* 65, no. 253 (1990), pp. 323–40; and Ted Gioia, *The Imperfect Art* (New York: Oxford University Press, 1988), pp. 19–49.

24. Billie Holiday with William Dufty, *Lady Sings the Blues* (New York: Penguin, 1984), p. 39. There is a certain irony here for anyone who wants to fit Holiday into the Romantic archetype, since she is talking about commercial songs by white composers.

25. See chaps. 3–5 of Peter Kivy, *Sound Sentiment* (Philadelphia: Temple University Press, 1989); this incorporates his earlier book *The Corded Shell.*

26. See Simon Frith, *Sound Effects* (New York: Pantheon, 1981), pp. 202–34.

27. Attempts to legitimize rock by association with folk music first arose among rock critics; see Simon Frith, " 'The Magic That Can Set You Free': The Ideology of Folk and the Myth of the Rock Community," in *Popular Music,* vol. 1, ed. Richard Middleton and David Horn (Cambridge: Cambridge University Press, 1981), pp. 159–68.

28. Peter Wicke, *Rock Music: Culture, Aesthetics, and Sociology,* trans. Rachel Fogg (Cambridge: Cambridge University Press, 1990), chaps. 5 and 7.

29. Friedrich Nietzsche, *Will to Power,* trans. Walter Kaufmann and R. J. Hollingdale (New York: Vintage/Random House, 1968), p. 429 (section 811).

30. Jeremy Bentham, "Reward Applied to Art and Science," *The Works of Jeremy Bentham,* vol. 2, ed. John Bowring (New York: Russell & Russell, 1962), p. 253.

31. See Edward C. Banfield, *The Democratic Muse* (New York: Basic Books, 1984).

32. Ezra Pound, *ABC of Reading* (Norfolk, Conn.: New Directions, n.d.), p. 61.

READING FOR INFORMATION

1. Explain why the pioneers of rock were neither Romantic archetypes nor rebels.

2. To what extent were early rockers influenced by an authentic oral tradition?

3. According to Gracyk, why is it that rock "has no special connections to Romanticism"?

4. Does Gracyk find links between rock and folk music? What are they?

5. What are the consequences of treating rock like the fine arts?

READING FOR FORM, ORGANIZATION, AND EXPOSITORY FEATURES

1. Gracyk has written an essay of analysis and evaluation. Which of the organizational patterns described in Chapter 4—cause and effect, comparison and contrast, structure of the reading source, or argument—does he use?

2. What types of sources does Gracyk draw upon, and what function do the sources serve?

3. Give examples of the various types of evidence—facts, statistics, references to authorities—that Gracyk uses to support his position.

READING FOR RHETORICAL CONCERNS

1. Describe the organizational features that make Gracyk's article easy to follow.
2. Is Gracyk's argument one-sided, or does he concede alternative viewpoints? Underline passages pertaining to alternate views.
3. Underline words that reveal Gracyk's tone. How would you characterize the tone?

WRITING ASSIGNMENTS

1. After reading Gracyk's article, what do you think of Camille Paglia's idea about training rock musicians in colleges and universities? Write a brief essay expressing your views.
2. Write an essay in which you argue point A or point B.
   A. Grants and scholarships should fund artists and musicians who take risks, those whose work is genuinely avant-garde or political in nature.
   B. Grants and scholarships should fund artists and musicians who express mainstream values and produce art music that appeals to the general public.
3. Write an essay in which you agree or disagree with Gracyk's statement: "If there is any element of Romanticism that we ought to keep out of art education, it is the notion of the artistic genius as a superior soul requiring special nourishment, for this is probably one of the great obstacles to full enjoyment and participation in the arts by large numbers of our students" (paragraph 39).

All Junk, All the Time

Richard Brookhiser

Richard Brookhiser is a senior editor of National Review *and also writes a column for* The New York Observer. *He has published numerous articles and books, including* The Way of the Wasp: How It Made America and How It Can Save It . . . So To Speak *and* Founding Father: Rediscovering George Washington.

Brookhiser, Richard. "All Junk, All the Time." *National Review* 25 Nov. 1996: 73–74. © 1996 by National Review, Inc., 215 Lexington Avenue, New York, NY 10016. Reprinted by permission.

PREREADING

The title of the article is referring to rock music. Write your reaction. Is there any rock music you would call "junk"? Why or why not? Why do you suppose Brookhiser considers rock to be worthless?

1   Like a turtle egg buried on the beach, the thought warmed, out of sight, all summer. The Olympics and the political conventions helped it grow, but the key stimulus was a passing sentence in a *New York Times Magazine* article on megachurches, which are evangelical churches that number their congregations in the thousands. The article was discussing the music used in the services, and said something to the effect that the megachurches favored rock. Just like the conventions. Just like the Olympics. Just like everyone everywhere.

2   Megachurches keep their eye on eternity. In the here and now, rock is triumphant and universal. Its empire will only expand, ferreting out the few nooks it does not yet command, and filling them. Francis Fukuyama alerted us (wrongly) to the End of History. But rock has ended the history of music. There are no ideological, religious, or ethnic redoubts. I once read a profile of the commander of a Salvadoran death squad. He was a Deadhead. Iranian mullahs, Chinese Communists, skinheads, rabbis expecting the return of Menachem Schneerson, Papuan savages dressed only in penis wrappers, all listen, openly or in secret, or their children will.

3   What is rock? A certain set of musicians—drums, guitars, a voice or two. A beat that, well, rocks. Lyrics. Pare down the music until it almost vanishes, as in rap; soften the beat until it becomes easy listening; give the songwriter the equipment and the ambitions of Brian Wilson: but the form never quite disappears. It hasn't changed for forty years, and it never will, because it is so easy to do well enough.

4   Consider the elements.

5   *Music.* The guitar is the ultimate E-Z-2-Play instrument. Why else was it the lyre of the American peasantry? If rock depended on some instrument—trumpet, clarinet, fiddle, piano—that required some tone of the lips or lightness of the fingers to play even barely competently, its pool of potential performers would have shrunk by 90 percent. There is only one instrument easier to fake: drums. The low standards also apply to rock vocalists. Remember Mick Jagger when he was in his prime? Heard

608 Rock Music and Cultural Values

him now, when he sounds like a voice on the subway PA system? Mr.
Jagger could actually move his notes around, but they were always harsh
and homely notes. That's OK—they were good enough for rock.

Words. The rock critic Elizabeth Wurtzel, reviewing an album of 6
covers of Cole Porter songs by rock musicians, hoped the experience
might inspire rock songwriters to be a little more careful of their rhyme
schemes. Wrong! The whole point is not to have to worry about rhyme
schemes. If you start worrying, not everyone will be able to do it. So rock
will keep on rhyming "pain" and "shame," and "stop" and "stuck."

Dancing. I was in fifth and sixth grade just after kids stopped tak- 7
ing solemn little lessons, in gym class or after school, in the box step and
the cha-cha. Those who still dance these, and all the other dances of
mankind, do it, like fox hunters or Greek scholars, as a passion or a hobby.
To fulfill the necessities of social intercourse, it will never be necessary
to take a dance lesson again. Slow dancing to rock is what you hope to be
doing horizontally with your clothes off afterward. Fast dancing is—well,
look at it, at any wedding or bar mitzvah, where even the grown-ups
shake their aged hams. The abolition of dance steps was a great relief to
the awkward, especially the men, who once had to lead—no more visu-
alizing the points of the compass, no more shame when you crunched the
foot you were supposed to be guiding.

Entrepreneurs. There is a final way in which rock is easy, which im- 8
pels the other three. It is easy to make a buck selling it. Because the
product is so generic, primitive, and witless, the distributors and marketers can know nothing, ingest huge quantities of drugs, and still not be
too addled to make millions. The fields I know best are journalism, publishing, and politics, and so I do know something about laziness and empty
pretensions. But if there were ever a land of opportunity for the feckless,
the modern music industry is it.

Rock is a form of popular culture that aims downward in terms of 9
class and age, instead of aiming up. Rather than aspiring, it *de*spires. As-
tronomers speak of the red shift, the change in the spectrum of the light
of receding galaxies. Rock is redneck shift. The preceding phase of popular music, encompassing jazz, dance bands, and show tunes, was urban
and adult. Rock is kids channeling the rhythms of bumpkins.

But the worst thing about rock is not that it fails the culture, but that 10
it fails on its own terms. Popular music is a marker and a memory aid. Most

of the important events in life—romance, courtship, celebration—are accompanied by it. We remember them because of their importance to us, no matter what was on the radio. But if the music is crude and blank, does not some of its crudity and blankness infect the experience, and the memory?

And while popular music mostly amplifies pre-existing emotions, at its best it can tug us, tease us, make us grow. Not rock. For all its supposedly revolutionary ethos, rock is a binary switch of angst and hormones—Kafka without humor, or centerfolds in notes. The emotions that unsettle, like stones under a sleeping bag—hope, regret—are beyond its ken. And they are beyond our ken, to the extent rock stuffs our ears. 11

It's Bottom 40, all junk, all the time. And it's here to stay. 12

READING FOR INFORMATION

1. How does Brookhiser define rock music?
2. Summarize the four reasons why "rock is easy."
3. Why is pop music superior to rock?

READING FOR FORM, ORGANIZATION, AND EXPOSITORY FEATURES

1. What is the function of paragraphs 1 and 2? How do they relate to the rest of the article?
2. What devices or aids pull readers into the conversation and help them follow Brookhiser's argument?
3. Do you think Brookhiser gives sufficient weight to opposing views. Why or why not?

READING FOR RHETORICAL CONCERNS

1. What incidents motivated Brookhiser to write the piece?
2. How do you think Brookhiser's *National Review* readers reacted to his position?
3. How would you characterize Brookhiser's tone of voice? Is it appropriate for his rhetorical purpose?

WRITING ASSIGNMENTS

1. Simon Frith tells us that one of the social functions of pop music is that it gives shape and voice to our emotions. He says that "we get to know ourselves via the music." Write an essay in which you compare and contrast

Frith's views in "Toward an Aesthetic of Pop Music" with Brookhiser's views as expressed in this selection.

2. Write an essay in which you contrast Brookhiser's views with those of Camille Paglia in "Rock as Art."

3. Write an essay analyzing and evaluating Brookhiser's argument.

Redeeming the Rap Music Experience

Venise Berry

Venise Berry is an assistant professor in the School of Journalism and Mass Communication at the University of Iowa. She is the co-editor of Mediated Messages and African-American Culture: Contemporary Issues. *She has published book chapters in* Adolescents and Their Music, Cecilia Reclaimed: Feminist Perspectives on Gender and Music, Viewing War: How the Media Handled the Persian Gulf, *and* Men, Masculinity, and the Media, *and she is the author of the novel,* So Good *(1996).*

PREREADING

React to the title of the article. What is your opinion of rap music? Do you think it needs to be redeemed? Freewrite your reactions.

You know—parents are the same no matter time nor place.
They don't understand that us kids are gonna make some
  mistakes.
So to you other kids all across the land, there's no need to
  argue—
    PARENTS JUST DON'T UNDERSTAND!
      (DJ Jazzy Jeff and The Fresh Prince 1988)

INTRODUCTION

When rap music first appeared on the scene, music critics said   1
it wouldn't last, record companies felt it was too harsh and
black-oriented to cross over, and parents dismissed it as the latest fad.

Berry, Venise. "Redeeming the Rap Music Experience." *Adolescents and Their Music.* Ed. Jonathan S. Epstein. New York: Garland, 1994. 165–87. Reprinted by permission of the publisher.

Ten years later, rap has become a powerful and controversial force in American popular culture. Rap music has grown significantly from its humble street beginnings in Harlem and the South Bronx. It now encompasses a dominant media paradigm through traditional music vehicles like cassettes and CDs, as well as television coverage in videos and talk shows, rappers as actors, film themes, concerts, advertising, and other promotional components.

On *Billboard's* top 200 album list on January 18, 1992, rappers   2
were found as high as #3 and as low as #184. Despite, or maybe because of, the controversies, groups such as Hammer, Public Enemy, Ice Cube, Ghetto Boyz, Salt N' Pepa, 2 Live Crew, NWA, Tone Loc, and Queen Latifah have reached mainstream popularity, and each success pushes the rap genre into new directions. Rap music is constantly testing the boundaries of commercialism, sexism, radicalism, feminism, and realism, and a growing concern over the music's disrespect for traditional boundaries keeps it on the cutting edge.

Current literature on rap music has taken varied approaches, from   3
content analyses which analyze and critique images and messages, to trade articles which offer promotional information on the artists and their music. One of the most important, yet least explored, areas in this discourse is the relationship between the music and its fans; particularly those whom it represents: black urban youths.

This chapter will explore three controversial issues in rap music: 4
sex, violence, and racism, in relation to the social, cultural, and historical reality of urban black American youth. My analysis will draw on both secondary and primary sources. It will incorporate related articles and previous literature, as well as worksheet responses collected from black high school participants in the Upward Bound Program at Huston-Tillotson College in Austin, Texas, between 1987 and 1989 and personal comments from an October 17, 1990, discussion group with twenty-four of the Upward Bound juniors and seniors.

In developing a conceptual framework for this examination of rap   5
music experience, it is necessary to distinguish between the pop-cultural and pop-crossover domains. The pop-cultural domain involves rap music, which, despite its popularity, maintains a black cultural focus in its message and style. For example, rap groups like NWA, Ice T, KRS One, Public Enemy, Ice Cube, and Queen Latifah are popular rappers with messages and styles that reflect an overt black consciousness.

In contrast, the pop-crossover domain involves rap music which   6
follows a more commercialized format. The message and style of these

rap songs are more generalizable and acceptable to mainstream audiences. Hammer, Salt N' Pepa, DJ Jazzy Jeff and the Fresh Prince, Tone Loc, and Kid and Play are examples of pop-crossover rap artists. The distinction between these two rap domains is important in recognition of their place in the American popular culture movement. The popularity of one helps to fuel the popularity of the other, just as the acceptable nature of one limits the acceptable nature of the other.

This research evolves from a broad sociocultural ideology, focusing   7 on the wish to understand the meaning and place assigned to popular culture in the experience of a particular group in society—the young, black, urban minority. It supports the pluralist approach, which considers rap music an example of how media systems, despite their attempt to control, are basically nondominant and open to change, and can be used effectively to present alternative views. Gurevitch (1982) has examined pluralism as a component of democracy and emancipatory media. Their work advocates the idea of media as public vehicles used for enhancing and encouraging self-expression and self-consciousness by a culture. As this chapter will highlight, cultural rap is just such a vehicle.

BLACK MUSIC AS CULTURAL COMMUNICATION

In the work of Standifer (1980), the musical behaviors of black society are   8 explained as "movement with existence." From spirituals to rap, black music style is a communicative process interwoven deep within the black American experience. For example, the spiritual served as an underground form of communication and a mechanism for emotional release. Natural words and phrases had secret meanings for slave communities. According to Cone (1972), words and phrases which seemed harmless were filled with latent meanings, such as, "De promise land on the other side of Jordan," which meant "freedom north" and later "Canada," rather than "heaven" as slave owners were led to believe.

B.B. King has told the story of how blues evolved from the unan-   9 swered prayers of slaves. He explained that slaves sang to God, but remained oppressed. As a result they began to lose at least part of their faith, and started to sing what was on their minds: the blues. Walton (1972) agrees, defining the blues as a composition grounded in individual experience and one with which the audience tends to identify.

When avant-garde jazz emerged, it was in protest to mainstream-   10 appropriated music styles such as ragtime and boogie-woogie. Kofsky (1970) explains that the revolutionary jazz style used the piano as a distraction, abandoning the traditional diatonic scale, and incorporating an atonal key structure in direct opposition to Western music form. He says the harsh and abrasive music represented the dissatisfaction of Black Americans with what they had been promised, but ultimately denied: a chance to have the American dream.

Soul music in the 1960s and 1970s presented itself as a blatantly 11 rebellious black musical genre. It created for black American culture a sense of heightened black consciousness, unity and pride. Soul music, ultimately, served as a powerful catalyst for protest and social change during the civil rights and black power movements (Maultsby, 1983).

Finally, today's rap music style reflects the distinct experience of 12 urban black culture. Black slang, street attitude, and fashion are reflected in powerful spoken song. Name-brand tennis shoes, sweatsuits, and an exorbitant display of gold chains and rings create a sense of appropriated success. The heavy beat, incessant scratching, aggressive delivery, and lyrical storyline present a message of anger and frustration from urban existence.

Just as socially, culturally, and historically music has always been es- 13 sential to the evolution of the black American experience, an essential part of contemporary black culture is the urban environment which manifests itself within the context of rap music. Several scholars have discussed the power of rap music as a mechanism of communication involving the struggle for a recognized black cultural empowerment.

Dyson (1991) examines performance, protest, and prophecy in the 14 culture of hip hop. He suggests that it is difficult for a society that maintains social arrangements, economic conditions, and political choices so that it can create and reproduce poverty, racism, sexism, classism, and violence to appreciate a music that contests and scandalizes such problems. He fears that the pop success of rap artists often means mainstream dilution; the sanitizing of rap's expression of urban realities, resulting in sterile hip hop devoid of its original fire and offensive to no one.

The communicative power of rap music is traced back to an African 15 tradition called "nommo" by Stephens (1991). Nommo refers to the supernatural power of the spoken word. The rhyme and rhythm which are part of African-American speech, literature, music, and dance are essential elements of nommo. He says it is believed in Africa that nommo can create changes in attitude. It can evoke unity, identity, and an atmosphere where everyone can relate.

Perkins (1991) explains how the ideology of the Nation of Islam has 16 become an important element of rap music's message. Perkins feels that rap artists such as Public Enemy and KRS One are social revolutionaries and their role is to carry the black nationalist tradition forward by heightening awareness, stimulating thought, and provoking the true knowledge of self.

The messages in rap music have also been compared to the messages in blues by Nelson (1991). She contrasts themes such as poverty and despair that appear in both and discusses how both musical forms are based on truth and reality. Dixon (1989) speaks about the context of rap music as truth. He feels rap music " . . . unites the listeners of the music into a common group with clear and readily identifiable racial, cultural, economic, and political/sexual shared concerns and emerges as the voice of its adherents." [17]

Finally, the issue of rap as historical account is raised by Shusterman (1991). He says, "Many rappers have taken their place as insightful inquirers into reality and teachers of truth, particularly those aspects of reality and truth which get neglected or distorted by establishment history books and contemporary media coverage." Shusterman attributes the audible voice of rap music in popular culture to its commercial success in the mass media, which has enabled renewed artistic investment as an undeniable source of black cultural pride. [18]

RAP MUSIC, URBAN REALITY, AND POPULAR CULTURE

Popular culture is made by subordinated peoples in their own interests out of resources that also, contradictorily, serve the economic interests of the dominant. Popular culture is made from within and below, not imposed from without and above as mass cultural theorists would have it. There is always an element of popular culture that lies outside of social control, that escapes or opposes hegemonic forces. [19]

The power and promise of rap music rests in the bosom of urban America; an environment where one out of twenty-two black males will be killed by violent crimes, where the black high-school dropout rate is as high as 72 percent and where 86 percent of black children grow up in poverty. Years of degradation, welfare handouts, institutional racism, and discrimination have created a community where little hope, low self-esteem and frequent failure translate into drugs, teen pregnancy, and gang violence. These are the social, cultural, and economic conditions which have spurred rap's paradoxical position within American popular culture. [20]

The relationship between low socioeconomic status and the negative self-evaluation of black urban youth results in problems of low [21] self-esteem. These feelings are prominent because of limited opportunities, unsatisfied needs, instability, estrangement, racial prejudice, and discrimination (Hulbary, 1975). As these youth struggle with questions of independence and control in their environment, they embrace a sense of powerlessness. Mainstream society tends to view the lifestyles of low-income communities as deviant. The poor are believed to be perpetuating their own poverty because of their nonconforming attitudes and unconventional behavior (Gladwin, 1967). Poussaint and Atkinson (1972) suggest that the stereotypes of deviance, a lack of motivation, and limited educational achievements ultimately become a part of their identity.

22   The youth movement which is evident in popular culture has, therefore, brought about only illusions for many urban American youth. The term "youth," which came to mean a specific attitude including pleasure, excitement, hope, power, and invincibility, was not experienced by these kids. Their future was mangled by racism, prejudice, discrimination, and economic and educational stagnation. As Bernard (1991) suggests, they found themselves in a gloomy darkness without friendship, trust, or hope; backed into a corner where life is all about self.

23   As a product of the black urban community, rap music is indisputably entangled with the struggle for black identity and legitimacy within mainstream society. Although rap music is undergoing significant changes, much of it remains true to its aesthetic purpose of bringing to the forefront the problematic nature of urban American experience.

24   Cultural rap music is, therefore, often seen in a negative light. The "culture of rap music" has been chracterized as a "culture of attitude" by Adler (1990), who suggests that attitude is something civilized society abhors and likes to keep under control. He concludes that the end of attitude is nihilism, which by definition leads nowhere, and that the culture of attitude is repulsive, mostly empty of political content.

25   Costello and Wallace (1990), in *Signifying Rappers*, say that vitalists have argued for forty years that postwar art's ultimate expression will be a kind of enormous psychosocial excrement and the real aesthetic (conscious or otherwise) of today's best serious rap may be nothing but the first wave of this great peristalsis.

26   Negative images of rap are dominant in the news. The 2 Live Crew controversy in Florida concerning sexually explicit lyrics made big headlines, along with the charity basketball game by rap artists in New York which resulted in nine kids being trampled to death. Violence has also been reported at movies where rap themes are prominent. And, the music

of defiant rap groups like NWA (Niggas with Attitude) have been considered radical and extremist. They made history as the first musical group to receive a warning from the FBI about the negative content of their song, "Fuck the Police," which encourages a lack of respect for the system.

Urban black American culture exists within a large infrastructure, 27 segmented by various negative individual and situational environments. The relationship between the rap fan and his or her music, therefore, involves the larger contextual environment of the urban street. At the same time, it is important to recognize how the mainstream success of the rap genre has made urban language, style, dance, and attitude viable components of popular cultural form.

THE ISSUE OF SEX

The 2 Live Crew appeared in the public eye in 1986 with their first 28 album, *The 2 Live Crew Is What We Are*. Their most successful hit, which is now considered tame, was entitled, "Hey, We Want Some Pussy." It sold a half-million copies without the backing of a major record company. The Crew's next album took sexual rap to a new level. *Move Something* sold more than a million copies and included songs like, "Head," "Booty and Cock," and "Me so Horny."

It was their third album, *As Nasty as We Wanna Be*, which made 29 the group a household name. On June 6, 1990, U.S. District Judge Jose Gonzales, Jr., said the album was "utterly without any redeeming social value." The obscenity issue created a media bonanza for 2 Live Crew and boosted the sale of their album to more than two million copies.

Luther Campbell, leader of the group, has been on a number of 30 talk shows and in many articles defending his right to produce sexually explicit rap music. In an interview in *Black Beat* magazine, he called the lyrics funny. "The stuff on our X-rated albums is meant to be funny. We sit down and laugh about our lyrics. We don't talk about raping women or committing violence against them or anything like that" (Henderson, February 1990).

An analysis by Peterson-Lewis (1991) presents a different per- 31 spective: ". . . their lyrics lack the wit and strategic use of subtle social commentary necessary for effective satire; thus they do not so much debunk myths as create new ones, the major one being that in interacting with black women 'anything goes.' Their lyrics not only fail to satirize the myth of the hypersexual black, they also commit the moral blunder of sexualizing the victimization of women, black women in particular."

Campbell adds that the group's lyrics are a reflection of life in America's black neighborhoods. Yet he admits he won't let his seven-year-old daughter listen to such music. While 2 Live Crew served as the thrust of the controversy, the negative images of women in this society have been a concern of feminists for many years, through various media forms. 32

Peterson-Lewis goes on to question the extent of the ethical and moral responsibilities of artists to their audiences and the larger public. She focuses her argument on the constitutionality and racially motivated persecution and prosecution of 2 Live Crew, which she feels overshadowed the real criticism—the sexually explicit nature of their lyrics and their portrayal of women as objects for sexual assault. 33

Frankel (1990) agrees that the 2 Live Crew situation took away the real focus. She says the attack on the 2 Live Crew group made it an issue of censorship, racism, and free speech, rather than an issue of disgust at how women are portrayed, especially since an act like Andrew Dice Clay, who also promotes women and sex from a negative perspective, has not been sanctioned by the law. 34

Even though the controversy about sexually explicit lyrics in rap music has become a heated issue, out of a list of the top fifty rap groups, only about 10 percent can actually be identified as using truly obscene and violent lyrics in relation to women. An analysis of the number of more generally negative images of females as loose and whorish would probably double that percentage. 35

In a discussion on the subject of sex in rap with a group of Upward Bound high school juniors and seniors, there was a split on the 2 Live Crew issue. Bené said their records contain too much profanity and are obscene, so maybe they should be sold in X-rated stores. Steve felt that fifteen- and sixteen-year-olds are able to drive, and if they can be trusted with their lives in a car, why not be trusted to select their own music? Tamara compared the group's lyrics to the Playboy channel or magazine, and wondered why access to 2 Live Crew's music is not limited as well. Marty said that teenagers are still going to get the album if they want it, despite warning labels. Finally, Dewan explained that the warning labels can't stop the sexual things teens think in their minds. 36

When asked about record censorship, most of them felt that some kind of censorship was acceptable for kids ages twelve and under. But they also cited television, movies, and magazines as the places where they usually receive new sexual information, rather than music. 37

Female rappers like Salt N' Pepa, Queen Latifah, Yo Yo, and MC Lyte have stepped forward to dispel many of the negative images of 38 women with their own lyrical rhetoric and aggressive performance style. Yo Yo, a popular nineteen-year-old female rapper, says that she got into rap to help improve women's self-esteem because a lot of black women don't believe in themselves. She has created an organization for teenage women called the Intelligent Black Women's Coalition (IBWC), which speaks on issues of social concern.

In direct opposition to positive female rappers are the contro- 39 versial groups, Bytches wit' Problems and Hoes wit' Attitude. According to Lyndah and Michelle of Bytches wit' Problems, "There's a little bitch in all women, and even some men . . . and we're just the bitches to say it" (October 1991). Lyndah and Michelle's new album, *B.Y.T.C.H.E.S.*, reflects another side of black urban reality. They feel they can say what they want just like men do, which is evident from their songs "Two Minute Brother," "Fuck a Man," and "Is the Pussy still Good." Their definition of a bitch is "a powerful woman in control of her life, going after what she wants and saying what's on her mind" (October 1991).

The female trio, Hoes wit' Attitude, has been called the raunchiest 40 all-girl rap group. With hit songs like "Eat This," "Little Dick," and "Livin' in a Hoe House," they constantly test their motto, "If men can do it we can too." The girls, 2 Jazzy, Baby Girl, and D. Diva, argue that "hoein' is the oldest profession, whether you're sellin' your body or something else. A hoe is a business woman. We're in business, the business of selling records."

When asked about their perceptions of such aggressive female im- 41 ages, the discussion group of Upward Bound students again split. Lani-etra said, "All women are not like that and the words they use to describe themselves are not necessary." Louis felt rappers don't actually use the lyrics they sing about as a personal thing with another person, they are using the lyrics to warn people about the females and males of today. Tonje added concern that such rap music makes females seem like sex objects that can only be used to satisfy a man's needs.

These youth easily identified specific popular songs which had mes- 42 sages that were positive and negative in relation to sex. The top three songs named as "good for moral thinking" were "Let's Wait Awhile" by Janet Jackson; "Growing Up" by Whodini; and "I Need Love" by L L Cool J. The top three songs listed as "bad for moral thinking about sex" were "Hey, We Want some Pussy" by the 2 Live Crew; "I Want Your Sex" by George Michael; and "Kanday" by L L Cool J.

THE ISSUE OF VIOLENCE

Another prominent issue which seems to follow the rap music phenom- 43
enon is violence. On December 28, 1991, nine youths were trampled to
death at a charity basketball game with rap artists at City College in New
York. On July 12, 1991, Alejandra Phillips, a supermarket clerk, was shot
outside a theater showing of *Boyz N' the Hood.* Cultural rap is often connected with such negative images of the black underclass. Pictures of
pimps, drug dealers, and gang members riding around with rap music
blasting loudly are prevalent in the media. Scholars like Jon Spencer have
questioned the link between rap and rape made by Tipper Gore's editorial in *The Washington Post,* "Hate, Rape, and Rap" and the juxtaposi-
tioning of the 2 Live Crew's lyrics with the rape of a New York jogger in
Central Park. Spencer suggests that when people see the word "rap" they
read the word "rape," and they often view "rappists" as rapists.

One of the groups most publicized when exploring violence are 44
NWA (Niggas with Attitude). NWA consists of five L.A. rappers whose
controversial lyrics include topics like gang banging, drive-by shootings,
and police confrontations. MTV refused to air their video, "Straight Outta
Compton," because they said it "glorified violence." The ex-leader of the
group, Ice Cube, says the group's lyrics deal with reality and violence is
their reality. "Our goals are to show the audience the raw reality of life.
When they come out the other end they gonna say, 'damn, it's like that
for real?' And, we're gonna make money" (Hochman 1989).

Williams (1990) disagrees that rap images and music are represen- 45
tative of the beliefs and ethics of black communities. He says when
women are treated like sex slaves and ideas like "materialism is God" are
put forth, they are not true visions of black America or black culture, but
a slice of the worst of a small element of black culture that is not em-
blematic of the black community at large.

The positive efforts of black rappers to eliminate violence in their 46
music and neighborhoods have not received as much publicity as the
negative. For example, various popular rap stars from the West Coast
such as NWA, Hammer, Young MC, and Digital Underground came together to record a single entitled "We're All in the Same Gang." It was a
rap song that spoke out against the senseless violence of gangs.

The East Coast's "Stop the Violence" campaign raised more than 47
$300,000 for youth-oriented community programs in New York. More
than a dozen rappers, like Ice T, Tone Loc, and King Tee participated in

the "Self Destruction" record and video which addressed the need to end black-on-black crime. The powerful lyrics and images of the song brought a new positive black urban consciousness into focus. As the song points out:

> Back in the sixties our brothers and sisters
>   were hanged, how could you gangbang?
> I never ran from the Ku Klux Klan, and I shouldn't have to
>   run from a black man.
> 'Cause that's self-destruction, self-destruction, you're
>   headed for self-destruction.

Kids are forced to learn from the rhythm of life around them. Rap 48 songs often include graphic images of drug dealers. The drug dealer is a very real personality in low-income neighborhoods. When asked to write down three questions they would include on a drug survey, Tamara asked, "Why do they (adults, authorities) allow the pushers to sell drugs on the corner by my school?" She later told me that it was very obvious what happens on that corner, but nobody bothers to do anything about it, so kids come to accept it too.

There is an obvious struggle going on in these kids' lives that links 49 them to the conflict-oriented nature of cultural rap. The violent urban environment which is a prominent theme in rap music is also a prominent reality. One example of that reality came from a worksheet concerning a rap tune called "Wild Wild West" by Kool Moe Dee. In the song, Kool Moe Dee raps about how he and his buddies stop others (including gangs) from coming into their neighborhoods and terrorizing people. He talks about taking control of his environment in a fashion appropriate to the Old West. In response to the song, Mary said she could relate to it because in her neighborhood, people are always getting into other people's personal business. Tim also knew what Kool Moe Dee was talking about because he and his homeboys (friends) were always scuffling (fighting) with somebody for respect. Michael said the song means that kids are growing up too hard in the streets. He added, "My school and neighborhood are a lot like that." Finally, James said he had a friend who got shot at a party "because of the way he looked at a guy and that's just how it is."

On a more positive side, several of the kids have come to understand 50 and change these negatives through their own raps. The Get It Girl Crew, four young ladies who love to rap, wrote the rap below as a testimony of their spirit and hope for the future.

Tricky B, Lady J, Lady Love and Kiddy B from up above,
we're the Get It Girl Crew and we're doing the do.
And, yes when we're on the mic we're talking to you,
homeboys and homegirls, with your jheri curls,
we'll blow you away, knock out those curls.
This is a rap for World Wide peace,
listen to my rhyme while my beat's released.
White and black, we're not the same color,
but in this world we're sisters and brothers.
I'll say this rhyme till my dying day,
I'd rather be dead, dead in my grave.
You talk about me and put my name down,
but when I take revenge I put your face in the ground.
This is Baby Rock in the place to be,
throwing a def rap on the M.I.C.
The Get It Girl Crew, there is none finer,
'cause we're the freshest and we're on fire.
We're the Get It Girl Crew with strength from above
We need peace, unity and love!

THE ISSUE OF RACISM

The issue of race in America is not a silent one today. Separate ideologies 51
of black power and white supremacy are prominent and dividing the nation even further as indicated by an ex-KKK leader, David Duke, running
for public office, the travesty of Rodney King's beating and trial in Los
Angeles that ignited riots, and the powerful slogan of Malcolm X, "By
any means necessary," as reemerging popular black ideology.

According to Pareles (1992), rap often sounds like a young black man 52
shouting about how angry he is and how he's going to hurt people. Pareles
says, "Rap's internal troubles reflect the poverty, violence, lack of education, frustration and rage of the ghetto. . . . Hating rap can be a synonym
for hating and fearing young black men who are also the stars of rap."

Samuels (1991) voices concern about the acceptance of racism in 53
this country through rap. He writes, "Gangster and racist raps foster a
voyeurism and tolerance of racism in which black and white are both
complicit, particularly when whites treat gangster raps as a window into
ghetto life."

Until recently, Public Enemy was the rap group who seemed to be 54
in the middle of the racist controversy. In response to the negative environment in the United States concerning race relations, rapper Chuck
D (1990) of Public Enemy makes statements such as "a black person is

better off dealing with a Klansman than a liberal." He goes on to quote Neely Fuller, Jr.'s; definition of a white liberal: "a white person who speaks and/or acts to maintain, expand and/or refine the practice of white supremacy (racism) by very skillfully pretending not to do so." Public Enemy has also called for the reorganization of the Black Panther party, a group considered radical in the 1960s that advocated violence and racism.

Public Enemy emerged into the headlines as racist when an ex-member, Professor Griff, made several statements that were considered anti-Semitic in a speech. Griff's comment involved his belief that Jews financed the slave trade and are responsible for apartheid in South Africa. He went on to ask, "Is it a coincidence that Jews run the jewelry business and it's named jew-elry?" (Dougherty, 1990.) 55

After firing Professor Griff, Chuck D responded to his comments in *Billboard* magazine. "We aren't anti-Jewish. We're pro-black," he said. "We're pro-culture, we're pro-human race. You can't talk about attacking racism and be racist" (Newman, 1989). According to Chuck D, the group is not here to offend anyone, but to fight the system which works against blacks twenty-four hours a day, 365 days a year. He adds, "We're not racists, we're nationalists, people who have pride and want to build a sense of unity amongst our own" (Newman, 1989). 56

Ice Cube is the second most prominent rapper to be labelled racist because of several controversial songs on his hit album, *Death Certificate.* He calls Koreans "Oriental one-penny motherfuckers" and lambasts members of his old group, NWA, about their Jewish manager. He raps, "Get rid of that Devil, real simple, put a bullet in his temple, 'cause you can't be the nigger for life crew, with a white Jew telling you what to do." In response to the criticism, Ice Cube says people need to pay heed to the frustration as they [black men] demand respect. 57

Ideology from the Nation of Islam, which is often called racist, is a major part of the controversy. Many rappers are reviving the words of black leaders like Elijah Muhammad and Louis Farrakhan, calling the white society devils and snakes, and advocating a new black solidarity. Several popular rappers are actually emerging from the Nation of Islam calling themselves "The 5 Percenters." These artists base their raps on the Islamic belief that only about 5 percent of the black nation knows that the black man *is* God and it's their duty to teach others. 58

Finally, racism is sometimes attributed to the Afrocentric voice; the pro-black attitude. The controversial KRS-One (Knowledge Reigns Supreme over Nearly Everyone) condemns gang violence, poor educational 59 systems, and drug use, but his attack on the "white system" has been called racially motivated. At fourteen, KRS One was a homeless runaway sleeping on steaming New York City sidewalk grates. At twenty-four, he has become a popular, positive rap star and educator. Queen Latifah is one of the most positive and powerful black female rappers. Her albums are rich in African cultural ideology and images as she dresses in African garb and tells kids that all black men and women are kings and queens. Queen Latifah believes that the only way to fight bigotry is to teach black children their history.

Cultural rap is so direct and angry that it can be frightening to those 60 who don't understand the frustration of these storytellers. For example, the decision not to honor the birthday of Martin Luther King, Jr., as a holiday in Arizona brought forth a rap from NWA with the theme "Gonna find a way to make the state pay" and the video portrayed the violent murders of several Arizona officials. Militant rapper Paris, on his album debut, *The Devil Made Me Do It,* presents a powerful, hard-edged commentary on the murder of Yousuf Hawkins in Bensonhurst called "The Hate that Hate Made." And the logo of Public Enemy shows the black male youth as a hunted animal with the motto "Kill or Be Killed." The image of a black silhouette is chilling within the crosshairs of a gun.

When Upward Bound students were asked to respond to the work- 61 sheet question, "How has growing up black, in your opinion, made a difference in your life?" a theme ran through the responses: the need to struggle or fight. Carlos, for instance, said being black causes him to struggle more for what he wants. He said, "At school, on TV, everywhere, other people get the things they want, but not me." Titus and Karon felt they had to fight a lot because of the color of their skin. "Fighting," according to Titus, "not only with people of other races." Damon explained, "Color really doesn't matter, but just because I'm black people expect me to be able to play sports and fight." When Damon went on to list the things which he felt might hinder him in his future success, his list included skin color, money, and friends.

As a whole, the group split on the issue of whether or not they felt 62 their skin color would affect their future. About half agreed with the statement "In the past, my skin color would have hindered my success, but that is not true today," and the other half disagreed.

When asked if they see Public Enemy, NWA, and other black- 63 conscious rappers as role models and heroes, the group said yes unanimously. As William explained, "They say what's going on in their hearts and that's what needs to be said." John added, "When brothers keep the pain inside they explode and that happens a lot around here." Nichole says she owns all of Public Enemy's tapes and she feels their music is important to help white people understand how black people feel about what's happening in black communities.

CONCLUSION

The history of black music is a history of adaptation, rebellion, accultur- 64 ation, and assimilation. An essential part of black music rests inherently in black experience. As we look closely, we realize that black music has always been a communicative response to the pressures and challenges within black American society.

The cultural rap music experience exists within the realm of spe- 65 cific environmental contexts. For the black urban adolescent, the environment manifests itself through their most popular music choice: rap. As they listen, they construct both shared and personal realities. Rappers rising from this context are empowering storytellers. Their oral wit and unique street style create a purposeful presence for inner-city ideology. Rap music has become the champion of an otherwise ignored and forgotten reality. Through critical spoken song, rappers are forcing cultural realities into the public arena. Rap music, therefore, serves not only as a mirror to this problematic community, but as a catalyst for it, providing legitimacy and hope.

Within popular culture, rap music has increased the sense of aware- 66 ness outside urban black America and interrupted normal flow of the commercialization process with a large dose of substance. Cultural musics, such as rap, often get caught in a repetitive cycle of acculturation, and are gradually absorbed into the pop mode. But, in opposition to pop-crossover rap, cultural rap has somehow managed to maintain elements which lie outside of social control, and escape the oppressive hegemonic forces.

Fiske's (1989) observations about such resistance and popular cul- 67 ture can be applied to the rap phenomenon. "The resistances of popular culture are not just evasive or semiotic; they do have a social dimension at the micro-level. And at this micro-level, they may well act as a constant erosive force upon the macro, weakening the system from within so that it is more amenable to change at the structural level." This is the power and promise of cultural rap.

The negative climate toward rap has been challenged by various 68 scholars as inaccurate and inadequate. Spencer (1991) believes that the current emergence of rap is a by-product of the "emergency of black." He connects rap ideology to the racial concerns of scholar Manning Marable, saying, "This emergency still involves the dilemma of the racial color-line, but it is complicated by the threat of racial genocide, the obliteration of all black institutions, the political separation of the black elite from the black working class, and the benign decimation of the 'ghetto poor,' who are perceived as nonproduction and therefore dispensable."

Dyson (1991) views rap music as a form of profound musical, cul- 69 tural, and social creativity. He says, "It expresses the desire of young black people to reclaim their history, reactivate forms of black radicalism, and contest the powers of despair, hopelessness, and genocide that presently besiege the black community. . . . It should be promoted as a worthy form of artistic expression and cultural projection, and as an enabling source of community solidarity."

Finally, Stephens (1991) sees rap music as a "crossroad to a new 70 transnational culture." He believes that "by conceptualizing rap as an intercultural communication crossroads located on a racial frontier, we can conceive how rap's non-black constituents use this artform as an interracial bridge, even as many blacks by defining it as 'only black' attempt to use it as a source of power and exclusive identity formation."

In considering such a transnational culture, the source of rap's pop- 71 ularity for white youth is then, less difficult to ascertain. It is obvious, however, that the rebellious nature of rap in many way parallels the rebellious nature of original rock and roll. Grossberg (1987), in discussing rock and roll today, says that the practice of critical encapsulation divides the cultural world into Us and Them. "While being a rock and roll fan," he goes on to explain, "sometimes does entail having a visible and self-conscious identity (such as punks, hippies, or mods), it more often does not appear visibly, on the surface of a fan's life, or even as a primary way in which most fans would define themselves."

Rap is also seen as an icon of resentment to the white status quo. 72 According to Spencer, as in any situation where an icon such as rap is attacked, there is always the potential that the attention will grant the music even further symbolic potency and, as a result, increase the population of listeners who subscribe to its newly broadened symbolism of protest.

As rock music sinks deeper into the mainstream, cultural rap music has 73 risen as a new rebellious youth movement. Self-understanding and practice are important elements in the cultural mirror of rap music style and it has fostered a liberating transcultural understanding. This rap experience becomes an all-encompassing one, which includes the outward projection and acceptance of rebellious identity and beliefs for all who listen.

I believe that through rap music, low-income black youth are able 74
to develop empowering values and ideologies, strengthen cultural interaction and establish positive identities. Rap music acts as a distinguishing mechanism as well as an informative cultural force for the
mainstream system, similar to other cultural musics such as heavy metal
and punk. As an integral part of the urban experience, the rap genre
serves as a bridge from favorite songs and artists to personal and social
realities. It is easy to see why mainstream society would feel uncomfortable with the sudden popularity of traditionally negative images like
dope dealers, pimps, and prostitutes in rap music. Yet these are very
real images and messages in the everyday world of the rapper and his
original fan: the black urban youth.

Rap music offers itself up as a unique and cohesive component of 75
urban black culture and is a positive struggle for black signification within popular culture. While there remain conflicts between negative and
positive, right and wrong, good and bad, the rap dynamic is an explicit
means of cultural communication fostering a crucial awareness of a
reawakening urban reality.

REFERENCES

Adler, Jerry, "The Rap Attitude," *Newsweek,* March 19, 1990, p. 59.

Bernard, James, "Bitches and Money," *The Source.* November 1991, p. 8.

Berry, Venise, "The Complex Relationship between Pop Music and Low-Income Black
   Adolescents: A Qualitative Approach," Dissertation, The University of Texas at Austin,
   May 1989.

Chuck D, "Black II Black," *SPIN,* 6, October 1990, pp. 67–68.

Cocks, Jay, "A Nasty Jolt for the Top Pops," *Time,* July 1, 1991, p. 78.

Cone, James, *The Spirituals and the Blues,* New York: Seabury Press, 1972.

Costello, Mark, and David Foster Wallace, *Signifying Rappers: Rap and Race in the
   Urban Present,* New York: The Ecco Press, 1990.

Dixon, Wheeler, "Urban Black American Music in the Late 1980s: The 'Word' as Cultural
   Signifier," *The Midwest Quarterly,* 30, Winter 1989, pp. 229–241.

Dougherty, Steve, "Charges of Anti-Semitism Give Public Enemy a Rep That's Tough to
   Rap Away," *People Weekly,* 33, March 5, 1990, pp. 40–41.

Dyson, Michael, "Performance, Protest and Prophecy in the Culture of Hip Hop," *Black
   Sacred Music: A Journal of Theomusicology,* 5, Spring 1991, p. 24.

Fiske, John, *Reading the Popular,* Boston: Unwin Hyman, 1989.

Frankel, Martha, "2 Live Doo Doo," *SPIN,* 6, October 1990, p. 62.

Garland, Phyl, *The Sound and Soul: Story of Black Music,* New York: Simon and
   Schuster, 1971.

Gates, David, "Decoding Rap Music," *Newsweek,* March 19, 1990, pp. 60–63.

Gladwin, Thomas, *Poverty U.S.A.,* Boston: Little, Brown, 1967.

Green, Kim, "Sisters Stompin' in the Tradition," *Young Sisters and Brothers*, November 1991, pp. 51–53.

———, "The Naked Truth," *The Source*, November 1991, pp. 33–36.

Grossberg, Lawrence, "Rock and Roll in Search of an Audience," in *Popular Music and Communication*, Ed. James Lull, Beverly Hills: Sage Publishing, 1987, pp. 175–198.

Gurevitch, Michael, *Culture, Society and the Media*, London: Methuen, 1982.

Haring, Bruce, "Lyric Concerns Escalate," *Billboard*, 101, November 11, 1989, p. 1.

Henderson, Alex, "New Rap Pack: Public Enemy," *Black Beat*, 20, January 1989, p. 44.

———, "2 Live Crew," *Black Beat*, 21, February 1990, p. 15–16.

———, "LA Rap All Stars: We're All in the Same Gang," *Black Beat*, 21, December 1990, p. 16.

Hochman, Steve, "NWA Cops an Attitude," *Rolling Stone*, 555, June 29, 1989, p. 24.

Hulbary, William, "Race, Deprivation and Adolescent Self-Images," *Social Science Quarterly*, 56, June 1975, pp. 105–114.

Kofsky, Frank, *Black Nationalism and the Revolution in Music*, New York: Pathfinder Press, 1970.

Kot, Greg, "Rap Offers a Soundtrack of Afro-American Experience," *Chicago Sunday Times*, February 16, 1992, Section 13, pp. 5, 24–25.

Leland, John, "Cube on Thin Ice," *Newsweek*, December 2, 1991, p. 69.

Levine, David, "Good Business, Bad Messages," *American Health*, May 1991, p. 16.

Logan, Andy, "Around City Hall," *The New Yorker*, January 27, 1992, pp. 64–65.

Lyndah and Michelle (Bytches wit' Problems), "A Bitch Is a Badge of Honor for Us," *Rappages*, 1, October 1991, p. 46.

Maultsby, Portia, "Soul Music: Its Sociological and Political Significance in American Popular Culture," *Journal of Popular Culture*, 17, Fall 1983, pp. 51–60.

Miller, Trudy, " '91 Holiday-Week Biz 3.7% Jollier than '90," *Billboard*, February 1, 1992, p. 46.

Mills, David, "The Obscenity Case: Criminalizing Black Culture," *Washington Post*, June 17, 1990, pp. G1, G8–G9.

———, "Five Percent Revolution," *Washington Post*, January 6, 1991, pp. G-1, G-6.

Nelson, Angela, "Theology in the Hip Hop of Public Enemy and Kool Moe Dee," *Black Sacred Music: A Journal of Theomusicology*, 5, Spring 1991, pp. 51–60.

Newman, Melinda, "Public Enemy Ousts Member over Remarks," *Billboard*, 101, July 1, 1989, pp. 1, 87.

"Paralyzed Man Files Suit over Boyz N' the Hood," *Jet*, 18, April 20, 1992, p. 61.

Pareles, Jon, "Fear and Loathing Along Pop's Outlaw Trail," *New York Times*, February 2, 1992, pp. 1, 23.

Perkins, William, "Nation of Islam Ideology in the Rap of Public Enemy," *Black Sacred Music: A Journal of Theomusicology*, 5, Spring, 1991, pp. 41–51.

Peterson-Lewis, Sonja, "A Feminist Analysis of the Defenses of Obscene Rap Lyrics," *Black Sacred Music: A Journal of Theomusicology*, 5, Spring 1991, pp. 68–80.

Poussaint, Alvin, and Carolyn Atkinson, "Black Youth and Motivation," in *Black Self Concept*, Ed. James Banks and Jean Grambs, New York, McGraw-Hill, 1972, pp. 55–69.

Riley, Norman, "Footnotes of a Culture at Risk," *The Crisis*, 93, March 1986, p. 24.

Roberts-Thomas, K., "Say It Loud I'm Pissed and I'm Proud," *Eight Rock*, 1, Summer 1990, pp. 28–31.

Rogers, Charles, "New Age Rappers with a Conscience," *Black Beat*, 20, April 1989, pp. 41, 75.

Royster, Phillip, "The Rapper as Shaman for a Band of Dancers of the Spirit: 'U Can't Touch This,'" *Black Sacred Music: A Journal of Theomusicology*, 5, Spring 1991, pp. 60–68.

Samuels, David, "The Rap on Rap," *The New Republic*, 205, November 11, 1991, pp. 24–26.

Shusterman, Richard, "The Fine Art of Rap," *New Literary History*, 22, Summer 1991, pp. 613–632.

Singletary, Sharon, "Livin' in a Hoe House?" *Rappages*, 1, October 1991, p. 60.

Spencer, Jon Michael, "The Emergency of Black and the Emergence of Rap: Preface," *Black Sacred Music: A Journal of Theomusicology*, 5, Spring 1991, pp. v–vii.

Standifer, James, "Music Behavior of Blacks in American Society," *Black Music Research Journal*, 1, 1980, pp. 51–62.

Stephens, Gregory, "Rap Music's Double Voiced Discourse: A Crossroads for Interracial Communication," *Journal of Communication Inquiry*, 15, Summer 1991, p. 72.

Stephens, Ronald, "Three Waves of Contemporary Rap Music," in *Black Sacred Music: A Journal of Theomusicology*, 5, Spring 1991, pp. 25–41.

"Top 200 Albums," *Billboard*, January 18, 1992, p. 86.

Walton, Ortiz, *Music Black, White and Blue*, New York: William Morrow and Co., 1972.

Williams, Juan, "The Real Crime: Making Heroes of Hate Mongers," *Washington Post*, June 17, 1990, pp. G-1, G-8.

READING FOR INFORMATION

1. Underline Berry's statement of intent. What will she explore in the essay?

2. Differentiate between pop-cultural and pop-crossover domains.

3. Explain how spirituals, the blues, jazz, soul, and rap are forms of cultural communication.

4. Why is "cultural rap" viewed negatively?

5. How did the Upward Bound students view 2 Live Crew (paragraph 36), record censorship (paragraph 37), and aggressive female images in rap (paragraph 41)?

6. Explain how black rappers have tried to eliminate violence in their music and neighborhoods.

7. Has anyone challenged the negative climate toward rap?

READING FOR FORM, ORGANIZATION, AND EXPOSITORY FEATURES

1. Comment on Berry's opening paragraphs. Are they effective? Why or why not?

2. What types of evidence (facts, statistics, references to authorities, and so forth) does Berry use to develop and support her argument?

3. Describe the features of the article that help the reader follow Berry's train of thought.

READING FOR RHETORICAL CONCERNS

1. Describe Berry's rhetorical goal. Do you think she achieves it?
2. Do you think Berry gives sufficient weight to opposing views? Why or why not?
3. Compare Berry's intended audience to Brookhiser's.

WRITING ASSIGNMENTS

1. Write an essay in which you agree or disagree with Berry's views on popular culture:

   Popular culture is made by subordinated peoples in their own interests out of resources that also, contradictorily, serve the economic interests of the dominant. Popular culture is made from within and below, not imposed from without and above as mass cultural theorists would have it. There is always an element of popular culture that lies outside of social control, that escapes or opposes hegemonic forces. (paragraph 19)

2. Write a short evaluative essay about whether or not Berry's assessment of the subject of sex in rap is accurate.
3. Write a brief essay describing the cultural conditions out of which rap emerges.
4. Write a critical response to Berry's claim that rap music is not only the mirror to black urban adolescents, it also provides them with "legitimacy and hope" (paragraph 65).

SYNTHESIS WRITING ASSIGNMENTS

1. Drawing on selections by Frith, Gracyk, and Berry, write an essay in which you synthesize the three critics' ideas about the value of rock music. Address your essay to an audience of students who have read the texts.
2. Drawing on selections by Frith and Berry, write an essay in which you demonstrate how rap music serves social functions for urban African-American youth. Address your essay to an audience of students who have not read the texts.
3. Write an essay explaining why Brookhiser would object to Paglia's, Gracyk's, and Berry's views on rock music. Address your essay to an audience of students who have read the texts.

4. Drawing on selections by Paglia, Gracyk, and Berry, either challenge or support the claim that rock is the music of rebellion. Address your essay to an audience of students who have not read the texts.

5. Draw upon selections by Frith, Paglia, Gracyk, and Berry to write a critical response to the selection by Brookhiser.

6. Gracyk claims that Paglia, like Nietzsche, "does not regard the masses as capable of appreciating true art when they encounter it" (paragraph 4). Would the same criticism apply to Frith, Brookhiser, and Berry? Write an essay in response. Address your essay to an audience of students who have read the texts.

7. Drawing on the selections in Chapter 12, write an essay explaining to your readers the relationship between pop and rock music and the commercial marketplace. Is the music "authentic" expression, or is it created only for the mainstream and compromised for profit?

CHAPTER

t h i r t e e n

Literatures of Diaspora:
Fiction and Nonfiction

Within the humanities, the various disciplines of literary criticism, theater arts, history of art, and musicology attempt to assess the cultural products of human civilization. Courses in literature, drama, art, and music train students to analyze, interpret, and evaluate meaningful "texts." We use the word "text" in a broad sense to refer to any composition, whether of words, as in poetry, drama, and prose fiction or nonfiction; of color, line, and texture, as in painting, sculpture, and architecture; or of sound and movement, as in music and dance, film, and television. The questions one might ask about one sort of text resemble those one might ask about other sorts. They concern the selection and arrangement of appropriate materials; the tone, attitude, and point of view that govern their selection and arrangement; similarities to and comparisons and contrasts with other texts; and further questions about relationships between texts and the sociocultural contexts of their production and reception.

One aim of literary criticism, art history, and music theory is to make the meaning of such "texts" more accessible to us. This aim is especially visible when the text displays a social, historical, or cultural otherness whose assumptions differ from ours. Shakespeare's plays, for example, profit from a critical and historical analysis that illuminates differences between early modern attitudes and our own. Sometimes the technical jargon of an analysis may have the opposite effect: It may make the object of study appear more impenetrable than ever. A musicological study of flats and sharps, harmonies and counterpoints, arpeggios and staccatos in

631

one of Mozart's string quarters may distance us entirely from the sound of the music. If we reflect upon its purpose, however, we may find that it evokes complexity only because the process of understanding any worthwhile text is correspondingly complex. It does not seek to replace an experience of the work of art. It seeks, rather, to explore the ramifications of that experience as they connect with social, historical, moral, political, philosophical, ideological, psychological, aesthetic, and other experiences. The outcome of good criticism shows us that what we take for granted in a text may be not so simple after all.

If academic approaches to expressive forms demonstrate the otherness, difference, and complexity of those forms, many of the texts that they study deal with otherness, difference, and complexity in a primary way. Fiction, nonfiction, poetry, drama, painting, sculpture, photography, film, television, song, dance, and instrumental music all provide us with glimpses into other worlds. They can represent customs, conventions, ways of life, and human experiences that different audiences might not otherwise have. Or, if they represent a world accessible to their audience, they do so best when they afford a new perspective on that world.

The selections in this chapter deal with otherness, difference, and accessibility by focusing on a range of fictional and nonfictional texts from a heterogeneous world culture. The word "diaspora" refers to the scattering and dispersion of people with a common ethnic origin. The first selection is a short story by the South American writer Isabel Allende, now a resident of the United States, and it concerns the dubious rise to prosperity and prestige of an oddly matched couple—she is Scotch, he is Spanish—amid varied immigrant and indigenous groups in Latin America. The second selection is a controversial account of tensions between displaced Palestinians and Jews by an Israeli writer, David Grossman, who uses literary techniques of dramatic dialogue, storytelling, and interlocking structure to represent a real-life situation. In the third selection, Ronald Takaki, a professional historian, uses similar techniques to describe patterns of Japanese immigration to America in the nineteenth century. The last two selections are works of fiction. Bharati Mukherjee's short story narrates the assimilation of an illegal immigrant from the West Indies into the academic community of Ann Arbor, Michigan. Alice Walker's short story depicts the bonds that relate three generations of African-American women to their ancestors despite the scattering of their origins and dispersion of their roots.

The Proper Respect

Isabel Allende

Isabel Allende, niece of the assassinated Marxist president of Chile, Salvador Allende, has worked as a journalist in Chile, Venezuela, and the United States. Currently residing in California, she has written best-selling novels, including The House of the Spirits *(1982),* Love and Shadows *(1985),* Eva Luna *(1987),* Infinite Plan *(1991), and* Paula *(1994); nonfiction such as* Paths of Resistance: The Art and Craft of the Political Novel *(1989); and many short stories.*

PREREADING

To an even greater extent than the mixed peoples of North America, the population of South America represents a multicultural patchwork of ethnic and national origins. Though significantly influenced by Spain and the Spanish language, its racial composition includes Native American, Asians, Africans, Middle Easterners, and Europeans, with sometimes profound cultural differences among them. Consult an atlas, an almanac, and a world encyclopedia to learn more about these differences.

They were a pair of scoundrels. He had the face of a pirate, and 1 he dyed his hair and mustache jet black; with time, he changed his style and left the gray, which softened his expression and lent him a more circumspect air. She was fleshy, with the milky skin of reddish blondes, the kind of skin that in youth reflects light with opalescent brush strokes, but with age becomes crinkled paper. The years she had spent in the oil workers' camps and tiny towns on the frontier had not drained her vigor, the heritage of her Scots ancestors. Neither mosquitoes nor heat nor abuse had spoiled her body or diminished her desire for dominance. At fourteen she had run away from her father, a Protestant pastor who preached the Bible deep in the jungle; his was a totally futile

Reprinted with the permission of Scribner, a Division of Simon & Schuster, from *The Stories of Eva Luna* by Isabel Allende, translated from the Spanish by Margaret Sayers Peden (New York: Macmillan, 1991) 225–33. Copyright © 1989 by Isabel Allende. English translation copyright © 1991 by Macmillan Publishing Company.

labor, since no one understood his English palaver and, furthermore, in those latitudes words, even the word of God, were lost in the jabbering of the birds. At fourteen the girl had reached her full growth and was in absolute command of her person. She was not sentimental. She rejected one after another of the men who, attracted by the incandescent flame of her hair, so rare in the tropics, had offered her their protection. She had never heard love spoken of, and it was not in her nature to invent it; on the other hand, she knew how to make the most of the only commodity she possessed, and by the time she was twenty-five she had a handful of diamonds sewed into the hem of her petticoat. She handed them over without hesitation to Domingo Toro, the bull of a man who had managed to tame her, an adventurer who trekked through the region hunting alligators and trafficked in arms and bootleg whiskey. He was an unscrupulous rogue, the perfect companion for Abigail McGovern.

In their first years together, the couple had fabricated bizarre 2 schemes for accumulating capital. With her diamonds, his alligator hides, funds he had obtained dealing contraband, and chicanery at the gaming tables, Domingo had purchased chips at the casino he knew were identical to those used on the other side of the border where the value of the currency was much stronger. He filled a suitcase with chips, made a brief trip, and traded them for good hard cash. He was able to repeat the operation twice more before the authorities became suspicious, and even when they did they could not accuse him of anything illegal. In the meantime, Abigail had been selling clay pots and bowls she bought from the Goajiros and sold as archeological treasures to the gringos who worked with National Petroleum—with such success that soon she branched out into fake Colonial paintings produced by a student in his cubbyhole behind the cathedral and preternaturally aged with sea water, soot, and cat urine. By then Abigail, who had outgrown her roughneck manners and speech, had cut her hair and now dressed in expensive clothes. Although her taste was a little extreme and her effort to appear elegant a little too obvious, she could pass as a lady, which facilitated social relationships and contributed to the success of her business affairs. She entertained clients in the drawing rooms of the Hotel Inglés and, as she served them tea with the measured gestures she had learned by imitation, she would natter on about big-game hunting and tennis tournaments in hypothetical places with British-sounding names that no one could locate on a map. After the third cup she would broach in a confidential tone the subject of the meeting. She would show her guests photographs of the purported antiquities, making it clear that her proposal was to save those

treasures from local neglect. The government did not have the resources
to preserve these extraordinary objects, she would say, and to slip them
out of the country, even though it was against the law, constituted an act
of archeological conscience.

Once the Toros had laid the foundations for a small fortune, Abigail's   3
next plan was to found a dynasty, and she tried to convince Domingo of
the need to have a good name.

"What's wrong with ours?"   4

"No one is called Toro, that's a barroom name," Abigail argued.

"It was my father's name, and I don't intend to change it."

"In that case, we will have to convince the world that we are
wealthy."

She suggested that they buy land and plant bananas or coffee, as so-   5
cial snobs had done before them; but he did not like the idea of moving
to the interior, a wild land fraught with the danger of bands of thieves,
the army, guerrillas, snakes, and all the diseases known to man. To him
it seemed insane to head off into the jungle in search of a future when a
fortune was theirs for the taking right in the capital; it would be less risky
to dedicate themselves to commerce, like the thousands of Syrians and
Jews who had debarked with nothing but misery in the packs slung over
their backs, but who within a few years were living in the lap of luxury.

"No small-time stuff!" objected Abigail. "What I want is a re-   6
spectable family; I want them to call us *don* and *doña* and not dare speak
to us without removing their hats."

But Domingo was adamant, and finally she accepted his decision.   7
She nearly always did, because anytime she opposed her husband, he
punished her by withdrawing communication and sexual favors. He would
disappear from the house for days at a time, return hollow-eyed from his
clandestine mischief, change his clothes, and go out again, leaving Abigail at first furious and then terrified at the idea of losing him. She was a
practical person totally devoid of romantic notions, and if once there had
been a seed of tenderness in her, the years she had spent on her back had
destroyed it. Domingo, nevertheless, was the only man she could bear to
live with, and she was not about to let him get away. The minute Abigail
gave in, Domingo would come home and sleep in his own bed. There
were no noisy reconciliations; they merely resumed the rhythm of their
routines and returned to the complicity of their questionable dealings.
Domingo Toro set up a chain of shops in poor neighborhoods, where he
sold goods at low prices but in huge quantities. The stores served as a
screen for other, less legal, activities. Money continued to pile up, and

they could afford the extravagances of the very wealthy, but Abigail was not satisfied: she had learned that it is one thing to have all the comforts but something very different to be accepted in society.

"If you had paid attention to me, they wouldn't be thinking of us   8
as Arab shopkeepers. Why did you have to act like a ragpicker?" she protested to her husband.

"I don't know why you're complaining; we have everything."

"Go ahead and sell that trash, if that's what you want, but I'm going to buy racehorses."

"Horses? What do you know about horses, woman?"

"I know that they're classy. Everyone who is anyone has horses."

"You'll be the ruin of us."

For once Abigail had her way, and in a very short time had proved   9
that her idea was not a bad one. Their stallions gave them an excuse to mingle with the old horse-breeding families and, in addition, were extremely profitable, but although the Toros appeared frequently in the racing section, their names were never in the society pages. Disheartened, Abigail compensated with even more vulgar ostentation. She bought a china service with her hand-painted portrait on every piece, cut-glass goblets, and furniture with raging gargoyles carved on the feet. Her prize, however, was a threadbare armchair she passed off as a Colonial relic, telling everyone it had belonged to El Libertador, which was why she had tied a red cord across the arms, so no one would place his unworthy buttocks where the Father of the Nation had sat. She hired a German governess for her children, and a Dutch vagabond who affected an admiral's uniform as custodian of the family yacht. The only vestiges of their past life were Domingo's buccaneer's tattoos and an old injury to Abigail's back, a consequence of spread-legged contortions during her oil-field days; but long sleeves covered his tattoos, and she had a silk-padded iron corset made to prevent pain from infringing upon her dignity. By then she was obese, laden with jewels, the spit and image of Nero. Greed had wrought the physical havoc her jungle adventures had not imposed upon her.

For the purpose of attracting the most select members of society,   10
every year the Toros hosted a masked ball at Carnival time: the Court of Baghdad with the elephant and camels from the zoo and an army of waiters dressed as Bedouins; a Bal de Versailles at which guests in brocade gowns and powdered wigs danced the minuet amid beveled mirrors; and other scandalous revels that became a part of local legend and gave rise to violent diatribes in leftist newspapers. The Toros had to

post guards before the house to prevent students—outraged by such extravagance—from painting slogans on the columns and throwing excrement through the windows, alleging that the newly rich filled their bathtubs with champagne, while to eat, the newly poor hunted cats on the rooftops. Such lavish displays had afforded the Toros a degree of respectability, because by then the line that divided the social classes was vanishing; people were flocking into the country from every corner of the globe, drawn by the miasma of petroleum. Growth in the capital was uncontrolled, fortunes were made and lost in the blink of an eye, and it was no longer possible to ascertain the ancestry of every individual. Even so, the old families kept their distance from the Toros, despite the fact they themselves had descended from other immigrants whose only merit was to have reached these shores a half-century sooner. They attended Domingo and Abigail's banquets and sometimes sailed around the Caribbean in the yacht piloted by the firm hand of the Dutch captain, but they did not return the invitations. Abigail might have been forced to resign herself to second-class status had an unforeseen event not changed their luck.

On a late August afternoon Abigail had awakened unrefreshed from 11 her siesta; it was unbearably hot and the air was heavy with presages of a coming storm. She had slipped a silk dress over her corset and ordered her chauffeur to drive her to the beauty salon. They drove through the heavy traffic with the windows closed, to forestall any malcontent who might spit at the *señora* through an open window—something that happened more and more frequently. They stopped before the salon at exactly five o'clock, which Abigail entered after instructing the chauffeur to come for her one hour later. When he returned to pick her up, Abigail was not there. The hairdresser said that about five minutes after she had arrived, the *señora* had said she had a brief errand to run, and had not returned. Meanwhile, in his office Domingo Toro had received a call from the Red Pumas, an extremist group no one had heard of until then, announcing that they had kidnapped his wife.

That was the beginning of the scandal that was to assure the Toros' 12 reputation. The police had taken the chauffeur and the hairdressers into custody, searched entire barrios, and cordoned off the Toros' mansion, to the subsequent annoyance of their neighbors. During the day a television van blocked the street, and a throng of newspaper reporters, detectives, and curiosity seekers trampled the lawns. Domingo Toro appeared on television, seated in a leather chair in his library between a globe of the world and a stuffed mare, imploring the kidnappers to release the mother of his children. The cheapgoods magnate, as the press had labeled him, was offering a million in local currency in exchange for his wife—an inflated amount considering that a different guerrilla group had obtained only half that much for a Middle East ambassador. The Red Pumas, however, had not considered the sum sufficient, and had doubled the ransom. After seeing Abigail's photograph in the newspaper, many believed that Domingo Toro's best move would be to pay the ransom—not for the return of his wife, but to reward the kidnappers for keeping her. Incredulity swept the nation when the husband, after consultations with bankers and lawyers, accepted the deal despite warnings by police. Hours before delivering the stipulated sum, he had received a lock of red hair through the mail, with a note indicating that the price had gone up another quarter of a million. By then, the Toro children had also appeared on television, sending desperate filial messages to their mother. The macabre auction was daily rising in pitch, and given full coverage by the media.

The suspense ended five days later, just as public curiosity was 13 beginning to be diverted by other events. Abigail was found, bound and gagged, in a car parked in the city center, a little nervous and bedraggled but without visible signs of harm and, if anything, slightly more plump. The afternoon that she returned home, a small crowd gathered in the street to applaud the husband who had given such strong proof of his love. In the face of harassment from reporters and demands from the police, Domingo Toro had assumed an attitude of discreet gallantry, refusing to reveal how much he had paid, with the comment that his wife was beyond price. People wildly exaggerated the figure, crediting to him a payment much greater than any man would have given for a wife, least of all his. But all this speculation had established the Toros as the ultimate symbol of opulence; it was said they were as rich as the President, who for years had profited from the proceeds of the nation's oil and whose fortune was calculated to be one of the five largest in the world. Domingo and Abigail were raised to the peak of high society, the inner sanctum from which they had previously been excluded. Nothing clouded their triumph, not even public protests by students, who hung banners at the University accusing Abigail of arranging her own kidnapping, the magnate of withdrawing millions from one pocket and putting them into another without penalty of taxes, and the police of swallowing the story of the Red Pumas in order to frighten the populace and justify purges against opposition parties. But no evil tongue could destroy the glorious result of the kidnapping, and a decade later the Toro-McGoverns were known as one of the nation's most respectable families. 🐚

READING FOR INFORMATION

1. Explain the differences between settling on a plantation and living in the capital as Domingo Toro perceives them in paragraph 5. What businesses does he conduct in paragraph 7?
2. Summarize the events that precede Abigail's disappearance in paragraph 11. Does she appear to shape the event?
3. List the major details that suggest a time frame for the story. When do you think it takes place?

READING FOR FORM, ORGANIZATION, AND EXPOSITORY FEATURES

1. Summarize from paragraph 2 the process and intention of Abigail's first efforts to pass as a lady.
2. Explain in your own words what the "vestiges of their past life" signify in paragraph 9.
3. List the details in paragraphs 12 and 13 that suggest the couple has staged Abigail's kidnapping.

READING FOR RHETORICAL CONCERNS

1. Explain in your own words what the narrator means by characterizing Abigail in paragraph 7 as "a practical person totally devoid of romantic notions." What does her practicality suggest about her motivations for seeking respect?
2. Describe the narrator's tone in paragraph 12. What is the significance of identifying Domingo as a "cheapgoods magnate" and of emphasizing his inflated ransom?
3. Describe the narrator's tone in paragraph 13.

WRITING ASSIGNMENTS

1. Write an analytical profile of the narrator. Does he or she admire the Toros? trust them? sympathize with their efforts? How does the narrator encourage the reader to adopt a skeptical attitude?

2. Write an analytical critique of how the story represents mass culture and popular opinion. What implications does the multicultural diversity of the setting have for the Toros' success? How do the Toros manipulate media and appearances, and what does their manipulation imply about those taken in by it? Though the story is set in Latin America, could its outcome happen elsewhere?

Sleeping on a Wire

David Grossman

David Grossman is an Israeli novelist, journalist, dramatist, and nonfiction writer whose works have won many awards. His first novel, The Smile of the Lamb, *received the Israeli Publishers' Association Prize in 1985.*

PREREADING

Grossman's essay records conversations with and among six groups of Arab-Israelis, non-Jewish citizens of the State of Israel who feel their Arab identities diminished in a homeland designated for Jewish sovereignty after the Holocaust. Tensions between Arabs and Jews have flared since the chartering of Israel by the United Nations in 1948. Consult entries in encyclopedias, almanacs, and historical digests in your college library to learn more about Israel's troubled internal history in recent decades.

"The Jews don't know enough about us. They don't even want to   1
know that there's another nation here. Who really cares what I feel? Who will want to read your book about us? But it's our fault, too, for not even trying to let you know who we are. We didn't bother. Maybe because we have a feeling that the authorities know everything about us anyway. They're the bosses, you know, the security agents, the state, the Ministry of Education, and it's as if they've already settled everything for us in advance. They've already planned out our future, and all that's left for us is

Excerpt from *Sleeping on a Wire: Conversations with Palestinians in Israel* by David Grossman, translated by Haim Watzman (New York: Farrar, Straus & Giroux, 1993) 3–21. Translation copyright © 1993 by Haim Watzman. Reprinted by permission of Farrar, Straus, & Giroux, Inc.

to toe the line. And we really toe it. That's how we've demeaned and wronged ourselves.

"But the Jews have to know what we're really thinking. We've already framed our ambitions, and they contain nothing that can harm the Jews. They can be stated openly and without theatrics: We're not in love with the Jews, not happy, not 'How wonderful, they're here'; but they're here, and we'll have to live with that. And if we aren't honest with ourselves, we're done for. If we make a big show of it and try to act as if everything's fine, we'll have internalized all of Western politics, and our identity will be lost completely."

—Mohammed Daroushe, twenty-eight, Iksal

PROLOGUE

One hot night in July 1991, I visited a summer camp in the Lavie Forest. Israeli boys and girls, Jews and Arabs, were standing and debating the state's treatment of its Arab citizens, the Arab's disregard of Israel's complex predicament, the way the army fights the intifadah. With righteous wrath and youthful charm they hammered home their arguments, worn from overuse. As I watched them, I could not tell by sight who was Jewish and who was Arab. Their features are similar, their clothes and hair styled by the dictates of the same fashions; even their body language is the same, as is the Hebrew they speak. Only the accent is different. I recalled that I had already participated in such an event—when I was their age, more or less, in a Jewish-Arab summer camp in Acre. Then, more than twenty years ago, we might have been distinguished from each other by our dress, language, and degree of contentiousness during a debate, but what has not changed since then is the sharpness of mutual emotion, the powerful need to have this particular individual understand you and confirm your feelings—and the awkwardness and illusion, because at times he is close by, that individual, and then suddenly he is far away, and how can someone so close to me be so wrong about me; how can someone so distant know me so well?

The circle of disputants opened abruptly. A boy of perhaps fourteen, who stood on the outside, was thrust toward me, and a trail of whispers rose and swooped after him. "He's the one who ran away," someone said in an undertone, and the debate instantly died.

"We sat with him all day, three Jews, three Arabs," a boy named Itai explained. "We talked with him, made him think."

The boy, M., listened to what was being said about him. He was a   6
somewhat clumsy, pale type, his movements guarded, his gaze older than
his age.

"It hurt me that M. ran away," said Sana,[1] from Acre. "It was im-   7
portant to me that he stay here, that we change preconceptions together. Because there were two Jewish girls here, right-wing, and they
decided to go home . . . "

Murmurs of agreement, Jewish and Arab, and a slight, common   8
sense of pride. I asked M. why he had come to the camp.

"To have a good time. For a vacation," he responded, caught up in   9
himself but apparently not at all put off by the interest he was attracting.
"I read that it was a camp for Jews and Arabs, but I didn't realize it was
Jews and Arabs together so much. And I—before that, what can I say,
being with Arabs really didn't grab me." While he spoke the others were
silent, drawn by the confession. "So I came, and right away I saw that it's
really together. More than I thought. Them and us together all the time.
Even at night. And I started feeling uneasy."

An Arab boy named Basel asked if he had known Arabs before.   10

"Yes. I was with Arabs once, but not like this. I was with my grandfather's laborers. But with them it was different, and here it became clear
to me—I didn't especially like the idea of sleeping together, me and
them, in the same tent."

"It didn't bother me to sleep together with Jews," Basel objected.

"I . . . " M. hesitated. "At night I couldn't take it anymore . . . I
went behind the tents, until I found a hole in the fence, and I left."

I thought of the way through the forest to the camp—a steep, nar-   11
row road between pine trees, the caves, the jagged rocks.

"We warned him not to leave," Itai said. "The forest is full of old
wells you could fall into at night."

"It was after nine o'clock," M. continued in a low voice, in awe of
himself, as if only as he spoke did he comprehend what had actually happened. "It was pitch black. No one saw me leave. I went through the
fence, hunched over, so they wouldn't see, into the forest."

The young people were transfixed by his white face. The strange   12
story stripped them of their youthful cockiness, and for a moment they
looked like children. Beyond the small, tight circle, the camp seemed
like a far-off memory. Light bulbs weakly illuminated the cots, adolescents
walked down the path from the shower; in one of the tents a boy preened

---

[1] Out of consideration for the reader who does not know Arabic, names and terms from that language are not transliterated "scientifically."

in front of a girl, and on the bed right next to them another girl lay on her belly, buried in a book.

"But what exactly were you scared of?" Sana whispered, a lock of hair in her mouth.

"I was scared, you think I know why? That they might rob me. That they'd do something to me . . . I felt really uneasy about it," he said, shrugging his shoulders apologetically. "I mean, about the tent, being the only Jew, and everyone around me an Arab. That we have to be together, for real."

"And did you know where you were going?" asked a voice out of the darkness.

"More or less . . . not exactly. I walked to where I thought there'd be a main road, and I thought I'd wait until morning and find a bus to go home to Jerusalem."

"Did you know the way?"

"I knew I had to go down. I got so mixed up."

"Did you find the road?"

"The police found me by the road."

"They found him in a total daze, crying," whispered a girl behind me.

"How long did you wander like that?"

"I don't know."

"Weren't you scared in the forest?"

"Sure I was scared," M. said, "but I was more scared in the tent."

It was morning in the *midafeh*—the room where guests are received—in the house of Hassan Ali Masalha in Kafr Kara. Passions flared among the men seated on mats; the elder Hassan Masalha was debating with his son. The former was saying, "The Palestinians have only lost and will continue to lose from the intifadah." His son jumped up, mortified at his father's words: "What is economic loss? That's a loss? In the territories they have culture now? *There* they have principles! *There* they have no crime! *There* there are no drugs!" The old man, reclining comfortably on a thin mattress, an embroidered pillow under his forearm, dismissed his son's words with a single wave of his hand. Another elder, Fahmi Fanaka, leaned over to me and whispered, "The Palestinians will have a state, but for us, the train has already passed us by." As I wrote this down, the windows in the large, unfurnished room suddenly shook from a sonic boom. An unfamiliar expression passed over the faces of all those present, skipping like a spark from eye to eye. "It's only an airplane," I said to the man next to me, reassuring him, as we do in

Jerusalem when there is a loud explosion. "I know," the man replied quietly. "It's probably going to Lebanon." I wanted to ask him another question, but the commotion resumed, the debate between the old father and his angry son, and I forgot the incident.

In Beit Hanina, to the north of Jerusalem, in a small apartment 15 full of burgeoning plants, Adel Mana—who was born in the Galilee village of Majd el-Krum—told me the story of his childhood, and then I remembered.

A long, harsh story. The village resisted the Israeli Army in 1948, and 16 after it was overcome, the army gathered all its inhabitants in the central square. According to Adel Mana, the soldiers shot four of those who had participated in the fighting. Afterward they put several hundred of the villagers on buses and took them to Wadi Ara, where they let them off at some unknown point in the middle of the night and said, Eastward, and whoever returns gets shot. Mana himself was then a one-year-old baby. He wandered with his parents to Nablus, to Jordan, to Syria, and to Lebanon. His first memories are from there, how other members of the family joined them in the refugee camp, how his father would steal into Israel to get money from his grandmother and sisters who had remained in Majd el-Krum, or sometimes to help them press the olives or harvest wheat in the summer.

"At the beginning of '51 we 'made *aliya*,'" he related. "We did what 17 you call 'illegal immigration.' We came in a boat from Sidon to Acre with a few other families from the village. My uncle, Father's brother, was uncertain whether to join us. Of course, he wanted to return to the village, but he was afraid of what they would do to him here. He was also afraid because many were killed when they tried to cross the border. When we set off, he stayed there, in Ein el-Hilweh."

"And then what happened?"

"He married, and he has a family there. We twice submitted re- 18 quests to the army to allow him to visit us. They were approved and he came. The last time was in '82. After that they didn't allow it anymore. Now we are almost unable to maintain contact with him. If we can, we send him letters. That's all. If we hear that the air force bombed Lebanon, obviously the first thing we think is, What about him, what about his children?"

It was then, some weeks later, that I caught the glances of the men 19 in the *midafeh*.

In Nazareth I spoke to Lutfi Mashour, editor of the weekly news- 20 paper *As-Sinara*: "My wife is from Bethlehem. She is the spoils I brought home from the Six-Day War, so you see that something good also came out of the occupation. My daughters have a grandfather there, my wife's father. Once the grandfather went to the civil administration to request that they renew his driver's license. He is eighty-five, but his health is excellent and he wants to continue to drive. He came to the administration's headquarters and saw Arabs kneeling down. Not on two knees, only on one. A soldier told him, Kneel like them. Grandfather said, 'I'm already eighty-five years old, and you can shoot me, but I won't kneel down.' The soldier let him be, but said, 'Because of that you'll go to everyone and collect their identity cards.' There were about three hundred people there. Grandfather, eighty-five years old, had to be insulted like that, to have a young soldier use him as an errand boy, and to take the cards from his kneeling brothers. He told the soldier, 'You have power and I'll do it, but why are you forcing them to kneel?' The soldier said, 'How else could I keep an eye on them all?' 'Bring an empty barrel and stand on it.' 'I should go to all that effort for them?' The soldier laughed.

"This is what my daughters have to hear. These are girls who were 21 born in the State of Israel, and every day they hear a new story from Grandfather, from their uncles, and they're fed up. I should tell you that we have decided to send them overseas to study, because if they stay here, I don't know what will happen to them. They've been through the seven circles of hell since they were small, through insults and curses, through substandard schools, through searches and roadblocks at the airport, and now these stories about their grandfather. I'm telling you that if they stayed here a little longer, we would lose control of them. Had I been in their position, I would have lost control long ago, and I don't know what will happen to them in the future. Don't you know, there's a new generation here. A generation that did not experience our fears, that isn't intimidated by you."

At such moments, almost incidentally, a full, three-dimensional 22 picture took shape as if it were crystallizing in a glass. I really should have recognized it. After all, like everyone else I knew that the Arabs who live in Israel have extensive links with the Palestinians in the territories and in the Arab countries. I knew the historical background, that about 160,000 Arabs remained here after the 1948 war and almost 600,000 of their relatives fled or were expelled. I remembered well the longings of the refugees in the camps for the cities and villages from which they were uprooted, and for their relatives there. But only at the sound of those slight, involuntary sighs, or at the sight of the faces of

the men around me draining of blood when an airplane passed overhead, could I for the first time feel it within myself, without putting up
any defenses. Those moments were repeated again and again—like the
story of the cousin who disappeared in Nablus, arrested by the army for
interrogation; for an entire week his whereabouts were unknown. An
entire family, in Israel and in Nablus, went mad with worry. And the
aunt, in whose house the search was conducted, from whom the entire
family's picture albums, all those precious moments, were confiscated.
And how you almost die before you find out exactly what names are
behind the laconic news on the radio of dead and wounded in "distur-
bances" in Jenin or in Ramallah, or what goes through your head when
the newscaster reports that "all our planes have returned safely."

"My Palestinian brother there," said Hassan Ali Masalah from Kafr   23
Kara, the old man, paunchy and smiling, "is not against my country; he
is only against your regime there. He wants to live. They shouldn't kill
my brother. They should respect him, and I will respect them. Blood is
not water." "How is it that you Jews don't understand such a thing," a
young leader of the intifadah in Barta'a said to me. "You, because of
blood ties, are willing to fly to Africa and bring 15,000 Ethiopians in a
single day, simply because two thousand years ago they were your relatives. And if they kill a Jew in Brooklyn or in Belgium, all of you immediately shout and cry."

When the realization finally penetrates, through all the functional   24
layers of protection, how much the Palestinians in Israel and in the territories are in many ways a single living body, a single organic tissue, one
wonders at the powers of forbearance needed by the Arabs in Israel in
order to continue to exercise self-restraint. And one wonders, Do they
consider what this restraint implies for themselves, and the significance
of their collaboration in Israel's daily routine? How do they excuse the fact
that their taxes finance that plane, and the bombs hanging from it, and
the soldier in Bethlehem who laughs at Grandfather: "I should go to all
that effort for them?"

"No, I'm not at all comfortable with the response of Israeli Arabs to   25
the intifadah," said Azmi Bishara, born in Nazareth, chairman of the Philosophy Department at Bir Zeit University in the West Bank. "It is not
the same struggle. Certainly not the same price. It's not even a struggle
parallel to the struggle in the territories. Jenin is under curfew, starving,
and Nazareth, twenty minutes away, is living normally. But what? We
have *solidarity* with them.

"It makes me feel horrible. It makes me feel sick. Because I think 26
that somewhere between Palestinian nationalism and the pitiful opportunism of the Arab mayors there is a path that can guide us as citizens in the State of Israel. Citizens who allow ourselves a little more
'solidarity' with the inhabitants of the territories. So I start behaving
a little more like the Israeli left—what's wrong with that? So I won't
be ashamed to march 50,000 Arabs through Tel Aviv. Just like Martin Luther King, Jr., wasn't ashamed of 50,000 blacks in Washington.
I have no problem with them calling me a nationalist. I'm not a nationalist. These slogans are not nationalism. They are in every respect
the slogans of good citizens. If the Tempo softdrink factory lays off all
its Arab workers, I will call on the Arab population of Israel to boycott it completely! If they don't want me, why should I drink their
Maccabee beer?"

"You mean an internal Arab boycott?"

"Not a boycott as Arabs! Not a boycott as Palestinians! As Israelis! 27
And as an Israeli I won't be ashamed to have a black crowd march through
Tel Aviv and upset the city. The inhabitants of the territories can't do it,
but we can. I should have and could have organized marches at the beginning of the intifadah. There was enough anger then for a step like
that. But our leadership died of fear. Our leadership is afraid that all
those nice Jews who are responsible for the 'sector' [he spits that word
out the same way he did "solidarity"] will smile at us and say in a nice
voice, 'You want to be like they are in the territories? Go on, do something, and then we will treat you just like we treat them. And remember
not to take anything for granted in our attitude toward you, Israeli Arabs.
When it comes down to it, you are tolerated guests here. And guests can
be shown the door.'"

He is thirty-five years old, black-haired, with a dark face and a thick 28
mustache. At age sixteen he founded the National Committee of Arab
High School Students in Israel, the first nationwide organization of Arab
youth. In the mornings, instead of going to school, the young Bishara
grabbed his satchel and set out on "working tours" of the villages in Wadi
Ara and the southern Triangle, organizing high-school students to fight
for equality in education. "We closed down the schools a few times, a
very militant story. We could decide just like that to shut down a school,
no problem. Remember that it wasn't an easy time—in '74 we went
around with *kaffiyehs*. That was when Arafat addressed the United Nations and the Egyptian Army crossed the Suez Canal. We had a lot of
Palestinian sensibility.

"Today? Today there's a difference between us and the Palestini- 29 ans in the territories. Our experience is different from theirs. The sensibility is different, too. They can conduct a violent struggle against you. We can't anymore. Not because of the Shin Bet [the internal security service], but because we ourselves are no longer able to see this as a possibility. It is already contrary to the temperament of our population, which has lived with you for decades and is already part of the economy and the way of life and a million other things. The Arabs here are an integral part of your story, even if you haven't fathomed this yet. When the intifadah began, we had to make a quick and clear decision: are we part of it or not part of it? Period. And we discovered that our aspirations branched off at this point from the aspirations of the Palestinians in the territories.

"But in one thing there is no distinction: as far as you're concerned, 30 both we and they are strangers here. Unwanted here. Rejected. And for this reason I say that the old way that Israeli Arabs think about Israel is bankrupt. It can't be allowed to go on. Precisely because of the alienation that you impose on me, precisely because I am frightened, precisely because in your opinion nothing can be taken for granted in your attitude toward us, so I'm also allowed not to have my attitude toward you taken for granted.

"When Martin Luther King put together his movement for equal 31 rights in America in the sixties, he called for total equality, period. Equality that would go as far as positive discrimination in favor of the blacks, in order to correct the injustice of decades. Together with that he had no problem shouting, 'I am proud to be an American,' in other words, as a black man, the country was his, too. The flag was also his. The blacks emphasized that they were no less American than others. Now I ask myself if the American Indians could do such a thing. Can an Indian shout with all his heart, 'I am proud to be an American'?"

"And you, in this metaphor, are the Indian?"

"I think so. From that point of view I am like the Palestinian in the 32 territories. Neither of us is wanted here. Both of us are ignored. And on top of that I'm caught in the perfect paradox—I have to be a loyal citizen of a country that declares itself not to be my country but rather the country of the Jewish people."

Vehement in expression, emotional, a dissenter from birth, his 33 movements untempered, Bishara looks as if a struggle is always going on within him. He lives in Nazareth, in Jerusalem, in Bir Zeit. He likes big cities and divided people. "The most dangerous people are healthy people at one with themselves, people without contradictions—I'm wary of them. I also liked Berlin when it was divided. Now I can't set foot in it. It disappointed me. It became normal."

"And do you feel a link to the land here, to the country?" I asked. 34 "A link to nature? To the view? Is there any place in the country that you especially like?"

He let out a long laugh, a laugh to himself. "You want me to feel 35 something for Karmiel? For Afula? Nothing is as gray as those places. However you look at them. Or Migdal Ha-emek. Would I take a tour of Migdal Ha-emek? You'll find that resistance stronger in me than in Israeli Arabs who have already assimilated the situation and their experience, who have married here, who have children, who go for weekends at the beach. I don't go for weekends at the beach. I don't recognize the beaches in this country. I hate the Israeli beach bum. He reeks of insolence and violence and swagger, and I can't stand it. I feel very foreign among Israelis. It's not just that I have white spots on the map where the Jewish settlements are; I've also got a great emptiness of nature. They always talk about the Palestinians' links with nature and the land. I have no link with nature, not to woods, not to mountains; I don't know the names of the plants and trees as even my Israeli friends do. In Arabic poetry in Israel the names of all the plants appear, the *za'atar* and the *rihan,* but I don't know them, can't tell them apart, and I don't care about them. For me nature is, somehow, the Jewish National Fund. All the forests and flora are the JNF. It's all artificial and counterfeit. Can you see me wandering the mountains, hiking for the fun of it, and suddenly the Green Patrol [charged with guarding state lands] comes and asks me what I'm doing here?"

When I met Bishara for the first time, years ago, there was some- 36 thing forbidding in his appearance. I force myself to write this because it is part of the subject as a whole. There's something forbiddingly Arab, I thought—his face is dark, his mustache thick—in the belligerence I attributed to him, all this formed part of the rough outline of the archetypical foreign and frightening Arab. Since then, every time our paths meet, I reflect on that. There is a special joy—joy in the victory of the weak, in the unraveling of any stereotype.

I asked how, in his opinion, Palestinians in the territories relate to 37 the dilemma of the Arabs who live in Israel.

"They look down on us. Yes, yes. Before the intifadah it was the 38 opposite—there was admiration. For a while even phony admiration. Admiration that was meant to inflate the Israeli-Arab experience. Yet I am not proud of anything. What do I have to be so proud of? Of the fact that the Arabs in Israel have not produced anything of significance? No culture, no elite, nothing. Their intellectual life is shocking. What is there for them to be proud of? Of their pursuit of lucrative professions, of money and more money? Of the lack of any intellectual dimension? There is not a single intellectual I can be proud of. Not a philosopher, not a single writer I'm proud of. They're all dwarfs. Look at Emile Habibi, who makes an ideology out of the 'Israeli-Arab experience,' and every time he talks he declares, 'We've stayed here for forty-three years!' What do you mean you've stayed? What's the big deal? But for him staying is a *conspiracy*. Do you understand? [He lowers his voice and whispers.] Some people got together and held meetings and consultations, and after a month of uncertainty they decided to remain in the State of Israel, to keep the flame burning . . . After all, our whole story, of the Arabs in Israel, is no more than the struggle to survive. That's not such a heroic struggle. It was largely a story of cringing, lots of toadying and opportunism, and imitation of the Israelis. And when the Arabs here finally started feeling a little more sure of themselves, they had already turned into Israelis. What Israeli-Arab symbols are there that a man like me can identify with? Nothing. Even when you think that there's an authentic phenomenon like the Islamic Movement, it turns out to be counterfeit. I debated their leader, Sheikh Abdallah Nimr Darwish, in Haifa. An open debate before an audience. I was astounded at how little he understands Islam. Superficial. He doesn't know it. For him, Islam is only a political tool.

"So where is all the talk about our pride, about our heroism? Lis- 39 ten to a heroic story: Once there was a protest rally in the Communists' Friendship House in Nazareth, and the police surrounded the building. The next day the headline in the Communist newspaper was THE SECOND SIEGE OF BEIRUT! Do you understand? They surrounded the Friendship House in Nazareth! When it comes down to it, the Arabs of Israel, with the exception of the six who fell on Land Day[2] in 1976, didn't pay much. In other words, it's impossible, it's disgraceful to compare them to the Arabs in the territories. You should see it there; when someone gives a speech, he is the spokesman for an entire history. There are symbols, there's rhetoric, pathos, spark. On our side you hear half a sentence and feel that where we are everything is empty. Our history is cut off."

When he came to our meeting, Bishara was upset. A short while 40 before he had been with his sister in a restaurant in East Jerusalem. His

[2] An annual day of protest by Palestinian Israelis against Israeli government confiscation of Arab land.

sister is a doctor and lives in Beit Jalla, near Bethlehem. Her Citroën has the blue license plates that show it is from the territories. But there was a little sticker with the word DOCTOR in Hebrew on the windshield. That was enough to get the car torched. "And imagine," he snorted, "there I was helping the guys from the Border Guard put out the fire; it was very embarrassing!"

He was nevertheless able to laugh at the circumstances there, and 41 at himself. So I did not restrain myself from saying to him, "Here they gave you the spark you were looking for." Afterward I asked him whether he was angry at the arsonists.

"On the contrary," he said immediately, "I was pleased that they are so good at spotting Israeli cars."

I already knew, after about a month of visits and conversations, that 42 I would almost always get an unexpected response. That the status of the Arab who lives in Israel is so tangled and twisted that I had to stop trying to anticipate, and only listen, to open myself to the complexity, to try to make room for it. Make room for them within us. How does one do that? It is precisely the thing that we, the majority, forbid them with such deft determination.

And here, something like a nervous security guard began running 43 around inside me, reorganizing the broken ranks. It seems to me that the words "make room for them" are what set him off. He is part of me, I've encountered him several times in the past month. Right now he demands to know exactly what I meant—just how much room to make for them? And at whose expense? And is it necessary to open the discussion just now, while the peace talks are in progress? And when the country is trying, with its remaining strength, to absorb a huge wave of immigration? He speaks, and something unpleasant is slowly revealed to me: that when, for example, Azmi Bishara says he wants to march a black crowd through Tel Aviv, something in me recoils. Contorts. And suddenly I am the one facing the test. How real and sincere is my desire for "coexistence" with the Palestinians in Israel? Do I stand wholeheartedly behind the words "make room for them among us"? Do I actually understand the meaning of Jewish-Arab coexistence? And what does it demand of me, as a Jew in Israel? How much room am I really willing to make for "them" in the Jewish state? Have I ever imagined, down to the smallest living detail, a truly democratic, pluralistic, and egalitarian way of life in Israel? These questions race at me, and caught me unprepared—an abstract, perhaps simplistic picture of life with the Arabs was impressed on me from the start, and because of it, apparently, I set out on this journey. I certainly wanted to persuade others it was an imperative, and here, the outer layer of these abstract declarations was quickly torn away, and from within its contents burst forth—demanding, threatening, enticing, shaking the defenses— ✍

READING FOR INFORMATION

1. List the problems between Jews and Arabs that Grossman emphasizes both directly and indirectly in paragraph 3.
2. Summarize Grossman's historical account of relationships among Arabs, Arab Palestinians, and Jews in paragraph 22.
3. In paragraph 29, what distinction does Grossman's interlocutor draw between Arab citizens inside the State of Israel and Arab Palestinians outside the state in Israeli-occupied territories? What comparisons does he make with Native Americans and African Americans in paragraph 31?

READING FOR FORM, ORGANIZATION, AND EXPOSITORY FEATURES

1. In paragraph 11, Grossman writes of his conversation with the runaway Jewish boy that "as if only as he spoke did he comprehend what had actually happened." How does Grossman show that such a comprehension in this and other dialogues occurs within the act of speaking, so that speakers themselves learn something about their predicaments that they had not grasped before?
2. Grossman records the substance of six conversations with Arab Israelis. What transitions does he provide between those conversations in paragraphs 19, 22, and 24?
3. In paragraph 36, how does Grossman imply a change in his attitude about Professor Bishara? Summarize Grossman's account of his own feelings in paragraphs 42 and 43.

READING FOR RHETORICAL CONCERNS

1. Explain how the personal statement of the Arab Mohammed Daroushe in paragraphs 1 and 2 functions as a preface to the essay. Paraphrase Daroushe's representation of Arab ambivalence in paragraph 2.
2. Paraphrase the grounds in paragraphs 14 and 23 on which the Arab Israelis criticize Palestinians in the occupied territories. Describe Professor Bishara's characterization of their attitude in paragraphs 26 and 38.

3. Summarize features of the incident involving Professor Bishara's sister in paragraphs 39 and 40 that color his conversation with Grossman.

WRITING ASSIGNMENTS

1. Write an analytical essay about Grossman's representation of each speaker in the text. Describe the attitude that he projects toward each, and estimate the sympathy or detachment that he feels. How does Grossman imply relationships among them?
2. Write an evaluative essay about the literary techniques that Grossman uses to report on the affairs of real people and the outcomes of historical events. Does Grossman distort his representation with dramatic effects, or does he enhance its moral significance with deeper insight?

A Different Mirror

Ronald Takaki

Ronald Takaki is a professor and Chair of the Department of Ethnic Studies at the University of California, Berkeley. He is the author of Iron Cages: Race and Culture in Nineteenth-Century America *(1979),* Strangers from a Different Shore: A History of Asian Americans *(1989),* A Different Mirror *(1993),* From Different Shores: Perspectives on Race and Ethnicity in America, *and other historical studies.*

PREREADING

In paragraph 5 of the following essay, Takaki cites an article in *Time* magazine that reports that "white Americans will become a minority group" within the next century. How might our knowledge of past history illuminate this future? What kinds of attention should historians pay to accounts about the multicultural foundation, growth, and development of the United States? How might personal narratives contribute to this history? Freewrite some responses to these questions.

From Ronald Takaki, *A Different Mirror: A History of Multicultural America* (Boston: Little, Brown, 1993) 1–2, 14–17, and 246–51. Copyright © 1993 by Ronald Takaki. By permission of the author.

A DIFFERENT MIRROR

I had flown from San Francisco to Norfolk and was riding in a   1
taxi to my hotel to attend a conference on multiculturalism.
Hundreds of educators from across the country were meeting to discuss the need for greater cultural diversity in the curriculum. My driver and I chatted about the weather and the tourists. The sky was
cloudy, and Virginia Beach was twenty minutes away. The rearview
mirror reflected a white man in his forties. "How long have you been
in this country?" he asked. "All my life," I replied, wincing. "I was born
in the United States." With a strong southern drawl, he remarked: "I
was wondering because your English is excellent!" Then, as I had many
times before, I explained: "My grandfather came here from Japan in
the 1880s. My family has been here, in America, for over a hundred
years." He glanced at me in the mirror. Somehow I did not look "American" to him; my eyes and complexion looked foreign.

Suddenly, we both became uncomfortably conscious of a racial   2
divide separating us. An awkward silence turned my gaze from the mirror to the passing landscape, the shore where the English and the
Powhatan Indians first encountered each other. Our highway was on
land that Sir Walter Raleigh had renamed "Virginia" in honor of Elizabeth I, the Virgin Queen. In the English cultural appropriation of
America, the indigenous peoples themselves would become outsiders
in their native land. Here, at the eastern edge of the continent, I mused,
was the site of the beginning of multicultural America. Jamestown, the
English settlement founded in 1607, was nearby: the first twenty
Africans were brought here a year before the Pilgrims arrived at Ply-
mouth Rock. Several hundred miles offshore was Bermuda, the
"Bermoothes" where William Shakespeare's Prospero had landed and
met the native Caliban in *The Tempest*. Earlier, another voyager had
made an Atlantic crossing and unexpectedly bumped into some islands
to the south. Thinking he had reached Asia, Christopher Columbus
mistakenly identified one of the islands as "Cipango" (Japan). In the
wake of the admiral, many peoples would come to America from different shores, not only from Europe but also Africa and Asia. One of
them would be my grandfather. My mental wandering across terrain
and time ended abruptly as we arrived at my destination. I said good-
bye to my driver and went into the hotel, carrying a vivid reminder of
why I was attending this conference.

Questions like the one my taxi driver asked me are always jarring,   3
but I can understand why he could not see me as American. He had a narrow but widely shared sense of the past—a history that has viewed American as European in ancestry. "Race," Toni Morrison explained, has
functioned as a "metaphor" necessary to the "construction of Americanness": in the creation of our national identity, "American" has been defined as "white."[1]

But America has been racially diverse since our very beginning on   4
the Virginia shore, and this reality is increasingly becoming visible and
ubiquitous. Currently, one-third of the American people do not trace
their origins to Europe; in California, minorities are fast becoming a majority. They already predominate in major cities across the country—
New York, Chicago, Atlanta, Detroit, Philadelphia, San Francisco, and
Los Angeles.

This emerging demographic diversity has raised fundamental ques-   5
tions about America's identity and culture. In 1990, *Time* published a
cover story on "America's Changing Colors." "Someday soon," the magazine announced, "white Americans will become a minority group." How
soon? By 2056, most Americans will trace their descent to "Africa, Asia,
the Hispanic world, the Pacific Islands, Arabia—almost anywhere but
white Europe." This dramatic change in our nation's ethnic composition
is altering the way we think about ourselves. "The deeper significance of
America's becoming a majority nonwhite society is what it means to the
national psyche, to individuals' sense of themselves and their nation—
their idea of what it is to be American."[2]

. . . Our diversity was tied to America's most serious crisis: the   6
Civil War was fought over a racial issue—slavery. In his "First Inaugural
Address," presented on March 4, 1861, President Abraham Lincoln
declared: "One section of our country believes slavery is *right* and
ought to be extended, while the other believes it is *wrong* and ought
not to be extended." Southern secession, he argued, would be anarchy.
Lincoln sternly warned the South that he had a solemn oath to defend
and preserve the Union. Americans were one people, he explained,
bound together by "the mystic chords of memory, stretching from
every battlefield and patriot grave to every living heart and hearth-
stone all over this broad land." The struggle and sacrifices of the War
for Independence had enabled Americans to create a new nation out
of thirteen separate colonies. But Lincoln's appeal for unity fell on
deaf ears in the South. And the war came. Two and a half years later,

at Gettysburg, President Lincoln declared that "brave men" had fought and "consecrated" the ground of this battlefield in order to preserve the Union. Among the brave were black men. Shortly after this bloody battle, Lincoln acknowledged the military contributions of blacks. "There will be some black men," he wrote in a letter to an old friend, James C. Conkling, "who can remember that with silent tongue, and clenched teeth, and steady eye, and well-poised bayonet, they have helped mankind on to this great consummation. . . . " Indeed, 186,000 blacks served in the Union Army, and one-third of them were listed as missing or dead. Black men in blue, Frederick Douglass pointed out, were "on the battlefield mingling their blood with that of white men in one common effort to save the country." Now the mystic chords of memory stretched across the new battlefields of the Civil War, and black soldiers were buried in "patriot graves." They, too, had given their lives to ensure that the "government of the people, by the people, for the people shall not perish from the earth."[3]

Like these black soldiers, the people in our study have been actors 7 in history, not merely victims of discrimination and exploitation. They are entitled to be viewed as subjects—as men and women with minds, wills, and voices.

> In the telling and retelling
>   of their stories,
> They create communities
>   of memory.

They also re-vision history. "It is very natural that the history written by the victim," said a Mexican in 1874, "does not altogether chime with the story of the victor." Sometimes they are hesitant to speak, thinking they are only "little people." "I don't know why anybody wants to hear my history," an Irish maid said apologetically in 1900. "Nothing ever happened to me worth the tellin'."[4]

But their stories are worthy. Through their stories, the people who 8 have lived America's history can help all of us, including my taxi driver, understand that Americans originated from many shores, and that all of us are entitled to dignity. "I hope this survey do a lot of good for Chinese people," an immigrant told an interviewer from Stanford University in the 1920s. "Make American people realize that Chinese people are humans. I think very few American people really know anything about Chinese." But the remembering is also for the sake of the children. "This story is dedicated to the descendants of Lazar and Goldie Glauberman," Jewish immigrant Minnie Miller wrote in her autobiography. "My history is bound up in their history and the generations that follow should know where they came from to know better who they are." Similarly, Tomo Shoji, an elderly Nisei woman, urged Asian Americans to learn more about their roots: "We got such good, fantastic stories to tell. All our stories are different." Seeking to know how they fit into America, many young people have become listeners; they are eager to learn about the hardships and humiliations experienced by their parents and grandparents. They want to hear their stories, unwilling to remain ignorant or ashamed of their identity and past.[5]

The telling of stories liberates. By writing about the people on   9 Mango Street, Sandra Cisneros explained, "the ghost does not ache so much." The place no longer holds her with "both arms. She sets me free." Indeed, stories may not be as innocent or simple as they seem to be. Native-American novelist Leslie Marmon Silko cautioned:

> I will tell you something about stories . . .
> They aren't just entertainment.
>   Don't be fooled.

Indeed, the accounts given by the people in this study vibrantly recreate moments, capturing the complexities of human emotions and thoughts. They also provide the authenticity of experience. After she escaped from slavery, Harriet Jacobs wrote in her autobiography: "[My purpose] is not to tell you what I have heard but what I have seen—and what I have suffered." In their sharing of memory, the people in this study offer us an opportunity to see ourselves reflected in a mirror called history.[6]

In his recent study of Spain and the New World, *The Buried*   10 *Mirror*, Carlos Fuentes points out that mirrors have been found in the tombs of ancient Mexico, placed there to guide the dead through the underworld. He also tells us about the legend of Quetzalcoatl, the Plumed Serpent: when this god was given a mirror by the Toltec deity Tezcatlipoca, he saw a man's face in the mirror and realized his own humanity. For us, the "mirror" of history can guide the living and also help us recognize who we have been and hence are. In *A Distant Mirror*, Barbara W. Tuchman finds "phenomenal parallels" between the "calamitous 14th century" of European society and our own era. We can, she observes, have "greater fellow-feeling for a distraught age" as we painfully recognize the "similar disarray," "collapsing assumptions," and "unusual discomfort."[7]

But what is needed in our own perplexing times is not so much a   11 "distant" mirror, as one that is "different." While the study of the past can provide collective self-knowledge, it often reflects the scholar's particular perspective or view of the world. What happens when historians leave out many of America's peoples? What happens, to borrow the words of Adrienne Rich, "when someone with the authority of a teacher" describes our society, and "you are not in it"? Such an experience can be disorienting—"a moment of psychic disequilibrium, as if you looked into a mirror and saw nothing."[8]

Through their narratives about their lives and circumstances, the   12 people of America's diverse groups are able to see themselves and each other in our common past. They celebrate what Ishmael Reed has described as a society "unique" in the world because "the world is here"— a place "where the cultures of the world crisscross." Much of America's past, they point out, has been riddled with racism. At the same time, these people offer hope, affirming the struggle for equality as a central theme in our country's history. At its conception, our nation was dedicated to the proposition of equality. What has given concreteness to this powerful national principle has been our coming together in the creation of a new society. "Stuck here" together, workers of different backgrounds have attempted to get along with each other

> People harvesting
> Work together unaware
> Of racial problems,

wrote a Japanese immigrant describing a lesson learned by Mexican and Asian farm laborers in California.[9]

Finally, how do we see our prospects for "working out" America's   13 racial crisis? Do we see it as through a glass darkly? Do the televised images of racial hatred and violence that riveted us in 1992 during the days of rage in Los Angeles frame a future of divisive race relations—what Arthur Schlesinger, Jr., has fearfully denounced as the "disuniting of America"? Or will Americans of diverse races and ethnicities be able to connect themselves to a larger narrative? Whatever happens, we can be certain that much of our society's future will be influenced by which "mirror" we choose to see ourselves. America does not belong to one race or one group, the people in this study remind us, and Americans have been constantly redefining their national identity from the moment of first contact on the Virginia shore. By sharing their stories, they invite us to see ourselves in a different mirror.[10]

PACIFIC CROSSINGS: SEEKING THE LAND OF MONEY TREES

During the 1890s, American society witnessed not only the Wounded 14 Knee massacre and the end of the frontier, but also the arrival of a new group of immigrants. Unlike the Irish, the Japanese went east to America. But they, too, were pushed here by external influences. During the nineteenth century, America's expansionist thrust reached all the way across the Pacific Ocean. In 1853, Commodore Matthew C. Perry had sailed his armed naval ships into Tokyo Bay and forcefully opened Japan's doors to the West. As Japanese leaders watched Western powers colonizing China, they worried that their country would be the next victim. Thus, in 1868, they restored the Meiji emperor and established a strong centralized government. To defend Japan, they pursued a twin strategy of industrialization and militarization and levied heavy taxes to finance their program.

Bearing the burden of this taxation, farmers suffered severe eco- 15 nomic hardships during the 1880s. "The distress among the agricultural class has reached a point never before attained," the *Japan Weekly Mail* reported. "Most of the farmers have been unable to pay their taxes, and hundreds of families in one village alone have been compelled to sell their property in order to liquidate their debts." Thousands of farmers lost their lands, and hunger stalked many parts of the country. "What strikes me most is the hardships paupers are having in surviving," reported a journalist. "Their regular fare consists of rice husk or buckwheat chaff ground into powder and the dregs of bean curd mixed with leaves and grass."[11]

Searching for a way out of this terrible plight, impoverished farm- 16 ers were seized by an emigration *netsu,* or "fever." Fabulous stories of high wages stirred their imaginations. A plantation laborer in the Kingdom of Hawaii could earn six times more than in Japan; in three years, a worker might save four hundred yen—an amount equal to ten years of earnings in Japan. When the Japanese government first announced it would be filling six hundred emigrant slots for the first shipment of laborers to Hawaii, it received 28,000 applications. Stories about wages in the United States seemed even more fantastic—about a dollar a day, or more than two yen. This meant that in one year a worker could save about eight hundred yen—an amount almost equal to the income of a governor in Japan. No wonder a young man begged his parents: "By all means let me go to America." Between 1885 and 1924, 200,000 left for Hawaii and 180,000 for the United States mainland. In haiku, one Japanese migrant captured the feeling of expectation and excitement:

> Huge dreams of fortune
> Go with me to foreign lands,
> Across the ocean.

To prospective Japanese migrants, "money grew on trees" in America.[12]

PICTURE BRIDES IN AMERICA

Initially, most of the migrants from Japan were men, but what became   17
striking about the Japanese immigration was its eventual inclusion of a significant number of women. By 1920, women represented 46 percent of the Japanese population in Hawaii and 35 percent in California. Clearly, in terms of gender, the Japanese resembled the Irish and Jews rather than the Chinese. This difference had consequences for the two Asian groups in terms of the formation of families. In 1900, fifty years after the beginning of Chinese immigration, only 5 percent were women. In this community composed mostly of "bachelors," only 4 percent were American-born. "The greatest impression I have of my childhood in those days was that there were very few families in Chinatown," a resident recalled. "Babies were looked on with a kind of wonder." On the other hand, in 1930, 52 percent of the Japanese population had been born in America. But why did proportionately more women emigrate from Japan than China?[13]

Unlike China, Japan was ruled by a strong central government that   18
was able to regulate emigration. Prospective immigrants were required to apply to the government for permission to leave for the United States and were screened by review boards to certify that they were healthy and literate and would creditably "maintain Japan's national honor." Japan had received reports about the Chinese in America and was determined to monitor the quality of its emigrants. Seeking to avoid the problems of prostitution, gambling, and drunkenness that reportedly plagued the predominantly male Chinese community in the United States, the Japanese government promoted female emigration. The 1882 Chinese Exclusion Act prohibited the entry of "laborers," both men and women, but militarily strong Japan was able to negotiate the 1908 Gentlemen's

Agreement. While this treaty prohibited the entry of Japanese "laborers," it allowed Japanese women to emigrate to the United States as family members.[14]

Through this opening in immigration policy came over sixty thou- 19 sand women, many as "picture brides." The picture bride system was based on the established custom of arranged marriage. In Japanese so- ciety, marriage was not an individual matter but rather a family concern, and parents consulted go-betweens to help them select partners for their sons and daughters. In situations involving families located far away, the prospective bride and groom would exchange photographs before the initial meeting. This traditional practice lent itself readily to the needs of Japanese migrants. "When I told my parents about my desire to go to a foreign land, the story spread throughout the town," picture bride Ai Miyasaki later recalled. "From here and there requests for marriage came pouring in just like rain!" Similarly, Riyo Orite had a "picture marriage." Her marriage to a Japanese man in America had been arranged through a relative. "All agreed to our marriage, but I didn't get married immedi- ately," she recalled. "I was engaged at the age of sixteen and didn't meet Orite until I was almost eighteen. I had seen him only in a picture at first. . . . Being young, I was unromantic. I just believed that girls should get married. I felt he was a little old, about thirty, but the people around me praised the match. His brother in Tokyo sent me a lot of beautiful pic- tures [taken in the United States]. . . . My name was entered in the Orites' *koseki* [family register]. Thus we were married."[15]

The emigration of Japanese women occurred within the context of 20 internal economic developments. While women in China were restrict- ed to farm and home, Japanese women were increasingly entering the wage-earning work force. Thousands of them were employed in con- struction work as well as in the coal mines where they carried heavy loads on their backs out of the tunnels. Young women were leaving their fam- ily farms for employment in textile mills where they worked sixteen-hour shifts and lived in dormitories. By 1900, 60 percent of Japan's industrial laborers were women. While it is not known how many of the women who emigrated had been wage-earners, this proletarianization of women already well under way in Japan paved the way for such laborers to con- sider working in America.[16]

Japanese women were also more receptive to the idea of traveling 21 overseas than Chinese women. The Meiji government required the edu- cation of female children, stipulating that "girls should be educated . . . alongside boys." Emperor Meiji himself promoted female education.

Japanese boys as well as girls, he declared, should learn about foreign countries and become enlightened about the world. Female education included reading and writing skills as well as general knowledge. Japanese women, unlike their Chinese counterparts, were more likely to be literate. "We studied English and Japanese, mathematics, literature, writing, and religion," recalled Michiko Tanaka. Under the reorganization of the school system in 1876, English was adopted as a major subject in middle school. This education exposed Japanese women to the outside world. They also heard stories describing America as "heavenly," and some of the picture brides were more eager to see the new land than to meet their husbands. "I wanted to see foreign countries and besides I had consented to marriage with Papa because I had the dream of seeing America," Michiko Tanaka revealed to her daughter years later. "I wanted to see America and Papa was a way to get there." "I was bubbling over with great expectations," said another picture bride. "My young heart, 19 years and 8 months old, burned, not so much with the prospects of reuniting with my new husband, but with the thought of the New World."[17]

The emigration of women was also influenced by Japanese views on gender. A folk saying popular among farmers recommended that a family should have three children: "One to sell, one to follow, and one in reserve." The "one to sell" was the daughter. Of course, this was meant only figuratively: she was expected to marry and enter her husband's family. "Once you become someone's wife you belong to his family," explained Tsuru Yamauchi. "My parents said once I went over to be married, I should treat his parents as my own and be good to them." One day, Yamauchi was told that she would be going to Hawaii to join her future husband: "I learned about the marriage proposal when we had to exchange pictures." Emigration for her was not a choice but an obligation to her husband.[18]

Whether a Japanese woman went to America depended on which son she married—the son "to follow" or the son "in reserve." Unlike the Chinese, Japanese farmers had an inheritance system based on impartible inheritance and primogeniture. Only one of the sons in the family, usually the eldest, inherited the family's holdings: he was the son who was expected "to follow" his father. In the mountainous island nation of Japan, arable land was limited, and most of the farm holdings were small, less than two and a half acres. Division of a tiny family holding would mean disaster for the family. As the possessor of the family farm, the eldest son had the responsibility of caring for his aged parents and hence had to stay home. The second or noninheriting son—the one held "in reserve" in case something happened to the first son—had to leave the family farm and find employment in town. This practice of relocating within Japan could easily be applied to movement abroad. Thus, although the migrants included first sons, they tended to be the younger sons. Unlike Chinese sons who had to share responsibility for their parents, these Japanese men were not as tightly bound to their parents and were allowed to take their wives and children with them to distant lands.[19]

But whether or not women migrated was also influenced by the needs in the receiving countries. In Hawaii, the government initially stipulated that 40 percent of the Japanese contract labor emigrants—laborers under contract to work for three years—were to be women. During the government-sponsored contract labor period from 1885 to 1894, women constituted 20 percent of the emigrants. During the period from 1894 to 1908, thousands of additional women sailed to Hawaii as private contract laborers. Planters viewed Japanese women as workers and assigned 72 percent of them to field labor. Furthermore, they promoted the Japanese family as a mechanism of labor control. In 1886, Hawaii's inspector-general of immigration reported that Japanese men were better workers on plantations where they had their wives: "Several of the planters are desirous that each man should have his wife." After 1900, when Hawaii became a territory of the United States, planters became even more anxious to bring Japanese women to Hawaii. Since the American law prohibiting contract labor now applied to the islands, planters had to find ways to stabilize their labor force. Realizing that men with families were more likely to stay on the plantations, managers asked their business agents in Honolulu to send "men with families."[20]

Meanwhile, Japanese women were pulled to the United States mainland where they were needed as workers by their husbands. Shopkeepers and farmers sent for their wives, thinking they could assist as unpaid family labor. Wives were particularly useful on farms where production was labor intensive. "Nearly all of these tenant farmers are married and have their families with them," a researcher noted in 1915. "The wives do much work in the fields."[21]

As they prepared to leave their villages for Hawaii and America, many of these women felt separation anxieties. One woman remembered her husband's brother saying farewell: "Don't stay in the [United] States too long. Come back in five years and farm with us." But her father quickly remarked: "Are you kidding? They can't learn anything in five years. They'll even have a baby over there. . . . Be patient for twenty years." Her father's words shocked her so much that she could not control her tears: suddenly she realized how long the separation could be. Another woman recalled the painful moment she experienced when her parents came to see her off: "They did not join the crowd, but quietly stood in front of the wall. They didn't say 'good luck,' or 'take care,' or anything. . . . They couldn't say anything because they knew, as I did, that I would never return." As their ships sailed from the harbor many women gazed at the diminishing shore:

> With tears in my eyes
> I turn back to my homeland,
> Taking one last look.[22]

NOTES

1. Toni Morrison, *Playing in the Dark: Whiteness in the Literary Imagination* (Cambridge, Mass., 1992), p. 47.

2. William A. Henry III, "Beyond the Melting Pot," in "America's Changing Colors," *Time,* vol. 135, no. 15 (April 9, 1990), pp. 28–31.

3. Abraham Lincoln, "First Inaugural Address," in *The Annals of America,* vol. 9, *1863–1865; The Crisis of the Union* (Chicago, 1968), p. 255; Lincoln, "The Gettysburg Address," pp. 462–463; Abraham Lincoln, letter to James C. Conkling, August 26, 1863, in *Annals of America,* p. 439; Frederick Douglass, in Herbert Aptheker (ed.), *A Documentary History of the Negro People in the United States* (New York, 1951), vol. 1, p. 496.

4. Weber (ed.), *Foreigners in Their Native Land,* p. vi; Hamilton Holt (ed.), *The Life Stories of Undistinguished Americans as Told by Themselves* (New York, 1906), p. 143.

5. "Social Document of Pany Lowe, interviewed by C. H. Burnett, Seattle, July 5, 1924," p. 6, Survey of Race Relations, Stanford University, Hoover Institution Archives; Minnie Miller, "Autobiography," private manuscript, copy from Richard Balkin; Tomo Shoji, presentation, Ohana Cultural Center, Oakland, California, March 4, 1988.

6. Sandra Cisneros, *The House on Mango Street* (New York, 1991), pp. 109–110; Leslie Marmon Silko, *Ceremony* (New York, 1978), p. 2; Harriet A. Jacobs, *Incidents in the Life of a Slave Girl, written by herself* (Cambridge, Mass., 1987; originally published in 1857), p. xiii.

7. Carlos Fuentes, *The Buried Mirror; Reflections on Spain and the New World* (Boston, 1992), pp. 10, 11, 109; Barbara W. Tuchman, *A Distant Mirror: The Calamitous 14th Century* (New York, 1978), p. xiii, xiv.

8. Adrienne Rich, *Blood, Bread, and Poetry: Selected Prose, 1979–1985* (New York, 1986), p. 199.

9. Ishmael Reed, "America: The Multinational Society," in Rick Simonson and Scott Walker (Eds.), *Multi-cultural Literacy* (St. Paul, 1988), p. 160; Ito, *Issei,* p. 497.

10. Arthur M. Schlesinger, Jr., *The Disuniting of America: Reflections on a Multicultural Society* (Knoxville, Tenn., 1991); Carlos Bulosan, *America Is in the Heart: A Personal History* (Seattle, 1981), pp. 188–189.

11. *Japan Weekly Mail*, December 20, 1884, reprinted in Nippu Jiji, *Golden Jubilee of the Japanese in Hawaii, 1885–1935* (Honolulu, 1935), n.p.; Yuji Ichioka, *The Issei: The World of the First Generation Japanese Immigrants, 1885–1924* (New York, 1988), p. 45. Ichioka's is the best book on the subject.

12. Kazuo Ito, *Issei: A History of the Japanese Immigrants in North America* (Seattle, 1973), pp. 27, 38, 29. Ito's study is a massive and wonderful compilation of stories, oral histories, and poems. It is indispensable.

13. Victor and Brett de Bary Nee, *Longtime Californ': A Documentary Study of an American Chinatown* (New York, 1972), p. 148.

14. Robert Wilson and Bill Hosokawa, *East to America: A History of the Japanese in the United States* (New York, 1980), pp. 47, 113–114.

15. Eileen Sunada Sarasohn (ed.), *The Issei: Portrait of a Pioneer, An Oral History* (Palo Alto, Calif., 1983), pp. 44, 31–32.

16. Thomas C. Smith, *Nakahara: Family Farming and Population in a Japanese Village, 1717–1830* (Stanford, Calif., 1977), pp. 134, 152, 153; Sheila Matsumoto, "Women in Factories," in Joyce Lebra *et al.* (eds.), *Women in Changing Japan* (Boulder, Colo., 1976), pp. 51–53; Sharon L. Sievers, *Flowers in Salt: The Beginnings of Feminist Consciousness in Modern Japan* (Stanford, Calif., 1983), pp. 55, 62, 66, 84; Yukiko Hanawa, "The Several Worlds of Issei Women," unpublished M.A. thesis, California State University, Long Beach, 1982, pp. 31–34; Yasuo Wakatsuki, "Japanese Emigration to the United States, 1866–1924," *Perspectives in American History*, vol. 12 (1979), pp. 401, 404; Wilson and Hosokawa, *East to America*, p. 42.

17. Hanawa, "Several Worlds," pp. 13–16; Susan McCoin Kataoka, "Issei Women: A Study in Subordinate Status," unpublished Ph.D. thesis, University of California, Los Angeles, 1977, p. 6; Akemi Kikumura, *Through Harsh Winters: The Life of a Japanese Immigrant Woman* (Novato, Calif., 1981), pp. 18, 25; Emma Gee, "Issei: The First Women," in Emma Gee (ed.), *Asian Women* (Berkeley, Calif., 1971), p. 11.

18. Tsuru Yamauchi is quoted in Ethnic Studies Oral History Project (ed.), *Uchinanchu: A History of Okinawans in Hawaii* (Honolulu, 1981), pp. 490, 491; the folk saying can be found in Tadashi Fukutake, *Japanese Rural Society* (Ithaca, N.Y., 1967), p. 47.

19. Fukutake, *Japanese Rural Society*, pp. 6, 7, 39, 40, 42; Victor Nee and Herbert Y. Wong, "Asian American Socioeconomic Achievement: The Strength of the Family Bond," *Sociological Perspectives*, vol. 28, no. 3 (July 1985), p. 292.

20. Katherine Coman, *The History of Contract Labor in the Hawaiian Islands* (New York, 1903), p. 42; Allan Moriyama, "Causes of Emigration: The Background of Japanese Emigration to Hawaii, 1885–1894," in Edna Bonacich and Lucie Cheng (eds.), *Labor Immigration under Capitalism: Asian Workers in the United States before World War II* (Berkeley, Calif., 1984), p. 273; Republic of Hawaii, Bureau of Immigration, *Report* (Honolulu, 1886), p. 256; manager of the Hutchinson Sugar Company to W. G. Irwin and Company, February 5, 1902, and January 25, 1905, Hutchinson Plantation Records; for terms of the Gentlemen's Agreement, see Frank Chuman, *The Bamboo People: The Law and Japanese-Americans* (Del Mar, Calif., 1976), pp. 35–36.

21. H. A. Millis, *The Japanese Problem in the United States* (New York, 1915), p. 86.

22. Sarasohn (ed.), *Issei*, p. 34; Yuriko Sato, "Emigration of Issei Women" (Berkeley, 1982), in the Asian American Studies Library, University of California, Berkeley; Ito, *Issei*, p. 34.

READING FOR INFORMATION

1. In paragraph 6, Takaki refers to the American Civil War as a struggle "to defend and preserve the Union." Summarize the ideas about "union" that motivate his discussion. What use does Takaki make of Lincoln's phrase "the mystic chords of memory"?

2. List features of Japanese history in paragraphs 14 and 15 that Takaki regards as important for understanding patterns of Japanese emigration to America.

3. Summarize Japanese views on gender that Takaki discusses in paragraphs 22 and 23 as they bear upon the history of Japanese emigration. How do Takaki's stories about "picture brides" relate to those views?

READING FOR FORM, ORGANIZATION, AND EXPOSITORY FEATURES

1. List the immigrant groups that Takaki mentions in paragraphs 6–8. Could you add other groups to this list? Why does Takaki propose that their stories are worth telling?

2. Describe the use that Takaki makes of statistics in paragraph 17. How does he interpret them to fashion an account of distinctive features about Japanese immigration?

3. Summarize the contrasts between Chinese and Japanese patterns of immigration that Takaki develops in paragraphs 18 and 20. Describe the major features of this contrast.

READING FOR RHETORICAL CONCERNS

1. Explain why Takaki begins his essay in paragraphs 1 and 2 with a personal account of his conversation with a taxicab driver. How does that account color his scholarly presentation of historical materials in the rest of the essay?

2. In paragraphs 10 and 11, Takaki cites two recent books with *Mirror* in their titles and suggests that his use of the world will differ from theirs. Explain how it differs. What role does he attribute to the idea of "mirroring" in the study of history?

3. Paraphrase Takaki's discussion of the family as a "mechanism of labor control" in paragraph 24. Describe Takaki's attitude toward that development.

WRITING ASSIGNMENTS

1. Write an argumentative essay about how American history should record patterns of racial diversity since the beginning. Reflect upon your own racial roots and comment upon how they are represented in American history.

2. Write a comparison and contrast essay drawing points of similarity and difference between Takaki's case history of Japanese picture brides and the case history of women in some other immigrant group who arrived in America with expectations of marrying and raising a family.

Jasmine

Bharati Mukherjee

Bharati Mukherjee was born in Calcutta and currently teaches English at the University of California, Berkeley. She has published many short stories, four novels, including The Tiger's Daughter *(1972),* Darkness *(1985),* Jasmine *(1989), and* The Holder of the World *(1993); and two works of nonfiction written with her husband, Clark Blaise,* Days and Nights in Calcutta *(1977) and* The Sorrow and Terror *(1987).*

PREREADING

Inquire at the reference desk of your college library to obtain a copy of the Immigration Reform and Control Act of 1986. Designed to restrict the flow of illegal immigrants into the United States, it imposes harsh penalties on employers who knowingly hire undocumented aliens. Read its provisions, and freewrite on some of the likely consequences of this act, including subtle and sometimes blatant racism, economic hardships, and class tensions.

Jasmine came to Detroit from Port-of-Spain, Trinidad, by way 1 of Canada. She crossed the border at Windsor in the back of a gray van loaded with mattresses and box springs. The plan was for her to hide in an empty mattress box if she heard the driver say, "All bad weather seems to come down from Canada, doesn't it?" to the customs man. But she didn't have to crawl into a box and hold her breath. The customs man didn't ask to look in.

The driver let her off at a scary intersection on Woodward Avenue 2 and gave her instructions on how to get to the Plantations Motel in

From Bharati Mukherjee, *The Middleman and Other Stories* (New York: Ballantine Books, 1988) 123–35. Copyright © 1988 by Bharati Mukherjee. Used by permission of Grove/Atlantic, Inc.

Southfield. The trick was to keep changing vehicles, he said. That threw off the immigration guys real quick.

Jasmine took money for cab fare out of the pocket of the great big   3
raincoat that the van driver had given her. The raincoat looked like something that nuns in Port-of-Spain sold in church bazaars. Jasmine was glad to have a coat with wool lining, though; and anyway, who would know in Detroit that she was Dr. Vassanji's daughter?

All the bills in her hand looked the same. She would have to be   4
careful when she paid the cabdriver. Money in Detroit wasn't pretty the way it was back home, or even in Canada, but she liked this money better. Why should money be pretty, like a picture? Pretty money is only good for putting on your walls maybe. The dollar bills felt businesslike, serious. Back home at work, she used to count out thousands of Trinidad dollars every day and not even think of them as real. Real money was worn and green, American dollars. Holding the bills in her fist on a street corner meant she had made it in okay. She'd outsmarted the guys at the border. Now it was up to her to use her wits to do something with her life. As her Daddy kept saying, "Girl, is opportunity come only once." The girls she'd worked with at the bank in Port-of-Spain had gone green as bananas when she'd walked in with her ticket on Air Canada. Trinidad was too tiny. That was the trouble. Trinidad was an island stuck in the middle of nowhere. What kind of place was that for a girl with ambition?

The Plantations Motel was run by a family of Trinidad Indians who   5
had come from the tuppenny-ha'penny country town, Chaguanas. The Daboos were nobodies back home. They were lucky, that's all. They'd gotten here before the rush and bought up a motel and an ice cream parlor. Jasmine felt very superior when she saw Mr. Daboo in the motel's reception area. He was a pumpkin-shaped man with very black skin and Elvis Presley sideburns turning white. They looked like earmuffs. Mrs. Daboo was a bumpkin, too; short, fat, flapping around in house slippers. The Daboo daughters seemed very American, though. They didn't seem to know that they were nobodies, and kept looking at her and giggling.

She knew she would be short of cash for a great long while. Be-   6
sides, she wasn't sure she wanted to wear bright leather boots and leotards like Viola and Loretta. The smartest move she could make would be to put a down payment on a husband. Her Daddy had told her to talk to the Daboos first chance. The Daboos ran a service fixing up illegals with islanders who had made it in legally. Daddy had paid three thousand back in Trinidad, with the Daboos and the mattress man getting part of it. They should throw in a good-earning husband for that kind of money.

The Daboos asked her to keep books for them and to clean the ₇ rooms in the new wing, and she could stay in 16B as long as she liked. They showed her 16B. They said she could cook her own roti; Mr. Daboo would bring in a stove, two gas rings that you could fold up in a metal box. The room was quite grand, Jasmine thought. It had a double bed, a TV, a pink sink and matching bathtub. Mrs. Daboo said Jasmine wasn't the big-city Port-of-Spain type she'd expected. Mr. Daboo said that he wanted her to stay because it was nice to have a neat, cheerful person around. It wasn't a bad deal, better than stories she'd heard about Trinidad girls in the States.

All day every day except Sundays Jasmine worked. There wasn't just ₈ the bookkeeping and the cleaning up. Mr. Daboo had her working on the match-up marriage service. Jasmine's job was to check up on social security cards, call clients' bosses for references, and make sure credit information wasn't false. Dermatologists and engineers living in Bloomfield Hills, store owners on Canfield and Woodward: she treated them all as potential liars. One of the first things she learned was that Ann Arbor was a magic word. A boy goes to Ann Arbor and gets an education, and all the barriers come crashing down. So Ann Arbor was the place to be.

She didn't mind the work. She was learning about Detroit, every ₉ side of it. Sunday mornings she helped unload packing crates of Caribbean spices in a shop on the next block. For the first time in her life, she was working for a black man, an African. So what if the boss was black? This was a new life, and she wanted to learn everything. Her Sunday boss, Mr. Anthony, was a courtly, Christian, church-going man, and paid her the only wages she had in her pocket. Viola and Loretta, for all their fancy American ways, wouldn't go out with blacks.

One Friday afternoon she was writing up the credit info on a ₁₀ Guyanese Muslim who worked in an assembly plant when Loretta said that enough was enough and that there was no need for Jasmine to be her father's drudge.

"Is time to have fun," Viola said. "We're going to Ann Arbor."

Jasmine filed the sheet on the Guyanese man who probably now ₁₁ would never get a wife and got her raincoat. Loretta's boyfriend had a Cadillac parked out front. It was the longest car Jasmine had ever been in and louder than a country bus. Viola's boyfriend got out of the front seat. "Oh, oh, sweet things," he said to Jasmine. "Get in front." He was a talker. She'd learned that much from working on the matrimonial match-ups. She didn't believe him for a second when he said that there were dudes out there dying to ask her out.

Loretta's boyfriend said, "You have eyes I could leap into, girl."   12

Jasmine knew he was just talking. They sounded like Port-of-Spain   13
boys of three years ago. It didn't surprise her that these Trinidad country boys in Detroit were still behind the times, even of Port-of-Spain.
She sat very stiff between the two men, hands on her purse. The Daboo
girls laughed in the back seat.

On the highway the girls told her about the reggae night in Ann   14
Arbor. Kevin and the Krazee Islanders. Malcolm's Lovers. All the big
reggae groups in the Midwest were converging for the West Indian Students Association fall bash. The ticket didn't come cheap but Jasmine
wouldn't let the fellows pay. She wasn't that kind of girl.

The reggae and steel drums brought out the old Jasmine. The rum   15
punch, the dancing, the dreadlocks, the whole combination. She hadn't
heard real music since she got to Detroit, where music was supposed to
be so famous. The Daboos girls kept turning on rock stuff in the motel
lobby whenever their father left the area. She hadn't danced, really
danced, since she'd left home. It felt so good to dance. She felt hot and
sweaty and sexy. The boys at the dance were more than sweet talkers;
they moved with assurance and spoke of their futures in America. The
bartender gave her two free drinks and said, "Is ready when you are,
girl." She ignored him but she felt all hot and good deep inside. She knew
Ann Arbor was a special place.

When it was time to pile back into Loretta's boyfriend's Cadillac,   16
she just couldn't face going back to the Plantations Motel and to the
Daboos with their accounting books and messy files.

"I don't know what happen, girl," she said to Loretta. "I feel all crazy
inside. Maybe is time for me to pursue higher studies in this town."

"This Ann Arbor, girl, they don't just take you off the street. It *cost*
like hell."

She spent the night on a bashed-up sofa in the Student Union. She   17
was a well-dressed, respectable girl, and she didn't expect anyone to question her right to sleep on the furniture. Many others were doing the same
thing. In the morning, a boy in an army parka showed her the way to the
Placement Office. He was a big, blond, clumsy boy, not bad-looking except for the blond eyelashes. He didn't scare her, as did most Americans.
She let him buy her a Coke and a hotdog. That evening she had a job with
the Moffits.

Bill Moffitt taught molecular biology and Lara Hatch-Moffitt, his   18
wife, was a performance artist. A performance artist, said Lara, was very
different from being an actress, though Jasmine still didn't understand

what the difference might be. The Moffitts had a little girl, Muffin, whom Jasmine was to look after, though for the first few months she might have to help out with the housework and the cooking because Lara said she was deep into performance rehearsals. That was all right with her, Jasmine said, maybe a little too quickly. She explained she came from a big family and was used to heavy-duty cooking and cleaning. This wasn't the time to say anything about Ram, the family servant. Americans like the Moffitts wouldn't understand about keeping servants. Ram and she weren't in similar situations. Here mother's helpers, which is what Lara called her—Americans were good with words to cover their shame—seemed to be as good as anyone.

Lara showed her the room she would have all to herself in the fin- 19 ished basement. There was a big, old TV, not in color like the motel's and a portable typewriter on a desk which Lara said she would find handy when it came time to turn in her term papers. Jasmine didn't say anything about not being a student. She was a student of life, wasn't she? There was a scary moment after they'd discussed what she would expect as salary, which was three times more than anything Mr. Daboo was supposed to pay her but hadn't. She thought Bill Moffitt was going to ask her about her visa or her green card number and social security. But all Bill did was smile and smile at her—he had a wide, pink, baby face—and play with a button on his corduroy jacket. The button would need sewing back on, firmly.

Lara said, "I think I'm going to like you, Jasmine. You have a some- 20 thing about you. A something real special. I'll just bet you've acted, haven't you?" The idea amused her, but she merely smiled and accepted Lara's hug. The interview was over.

Then Bill opened a bottle of Soave and told stories about camping 21 in northern Michigan. He'd been raised there. Jasmine didn't see the point in sleeping in tents; the woods sounded cold and wild and creepy. But she said, "Is exactly what I want to try out come summer, man. Campin and huntin."

Lara asked about Port-of-Spain. There was nothing to tell about 22 her hometown that wouldn't shame her in front of nice white American folk like the Moffitts. The place was shabby, the people were grasping and cheating and lying and life was full of despair and drink and wanting. But by the time she finished, the island sounded romantic. Lara said, "It wouldn't surprise me one bit if you were a writer, Jasmine."

Ann Arbor was a huge small town. She couldn't imagine any kind 23 of school the size of the University of Michigan. She meant to sign up for courses in the spring. Bill brought home a catalogue bigger than the phonebook for all of Trinidad. The university had courses in everything. It would be hard to choose; she'd have to get help from Bill. He wasn't like a professor, not the ones back home where even high school teachers called themselves professors and acted like little potentates. He wore blue jeans and thick sweaters with holes in the elbows and used phrases like "in vitro" as he watched her curry up fish. Dr. Parveen back home— he called himself "doctor" when everybody knew he didn't have even a Master's degree—was never seen without his cotton jacket which had gotten really ratty at the cuffs and lapel edges. She hadn't learned anything in the two years she'd put into college. She'd learned more from working in the bank for two months than she had at college. It was the assistant manager, Personal Loans Department, Mr. Singh, who had turned her on to the Daboos and to smooth, bargain-priced emigration.

Jasmine liked Lara. Lara was easygoing. She didn't spend the time 24
she had between rehearsals telling Jasmine how to cook and clean American-style. Mrs. Daboo did that in 16B. Mrs. Daboo would barge in with a plate of stale samosas and snoop around giving free advice on how mainstream Americans did things. As if she were dumb or something! As if she couldn't keep her own eyes open and make her mind up for herself. Sunday mornings she had to share the butcher-block workspace in the kitchen with Bill. He made the Sunday brunch from new recipes in *Gourmet* and *Cuisine.* Jasmine hadn't seen a man cook who didn't have to or wasn't getting paid to do it. Things were topsy-turvy in the Moffitt house. Lara went on two- and three-day road trips and Bill stayed home. But even her Daddy, who'd never poured himself a cup of tea, wouldn't put Bill down as a woman. The mornings Bill tried out something complicated, a Cajun shrimp, sausage, and beans dish, for instance, Jasmine skipped church services. The Moffitts didn't go to church, though they seemed to be good Christians. They just didn't talk church talk, which suited her fine.

Two months passed. Jasmine knew she was lucky to have found a 25
small, clean, friendly family like the Moffitts to build her new life around. "Man!" she'd exclaim as she vacuumed the wide-plank wood floors or ironed (Lara wore pure silk or pure cotton). "In this country Jesus givin out good luck only!" By this time they knew she wasn't a student, but they didn't care and said they wouldn't report her. They never asked if she was illegal on top of it.

To savor her new sense of being a happy, lucky person, she would put 26
herself through a series of "what ifs": what if Mr. Singh in Port-of-Spain

hadn't turned her on to the Daboos and loaned her two thousand! What if she'd been ugly like the Mintoo girl and the manager hadn't even offered! What if the customs man had unlocked the door of the van! Her Daddy liked to say, "You is a helluva girl, Jasmine."

"Thank you, Jesus," Jasmine said, as she carried on.

Christmas Day the Moffitts treated her just like family. They gave 27 her a red cashmere sweater with a V neck so deep it made her blush. If Lara had worn it, her bosom wouldn't hang out like melons. For the holiday weekend Bill drove her to the Daboos in Detroit. "You work too hard," Bill said to her. "Learn to be more selfish. Come on, throw your weight around." She'd rather not have spent time with the Daboos, but that first afternoon of the interview she'd told Bill and Lara that Mr. Daboo was her mother's first cousin. She had thought it shameful in those days to have no papers, no family, no roots. Now Loretta and Viola in tight, bright pants seemed trashy like girls at Two-Johnny Bissoondath's Bar back home. She was stuck with the story of the Daboos being family Village bumpkins, ha! She would break out. Soon.

Jasmine had Bill drop her off at the RenCen. The Plantations Motel, 28 in fact, the whole Riverfront area, was too seamy. She'd managed to cut herself off mentally from anything too islandy. She loved her Daddy and Mummy, but she didn't think of them that often anymore. Mummy had expected her to be homesick and come flying right back home. "Is blowin sweat-of-brow money is what you doing, Pa," Mummy had scolded. She loved them, but she'd become her own person. That was something that Lara said: "I am my own person."

The Daboos acted thrilled to see her back. "What you drinkin, Jas- 29 mine girl?" Mr. Daboo kept asking. "You drinkin sherry or what?" Pouring her little glasses of sherry instead of rum was a sure sign he thought she had become whitefolk-fancy. The Daboo sisters were very friendly, but Jasmine considered them too wild. Both Loretta and Viola had changed boyfriends. Both were seeing black men they'd danced with in Ann Arbor. Each night at bedtime, Mr. Daboo cried. "In Trinidad we stayin we side, they stayin they side. Here, everything mixed up. Is helluva confusion, no?"

On New Year's Eve the Daboo girls and their black friends went to 30 a dance. Mr. and Mrs. Daboo and Jasmine watched TV for a while. Then Mr. Daboo got out a brooch from his pocket and pinned it on Jasmine's red sweater. It was a Christmasy brooch, a miniature sleigh loaded down with snowed-on mistletoe. Before she could pull away, he kissed her on the lips. "Good luck for the New Year!" he said. She lifted her head and saw tears. "Is year for dreams comin true."

Jasmine started to cry, too. There was nothing wrong, but Mr. 31
Daboo, Mrs. Daboo, she, everybody was crying.

What for? This is where she wanted to be. She'd spent some damned 32
uncomfortable times with the assistant manager to get approval for her
loan. She thought of Daddy. He would be playing poker and fanning himself with a magazine. Her married sisters would be rolling out the dough
for stacks and stacks of roti, and Mummy would be steamed purple from
stirring the big pot of goat curry on the stove. She missed them. But. It felt
strange to think of anyone celebrating New Year's Eve in summery clothes.

In March Lara and her performing group went on the road. Jas- 33
mine knew that the group didn't work from scripts. The group didn't use
a stage, either; instead, it took over supermarkets, senior citizens' centers,
and school halls, without notice. Jasmine didn't understand the performance world. But she was glad that Lara said, "I'm not going to lay a
guilt trip on myself. Muffie's in super hands," before she left.

Muffie didn't need much looking after. She played Trivial Pursuit 34
all day, usually pretending to be two persons, sometimes Jasmine, whose
accent she could imitate. Since Jasmine didn't know any of the answers,
she couldn't help. Muffie was a quiet, precocious child with see-through
blue eyes like her dad's, and red braids. In the early evenings Jasmine
cooked supper, something special she hadn't forgotten from her island
days. After supper she and Muffie watched some TV, and Bill read. When
Muffie went to bed, Bill and she sat together for a bit with their glasses
of Soave. Bill, Muffie, and she were a family, almost.

Down in her basement room that late, dark winter, she had trouble 35
sleeping. She wanted to stay awake and think of Bill. Even when she fell
asleep it didn't feel like sleep because Bill came barging into her dreams
in his funny, loose-jointed, clumsy way. It was mad to think of him all the
time, and stupid and sinful; but she couldn't help it. Whenever she put
back a book he'd taken off the shelf to read or whenever she put his
clothes through the washer and dryer, she felt sick in a giddy, wonderful
way. When Lara came back things would get back to normal. Meantime
she wanted the performance group miles away.

Lara called in at least twice a week. She said things like, "We've fi- 36
nally obliterated the margin between realspace and performancespace."
Jasmine filled her in on Muffie's doings and the mail. Bill always closed
with, "I love you. We miss you, hon."

One night after Lara had called—she was in Lincoln, Nebraska— 37
Bill said to Jasmine, "Let's dance."

She hadn't danced since the reggae night she'd had too many rum 38
punches. Her toes began to throb and clench. She untied her apron and
the fraying, knotted-up laces of her running shoes.

Bill went around the downstairs rooms turning down lights. "We 39
need atmosphere," he said. He got a small, tidy fire going in the living
room grate and pulled the Turkish scatter rug closer to it. Lara didn't
like anybody walking on the Turkish rug, but Bill meant to have his way.
The hissing logs, the plants in the dimmed light, the thick patterned rug:
everything was changed. This wasn't the room she cleaned every day.

He stood close to her. She smoothed her skirt down with both 40
hands.

"I want you to choose the record," he said.

"I don't know your music."

She brought her hand high to his face. His skin was baby smooth.

"I want *you* to pick," he said. "You are your own person now."

"You got island music?"

He laughed, "What do you think?" The stereo was in a cabinet 41
with albums packed tight alphabetically into the bottom three shelves.
"Calypso has not been a force in my life."

She couldn't help laughing. "Calypso? Oh, man." She pulled dust 42
jackets out at random. Lara's records. The Flying Lizards. The Violent
Fems. There was so much still to pick up on!

"This one," she said finally.

He took the record out of her hand. "God!" he laughed. "Lara must 43
have found this in a garage sale!" He laid the old record on the turntable.
It was "Music for Lovers," something the nuns had taught her to fox-trot
to way back in Port-of-Spain.

They danced so close that she could feel his heart heaving and crash- 44
ing against her head. She liked it, she liked it very much. She didn't care
what happened.

"Come on," Bill whispered. "If it feels right, do it." He began to
take her clothes off.

"Don't Bill," she pleaded.

"Come on, baby," he whispered again. "You're a blossom, a flower."

He took off his fisherman's knit pullover, the corduroy pants, 45
the blue shorts. She kept pace. She'd never had such an effect on a
man. He nearly flung his socks and Adidas into the fire. "You feel so
good," he said. "You smell so good. You're really something, flower of
Trinidad."

"Flower of Ann Arbor," she said, "not Trinidad."

She felt so good she was dizzy. She'd never felt this good on the is- 46
land where men did this all the time, and girls went along with it always
for favors. You couldn't feel really good in a nothing place. She was thinking this as they made love on the Turkish carpet in front of the fire: she
was a bright, pretty girl with no visa, no papers, and no birth certificate.
No nothing other than what she wanted to invent and tell. She was a girl
rushing wildly into the future.

His hand moved up her throat and forced her lips apart and it felt 47
so good, so right; that she forgot all the dreariness of her new life and gave
herself up to it. ✍

READING FOR INFORMATION

1. List the business and commercial enterprises of the Daboo family in
   paragraphs 5, 6, and 8. What attitude does the narrator project toward
   those activities?
2. List the various racial and ethnic groups with which Jasmine has contact
   in paragraphs 5, 9, 10, 17, and 18.
3. Paraphrase and compare the story's representations of Christmastime with
   the Hatch-Moffits, the Daboos, and Jasmine's parents in paragraphs 27, 30,
   and 32.

READING FOR FORM, ORGANIZATION, AND EXPOSITORY FEATURES

1. Summarize the features of Lara's first meeting with Jasmine in paragraphs
   18, 19, 20, and 22. Why does Lara assume that Jasmine is a student actress
   and writer?
2. Explain why in paragraph 24 Jasmine thinks that the Hatch-Moffit
   household is "topsy-turvy."
3. Explain the significance of Bill's "Learn to be more selfish" in paragraph 27, of Jasmine's "But" in paragraph 32, and of Lara's "guilt trip"
   in paragraph 33.

READING FOR RHETORICAL CONCERNS

1. Describe Jasmine's attitude toward the Daboo family in paragraph 5. Why
   does she feel superior to them?
2. Summarize the account of Jasmine's upbringing in Jamaica as related in
   paragraphs 3, 4, 6, and 18.
3. Explain the significance of Bill's "If it feels right, do it" in paragraph 44.

WRITING ASSIGNMENTS

1. Write a critical analysis of the story's action from the points of view of the Daboos, the Hatch-Moffits, and Jasmine. Comment upon the narrator's implied attitude toward each of these points of view.
2. Write a critical evaluation of Jasmine's character. Is she an outright opportunist? Or does she acquiesce to her crises, accepting the provisional good that comes to her? To what extent does she control what's happening to her? In the final scene, who seduces whom?

Everyday Use

Alice Walker

Alice Walker (b. 1944) was born in Eatonton, Georgia, the daughter of a share-cropper and a maid. After graduating from Sarah Lawrence College, she began publishing novels, poems, short stories, and essays. Her novels include The Third Life of Grange Copeland *(1970),* Meridian *(1976), and* The Color Purple *(1982, winner of the Pulitzer Prize). She has also served as contributing editor for* Ms. *magazine and has taught and lectured at several colleges and universities.*

PREREADING

Do you or your family cherish any artifacts that through time have acquired value as works of art in your own or others' eyes? They may include everyday objects of clothing, furniture, or tools or special ones such as fancy pottery, jewelry, or ornaments. Try to describe them in a way that will communicate to others the qualities that make them valuable to you. Freewrite your response as though you were composing a letter to a friend.

 for your grandmama

I will wait for her in the yard that Maggie and I made so clean and   1
wavy yesterday afternoon. A yard like this is more comfortable than most
people know. It is not just a yard. It is like an extended living room. When

Alice Walker, "Everyday Use." From *In Love and Trouble: Stories of Black Women* (San Diego: Harcourt Brace Jovanovich Publishers, 1973) 47–59. Copyright © 1973 by Alice Walker. Reprinted by permission of Harcourt Brace & Company.

the hard clay is swept clean as a floor and the fine sand around the edges lined with tiny, irregular grooves, anyone can come and sit and look up into the elm tree and wait for the breezes that never come inside the house.

Maggie will be nervous until after her sister goes: she will stand   2 hopelessly in corners, homely and ashamed of the burn scars down her arms and legs, eying her sister with a mixture of envy and awe. She thinks her sister has held life always in the palm of one hand, that "no" is a word the world never learned to say to her.

You've no doubt seen those TV shows where the child who has   3 "made it" is confronted, as a surprise, by her own mother and father, tottering in weakly from backstage. (A pleasant surprise, of course: What would they do if parent and child came on the show only to curse out and insult each other?) On TV mother and child embrace and smile into each other's faces. Sometimes the mother and father weep, the child wraps them in her arms and leans across the table to tell how she would not have made it without their help. I have seen these programs.

Sometimes I dream a dream in which Dee and I are suddenly   4 brought together on a TV program of this sort. Out of a dark and soft-seated limousine I am ushered into to a bright room filled with many people. There I meet a smiling, gray, sporty man like Johnny Carson who shakes my hand and tells me what a fine girl I have. Then we are on the stage and Dee is embracing me with tears in her eyes. She pins on my dress a large orchid, even though she has told me once that she thinks orchids are tacky flowers.

In real life I am a large, big-boned woman with rough, man-working   5 hands. In the winter I wear flannel nightgowns to bed and overalls during the day. I can kill and clean a hog as mercilessly as a man. My fat keeps me hot in zero weather. I can work outside all day, breaking ice to get water for washing; I can eat pork liver cooked over the open fire minutes after it comes steaming from the hog. One winter I knocked a bull calf straight in the brain between the eyes with a sledge hammer and had the meat hung up to chill before nightfall. But of course all this does not show on television. I am the way my daughter would want me to be: a hundred pounds lighter, my skin like an uncooked barley pancake. My hair glistens in the hot bright lights. Johnny Carson has much to do to keep up with my quick and witty tongue.

But that is a mistake. I know even before I wake up. Who ever   6 knew a Johnson with a quick tongue? Who can even imagine me looking a strange white man in the eye? It seems to me I have talked to them always with one foot raised in flight, with my head turned in whichever way is farthest from them. Dee, though. She would always look anyone in the eye. Hesitation was no part of her nature.

"How do I look, Mama?" Maggie says, showing just enough of her 7 thin body enveloped in pink skirt and red blouse for me to know she's there, almost hidden by the door.

"Come out into the yard," I say.

Have you ever seen a lame animal, perhaps a dog run over by some 8 careless person rich enough to own a car, sidle up to someone who is ignorant enough to be kind to him? That is the way my Maggie walks. She has been like this, chin on chest, eyes on ground, feet in shuffle, ever since the fire that burned the other house to the ground.

Dee is lighter than Maggie, with nicer hair and a fuller figure. She's a 9 woman now, though sometimes I forget. How long ago was it that the other house burned? Ten, twelve years? Sometimes I can still hear the flames and feel Maggie's arms sticking to me, her hair smoking and her dress falling off her in little black papery flakes. Her eyes seemed stretched open, blazed open by the flames reflected in them. And Dee. I see her standing off under the sweet gum tree she used to dig gum out of; a look of concentration on her face as she watched the last dingy gray board of the house fall in toward the red-hot brick chimney. Why don't you do a dance around the ashes? I'd wanted to ask her. She had hated the house that much.

I used to think she hated Maggie, too. But that was before we raised 10 the money, the church and me, to send her to Augusta to school. She used to read to us without pity; forcing words, lies, other folks' habits, whole lives upon us two, sitting trapped and ignorant underneath her voice. She washed us in a river of make-believe, burned us with a lot of knowledge we didn't necessarily need to know. Pressed us to her with the serious way she read, to shove us away at just the moment, like dimwits, we seemed about to understand.

Dee wanted nice things. A yellow organdy dress to wear to her grad- 11 uation from high school; black pumps to match a green suit she'd made from an old suit somebody gave me. She was determined to stare down any disaster in her efforts. Her eyelids would not flicker for minutes at a time. Often I fought off the temptation to shake her. At sixteen she had a style of her own: and knew what style was.

I never had an education myself. After second grade the school was 12 closed down. Don't ask *me* why: in 1927 colored asked fewer questions than they do now. Sometimes Maggie reads to me. She stumbles along good-naturedly but can't see well. She knows she is not bright. Like good looks and money, quickness passed her by. She will marry John Thomas (who has mossy teeth in an earnest face) and then I'll be free to sit here and I guess just sing church songs to myself. Although I never was a good singer. Never could carry a tune. I was always better at a man's job. I used to love to milk till I was hooked in the side in '49. Cows are soothing and slow and don't bother you, unless you try to milk them the wrong way.

I have deliberately turned my back on the house. It is three rooms, 13 just like the one that burned, except the roof is tin; they don't make shingle roofs any more. There are no real windows, just some holes cut in the sides, like the portholes in a ship, but not round and not square, with rawhide holding the shutters up on the outside. This house is in a pasture, too, like the other one. No doubt when Dee sees it she will want to tear it down. She wrote me once that no matter where we "choose" to live, she will manage to come see us. But she will never bring her friends. Maggie and I thought about this and Maggie asked me, "Mama, when did Dee ever *have* any friends?"

She had a few. Furtive boys in pink shirts hanging about on wash- 14 day after school. Nervous girls who never laughed. Impressed with her they worshiped the well-turned phrase, the cute shape, the scalding humor that erupted like bubbles in lye. She read to them.

When she was courting Jimmy T she didn't have much time to pay 15 to us, but turned all her faultfinding power on him. He *flew* to marry a cheap city girl from a family of ignorant flashy people. She hardly had time to recompose herself.

When she comes I will meet—but there they are!   16

Maggie attempts to make a dash for the house, in her shuffling way, but I stay her with my hand. "Come back here," I say. And she stops and tries to dig a well in the sand with her toe.

It is hard to see them clearly through the strong sun. But even the 17 first glimpse of leg out of the car tells me it is Dee. Her feet were always neat-looking, as if God himself had shaped them with a certain style. From the other side of the car comes a short, stocky man. Hair is all over his head a foot long and hanging from his chin like a kinky mule tail. I hear Maggie suck in her breath. "Uhnnnh," is what it sounds like. Like when you see the wriggling end of a snake just in front of your foot on the road. "Uhnnnh."

Dee next. A dress down to the ground, in this hot weather. A dress 18
so loud it hurts my eyes. There are yellows and oranges enough to throw
back the light of the sun. I feel my whole face warming from the heat
waves it throws out. Earrings gold, too, and hanging down to her shoulders. Bracelets dangling and making noises when she moves her arm up
to shake the folds of the dress out of her armpits. The dress is loose and
flows, and as she walks closer, I like it. I hear Maggie go "Uhnnnh" again.
It is her sister's hair. It stands straight up like the wool on a sheep. It is
black as night and around the edges are two long pigtails that rope about
like small lizards disappearing behind her ears.

"Wa-su-zo-Tean-o!" she says, coming on in that gliding way the dress 19
makes her move. The short stocky fellow with the hair to his navel is all
grinning and he follows up with "Asalamalakim, my mother and sister!"
He moves to hug Maggie but she falls back, right up against the back of
my chair. I feel her trembling there and when I look up I see the per-
spiration falling off her chin.

"Don't get up," says Dee. Since I am stout it takes something of a 20
push. You can see me trying to move a second or two before I make it.
She turns, showing white heels through her sandals, and goes back to the
car. Out she peeks next with a Polaroid. She stoops down quickly and
lines up picture after picture of me sitting there in front of the house with
Maggie cowering behind me. She never takes a shot without making
sure the house is included. When a cow comes nibbling around the edge
of the yard she snaps it and me and Maggie *and* the house. Then she puts
the Polaroid in the back seat of the car, and comes up and kisses me on
the forehead.

Meanwhile Asalamalakim is going through motions with Maggie's 21
hand. Maggie's hand is as limp as a fish, and probably as cold, despite
the sweat, and she keeps trying to pull it back. It looks like Asalamalakim
wants to shake hands but wants to do it fancy. Or maybe he don't know
how people shake hands. Anyhow, he soon gives up on Maggie.

"Well," I say. "Dee." 22

"No, Mama," she says. "Not 'Dee,' Wangero Leewanika Kemanjo!"

"What happened to 'Dee'?" I wanted to know.

"She's dead," Wangero said. "I couldn't bear it any longer, being
named after the people who oppress me."

"You know as well as me you was named after your aunt Dicie," I
said. Dicie is my sister. She named Dee. We called her "Big Dee" after
Dee was born.

"But who was *she* named after?" asked Wangero.

"I guess after Grandma Dee," I said.

"And who was she named after?" asked Wangero.

"Her mother," I said, and saw Wangero was getting tired. "That's about as far back as I can trace it," I said. Though, in fact, I probably could have carried it back beyond the Civil War through the branches.

"Well," said Asalamalakim, "there you are."

"Uhnnnh," I heard Maggie say.

"There I was not," I said, "before 'Dicie' cropped up in our family, so why should I try to trace it that far back?"

He just stood there grinning, looking down on me like somebody in- 23
specting a Model A car. Every once in a while he and Wangero sent eye signals over my head.

"How do you pronounce this name?" I asked.

"You don't have to call me by it if you don't want to," said Wangero.

"Why shouldn't I?" I asked. "If that's what you want us to call you, we'll call you."

"I know it might sound awkward at first," said Wangero.

"I'll get used to it," I said. "Ream it out again."

Well, soon we got the name out of the way. Asalamalakim had a 24
name twice as long and three times as hard. After I tripped over it two or three times he told me to just call him Hakim-a-barber. I wanted to ask him was he a barber, but I didn't really think he was, so I didn't ask.

"You must belong to those beef-cattle peoples down the road," I 25
said. They said "Asalamalakim" when they met you, too, but they didn't shake hands. Always too busy: feeding the cattle, fixing the fences, putting up salt-lick shelters, throwing down hay. When the white folks poisoned some of the herd the men stayed up all night with rifles in their hands. I walked a mile and a half just to see the sight.

Hakim-a-barber said, "I accept some of their doctrines, but farm- 26
ing and raising cattle is not my style." (They didn't tell me, and I didn't ask, whether Wangero (Dee) had really gone and married him.)

We sat down to eat and right away he said he didn't eat collards and 27
pork was unclean. Wangero, though, went on through the chitlins and corn bread, the greens and everything else. She talked a blue streak over the sweet potatoes. Everything delighted her. Even the fact that we still used the benches her daddy made for the table when we couldn't afford to buy chairs.

"Oh, Mama!" she cried. Then turned to Hakim-a-barber. "I never 28
knew how lovely these benches are. You can feel the rump prints," she said, running her hands underneath her and along the bench. Then she

gave a sigh and her hand closed over Grandma Dee's butter dish. "That's it!" she said. "I knew there was something I wanted to ask you if I could have." She jumped up from the table and went over in the corner where the churn stood, the milk in it clabber by now. She looked at the churn and looked at it.

"This churn top is what I need," she said. "Didn't Uncle Buddy   29
whittle it out of a tree you all used to have?"

"Yes," I said.

"Uh huh," she said happily. "And I want the dasher, too."

"Uncle Buddy whittle that, too?" asked the barber.

Dee (Wangero) looked up at me.

"Aunt Dee's first husband whittled the dash," said Maggie so low you almost couldn't hear her. "His name was Henry, but they called him Stash."

"Maggie's brain is like an elephant's," Wangero said, laughing. "I   30
can use the churn top as a centerpiece for the alcove table," she said, sliding a plate over the churn, "and I'll think of something artistic to do with the dasher."

When she finished wrapping the dasher the handle stuck out. I took   31
it for a moment in my hands. You didn't even have to look close to see where hands pushing the dasher up and down to make butter had left a kind of sink in the wood. In fact, there were a lot of small sinks; you could see where thumbs and fingers had sunk into the wood. It was beautiful light yellow wood, from a tree that grew in the yard where Big Dee and Stash had lived.

After dinner Dee (Wangero) went to the trunk at the foot of my bed   32
and started rifling through it. Maggie hung back in the kitchen over the dishpan. Out came Wangero with two quilts. They had been pieced by Grandma Dee and then Big Dee and me had hung them on the quilt frames on the front porch and quilted them. One was in the Lone Star pattern. The other was Walk Around the Mountain. In both of them were scraps of dresses Grandma Dee had worn fifty and more years ago. Bits and pieces of Granpa Jarrell's Paisley shirts. And one teeny faded blue piece, about the size of a penny matchbox, that was from Great Grandpa' Ezra's uniform that he wore in the Civil War.

"Mama," Wangero said sweet as a bird. "Can I have these old quilts?"   33

I heard something fall in the kitchen, and a minute later the kitchen   34
door slammed.

"Why don't you take one or two of the others?" I asked. "These old things was just done by me and Big Dee from some tops your grandma pieced before she died."

"No," said Wangero. "I don't want those. They are stitched around the borders by machine."

"That'll make them last better," I said.

"That's not the point," said Wangero. "These are all pieces of dresses Grandma used to wear. She did all this stitching by hand. Imagine!" She held the quilts securely in her arms, stroking them.

"Some of the pieces, like those lavender ones, come from old clothes her mother handed down to her," I said, moving up to touch the quilts. Dee (Wangero) moved back just enough so that I couldn't reach the quilts. They already belonged to her.

"Imagine!" she breathed again, clutching them closely to her bosom.

"The truth is," I said. "I promised to give them quilts to Maggie, for when she marries John Thomas."

She gasped like a bee had stung her.

"Maggie can't appreciate these quilts!" she said. "She'd probably 35 be backward enough to put them to everyday use."

"I reckon she would," I said. "God knows I been saving 'em for long enough with nobody using 'em. I hope she will!" I didn't want to bring up how I had offered Dee (Wangero) a quilt when she went away to college. Then she had told me they were old-fashioned, out of style.

"But they're *priceless!*" she was saying now, furiously; for she has a temper. "Maggie would put them on the bed and in five years they'd be in rags. Less than that!"

"She can always make some more," I said. "Maggie knows how to quilt."

Dee (Wangero) looked at me with hatred. "You just will not un- 36 derstand. The point is these quilts, *these* quilts!"

"Well," I said, stumped. "What would *you* do with them?"

"Hang them," she said. As if that was the only thing you *could* do with quilts.

Maggie by now was standing in the door. I could almost hear the 37 sound her feet made as they scraped over each other.

"She can have them, Mama," she said, like somebody used to never winning anything, or having anything reserved for her. "I can 'member Grandma Dee without the quilts."

I looked at her hard. She had filled her bottom lip with checker- 38 berry snuff and it gave her face a kind of dopey, hangdog look. It was Grandma Dee and big Dee who taught her how to quilt herself. She stood there with her scarred hands hidden in the folds of her skirt. She looked at her sister with something like fear but she wasn't mad at her. This was Maggie's portion. This was the way she knew God to work.

When I looked at her like that something hit me in the top of my head 39 and ran down to the soles of my feet. Just like when I'm in church and the spirit of God touches me and I get happy and shout. I did something I never had done before: hugged Maggie to me, then dragged her on into the room, snatched the quilts out of Miss Wangero's hands and dumped them into Maggie's lap. Maggie just sat there on my bed with her mouth open.

"Take one or two of the others," I said to Dee.

But she turned without a word and went out to Hakim-a-barber.   40

"You just don't understand," she said, as Maggie and I came out to the car.

"What don't I understand?" I wanted to know.

"Your heritage," she said. And then she turned to Maggie, kissed her, and said, "You ought to try to make something of yourself, too, Maggie. It's really a new day for us. But from the way you and Mama still live you'd never know it."

She put on some sunglasses that hid everything above the tip of her 41 nose and her chin.

Maggie smiled; maybe at the sunglasses. But a real smile, not scared. 42 After we watched the car dust settle I asked Maggie to bring me a dip of snuff. And then the two of us sat there just enjoying, until it was time to go in the house and go to bed. 🍃

READING FOR INFORMATION

1. List examples of Dee's superior attitude toward others, and describe instances where she flaunts her newly acquired tastes and refinement.

2. List corresponding examples of Maggie's sense of inferiority and low self-esteem. Is there any evidence that Maggie still has a nucleus of self-confidence that may help her to survive and triumph?

3. Explain in your own words any family resemblances that link Mama and her two daughters, and recount any sharp differences that distinguish them. Note important differences in the characters' responses to the burning of the old house in paragraph 9.

READING FOR FORM, ORGANIZATION, AND EXPOSITORY FEATURES

1. Circle usages of the word "style" in paragraphs 11 and 35. Explain how each context modifies the meaning of the word. Underline references to reading and education in paragraphs 10, 12, 35, and 40. Explain how each context modifies the significance of those activities.

2. Explain why the word "choose" appears in quotation marks in paragraph 13. Explain what Maggie's "uhnnnh" means in paragraphs 17, 18, and 22. Does this word change its meaning in different contexts?

3. Paraphrase Dee's argument about the value of the quilts in paragraphs 34, 35, and 36. What attitude does she project about her own taste and refinement? Rewrite the dialogue in these paragraphs as a statement that clarifies the differences in attitudes.

READING FOR RHETORICAL CONCERNS

1. Recount Mama's description of her own appearance and physique in paragraphs 5, 12, and 20.

2. Compare and contrast Mama's self-descriptions with her descriptions of each daughter's appearance in paragraphs 2, 7, 8, 9, 11, 12, 18, and 38.

3. Describe how ironically the narrator treats the names of her daughter and Hakim-a-barber in paragraphs 22, 24, 26, 29, 32, 34, and 35.

WRITING ASSIGNMENTS

1. On one level, this story depicts a mother's progress from a world of fantasy where she idolizes one daughter at the other's expense into a world of reality where she becomes critical of that daughter and appreciative of the other. Write an analytical essay about her progress and the experiences that influence it.

2. On another level, the story encourages us to make positive value judgments about culture and possessions, history, and human relationships. It also encourages us to recognize mistaken value judgments about them. The artistic worth of the quilts focuses all of these meanings. Write an analytical essay about the characters' various assumptions concerning the quilts and about how their judgments of their value define their own individuality.

SYNTHESIS WRITING ASSIGNMENTS

1. Drawing on selections by Takaki and Mukherjee, write a five- to six-page essay in which you synthesize their representational views about the immigrant experience in America. Address your essay to an audience of classmates from high school with whom you have not been in contact since starting college.

2. Drawing on selections by Allende and Takaki, write a five- to six-page essay in which you compare and contrast the experiences of different ethnic groups as they interact with one another in North and South America.

What conditions drive members of these groups to different forms of economic survival? Address your essay to an audience of students who have not read these texts.

3. Drawing on selections by Mukherjee and Walker, write a five- to six-page essay in which you respond to the characters' various efforts, both successful and unsuccessful, to preserve their ethnic identities. Address your essay to members of the academic community at large as a critical review in your college newspaper.

4. Drawing on selections by Grossman and Takaki, write a five- to six-page essay in which you analyze the writers' appropriation of fictional techniques (narrative, dialogue, vivid description) to represent nonfictional experience. Address your essay to an audience of students who have read these texts.

5. Drawing on selections by Allende and Mukherjee, write a five- to six-page essay in which you evaluate their narrative representations of outsiders' efforts to succeed as insiders in multicultural societies. Address your essay to members of the academic community at large as a critical review in your college newspaper.

6. Drawing on selections by Allende and Grossman, write a five- to six-page argumentative essay in which you challenge their claims about multicultural diversity, pro and con, in their respective locales (Latin America and the Middle East). Do these writers suggest that peaceful coexistence is possible or impossible in such settings? Address your essay to a local political representative whose views you might wish to influence.

Appendix:
Documenting Sources

MLA DOCUMENTATION STYLE

Every chapter in this book contains sample essays or research papers written according to the MLA (Modern Language Association) rules for page format (margins, page numbering, titles, and so forth) and source documentation. In addition to providing many sample pages that illustrate MLA style, we describe how to type papers in MLA format (pp. 72–74); use parenthetical documentation to cite sources that you summarize (pp. 23–29), paraphrase (pp. 16–22), or quote (pp. 30–35); and construct a works cited list (p. 57). Most of our examples, however, are based on the articles and book excerpts that are reprinted in the anthology section of this book. As a college student, you may need to document materials that differ from our earlier examples and follow a different format. You may need, for instance, to document a television newscast, a pamphlet, or a personal interview. The first section of the Appendix explains how to document many different types of sources. For an exhaustive discussion of MLA documentation style, see the *MLA Handbook for Writers of Research Papers.*

Documentation Models for Books

When documenting books, arrange the documentary information in the following order:

1. Author's name
2. Title of the part of the book (if you are referring to a section or chapter)
3. Title of the book
4. Name of the editor or translator
5. Edition
6. Number of volumes
7. Name of the series if the book is part of a series
8. City of publication

9. Abbreviated name of the publisher
10. Date of publication
11. Page numbers (if you are referring to a section or chapter)

Book with one author

> Kennedy, William J. <u>Rhetorical Norms in Renaissance
> Literature</u>. New Haven: Yale UP, 1978.

Two or more books by the same author (alphabetize by title)

> Kennedy, William J. <u>Jacopo Sannazaro and the Uses of
> the Pastoral</u>. Hanover, NH: UP of New England,
> 1983.
> ---. <u>Rhetorical Norms in Renaissance Literature</u>. New
> Haven: Yale UP, 1978.

Book with two authors

> Lambert, William W., and Wallace E. Lambert. <u>Social
> Psychology</u>. Englewood Cliffs: Prentice, 1964.

Book with three authors

> Kitch, Sally, Carol Knock, and Fran Majors. <u>The Source-
> Book</u>. New York: Longman, 1981.

Book with more than three authors

> Glock, Marvin D., et al. <u>Probe: College Developmental
> Reading</u>. 2nd ed. Columbus, OH: Merrill, 1980.

Book with a corporate author

> Boston Women's Health Book Collective. <u>Our Bodies, Our-
> selves: A Book by and for Women</u>. New York: Simon,
> 1971.

Book with an anonymous author

> <u>Writers' and Artists' Yearbook, 1980</u>. London: Adam and
> Charles Black, 1980.

Book with an editor instead of an author

> Bronfenbrenner, Urie, ed. <u>Influences on Human Develop-
> ment</u>. Hinsdale, IL: Dryden, 1972.

Book with two or three editors

> McQuade, Donald, and Robert Atwan, eds. <u>Popular Writing in America</u>. 3rd ed. New York: Oxford UP, 1985.

Book with more than three editors

> Kermode, Frank, et al., eds. <u>The Oxford Anthology of English Literature</u>. 2 vols. New York: Oxford UP, 1973.

Book with a translator

> de Beauvoir, Simon. <u>Force of Circumstance</u>. Trans. Richard Howard. Harmondsworth, Middlesex, Eng.: Penguin, 1968.

Book with more than one edition

> Hodges, John C., and Mary E. Whitten. <u>Harbrace College Handbook</u>. 9th ed. New York: Harcourt, 1984.

Book that has been republished

> Conroy, Frank. <u>Stop-time</u>. 1967. New York: Penguin, 1977.

Parts of Books

Section, chapter, article, or essay in a book with one author

> Chomsky, Noam. "Psychology and Ideology." <u>For Reasons of State</u>. New York: Vintage, 1973. 318-69.

Introduction, preface, or foreword written by someone other than the book's author

> Piccone, Paul. General Introduction. <u>The Essential Frankfurt Reader</u>. Ed. Andrew Arato and Eike Gebhardt. New York: Urizen, 1978. xi-xxiii.

Essay or article reprinted in a book

> Wimkoff, Meyer F., and Russell Middleton. "Type of Family and Type of Enemy." <u>American Journal of Sociology</u> 66 (1960): 215-24. Rpt. in <u>Man in</u>

<u>Adaptation: The Cultural Present</u>. Ed. Yehudi A.
Cohen. Chicago: Aldine, 1968. 384-93.

Essay, article, short story, or poem in an anthology

Cornish, Sam. "To a Single Shadow Without Pity." <u>The
New Black Poetry</u>. Ed. Clarence Major. New York:
International, 1969. 39.

Novel or play in an anthology

Gay, John. <u>The Beggar's Opera</u>. <u>Twelve Famous Plays of
the Restoration and Eighteenth Century</u>. Ed. Cecil
A. Moore. New York: Random, 1960. 573-650.

Signed article in a reference work

Goris, Jan-Albert. "Belgian Literature." <u>Colliers Ency-
clopedia</u>. 1983 ed.

Unsigned article in a reference work

"Solar Energy." <u>The New Columbia Encyclopedia</u>. 4th ed.
1975.

Documenting a Book Without Complete Publication Information or Pagination

Supply as much of the missing information as you can, enclosing the information you supply in square brackets to show your reader that the
source did not contain this information. For example: Metropolis: U of
Bigcity P, [1971]. Enclosing the date in brackets shows your reader that
you found the date elsewhere: another source that quotes your source,
the card catalog, your professor's lecture, and so on. If you are not certain of the date, add a question mark. For example: [1971?]. If you only
know an approximate date, put the date after a "c." (for *circa* "around").
However, when you cannot find the necessary information, use one of the
following abbreviation models to show this to your reader. These examples document material taken from page 42 of a source.

No date

Metropolis: U of Bigcity P, n.d. 42.

No pagination

    Metropolis: U of Bigcity P, 1971. N. pag.

No place of publication

    N.p.: U of Bigcity P, 1971. 42.

No publisher

    Metropolis: n.p., 1971. 42.

Neither place nor publisher

    N.p.: n.p., 1971. 42.

        For example: <u>Photographic View Album of Cambridge</u>.
        [England]: N.p., n.d. N. pag.

Cross-References

If you cite two or more articles from the same anthology, list the anthology itself with complete publication information, then cross-reference the individual articles. In the cross-reference, the anthology editor's last name and the page numbers follow the article author's name and the title of the article. In the example below, the first two entries are for articles reprinted in the third entry, the anthology edited by Kennedy, Kennedy, and Smith.

    Duff, Raymond G., and A. G. M. Campbell. "Moral and
        Ethical Dilemmas in the Special-Care Nursery."
        Kennedy, Kennedy, and Smith 406-12.
    Hentoff, Nat. "The Awful Privacy of Baby Doe." Kennedy,
        Kennedy, and Smith 417-24.
    Kennedy, Mary Lynch, William J. Kennedy, and Hadley M.
        Smith, eds. <u>Writing in the Disciplines</u>. Englewood
        Cliffs: Prentice Hall, 1987.

Documentation Models for Periodicals

When documenting articles in a periodical, arrange the documentary information in the following order:

1. Author's name
2. Title of the article

3. Name of the periodical

4. Series number or name

5. Volume number (followed by a period and the issue number, if needed)

6. Date of publication

7. Page numbers

Article in a scholarly/professional journal; each issue numbers its pages separately

> Maimon, Elaine P. "Cinderella to Hercules: Demytholo-
> gizing Writing Across the Curriculum." <u>Journal of
> Basic Writing</u> 2.4 (1980): 3-11.

Article in a scholarly/professional journal; the entire volume has continuous page numbering

> Slack, Warner V., and Douglas Porter. "The Scholastic
> Aptitude Test: A Critical Appraisal." <u>Harvard Edu-
> cational Review</u> 50 (1980): 154-75.

Signed article in a weekly or monthly magazine

> Golden, Frederic. "Heat Over Wood Burning: Pollution
> from Home Stoves Is Nearing Crisis Proportions."
> <u>Time</u> 16 Jan. 1984: 67.

Unsigned article in a weekly or monthly magazine

> "Planning Ahead: Proposals for Democratic Control of
> Investment." <u>Dollars and Sense</u> Feb. 1983: 3-5.

Signed article in a newspaper (in an edition with lettered sections)

> Miller, Marjorie. "Britain Urged to Legalize Cloning of
> Human Tissue." <u>Los Angeles Times</u> 9 Dec 1998: A1.

Unsigned article in a newspaper (in a daily without labeled sections)

> "Breast Cancer Study to Begin on Long Island." <u>Ithaca
> Journal</u> 14 Jan. 1984: 2.

Editorial or special feature (in an identified edition with numbered sections)

> "The Limits of Technology." Editorial. <u>New York Times</u> 3
> Jan. 1999, early ed., sec. 4: 8.

Review

> Hoberman, J. "The Informer: Elia Kazan Spills His
> Guts." Rev. of <u>Elia Kazan: A Life</u>, by Elia Kazan.
> <u>Village Voice</u> 17 May 1988: 58-60.

Article whose title contains a quotation

> Nitzsche, Jane Chance. "'As swete as is the roote of
> lycorys, or any cetewale': Herbal Imagery in
> Chaucer's Miller's Tale." <u>Chaucerian Newsletter</u>
> 2.1 (1980): 6-8.

Article from Dissertation Abstracts International (DAI)

> Webb, John Bryan. "Utopian Fantasy and Social Change,
> 1600-1660." Diss. SUNY Buffalo, 1982. <u>DAI</u> 43
> (1982): 8214250A.

Documentation Models for Other Written Sources

Government publication

> U. S. Dept. of Energy. <u>Winter Survival: A Consumer's
> Guide to Winter Preparedness</u>. Washington: GPO,
> 1980.

Congressional Record

> <u>Cong. Rec.</u> 13 Apr. 1967: S505457.

Pamphlet

> Hopper, Peggy, and Steve Soldz. <u>I Don't Want to Change
> My Lifestyle--I Want to Change My Life</u>. Cambridge,
> MA: Root and Branch, 1971.

Dissertation

> Boredin, Henry Morton. "The Ripple Effect in Classroom
> Management." Diss. U of Michigan, 1970.

Personal letter

> Siegele, Steven. Letter to the author. 13 Jan. 1983.

Published letter

> Bloom, Ira Mark. Letter. <u>New York Times</u> 9 Oct. 1985: A22.

Public document

> U. S. Depart. of Agriculture. "Shipments and Unloads of Certain Fruits and Vegetables. 1918-1923." <u>Statistical Bulletin</u> 7 Apr. 1925: 10-13.

Information service

> Edmonds, Edward L., ed. <u>The Adult Student: University Challenge</u>. Charlottetown: Prince Edward Island U, 1980. ERIC ED 190 008.

Documentation Models for Online Sources That Are Also Available in Print

The World Wide Web offers electronic versions of many publications that are available in print, ranging from newspaper articles to full-length books. Entries for sources that have electronic addresses (URLs) should include as many of the following items as are available:

1. Author
2. Title of the source (book, article, poem, or other source type)
3. Editor, compiler, or translator (if relevant)
4. Complete publication information for the print version
5. Title of the Web site (if no title is given, provide a label such as "Home page") or name of the database
6. Name of the Web site editor or compiler (if available)
7. Version number of the source (if relevant)
8. Date of electronic publication (latest update)
9. Number of total pages, paragraphs, or sections (if available)
10. Organization or institution associated with the Web site
11. Date when the researcher collected the information from the Web site
12. Electronic address, or URL, of the source (enclosed in angle brackets)

Each of the elements listed above should follow the format specifications on pages 689–96. For example, article titles should be placed in quotation marks while book titles should be underlined.

Book

> Shaw, Bernard. <u>Pygmalion</u>. 1912 Bartleby Archive. 6 Mar.
> 1998. <http://www.columbia.edu/acis/bartleby/shaw/>.

Poem

> Carroll, Lewis. "Jabberwocky." 1872. 6 Mar. 1998.
> <http://www.jabberwocky.com/carroll/jabber/
> jabberwocky.html>.

Article in a journal

> Rehberger, Dean. "The Censoring of Project #17: Hypertext
> Bodies and Censorship." <u>Kairos</u> 2.2 (Fall 1997): 14
> sec. 6 Mar. 1998 <http:english.ttu.edu/kairos/2.2/
> index_f.html>.

Article in a magazine

> Viagas, Robert, and David Lefkowitz. "Capeman Closing
> Mar. 28." <u>Playbill</u> 5 Mar. 1998. 6 Mar. 1998.
> <http:www1.playbill.com/cgi-bin/plb/news?cmd=
> show&code=30763>.

Documentation Models for Sources That Are Only Available Online

Certain electronic sources are available only online (on the World Wide Web, at Gopher sites, etc.). A myriad of organizations and individuals maintain Web sites that provide information that is not published in print form. For sources that do not appear in print, MLA works-cited entries should include as many of the following items as possible:

1. Author
2. Title of the source (essay, article, poem, short story, or other source type); or title of a posting to an online discussion, followed by the label "Online posting"
3. Editor, compiler, or translator (if relevant)

4. Title of the Web site (if no title is given, provice a label such as "Home page")
5. Name of the Web site editor or compiler (if available)
6. Version number of the source (if relevant)
7. Date of electronic publication (latest update) or of posting
8. Name of discussion list or forum (for a posting only)
9. Number of total pages, paragraphs, or sections (if available)
10. Organization or institution associated with the Web site
11. Date when the researcher collected the information from the Web site
12. Electronic address, or URL, of the source (enclosed in angle brackets)

All elements within entries should follow the format guidelines present-ed on pages 689–96. For example, article titles should be placed in quo-tation marks, while book titles should be underlined.

Posting to a discussion list

```
Grumman, Bob. "Shakespeare's Literacy." Online posting.
    6 Mar. 1998. Deja News. 13 Aug. 1998 <humanities
    .lit.author.>.
```

Scholarly project

```
Voice of the Shuttle: Web Page for Humanities Research.
    Ed. Alan Liu. 3 March 1998. U. California, Santa
    Barbara. 8 Mar. 1998. <http://humanitas.ucsb.edu/>.
```

Professional site

```
The Nobel Foundation Official Website. The Nobel Foun-
    dation. Dec. 1998. 28 Feb. 1999. <http://www
    .nobel.se/>.
```

Personal site

```
Thiroux, Emily. Home page. 7 Mar. 1998. 12 Jan. 1999.
    <http://academic.csubak.edu/home/acadpro/
    departments/english/engthrx.htmlx>.
```

Synchronous communication (such as MOO, MUD, and IRC)

```
"Ghostly Presence." Group discussion. telnet 16 Mar.
    1997. <moo.du.org:8000/80anon/anonview/1 4036#
    focus>.
```

Gopher site

> Banks, Vickie, and Joe Byers. "EDTECH." 18 Mar. 1997.
>   <gopher://ericyr.syr.edu:70/00/Listervi/EDTECH/
>   README>.

FTP (file transfer protocol) site

> U.S. Supreme Court directory. 6 Mar. 1998.
>   <ftp://<ftp.cwru.edu/U.S.Supreme.Court/>.

Some electronic sources are "portable," as is a CD-ROM for example, and may or may not have print versions. Other electronic sources do not have URLs. In each case, use the style that applies, listing the publication medium (CD-ROM, for example) and publisher and the computer network or service for an online source (for example, a computer database such as PsychINFO reached through CompuServe). Give the electronic publication information after the author, title, editor or compiler, and print publication information.

> Stucky, Nathan. "Performing Oral History: Storytelling
>   and Pedagogy." <u>Communication Education</u> 44.1
>   (1995): 1-14. <u>CommSearch</u> 2nd ed. CD-ROM. Electron-
>   ic Book Technologies. 1995.

Documentation Models for Nonprint Sources

Film

> <u>Rebel without a Cause</u>. Dir. Nichols Ray. With James
>   Dean, Sal Mineo, and Natalie Wood. Warner Broth-
>   ers, 1955.

Television or radio program

> <u>Comet Halley</u>. Prod. John L. Wilhelm. PBS. WNET, New
>   York. 26 Nov. 1986.

Personal (face-to-face) interview

> Warren, Charles. Personal interview. 26 Apr. 1985.

Telephone interview

> Springsteen, Bruce. Telephone interview. 1 Oct. 1984.

Performance of music, dance, or drama

> Corea, Chick, dir. <u>Chick Corea Electrik Band</u>. Cornell
> U., Ithaca, New York. 15 Oct. 1985.

Lecture

> Gebhard, Ann O. "New Developments in Young Adult Liter-
> ature." New York State English Council. Buffalo,
> NY. 15 Nov. 1984.

Recording: CD

> Green Day. <u>Dookie</u>. Reprise, 1994.

Recording: Cassette

> Tchaikovsky, Piotr Ilich. Violin Concerto in D, op. 35.
> Itzhak Perlman, violinist. Audiocassette. RCA,
> 1975.

Recording: LP

> Taylor, James. "You've Got a Friend." <u>Mud Slide Slim
> and the Blue Horizon</u>. LP. Warner, 1971.

Videotape

> <u>The Nuclear Dilemma</u>. BBC-TV. Videocassette. Time-Life
> Multimedia, 1974.

Computer program

> <u>WordPerfect</u>. Vers. 5.1. Diskette. Orem, UT: WordPerfect
> Corp., 1990.

Work of art

> da Vinci, Leonardo. <u>The Virgin, the Child and Saint
> Anne</u>. Louvre, Paris.

Map or chart

> <u>Ireland</u>. Map. Chicago: Rand, 1984.
> <u>Adolescents and AIDS</u>. Chart. New York: Earth Science
> Graphics, 1988.

Cartoon

```
Addams, Charles. Cartoon. New Yorker 16 May 1988: 41.
```

Content Endnotes

In addition to a Works Cited list, MLA style provides for a list of comments, explanations, or facts that relate to the ideas discussed in the essay but do not fit into the actual text. You may occasionally need these *content endnotes* to provide information that is useful but must, for some reason, be separated from the rest of the essay. The most common uses of endnotes are listed below.

1. Providing additional references that go beyond the scope of the essay but could help the reader understand issues in more depth
2. Discussing a source of information in more detail than is possible in a Works Cited list
3. Acknowledging help in preparing an essay
4. Giving an opinion that does not fit into the text smoothly
5. Explaining ideas more fully than is possible in the text
6. Mentioning concerns not directly related to the content of the essay
7. Providing additional *necessary* details that would clutter the text
8. Mentioning contradictory information that goes against the general point of view presented in the essay
9. Evaluating ideas explained in the essay

In MLA style, endnotes are listed on separate pages just before the Works Cited list. The first page of the endnote list is titled Notes. Notes are numbered sequentially (1, 2, 3 . . .), and a corresponding number is included in the text of the essay, typed halfway between the lines (in superscript), to show the material to which the endnote refers. Notice in the example below that the reference numeral (that is, the endnote number) is placed in the text of the essay immediately after the material to which it refers. Usually, the reference numeral will appear at the end of a sentence. No space is left between the reference numeral and the word or punctuation mark that it follows. However, in the Notes list, one space is left between the numeral and the first letter of the note. Notes are numbered according to the order in which they occur in the essay.

Any source that you mention in an endnote must be fully documented in the Works Cited list. Do not include this complete documentation in the endnote itself. Never use endnotes as a substitute for the Works Cited list, and do not overuse endnotes. If possible, include all information in the text of your essay. For most essays you write, no endnotes will be necessary.

The following excerpts from the text of an essay and its list of end-notes illustrate MLA endnote format.

For example, in your text you would type

> For hundreds of years, scientists thought that the sun's energy came from the combustion of a solid fuel such as coal.[1] However, work in the early twentieth century convinced researchers that the sun sustains a continuous nuclear fusion reaction.[2] The sun's nuclear furnace maintains a temperature. . .

The notes on the Notes page would be formatted with the first line of each note indented five spaces.

> [1] Detailed accounts of pre-twentieth-century views of solar energy can be found in Banks and Rosen (141-55) and Burger (15-21).
>
> [2] In very recent years, some scientists have questioned whether or not the sun sustains a fusion reaction at all times. Experiments described by Salen (68-93) have failed to detect the neutrinos that should be the byproducts of the sun's fusion. This raises the possibility that the sun turns off and on periodically.

APA DOCUMENTATION STYLE

While MLA documentation style is an important standard in the humanities, APA (American Psychological Association) style is used widely in the social sciences. APA style differs from MLA style in many details, but both share the basic principles of including source names and page numbers (APA also adds the publication date) in parentheses within the text of the paper and of listing complete publication information for each source in an alphabetized list. Below is a point-by-point comparison of APA and MLA styles. For a complete explanation of APA style, consult the *Publication Manual of the American Psychological Association*. Pages 176–88 of this book contain a sample student paper written in APA style.

Parenthetical Documentation

MLA

Give the last name of the author and the page number if you are quoting a specific part of the source. For example:

```
The question has been answered before (Sagan 140-43).

Sagan has already answered the question (140-43).
```

APA

Give the last name of the author, the publication date, and the page number if you are quoting a specific part of the source. For example:

```
The question has been answered before (Sagan, 1980, pp.
140-143).

Sagan (1980) has already answered the question (pp.
140-143).
```

MLA

Omit the abbreviation for page. Drop redundant hundreds digit in final page number. For example:

```
Walsh discusses this "game theory" (212-47).
```

APA

Use the abbreviation "p." for "page" or "pp." for "pages" to show page citation. Retain redundant hundreds digit in final page number. For example:

```
Walsh (1979) discusses this "game theory" (pp.
212-247).
```

MLA

Omit commas in parenthetical references. For example:

```
The question has been answered before (Sagan 140-43).
```

APA

Use commas within parentheses. For example:

```
The question has been answered before (Sagan, 1980, pp.
140-143).
```

MLA

Use a shortened form of the title to distinguish between different works by the same author. For example:

```
Jones originally supported the single-factor theory
(Investigations) but later realized that the phenomenon
was more complex (Theory).
```

APA

Use publication date to distinguish between different works by the same author. For example:

```
Jones originally supported the single-factor theory
(1972) but later realized that the phenomenon was more
complex (1979).
```

List of Sources

MLA

The title of the page listing the sources is Works Cited.

APA

The title of the page listing the sources is References.

MLA

Indent the second and subsequent lines five spaces.

APA

Indent the first line five spaces.

MLA

Use the author's full name. For example:

```
Sagan, Carl.
```

APA

Use the author's last name, but only the initials of the author's first and middle names. For example:

```
Sagan, C.
```

MLA

Use the word "and" when listing more than one author.

APA

Use an ampersand (&) when listing more than one author.

MLA

When there are two or more authors, invert the first author's name, insert a comma and the word "and," and give the second author's first name and surname in the common order. For example:

```
Kennedy, Mary Lynch, and Hadley M. Smith.
```

APA

When there are two or more authors, invert all the names. After the first author's name, insert a comma and an ampersand (&). For example:

```
Kennedy, M. L., & Smith, H. M.
```

MLA

Capitalize major words in the titles of books and periodicals. For example:

<u>The Beginner's Guide to Academic Writing and Reading: A New Approach.</u>
<u>Reading Research Quarterly.</u>

APA

Capitalize only the first word and all proper nouns of the titles (and subtitles) of books. Capitalize all major words in the titles of periodicals. Underline punctuation that ends titles. For example:

<u>The beginner's guide to academic writing and reading: A new approach.</u>
<u>Reading Research Quarterly.</u>

MLA

List book data in the following sequence: author, title of book, city of publication, shortened form of the publisher's name, date of publication. For example:

```
Fries, Charles C. Linguistics and Reading. New York:
     Holt, 1962.
```

APA

List book data in the following sequence: author, date of publication, title
of the book, place of publication, publisher. For example:

```
Fries, C. C. (1962). Linguistics and reading. New
     York: Holt, Rinehart & Winston.
```

MLA

List journal article data in the following sequence: author, title of the article, title of the journal, volume number, date of publication, inclusive
pages. For example:

```
Booth, Wayne C. "The Limits of Pluralism." Critical
     Inquiry 3 (1977): 407-23.
```

APA

List journal article data in the following sequence: author, date of publication, title of the article, title of the journal, volume number, inclusive
pages. For example:

```
Booth, W. C. (1977). the limits of pluralism.
     Critical Inquiry, 3, 407-423.
```

MLA

List the data for an article in an edited book in the following sequence:
author of the article, title of the article, title of the book, editor of the
book, place of publication, publisher, date of publication, inclusive pages.
For example:

```
Donaldson, E. Talbot, "Briseis, Briseida, Criseyde,
     Cresseid, Cressid: Progress of a Heroine."
     Chaucerian Problems and Perspectives: Essays Pre-
     sented to Paul E. Beichner, C.S.C. Eds. Edward
     Vasta and Zacharias P. Thundy. Notre Dame: Notre
     Dame UP, 1979. 3-12.
```

APA

List the data for an article in an edited book in the following sequence:
author of the article, date, title of the article, name of the editor, title of

the book, inclusive pages, place of publication, and publisher. For example:

> Donaldson, E. T. (1979). Briseis, Briseida, Criseyde, Cresseid, Cressid: Progress of a heroine. In E. Vasta & Z. P. Thundy (Eds.), <u>Chaucerian problems and perspectives: Essays presented to Paul E. Beichner, C.S.C.</u> (pp. 3-12). Notre Dame: Notre Dame University Press.

Note: The proper names in the article title are capitalized, as is the word following the colon.

MLA

Use a shortened form of the publisher's name unless this would cause confusion. Abbreviate University Press as UP (U for University, and P for Press).

APA

Use the complete name of the publisher, but drop the terms Publishers, Incorporated, and Company. Do not delete Books and Press from a publisher's name; for example, Guilford Press.

Content Endnotes

MLA

Title the list of endnotes: Notes.

APA

Title the list of endnotes: Footnotes.

MLA

Place the endnote list immediately before the Works Cited page.

APA

Place the endnote list immediately after the References page.

MLA

Skip one space between the reference numeral and the endnote. For example:

[1] For more information, see Jones and Brown.

APA

Do not skip any space between the reference numeral and the endnote. For example:

[1]For more information, see Jones (1983) and Brown (1981).

R H E T O R I C A L
index

Antecedent-Consequent Plan

Comparison Plan

Description Plan

Time-Order Plan

Response Plan

index